Visual Basic 4 Performance Tuning and Optimization

Keith Brophy & Timothy Koets

SAMS PUBLISHING

201 West 103rd Street
Indianapolis, Indiana 46290

This book is dedicated to our wonderfully supportive families. We would like to specifically mention two special sources of inspiration.

Mr. Brophy: To Grandma Hodell, who helped teach me at a young age that determination is everything. As we'd search for elusive Petoskey stones on the beach, just as I'd start to weary of the search, I'd be gently reminded that diligent persistence often unearths great rewards. More often than not, soon after we'd find a prize Petoskey. With her wisdom and determination, my grandmother would make a great Visual Basic programmer!

Mr. Koets: To Grandpa Koets, who has inspired me with his wisdom, perseverance, and love. He has taught me by his example how to make the most of my pursuits and strive for excellence in my life. To him I am deeply grateful.

FIRST EDITION

International Standard Book Number: 0-672-30796-0

Library of Congress Catalog Card Number: 95-70087

99 98 97 96 4 3 2 1

Interpretation of the printing code: the rightmost double-digit number is the year of the book's printing; the rightmost single-digit, the number of the book's printing. For example, a printing code of 96-1 shows that the first printing of the book occurred in 1996.

Composed in AGaramond and MCPdigital by Macmillan Computer Publishing

Printed in the United States of America

Publisher and President: *Richard K. Swadley*
Acquisitions Manager: *Greg Wiegand*
Development Manager: *Dean Miller*
Managing Editor: *Cindy Morrow*
Marketing Manager: *Gregg Bushyeager*

Acquisitions Editor
Christopher Denny

Development Editor
L. Angelique Brittingham

Software Development Specialist
Steve Straiger

Production Editor
Kitty Wilson

Copy Editors
Kimberly K. Hannel
Joe Williams

Technical Reviewer
John W. Charlesworth

Editorial Coordinator
Bill Whitmer

Technical Edit Coordinator
Lynette Quinn

Formatter
Frank Sinclair

Editorial Assistants
Sharon Cox
Andi Richter
Rhonda Tinch-Mize

Cover Designer
Tim Amrhein

Book Designer
Alyssa Yesh

Production Team Supervisor
Brad Chinn

Production
Mary Ann Abramson, Georgiana Briggs, Michael Brumitt, Jeanne Clark, Tim Griffin, Jason Hand, Mike Henry, Ayanna Lacey, Kevin Laseau, Paula Lowell, Steph Mineart , Cheryl Moore, Nancy Price, Brian-Kent Proffitt, Erich Richter, Bobbi Satterfield, SA Springer, Andrew Stone, Susan Van Ness, Colleen Williams

Overview

Contents

VB
4

VB
4

VB
4

Acknowledgments

We would like to gratefully acknowledge Sams Publishing for the opportunity to author this book and their firm belief in the need for it. Many people had a hand in this book and we couldn't have done it without them. We'd like to thank Chris Denny, acquisitions editor, Angelique Brittingham, development editor, John Charlesworth, technical editor, and Kitty Wilson, production editor, and the rest of the SAMS family for all their support and assistance.

We would also like to thank the many fervent critics of Visual Basic in the early days of the product who were adamant in claiming that Visual Basic was "not a real language," or "a language without adequate performance for any real-world task." Although they were off the mark, their words served as a motivation for us to explore the bounds of Visual Basic and helped inspire this work.

And just as we each brought some unique experience with us to this task, we also each have our own teams to thank. Without their direct or indirect influence, we couldn't have done it!

Mr. Brophy: I would like to thank my friends and family for their support and understanding during this endeavor. Particular thanks go to my special running friends with whom I've shared many long hours pounding the trails; they've helped to energize and inspire me. To Tim, an endlessly patient co-author as well as a terrific friend. To Mom and Dad, the world's most supportive parents! To my mother-in-law, Ginger, who came to the rescue many times by watching over the kids as deadlines became tight. To my very special wife, Sue, who not only was an excellent administrative assistant for this book, but its greatest believer as well. This is her book too, even if her name's not on the cover. And finally, to Ginny, Emma, and Ben, who have been content to let Daddy take long hours away from playtime to spend at the computer. They've understood that a book and the knowledge it conveys is a very special and magical thing, and therefore have accepted this undertaking.

Mr. Koets: I would to thank my family and friends who supported and encouraged me while writing this book. I spent many late nights and weekends writing and programming as this book came together. I deeply appreciate their patience and understanding during those intense and sometimes stressful times. I especially thank my dad for letting me win a few points out on the tennis court over the summer; my mom, who always loves and supports me and makes sure I eat my vegetables; Michelle, who fills my heart with love and with whom I am happy and honored to share life; and God, who has blessed me with the strength, knowledge, and ability to complete this project. Finally, I want to thank Keith Brophy, who has not only been a great teammate in the writing this book, but has become a great friend as well.

About the Authors

Keith Brophy

Keith Brophy is a Software Release Coordinator at X-Rite, Incorporated, in Grandville, Michigan, a leading worldwide provider of Color and Appearance quality control software and instrumentation. Prior to that he was a software designer/lead developer at IBM's System Integration and Federal Systems Divisions in Manassas, Virginia, near Washington, D.C. Mr. Brophy has many years of experience in the design, development, and testing of projects large and small, including extensive experience in Visual Basic, databases, distributed systems, and performance analysis. He also serves as an adjunct faculty member at Grand Rapids Community College where he teaches Advanced Visual Basic. Mr. Brophy was a contributing author for *Visual Basic 4 Unleashed* (Sams, 1995) and served as technical editor on *Real-World Programming with Visual Basic* (Sams, 1995) and the revised edition of *Teach Yourself Visual Basic 4 in 21 Days* (Sams, 1995). He has a B.S. in computer science from the University of Michigan at Ann Arbor, and an M.S. in information systems from Strayer College in Washington, D.C.

Timothy Koets

Timothy Koets is a software engineer at X-Rite, Incorporated, in Grandville, Michigan, a leading worldwide provider of Color and Appearance quality control software and instrumentation. Prior to this, Mr. Koets was a computer systems engineer in the Systems Engineering and Integration division of Martin Marietta in the Washington, D.C., area. In addition to developing Visual Basic applications, Mr. Koets has experience in many other areas, including Visual C++, computer networking, client/server application design, parallel processing, and performance analysis. As a graduate student, Mr. Koets has taught electrical engineering and computer programming laboratory classes. He has also served as an instructor for Lotus Notes, a client/server database management product. Mr. Koets was a contributing author for *Visual Basic 4 Unleashed* (Sams, 1995). He has a B.S. in Electrical Engineering and an M.S. in Electrical Engineering from Michigan Technological University in Houghton, Michigan.

Introduction

Welcome to the world of Visual Basic performance tuning and optimization! If you've done much programming in Visual Basic, you have likely realized that performance gremlins are a frequent companion of the Visual Basic developer. However, it is possible to write efficient, high-performance Visual Basic programs. Better yet, this is achievable by the ordinary programmer, not just the Visual Basic guru who has been weaned on the Windows API. The world of performance encompasses a vast arena of interrelated issues and considerations. This book opens a door to this world by providing a look at some of the most fundamental Visual Basic performance considerations that every programmer should be aware of, and then leads you down the road, step by step, to implementing such optimizations in your own programs.

All developers want to provide the best applications possible to their users. Great attention is paid during the development of programs to user interface appearance, ease of use, and program functionality. However, performance optimization of programs is often regarded as an "extra frill" with little payback or an esoteric concept to be explored by computer hackers. Reality dictates that the role of performance tuning should be much more central than a back-seat issue. Visual Basic, in particular, brings issues of performance to the forefront. For reasons discussed in detail in the chapters to come, the powerful and rapid Visual Basic programming model can also induce certain performance penalties. All too often these penalties are viewed as inevitable, but in many cases performance can be optimized to circumvent them. Knowledge of such performance issues leads to programs with faster user response time that enable the users to carry out their tasks more efficiently. In other words, awareness and application of optimization allow the developer to deliver *better programs* to the end user.

This book addresses performance tuning from this fundamental standpoint. It is intended to guide Visual Basic developers to faster, more responsive, more robust, and therefore better applications. This can only be accomplished by a developer with a well-grounded understanding of the Visual Basic performance techniques that are introduced in this book. These techniques are designed to help your programs circumvent the behaviorisms inherent to Windows and Visual Basic that can degrade application performance.

Much of the material that has previously appeared on performance has focused on very specific areas or addressed the topic at a very low level that perhaps has left many programmers feeling that good optimization of their programs is out of reach. To the contrary, many important optimization concepts are easily applied, and years of Windows experience *does not* have to be a prerequisite for understanding most of the important performance considerations of Visual Basic. In that light, the purpose of this book is not to provide an intricate understanding of Windows internals, complex theoretical performance algorithms, or an intensive analysis of why Microsoft implemented Visual Basic as they did. Rather, the intent is to explain how a developer can produce a better product by working with an awareness of Visual Basic optimization concepts.

Analogy: Focusing on What's Important in Visual Basic Performance

Picture yourself strolling down a bustling New York City street, and unwittingly wandering under a piano that is being lowered from the 60th floor of an apartment building. Furthermore, the rope used to lower the piano is dangerously frayed. In this situation, it would be helpful to have someone holler "get out, the piano is about to fall!" It would be less helpful (and more dangerous!) if a scholar were to approach you with an armful of books and deliver an extensive discourse on Sir Isaac Newton's theory in the area of mechanics and gravity while the piano continues to sway overhead.

This book provides the vital information needed to get you out from under the "Visual Basic performance piano" immediately, rather than swamp you with an onslaught of details that ensures that you'll remain under the teetering piano for some time to come! The performance issues are presented in a simple, straightforward manner without burdening you with detailed Windows internal minutiae if it does not add to Visual Basic optimization skills. This approach is used to ensure that the focus remains solely on the concepts that will help you produce better programs.

Who Should Use This Book?

This book is intended for anyone involved with the development of Visual Basic applications. This includes, but is not limited to, the following types of readers:

- *Current Windows commercial application developers.* Since your applications are used by a wide body of users, it is crucial that you design your applications to be as efficient as possible. An application that is designed poorly or performs inefficiently can be a direct reflection on the company or business you work for. It is therefore of paramount importance that you understand how to maximize the efficiency of your Visual Basic applications.
- *Corporate application developers.* You are often responsible for writing in-house software that must respond to the needs of your company's operations by providing key operational programs or productivity tools. Performance is also very important to your software. Software that performs poorly can have a direct impact on business operations and productivity.
- *Software development management.* You should have an understanding of performance issues in Visual Basic if you help make decisions about the software you produce for your end users or customers. Having an understanding of the areas of optimization most needed or commonly applied in applications will help you to better determine what is acceptable or unacceptable to the customer.

You may be a reader who does not fit any of these categories. You may be a programmer who isn't responsible to anyone else or just might be interested in Visual Basic. If so, this book is for you, as well. Anyone who programs in Visual Basic or wonders how to optimize Visual Basic applications will learn much from reading this book.

How This Book Is Organized

This book is organized into eight parts that center around two themes—optimization *concepts* and optimization *strategies*. Optimization concepts help you to better understand performance tuning and optimization at a philosophical level. Optimization strategies present specific techniques you can apply directly to your Visual Basic applications, accompanied by sample programs that illustrate these techniques.

Optimization Concepts

When one sets out to slay performance gremlins and eliminate performance bottlenecks, it helps to have an overall understanding of the fundamental performance tuning concepts. That is the focus of the first two parts of this book, "Optimization Concepts: Understanding Optimization," and "Optimization Concepts: Applying Optimization." These two parts present you with sufficient background to understand the performance strategies and techniques that follow in later chapters. In addition, this section will give you the background needed to tackle specific performance analysis challenges in your own applications. A discussion of understanding optimization includes a look at the general issues of what performance is, when to optimize, and where to optimize. This leads to discussion of implementing performance tuning changes in applying optimization. Specific issues that apply to all performance tuning tasks are addressed, such as how to take measurements, accuracy of performance measurements, a methodology for implementing changes, and a discussion of utilities and routines that can aid in this task. Some of the referenced utilities and all the routines are included with this book. Any important optimization principle covered is highlighted as a performance tip, all of which are summarized in the Epilogue of the book. This collection of tips can be used as a convenient reference when you're doing actual performance tuning work.

Optimization Strategies

After a foundation has been laid for understanding Visual Basic performance, the parts based on the second theme, *optimization strategies,* provide performance enhancement techniques through a series of discussions of specific optimization examples. Armed with the conceptual background from the optimization concepts sections of the book, the many various topics that can be affected by performance bottlenecks are tackled. These diverse areas include programming language topics, the use of controls, graphics approaches, system environment issues, object creation and manipulation, and dynamic link library issues. Code optimizations are demonstrated through code examples illustrating "before" and "after" code as well as the normalized timings of each case. All examples are included on the CD-ROM that accompanies this book so that you can run the examples yourself, inspect and modify the code, and conduct further timings of your own. Since performance tuning can be very application specific, these sample programs can serve as an important tool chest of optimization tests for you to use on your own projects. Any performance technique is pointed out as a tip, and all the tips are summarized in the Epilogue of the book. This collection of tips can be used as a reference when you're doing actual performance tuning work.

Chapter Format: Analogies, Signs, Questions, and Quizzes

Throughout many of the chapters in this book, you will find analogies to help you better understand a concept being discussed. These analogies use some real-world concept to make the topic being discussed more clear.

In addition to various analogies, at the end of each chapter is a summary and "Obey the Signs" guidelines, questions, quizzes, and workshops. The chapter summary recaps important points presented throughout the chapter. The "Obey the Signs" section includes "Wrong Way" and "Beware of Falling Rocks" guidelines. The "Wrong Way" guidelines indicate common misstatements, myths, or misrepresentations that people often blindly follow but that should be avoided. The "Beware of Falling Rocks" guidelines convey performance statements that are commonly overlooked or must be considered in performance assessment. Both types of guidelines point out important concerns and issues relevant to the subject matter of the chapter in which they are presented. Following the "Obey the Signs" section at the end of the chapter is the chapter's "Q&A" section. Questions and corresponding answers are provided to reinforce key concepts presented in the chapter. Finally, for those wishing further pursuit of a topic, workshops, and in some chapters, quizzes provide directions to explore a topic in more detail.

Tools You Need to Use This Book

This book is accompanied by a CD-ROM that includes all the sample programs found in this book. In addition, there are many common code routines and utilities contained on the CD-ROM that you can use in your own performance tuning and assessment tasks. In order to change and explore the sample application programs, you should have a copy of Visual Basic 4.0, preferably the Professional or Enterprise Edition, and Windows 95 or Windows NT, which are required to build Visual Basic 4.0 32-bit programs. 16-bit versions of source code and executables are included on the CD-ROM as well.

Typographical Conventions Used in This Book

This book has a number of typographical conventions to make it easier and more enjoyable. The following conventions are used:

- `monospace` Listings, code segments, commands, options, functions, and other elements of code appear in a special monospace font.
- *`italic monospace`* Placeholders in code appear in italic monospace typeface.
- *italics* Italics are used to introduce new terms or emphasize important points.

When a code line is too long to appear in this book as a single line, the ➥ symbol is used to indicate that the two "lines" should be considered as one. If the ➥ symbol appears before a "line," you should read that line as a continuation of the preceding line.

What You Gain by Reading This Book

After you have read this book, you will be able to address your own Visual Basic application performance problems. You'll have the combined knowledge of general optimization concepts and then specific topical optimization strategies. You will have skills to analyze and understand the scope of performance bottlenecks. You will have specific optimization techniques which you can apply directly to your own code, with relevant code samples to draw on. Of course, you may not be able to remember all of the thousands of lines of sample code during your own daily dances with Visual Basic without referencing the book. Hopefully you will, however, have a clear recollection of many of the performance tips provided throughout the book, and summarized again in the appendix.

It is expected that upon completion of *Visual Basic 4 Performance Tuning and Optimization,* you will find it natural to keep these basic considerations in mind during your daily routine. You'll be better suited to understand performance with a greater general knowledge of performance issues. You'll make better choices in the constant stream of daily decisions programmers are faced with by building on the tips in the book. And you'll have a clear source to turn to if you wish to reference specific optimization techniques. You may not be able to dodge every performance gremlin that pops up in your program, but you will be able to eliminate some of the most persistent ones, and you can look the remainder square in the eye with a better understanding of why they stalk you. The end result should be faster, more robust, better programs for your end user. And that's what performance is really all about!

Part I

Optimization Concepts: Understanding Optimization

Welcome to the world of performance tuning and optimization! Before you explore the various ways of making your applications faster and more robust, it is important to understand the fundamentals. Part I introduces you to the basic ideas on which this book is founded as well as provides you with insight and advice that will aid you as you learn specific optimization techniques and strategies.

Chapter 1, "What Is Performance?," gives you a detailed explanation of what performance tuning and optimization are really all about. Chapter 1 gives a definition of performance, explains the trade-offs inherent in performance, and shows you how to determine what an acceptable performance level is.

Chapter 2, "When to Optimize," addresses when it may or may not be appropriate to carry out a performance optimization. Fixing a performance bottleneck can affect an application in terms of maintainability, debugging ease of use, and reusability, and it can even conflict with other optimizations. The programmer must understand these issues and trade-offs in making the decision of whether to optimize.

Chapter 3, "Where to Optimize," shows you how to determine where you need to focus your optimization efforts. Furthermore, this chapter points out various ways to improve the user's perception of the performance of the application. During those parts of your application that execute more slowly, for example, you can give the user visual aids to prevent him or her from waiting through a time-intensive operation with nothing to do. This chapter gives you a better idea of where to focus your optimization efforts and how to make the user as satisfied as possible with your application.

These chapters each present various concepts to help you better understand the optimization process and the issues behind it, giving you a well-rounded and practical foundation on which the rest of the book will build.

What Is Performance?

The term *application performance* is traditionally used to refer to the amount of time a user must wait for some program action to take place. For example, the time it takes a program to fully display the first window the user can interact with after a program starts, to retrieve database data and update a display after a user clicks on a command button, or to carry out a series of complex financial calculations and show the final result are all speed issues. The process of making changes to improve speed is commonly called *performance tuning*. The end result of performance tuning is to provide better programs to the end user by enhancing speed.

Performance Enhancements and Expectations

Performance problems have been around as long as there have been computers. The issue of wanting more processing with a faster turnaround time is a constant in this rapidly changing industry. However, the outer boundaries of performance limits march in step with the evolution of hardware and software technology. Notebook computers now surpass the speed of room-sized computers of a few decades ago, and still we want better performance.

The amount of available RAM in a PC often has a significant impact on system performance. The original 640KB memory capability of early PCs was once considered an amount that only researchers and advanced power users would need. Now 4MB systems are on their way to obsolescence because of inadequate performance. Many would say that a 33MHz 486 with 8MB of memory is needed as a minimum to run applications under Windows 95 with adequate performance, and some would place the minimum requirement for a system with adequate performance even higher.

What explains this constant thirst for performance? Are users getting ever greedier? Actually, users are just trying to keep up with the possibilities brought about by the creation of new software. As operating-environment software, such as Windows, offers more capabilities and a graphical interface, it gets more complex and requires more memory to provide adequate performance. Likewise, tools such as Visual Basic enable programmers to assemble sophisticated, memory-intensive, graphics-oriented packages that were not even feasible to build just a few years ago. Such programs, in turn, often demand more memory and CPU horsepower for adequate performance than their less sophisticated DOS counterparts of the past.

And the more users can do, the more they want to do. If a customer group has a program that provides ready access to 10,000 records with another 90,000 backed up on less-accessible tape, it is natural that as technology evolves, they will want the program modified to provide ready access to all 100,000 records. After that has been accomplished, they might realize that they could benefit from a global company network that provides instant access to 1,000,000 records. In this manner, people are always extending the boundaries of what their computers and applications can do. As long as this evolutionary path continues, there is no end in sight. Performance will continue to be a key issue in all areas of computing.

The aim of performance tuning is to provide better programs to the end user. Performance is the measurement of how fast and reliable the program is. Performance is a factor both of the environment in which an application runs and of how the application itself was written. As the application developer, you have control over the second factor but not the first. You generally cannot mandate an upgrade to a different operating system or faster hardware for any user of your application. You can, however, often improve the performance of your applications by changing its code.

This process of making changes to improve the speed, resource utilization, or robustness of a program is commonly called *optimization.* As previously defined, *performance tuning* is the process of making changes to enhance program speed. In practice, the terms performance tuning and optimization are often used interchangeably. However, performance tuning is actually one part of the optimization process, which also involves steps to increase program robustness and improve resource utilization. Taken together, these steps make up optimization—the act of improving performance and resource-related behavior of the program through code or configuration changes.

The Cost of Poor Performance

The end user pays for poor performance. In some cases, if the end user is frustrated enough, the developer and company might ultimately pay, too, when the end user refuses to use the product. Perhaps more common than such a dramatic case, however, is the situation in which the end user tolerates a poorly performing program day after day. The developer might be on to the next product, happily coding away, believing "That widget application I did last year was awesome!" The end user, on the other hand, might spend most coffee breaks complaining to co-workers about the fact that "It takes that dumb widget program 5 minutes just to load!" The bottom line is, if the end user perceives he or she has a performance problem, *he or she has a problem.* The ultimate judge of determining acceptable performance is the end user.

Users' Psychological Perception of Performance

The developer must often act as an advocate for the user in gauging performance because the developer knows (or at least *thinks* he or she knows) what is and is not technically achievable. Likewise, a user's satisfaction point is—perhaps—unreachable, because a user's ideal performance speed would be a zero wait time! However, if an application is usable, performs well enough that users are content to use it, and has taken advantage of available technology to provide the fastest performance reasonably achievable, it can be viewed as an application with adequate performance.

The determination of when this goal has been reached is subjective. There is a real danger in not representing the user's viewpoint when considering performance in this manner. For example, a developer of a recipe-management application might think performance is just fine when a hierarchical, bitmap-based list box loads in less than 10 seconds. However, if the developer reached that conclusion based on a sample database of 50 recipes and the project ships to customers who work with databases of 50,000 recipes, they might feel differently. When the list box takes 15 minutes to load for customers, it will become obvious that performance was not successfully addressed from their standpoint.

The user's opinion of the performance of an application is also shaped largely by expectations and past experience. If the same application is provided to two businesses, workers might react to it very differently. If one business has just switched its workers from mainframe-connected terminals to PCs, and your new application is the first PC application they have ever used, they might be delighted with the performance. Compared to their terminal experience, it seems to blaze if they only have to wait 5 seconds to retrieve data instead of the 30 seconds they were used to!

On the other hand, if the other business has a group of users used to working with fast, local spreadsheets on the PC, and then they are introduced to a networked PC program that takes 5 seconds to retrieve data, they might be very unhappy. In the first case, the developer should consider himself fortunate. In the second case, the users should be educated to realize that network database applications will have performance that is not on par with that of local applications so they can downscale their expectations to be more realistic.

In many cases, even if there are performance constraints the developer can do nothing to fix, the satisfaction level of the user can still be increased by distracting them during times of system inactivity. For example, displaying a *splash screen*, or colorful startup screen, in front of the user gives him something to look at and diverts his attention while a more complex form with many controls loads.

Tactics such as assessing performance from the standpoint of real-world use, educating the user to shape expectations, and distracting the user from performance through avenues such as splash screens are all important parts of the strategy of addressing users' performance concerns. In this manner, improving performance can involve steps in addition to direct performance tuning. The reception your program receives will involve the emotions and reactions of your users, not to mention the ultimate speed of your application, on their computers. Therefore, performance addresses subjective perception considerations as well as objective measurable behavior.

The Challenge of Producing Meaningful Performance Assessments

Performance is typically evaluated by collecting *timings*. Timings are timed measurements of various areas of code. Such tasks in timings can be used to gauge how long the computer takes to carry out each respective area. They can be used to compare one area of code to another to see which areas are the best candidates for optimization. Alternatively, timings can be used to compare one area of code to itself, both before and after optimization to assess optimization improvements. In some cases, comparisons might be performed between different code techniques to determine which of various alternate methods is preferable. These timings might be collected from the application itself or from test applications that highlight various characteristics of the target application.

Initial testing often consists of looking at an application simply to determine if it is fast enough to satisfy the users' needs. At this phase, informal timings, such as wristwatch timings or simple

observations, are sometimes used to determine if performance is adequate or more research is warranted. In some cases, more formal timings with advanced tools might be carried out initially on the test application. This would be the case if there were reason to suspect that a performance problem might be present, if the impact of a performance problem could be critical, if there were a need to determine if performance is slower than in previous releases, or to gauge internal performance of areas not easily viewed as separate, measurable activities by the user.

More intensive testing and analysis is typically undertaken when a decision has been made that there is a performance problem and therefore a need to optimize the application. This phase of testing involves comparing two or more alternate code methods side by side to gauge their relative performance. Typically, you would use more formal timing methods here, using timers and other tools rather than relying on casual observations—in this case, a choice will be made based on results. The purpose of such testing is to make a decision between alternatives that will be used in subsequent optimization of the code, or to verify the amount of improvement gained from an optimization step. However, there are many considerations to keep in mind when carrying out performance analysis that can complicate the task considerably.

Many Factors Affect Performance

Nothing would seem to be easier on the surface than choosing the speediest race car at the conclusion of the Indy 500, or the fastest endurance runner at the finish line of the Boston Marathon. Simply point to the contestant that reached the finish line first and is carrying the trophy around, and you can say "That one is the fastest!" *Or can you…?* If you call the same field of contestants back to the starting line and re-run the race, the results might be completely different. A safer statement to make about who's the fastest is "That one *was* the fastest in the last race!"

Although computers are more predictable than highly tuned race cars and exhausted runners, in some respects the process of gauging the performance of Visual Basic code shares the same inability to predict future results based on one outcome. The results of a trial run can vary with successive trials, subject to the influence of the environment; and coming up with a fair race that is not slanted to the benefit of any one competitor is a constant concern.

One Performance Measurement Is Not Conclusive

Everything from memory to disk access speed, system swap file configuration, other programs running, other Windows configuration issues, and potentially hundreds more issues both minor and major beyond just your application code can affect the speed of your application. The developer must identify any areas of major significance and isolate them out of the test as much as possible. Unfortunately, if all these factors were removed from the test, there would be no PC hardware or operating environment left on which to test! Therefore, performance assessment includes understanding the impact of the environment and determining which factors should be eliminated or isolated before gathering timings.

Careful attention to the environment you are conducting the test on and the kind of test you are performing is necessary to carry out meaningful optimization. It does little good, for instance, to test the performance of your program on a system where an unrelated mail program automatically checks for mail every 60 seconds in the background if that is a situation your user will never face. As a matter of fact, the background mail program could introduce system performance factors that could skew your test results. Likewise, if your application only carries out one text box assignment when a form loads, viewing performance of a test application that carries out 100 successive text box assignments on the same form might not be the most relevant.

It is for this same reason that industry-standard benchmark programs are of little use for many application-specific purposes. An *industry benchmark* is a program that can be run across systems to assess performance of such areas as video drivers or floating-point manipulation speed. Many of these programs are used widely throughout the industry for system comparisons. Because they are often emphasized in various industry forums as magical performance indicators of PCs, novices often think the answer to their puzzles over performance lies partly in obtaining an industry benchmark. Most often, such industry benchmarks are of little relevance for the application developer looking at his own specific applications.

The industry benchmarks are good, for example, for telling system vendors and potential customers which systems have the fastest video update capabilities. They do not, however, necessarily tell an individual which system his own unique application will run the most quickly on, because his program consists of different code and results in different system interactions (disk access, video update frequency, memory management) than the benchmark program. And they certainly will not tell you how fast your program is or where it can be optimized. The only way to find that out is with careful research, trial and experimentation, and informed thought aimed at the user's own specific application.

Timing Methods Can Affect Performance Assessments

Even the method used to time various performance alternatives can affect the conclusions that are reached. For example, there are different methods of timing code execution available to the programmer. The crudest of these is simply using a wristwatch. The human error inherent in this method, however, can introduce a time skew ranging from 1 second to several seconds. Other code-based methods could take advantage of Visual Basic time-of-day functions, VB timer capabilities, or Windows API timer functions such as `timeGetTime` (a 32-bit multimedia function).

The choice of a timing method can be very important. For example, some timing methods yield times based on timers that are updated every millisecond, whereas others produce times that are only updated every 55 milliseconds or more. Obviously it would be a poor choice to

use a timing method that only records time values that are updated every 55 milliseconds to measure some code activity that only is a few milliseconds in duration. These timer considerations are discussed in considerably more detail in Chapter 4, "Timing Methods." The bottom line is that a thorough understanding of the ramifications of the timing method used is required.

Analogy: Using the Right Timer for the Job

Consider how you might time some common household tasks. If you wanted to spend 30 minutes reading, you could probably listen for the chimes of the grandfather clock in the other room that ring every 15 minutes and be reasonably sure this system would satisfy your need to be notified of a certain time frame. On the other hand, if you wanted to make some soup that needed to simmer on the stove for 5 minutes, but you relied on the grandfather clock chimes that only occur every 15 minutes to guide you as to when it was finished, this method of timing could lead to dire results!

Like the grandfather clock, some timing methods, such as the 55-millisecond-update Visual Basic `Timer` function, might be perfectly adequate for many of your needs. However, for very precise performance assessment, the `Timer` function might not provide the required resolution or frequency of updates.

Fair Tests Are Required

Another key issue in comparison testing is that tests should be fair. You need to ensure that if you are comparing two code methods, they are truly similar methods for comparison of the alternatives under consideration. For example, if you were deciding between use of a text box or a label, comparing the following two code fragments would enable you to accurately judge two potentially interchangeable methods:

- Text box test code:

```
txtAuthors = "Keith Brophy and Tim Koets"
```

- Label test code:

```
lblAuthors = "Keith Brophy and Tim Koets"
```

On the other hand, the following test would be unfair because it would use the most efficient text box update method but would not accurately reflect the most efficient label method available:

- Text box test code:

```
txtAuthors = "Keith Brophy and Tim Koets"
```

- Label test code:

```
lblAuthors.caption = "Keith Brophy "
lblAuthors.caption = lblAuthors.caption & " and Tim Koets"
```

It would be inaccurate to draw the conclusion from the second test that the text box control is superior to the label control for displaying text. The label method should be optimized to make its assignment all in one statement:

```
"lblAuthors = "Keith Brophy and Tim Koets"
```

Then there can be a fair test between alternatives because you are comparing reasonably optimized program options as opposed to an optimized code technique and a dissimilar non-optimized code technique.

This does not mean that you must always compare identically structured code methods, or apples to apples. Although you will generally want to avoid comparing drastically different approaches, you might at times need to compare firm apples to mushy apples, or approaches that have the same intent but not necessarily the same number of statements. One such alternative might be comparing a text box update to a list box update, as in the following fair test:

- Text box test code:

  ```
  txtAuthors = "Keith Brophy and Tim Koets"
  ```

- List box test code:

  ```
  lstAuthors.Clear
  lstAuthors.AddItem "Keith Brophy and Tim Koets"
  ```

In this case, the text box update replaces all the old text with the new entry. The list box update does not get rid of old entries unless a clear method is carried out. Therefore, if for some application-specific reason you were contemplating using a list box in place of a text box to display text, the list box would need an extra `Clear` statement. In comparing the text box methods to the list box method for text display, the list clear would be a necessary part of the test to compare the two alternatives.

The Visual Basic Performance Paradox

The paradox of Visual Basic programming is that the very characteristics that merit its praise as a wonderful development language can also lead it to be criticized as a language with performance drawbacks. Visual Basic enables developers to piece together programs with tremendous ease and minimal time investment. However, the same ease of use and rapid-application-development technology that make that rapid assembly possible can introduce many difficulties from a performance and optimization standpoint.

This ease-of-use/performance penalty trade-off occurs in many specific areas. It is important to understand that these trade-off areas exist in order to carry out effective performance analysis. Although in many cases these factors are interrelated, it is illuminating to consider them somewhat independently. These key areas in which the trade-off occurs are

- Custom control layers
- Ease of technology incorporation

- Interpreted language
- High-level, layered building-block tool
- Ease of programming

Custom Control Layers

Visual Basic programs are often built with many custom controls. These custom controls consist of pre-packaged code available to the user in a consolidated library in OCX or VBX form. Controls are typically written in a generic manner to provide maximum flexibility in the widest variety of application uses. Any one application typically exercises only a subset of the properties and methods available and uses only a fraction of the flexibility built into the control. This means that each use of a control might carry with it more of an automatic performance overhead penalty than if the user had built a customized control or designed a direct implementation from the ground up.

When a control is used, for example, the internal logic of the control itself might carry out checks to make branching decisions based on property-value states. However, the specific property-value states that the code checks for might never be true for a given application. This all happens at a low level that you as a Visual Basic programmer never see, but it nevertheless affects the speed of the application. If you had implemented the logic in the controls directly, whether in your own non-generic control or in the Visual Basic application itself, you would have implemented only the exact conditional checks pertinent to your specific application. In this manner, you might have avoided some of the potential overhead inherent in control use.

Ease of Technology Incorporation

The ease of component incorporation in Visual Basic also means that Visual Basic programs, as much as (or more than) programs of any other language, are likely to leverage areas of technology beyond the programming language itself. The odds are very high that a Visual Basic program makes use of a database, mail support, or multimedia, or generates graphs. In each of these cases, the user's performance perception is based on the performance of the underlying technologies—database engine speed, network load impact, the mail interface and mail server, network speed, CD speed, and the graphics engine—as well as on the application itself.

Interpreted Language

Visual Basic is an *interpreted language.* When a Visual Basic program is running, the instructions in the Visual Basic executable file are not carried out directly by the PC's processor. Rather, the instructions are passed on as data to yet another program, the Visual Basic runtime interpreter, that is started along with the Visual Basic application. The following are runtime interpreter filenames for various versions of Visual Basic:

Visual Basic 3.0	VBRUN300.DLL
Visual Basic 4.0 16-bit	VB40016.DLL
Visual Basic 4.0 32-bit	VB40032.DLL

A *compiled language* such as C, Pascal, or Delphi stores executable programs as a sequence of instructions that can be directly carried out by the PC's processor without assistance from another runtime program, avoiding the overhead of the interpreter. Many people have said that the performance penalty for the interpreter is relatively small because the Visual Basic runtime program performs its interpretation very quickly and much of the time in a program is actually spent waiting on areas such as system and database response rather than on raw processing of the application's instructions. Nevertheless, there is no denying that an extra level of activity must take place to execute the program.

A High-Level, Layered, Building-Block Tool

Windows resource management is complicated by the presence of a high-level interpreted language. In the traditional Windows languages C and C++, management of Windows resources is directly available through the use of the Windows Application Programming Interface, or API. In Visual Basic, the developer is still able to take advantage of this low-level management, but also must depend on the fact that the Visual Basic interpreter is automatically carrying out its own level of resource and memory management in support of the forms and code that have been defined. Forms are easy to define because the developer does not have to deal with these low-level issues. Visual Basic addresses these issues as out of sight, out of mind.

The Visual Basic programming language makes the task of the developer wonderfully easy because it enables him to work at a high level by moving the tedious work of programming out of the way to lower layers. Resource and memory management are carried out at a lower layer by controls and the Visual Basic interpreter; ultimate machine code paths are determined at lower layers by the interpreter and custom control library code; instructions are fed to the CPU at runtime by the interpreter; and so on. The beauty of Visual Basic carries with it an unavoidable penalty: The typical Visual Basic developer is shielded by the layers from low-level details, and it can be these low-level details that affect performance.

Ease of Programming and Impact on Performance

There is another penalty area of Visual Basic development that is usually conspicuously absent from many industry discussions on Visual Basic performance, but can be one of the most significant factors that influences performance. Here it is, stated for the record:

It is easy to write sloppy programs in Visual Basic.

Now that the secret is out, let's address the problem. Visual Basic is an exciting, powerful language that has shaped the way Windows software development takes place. Nevertheless, it is important to recognize that Visual Basic can still be used in a sloppy, inefficient manner. This is true with any language, but in some respects it is even more true in a Visual Basic application because it is so easy to rapidly "crank out code." A Visual Basic application will very likely have room for improvement in simple code-organization areas such as variable declarations, use of logic, iteration methods, and removal of dead code (code that never gets executed).

Inefficient code can be a serious problem in Visual Basic applications produced in certain development environments for several reasons. At the top of the list is the fact that Visual Basic is an easy language to begin programming in right away. Even those without prior knowledge of the language find the syntax quick to master with its clear identifiers (for example, `End` will end a program, as one might expect!) and lack of complexity (no pointers to deal with explicitly). However, this ease of use enables programmers to piece together programs rapidly in a "first-come, first-served" manner, using the first syntax that gets the job done without considering the ramifications.

Likewise, Visual Basic programs can be built in a piecemeal fashion. A snippet of code can be associated with one control, and later a snippet added for another control, with a variable thrown in here or there in the mix. This makes for an easy and painless development path as you add a piece of functionality at a time, but can lead to tangled, unorganized code in the end if planning and discipline are not used along the way.

Similarly, Visual Basic is the classic example of an "I'll do it later" language. It is so easy to implement functionality that it is natural for a programmer to add a quick-and-dirty piece of code. Quick code insertions frequently are used to get a prototype user-interface feature running or to see if a concept works. However, this type of coding is usually done with an emphasis on plugging it in with a minimal time investment in order to view the new functionality as soon as possible.

Such code is rarely optimized or elegantly written. Of course, the developer taking these shortcuts usually plans to revisit the code and implement it more elegantly in the future. But it is easy for the developer to forget (or choose to forget!) to go back and optimize the code once a working program is in hand.

All the performance problems mentioned here are areas that can be avoided by planning, discipline, and up-front design. These problems don't just go away with experience, however. In the real world, there often remain situations when code must be quick, dirty, and done yesterday rather than today. The inevitable fallout from this mix is that there is often code that cries out for optimization.

Alternative Languages

Until very recently, in the minds of many seasoned programmers, there were two fundamental approaches to Visual Basic application performance problems:

- Write *part* of it in another, faster language
- Write *all* of it in another, faster language

Needless to say, there can be a great deal of work and inconvenience in either of these approaches, and they mitigate the advantages of using Visual Basic in the first place! The world will never know how many potential Visual Basic programs never reached fruition because of the purveyor of doom to be found in every company grumbling and overreacting "It'll never be fast enough in VB… we must rewrite it in C++!" This is *not* to say that there are never situations when another language alternative is warranted. However, in many cases there are optimization steps that can be taken short of turning to such drastic measures.

Visual Basic Versus Other Languages

One issue that often arises in discussions of Visual Basic performance is C++ versus Visual Basic or Delphi versus Visual Basic. All too often discussions on language performance issues, however, lose sight of the forest for the trees as participants get bogged down in emotional views of particular languages based on their own subjective language experience. There have been industry demonstrations of highly optimized Visual Basic applications outperforming similar, non-optimized C++ applications. However, most seasoned developers would agree that programs written in C or C++ will, unless special circumstances prevail, have faster performance than Visual Basic programs. However, more important than the issue of which language is faster is the question "Can a Visual Basic program have acceptable performance for the user?" The answer is, in most cases, yes.

Analogy: If It's Fast Enough, Faster Alternatives Don't Matter

I often ride a bike the two miles between my house and work. I like the sensation of the wind in my face and the feeling of speed as I travel the bike trail. I also need to get to work on time. The bike serves both of these purposes well.

I could get to work faster if I flew a helicopter. My speed would be greatly increased, although my perception of speed might not be without the wind in my face. However, it would take me so long to learn to manipulate the many controls in the cockpit that I might never get off the ground in the first place. I can't argue with anyone who says I *could in theory* get to work faster if I commuted by helicopter. In my case, there is no need or motivation to incur the extra work this would involve, so I'll stick with the bike

(and won't be swayed by my friends who tell me I'm not really living until I'm traveling by helicopter).

It's true that certain languages provide inherent performance advantages over others. However, this is not the only, or the most important, issue in looking at the performance of a language. The more relevant issue is "is this the best language for my needs as a developer, and is the performance I can get out of using that language suitable for the needs of my user?" If you are currently a Visual Basic programmer, it is very likely that it is because you want to take advantage of the ease of development it provides. Therefore, the most important issue to you is *not* which language is fastest, but what you have to do to write Visual Basic programs that have an acceptable performance level.

Industry-Standard Advice: Write a DLL in Another Language (Give Up!)

Whereas guidelines on proper use of VB syntax and controls might be the Visual Basic performance battle cry, the white-flag-waving surrender of "Write a DLL in another language!" often seems to follow closely on its heels. A DLL, or dynamic link library, is a library of code routines distributed as a separate file that can be called from another program. A Visual Basic program can often gain considerable speed by implementing key pieces in a block of performance-tuned, carefully crafted code that is packaged into a dynamic link library generated from another language. This is especially true of certain types of code such as algorithms that involve many mathematical computations or make extensive use of floating-point numbers. Often these routines can be carried out much more efficiently in another language. However, this approach should be an avenue of last resort, not of first resort. Backing away from Visual Basic and into another language mitigates the very reasons that Visual Basic was used as the target language in the first place—ease of use and rapid development.

Why Isn't Optimization Viewed As an Easy Answer?

You might ask why addressing Visual Basic performance problems has historically often focused on simply moving to another language. The answer is that this is an easy reaction! The "use another language" response is a clear, straightforward, cut-and-dried issue our minds can deal with in a logical fashion. The logic is so clear that with a little imagination you can even picture the solution as a code statement:

```
If My_VB_Program < Acceptable_Performance then
       Call Have_C_Programmers_Redo_It
End If
```

The routine `Have_C_Programmers_Redo_It` might not be easy to carry out, but at least you know what it is you need to implement to reach your solution!

On the other hand, use your imagination and try to picture what's involved in the performance-tuning approach:

```
If My_VB_Program < Acceptable_Performance then
        Call Tune_And_Tweak_And_Pray
End If
```

Where do we even start to implement the routine `Tune_And_Tweak_And_Pray`? Does anyone know how to implement it? Is this approach even a process that can be sequentially carried out in the same fashion every time?

The answer, of course, is no. The second approach is much murkier and much less cut-and-dried. Performance tuning and optimization are not always clear-cut issues; they can be quite complex and have many interdependencies.

One striking example of this occurred at a recent computer conference. A speaker was presenting findings on Visual Basic performance and went through a series of "this technique will be faster," "this technique will be slower" examples, demonstrating the programs on a large overhead screen for the audience to observe. Unfortunately (and we would imagine to his consternation), example after example did just the opposite of what he predicted. The speaker would say "technique A will be faster than B" and proceed to the demo, which would show technique B outperforming technique A!

These contradictions were not due to a lack of homework by the speaker. Rather, they were due to the evasive nature of performance. Findings that had been verified by the speaker on his office PC did not hold true on the PC used for the demonstration, which had a different hardware configuration and a different Windows-compatible operating system. The speaker's presentation was a good example of the fact that it is often difficult to make absolute statements about performance—often the best that can be done is to make relative statements with respect to a given environment.

Stated another way, this book—and for that matter, any performance-tuning reference—cannot provide tips in the form of "carry out technique A and increase the performance of your program by 2 seconds." Performance is too complex a beast for anyone to state optimization techniques in absolute terms. A multitude of factors can affect the behavior and timing of a Windows program. Just a few of these factors include the version of the operating system, the amount of RAM, the size of a swap file, the use of disk caching, the speed of processor used, other programs currently running on the system, other dynamic link libraries loaded into memory before program startup, and wallpaper used for the desktop!

However, performance insights can be shared in relative terms: "Technique A is faster than technique B by factors ranging from 30 to 60 percent as tested on the following systems...." This can be supplemented by an explanation of underlying concepts: "The reason technique A is faster than technique B is that it avoids the following overhead...." The recipient of the technique should also be provided with a general framework for understanding performance issues.

This is the approach that must be used to effectively convey an understanding of performance enhancements, and the approach that this book uses. However, it is not an approach that is easily conveyed in a quick sound bite, hallway discussion, or concluding paragraph of an article, such as "Use a DLL." This, perhaps, explains why using another language is well known as the *de facto* optimization step for Visual Basic applications. There has been less insight (until recently) into the gains that can be made with specific optimization steps *within* the Visual Basic environment.

Summary

This chapter provides a broad and general overview into the far-reaching world of performance. Performance and optimization are defined, and the consequences of poor performance and the importance of considering user perception of performance are addressed. Some background is provided on why Visual Basic programs can run into performance problem areas, and why switching to another programming language should not always be the first alternative for performance tuning.

Performance assessment can be a complex and challenging task; this endeavor is discussed in detail. One of the keys to performance assessment is carrying out meaningful and relevant performance assessments as opposed to assessments that don't focus on true performance bottlenecks. Various considerations to ensure that this occurs are mentioned. This material provides a foundation for understanding and assessing performance and carrying out the optimization of Visual Basic programs. Subsequent chapters build on this foundation with more specific techniques and examples.

Obey the Signs

Wrong Way: The first step toward improving performance is moving code to a DLL in another language.

There are many optimization steps that can be used other than moving code to a dynamic link library to speed performance. The DLL route can involve considerable development time, and should be viewed as an avenue of last resort rather than the first optimization technique to consider.

Wrong Way: The best way to determine the faster of two code approaches is to take one set of timings for each method and choose the faster of the two.

As this chapter discusses, there are many factors that affect performance and that affect which type of performance assessment is appropriate for any one performance problem. Careful consideration should be given to how two code approaches will be compared. A series of tests might be required to define all the issues. Even if a single test can be used, it should be run multiple times on multiple platforms. Test results can differ

between systems, as well as even from one execution to another on the same system, due to the many factors affecting system performance.

Beware of Falling Rocks: Don't count on the performance-analysis road always being clearly marked!

Visual Basic performance analysis is often not straightforward because there are so many interrelated factors that affect performance. Among system settings, PC hardware, windows configuration, component usage, and program structure, a multitude of factors can affect how quickly and efficiently an application operates.

Q&A

Q Are performance considerations the same for Visual Basic as they are for other languages?

A No. Actually, the ease of use of Visual Basic in some cases comes at the penalty of decreased performance if special attention is not paid to optimization. Performance considerations are present in any language, but the VB developer must be especially aware of them.

Q Does Visual Basic isolate the application from performance penalties of incorporated technologies such as multimedia and database features?

A No. To the contrary, Visual Basic makes it easy to incorporate such technologies through important features such as the ease of component integration and networked database access. Therefore, Visual Basic does not isolate the application from these penalties. It is more likely to pull these penalties into the application than are some other development tools because Visual Basic makes it much easier to incorporate these technologies in the first place.

Q Should the correct focus of performance analysis and optimization be to provide the absolute fastest performance technically possible for a given application before pronouncing it finished?

A Absolutely not. The correct focus of performance analysis and optimization is to better satisfy the needs of the end user. Performance should be tuned to the point where it is satisfactory to the end user. If an end user has a choice between receiving an acceptably performing program today or waiting six more months for a program that loads $^{1}/_{1000}$ second faster, you would better serve the needs of the end user by bypassing the last stage of optimization.

Q Is it sufficient to carry out performance testing only on the slowest possible platform and ensure that the application performs adequately there?

A No. If you *must* choose just one platform on which to carry out performance testing, the slowest platform is the one to select (for example, test on a 386 rather than a

Pentium). On the other hand, you really should test on a variety of platforms to ensure the fullest possible results. Depending on the implementation, there can be cases where problems occur on a faster processor (such as flashing and removing a message too quickly) that will not be present on a slower processor. Likewise, there are many hardware factors that affect performance beyond just the CPU, such as the amount of memory and the speed of the network card. The safest approach in performance assessment is to carry out critical tests on a variety of platforms.

Q Does the developer need to be concerned with code statements that take less than a couple hundred milliseconds to execute, because a couple hundred milliseconds is not a very noticeable wait time for a user?

A Yes. Even though such code statements complete very quickly *by themselves,* the performance impact the end user notices is the sum total of all of the code statements. Therefore, the difference in a few milliseconds between two code methods, when multiplied by many statements, can be very noticeable.

Workshop

Write a program that takes a timing before and after 1000 iterations of a loop and produces a total time summary much like the example that appears in this chapter. Plug in various types of operations inside the loop, such as label assignments, text box assignments, and form caption assignments. Consider whether you can make any *conclusive* statements from your findings, and how many test trials you must carry out before you get an intuitive feel for which operations are faster.

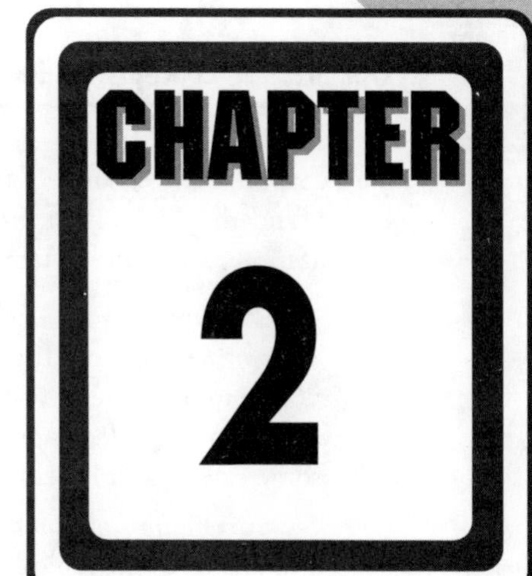

When to Optimize

Any programmer who has ever tried to make an application perform better would probably agree that software optimization is more of an art than a science. Optimization never seems to be as simple as thought at the outset, and the results are not always pleasing to the user. This is due, in part, to the fact that optimization isn't simply a set of rules and techniques that can be applied the same way to all applications with equally predictable results. A wide body of general optimization techniques exist, and the practical application of these techniques varies widely with the programming languages being used, the operating system and hardware platforms being targeted, and the expectations of the end user.

This chapter analyzes some of the factors that complicate this process. The developer should understand these factors in order to appreciate the magnitude and scope of the software-optimization process and its ramifications. Following is a brief summary of the topics addressed:

- *Software optimization is not just a set of techniques that can be applied at the end of software development.* If you wait until you have written all of your code and then decide to optimize it, you are not likely to have a product with the highest possible efficiency. In order to properly optimize an application, you must optimize code, to some extent, as it is being written.
- *Software optimization must be based on how users will use the application.* Considerations such as the typical user's usage patterns, the amount of data processed by the application, and the various system configurations on which the application is run are essential specifications to consider when both writing and optimizing an application.
- *It is not always a good idea to optimize.* Optimization can often run counter to other, equally important, issues such as maintainability, debugging ease, code structure, expandability, and code reuse. You must, therefore, weigh the benefits of optimization against these other, competing, factors.
- *Some optimization methods can contradict each other.* You cannot always apply a single set of optimization techniques to an application without the potential of producing side effects in other areas of the application. This, therefore, makes a fundamental understanding of performance techniques essential. Blindly applying performance techniques without understanding the full scope and ramifications of those techniques can lead to trouble.

This chapter will help you to better determine when it might or might not be a good idea to optimize. In Chapter 3, "Where to Optimize," the focus changes from *when* to optimize to *where* to optimize an application. Keep in mind that these issues not only apply to Visual Basic applications, but to any Windows application regardless of language used.

Optimize As You Develop

When writing software, developers are almost always under tight deadlines. When the pressure is on, the developer is constantly facing the temptation to take shortcuts. At the beginning of development, when the programmer or program manager determines the requirements of the software and works out the specifications, the temptation for the programmer is to shortcut these steps and get down to writing code right away. When the actual coding effort begins, the developer is further tempted to simply get something working and worry about its efficiency later.

When writing software with a language such as Visual Basic, it's especially easy to succumb to this temptation. One of Visual Basic's primary strengths is its easy-to-use language, which is well suited for programmers who do not have extensive programming backgrounds. One reason Visual Basic is easier to learn and apply than a language such as C or C++, for example, is that Visual Basic is not as structured and demanding on the programmer. Unfortunately, this lack of rigidity makes it easy to get away with writing inefficient and sloppy code. More of a burden is placed on the developer to write structured, maintainable, and efficient code.

In reality, human nature often prevails, and Visual Basic applications tend to be poorly written. One of the biggest complaints critics have about Visual Basic is that the applications run too slowly. Interestingly, another big complaint is that Visual Basic applications are overloaded with too many controls. These two complaints are essentially symptomatic of the same problem, namely the failure of the programmer to judiciously and carefully write code. Although Visual Basic is indeed easier to program, the developer still needs to write code intelligently and efficiently. Specifically, the programmer must learn to optimize *as* he/she develops code rather than do all the optimization *after* the program is written.

In order to optimize software *as* you develop, you must first understand *when* to optimize, *where* to optimize, and *how* to optimize. As you read this book, you will develop the skills necessary not only to optimize code that is inefficient, but to write efficient code right from the start. The concepts introduced in this book will hopefully become habits that you will exercise automatically when programming. If you master these techniques and use them when writing code, you will not have to invest large amounts of time optimizing and tuning your code after you have written it.

When an application is put together hastily, without regard to performance, the developer often finds that when the program is finished, the performance is unacceptable to the users. A typical problem is that the developer writes the application on a computer with large amounts of memory and processor power and does not take into account users who use much less powerful systems. When the application is released to such users, the complaints are usually quite loud. The developer must then go back and figure out how to make the code more efficient. Without any training or education in how to optimize Visual Basic applications, the developer can often be at a loss to make the program much more efficient. Unfortunately, many developers resort to taking functionality out of the application and stripping down valuable features.

Another potential problem is that developers, in their attempts to optimize a poorly written application, sometimes further compromise the integrity of the code. They might actually introduce additional bugs into the application that are difficult to fix due to the poor overall quality of the code. Therefore, it is critical that developers write high-quality, efficient code throughout the development process to avoid such problems.

Analogy: Building on a Soggy Foundation

If a house is built on a soggy foundation and starts to collapse here and there, rebuilding only certain parts of the house can put more stress on other areas of the house that are weak, resulting in an even bigger disaster. Often, the foundation has to be fully rebuilt at the cost of tearing down the superstructure of the house.

This is the danger of poorly designed code. If the application is unacceptably slow, sometimes the only recourse is to redesign the entire application. This is why it is so important to write efficient code right from the start.

Now that you know the importance of optimizing during development, remember this caveat: You must also be careful to avoid investing too much time optimizing at a level of detail that is counterproductive to the project. If you engage in micro-optimizing code, you can spend too much time being concerned about optimization techniques without knowing their overall impact on the user. A developer can, for example, spend three days optimizing a sorting algorithm in an area of the application that is later found to be rarely used by the end user. Therefore, although a general optimization strategy is desired, you must be careful not to spend too much time worrying about details that might not end up being as significant as expected.

Therefore, when you write code, take time to think about what your code is doing. Be thinking about how best to *write* your code in an optimal way, not just to *modify* your code to run efficiently. You should be able to apply the techniques in this book and minimize the burden of having to tune your applications after they have been written. Having done so, you can avoid facing the possibility of settling for an inefficient application that could potentially be much more efficient.

Optimization and the User

In order to better understand when to optimize, the developer should work closely with testers and users to see just how the application is being used. The developer might be unable to predict just how the user will use the application during a typical day, and might therefore completely overlook areas of the application with which the user will be dissatisfied. For example, if the application accesses a database, the developer might never think about how the application will behave if the user has more than 20,000 records. In fact, the application might never have been tested for that many records. Areas of poor performance caused by a large database size might never have surfaced to the developer, who had only 100 records in the database when he/she tested it.

Another important concern the developer should understand up front is the variety of configurations in which the user might run the application. Each configuration might behave differently in terms of performance, and each one needs to be considered independently. Often during development, the programmer fails to anticipate a unique type of configuration a user may have. If this particular configuration bogs down performance and is the only configuration the user wants to use, he/she will be very unhappy with the program.

Although the other users might not use that specific configuration and may be happy with the performance of the application, that one overlooked configuration could cause much anxiety to you, the developer, after you release the application.

The most effective way to overcome the failure to anticipate the user's pattern of usage for your application is to continually elicit tester feedback, optimizing and evaluating each major feature or component of functionality in the application. As features and major components of functionality are added into the application over time, the programmer must keep current with the usage patterns and expectations of the users.

Optimization Versus Maintainability

Although the goal of optimization is to make the application run faster, certain trade-offs can make various types of optimization prohibitive. One such trade-off is optimization versus maintainability. You can spend so much time tuning and modifying your code that it becomes extremely difficult to understand. For example, you might have an algorithm that is fairly simple to understand but can be made to execute faster. If the modifications you must make to that algorithm to increase performance obscure the clarity of the algorithm, you might pay a higher price in maintaining the code through the life of the software than you benefit from the performance improvement.

Again, a balance must be struck. The user does not care how well the code is written, only that the application meets his needs, operates correctly and efficiently, and can be delivered in a reasonable amount of time. If, however, the program has been tuned to the extent that it is extremely difficult to maintain, the user might be dissatisfied because the developer has difficulty performing maintenance and providing a new release of the software in a reasonable amount of time, resulting in delays and the possible introduction of bugs into the software.

The following example demonstrates this concept. The code in Listing 2.1 calculates the number of seconds in the current month.

Listing 2.1. Calculating the number of seconds in the current month (unoptimized).

```
Dim intDays as Integer
Dim intHours as Integer
Dim intMinutes as Integer
Dim intSeconds as Integer

intDays = DaysInMonth(Month(Now))          // This is a user-defined function
intHours = Days * 24
intMinutes = intHours * 60
intSeconds = intMinutes * 60
Print "There are " & intSeconds & " seconds in the current month."
```

Consider the same calculation, using a different approach, as shown in Listing 2.2.

Listing 2.2. Calculating the number of seconds in the current month (optimized).

```
Print "There are " & DaysInMonth(Month(Now)) * 86400 & " seconds in the
       current month."
```

Suppose you are the one who maintains the application in which either segment of code could be found. If you needed to change the code so that instead of displaying the number of seconds in the month it displayed the number of minutes, which listing would you choose? You would probably choose the first implementation. Even though the second implementation is more efficient, the fact that the first approach is easier to maintain and understand makes it the natural choice.

In order to change Listing 2.2, you need to figure out the significance of the number 86,400 and what value you would need to substitute for it. In Listing 2.1, you could simply display the variable `intMinutes` instead of `intSeconds` and be finished! Do you see the trade-off? As a developer, particularly in a team environment, one of your goals is most likely to write code that others on the team can maintain. You, and perhaps your fellow teammates, will have to decide whether it's appropriate to sacrifice ease of maintenance for increased efficiency. Chapter 8, "The Brophy/Koets Optimization Methodology," shows you how to make this decision in a quantitative fashion.

Aside from general optimization techniques you automatically apply while you write code, you should avoid overhauling significant portions of your application until you have first determined the impact that the section of code under analysis has on overall performance. When you are convinced that the portion under study, if optimized, will improve the execution time of the application in a significant way, you should perform the optimization. In order to decrease the difficulty that might result in maintaining the code after you optimize it, you should be sure to document very carefully how you are modifying the section of code to increase performance.

As you weigh the relative merits of optimization at the cost of maintenance, consider the following questions:

- Will the application require maintenance?
- What changes do you anticipate being made to the application?
- What will be the frequency of future updates and releases of the application?
- Will the maintainers of the code be as familiar with the code as you are, or will they be totally unacquainted with it?
- How much of a performance improvement do you realize by optimizing the code?
- Are there any other effects on the user?

Optimization Versus Debugging Ease

Another trade-off that comes with optimization is the potential for increased difficulty in debugging the application you have optimized. This underscores the importance of simple optimization techniques and the necessity to avoid major performance overhauls until the code works properly and runs correctly. While writing code, the experienced VB programmer will apply fundamental optimization techniques as he/she develops the code. If done correctly, debugging should not pose a major problem. The difficulty in debugging comes in later when those major overhauls to improve performance are enacted on the code base, resulting in bugs that might be more difficult to determine and isolate.

Consider the code example in Listing 2.3. It takes text from various text boxes on a form and prepares a string to be sent to a message box.

Listing 2.3. String assembly (unoptimized).

```
Dim strLastName as String
Dim strFirstName as String
Dim strName as String
Dim strOutput as String
Dim intAge as Integer
Dim intNumKids as Integer

strLastName = txtLastName.Text
strFirstName = txtFirstName.Text
strName = strLastName & ", " & FirstName
intAge = Val(txtAge.Text)
intKidCount = Val(txtKids.Text)
strOutput = strName & "is " & intAge & " years old and has &
        intNumKids & " children."
MsgBox strOutput
```

Now consider an optimized version of the same coding task, shown in Listing 2.4.

Listing 2.4. String assembly (optimized).

```
MsgBox txtLastName & ", " & txtFirstName & " is " & txtAge &
➥" years old and has " & txtKids & " children."
```

As you can see, Listing 2.3 breaks every piece of the text to be displayed into separate variables. Listing 2.4 does not do so; it avoids the use of any variables, making it more efficient because the interpreter doesn't have to allocate memory for the variables and assign values to them.

Now assume that, for some reason, the output message is not correct. Suppose there is some kind of error in the construction of the string—not the kind of error that Visual Basic would detect, such as a syntax error, but a logical error in the code that produces an incorrect result.

Now suppose you have been assigned to debug the code. Which listing would you choose? By a simple examination of the code, you can see that Listing 2.3 is easier to debug. It allows for a clear examination of each temporary variable rather than forcing you to wade through one big line of code without the capability to examine any one part of the expression clearly through a variable.

In terms of performance, Listing 2.4 is more efficient, because it doesn't use any temporary variables, avoiding the necessity of allocating more memory for the task. It also has fewer statements for the interpreter to execute. In this case, you might decide that the code is so simple to understand that it is best to write it in the most optimal way possible and use the optimized listing. On the other hand, you might be concerned about maintaining the code later on and might want to consider the unoptimized listing. As a developer, you must make this decision.

As another example, consider an application in which the programmer utilizes a third-party custom control that provides calendar support. The programmer builds the application using the calendar custom control as a part of the application's foundation. When the program runs and is verified to work correctly, the programmer might decide that the custom control slows down the application too much. What should the programmer do?

The programmer might decide to do away with the custom control and instead manufacture his own calendar through the use of a simple image control and graphics methods such as `Line`. In doing so, the programmer would substitute the stable custom control with a potentially less stable, manual implementation. This solution might indeed make the application run faster, but it also might make the foundation less stable, introducing bugs into the application that are a direct or indirect result of all the programmer-designed code that has been introduced—code that has not been thoroughly tested and fully developed as with a custom control. Because a stable part of the foundation has been replaced with something less stable, time and effort will be required to make sure the programmer's calendar solution is just as stable as the custom control. Until the foundation is judged to be that stable, the developer incurs the cost of doing the debugging.

You should be able to see the trade-off between increased performance and increased difficulty in debugging. This same example can also be applied to the increased difficulty of maintaining the code, as performance has been improved at the cost of more code—code that must be maintained, and whose interface to the remainder of the code must be assimilated properly. You can see that various techniques to improve performance might or might not be worth the cost of maintenance and debugging. Often, the programmer must simply experiment with various techniques and arrive at the correct compromise. Although this book provides you with the expertise to do so, optimization is typically a judgment call on a case-by-case basis; and such judgment comes with experience.

When considering whether to optimize based on debugging ease, consider these questions:

- How much performance do you gain by making the code more efficient?
- How much more difficult will the code be to debug?
- Have you considered maintenance in addition to debugging, as the two can be closely related?
- Are there any other effects on the user?

Optimization Versus Code Reuse

Yet another issue to be concerned with in determining when to optimize is code reuse. Code reuse is more possible and practical with Visual Basic 4.0's ability to create classes using *class modules*. Class modules can be used to effectively exploit code reuse so that classes can be shared among various applications. Objects can also be exposed through OLE Automation servers to promote reuse.

When performance optimizations are applied to reusable code, the programmer must avoid obscuring the interface between the reusable code module and the outside world. Reusable code should have a very simple interface, providing a simple set of functions or properties and methods to the user. When using the class module, the programmer can create properties and methods and hide all of the variables internal to the module. In this way, the interface behaves very much like an OCX or a VBX. This is clearly the best way to create reusable components in Visual Basic. Developers can also create modules that consist of commonly used functions that are generic enough to be used in any application.

This is very much patterned after the object-oriented methodology common in languages such as C++. The more object-oriented the reusable code is, the easier it is for those trying to use it and apply it to their own applications. Reusable code must have a clean, well-defined user interface and avoid implied or assumed conditions that are not readily obvious to the user of the code. For example, a function that relied on the use of a global variable, rather than simply on variables that were passed into the function, would not have an obvious interface to the user.

When performance improvements are made to reusable code, this clean interface might break down. This is the condition the developer must avoid or make compromises on based on the benefits of the performance improvements realized. For instance, you might have a function that can be made to run much faster if you know that certain conditions never occur. Assume for the moment that if the reusable function does not need to check for the existence of those conditions, it can run faster. If the programmer assumes that these conditions will never exist, the code might indeed run faster, but might not work properly with the minority of applications in which the conditions do exist. Because those conditions were assumed not to occur, the programmer has effectively cut down on the scope of reuse of the code while improving the performance. Thus the trade-off comes clearly into view.

When you see potential conflicts between optimization and code reuse, ask yourself the following questions:

- Is the interface to the reusable component well defined before it is optimized?
- How does the interface get degraded, if at all, after it's optimized?
- Have you compromised error correction, validation, or any other component that is important when code must be reused? Are these acceptable compromises?
- Are there any effects that the user sees? If so, are they acceptable?

The example in Listing 2.5 demonstrates the principles of optimization versus debugging ease, optimization versus maintainability, and optimization versus code reuse. The example demonstrates how, by making an optimization in code, the code becomes more difficult to maintain, debug, and reuse.

Listing 2.5. Unoptimized code.

```
'In the form module...

Private Sub cmdOK_Click()

    Dim x As Single
    Dim y As Single
    Dim z As Single
    Dim ans As Single

    ' Set the parameters
    x = Val(txtX)
    y = Val(txtY)
    z = Val(txtZ)

    ' Call the calculation function
    ans = CalculateResult(ByVal x, ByVal y, ByVal z)

    ' Display the answer to the user
    lblResult = ans

End Sub

' In the code module...
Public Function CalculateResult(ByVal x As Single, ByVal y As Single,
➥ByVal z As Single) As Single

    CalculateResult = x ^ 3 + 2 / y - z

End Function
```

This listing consists of a function that requires three single-precision, floating-point numbers as input parameters and returns a single. The function is in a separate code module and is called as a result of the `Click` event of a form's OK command button.

Notice that the input parameters to the function are passed using the ByVal keyword. This means that copies of these variables are created and passed to the function. If those variables are modified inside the function, the original values are not changed—just the copies within the function. This ensures that the data being passed to the function is protected at the cost of making copies of the variables.

Note, however, that the copies of those variables are never modified by the function. Theoretically, therefore, it is not necessary to use the ByVal keyword (but it is safer). In this case, the programmer who wants to optimize the application decides to eliminate the ByVal keyword and use public (or *global*) variables rather than input parameters. The revised code is shown in Listing 2.6.

Listing 2.6. Optimized code.

```
' In the form module...
Private Sub cmdOK_Click()

    Dim ans As Single

    ' Set the parameters
    x = Val(txtX)
    y = Val(txtY)
    z = Val(txtZ)

    ' Call the calculation function
    ans = CalculateResult()

    ' Display the answer to the user
    lblResult = ans

End Sub


' In the code module...

Option Explicit

Public x As Single
Public y As Single
Public z As Single

Public Function CalculateResult() As Single

    CalculateResult = x ^ 3 + 2 / y - z

End Function
```

In this version of the code, notice that all the input parameters must be declared as public variables. The program will run faster because Visual Basic does not have to make copies of the variables before executing the function. Note, however, the trade-offs that the programmer has just made:

- *Maintainability.* Although the program might run faster, suppose a total stranger to the code had to modify the function so that, instead of modifying the set of public variables set inside the function, it needed to modify a host of other variables as well. In order to do this, the programmer would have to declare all the other variables as public before the function could modify them. This would be a painstaking effort and could cause many unpleasant side effects in the application. If the function were left in the form shown in Listing 2.5, however, the programmer could just go to where the function gets called and pass in different variables as appropriate. So in making the program more optimized, the programmer could potentially make life more difficult for himself or others down the road.
- *Debugging ease.* Furthermore, the optimized version of the code makes it more difficult to debug the application. Suppose that while the function is executing, one of the public variables gets changed by code elsewhere in the application. Because the variables are not private to the subroutine but are public to the entire application, the programmer cannot be certain the variables won't change during the execution of the function. This makes it very difficult to debug the function if the values are incorrect. If the code were left alone as in Listing 2.5, the data would not change and the return value of the function could be delivered with confidence.
- *Code reuse.* The third compromise the developer must make in optimizing the code is in the area of code reuse. If this function is in a module of common routines that others might want to use in their programs, they might not be aware of the existence of the public variables. Because they are not clearly specified as input parameters, the programmer who wants to reuse the function must create the public variables and know how they are modified. This makes reuse more difficult because the programmer who reuses the code must delve into the subroutine to figure out how to use it rather than simply use it without knowing the details of how it works. If the interface is clearly specified and all the variables are explicitly passed into and out of the function, reuse is much easier and more productive. Therefore, the optimizer must once again make a trade-off in the area of reusability.

Optimization Versus Optimization

Finally, consider the case where making an optimization on one part of the code reduces the benefits or effects of optimizations made on other parts of the code. At times, the programmer can make so many optimizations that eventually one optimization technique interferes with another. This is especially noticeable when you're optimizing large sections of code that frequently interact with each other. Consider once more the analogy of the house built on a shaky foundation. In an attempt to make one section of the foundation stronger, the builder might put more stress on other parts of the foundation. Even though those other parts of the foundation are just as strong, they might not be able to bear the added stress. As a result, the foundation as a whole might not be as strong as it was originally. The same thing can happen to an application when it's being optimized.

The only way to adequately determine whether to apply such optimizations is, first, to understand the effects of any changes made in an application in order to improve performance. Are there other sections of code where performance will decrease as a result of the changes you would like to make? Second, you should be sure to take measurements of the performance before and after the optimization is made to see how much it actually improves the application. This can usually not be determined up front, and if the optimization does not improve the speed of the application very much, it might not be worth implementing because it might degrade maintenance and debugging capabilities.

You might find that performance is worse because of your optimizations if the technique you thought would speed up the application actually does the reverse. It is also possible that the technique does speed up the application, but that other areas perform worse and overshadow the improvement you have just made. Because you might want to revert back to an earlier state, it is imperative that every optimization method employed be well documented and that the original state be saved. That way, the programmer can go back to the original state of the code if necessary.

Summary

This chapter covers some important issues to consider in determining when to optimize code. It emphasizes the need for the programmer to think about the most efficient and optimal way to write code before actually writing it. In doing so, the programmer avoids writing sloppy, inefficient code that might need to be heavily optimized later. You can save a lot of time later if you write code efficiently the first time through. This is especially important when using a language such as Visual Basic because there is no optimizing compiler that will handle a great deal of the optimization for you and compensate for some areas of inefficient source code.

You must take into account the cost of optimization when making the decision of when to optimize. The cost of optimization can be seen in many ways, each of which is discussed in this chapter. Some of the trade-offs include more difficult code maintenance, debugging, and code reuse. Furthermore, one optimization scheme can conflict with another, resulting in a lower overall performance.

Optimization sometimes takes code that is fairly easy to understand and makes it more complex or difficult to follow. This, in turn, can make the program more difficult to maintain, either for yourself or for someone totally new to the code. Although this can be minimized by careful documentation of the optimization stages, the trade-off does exist between making an application efficient and making its code less cryptic and easier to understand.

Likewise, optimization often makes code difficult to debug. This trade-off goes hand in hand with maintenance, as code that is more difficult to understand is typically more error prone and more difficult to debug. If the programmer is careful to test the application in light of the applied optimization technique, his chances of having fewer errors are greatly improved.

Yet another area of compromise is code reuse. The goal in Visual Basic, as in any other language, is often to write reusable components of software so that they can be applied in a wide variety of projects. Optimization strategies often include techniques that can break down the modeling goals for code reuse, particularly the well-defined interface between modules. Care must be taken to preserve this interface as much as possible, avoiding any implied conditions for the programmer reusing the code.

Often, performance can be increased by decreasing the reusability of the code. If you decide to do so, it is very important to thoroughly document any such modifications. If, for example, the performance of an application could be improved if a reusable component relied on some global variables within the application, it would be very important to document the reliance of the reusable component on those global variables. That way, when other applications go to use the component, this assumption will be clearly stated. Still, such a modification, while improving performance, decreases the ease of use and reusability of the code. You must make a decision about this trade-off.

Knowing when to optimize and knowing the cost of doing so is very important. It gives the programmer a clearer idea of when optimization is appropriate and when it might not be. Now that you have seen *when* it can be appropriate to optimize, you're ready for Chapter 3, where you'll learn *where* to optimize an application.

Obey the Signs

Wrong Way: Hold off on optimizing anything until you have finished writing your application.

Although it is true that the developer must beware not to invest too much time optimizing up front, it is essential that he/she write efficient code along the way. As you write code, think about optimization. Don't worry about optimizing big sections of code right away, because you need to see the big picture before you start divvying up optimization tasks. Follow the optimization guidelines presented in this book while writing your code, and your burden will be much lighter further along in the development cycle of your applications.

Wrong Way: You can never optimize your code enough.

You might get the impression that optimization is a task that never ends. Although developers should always look for ways to optimize applications, you must remember that sometimes performance can only be improved so much, at the cost of the factors mentioned in this chapter as well as issues such as cost, manpower, and length of time to release software.

Analogy: Law of Diminishing Returns

There is a law of diminishing returns on software performance, much like the law of diminishing satisfaction when buying popcorn in a theater. The graph in Figure 2.1 helps to illustrate this principle, using the example of eating popcorn.

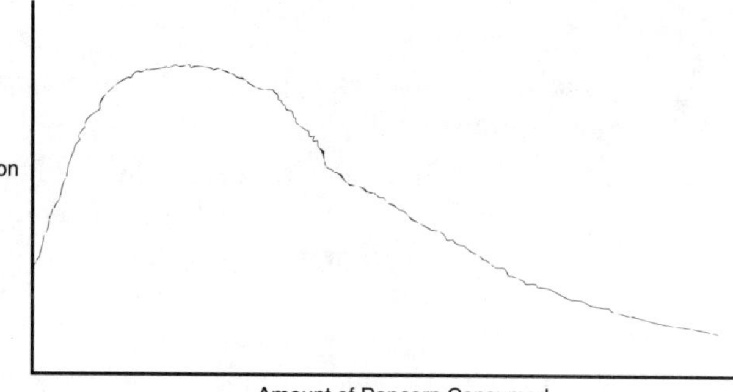

Figure 2.1.
The law of diminishing returns.

You derive a great deal of satisfaction with the first couple handfuls of popcorn, but as you consume more and more of it, your satisfaction level drops off. If you continue to eat too much, your satisfaction level will go back down and might even drop below that of when it first began.

The same principle applies to software optimization. If you prioritize optimizations in order of importance, the first several optimization stages will return large benefits. As you continue to optimize areas that have less and less of an impact, the amount of return you get for the resources invested will begin to diminish. Eventually, because of slipping software-release dates or problems with decreased maintainability and an increase in bugs due to optimization, the benefit from optimization might actually be worse than when you started. Therefore, the judicious application of software optimization cannot be overemphasized. If you can hit the top of the satisfaction curve, you'll be able to do a pretty good job assessing how far is too far.

Wrong Way: Because of the way Visual Basic works, the applications you develop with VB will always be poor in terms of performance.

Some Visual Basic critics constantly speak of how poor Visual Basic performance is. Often, this is true because of inefficient code, which can be true in any language and not just Visual Basic. Visual Basic applications do not have to be slow or require large amounts of memory and resources if the programmers writing the applications are careful to design and write their applications in an optimized, efficient manner.

It can be easy for the Visual Basic programmer to get lazy because of the easy programming environment and write code carelessly, adding custom controls left and right to minimize the amount of work he/she needs to do. For some applications, this is acceptable and desirable. But as a rule, in any application intended for a wide body of users where performance and resource use is important, both the programmer and the user will pay the price for an application not designed with performance in mind. Visual Basic applications are positioned to meet user expectations just as effectively as applications written in any other language when good programming techniques are applied.

Q&A

Q Why can't programmers wait until they have written an application before they consider optimizing it?

A Although some might claim it is best to disregard optimization until the end of the development cycle, this can lead to disaster. If a programmer totally disregards the performance of an application until it is completely written, he/she might be in for an enormous, if not impossible, amount of work. If, on the other hand, he/she is conscientious to optimize to some extent while writing the application, the optimization task at the end will be much simpler and hopefully much less significant.

Q Can optimization be over-emphasized during development?

A Absolutely. Although optimizing during development is very important, care must be taken not to over-invest effort. Simple optimization tasks—such as using integers instead of floating-point numbers and minimizing the number of controls on a form—are appropriate, but an over-emphasis on optimizing functional units of code might be counterproductive, especially if those components are completely changed or redesigned during the development process.

Q Does optimization come at a price?

A As with anything worthwhile in life, there is a price to pay. Optimization often comes at the cost of reduced program maintainability, reduced reusability of components within the application, and increased effort to debug an application during development. The developer must be wise enough to determine whether the optimization is worth the cost.

Workshop

During your next development cycle, ask yourself who will make the judgment on whether your application has acceptable performance. You as the developer? Beta testers? The end users?

Where to Optimize

Optimization can be a time-consuming process, so knowing where to optimize is very important. You can spend a great deal of time optimizing part of an application that is not critical to performance. Likewise, you can overlook areas of code that are very critical to performance. If you do not have a good understanding of which parts of an application are critical to performance and which parts are not, you will be shooting in the dark when optimizing and will be likely to optimize areas you think are critical with no quantitative justification for doing so. This chapter provides some insight into where optimization must take place in a program. When you're considering where to optimize, it is useful to break optimization into two main categories: *actual speed*, representing how fast your program performs calculated operations, database access, form loads and unloads, graphical painting, file I/O, and so on; and *perceived speed*, representing how fast your application appears to run to the user. These two categories provide an optimization framework that enables the programmer to break down performance tasks into two separate areas, concentrating on each one as appropriate. Each category represents a different way of optimizing the application. Both are covered in this chapter.

In order to determine where to optimize an application, you must first understand some fundamental concepts regarding the way Visual Basic and Microsoft Windows work together. These fundamentals should be understood before any specific optimization strategies are discussed. This chapter presents some of these fundamentals to give you a better understanding of how Visual Basic and Windows work together to execute a program you create.

The first fundamental you should understand is the *way* Visual Basic executes code. This will help you to write code more efficiently because you will better understand how the computer responds to each line of code you create. A second fundamental concept is how Visual Basic applications use the available memory that Windows provides. This is important because the performance of the application is often directly related to the memory it requires. If, for example, you create a form with 50 controls versus a form with only 10, the form with 50 controls will use more memory and is therefore likely to take more time to display. Both of these concepts are briefly discussed in this chapter.

In determining where to optimize, you should carefully examine the application's code and the way it uses memory. Having done so, you may find several areas suitable for optimization. Because time is almost always a scarce resource, the potential optimization areas should be prioritized so that areas most critical to overall performance are addressed first, followed by less critical areas in order of decreasing priority. Programmers can use profiling tools and simple analysis to determine which segments of code are executed most often. As a general rule, you should spend the greatest amount of time optimizing the code that has the largest impact on the user. Therefore, knowing which segments of code get executed the most is critical. These topics are discussed in greater detail in this chapter.

The Optimization Framework—Actual Speed

The actual speed of an application is the most important factor to consider when optimizing an application. Although the perceived speed can usually be improved (and should be), you should focus the majority of your optimization efforts on improving the *actual* speed of the application. The primary focus of this book is on doing just that.

With the power and speed of the microprocessors on the market today, the performance of applications being run under Microsoft Windows is usually not limited by processor speed.

Most applications are limited by other factors, such as the amount of memory, the size and speed of the hard disk, and the type and speed of the video card, network, and other input/output devices with which the application interfaces. The Windows environment itself imposes significant demands on memory and video performance. This demand, combined with the added demands of your application, makes performance a significant issue. When the objective is to improve the actual speed of an application, therefore, one must be just as concerned with the environment surrounding the application as with the speed of the code itself.

The best way to determine what slows down an application is to *profile* it, both by simple human observation as well as by taking specific timings of every critical operation, if necessary, to accurately determine the speed. The areas to optimize should be based on how often the user causes a given segment of code to execute, and what percentage of total execution time it takes to execute that segment. Either factor *by itself,* however, is not necessarily an indicator that optimization is required.

Consider this example: An application has a subroutine that is called every time the user presses a key. If the programmer performs a simple optimization that takes 100 milliseconds off the execution time of the procedure that handles keystrokes, the optimization might be noticeable to the user and make the application more responsive. That same programmer, on the other hand, could spend a great amount of time and effort optimizing a routine that repairs a corrupt database. If that routine is only called once a year by the typical user, however, the extensive optimization effort that had to be carried out might not be justified. The user doesn't exercise the operation on a regular basis, so this will not likely be a major source of trouble for the user.

In Windows applications, and Visual Basic applications in particular, most of the delay in an application results from loading resources into memory, drawing and painting windows and controls on those windows, accessing files over a network, working with database files, performing complex string manipulations or mathematical calculations, and carrying out processes such as object linking and embedding (OLE). Some of these processes, particularly areas such as string manipulation and mathematical calculations, are directly related to the way code is constructed. Performance can often be improved in these cases simply by modifying the code to make it more efficient. The other issues, however, often relate to memory and the amount of available system resources. Although these issues can also involve modifying code, here the scope is more broad. Improving performance, for example, might involve reducing the number of controls on a form, or perhaps cutting down on the amount of storage space the program requires to perform operations in code.

In order to better understand where to optimize and how one might go about doing so, it can be useful to think of optimizing an application as a two-phase process. One phase consists of spending time working through the code, thinking of ways to cut down the amount of code and the time it takes to execute it. The other phase consists of spending time optimizing to cut back on resources, memory consumption, and resource usage. Although the two are not necessarily distinct and both must be considered, dealing with them separately might help you understand how they relate.

The Optimization Framework—Perceived Speed

As discussed earlier, the perceived speed of an application is a measure of how fast the application *seems* to execute to the user. This is important because parts of an application that take large amounts of time to execute can appear to take less time when the program distracts or otherwise keeps the user occupied while those parts complete. Incorporating these distractions is a common practice in most commercial applications. A simple title dialog box, sometimes referred to as a *splash screen*, can present the user with something to observe while the application loads, as is the case with popular applications such as Microsoft Word and Microsoft Excel.

Typically, the developer should focus on improving the perceived speed only after the actual speed has been improved as much as possible. When the developer determines that the actual speed will be unacceptable in certain areas of the application, and performance improvements have been taken as far as practically possible, techniques should be used to increase the perceived speed of the application.

Most often, this consists of giving the user something to do while forms load, calculations take place, and complex algorithms complete. Various techniques can be used, including progress indicators, title windows, information dialog boxes, and animation. Many commercial applications now have setup programs that display useful information while the application goes through the installation procedure. This is one way of making the time for the application to set up seem shorter. Progress indicators give the user an idea of how far along an operation is; the user can examine the progress of an operation and feel at ease because he/she is more informed. Animation is also used for this purpose (for example, when you're copying files in Windows 95, pages fly through the air during the copy process).

As an example, consider the splash screen shown in Figure 3.1. This title box might appear while the user is waiting for the main form in an application to load.

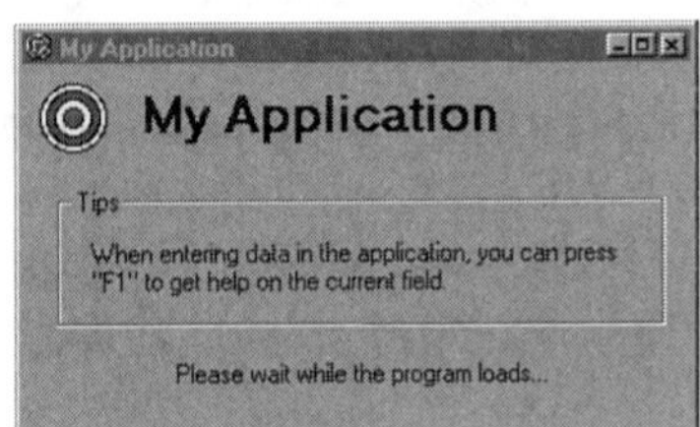

Figure 3.1.
A sample splash screen.

In order to implement this splash screen in code, the programmer might create the form and show it during the `Load` event of the application's main form. Consider the code in Listing 3.1 as a possible approach.

Listing 3.1. Splash screen implementation.

```
Public Sub Main()

    frmSplashScreen.Show                ' Show the splash screen
    Call Do_Initializations             ' Initialize the program
    Call Do_Database_Search             ' Search the database
    frmMain.Show                        ' Show the Main form
    Unload frmSplashScreen              ' Unload the splash screen when done

End Sub
```

The code in the startup subroutine of the application first shows the splash screen to the user. While the rest of the code in the subroutine is executed, the splash screen appears on the screen. At the very end of the subroutine when all of the initialization code is processed, the splash screen is unloaded from memory and disappears from the screen.

The use of splash screens and progress indicators should not be thought of as attempts at deceiving the user into thinking the program runs faster. Rather, these techniques should be thought of as opportunities to take advantage of user wait time to communicate information to them that improves the quality of the product. The ultimate goal of the application is to satisfy the needs of the user. If you, the programmer, do not have the time, resources, or capabilities required to improve the performance of an application further, these techniques are very helpful in cutting down negative reactions from the users. Almost every commercial application in existence has areas in which performance is slow, and the programmers of most of those applications applied these techniques to help overcome the users' annoyance.

How Visual Basic Executes Code

As already discussed, Visual Basic code is *interpreted*, not *compiled*. As a result, the VB programmer has more direct responsibility to ensure that the program gets the most done in the smallest number of computer clock cycles. With compiled languages such as C and C++, the programmer can be less concerned with performance because many of these compilers have the capability of optimizing code themselves to some extent.

Visual Basic code is saved in an intermediate format in an executable file rather than exactly as you type it in the design environment. Programmers refer to this intermediate format as *pseudo-code*, or *p-code*. Pseudo-code is not the actual code that gets executed by the computer. The Visual Basic language has an *interpreter* that must first translate the p-code code into a language the computer understands. The following analogy will make this clearer.

Analogy: Overhead of Communicating Through an Interpreter

Consider the following analogy. Suppose you speak English, but must convey instructions to someone who lives in France and does not speak English. You can communicate only through the telephone, and you can talk to only one person at any one time. To enable communication to take place, you have an interpreter who is between you and the person in France. Here is the progression of events:

1. You give the interpreter a call and tell him the first instruction in English. He interprets your instruction, word for word, into French.
2. He hangs up with you and then calls the person in France. When the Frenchman answers the phone, the interpreter reads him the instruction in his own language.
3. While the interpreter is talking to the Frenchman, you get the next instruction ready.
4. You then call the interpreter, reading him the next instruction. The interpreter once again interprets your instruction, word for word, from English into French.
5. Once again, he hangs up with you and calls the Frenchman, reading him the instruction in his own language.

This process would continue until all the instructions had been read, as Figure 3.2 illustrates.

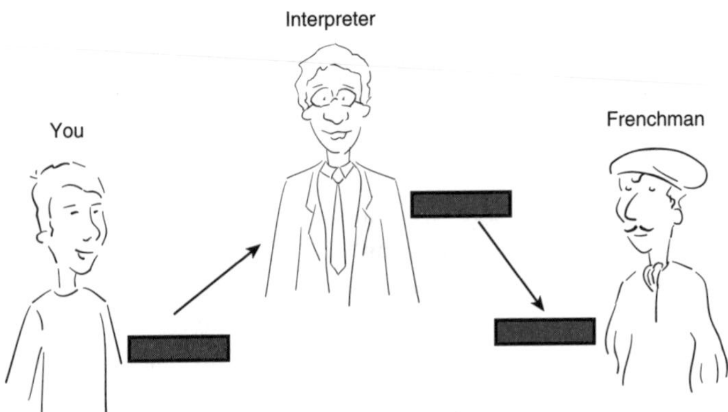

Figure 3.2.
Communicating through an interpreter.

This analogy helps describe what must happen in order for the computer to understand and execute instructions written in Visual Basic. Visual Basic communicates each line of code to the interpreter, which then translates the code into a series of instructions the computer understands.

Now let's consider what happens when you're using a compiled language.

Analogy: Efficiency of Compiling Instructions

Suppose there was another person in Japan who also wanted to convey instructions to the person in France. Instead of calling an interpreter for each and every command, waiting each time for the interpreter to notify the Frenchman, the Japanese caller does things differently. Here is the progression of events followed in this case:

1. He gives the *entire* list of instructions, written in Japanese, all at once over the phone to an individual we will call the "compiler."
2. The compiler takes the entire list of Japanese instructions and converts them to French. Rather than translating word for word, the compiler might change the instructions here and there to make them more readable to the Frenchman, and he might even reorganize them so that they can be read more efficiently and in less time. He translates the entire list before passing on his completed work.
3. After he hangs up with the person in Japan, the compiler calls the person in France, faxing the entire list of instructions at once to the Frenchman.

This analogy, illustrated in Figure 3.3, helps describe what must happen in order for the computer to understand and execute instructions written in a compiled language such as C. The compiler takes the source code, written in C, and compiles it into a lower-level language the computer can understand, optimizing code where appropriate. The compiler cannot compromise on the correctness of the instructions, but it can make the code run more efficiently.

Figure 3.3.
Communicating through a compiler.

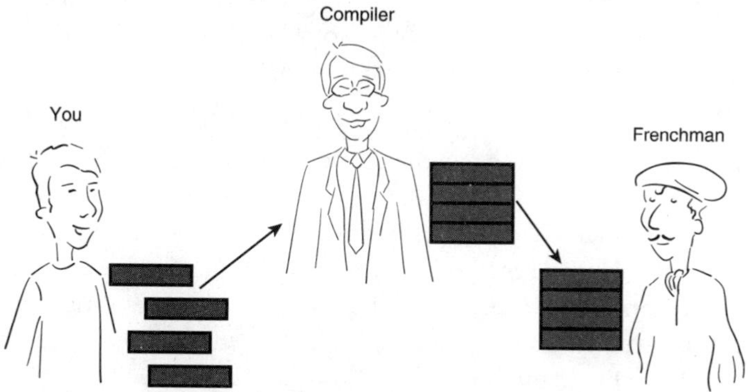

Can you see how the Frenchman could carry out the instructions more quickly working with the compiler rather than the interpreter? The interpreter must call the Frenchman every single time he sends an instruction, and then must hang up in order to call the American for another instruction. Not only that, but he must interpret each one

continues

individually. The overhead delay of calling the American, interpreting the command, calling the Frenchman, and giving him the command can take much more time than receiving the one call from the Japanese man, getting the entire list of commands, writing and reorganizing all of the commands into French, and faxing the instructions once to the Frenchman.

So how does this analogy apply in computer terms? When a Visual Basic application executes, the interpreter is called. One by one, the interpreter takes the Visual Basic statements, translates them into the computer's native language, and sends them along to the processor. The interpreter must interpret each Visual Basic statement in the application. All of the work the interpreter must do in order to execute each line of code adds overhead to the system. Extra clock cycles must be consumed to call the interpreter, and the interpreter needs time to get its work done. Using the analogy just presented, the overhead spoken of here is likened to dialing the interpreter's number and waiting for him to give every new instruction to the Frenchman.

A compiled language, on the other hand, is translated all at once and ahead of time. The compiler takes the entire list of instructions, translates them into the language the computer understands, and readies them in their entirety for the processor. Although the programmer must wait a while for the application to compile when building the application, the overhead while running the program is eliminated because the processor doesn't have to cycle through the interpreter every time an instruction is executed. Instead, the processor has the entire set of instructions ready to execute with no interpreter required.

This is why it is so important to minimize the amount of interpreting the interpreter must do while running a Visual Basic application. This does not necessarily mean, however, that you must write as little code as possible. With Visual Basic, certain code statements require more effort to interpret than others. The amount of interpretation depends on what the code statement is doing; generally, the more complex the command, the longer it will take to interpret it. Furthermore, the more information that command must manipulate, the more time it will take for the computer to process the information.

The most effective way to write efficient Visual Basic code is to keep the code simple and keep the amount of information the code must manipulate to a minimum. The information the code must manipulate is usually stored in *variables*, so the goal here is to keep the storage size of the variables and the frequency with which they are used to a minimum when writing code. Understanding how efficiently the interpreter handles various variable types and code statements is essential for optimizing. This topic is addressed in depth in Part III, "Optimization Strategies: Programming."

In Visual Basic, it is often better to break up routines into a greater number of simple variables such as integers and strings, each with a clear purpose, than to write fewer lines of code that are more complex, cryptic, and use more complex variables such as variants and floating-point numbers that require more memory and time to process. Later in the book, you will see the advantages of keeping code simple and keeping variables as simple and small as possible.

How Visual Basic Applications Use Memory

Now that you have a better understanding of how Visual Basic executes code and the ways you might go about making Visual Basic more efficient at doing so, it's time to explore how Visual Basic applications use memory. Writing efficient code is very important in Visual Basic, but programmers will often find that the most significant performance bottlenecks in their applications are due to inefficient memory usage.

One of the ways Visual Basic applications use memory is through their *resources.* Resources are entities used in Windows applications that are loaded into and consume memory. Resources include objects such as menus, command buttons, bitmaps, and list boxes. In Visual Basic, resources are consumed by the creation of *objects.* The two fundamental objects in Visual Basic are the *form* and the *control.* The Visual Basic programmer has discretion over how many forms are used in a project and how many controls are on each form. The programmer can also control how many forms are loaded into memory at any given time. Forms are often referred to as *containers* because all the controls placed on a form are the property of that form alone. If the form is removed from memory, all the controls on that form are removed as well.

As you might expect, a form with a large number of controls on it will most likely require more resources than a form with fewer controls. This depends, of course, on how many resources the controls require. A form with a lot of simple controls on it might not require as much memory as another form with a few complex controls.

When Visual Basic was first introduced, the programmer was forced to use the controls that Microsoft provided—controls such as text boxes, command buttons, timers, and list boxes. As Visual Basic became more popular, programmers began to bump into limitations imposed by these controls or find needs that the controls did not address. Programmers didn't want to have to write a lot of code to get around the limitations, and some limitations could not be overcome through Visual Basic. As a result, an array of third-party vendors emerged, each offering a wide variety of custom controls to Visual Basic programmers. Many of these controls are very powerful and take the capabilities of Visual Basic to new heights.

But no gain comes without a cost. Programmers soon realized that by using this wide variety of controls, the performance of their applications would drop off significantly unless the target machine had a sufficient amount of memory and processing power to satisfy the demands of the custom controls. Although a beneficial control might offer the programmer features he/she could not otherwise take advantage of, the amount of memory that the application demands increases with the complexity of the control.

The wise developer must continually make decisions on how many and what types of controls to use during development. One of the reasons Visual Basic has received poor press in terms of performance is that so many developers do not understand this trade-off. So they put as many custom controls on forms as they like, giving no regard whatsoever to the fact that their application, when finished, demands an extremely large amount of memory and runs very slowly.

Therefore, minimizing the amount of memory consumption of Visual Basic applications not only makes them run faster, because there is not as much data to load into memory when the application is started, but it is also more conducive to the stability of Windows and the capability to run other applications simultaneously. This book presents practical techniques to measure, pinpoint, and reduce the amount of memory and resources required by Visual Basic applications.

Prioritizing Areas of Optimization

The first step in trying to make an application run faster is to see how long it takes the application to perform its tasks. Specifically, the developer must profile the code, checking to see how much time certain commands, subroutines, functions, procedures, operations, algorithms, events, and methods take. When profiling the code, it is essential to exercise all possible cases and conditions so that a realistic profile can be taken and no areas are overlooked. You will learn more about profiling tools and strategies in subsequent chapters.

You must be careful never to blindly assume that the code that takes the longest cumulative time to execute must be inefficient. Just because a subroutine consumes a large amount of time in an application, for instance, does not necessarily mean it is inefficient. It simply means that the program spends most of its time in that subroutine, whether it gets carried out frequently and executes quickly, gets run infrequently but takes a long time, or is on some middle ground between the two extremes. In order to determine this, the developer must go deeper.

Depending on the profiling approach you use (whether it be user perception or using a Windows API timing call, the profiler that comes with Visual Basic, a commercial profiling tool, or some combination of these approaches), you should at least have some set of timings for every procedure in your application that is carried out frequently by the user or that has a key impact on them. The next step is to rank each of these procedures according to the amount of time they take to execute. Those are the procedures you must pay close attention to, as they are the ones in which modifications will have the most dramatic effect on the application's overall performance. Figure 3.4 shows a collection of procedures, each of which has been arranged in order of decreasing execution time.

In order to see how you might go about prioritizing a set of procedures in an application, consider the following example. Suppose you have an application that contains three subroutines. You wish to optimize the application, so you begin to examine the code. The three subroutines are shown in Listing 3.2.

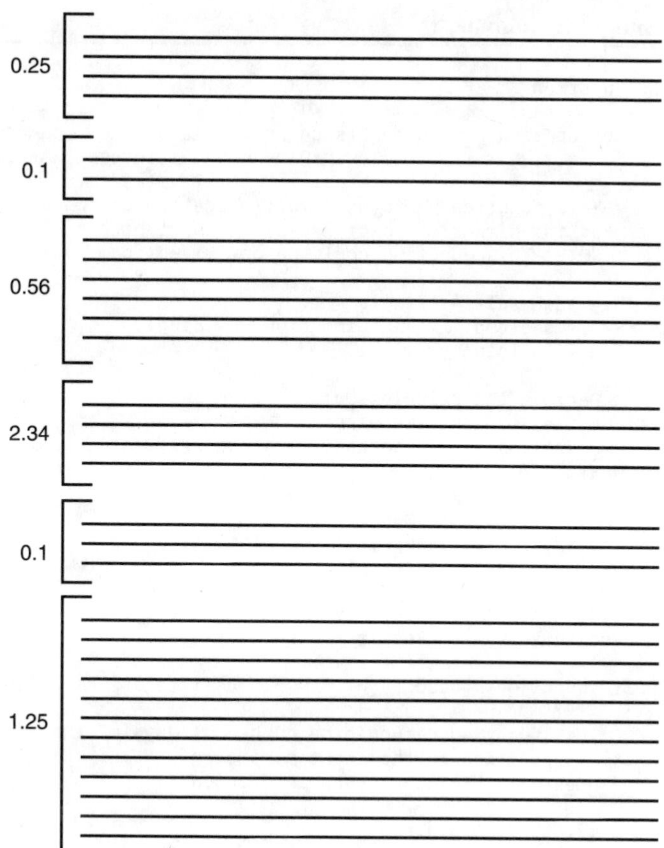

Figure 3.4.
Profiling.

Listing 3.2. Three subroutines to optimize.

```
Public Function Procedure_1(sngLeg1 As Single, sngLeg2 As Single) As Single

    ' This function calculates the hypotenuse of a right triangle
    ' using the Pythagorean theorem.
    ' NOTE: This function could be optimized in many ways.

    Dim sngHypotenuse As Single
    Dim sngTerm1 As Single
    Dim sngTerm2 As Single

    ' Calculate the hypotenuse of the right triangle
    sngTerm1 = sngLeg1 ^ 2
    sngTerm2 = sngLeg2 * sngLeg2
    sngHypotenuse = Sqr(sngTerm1 + sngTerm2)

    ' Return the result
    Procedure_1 = sngHypotenuse
```

continues

Listing 3.2. continued

```
End Function

Public Function Procedure_2(sngArray1() As Single, sngArray2() As Single,
                            intDimension As Integer) As Single

    ' This function performs a multiplication of two arrays
    ' of the dimension specified as an input parameter.
    ' NOTE: This function could be optimized in many ways.

    Dim sngResult As Single
    ReDim sngTemp(1 To intDimension) As Single
    Dim i As Integer

    ' Perform the calculation
    For i = 1 To intDimension
        sngTemp(i) = sngArray1(i) * sngArray2(i)
    Next

    For i = 1 To intDimension
        sngResult = sngResult + sngTemp(i)
    Next

    ' Return the result
    Procedure_2 = sngResult

Public Function Procedure_3(intMonth As Integer) As Integer

    ' This function returns the number of days of the month
    ' as specified in the input parameter.  NOTE: This function
    ' does not take leap years into account!

    Dim intDays As Integer

    Select Case intMonth
        Case 1, 3, 5, 7, 8, 10, 11, 12:
            intDays = 31
        Case 2:
            intDays = 28
        Case 4, 6, 9, 11:
            intDays = 30
        Case Else:
            intDays = 0
    End Select

    ' Return the result
    Procedure_3 = intDays

End Function
```

In order to help determine which procedure to optimize first, you must see which one takes the longest to execute. Suppose you obtain the results shown in Table 3.1 after timing these three subroutines.

Table 3.1. Timing results of the three subroutines.

Subroutine	*Elapsed Time (Normalized)*
`Procedure_1`	1.9
`Procedure_2`	53.4
`Procedure_3`	1.0

As you can see, the second subroutine requires the most time, followed by the first, and finally the third. You can see that you should focus on the second subroutine first, checking whether optimization can be carried out. Then you can look at the other two in order of decreasing execution time. It might turn out that no significant optimization can be carried out on the second subroutine, but the first subroutine can be optimized significantly. This approach, however, ensures that the code is examined in order of importance—namely, the amount of time it gets executed in the application.

After you have ordered the procedures in terms of percentage of total user impact—that is, execution time and frequency of use—you should take each procedure (starting with the one that gets the most execution time), break it down into components, and analyze each component separately, determining how long it takes each component to execute. The components might consist of each line of code or modular groups of code, as appropriate. In this way, you gain a good understanding of what each section is doing and how those sections individually contribute to the overall execution time.

Continue to break out sections of code within each procedure until the subsections are down to a low enough level to apply a clearly defined optimization technique (or set of techniques) to that subsection. Again, the developer should maintain a list of the sections and subsections that need to be optimized, prioritizing based on percentage of time executed in the application. After every procedure and module significant to the performance of the application has been fleshed out, you must make a judgment call on what procedures and sections to deal with first.

You must remember that some performance bottlenecks cannot be determined simply by looking at the code. For example, if your code contains a command that loads a form, as shown in the following code line, how long it will take to load it depends on the contents of the form:

```
frmMain.Show 1          ' Show the main form
```

If you have another line of code that moves to the first record in a database as shown in the next code line, the current position within the database, the size of the database, the type of database engine that is being used, and the location of the database (local versus on a network, for instance) are all important factors in determining performance:

```
mySnapshot.MoveFirst     ' Move to the first database record
```

Therefore, as each procedure is broken into sections, the programmer must be aware of the other elements that affect performance. The solution to increasing performance in a particular module might not lie in changing the code in that module, but perhaps in another module or on a form.

Summary

This chapter provides you with a general series of steps to determine where to optimize your code. It starts out by discussing the different ways of optimizing an application—namely, improving the actual speed of the application and the perceived speed of the application. It also discusses how Visual Basic code gets executed and what performance concerns you need to consider when writing Visual Basic code. The chapter also focuses on memory usage, explaining what resources are and how those resources consume memory. The importance of conserving memory is addressed.

The purpose of these sections is to give you a better understanding of what types of performance concerns you should focus on when programming in Visual Basic. When you have a better understanding of the typical culprits that degrade performance, you are more able to zero in on and isolate areas of the application that are suspect. You need to read between the lines when examining sections of code, and you must realize that performance problems can occur because of forces outside Visual Basic such as network speed, database access times, and loading delays due to memory demands.

Finally, the chapter introduces the concepts necessary to determine *where* to optimize, which essentially consist of taking a profile of every procedure in the application, logging cumulative time spent in each procedure, dividing the procedures with the highest user impact into smaller sections, and continuing to profile and subdivide those sections until easily defined optimization techniques can be applied. Specific optimization strategies and techniques are discussed in subsequent chapters.

Obey the Signs

Wrong Way: Improving the perceived speed of an application is necessary only if the application is written using Visual Basic.

Due to limited time and resources, optimization can typically be carried only so far. You reach a point at which you must be satisfied with the actual performance of an application. At that point, the perceived speed of an application can be improved through the use of splash screens, distracter dialogs, progress indicators, and the like. These techniques are not specific to Visual Basic; they are applied to many commercial applications in some way, shape, or form where performance lags. Performance factors are not limited to Visual Basic.

Beware of Falling Rocks: Do not spend time optimizing parts of the application that rarely get executed.

One common mistake a programmer makes is to optimize parts of the application that he/she *thinks* are performing poorly or that are commonly known to be so. The danger of blind optimization is that you might spend several hours optimizing a section of code that only gets executed 10 percent of the time. Making a segment of code 90 percent faster that only gets executed 10 percent of the time is not nearly as effective as making a similar code segment that gets executed 90 percent of the time 10 percent faster. That is why profiling your code is so important and goes hand in hand with optimization.

Wrong Way: You don't have to worry about optimization until the application is finished.

Although it is important to save broad performance optimizations until the application is complete and correct, don't forget to optimize your code as you write it, continually keeping in mind the tips and techniques presented in this book. The failure to write efficient code during development might cripple your application in the future, making it too time-consuming to optimize effectively and frustrating the user who will attempt to use it.

Q&A

Q Do you only need to worry about execution time in considering where to optimize in your application?

A Definitely not. The primary concern is that the user perceives that poor performance exists. Because the program is designed for the user, optimization must take place where the user feels the impact the most.

Q Because Visual Basic makes it easy to develop applications, isn't it logical that I don't need to worry about resources and memory and all those Windows concepts?

A Visual Basic certainly does make developing Windows applications easy, but with that ease comes the responsibility of being just as wise a programmer as when using any other language. Visual Basic is not a silver bullet—the programmer still must often concern himself with memory, resource usage, and optimization to satisfy the user's needs and expectations.

Q How do I prioritize my application for optimization?

A Get feedback from users and experiment with the application yourself. Concentrate on areas where users complain about poor performance. Isolate the code in which those areas are represented and prioritize each area based on execution time, frequency of execution, and the level of annoyance to the user. Subdivide each section of code further and further until you can apply a set of well-defined optimization techniques to an area of code. Continue this process in order of importance until all the important problem areas have been eradicated.

Workshop

Inspect a commercial application and, as a user, make a prioritized list of areas where you believe performance should be improved.

Optimization Concepts: Applying Optimization

The purpose of Part I is to introduce you to the world of performance tuning and optimization, providing you with a foundation of terms and concepts used throughout the remainder of the book. Part II expands on this foundation by discussing how to *apply* optimization.

Chapter 4, "Timing Methods," introduces you to the various ways you can measure the performance of your application. Different timing methods are introduced and are compared for 16-bit and 32-bit applications running in the 16-bit Windows operating systems—Windows 3.1 and Windows for Workgroups 3.11—and in the 32-bit Windows operating systems—Windows NT and Windows 95.

Chapter 5, "Collecting Performance Measurements," sheds light on how to collect and then interpret the timings taken using the timing methods discussed in Chapter 4. A set of results can be interpreted quantitatively by the use of statistical methods such as the average and standard deviation of a set of timing values. These values are then used to add significance to the set of timings. You will learn how to use these statistical methods and apply them to your own applications to make your measurements meaningful.

Chapter 6, "Factors That Affect Performance," discusses some of the factors that make consistent timings difficult to obtain. Measuring performance of programs running within an operating system such as Windows 95 can be made more complex by the very nature of multitasking operating systems. Many factors can affect the consistency of timings and thereby make conclusive results difficult to obtain. This chapter describes strategies for minimizing these factors, which helps make the resultant timings more consistent and reliable.

Chapter 7, "Supporting Utilities for Performance Analysis," presents a wide variety of utilities that will be of immense help to you in performance analysis. Most of the utilities are provided on the CD-ROM that accompanies this book, and many other commercial products are discussed, as well. These tools, together with a correct application of the concepts in this book, will make you very adept and skilled at evaluating applications to find performance bottlenecks, making performance optimizations, and measuring the impact of those optimizations.

Chapter 8, "The Brophy/Koets Optimization Methodology," presents a formal process you should follow for making changes in applications to improve performance. This methodology gives you an organized, logical, and fail-safe way of making performance changes. It is designed so that you can always fall back on the original software. If you make a change that does not give you the desired result, you can backtrack and try some other approach.

At the end of this section, you will have the methodologies, utilities, and methods needed to take, evaluate, and interpret timing results. The chapters in Part II are indispensable in applying optimization techniques to your applications.

Timing Methods

Chapter 1, "What Is Performance?" defines performance and outlines the challenges inherent in performance analysis. The purpose of this chapter is to present you with the timing tools available to measure performance. As a carpenter must become acquainted with the tools he uses, such as hammer and saw, so the performance analyst must be familiar with the variety of timers and profiling tools available to him through Windows and third-party vendors.

This chapter presents a simple case study that introduces you to the timing methods at your disposal for taking measurements. The case study is presented as a sample program on the CD-ROM that accompanies this book. It is not intended to show you any specific optimization technique, or for that matter even to represent any one optimization problem. Those samples will come in later chapters. Instead, this case study is intended to emphasize, at an introductory level, many of the key points that have been outlined so far:

- Selecting an appropriate level of performance assessment, including the method of timing it, is essential.
- Timings can differ from one trial to another.
- Optimization testing involves reaching a reasonable level of comfort (not necessarily conclusive findings applicable to all environments) when choosing between two methods.

A more theoretical explanation of these timing approaches is discussed later in the chapter after the presentation of the case study, followed by a brief explanation of additional, more advanced functions and tools available for performance assessment. This portion of the chapter discusses the following topics:

- Accuracy in timings
- Timing methods

This theoretical section begins with a discussion on the importance of taking accurate timings when assessing performance. Timing accuracy is the result of the *precision* and *resolution* of the timer being used. Both of these terms are defined and explained later in this chapter. If a timing method is not accurate enough, the results will be meaningless. At the same time, an extremely accurate timing might not be necessary, particularly if it requires a great deal of effort to implement. This chapter provides some insight into determining how much accuracy is suitable when taking timings in an application. The chapter then discusses the methods available to the Windows programmer for taking timings. The chapter introduces each method and discusses the relative merits of each.

Performance Case Study

Consider the simple case of a user—let's call him Bill—who wishes to compare the speed of two simple Visual Basic alternatives: assigning text to a text box versus clearing a list box and assigning text to it. Assume for the sake of this example that Bill has little prior background in performance analysis. Bill simply wants to know which operation is faster so he can choose between them in an application-specific situation when either method is feasible.

The two methods Bill is comparing are using the text box test code using the statement

```
txtInfo = "C++ is torture!"
```

versus using the list box test code:

```
lstInfo.Clear
lstInfo.AddItem "C++ is torture!"
```

Bill's application might have to carry out this assignment a few or a great many times after his form is loaded, depending on the user's actions. His initial performance testing, based on casual observation, seemed to show that there was no major performance problem in this area, so Bill doesn't want to devote an inordinate amount of time to this optimization. On the other hand, because this operation occurs frequently in his code, he wants to ensure that he is using the most efficient alternative.

Now it seems that Bill's task to assess these alternatives would be straightforward: He simply needs to decide which method is faster. However, because he lacks performance background, Bill will flounder in deciding how to collect relevant timings and which timer to use to gauge the performance. You will see his testing efforts evolve through the sequence of test techniques covered on the following pages as he refines his approach after each test. The application Bill assembles to carry out these tests is shown in Figure 4.1.

Figure 4.1.

Bill's test application.

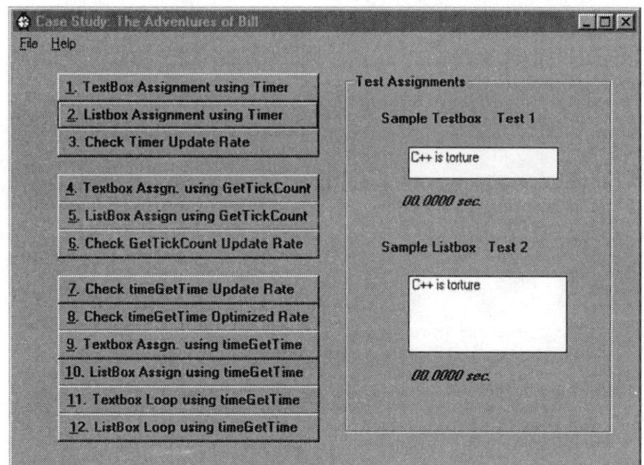

The steps that follow relate to Bill's use of his 32-bit test application under Windows 95. Of course it's to be expected that the time durations he obtains will be different on PCs with different speeds (Bill's results are from a 50MHz 486 with 8MB of RAM). The operating system can also make a significant difference in timings. If he were to carry out the same tests under Windows 3.1 or Windows NT, the timing results would differ significantly from the Windows 95 results shown in this chapter. Not only does performance differ between operating systems, but the supported resolution of standard timing methods can differ between operating systems. These issues are discussed in more detail later in the case study. For these initial steps, Bill proceeds with his 32-bit Windows 95 application.

SAMPLE APPLICATION NOTE

The corresponding sample application, Bill32.exe, as well as corresponding source code, is provided on the CD-ROM that comes with this book under the Chapter 4 directory. You will also notice two other related programs there: Bill16.exe and BillEn32.exe. Bill16.exe is a 16-bit version of the same program—all operations are the same except that this version does not carry out 32-bit API calls. BillEn32.exe is an enhanced version of Bill32.exe that exploits the resettable timer-resolution capabilities of Windows NT to provide more accurate timings, and is addressed later in the chapter.

Bill's first step is to write a simple test application with a block of code to measure text box assignment time and a block of code to measure list box assignment time. Bill's first-try code to measure the text box assignment time is shown in Listing 4.1. The code shown in this listing is associated with the command button labeled 1. TextBox Assignment using Timer in the test application.

Listing 4.1. Test 1: Using a timer to assess text box assignment performance.

```
Private Sub cmdTextBoxSet1_Click ()

    Dim sngStartTime As Single, sngEndTime As Single

    ' Indicate which test is to be carried out
    lblTextboxTest = "Test 1"

    ' Retrieve time in seconds since startup
    sngStartTime = Timer

    ' Make the assignment
    txtInfo = "C++ is torture"

    ' Retrieve the current time, and update total time for operation
    sngEndTime = Timer
    lblTextBoxTime = Format(sngEndTime - sngStartTime, "00.0000") & " sec."

End Sub
```

Notice that Bill makes use of the Visual Basic `Timer` function to retrieve the current time prior to the text box assignment operation. Then, after the assignment is carried out in the next statement, he again retrieves the time. The code then calculates the difference between the ending and starting times. This value, referred to as the *elapsed* time, is shown in a label control so that Bill can easily view the result.

Bill provides similar code to measure the speed of the list box assignment. This code is identical, except that the operation measured is the list box assignment and the total time for the operation is displayed on a different label on the screen. This sample is shown in Listing 4.2.

In the sample application this code is associated with the command button labeled 2. Listbox Assignment using Timer.

Listing 4.2. Test 2: Using a timer to assess list box assignment performance.

```
Private Sub cmdListBoxSet1_Click ()

    Dim sngStartTime As Single, sngEndTime As Single


    ' Indicate which test is to be carried out
    lblListBoxTest = "Test 2"


    ' Retrieve time in seconds since startup
    sngStartTime = Timer

    ' Make the assignment
    lstListBoxSet.Clear
    lstListBoxSet.AddItem "C++ is torture"

    ' Retrieve the current time, and update total time for operation
    sngEndTime = Timer
    lblListBoxTime = Format(sngEndTime - sngStartTime, "00.0000") & " sec."

End Sub
```

The user interface for this application is simple and clear, as you can see in Figure 4.1. It provides Bill with a button for each test and uses labels to display the results. Using a button for each test, rather than automatically launching the test from the `Form_Load` event, enables Bill to carry out the test repeatedly and easily to gather multiple timings. This shows good foresight in test-application design on Bill's part!

When Bill clicks on both the Visual Basic Timer text box and list box measurement command buttons, he is in for a surprise, as you can see from the results shown in Figure 4.1. On most PCs, his test program will show identical timings for both of the code techniques. And, on most PCs, the timing returned will be `0.0`! This timing is a confusing revelation to a first-time performance analyst such as Bill. His initial reaction is to wonder if an operation takes no time at all. If so, programs that use those operations should take no time at all either!

If only life were that easy.... Obviously, some of the CPU's time must be required to process the instruction, so to say the operation takes no time at all, as the value of `0` would indicate, cannot be accurate. Rather, the timing is `0` because of the stopwatch technology used to collect the timing data. The Visual Basic `Timer` function was used to record the instant in time right before the operation and the instant in time right after the operation.

Unfortunately, the `Timer` function does not have sufficient resolution to reflect minor variations in time. According to the documentation on the `Timer` function, which you can find in

the Visual Basic help file, it returns a time in seconds. The Visual Basic documentation does not elaborate on how often the timer behind the `Timer` function is updated. There is no indication if the timer will change every 0.1 second, every 0.5 second, or every 1 second. For example, if a program calls `Timer` at one moment in time and gets of value of `360.5`, and then calls it another 0.2 second later, you can't tell from the documentation if the timer will retrieve an updated value of `360.7`, or if the timer value updates less frequently and will still have the old value of `360.5`.

Bill's next alternative is to carry out a little experiment. He writes another type of test program to help him understand the `Timer` function, which yields some insights. (See Listing 4.3.) In the sample application this code is associated with the command button labeled 3. Check Timer Update Rate.

Listing 4.3. Test 3: Checking the update rate of `Timer`.

```
Private Sub cmdStart_Click()

    Dim intCounter As Integer    ' Count of unique timings returned
    Dim sngStarttime As Single   ' Starting time of test timings
    Dim sngCurtime As Single     ' Most current time of test timings
    Dim sngPrevtime As Single    ' Prior time retrieved during test timings


    ' Indicate which test is to be carried out
    lblListBoxTest = "Test 3"

    ' Clear listbox from any prior trials
    lstListBoxSet.Clear

    ' Save initial time that test began
    sngStarttime = Timer
    sngCurtime = Timer

    ' Intialize the number of unique timing events that have occurred
    intCounter = 0

    ' Hide the listbox that will be updated with timings, so
    '  that the process of updating it doesn't slow down the
    '  system from providing us with timings.
    lstListBoxSet.Visible = False
    Me.MousePointer = HOURGLASS

    ' Loop until 5 seconds have expired
    Do While (sngCurtime - sngStarttime) < 5
        ' Save old time for later comparison
        sngPrevtime = sngCurtime
        ' Get the new current time
        sngCurtime = Timer

        ' If the new time isn't same as old time, a new time value was provided
        If sngCurtime <> sngPrevtime Then
            ' Add it to the listbox and update the count
            lstListBoxSet.AddItem sngCurtime
```

```
            intCounter = intCounter + 1
        End If
    Loop

    ' Now show the listbox full of timings
    lstListBoxSet.Visible = True
    Me.MousePointer = DEFAULT

    ' Display the average number of unique time events that occurred
    ' over the 5 second period
    lblListBoxTime = "Avg. # Unique Times Retrieved Per Second:  " &
    ➥Format(intCounter / 5, "####.00")

End Sub
```

This program loops for 5 seconds, using a starting time and a current time retrieved in the loop to determine when 5 seconds have expired. During each loop, a new current time is retrieved from the `Timer` function. If this current time is a brand-new time, meaning it differs from the timing retrieved on the prior loop, the timer has updated since the last loop. When this occurs, the new timer value is placed in the list box for later viewing. In other words, this program will show how often the value returned by the timer updates over the 5 seconds it takes the program to loop.

The purpose of this test program was to help Bill understand how the timer works. However, he needed to be aware of timing issues even to write this program correctly and have it accurately record all the updated timer values. If the list box that is filled with updated timer values within the loop was not set to be initially invisible, the whole test would be flawed. Every time a new entry was added within the loop, the test code would incur the performance penalty of causing Windows to update the list box. This would slow down the loop. On some systems, it could even slow down the loop enough that the timer would update multiple times between loops, and the test program would miss catching all the timer updates.

As with many performance issues, a good way to picture this clearly is to consider an even slower performance case. For example, if the loop code included a network database retrieval statement that took 2 seconds to complete each time through the loop, the program would not be able to loop and collect timings any more frequently than once every 2 seconds. This would reveal nothing about how many unique timings the timer function can return during a second, because the loop would be cycling at a slower rate than the internal timer updates behind the `Timer` function.

Similarly, but of lesser performance significance, if the loop contained code to update and refresh a list box each time through and it takes Windows some time to carry out these tasks, by the time one loop completes, the `Timer` function's internal timer might have updated several times. The loop might not be fast enough to catch each unique value available from the `Timer` function over the course of a second.

Therefore, the program must not carry out any extra tasks within its own processing loops if it is to be fast enough to retrieve millisecond-level changes in times. For this reason, all unique timings collected during the loop are stored in a hidden list box (to suppress list box updates that take time and slow loop turnaround). Only after the loop has completed can the program show the list box without skewing the timing results.

As you can see, things are already starting to get a bit complicated! It might seem like a computer's speed ought to be fast enough that you shouldn't have to worry about a few lines of code slowing down the loop turnaround time and throwing off the timings you collect. Depending on the precision you need, that's usually not the case, however. The developer implementing performance-analysis programs must think carefully about such factors and overall objectives when structuring performance-assessment tests. A knowledge of how timers work and how code activities affect turnaround time is required even to implement a simple timer-analysis program such as this.

The results from this update test of Bill's are shown in Figure 4.2. When Bill observes the results of the Stopwatch Precision Check program, he finds that the Visual Basic `Timer` function is actually returning only around 18.2 unique timer values per second, as shown in the figure. Therefore, any operation that takes less than 1/18 second, such as the text box or list box updates carried out by Bill's original program, will be too quick to detect using the Visual Basic `Timer` function.

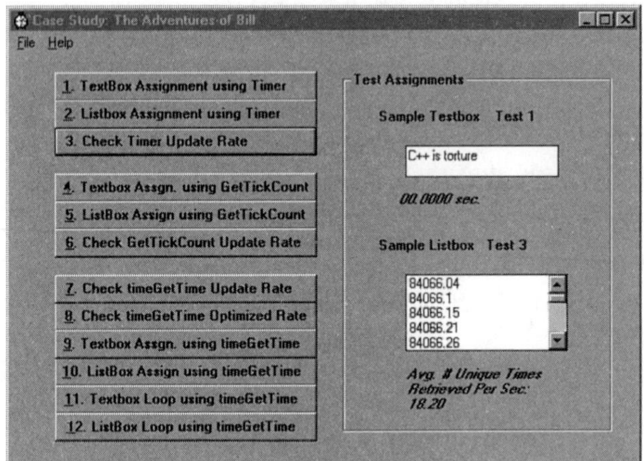

Figure 4.2.
Checking `Timer` function timer updates.

If you want to carry out more detective work, you can deduce that, because there are 1000 milliseconds in a second and you get approximately 18.2 unique timings in a second, the `Timer` function only updates about every 1000 / 18.2 milliseconds. In other words, the `Timer` function only provides updated values about every 55 milliseconds. Not coincidentally, there is a hardware timer interrupt that occurs about every 55 milliseconds. The timer updates behind the `Timer` function are based on this interrupt.

Therefore, the precision of the Visual Basic `Timer` function (as well as the Visual Basic `Timer` *control*) is constrained, at least on current PC platforms running Windows 3.1 and Windows 95, by the fact that the hardware interrupt provides updated values only about every 55 milliseconds. Because the assignment operations Bill was timing in his original program took less than 55 milliseconds, the `Timer` function returned the same time before the operation started and after it completed. Subtracting these values to produce an overall operation time would, of course, produce a timing of 0.

At this point, although Bill has an explanation for his original text box/list box update comparisons of 0, he is still no closer to having an answer to his original timing question of which method is faster. Because Bill is a fairly determined programmer, his next step is to browse the list of Windows API commands to see if he can go outside Visual Basic and use any of the timing commands built into Windows for more precise measurements.

A browse of the Windows API commands leads Bill to an interesting API function named `GetTickCount`. The documentation for this API call says it returns the number of *milliseconds* (great!) since Windows started running. At this point, Bill is flushed with the excitement of feeling like he's onto something, so he produces another test program.

This program is essentially the same as Bill's original assignment-comparison program except that it uses the `GetTickCount` function rather than the Visual Basic `Timer` function to retrieve timings. The code for the text box assignment test is shown in Listing 4.4. In the sample application, this code is associated with the command button labeled 4. Textbox Assign. using GetTickCount.

Listing 4.4. Test 4: Using `GetTickCount` to assess text box assignment performance.

```
' Windows API GetTickCount declaration added to Common.Bas declarations
Declare Function GetTickCount Lib "kernel32" () As Long


Private Sub cmdTextBoxSet2_Click ()

    Dim lngStartTime As Long, lngEndTime As Long


    ' Indicate which test is to be carried out
    lblTextboxTest = "Test 4"

    ' Retrieve time in milliseconds since startup
    lngStartTime = GetTickCount()

    ' Make the assignment
    txtInfo = "C++ is torture"

    ' Retrieve the current time, and update total time for operation
    lngEndTime = GetTickCount()
    lblTextBoxTime = Format((lngEndTime - lngStartTime) / 1000, "00.0000") &
    ➥ "     sec."

End Sub
```

Once again, Bill also provides similar code to measure the speed of the list box assignment. The code is identical except that the operation measured is the list box assignment, and the total time for the operation is displayed on a different label on the screen. (See Listing 4.5.) In the sample application, this code is associated with the command button labeled 5. ListBox Assign using GetTickCount.

Listing 4.5. Test 5: Using `GetTickCount` to assess list box assignment performance.

```
Private Sub cmdListBoxSet2_Click ()

Dim lngStartTime As Long, lngEndTime As Long

' Indicate which test is to be carried out
lblListBoxTest = "Test 5"

' Retrieve time in milliseconds since startup
lngStartTime = GetTickCount()

' Make the assignment
lstListBoxSet.Clear
lstListBoxSet.AddItem "C++ is torture"

' Retrieve the current time, and update total time for operation
lngEndTime = GetTickCount()
lblListBoxTime = Format((lngEndTime - lngStartTime) / 1000, "00.0000") & " sec."

End Sub
```

When Bill runs these tests, the results are once again timings of 0, as shown in Figure 4.3, and he is no closer to having a meaningful comparison than he was before!

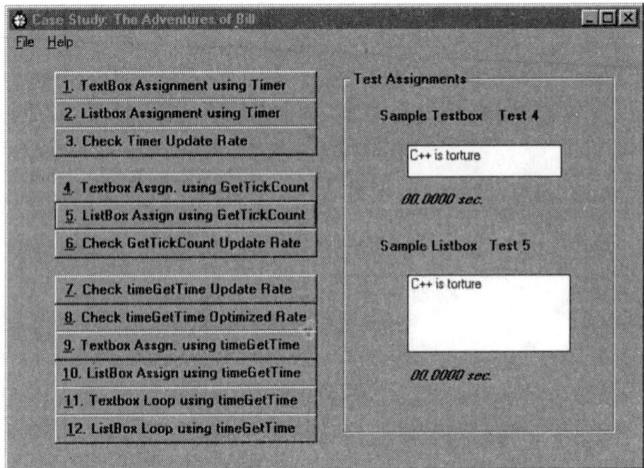

Figure 4.3.
Assignment timings from `GetTickCount`.

The underlying reason for the additional timings of 0 with this timer approach is the same. The documentation for the `GetTickCount` API indicates that this function call will provide the number of milliseconds since Windows startup; but it doesn't promise that the timer behind this function will update every millisecond. In other words, because the timer is not updating as often as once every millisecond, even if Bill's program calls this API function at 5 minutes, 15 seconds, and 3 milliseconds past system startup, and then again at 5 minutes, 15 seconds, and 10 milliseconds past system startup, the function could return exactly the same value! (Once again, Bill learns the lesson to never assume anything from documentation....)

To verify this theory, Bill puts together a test program similar to his first timer accuracy test program. His purpose is to observe how frequently per second updated timer values are really generated by `GetTickCount`. His program is essentially the same as the previous program he used to check `Timer` updates, with the only difference being that his new program utilizes `GetTickCount` as the timer function. (See Listing 4.6.) In the sample application this code is associated with the command button labeled 6. Check GetTickCount Update Rate.

Listing 4.6. Test 6: Checking the update rate of `GetTickCount`.

```
' Windows API GetTickCount declaration added to Common.Bas declarations
Declare Function GetTickCount Lib "kernel32" () As Long


Private Sub cmdStartGetTick_Click()

    Dim intCounter As Integer    ' Count of unique timings returned
    Dim lngStarttime As Long     ' Starting time of test timings
    Dim lngCurtime As Long      ' Most current time of test timings
    Dim lngPrevtime As Long      ' Prior time retrieved during test timings

    ' Indicate which test is to be carried out
    lblListBoxTest = "Test 6"

    ' Clear listbox from any prior trials
    lstListBoxSet.Clear

    ' Save initial time that test began
    lngStarttime = GetTickCount()
    lngCurtime = GetTickCount()

    ' Intialize the number of unique timing events that have occurred
    intCounter = 0

    ' Hide the listbox that will be updated with timings, so
    '  that the process of updating it doesn't slow down the
    '  system from providing us with timings.
    lstListBoxSet.Visible = False
    Me.MousePointer = HOURGLASS

    ' Loop until 5000 milliseconds have expired
    Do While (lngCurtime - lngStarttime) < 5000
```

continues

Listing 4.6. continued

```
        ' Save old time for later comparison
        lngPrevtime = lngCurtime
        ' Get the new current time
        lngCurtime = GetTickCount()

        ' If the new time isn't same as old time, a new time value was provided
        If lngCurtime <> lngPrevtime Then
            ' Add it to the listbox and update the count
            lstListBoxSet.AddItem Str(lngCurtime)
            intCounter = intCounter + 1
        End If
    Loop

    ' Now show the listbox full of timings
    lstListBoxSet.Visible = True
    Me.MousePointer = DEFAULT

    ' Display the average unique time events that occurred over
    ' the 5 second period
    lblListBoxTime = "Avg number of unique timings returned per second was " &
    ➥ Format(intCounter / 5, "####.00")

End Sub
```

The interface for this program and the results from a trial run are shown in Figure 4.4. As the results show, you can now reach similar conclusions about `GetTickCount` as you did for the `Timer` function—time values are not updated as frequently as every millisecond. Bill is still left at square one, with no way to derive the level of precision he needs to compare his operations.

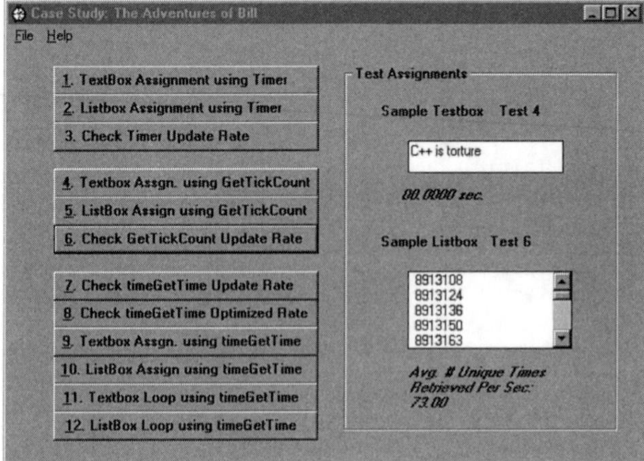

Figure 4.4.
Checking `GetTickCount` *timer updates.*

Because Bill is the stubborn sort, he doesn't throw in the towel, but digs deeper into the Windows API (or perhaps goes out and purchases *Visual Basic 4 Performance Tuning and Optimization*). Eventually he uncovers yet another function that is documented with the Windows 32-bit API. To Bill's surprise, however, it is grouped in a separate DLL named winmm.dll.

The winmm.dll is a dynamic link library (DLL) included with Windows 95 for multimedia support. Among the functions available through this DLL is one named `timeGetTime`. By now Bill regards everything with suspicion, and his first thought is that this function might be no more accurate than Visual Basic's `Timer` or the Windows API `GetTickCount`. But then he reads the encouraging words in the `timeGetTime` documentation that indicate that this timer has a default resolution of 1 millisecond under Windows 95 and a default resolution of 5 milliseconds under Windows NT that can be reset to a longer or shorter duration.

Finally it looks is if Bill is on to something! To be sure, this time he verifies the update frequency of the `timeGetTime` function before trying to get timings on the particular text box and list box assignments. He once again returns to his program that loops for 5 seconds and records the number of timer updates. He modifies the program as shown in Listing 4.7. It is essentially the same program as before, but it now uses the `timeGetTime` function to retrieve timings. In the sample application, this code is associated with the command button labeled 7. Check timeGetTime Update Rate.

Listing 4.7. Test 7: Checking the update rate of `timeGetTime`.

```
' timeGetTime declaration added to Common.Bas declarations.
' timeGetTime generally has  1 millisecond resolution on Win95
' and 5 millisecond resolution or longer on Windows  NT.

    Declare Function timeGetTime Lib "winmm" () As Long


Private Sub cmdStartTimeGetTime_Click()

   Dim intCounter As Integer    ' Count of unique timings returned
   Dim lngStarttime As Long     ' Starting time of test timings
   Dim lngCurtime As Long      ' Most current time of test timings
   Dim lngPrevtime As Long      ' Prior time retrieved during test timings

   ' Indicate which test is to be carried out
   lblListBoxTest = "Test 7"

   ' Clear listbox from any prior trials
   lstListBoxSet.Clear

   ' Save initial time that test began
   ' Retrieve time in milliseconds since startup into lngStartTime
   lngStarttime = timeGetTime()
   lngCurtime = timeGetTime()

   ' Intialize the number of unique timing events that have occurred
   intCounter = 0
```

continues

Listing 4.7. continued

```
    ' Hide the listbox that will be updated with timings, so
    ' that the process of updating it doesn't slow down the
    ' system from providing us with timings.
    lstListBoxSet.Visible = False
    Me.MousePointer = HOURGLASS

    ' Loop until 5000 milliseconds have expired
    Do While (lngCurtime - lngStarttime) < 5000
        ' Save old time for later comparison
        lngPrevtime = lngCurtime
        ' Get the new current time
        lngCurtime = timeGetTime

        ' If the new time isn't same as old time, a new time value was provided
        If lngCurtime <> lngPrevtime Then
            ' Add it to the listbox and update the count
            lstListBoxSet.AddItem Str(lngCurtime)
            intCounter = intCounter + 1
        End If
    Loop

    ' Now show the listbox full of timings
    lstListBoxSet.Visible = True
    Me.MousePointer = DEFAULT

    ' Display the average unique time events that occurred over
    ' the 5 second period.
    lblListBoxTime = "Avg. # Unique Times Retrieved Per Sec.:" &
    ➥Format(intCounter / 5, "####.00")

End Sub
```

See Figure 4.5 for the results from a trial run of this test. The results show a marked difference from the previous timer-function techniques attempted.

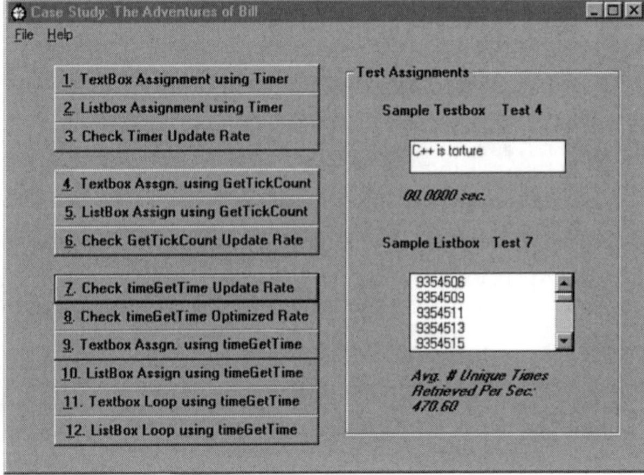

Figure 4.5.
Test 7: Checking `timeGetTime` timer updates.

Bill's reaction on reading these results is likely to be one of excitement—"over 400 unique timings captured in 1 second...whoooo-dooggiiie!"—but followed, after the warm glow of the moment fades, by puzzlement. The `timeGetTime` function has certainly proven to be more accurate, but now there are even more mysteries to consider. If `timeGetTime` is documented as being accurate to the millisecond under Windows 95, and there are 1000 milliseconds in a second, `timeGetTime` should return 1000 updated timings per second.

At this point, Bill's first instinct is to follow the trend of all too many in the computer industry and blame the problem on that all-encompassing scapegoat for every situation: flaky hardware! ("Well boss, I think we have a flaky motherboard with intermittent timing glitches...I told you that you should have gotten the top-of-the-line Pentium for me instead of that generic 486.")

After he reflects on his boss' likely reaction, however, he decides that further research is warranted. It turns out that such scapegoating was indeed unfounded. The `timeGetTime` function does indeed promise to deliver accuracy to the millisecond, *but it can only provide a unique value for each passing millisecond if it is called every millisecond.*

As you have seen before, if code is written in such a way that it calls `timeGetTime` only 5 times per second, it will only return 5 unique values per second. Likewise, if code is written in such a way that it only calls `timeGetTime` 852 times a second, the largest number of timings that `timeGetTime` could be expected to return is 852.

Thus, the bottleneck in retrieving unique, accurate-to-the-millisecond timings here is the code, not the hardware or the `timeGetTime` function! The code in Bill's test program doesn't loop fast enough (on this PC) to call `timeGetTime` as frequently as every millisecond.

This implies that speeding up the loop might help his program come closer to proving to-the-millisecond accuracy. Bill's original program takes each updated timing and tucks it into an invisible list box so that all the unique values can be inspected after the looping completes and the list box is made visible. However, even tucking each timing into the invisible list box takes some processing time itself for the CPU to handle, along with all the other code that supports the loop each time through.

Bill's mission now is to prove to himself that the `timeGetTime` function really does provide updated values every millisecond. His next step is to simply remove the piece of code that adds a timing to the invisible list box so that each loop can cycle through faster. This revised code is shown in Listing 4.8. The single line that was commented out to remove it from the execution path is indicated in bold. In the sample application, this code is associated with the command button labeled 8. Check timeGetTime Optimized Rate.

Listing 4.8. Test 8: Checking the update rate of `timeGetTime` with an enhanced loop.

```
' timeGetTime declaration added to Common.Bas declarations
' timeGetTime generally has 1 millisecond resolution on Win95
' and 5 milliseconds or longer on Windows NT.
```

continues

Listing 4.8. continued

```
    Declare Function timeGetTime Lib "winmm" () As Long

Private Sub cmdStartTimeGetTime2_Click()

    Dim intCounter As Integer    ' Count of unique timings returned
    Dim lngStarttime As Long     ' Starting time of test timings
    Dim lngCurtime As Long      ' Most current time of test timings
    Dim lngPrevtime As Long      ' Prior time retrieved during test timings

    ' Indicate which test is to be carried out
    lblListBoxTest = "Test 8"

    ' Clear listbox from any prior trials
    lstListBoxSet.Clear

    ' Save initial time that test began
    ' Retrieve time in milliseconds since startup into lngStartTime
    lngStarttime = timeGetTime()
    lngCurtime = timeGetTime()

    ' Intialize the number of unique timing events that have occurred
    intCounter = 0

    ' Hide the listbox that will be updated with timings, so
    '  that the process of updating it doesn't slow down the
    '  system from providing us with timings.
    lstListBoxSet.Visible = False
    Me.MousePointer = HOURGLASS

    ' Loop until 5000 milliseconds have expired
    Do While (lngCurtime - lngStarttime) < 5000
        ' Save old time for later comparison
        lngPrevtime = lngCurtime
        ' Get the new current time
        lngCurtime = timeGetTime

        ' If the new time isn't same as old time, a new time value was provided
        If lngCurtime <> lngPrevtime Then
            ' Add it to the listbox and update the count
            ' REM - NOW SKIPPED TO SPEED UP LOOP   lstTimes.AddItem Str(lngCurtime)

            intCounter = intCounter + 1
        End If
    Loop

    ' Now show the listbox full of timings
    lstListBoxSet.Visible = True
    Me.MousePointer = DEFAULT

    ' Display the average unique time events that occurred over
    ' the 5 second  period.
    lblListBoxTime = "Avg. # Unique Times Retrieved Per Sec.:" &
    ➥Format(intCounter / 5, "####.00")

End Sub
```

The results from a trial run of this modified program are shown in Figure 4.6. As you can see, these results are much closer to what Bill had expected.

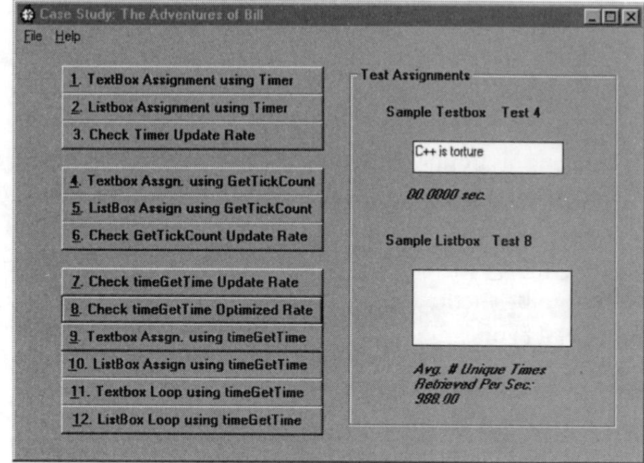

Figure 4.6.
Checking `timeGetTime` *timer updates with an enhanced loop.*

This time, the program using `timeGetTime` collected approximately 988 unique timings per second when running under Windows 95. This is still not perfect, but it's much closer to the anticipated accuracy of a timer update every millisecond. The fact that 988 rather than 1000 timings per second were retrieved can again be explained by considering that the overhead of the test code and other activity going on in the system might still cause the `timeGetTime` function to not be carried out as frequently as once every millisecond, and timer updates might occasionally be missed. As you'll see later in this chapter, the results of this timing will most likely be different under Windows NT because the resolution of this timer differs depending on the operating system used.

There are, of course, many other ways this accuracy can be programmatically verified to a further level. The particular method shown in this chapter was selected to illustrate key concepts. The remaining degrees of accuracy in question are now small enough that chasing them down and verifying them further doesn't necessarily provide any performance-analysis benefits for Bill.

This brings us back to the familiar refrain of performance assessment—it is important not to lose sight of the forest for the trees. The original question that motivates the performance research must always be kept clearly in sight. The amount of energy expended on performance-analysis research should be dictated by what it takes to achieve a reasonable answer.

There are so many factors that affect performance that sometimes it can take considerable effort to produce *definitive proof* that a research finding holds true across the board, even after you have reached an intuitive state of comfort with the findings. It is at this point that a consideration of your application's needs, your required level of assurance, and the law of diminishing returns should dictate when you declare your findings conclusive enough.

In Bill's case, his original question was the length of his assignment operations. To get this answer he needed a timer that would work at close to the millisecond level. It can be assumed that when Bill sees that he is getting 988 timings per second it is close enough to provide him with the assurance that he has found a timer with millisecond accuracy.

Now that Bill has finally convinced himself that he has a timer that can give him a more meaningful execution time than 0 seconds for his functions, he can return to his original mission. He once again modifies his original program to compare the two assignment methods, this time retrieving his timings with the `timeGetTime` function for the textbox assignment. (See Listing 4.9.) Similar modifications are carried out to the code that measures the time for the list box assignment. In the sample application, this code is associated with the command button labeled 9. Textbox Assgn. using timeGetTime. The code to carry out the list box timing using the same timing method is associated with the command button labeled 10. ListBox Assign using timeGetTime.

Listing 4.9. Using `timeGetTime` to assess text box assignment performance.

```
' timeGetTime  declaration added to Common.Bas declarations
' timeGetTime has generally 1 millisecond resolution on Win95, 5 milliseconds or
above NT.
    Declare Function timeGetTime Lib "winmm" () As Long

Sub cmdTextBoxSet3_Click ()

    Dim lngStartTime as long
    Dim lngEndTime as long

    ' Indicate which test is to be carried out
    lblTextboxTest = "Test 9"

    ' Retrieve time in milliseconds since startup into lngStartTime
    lngStartTime = timeGetTime()

    ' Make the assignment
    txtInfo = "C++ is torture"

    ' Retrieve the current time in milliseconds since startup into
    lngEndTime = timeGetTime()

   ' Update the total time the operation took
    lblTextBoxTime = Format((lngEndTime - lngStartTime ) / 1000, "00.0000") &
   ➥ " sec."

End Sub
```

The interface for the modified tests that time the two alternatives being compared is shown in Figure 4.7, along with results from a trial run.

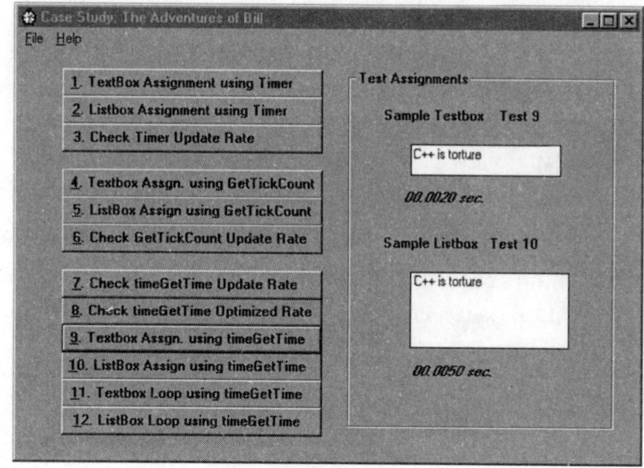

Figure 4.7.
Assignment timings from `timeGetTime`.

Now Bill finally has his answer about which technique is faster...er,...sort of...maybe. Unfortunately, this last disclaimer often accompanies initial performance findings. What is the reason for the uncertainty here? Well, if the text box test is run repeatedly on the specific PC used for the test, it gives different answers during the different trials! One test series yielded the following results, listed in units of seconds:

```
.007, .001, .002, .002, .002, .002, .001, .002, .003, .001, .002...
```

Then Bill turned his attention to his list box test, where the results were just as puzzling. Again, the individual times varied. One series of tests produced the following times, shown in units of seconds:

```
.003, .003, .003, .004, .005, .003, .002, .005, .005, .004, .003...
```

Now Bill is getting fairly accurate timings, but the timings vary from one trial to another. This is typical of a Windows system, which has a multitude of variables that affect performance. Caching, swap file activity, other programs running when the test application is running, video and other drivers, behavior of the operating system such as message processing and memory management, and even hardware factors can all influence the timing of a Windows program. This is true of both the cooperative multiprocessing Windows 3.1 and the scheduling-based, preemptive multiprocessing Windows 95 and Windows NT. It is to be expected that the duration of activity of the same Windows program might vary slightly from one moment to another, even under fairly controlled circumstances.

The good news is that the task facing Bill and other programmers concerned with performance is not hopeless. Coming up with a precise measurement could mean one or all of the following:

- Choosing a longer-duration benchmark where the activity measured is on the order of seconds rather than milliseconds. For example, time a loop of 1000 list box assignments instead of just 1. This doesn't eliminate system variance, but the effects of system variance on the overall test will be of less significance in a longer test. An occasional skew of 5 milliseconds for disk caching on a 50-millisecond test is very significant, but a skew of 5 milliseconds on a 5000-millisecond test is of less impact.
- Fine-tuning a benchmark even more (restructuring the benchmark code).
- Expending more energy observing what is going on elsewhere in the system (watching system messages, ensuring that other applications are not running, verifying resources, and so on).
- Coming up with a larger quantity of timings that will be more statistically significant for a given system.

For example, Bill just wants a general feel for whether the simple Text property assignment to the text box or the list box `Clear` and `Additem` methods will be quicker. The most ideal timing approach would be to simply count the number of CPU clock cycles required for each approach. Unfortunately, not only does he not have access to this information, but even if he did have it, the measured cycles would have to include Windows code as well as the specific technique measured, and also could potentially vary based on many system factors.

However, Bill does have statistics from a fairly accurate millisecond timer, and he has collected these results from several runs to get a feel for the average response time. The statistics he's already gathered indicate that the average time of assignment is less for the text box, especially after the first assignment has taken place. Bill's test is not the most controlled, or the most statistically precise, but it does provide him with the answer he needs to make his optimization decision and improve the application he will provide to his end user.

To get a larger sample size, one technique is to simply obtain an elapsed time for carrying out the assignment 1000 times instead of just once. The modified code to carry out this task for the text box is shown in Listing 4.10. The list box code is modified in a similar fashion to likewise loop and carry out 1000 assignments. The code for the text box loop test is associated with the button labeled 11. Textbox Loop using timeGetTime in the sample application. The code for the list box loop test is associated with the button labeled 12. ListBox Loop using timeGetTime.

Listing 4.10. Test 11: Using `timerGetTime` to assess text box assignment performance over 1000 assignments.

```
' timeGetTime declaration added to Common.Bas declarations
' timeGetTime generally has 1 millisecond resolution on Win95
' and 5 milliseconds or longer on Windows  NT.
    Declare Function timeGetTime Lib "winmm" () As Long

Private Sub cmdTextBoxSet4_Click()
```

```
    Dim lngStarttime As Long
    Dim lngEndTime As Long
    Dim I as Integer

    ' Indicate which test is to be carried out
    lblTextboxTest = "Test 11"

    ' Retrieve time in milliseconds since startup
    lngStarttime = timeGetTime()

    ' Make the assignment
    For i% = 1 To 1000
        txtInfo = "C++ is torture"
    Next i%

    ' Retrieve the current time in milliseconds since startup
    lngEndTime = timeGetTime()

    ' Update the total time the operation took
    lblTextBoxTime = Format((lngEndTime - lngStarttime) / 1000, "00.0000") &
    ➥" sec."

End Sub
```

The test carries out essentially the same activity as the earlier test except that now these assignments are carried out 1000 times, and total time for the 1000 assignments is derived by capturing a timing before and after the loop. The results for this enhanced test of 1000 assignments are shown in Figure 4.8.

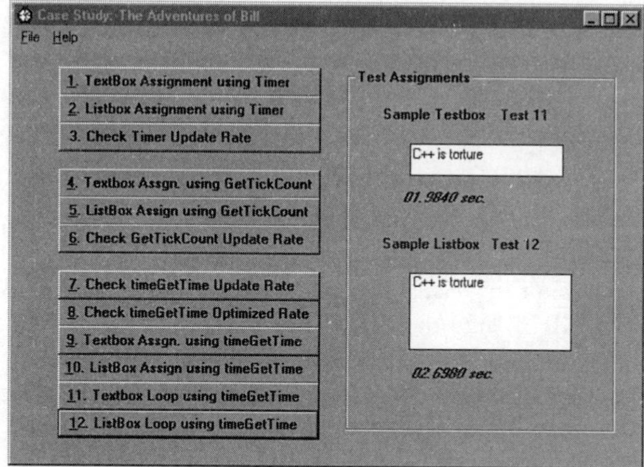

Figure 4.8.
Assignment timings from `timeGetTime` *with a 1000x loop.*

As the results show, when a timing is collected in this fashion it is easier to see who the winner is. The text box assignments take roughly 2 seconds, whereas the list box assignments take roughly 2.7 seconds. Although the numbers might change each time the test is run, the relative position, with text box updates quicker than list box updates, remains the same. The results are easier to see now that Bill is comparing more operations over longer periods of time.

As a matter of fact, if you are carrying out this type of "larger dose" test, the issue of timers becomes less important. Even a timer that updates only every 55 milliseconds could show you differences between the two techniques because now the operations being measured take nearly 2 seconds or more.

Another method to complete this test, therefore, would have been to repeat the same operation a significant number of times, accumulate the total time, and then divide the total time by the number of times the operation was executed. Because the total time would be much larger, `Timer` and `GetTickCount` would be perfectly suitable for a test such as this with a large number of samples.

For a case like Bill's, and unfortunately for most of the performance testing you are likely to do, there may not be one single method that is clearly the best for making an accurate performance assessment. There will always be at least one method, but there may be many, and it is not always clear which is the best. Furthermore, the results you obtain may not be consistent enough to enable you to make an objective conclusion. What does Bill really know with absolute certainty now? He knows that if he uses a program that loops 1000 times and does assignments on his particular system, the text box assignments will be faster. That's about it. He can be pretty sure that the same would hold true on other systems, but he doesn't have proof yet. Likewise, he now has a pretty good idea that even individual text box assignments are faster in general than individual list box clear/add item assignments, if done repeatedly.

Bill still has some questions about the speed of the first text box assignment versus the speed of the first list box assignment after a form is loaded. His initial findings over repeated trials seem to indicate that the first text box assignment took a slow 0.007 seconds, versus 0.003 for the list box. Bill must decide if this is important to his program, or if the performance of his program is affected more by repeated assignments made after his form is loaded.

Likewise, he must decide how much proof he needs that other systems will perform the same, and that his findings really hold true. His tests were carried out on his aging (six-month-old) 50MHz 486DX2 using Windows 95. He has a suspicion (generally correct!) that the relative performance of the Visual Basic language will hold true across different systems such as his boss's 135MHz Pentium running Windows NT and his grandmother's 33MHz 486 running Windows 3.1, but he won't really know for sure until he tests on their platforms. If a general feel is what Bill was after, he has it, and extensive follow-up research could be a waste of time if he has more pressing work to do. On the other hand, if he's betting his company on this decision, more tests are in order.

Making the Test Portable for 16-Bit Applications

As an added step, Bill decided to build the same test to run under the 16-bit environment. (See Bill16.exe on the CD-ROM that accompanies this book.) Available APIs are different between

16-bit and 32-bit systems: The `GetTickCount` call is made from a 16-bit DLL rather than a 32-bit DLL, and the `timeGetTime` function isn't available at all under any 16-bit DLL. Fortunately, Bill could easily set up his source code to be portable, so the same source code can be used to build either a 16-bit or a 32-bit version of his application.

This was easily carried out for the `GetTickCount` function, available both for 16-bit *and* 32-bit systems, with the following conditional compilation of Visual Basic:

```
#If Win32 Then ' 32-bit VB uses this Declare.
    Declare Function GetTickCount Lib "kernel32" () As Long
#Else   ' 16-bit VB uses this Declare.
   Declare Function GetTickCount Lib "User" () As Long
#End if
```

This conditional compilation will make the appropriate DLL declarations based on whether a 32-bit or a 16-bit application is being built. The source code in all tests that use the `GetTickCount` function doesn't have to change at all because the correct declaration is established and the calling conventions remain the same.

There are some API functions with which Bill cannot use this approach, however—namely, the 32-bit `timeGetTime` function, which has no 16-bit equivalent. For cases such as this, Bill declares the API only for 32-bit mode:

```
#If Win32 Then ' 32-bit VB uses this Declare.
   Declare Function timeGetTime Lib "winmm" () As Long
#End if
```

In this case, he also must modify all the code that makes this call so that the call is only allowed to take place in 32-bit applications. This is accomplished with a modification to each routine that uses `timeGetTime`, as shown in Listing 4.11.

Listing 4.11. Making code portable between 16-bit and 32-bit systems.

```
Private Sub cmdStartTimeGetTime_Click()

    Dim intCounter As Integer   ' Count of unique timings returned
    Dim lngStartTime As Long    ' Starting time of test timings
    Dim lngCurtime As Long      ' Most current time of test timings
    Dim lngPrevtime As Long     ' Prior time retrieved during test timings

    #If Win32 Then
        ' This API can be used in 32-bit apps
        ' Indicate which test is to be carried out
        lblListBoxTest = "Test 7"

        ' Clear listbox from any prior trials
        lstListBoxSet.Clear
        ' Save initial time that test began
        ' Retrieve time in milliseconds since startup into lngStartTime
        lngStartTime = timeGetTime()
        ....<more lines not shown here>
    #Else
```

continues

Listing 4.11. continued

```
        ' This 32-bit API cannot be used in 16-bit applications
        MsgBox "This test (timeGetTime) is only available in 32-bit
        ➥ applications!", , "Not Supported!"
    #End If

End Sub
```

Now the code will compile correctly for 32-bit or 16-bit applications and will run successfully in either environment. Either the DLL with the appropriate version will be called or, if the required DLL is not supported, a relevant error message will be displayed.

Bill now goes to use his new 16-bit test application, Bill16.exe, under Windows 95 to see how the timer update rates compare. He observes that the Visual Basic `Timer` function still has an update rate of about 55 milliseconds, and `GetTickCount` is roughly the same in the 16-bit version as in its 32-bit equivalent.

Windows NT Timing Resolutions

Bill then assumes that Windows NT would offer the same resolutions, and rushes over to his co-worker's Pentium that is running NT. Right away he's reminded that one should never make assumptions! The performance of Bill16.exe is the same for `Timer` updates, but `GetTickCount` update rates are even slower than the `Timer` update rates are now! Next he tries Bill32.exe, and sees that the update rates for `Timer`, `GetTickCount`, and `timeGetTime` are all about 10 milliseconds!

Bill is disappointed that 10-millisecond resolution seems to be the best he can do under NT, so he again searches for answers. Because he has by now purchased *Visual Basic 4 Performance Tuning and Optimization*, he turns to the collection of common timing routines in Chapter 7, "Supporting Utilities for Performance Analysis," and finds a routine built on a 32-bit Windows API that looks like it can solve his problem. That routine, `Common_SetOptimalTimer`, calls the API function `TimeGetDevCaps`, which retrieves the minimum available timing resolution. The procedure then uses the `timeBeginPeriod` function to reset the default resolution to the minimum available resolution just found. This reset, according to the documentation, affects only `timeGetTime` under Windows NT and will have no effect under Windows 95. It must, however, be paired with a `timeEndPeriod` call.

Bill places `Common_SetOptimalTimer` (from the Common.bas module found on the CD-ROM that accompanies this book) at the start of his code in his form load statement. (See Listing 4.12.) He uses this function along with `Common_FreeOptimalTimer` (see Listing 4.13) in his form unload because the underlying APIs require that they be used in pairs. As a matter of fact, `TimeBeginPeriod` and `TimeEndPeriod`, according to the documentation, should be used immediately before and after a timing. Therefore, a more standard and recommended tactic would be to cluster these calls around each timing operation. But for Bill's test application, placing the calls at form load and unload seems to give him the desired results.

Listing 4.12. The `Common_SetOptimalTimer` function.

```
Function Common_SetOptimalTimer() As Long

    ' Make sure app is using the lowest resolution timer (most frequent
    ' updates) available
    '
    ' Behavior:
    '           16 bit app under Windows 3.1, Windows 95, or Windows NT -
    '           Not applicable, has no effect, returns standard default
    '
    '           32 bit app under Windows 95 - Relevant 32bit API to reset
    '           time is supported, but has no effect
    '
    '           32 bit app under Windows NT - Using relevant 32bit API, will
    '           reset default timer resolution to the lowest available value.
    '
    '           NOTE: on 32 bit usage, every Common_SetOptimalTimer call should
    '           be paired with a Common_FreeOptimalTimer call. Refer to
    '           timeBeginPeriod documentation for details.
    '
    ' Returns the current timing resolution that will be used with
    ' Common_GetTiming, 0 if failure.

    #If Win32 Then
        Dim rc&
        ' This call retrieves minimum available timer value
        rc& = timeGetDevCaps(typTimeInfo, Len(typTimeInfo))

        ' This resets default timer resolution for Windows NT, has no effect
        ' for Windows 95
        rc& = timeBeginPeriod(typTimeInfo.wPeriodMin)
        If rc& <> 0 Then
            ' Something failed!
            Common_SetOptimalTimer = 0
        Else
            ' Note: Value is saved in module level variable
            ' typTimeInfo.wPeriodMin so that this resolution can be cleared
            ' later by Common_FreeOptimalTimer if needed
            Common_SetOptimalTimer = typTimeInfo.wPeriodMin
        End If
    #Else
        ' The 16-bit API GetTickCount timer only has a resolution of 55
        '  milliseconds under Windows 3.1.
        '  Results vary for this API for 16-bit apps under Windows NT
        '  and Windows 95.

        ' Common_GetTimer uses 16bit Toolhelp.DLL TimerCount API if
        ' possible, which has a resolution of 1 millisec. under
        ' Windows 3.1, and generally close to that for 16bit apps
        ' under 32bit Windows operating systems.
        Common_SetOptimalTimer = 1
    #End If

End Function
```

Listing 4.13. The `Common_FreeOptimalTimer` function.

```
Function Common_FreeOptimalTimer() As Long

    ' Clear the lowest resolution timer (most frequent updates)
    ' that was being used.
    ' Behavior:
    '           16 bit app under Windows 3.1, Windows 95, or Windows NT  -
    '           Not applicable, has no effect
    '
    '           32 bit app under Windows 95 - Relevant 32bit API to
    '           clear time is supported, but has no effect
    '
    '           32 bit app under Windows NT - Using relevant 32bit API, will
    '           clear last setting for timer resolution
    '
    '           NOTE on 32 bit usage: every Common_SetOptimalTimer call should
    '           be paired with a Common_FreeOptimalTimer call. Refer to     '
    '           timeBeginPeriod documentation for details.
    '
    ' RETURNS 0 on success

    #If Win32 Then
        ' This clears last timer setting for Windows NT, has no effect
        ' for Windows 95
        Common_FreeOptimalTimer = timeEndPeriod(typTimeInfo.wPeriodMin)
    #Else
        ' Nothing to free under 16 bit apps, indicate success
        Common_FreeOptimalTimer = 0
     #End If

End Function
```

With this reset of the Windows NT `timeGetTime` resolution, Bill rebuilds the application as BillEn32.exe and runs it again. He finds that the update rates for `Timer` and `GetTickCount` are the same, but the update rate for `timeGetTime` is now nearly 1 millisecond as gauged by his test application, as opposed to the 10 milliseconds he had when he used the default Windows NT resolution on that particular system. Bill now has a full understanding of the timing methods that are available to gauge his applications.

Case Study Summary

The progression that has been outlined through this series of performance-analysis steps is typical of performance assessment. This example focuses largely on assessing timing method update rates, but the approach is much the same regardless of which aspect of performance is being examined. Performance and optimization work typically results in putting major questions to rest at each phase, but in turn gives rise to additional questions and observations such as "Why is this?" or "I must do more to prove this definitively!"

Timing Method Accuracy

When you're measuring the amount of time it takes to execute a series of instructions, the accuracy of the timing method you use is very important. If the timing results you measure are not accurate enough, your results will probably not be worth very much to you. The shorter the amount of time it takes your code to execute, the more significant this issue becomes.

Timing accuracy is a combination of two factors: precision and resolution. *Precision* indicates how fast a timing method can retrieve the current time. If the timing method is slow in reporting back the current time, that time will be outdated by the time it gets back to you. And the more outdated the time gets, the less precise the time will be because you have to add in the delay in retrieving the time.

Resolution, the second factor in timer accuracy, indicates how often the underlying clock, or *tick*, is updated. A timing method whose clock has a very low resolution can also cause a timing to be inaccurate. Suppose, for example, that the timing method is based on a clock that updates only once every second. If the time it takes to execute an operation is 1.80 seconds, your timing will be very inaccurate. The timing method might only report 1 second, which introduces an 80 percent error! If, on the other hand, you had a clock that updated every millisecond, your percentage of error would drop considerably.

This section discusses and compares timing-method accuracy by taking a look at the resolution and precision of the available timing functions. Some practical solutions for increasing the accuracy of timing methods are discussed in Chapter 5, "Collecting Performance Measurements." It is helpful to keep the distinction between accuracy and precision in mind while reading this chapter, remembering that accuracy is a combination of the timer's precision *and* resolution.

Several functions can be used to measure time. Each of these functions might offer you a different level of resolution. Typically, the functions that provide greater resolution are more difficult to implement and require more effort. Others, such as the Visual Basic `Timer` function, are simply a matter of adding a single line of code in the right place.

Although each timing method can, in part, be characterized by its resolution, the precision of these timing methods is more difficult to quantify. The very nature of Windows works against precision. Programs written in Windows, unlike their DOS counterparts, are *event driven* rather than *procedure driven.* Procedure-driven code executes in a very predictable fashion, one line of code at a time, in a predetermined manner. The programmer usually is in full control of the environment. When the programmer decides it is time for the user to offer input, he allows the program to wait for the user to take an action such as entering data into a field. Consider the procedure-driven code example in Listing 4.14.

Listing 4.14. A procedure-driven code example.

```
DIM strFirstName AS STRING
DIM strLastName AS STRING

PRINT "Please enter your first name: ";
INPUT$ strFirstName
PRINT "Please enter your last name: ";
INPUT$ strLastName
```

This program was written using standard BASIC. Notice that after the program prints `Please enter your first name:`, the next line is an `INPUT$` statement. This command waits for the user to enter a string and assigns that string to the variable that follows the command. So, in this case, whatever the user typed would be assigned to `strFirstName`. Note that the programmer has total control over what the user types.

Now, suppose you wanted to perform the same task in Visual Basic. You would need to create a form with two text boxes, one for the first name and the other for the last name. One possible implementation is shown in Figure 4.9.

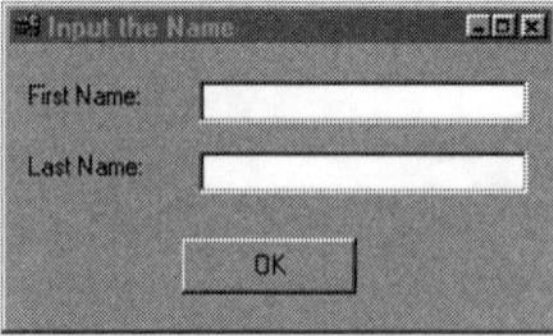

Figure 4.9.
An event-driven application example.

You could assign the names to the strings by responding to the `Click` event of the OK command button with the code shown in Listing 4.15.

Listing 4.15. Event-driven code.

```
Private Sub cmdOK_Click()

    ' Store the text in these two textboxes into global variables
    strFirstName = txtFirstName.Text
    strLastName = txtLastName.Text

End Sub
```

Can you see the difference between standard BASIC and Visual Basic? Notice that in Visual Basic, the program must *respond* to actions taken by the user, who can act upon the program in a variety of ways. In a procedure-driven application, however, the user must respond to the program in the manner the program dictates. When programming a Windows application,

the programmer must respond to the actions of the user without really knowing what he or she is going to do next. In a procedural environment, on the other hand, the user can only do what the programmer allows at any given moment.

In order for Windows applications to be event driven, the operating environment must inform the program of what is happening. For example, when the user clicks the OK button in the event-driven application shown in Figure 4.9, Windows must tell the Visual Basic application that the `Click` event has occurred. Windows does this by passing a message to Visual Basic, telling it that the user has clicked on the OK button with the mouse. Visual Basic then triggers the `cmdOK_Click()` event, executing the code that you, the programmer, have placed in that event subroutine.

Windows must rely on messages to respond to user actions, timers, screen drawing, operating-system maintenance, and so on. The number of messages Windows receives during any given span of time can fluctuate. At times, very few messages are being processed by Windows, and it spends most of its time waiting idly for the user to do something. At other times, the system is so busy that the user has to wait for Windows to take care of all its messages and background tasks before it can get back to satisfying the user's program. Have you ever tried to click on a button, had nothing happen, and clicked two or three more times on it, thinking it was ignoring your request?

What actually happens in this case is that every time you click on the button, Windows stores a click message in a queue for commands waiting to be processed. If other activities are taking place, the messages waiting to be processed simply wait their turn until Windows can get to them. Windows—and, for that matter, the CPU—can only process one instruction at a time. Therefore, Windows is either busy executing code or it is dispatching your messages to the appropriate piece of code to satisfy your needs. While code is busy executing, your messages wait to be processed and you, the user, wait as well.

In addition to system messages, Windows often has *background tasks* that must be processed, such as updating disk caches or virtual memory, updating the screen, or handling network access.

The same problem with time variability can also occur when you're using a timing method in your code. You might put the `Timer` statement at the beginning of a subroutine and another one at the end. If the elapsed time during those two calls varies, it is often due to the fact that every time you execute the body of code, Windows has a particular set of background tasks to process and, under certain conditions, Windows messages that must be addressed immediately. In Windows 95 and Windows NT, your application can even be preempted by other applications. The operating-system component called the *scheduler* is in charge of making sure each application gets appropriate execution turns, and can override your application. In other words, it might have more to do during one instance of the subroutine's execution than another.

Analogy: Executing Windows Applications

Assume that you usually go grocery shopping once a week. You find that if you shop at the beginning of the week, the store seems less busy. When you buy your goods and wait in line, you might only have an average of two or three customers ahead of you at any one time. When you go to the store on the weekend, however, it is very busy, and you might have many more people waiting in line ahead of you. Some of the customers have a lot of items to buy, whereas others might have only two or three items. You have no way of knowing how long you will wait.

Suppose your friend asks you to go out and buy some food for the week. Your friend, who wants you to get back as soon as you can, decides to time you. He expects you to be back in a reasonable amount of time, but he doesn't know exactly how long it will take you. He starts his stopwatch the minute you pull out of the driveway. Fortunately, the store turns out to be quite empty and you are able to get home quickly, much to your friend's satisfaction.

The following week, you go out shopping again. This time, however, the cashier has other customers to satisfy before he can get to you. Because of this, it takes you twice as long to return home. If your friend understands the nature of grocery shopping and waiting in line, he will accept the fact that, short of rescheduling your trip, the delay was beyond your control.

When Windows executes a program, it might take more time to execute the program in one instance than it does in another. This might be because Windows has more background tasks to process the second time than it did the first time the application was executed. Because of this variability, you can often receive inconsistent timings. This is one of the unpleasant realities of Windows programming: Windows can inherently reduce the accuracy of timings. Chapter 6, "Factors That Affect Performance," provides practical solutions to minimize the instability of Windows and make timings more accurate.

A Closer Look at Timing Methods

Now it's time for a more technical overview of the timing functions available to the Windows programmer. Most often, you want to choose a timing method that gives you as high a degree of resolution as possible. The Windows API provides the programmer with three simple function calls for this purpose, each of which is discussed in the following sections.

The Visual Basic *Timer* Function

The Visual Basic `Timer` function is an uncomplicated function that simply returns the number of seconds elapsed since midnight. The `Timer` function is very easy to use, takes no parameters, and requires no declarations. Here is an example:

```
sngStartTime = Timer
Call Process_Records
sngEndTime = Timer
```

Notice that the `Timer` *function* is not the same as the `Timer` *control*. The `Timer` control can be set to trigger an event every specified number of milliseconds. That control is not useful for performance measurement. The `Timer` *function*, on the other hand, is used to obtain the time since system startup, which we are using here.

Unfortunately, the `Timer` function is not very accurate for measurements of a short duration. The `Timer` function relies on a hardware timer that issues an interrupt about once every 55 milliseconds and is therefore limited to that level of resolution under the Windows operating system. Resolution is similar under Windows 95 and 16-bit applications under Windows NT. (This function appears to take a resolution of approximately 10 milliseconds on Windows NT 32-bit test cases.) Therefore, although the `Timer` function might be appropriate for timing long intervals, it is generally not accurate enough for individual operations. If, for example, you are timing code that takes less than 55 milliseconds, you might not get any measure whatsoever of the elapsed time.

Although the `Timer` function is not very accurate if your operations are less than a second, it is very easy to use and thus might be appropriate for timings in which its level of accuracy is not prohibitive to its use. If you can accept a skew of up to 55 milliseconds in your timings, and, in general, your operations to time take a second or longer, this timing method is acceptable.

The Windows API *GetTickCount* Function

`GetTickCount` is a Windows API function that retrieves the number of clock cycles, or ticks, that have elapsed since Windows was started. This function is also very easy to use. When you're running a 16-bit version of Windows, it requires the following declaration in a Visual Basic code module:

```
Declare Function GetTickCount Lib "User" () As Long
```

When running Windows NT or Windows 95, use the following declaration:

```
Declare Function GetTickCount Lib "Kernel32" () As Long
```

Note that the return value, in both cases, is of type *long*. In terms of implementing the function in code, `GetTickCount` essentially works the same way the `Timer` function does, as shown in the following code:

```
lngStartTime = GetTickCount()
Call Process_Records
lngEndTime = GetTickCount()
```

In the 16-bit versions of Windows, the `GetTickCount` function is accurate to the nearest 55 milliseconds, which is the same as the `Timer` function. This is due to the fact that both the `Timer` and `GetTickCount` functions use the same hardware interrupt to obtain their times. Therefore, their update rates are the same.

In Windows 95 and Windows NT applications, however, the resolutions of the `GetTickCount` function results are different. Results from testing varied from system to system and across operating systems. Results ranged from 1 millisecond for Windows 95, to over 55 milliseconds for 16-bit apps on Windows NT, to 10 seconds for 32-bit Windows NT apps, to 1 millisecond for 32-bit Windows NT apps that reset the timer resolution with `BeginTimePeriod`. Therefore, the `GetTickCount` function should be used with a clear understanding of the environment and the required and supported resolution for that particular environment.

The Windows API *TimerCount* Function

The `TimerCount` function is another timing function available under 16-bit versions of Windows. The Windows API help file states that the `TimerCount` function is accurate to the nearest millisecond, making it one of the best Windows API functions for taking timings in Windows 3.1 and Windows 3.11. The increased accuracy, however, comes at the cost of the additional code and variable declarations required to use the method. The extra code and variable usage isn't too bothersome, however, and in many cases might be worth the extra effort. The function requires the use of a user-defined type, as outlined in the following code:

```
Type TIMERINFO
     lngSizeSetup as Long       ' Specify size of user-defined type
     lngMillisec as Long        ' Milliseconds since task start
     lngNotUsed as Long         ' Milliseconds since virtual machine start
End Type
```

As you can see, the type consists of three long integers, for a total of 12 bytes (4 bytes per long integer). A value of 12 must therefore be used for the first field, indicating the size of the user-defined type. The second parameter is set when the function is called and is the value retrieved to show the number of milliseconds. The third parameter is used to indicate the number of milliseconds since the virtual machine start, which is normally not used—it is part of an advanced concept beyond the scope of this book. To use the `TimerCount` function, you must place the following `Declare` statement in a code module:

```
Declare Function TimerCount% Lib "toolhelp.dll" (typTimer as TIMERINFO)
```

Note that the function comes from the 16-bit TOOLHELP.DLL, but this function is only found in the TOOLHELP.DLL designed for Windows 3.1 and Windows 3.11. To use the function in code, you must declare a variable of type TIMERINFO and call the function as follows:

```
Dim typCurTime as TIMERINFO
typCurTime.lngSizeSetup = 12              ' Set up type size
If TimerCount(typCurTime) = 0 Then        ' If return code = 0, then
     MsgBox "Timer failed"                ' the function failed!
End If
```

The time will be available, in this case, in the `typCurTime.lngMillisec` member variable. Be aware of the return code condition—if it equals 0, the timer failed.

Although using this timer might require slightly more code, it is useful when timing short sequences of code that require a high degree of resolution to maximize accuracy in Windows 3.1 and 3.11. However, this function is not available as a 32-bit API, so such code will not be portable between 16-bit and 32-bit applications.

The Windows API *timeGetTime* Function

The most accurate timer for 32-bit applications (assuming that special high-resolution hardware timers have not been added to the system) is the Windows API `timeGetTime` function. This function is only available in 32-bit versions of Windows, namely Windows 95 and Windows NT. The Windows API help file states that the default accuracy of the `timeGetTime` function is 1 millisecond in Windows 95 and 5 milliseconds or longer in Windows NT, making it the most accurate timer of the three timers available. This function requires a simple declaration in a Visual Basic code module:

```
Declare Function timeGetTime Lib "winmm.dll" () As Long
```

and can be set equal to a variable of type long. It essentially works the same way the `Timer` function does:

```
lngStartTime = timeGetTime()
Call Process_Records
lngEndTime = timeGetTime()
```

The `timeGetTime` function is the most accurate timer of the three 32-bit alternatives because it relies on processing that provides more precision than the `GetTickCount` function. `timeGetTime` is more accurate because it uses an advanced capability in Windows called a "virtual timer device." This timer device uses extended Windows virtual memory capabilities to obtain its millisecond accuracy.

The resolution of 1 millisecond cannot be changed in Windows 95, but in Windows NT the default resolution can be 5 milliseconds or more, depending on the machine. The programmer can call the function `GetTimerCaps`, which returns the minimum and maximum resolutions that the timer can provide on the specific system in which the function is called. With this minimum value, the programmer can change the resolution of the timer by using the functions `timeBeginPeriod` and `timeEndPeriod`. The code in Listing 4.16 demonstrates the use of these functions. In this listing, the timer is set to the lowest resolution possible for that system.

Listing 4.16. Changing the `timeGetTime` resolution in Windows NT.

```
Private Sub cmdOK_Click()

     Type TIMECAPS
          wPeriodMin As Long
          wPeriodMax As Long
          End Type
```

continues

Listing 4.16. continued

```
    Dim typTimeInfo As TIMECAPS
    Dim rc&
    ' Get the default resolution
      rc& = timeGetDevCaps(typTimeInfo, Len(typTimeInfo))
    ' Set the resolution to the lowest possible value
      rc& = timeBeginPeriod(typTimeInfo.wPeriodMin)
    ' Get the start time
    lngStartTime = timeGetTime()
    ' Do the work
    Call Process_Information
    ' Take the end time
    lngEndTime = timeGetTime()

    ' Set the resolution back to the default value
      rc& = timeEndPeriod(typTimeInfo.wPeriodMin)

End Sub
```

If you delve into the depths of the Windows API, you might notice another function called `timeGetSystemTime`. This function is similar to the `timeGetTime` function except that it uses a structure to return the system time rather than returning a simple value. The `timeGetSystemTime` function requires more overhead and, as it is otherwise identical, is not presented in detail in this book. Refer to the Windows API help file for more information about the specific details of this function.

Table 4.1 shows a summary of each timer and its respective resolution. Use this as a convenient chart for determining which timer to use.

> **NOTE:** These are not presented as definitive statistics, but simply the results of test research. *Results are approximate, and might vary on your own system.*

Table 4.1. Summary of timers and their resolutions.

Timer	*16-Bit App*	*32-Bit App*	*Location*
	Windows 3.x, Windows 3.11, and WFW		
`VB Timer`	55 ms	N/A	VB function
`GetTickCount`	55 ms	N/A	KERNEL
`TimerCount`	1 ms	N/A	TOOLHELP.DLL
`timeGetTime`	N/A	N/A	N/A

Timer	*16-Bit App*	*32-Bit App*	*Location*
		Windows 95	
`VB Timer`	55 ms	55 ms	VB function
`GetTickCount`	1 ms	1 ms	KERNEL
`TimerCount`	1 ms	N/A	TOOLHELP.DLL
`timeGetTime`	N/A	1 ms	WINMM.DLL
		Windows NT with Default Resolution	
`VB Timer`	55 ms	10 ms	VB function
`GetTickCount`	62 ms	10 ms	KERNEL
`TimerCount`	1 ms	N/A	TOOLHELP.DLL
`timeGetTime`	N/A	10 ms*	WINMM.DLL
		Windows NT with `BeginTimePeriod` Min Res Set to 1 ms	
`VB Timer`	55 ms	10 ms	VB function
`GetTickCount`	62 ms	10 ms	KERNEL
`TimerCount`	1 ms	N/A	TOOLHELP.DLL
`timeGetTime`	N/A	1 ms*	WINMM.DLL

* In Windows 95, the default is 1 millisecond for `timeGetTime`. In Windows NT, the default is stated as 5 milliseconds or above, which can be changed through the functions `timeBeginPeriod` and `timeEndPeriod`.

Advanced Timer Methods

In addition to these basic timing functions, the Windows API provides a more sophisticated level of functionality for those interested in advanced performance monitoring. Specifically, four functions exist in the API for this purpose:

- `RegConnectRegistry`
- `RegQueryValueEx`
- `QueryPerformanceFrequency`
- `QueryPerformanceCounter`

The first two functions are used for setting the system registry object for monitoring the performance of system-defined objects such as processors, disks, and memory. Because we are primarily concerned with monitoring the performance of Visual Basic applications, these types of performance measurements are beyond the scope of this book. The functions themselves are very complex, deal with the system registry, and are used most often for advanced system performance monitoring utilities.

The second two functions, on the other hand, are more relevant for our purposes. The first function is used to check for the existence of a *high-resolution performance counter.* This type of counter provides high-resolution elapsed times that can be used to fine-tune specific sections of code. High-resolution counters might be found on some types of hardware devices that have separate timing logic more accurate than the computer's.

The `QueryPerformanceFrequency` function checks for the existence of such a counter and, if it exists, returns the frequency of the timer in counts per second. This value is dependent on the processor clock speed and might, in some cases, be equal to the frequency of the processor clock. If such a high-resolution timer exists, the `QueryPerformanceCounter` function can be used to retrieve the current value of the counter. This function can be used the same way the other functions are used (that is, wrapped around a section of code the user wants to time).

These two functions can therefore be used to gain even more accuracy than you get with the other timing methods discussed in this chapter. Provided that the high-resolution counter exists, these functions should be used for maximum accuracy. Otherwise, `timeGetTime` is the most accurate timer.

Common Timer Functions

Rather than calling these functions directly and having to account for the use of a 16-bit or 32-bit operating system, you can simply use the functions provided on the CD-ROM included with this book. They provide cross-system code portability between 32-bit and 16-bit applications with resolutions no worse than 55 ms. Table 4.2 shows a list of functions provided for your use for taking timings.

Table 4.2. Summary of common timing functions.

Common Function	*Description*
`Common_GetTimer`	Returns the current time using `timeGetTime` if you're running a 32-bit version of Windows and `GetTickCount` if you're using a 16-bit version. This ensures that the most accurate time is returned without the use of a high-resolution timer.
`Common_GetOptimizedTimer`	Sets the time resolution to the lowest available on the system. This only has an effect on Windows NT, where it will reset `timeGetTime` resolution to lower than the standard default. It returns the lowest resolution available.

Common Function	Description
`Common_FreeOptimizedTimer`	Frees up time-resolution overrides established with `Common_GetOptimizedTimer`.
`Common_GetHighResTimer`	Returns the current time from the high-resolution timer, if one exists. If such a timer does not exist, the function returns `0`.
`Common_GetHighResTimerFreq`	Returns a string indicating how often the high-resolution timer updates. If such a timer does not exist, the function returns `0`.

These functions are discussed in greater detail in Chapter 7. Keep in mind that if you use these functions, you won't have to worry about which timing methods to use and in which modes they operate. You will have a portable set of functions to apply on any operating-system platform that ensures that you have the most accurate timing method possible.

Other Profiling Tools

Thus far, this discussion has been limited to the tools available within Windows. Anyone with a copy of Visual Basic and Microsoft Windows can take advantage of these timing techniques. Another alternative is to consider more advanced tools that can be used to measure performance. These include the Microsoft Visual Basic profiler tools as well as various third-party tools. Often, these profiling tools can present timing results in a much more user-friendly way and can do the work of inserting timing code throughout your application. Some also can give a graphical analysis of the results and let you see easily what your program is doing at the click of a few buttons. With the advent of Visual Basic 4.0, Microsoft also provides its own profiling tool. These and other third-party alternatives are discussed in Chapter 7.

Summary

This chapter introduces you to the timing tools required for the programmer to take meaningful performance measurements. The chapter begins by providing an introductory case study to illustrate some basic timing issues and demonstrate some of the complexities inherent in carrying out even a series of simple performance tests.

This case study is followed by a discussion of timing methods in terms of timer precision and resolution. The ingredients that make a timing method accurate are discussed, and reasons that timing methods can be inaccurate are briefly introduced. Two vital factors, precision and resolution, are introduced and explained in the context of the Windows operating environment. Precision is a way to indicate how quickly the time is reported when requested. The less precise the timing method, the greater and less reliable the time. Resolution is a measure of the frequency with which the underlying clock or tick count gets updated. The smaller the amount of time it takes for a block of code to execute, the more important the resolution of the timer. If, for example, a timer is only accurate to the nearest 55 milliseconds, an operation that takes 30 milliseconds would very likely report 0 milliseconds total time for the measured operation. You would need a timer with a higher degree of resolution.

The chapter then focuses on the various timing methods you can use, pointing out the best timing methods to take advantage of either in Visual Basic or through the Windows API. Three functions—the Visual Basic `Timer` function, the `GetTickCount` Windows API function, and the `timerGetTime` Windows API function—are examined in some detail, pointing out the advantages and disadvantages of using each timing method. Advanced timing methods are also introduced briefly for those who require more advanced timing-analysis capabilities. In addition to the functions provided in the Windows API, profiling tools can save a great deal of time and can provide even more accurate measurements. Refer to Chapter 7 for a comprehensive review of the available profiling tools.

Obey the Signs

Wrong Way: The best way to determine the faster of two code approaches is to take one set of timings for each method and choose the faster of the two.

As this chapter shows, there are many factors that affect performance and that affect which type of performance assessment is appropriate for any performance problem. You should test various code approaches as consistently as possible. A series of tests might be required to determine the timings you need. Even if only one test is needed, the test should be run multiple times on multiple platforms. Test results can differ between systems, as well as even from one execution to another on the same system, due to the many factors affecting system performance.

Beware of Falling Rocks: Don't attempt to use a timer that only updates every 55 milliseconds to make a decision that hinges on differences of a couple milliseconds!

The various timing methods available under Visual Basic are based on timers that range from 1/18 second (55-millisecond) update rates to 1/1000 second (1-millisecond) update rates. The methods based on the timer with less-frequent updates (VB's `Timer` function and the Windows API `GetTickCount` function) might be adequate for many purposes if the duration of activity being timed is long enough that a difference of a few milliseconds is insignificant.

However, if the duration of the activity is so short that the only difference between alternatives is a few milliseconds, a more accurate timer should be used. Alternatively, the test could be restructured so a longer-duration trial based on multiple iterations of the method under test is carried out. If you are using a profile tool to carry out your comparisons (as discussed in Chapter 7), be sure you understand the capabilities and timings of the profiler.

Q&A

Q Do I need to worry about the details of which timer is best to use?

A Fortunately, you don't have to. The CD-ROM that accompanies this book contains a common code module that contains functions you can call to automatically pick the best timing method for you. Refer to the "Common Timer Functions" section in this chapter for more information.

Q What do I do if none of the timers give me sufficient accuracy?

A If this happens to you, you might be trying to time an operation that is simply too fast to measure. If you are comparing such an operation to alternatives, you might want to try executing them multiple times, perhaps in a loop, so that you can obtain more meaningful results.

Q Why are there so many timers with so many different resolutions?

A As Windows has evolved, various timing techniques have been implemented within each operating environment. To maintain backward compatibility, those functions could not be made obsolete. Therefore, a variety of alternatives exist. This chapter shows you which timing methods are most accurate, and it provides you with a set of common modules that makes this determination for you.

Collecting Performance Measurements

Thus far, you have examined performance and optimization, learned about their importance, and learned to determine when and where optimization should be applied. You have also looked at the various timing methods you can use to measure performance, primarily the Visual Basic `Timer` function, the Windows API `GetTickCount` function, and the `timeGetTime` function. You have also observed that each timing method varies in terms of its accuracy, due (in part) to the resolution of each timer. This chapter briefly describes how to use these timing methods within an application. You should gain insight into how and where to place timing functions in code, as well as where they are not appropriate. The major concepts covered in this chapter include using timing methods inside an application and making timings meaningful.

There are two ways to measure the impact of an optimization in code. The first approach is to build a Visual Basic application designed as a model to test some specific feature. Such cases are considered in Chapter 4, "Timing Methods," where simple applications are created that perform operations over and over and timings of bulk operations are used to evaluate performance improvements. The second approach is to measure the impact of an optimization in the target application itself. Since this approach actually modifies the application, this approach should be carried using a systematic methodology as outlined in Chapter 8, "The Brophy/Koets Optimization Methodology." This chapter considers the second approach, showing you how to integrate performance enhancements into the actual application.

Finally, the chapter addresses the issue of making timings meaningful. As briefly discussed in Chapter 4, one timing is sometimes not enough, as timing values can fluctuate. You must often make several passes at the same timing and average the set of data obtained. This chapter addresses this in more detail, providing insight into knowing how many sample timings to obtain and how to arrive at a reliable timing result from that set of data.

Using Timing Methods Inside an Application

This section discusses the techniques used in taking timings in various types of code-structure situations. Included on the CD-ROM that accompanies this book is a sample program that illustrates many of the concepts found in this section.

How to Time Events

When you're using any of the timer methods, the easiest way to take a timing of an event is to record the time at the beginning of the subroutine and then take another timing at the end, just before the exit. Listing 5.1 presents an outline representation of the code and function calls you would make when using the Visual Basic `Timer` function.

Listing 5.1. Timing a subroutine using the VB `Timer` function.

```
Private Sub GetFirstName ()

    Dim sngStartTime As Single, sngEndTime As Single

    ' Store the starting time
    sngStartTime = Timer

    ' Perform the operations
    Data1.Recordset.MoveNext
    txtFirstName.Text = Data1.Recordset!First_Name
```

```
    ' Store the ending time
    sngEndTime = Timer

    ' Report the total elapsed time
    Debug.Print "Elapsed time in GetFirstName function = " & _
                Format(sngEndTime - sngStartTime, "#####.0000") & " sec."

End Sub
```

Note that in this example, the total elapsed time is printed out in the debug window. Because you must be in the Visual Basic design environment to see the results, you might instead want to put the timings into a file or in a message box so you can run the executable directly. Listing 5.2 shows the same implementation using the `GetTickCount` API function call.

Listing 5.2. Timing a subroutine using the `GetTickCount` function.

```
' Windows API GetTickCount declaration added to common.bas declarations
Declare Function GetTickCount Lib " kernel32" () As Long


Private Sub GetFirstName()

    Dim lngStartTime As Long, lngEndTime As Long

    ' Store the starting time
    lngStartTime = GetTickCount()

    ' Perform the operations
    Data1.Recordset.MoveNext
    txtFirstName = Data1.Recordset!First_Name

    ' Store the ending time
    lngEndTime = GetTickCount()

    ' Report the total elapsed time
    Debug.Print "Elapsed time in GetFirstName function = " & _
                Format(lngEndTime - lngStartTime, "#####.0000") & " sec."

End Sub
```

Note that the code is virtually identical, except for the fact that the `GetTickCount()` function is used rather than the Visual Basic `Timer` function. Finally, Listing 5.3 contains the code for the `timeGetTime` function.

Listing 5.3. Timing a subroutine using the `timeGetTime` function.

```
' Windows API timeGetTime declaration added to common.bas declarations
Declare Function timeGetTime Lib "winmm" () As Long


Private Sub GetFirstName()

    Dim lngStartTime As Long, lngEndTime As Long

    ' Store the starting time
    lngStartTime = timeGetTime()

    ' Perform the operations
    Data1.Recordset.MoveNext
    txtFirstName = Data1.Recordset!First_Name

    ' Store the ending time
    lngEndTime = timeGetTime()

    ' Report the total elapsed time
    Debug.Print "Elapsed time in GetFirstName function = " & _
             Format(lngEndTime - lngStartTime, "#####.0000") & " sec."

End Sub
```

In these simple cases, the subroutine executes from start to finish. Often, however, there might be more than one exit point in the subroutine, and you might have error handling in the subroutine that triggers a `Goto` statement. In such cases, it is best to label a section of code that takes the final timing so that, no matter what path the sequence of code execution takes, the timing code is called.

> **NOTE:** Although the use of the `Goto` statement is usually discouraged as a programming practice because it makes for less maintainable code, it must be used when handling errors and, in specific cases such as this, is appropriate if used judiciously.

The code in Listing 5.4 uses the `Timer` function along with error handling and multiple subroutine exit points to make sure a timing is obtained regardless of the code path taken.

Listing 5.4. Timing a subroutine with multiple exit points using the `Timer` function.

```
Private Function GetEmployeeInfo(strLastName As String) As Boolean

      ' Set subroutine to goto error handling area
      On Error GoTo GetEmployeeInfo_Error

      ' Declare variables
      Dim sngStartTime As Single
      Dim sngEndTime As Single
```

```
        Dim RS As Recordset
        Dim DB As Database

        ' Assume the function is not successful until otherwise told
        GetEmployeeInfo = False

        ' Retrieve the start time
        sngStartTime = Timer

        ' Make sure last name has been provided as an input parameter
        If strLastName = "" Then
             MsgBox "You must supply a valid employee name!"
             GoTo GetEmployeeInfo_Exit
        End If

        ' Find the data based on the last name retrieved
        Set DB = Workspaces(0).OpenDatabase("C:\MYDB.MDB", False, False)

        ' Open the recordset as a snapshot
        Set RS = DB.OpenRecordset("SELECT * from tblEmployee WHERE Last_Name =
        ➥'" & strLastName & "'", dbOpenSnapshot)

        ' If no employees exist in the table, alert the user and exit
        If RS.RecordCount = 0 Then

             MsgBox "The employee you have requested is not in the table."
             GoTo GetEmployeeInfo_Exit

         ' Otherwise, get the first name and SSN of the employee
        Else
             ' Get the first name
             If Not IsNull(RS!First_Name) Then
                 txtFirstName = RS!First_Name
             Else
                 MsgBox "The first name is missing from the database!"
                 GoTo GetEmployeeInfo_Exit
             End If

             ' Get the SSN
             If Not IsNull(RS!SSN) Then
                 txtSSN = RS!SSN
             Else
                 MsgBox "The SSN is missing from the database!"
                 GoTo GetEmployeeInfo_Exit
             End If

        End If

        ' If the program reaches this statement, every call above was
        ' successful and we can denote the function as successful
        GetEmployeeInfo = True

GetEmployeeInfo_Exit:

        RS.Close
        DB.Close
```

continues

Listing 5.4. continued

```
        ' Retrieve the end time and display it
        sngEndTime = Timer

        Debug.Print "Elapsed Time in GetEmployeeInfo function = " & _
                    Format(sngEndTime - sngStartTime, "#####.0000") & " sec."

        Exit Function

GetEmployeeInfo_Error:

        ' This code gets executed if there is a program error
        Debug.Print "Error " & Err & ": " & Error$ & " has occurred."

        ' Return a failure code
        GetEmployeeInfo = False

        Resume GetEmployeeInfo_Exit

End Function
```

Note the use of additional labels to define the group of code that takes the end timing and the group of code that handles errors. Notice the use of the `Resume` statement that causes the subroutine to go to the exit section of code after the error condition has been handled. Observe also that during runtime, there is no possible code path to exit the function without obtaining the total elapsed time in the function.

How to Time Database Functions

When working with a database, either through a data control, recordset, or some other data object, it is often useful to obtain timings for various activities such as the amount of time it takes to open the database, move to the first record, perform some sort of query, or perform some action on a database table.

When you're determining the amount of time it takes to open a database, the time will vary based on the size of the database and what subset of the database is being loaded into memory. You must also take into consideration bound controls when working with databases. If, for example, you have several text boxes bound to various fields of a data control, the amount of time to open the database will increase because Visual Basic must also take the time to associate the appropriate bound data with each text box.

The method of timing code insertion is the same as in Listings 5.1 through 5.4, except that multiple timings can be taken in the same subroutine, if appropriate. Consider an application that shows information for a personnel database, as shown in Figure 5.1.

Note that, in this case, labels are used instead of text boxes for displaying the data on the form.

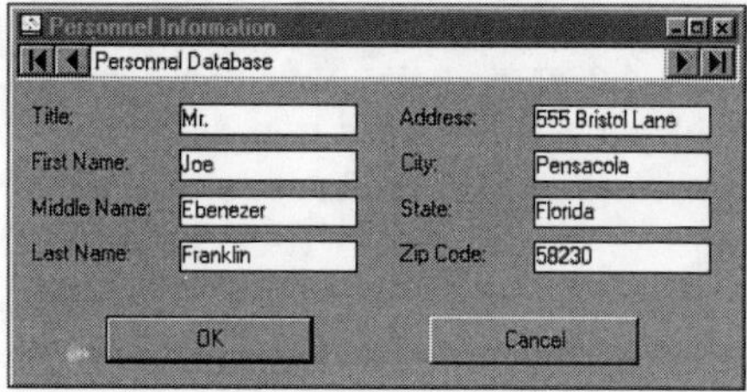

Figure 5.1.
The Personnel Database Browser application.

This provides the benefit of preventing the user from modifying the data, but introduces a problem because labels cannot be bound to databases. Therefore, you must assign the data to the labels manually. Listing 5.5 provides an example of taking multiple timings for a subroutine that queries the database for various values.

Listing 5.5. Taking timings for database operations.

```
Private Sub GetInfo()


Dim sngAddressStartTime As Single
    Dim sngAddressEndTime As Single
    Dim sngAddressTotalTime As Single

    Dim sngNameStartTime As Single
    Dim sngNameEndTime As Single
    Dim sngNameTotalTime As Single

    ' Place address data in the labels on the form
    sngAddressStartTime = Timer
    lblAddress.Caption = Data1.Recordset!Address
    lblCity.Caption = Data1.Recordset!City
    lblState.Caption = Data1.Recordset!State
    lblZipCode.Caption = Data1.Recordset!Zip_Code
    sngAddressEndTime = Timer

    ' Place name data in the labels on the form
    sngNameStartTime = Timer
    lblTitle.Caption = Data1.Recordset!Title
    lblFirstName.Caption = Data1.Recordset!First_Name
    lblMiddleName.Caption = Data1.Recordset!Middle_Name
    lblLastName.Caption = Data1.Recordset!Last_Name
    sngNameEndTime = Timer

    ' Calculate and display the elapsed times
    sngAddressTotalTime = sngAddressStartTime - sngAddressEndTime
    sngNameTotalTime = sngNameStartTime - sngNameEndTime

    Debug.Print "Elapsed time to display address info in GetInfo = " & _
            Format(sngAddressTotalTime, "#####.0000")

    Debug.Print "Elapsed time to display name info in GetInfo = " & _
            Format(sngNameTotalTime, "#####.0000")

End Sub
```

Note that in Listing 5.5, each set of database operations uses the Visual Basic `Timer` function at the beginning of the set of operations and at the end of the set. After the database calls, elapsed times are calculated and displayed in the debug window. Keep in mind that the `timeGetTime` function might be more appropriate to ensure timer accuracy.

How to Time Functions and Subroutines

When you must take timings of procedures (that is, functions or subroutines) that are called inside other procedures, you must decide whether to begin the timing in the calling procedure or inside the procedure being called. The first alternative, timing in the calling procedure, is shown in Listing 5.6.

Listing 5.6. Timing a function outside the code body.

```
Private Sub cmdOK_Click()

        Dim intSuccess as Integer
        Dim sngStartTime as Single, sngEndTime as Single

        sngStartTime = Timer
        intSuccess = Initialize_Database(txtName.Text)
        sngEndTime = Timer

        Debug.Print "Elapsed time calling and executing
                    ➥Initialize_Database = " &
                    ➥Format(sngEndTime - sngStartTime, "#####.0000")

End Sub

Private Function Initialize_Database(ByVal strName As String) As Integer

        Dim DB As Database
        Dim RS As Recordset
        Dim bDBOpen As Boolean
        Dim bRSOpen As Boolean

        On Error GoTo Initialize_Database_Error

        Set DB = Workspaces(0).OpenDatabase("RECORDS.MDB")
        bDBOpen = True

        Set RS = DB.OpenRecordset("tblAdministrative", dbOpenDynaset)
        bRSOpen = True

        RS.Edit
        RS!Date = Date$
        RS!Time = Time$
        RS!Name = strName$
        RS.Update
        Initialize_Database = True

Initialize_Database_Exit:
```

```
        ' Close the recordset and the database, and exit the function

        If bRSOpen Then
            RS.Close
        End If

        If bDBOpen Then
            DB.Close
        End If

        Exit Function

Initialize_Database_Error:

        MsgBox "Error " & Error$ & " has occurred!"
        Initialize_Database = False
        Resume Initialize_Database_Exit

End Function
```

The other alternative, to place the timing inside the procedure itself, is shown in Listing 5.7.

Listing 5.7. Timing a function inside the code body.

```
Private Sub cmdOK_Click()

        Dim intSuccess as Integer
        Dim strEmployeeName as String

        strEmployeeName = txtName

        intSuccess = Initialize_Database(strEmployeeName)

End Sub

Private Function Initialize_Database(ByVal strName As String) As Integer

    Dim DB As Database
    Dim RS As Recordset
    Dim sngStartTime As Single, sngEndTime As Single
    Dim bDBOpen As Boolean, bRSOpen As Boolean

    On Error GoTo Initialize_Database_Error

    sngStartTime = Timer

    Set DB = Workspaces(0).OpenDatabase("RECORDS.MDB")
    bDBOpen = True

    Set RS = DB.OpenRecordset("tblAdministrative", dbOpenDynaset)
    bRSOpen = True

    RS.Edit
    RS!Date = Date$
```

continues

Listing 5.7. continued

```
    RS!Time = Time$
    RS!Name = strName$
    RS.Update

    Initialize_Database = True

Initialize_Database_Exit:

    sngEndTime = Timer

    Debug.Print "Elapsed time executing Initialize_Database = " & _
                Format(sngEndTime - sngStartTime, "#####.0000")

    If bRSOpen Then
        RS.Close
    End If

    If bDBOpen Then
        DB.Close
    End If

    Exit Function

Initialize_Database_Error:

    MsgBox "Error " & Error$ & " has occurred!"
    Initialize_Database = False
    Resume Initialize_Database_Exit

End Function
```

As a general rule, it is advisable to put the timing code inside the procedure being called. There are two primary reasons for doing so. The first reason is that the procedure can be called from many places in the application. If you wanted to take a timing every time the procedure is called, you would have to wrap the timing code around each call. This would require a great deal of code duplication and extra effort on your part. You would have to worry about duplicating the code every single place the procedure was called throughout your application. If, on the other hand, you place the timing inside the procedure itself, you have to write the timing code only once for that procedure and are guaranteed that it will take place every time the procedure gets called.

Another reason you might want to consider putting the timing calls inside the procedure itself is the overhead in calling the procedure and the possibility of having to load the code module from memory. If you begin timing before you make the call to the procedure, you must incur the additional time that Visual Basic takes to jump to the subroutine. This penalty becomes even more costly if the code module must be loaded into memory.

Windows loads code into memory on a module-by-module basis. If the code that is calling a procedure exists in module A, and the procedure itself exists in module B, Windows will have to load that module into memory before it can execute the procedure. If your timings are placed in the calling procedure, they will incur the expense in the time it takes to load the module in which the procedure resides into memory *in addition to* the time it takes to jump to and execute the procedure. Consider, for example, the code in Listing 5.8, where you have two modules and are calling a subroutine.

Listing 5.8. Calling code in a different module.

```
Module A                                  Module B

Sub Main()                                Sub My_Subroutine()
   Call My_Subroutine                     ... body of code...
End Sub                                   End Sub
```

If module B is not in memory when `My_Subroutine` is called, it will take more time for the subroutine to execute from module A's point of view. If you take the timing in module A, it will take longer than if done in module B.

You might want to put the timing code in the calling procedure if you want to get an indication of how long it takes a function to execute if the module is not loaded into memory, but a great deal of effort would be needed to make sure the module was not loaded when the function was called. Furthermore, the delay would *most likely* only occur the first time—but not necessarily, as the module could get taken out of memory at some point. Thus, the inaccuracy of such an approach makes it prohibitive. Once again, the best approach is to keep timing measurements wrapped up inside the function calls themselves if it is the execution time of the functions, and not the calling overhead, that you are concerned with.

How to Time Simple Code Groups

Simple code groups include areas in a procedure where you simply want to time a group of code statements or perhaps even a single code statement. In cases when you want to test a specific set of code, it is often best, when possible, to build a *test loop* that executes the series of statements over and over again and takes the overall timing of the entire loop. This gives you a longer timing interval to compare against different methods, as the same operation is carried out repeatedly. It might be advisable to place this test loop code in its own executable in order to test it as a modular component. (See Chapter 6, "Factors That Affect Performance," for more information regarding performance assessment strategies and techniques.) Creating test applications that evaluate one piece of code in a loop of multiple trials can be much more accurate when you're doing comparison testing. Using timings with loops is discussed in the next section.

How to Time Loops

There are essentially two methods you can use when timing loops. You can place your timing code completely around the loop or you can place timing code inside the loop itself. Because loops usually execute the same group of code more than once, you must be careful when measuring timings inside the loop. The overhead you incur by taking a timing in the inner loop will be multiplied by the number of times you proceed through the loop. This additional overhead usually makes timing inside a loop at the same time as timing outside the loop prohibitive. On the other hand, it can be appropriate if, for some reason, you want to see how long specific runs through the loop take.

Consider the code in Listing 5.9. In this listing, timings are taken both inside and outside the code loop.

Listing 5.9. Taking timings inside and outside a loop.

```
Private Sub GetName()

       Const NAME_COUNT = 1000

       Dim sngInnerStartTime as Single, sngInnerEndTime as Single
       Dim sngOuterStartTime as Single, sngOuterEndTime as Single
       Dim iCount as Integer

       sngOuterStartTime = Timer
       For iCount = 1 to NAME_COUNT

              Call Get_Last_Name

              sngInnerStartTime = Timer
              Call Get_First_Name
              sngInnerEndTime = Timer

              Debug.Print "Get_First_Name elapsed time in GetName subroutine
                     ➥(iCount = " & iCount & ") = " &
                     ➥Format(sngInnerEndTime - sngInnerStartTime, "#####.0000")

              Call Create_Full_Name

              Call Store_Full_Name

       Next iCount
       sngOuterEndTime = Timer

       Debug.Print "Loop elapsed time in GetName subroutine = " &
                     Format(sngOuterEndTime - sngOuterStartTime, "#####.0000")

End Sub
```

Note that the overhead in setting the inner timer will make the outer timer less accurate. A measure of this overhead delay can be represented by

```
delay = outer_delay + iCount  * inner_delay
```

where `delay` is the total delay time, `outer_delay` is the delay in measuring the entire loop execution time, and `inner_delay` represents the delay in getting the time for the `GetName` function inside the loop. Because there is usually no practical reason to put the timings inside the loop, it is advisable not to do so unless absolutely necessary.

How to Time Conditional Code

Finally, you need to know how to take timings when working with conditional code. The simplest way to time a conditional code section is to put a timing statement before and after the conditional statement. This will work fine as long as you can guarantee that the program will reach the statement following the conditional structure. The code shown in Listing 5.10, for instance, would work fine.

Listing 5.10. Conditional code with correct timing.

```
Private Sub Check_Start(intStartFlag as Integer)

       Dim sngStartTime as Single, sngEndTime as Single

       sngStartTime = Timer

       If intStartFlag = False Then
              lstParts.Clear
              txtName.Text = ""
              txtSerialNum = ""
              timTimer.Interval = 3000
              timTimer.Enabled = True
              intStartFlag = True
       Else
              cmdProceed.Enabled = True
              timTimer.Enabled = False
       End If

       sngEndTime = Timer

       Debug.Print "Elapsed time in Get_First_Name subroutine where
                 ➥iStartFlag = " & iStartFlag & " = " &
                 ➥Format(sngEndTime - sngStartTime, "#####.0000")

End Sub
```

This code example works because there is no code within the conditional statement that would cause the program to exit without reporting the end timing. Also note that the particular branch that the loop took is printed in the debug window along with the elapsed time. This is very important, as the meaningfulness of the timing usually depends on which branch it took. Always remember to declare the branching activity when reporting the time so that you have as complete a picture as possible.

In Listing 5.11, the programmer did not properly design the subroutine to report the time for every condition in the subroutine.

Listing 5.11. Conditional code with incorrect timing.

```
Private Sub Check_Start(intStartFlag as Integer)

       Dim sngStartTime as Single, sngEndTime as Single

       sngStartTime = Timer

       ' If operation has not started yet, then start it
       If intStartFlag = False Then
              lstParts.Clear
              txtName.Text = ""
              txtSerialNum.Text = ""
              timTimer.Interval = 3000
              timTimer.Enabled = True
              intStartFlag = True
              Goto Check_Start_Exit             ' Exit the subroutine
       End If

       ' The operation has already started, so just initialize
       ' a few controls
       cmdProceed.Enabled = True
       timTimer.Enabled = False

       ' Take the ending time
       sngEndTime = Timer


Check_Start_Exit:

       MsgBox "We have started!"

       Debug.Print "Check_Start elapsed time = " &
                     Format(sngEndTime - sngStartTime, "#####.0000")

End Sub
```

In this case, the `Goto` statement causes the program to jump over the line of code that sets the ending time. Because the end time is never set, the time value would be wrong and would be reported incorrectly. This code is very poorly structured and is a good example of an improper use of the `Goto` command. It does, however, illustrate the potential problem of failing to set the end timing in a conditional code group and therefore reporting an inaccurate result. The same considerations are present with any of the keywords that can cause a non-sequential code flow in a routine, including `Exit Sub`, `Exit Func`, and `Raise`.

Making Timings Meaningful

You have examined the various timers you can use in your code, how precise they are, and how you should go about placing timing code in your application. The remainder of this chapter tells you how to derive meaning from the timing values you get in your application.

As you saw in Chapter 4, it is never wise to base a performance analysis on one timing. Often, in order to get a truly accurate picture, you must take many timings of the same event and collect a set of data. Because it takes time to collect a set of data, you must have a feel for how much data should be collected before an accurate determination of performance is achieved.

The process of taking more than one timing and obtaining meaningful results from a set of values requires the basic use of *statistical analysis*. In this section, you will be introduced to some simple statistical-analysis theory that will help you derive meaning from the timings you obtain.

Here are the three steps in obtaining an accurate timing value:

1. Collect a set of timings.
2. Calculate the *average*, *median*, and *standard deviation* of the timing set.
3. Decide whether the standard deviation is acceptable. If it is, take the average and use it as the final value. If it's not, repeat these steps after taking more readings.

As mentioned previously, one timing is almost never sufficient to accurately determine how long a portion of code takes to execute. The particular activity under evaluation should be timed again and again, because Windows can cause timings to vary during execution (see Chapter 6 for an extensive discussion on this subject).

The performance analyst should plan on getting at least 10 data points for any code being timed. Each sample should be taken under the same conditions, and the user's steps to get the code to execute should be the same. If they are not, the timings will vary. In Chapter 6, you'll learn how to make your performance measurements as accurate as possible. Until you read that chapter, let's assume that you have taken the timings in the correct manner and have a set of data that is as accurate as you've been able to make it. As already discussed, timings will always vary somewhat—it's simply the nature of Windows. This is why you would never want to take one timing and assume it will always be the same.

Are 10 timings sufficient? Are 100? How can you tell? Let's suppose you have written a database application and are taking timings in a subroutine that carries out the initialization of the database. Because you're really not sure how many readings to take, you take 10 readings, as shown in Table 5.1.

Table 5.1. A timing set with 10 values.

Timing	*Time (ms)*
1	230
2	20
3	40
4	180
5	130
6	120
7	20
8	110
9	150
10	30

After you have taken a certain number of timings, you can get some idea of the accuracy of the values by taking the average, the median (or middle value), and the standard deviation of the data set.

The *average* of a set of values is useful in order to see where the center of your values falls. The average is given as

$$\mu \equiv \frac{\sum_{i=1}^{N} Xi}{N}$$

where μ is the average, N is the number of variables, Xi is the ith value in the set, and Σ represents the summation of all values ranging from $i=1$ to N.

The *median* of a data set is the middle number in the set. If the set has an even number of values, it is the higher of the middle two values. If the set has an odd number of items, the median is the middle number. The median is useful to see where the middle number falls. The median can help determine whether a few values differ drastically from the rest of the set. If the median differs significantly from the average, the numbers will deviate significantly—perhaps because of a few stray values in the set.

The *standard deviation* of a set of numbers indicates how far the values drift from the norm. The standard deviation is given as

$$\sigma \equiv \sqrt{\frac{\sum_{i=1}^{N}(\mu - xi)^2}{N}}$$

where Σ is the standard deviation, μ is the average, *Xi* is the *i*th data point, and *N* is the total number of points. The standard deviation gives you an idea of how much your values drift around the median, or middle of the set. It is used to determine the amount in which the values drift.

For the values in Table 5.1, the average is calculated as

$$\frac{230+20+40+180+130+160+20+110+150+30}{10} = 107$$

If the set of values is organized in increasing order, the set consists of 20, 20, 30, 40, 110, 130, 150, 160, 180, and 230. Because there is an even number of values in the set, the median is the sixth value, or 130. The standard deviation is calculated as

$$\sqrt{\frac{(107-230)^2+(107-20)^2+(107-40)^2+...+(107-30)^2}{10}} = 75$$

Note that the median differs significantly from the average and the standard deviation seems quite high. Ideally, you would like to get the average and the median values to agree as much as possible and have as small a deviation as possible. So you take another set of readings, except this time, you take 20, as shown in Table 5.2.

Table 5.2. A timing set with 20 values.

Timing	*Time (ms)*
1	230
2	20
3	40
4	180
5	130
6	160
7	20
8	110
9	150
10	30

continues

Table 5.2. continued

Timing	*Time (ms)*
11	130
12	90
13	70
14	90
15	50
16	140
17	150
18	120
19	110
20	120

If the set of values is organized in increasing order, the set consists of 20, 20, 30, 40, 50, 70, 90, 90, 110, 110, 120, 120, 130, 130, 140, 150, 150, 160, 180, and 230. The results from the expanded data set produce an average of 107, a median of 120, and a standard deviation of 56. Notice that this time the median is closer to the average and the standard deviation has dropped by about 25 percent. Obviously, taking more readings gives you a lower standard deviation even though the average stays the same. This trend gives you more confidence in your average, as the standard deviation continues to drop. Just for fun, you take 10 more readings for a set of 30, as shown in Table 5.3.

Table 5.3. A timing set with 30 values.

Timing	*Time (ms)*
1	230
2	20
3	40
4	180
5	130
6	160
7	20
8	110
9	150
10	300
11	130

Timing	*Time (ms)*
12	90
13	70
14	90
15	50
16	140
17	150
18	120
19	110
20	120
21	90
22	100
23	120
24	90
25	100
26	120
27	100
28	40
29	90
30	120

If the set of values is organized in increasing order, the set consists of 20, 20, 40, 40, 50, 70, 90, 90, 90, 90, 90, 100, 100, 100, 110, 110, 120, 120, 120, 120, 120, 130, 130, 140, 150, 150, 160, 180, 230, and 300. This set of values produces an average of 107, a median of 110, and a standard deviation of 4.6. Now the median is very close to the average, and the standard deviation continues to drop. You are likely to conclude at this point, with confidence, that your timing is (on average) 107 milliseconds. In order to determine this, you had to continue taking data until you were able to see a trend in your results. As the trend was observed, you gained confidence in your results.

In order to determine these results, you must have a means of taking the average, standard deviation, and median of a set of data. Although this can be quite tedious to do by hand, it is very easy to accomplish with a spreadsheet application such as Excel, or with the TimeLog OLE Automation server utility discussed in Chapter 7, "Supporting Utilities for Performance Analysis."

Summary

In this chapter you have been presented with information on how to take performance measurements. The chapter discusses two specific issues:

- Using timing methods inside an application
- Making timings meaningful

The chapter points out the way to take timings in event procedures; when working with database functions; and when timing functions and subroutines, simple code groups, loops, and conditional code. Various issues to watch out for are pointed out along the way, and code listings guide you when implementing the timing measurements in your own applications.

The chapter also describes how to make timings meaningful and useful. Included in this discussion is an introduction to simple statistical techniques required to obtain meaningful results. Specifically, you have learned the necessity of taking more than one timing; how and why to take the average, median, and standard deviation of the set of timing values; and, as the data set size increases, to watch for trends in the data to determine the stability of the numbers being obtained. Ultimately, the analyst must come to the conclusion that the standard deviation has settled and the median and average agree to the point where there is enough confidence in the average timing value to use it as a benchmark for comparison.

In this and the past few chapters, it has been mentioned that Windows can make timings inherently inaccurate. Chapter 6 covers strategies and techniques to reduce this potential instability. Now that you have a better understanding of *how* to take performance measurements, you will be presented with steps to make sure your measurements are as consistent, relevant, and accurate as possible.

Obey the Signs

Wrong Way: One performance timing is sufficient to get a rough idea of performance.

Taking one timing of a process is almost as bad as not taking any timings at all. The very nature of how Windows operates virtually guarantees that your timings will be somewhat different every time they are taken. Make sure you take as many timings as possible, checking to make sure that the average and median values converge and that the standard deviation is acceptably low. If you base your performance analysis on one timing value, you might be surprised to find that, in the majority of cases, the actual amount of time is much higher or much lower than you expected.

Beware of Falling Rocks: Never rely on timer data that does not provide enough accuracy.

Using a timer with insufficient resolution might give you an overly optimistic view of the performance of your application, and you probably wouldn't optimize areas that

you should. This is why it is important to use as accurate a timing method as possible, using a timer with sufficient resolution for what you are testing.

Wrong Way: You can take enough data to be absolutely sure of an accurate performance measurement.

Although a careful analysis of timing values can make you reasonably confident of how long a routine takes to execute, make sure you don't become overconfident with any values you measure. This might sound contradictory to the previous statements, but you actually must make a compromise between the two. Make sure your values are reliable enough to warrant making decisions on whether to optimize. Keep in mind, however, that the increase in performance you obtain by optimizing the code might not be as dramatic on other systems on which you happen to test the application. Likewise, other systems might have other factors that affect performance but that are not present on your system.

Q&A

Q What do I do if I can't take enough readings to get reliable timings?

A If you do not see some sort of trend emerging from your data, it is likely that other factors are influencing your application, making the timings very unstable. There are things you can and should do to make sure those timing values are more stable. Refer to Chapter 6 for a more thorough consideration of these issues.

Q Why do I need to worry so much about how to put timing code in my applications?

A If you go through all the trouble of placing timing-analysis code in your application, you might as well do it right. Timing-analysis code can be left in the rest of the code throughout the development cycle. Normally, it is removed to improve performance in the final product, but in many cases the maintainability convenience might merit keeping it in. If you send your timing results to the debug window, you can leave the analysis code in the application for performance-tuning purposes. Although your application will run slightly more slowly than it would without the statements, the timing information will not be visible to the user when the compiled program is run. The timings are only visible when you run the application in the Visual Basic development environment.

You can also structure the code in such a way that a debug flag must be set in order for the timings to take place, although this still imposes a performance penalty since the flag checks are included in the compiled program. Alternatively, you can insert the timing code within a conditional compile, as presented in Chapter 4. With this approach, you can control whether timings are included in the compiled executable when you build the application. In any event, you must make sure your timing-analysis code works properly before you can depend on it.

Workshop

Calculate the average, median, and standard deviations of the following sets of timings. What lessons can you learn from the results?

Timing Set A

Timing	*Time (ms)*	*Timing*	*Time (ms)*
1	230	6	160
2	20	7	20
3	40	8	110
4	180	9	150
5	130	10	30

Timing Set B

Timing	*Time (ms)*	*Timing*	*Time (ms)*
1	100	6	60
2	140	7	90
3	50	8	110
4	180	9	170
5	130	10	40

Timing Set C

Timing	*Time (ms)*	*Timing*	*Time (ms)*
1	90	6	100
2	110	7	110
3	100	8	110
4	120	9	130
5	100	10	100

Timing Set D

Timing	*Time (ms)*	*Timing*	*Time (ms)*
1	110	6	100
2	100	7	110
3	110	8	110
4	110	9	100
5	110	10	110

Workshop Answers

Timing Set	*Average*	*Median*	*Standard Deviation*
A	107	130	75.4
B	107	110	48.6
C	107	110	11.6
D	107	110	4.8

From the results listed here, the last set gives you the most confidence. If you only relied on the average, it would appear that all the sets are equally reliable. Note, however, that the median slowly drifts toward the average and the standard deviation drops drastically. This is an indicator that you can rely on the average obtained.

Factors That Affect Performance

Thus far, this book has defined and discussed performance and optimization, pointed out when and where to optimize, and presented methods to properly measure performance. This chapter discusses some of the specific factors that make timings less accurate and proposes solutions to minimize the amount of instability in Windows that causes timings to be imprecise. By minimizing these instabilities, your timings will be more accurate and more reliable, which will lead to better performance-optimization choices.

In addition to the inherent issues in Windows that lead to fluctuating performance measurements, this chapter addresses other factors within the application that make timings inaccurate. These are not necessarily due to the Windows operating environment, but are instead a function of other components of your application. Issues such as network access, database size and complexity, and various application configurations can make timings fluctuate from one run of an application to another. You will be introduced to methods for reducing instability related to these factors.

The ability to *minimize,* not eliminate, factors that make timings fluctuate in an application is vital to a discussion of the issues in this chapter. Although you can certainly limit the causes of fluctuation, you can never totally eliminate them. The goal of this chapter is to give the analyst an understanding of the causes of inaccuracy in timings, and specifically where you might expect these variances in your applications. If you target a low-end user system throughout your analysis, you will have a realistic picture of what variances exist. Armed with this knowledge, you can then determine the *reliability* of various timings in your application and ascertain their usefulness based on that determination.

Factors Outside the Application That Limit Timing Accuracy

The Windows operating system and the computer hardware are the first two factors that tend to make timings unreliable. Some specific factors are listed in this section, each of which will be addressed in turn. The list is not necessarily prioritized by importance, as each issue can contribute individually to variations in measuring performance. Furthermore, with the advent of Windows 95, some of these issues are much less relevant. They are relevant, however, in previous versions of Windows.

Keep in mind that the significance of each of these issues depends, in part, on the specific hardware and operating system configuration of the computer being used. Because the purpose of performance analysis is to most adequately meet the user's performance expectations, you must take this into account and design and optimize to satisfy the worst-case scenario whenever possible.

Here is a summary of the issues that are addressed in this section:

- Available memory and CPU type
- Hard disk speed
- Swap file parameters
- Disk caching
- Windows multitasking
- Network loading and drive access
- Video cards and display speed

Each of these issues is addressed in turn. In each case, the issue is identified and explained, and strategies for reducing its negative impact on performance accuracy are addressed.

Available Memory and CPU Type

In the computer industry, systems that are at one moment leading-edge systems can become virtually obsolete in a matter of a few years. Hardware technology continues to improve rapidly in the '90s and outpaces improvements in software engineering. A good example of this is Intel's release of the Pentium processor. After the Pentium was first released, a very small amount of software took advantage of the increased processor speed and power. Some industry pundits even claim that today's software is not tapping the full potential of the Intel 80486 (or 486) processor, let alone the Pentium. Yet today you can still find a substantial number of users who are completely satisfied with the power and performance a 486 can provide.

One observable trend over the past several years has been an increase in the size of applications and the amount of memory they require to run adequately. For example, only a few years ago a PC with 4MB of RAM was adequate for most applications. Today, many packages are designed to run with a minimum of 8MB of memory. Any computer dealer will tell you that a system with 8MB of memory is the practical minimum to run powerful software today.

The fact that software continues to use more and more memory becomes more of a critical issue when users multitask these applications. Most users are not satisfied with the performance Windows 3.1 provides when simultaneously running two or three powerful applications such as Microsoft Word, Microsoft Excel, and Microsoft Access without large amounts of RAM. Users find that applications perform considerably better if their systems have from 4MB to 8MB of memory. The jump from 8MB to 16MB or higher improves performance even more, although the law of diminishing returns will begin to play a more prominent role as memory increases.

Windows 95 provides improved memory management over Windows 3.1, but even in Windows 95, more memory makes execution of programs more efficient. The absolute minimum requirement is 4MB of RAM to run Windows 95, but this is a bare minimum—Windows behaves quite sluggishly. A jump to 8MB, however, dramatically improves performance. 16MB is enough to make Windows 95 perform very well. But memory is still comparatively expensive, and often users must settle for less than what would be optimal.

In most cases, the developer cannot predict the amount of memory the user will have on a computer. Often, developers use powerful computers with great amounts of memory. As they design their applications, developers can forget that their users might not have computer systems with as much memory or processing power as they do. Developers are often surprised to find, upon releasing the software, that most of their users use computer systems with much less memory and power than the developers. As a result, their users complain about performance.

Therefore, the developer must be sure to test the application on a variety of computer configurations with different amounts of memory and different processors. Ultimately, the developer must decide on the minimum configuration and build to that level. He must be sure to communicate the minimum system requirements to the user. If you go to the store and pick up the latest game off the shelf, you will usually find on the side of the box a list of system requirements. These requirements are most likely determined to be the minimum requirements, and often the software checks to make sure those conditions exist before it will even run. You as a developer also must be aware of minimum requirements, stating them clearly to the user and treating the minimum configuration as the worst-case system. If you can satisfy user expectations on your low-end target system, performance is bound to improve as the amount of memory and processor type improve.

The average Visual Basic application has a tendency to consume a significant amount of memory, partially due to the way Visual Basic hides complex layers of functionality and provides the programmer with a simpler interface. If the computer does not have much memory to begin with, and the combined application demands are large, Windows must resort to moving parts of the application and its data out to the *hard drive*, a mechanical device that is considerably slower than fast, electronic memory. Furthermore, if the user is running many applications at the same time, memory will be further degraded, resulting in an additional drop in performance. The issues of multitasking and the hard drive are addressed in later sections. As a *general* rule, however, the smaller the amount of available memory, the worse a Windows application will perform.

When you're taking timings, the amount of available memory in the system and the type of processor will often result in differences in timings. The best way to minimize this impact is to make sure you have the same amount of memory and the same processor when trying to get meaningful timings across systems. For example, if you take a timing, make a performance improvement, and then take another timing, you want to make sure you use the same processor with the same amount of memory. Ideally, you should take the second timing on the same computer on which you took the first.

Analogy: Taking Trial Runs Under Consistent Conditions

Suppose you built yourself a kite and took it out to the park to try it out. On any particular day, you might encounter certain wind conditions. Furthermore, the park is likely to have trees and other such obstacles in the area where you are flying the kite. You give the kite a try on a particular day and decide it just doesn't get high enough—the kite keeps crashing to the ground even though the wind ought to be sufficient to get it high into the sky.

You decide to make some changes to the shape of the kite to streamline it and give it more lift. You go back out the next day with your new and improved kite to give it a try. Instead of going to the park you went to yesterday, you go to another park. You get out on the field, expecting much better performance from your kite. To your chagrin, however, you find that this kite performs even worse than the first one. In disgust, you storm off the field. As you walk out of the park, an expert kite flyer notices your disgust and comes over to talk to you.

As a more experienced kite flyer than you, he is quick to point out that the wind was much stronger yesterday than it is today. He also points out that the trees at the other park are much lower to the ground than the ones here. Suddenly, you realize his point. The wind and terrain conditions are different today and are, in fact, worse. Of course your kite won't fly any better, even though you have improved it.

So it often can be when you're optimizing an application on two different computers. Suppose your application performs poorly on computer A. You optimize it and then run it on computer B. If it performs worse on computer B, it does not necessarily mean your attempt at optimization has failed. It might simply mean you are running the application on a computer with less horsepower and/or memory. Just as you couldn't be sure whether your kite was actually better because of changing conditions, you cannot make an accurate determination in this case. Now if you were to fix up the kite and fly it on the same day, at the same park, and with the same wind conditions, you might indeed notice a speedup. If you optimize an application and run it on the same computer, you will also get a better picture of whether the optimization improves performance.

Therefore, you should minimize the impact of CPU and memory differences by always testing performance improvements on the same computer whenever possible. But beware. There are many other factors that can throw off timings, as you'll learn in the following section. Don't forget to take them *all* into account.

The choice of which computer platform to use in assessing performance is very important. You should know how the capabilities of your test PC relate to the minimum target PC and, if possible, measure performance on the minimum-targeted system. By doing so, you can make an effort to meet the needs of those users with computers at the bottom of the performance curve and can make sure your application runs at an acceptable performance level on those systems.

> **NOTE:** When taking timings, make sure the computer's memory and CPU configuration do not change. Avoid taking performance tests on different machines if your goal is to maintain consistency between timings. The best choice of a computer for performance analysis is one with the minimum configuration you will specify for your users.

Windows Memory Management in a Nutshell

In the last section, you learned that if not enough memory is available, Windows and the operating system often move data out to the hard disk. This is part of what Windows calls its *virtual memory system.* Although this chapter does not delve into the technical details of memory management, following is a brief explanation of how memory management works.

Essentially, the operating system attempts to hold as much data in the computer's memory (the RAM chips on the motherboard) as possible. As programs demand more and more memory, and more than one program is run at the same time, Windows begins to run out of on-board memory to hold the increased amount of data. As memory demands increase, there might simply not be enough RAM to hold all of the programs and their data. As a result, Windows can move the segments of memory not currently required out onto the hard drive. When those pieces are again needed, they are pulled back off the hard drive, possibly replacing other pieces in memory that must be exchanged.

Analogy: Expensive but Fast Versus Cheap but Slow Retrieval

Suppose you've been elected to bake a cake for an upcoming Christmas party. On some snowy afternoon, you decide to give it a try and you decide what you need. Fortunately, you already have some of the ingredients you need in your cupboard. The others you have to go out and buy. Once you have everything, you're ready to begin. In order to get your cake finished as quickly as possible, you want to have all the ingredients you need as close to you as possible, which in your case is on your counter. Rather than having to run to the cupboard for every single ingredient, it is more advantageous to get everything you need out in front of you ahead of time so that you can work faster and more efficiently.

When a computer runs a program, the user wants the program to run as quickly as possible, just as you want to make your cake as quickly as possible. Just as you want all the ingredients close by, so the computer wants its programs and data close by in memory so that it can access them quickly.

Unfortunately, you have a lot more cupboard space than you do counter space, so you can't possibly put everything out on the counter at once. Similarly, a computer system typically cannot store in memory all the data it needs at once. It must resort to placing some of the data out on the hard drive, which is bigger but slower. If you keep the ingredients you use the most out on the counter and put back the ingredients you haven't used for a while into the cupboard, you ensure that the ingredients out on the counter will be as useful to you as possible. Similarly, the computer also keeps the data and code it has used most recently in memory, while it keeps the code and data not currently required out on the hard drive.

> **NOTE:** You can improve the speed of many applications by adding memory.

Hard Drive Speed

The last section discusses the need for computers to place code and data on the hard disk rather than in memory when memory gets limited. The speed of the hard drive is therefore important when code and data must be moved back and forth. In fact, hard drive speed is an important factor when an application performs *any* type of file I/O, such as when working with local databases, text files, and other types of data files.

The faster the hard drive can read and write data to and from the hard disk, the better the performance. Just as in the case of the processor and memory, the hard drive and its controller similarly affect performance. When taking multiple timings in an application, the use of different hard drives on the same single-user system can lead to fluctuating results. To avoid this problem, use the same computer and the same hard drive on that computer when taking multiple timings. Otherwise, the performance differences among the hard drives can have a major impact on the performance results.

Hard drive *fragmentation* is another important issue. Drives that are highly fragmented offer poorer performance, especially in file I/O–intensive programs. When making comparisons between different optimizations, make sure these tests are done with the same level of drive fragmentation. It is, of course, always wise to keep fragmentation to a minimum before you even begin testing and optimizing.

> **NOTE:** Do not change the hard driveor controller if you want to maintain consistency between performance timings. If possible, use a hard drive with the slowest allowable access speed when assessing the worst-case user-performance level and a midrange-speed hard drive to gauge typical user performance.

Swap File Parameters

When Windows uses up all of the physical memory of the computer and needs more memory, it relies on its *swap file* to bring information into and out of memory.

Analogy: A Swap File Is Like a Desk Drawer

When working at his desk, an employee can eventually fill up the entire desk with as much paperwork as possible. When that happens, some of the paperwork must be put back away to make room for other things. In such a case, the employee might put some of the papers he isn't working with at the moment into a drawer. When he needs the

continues

> papers in the drawer, he can simply pull them back out and put other papers that are on the desk into the drawer, if necessary. Windows handles data in much the same way. When it runs out of physical memory for data storage, it relegates the data out to the swap file, making room in memory for other data. When the data in the swap file is once again needed, other data can be swapped in and out of the file as needed.

In the versions of Windows before Windows 95, the user had to specify the size of this swap file and whether the file is permanently fixed on the hard drive or is simply temporary. Windows 95, however, uses a different methodology for swap files so that there is no longer a distinction between a temporary and a permanent swap file. The only concern in Windows 95 is the size of the file, which Windows 95 can automatically set for the user. Windows 95 chooses the best swap file size, although it does enable the user to override the settings and set the minimum and maximum sizes manually if desired.

For those using Windows 3.*x* or Windows for Workgroups rather than Windows 95, however, the type of the swap file must be considered. The difference between a permanent swap file and a temporary one can have a drastic impact on performance, especially when memory is limited and swapping to the drive must take place frequently. A *permanent swap file* is faster because Windows always knows exactly where it is on the hard drive. It is never moved, has a fixed size, and is contiguous, not fragmented. These factors make it easier to manage. A *temporary swap file*, on the other hand, can move around on the hard drive and grow and shrink in size. Furthermore, the file can be broken into fragments, which means that the hard drive's read head must jump all over the hard drive's magnetic surface to read the data in the file, thus slowing down the data access time. The extra work needed to manage the temporary swap file also slows down the system somewhat.

If you're using a version of Windows previous to Windows 95, the best way to minimize the instability of performance timings is to keep the swap file the same type throughout testing. In other words, keep it either permanent or temporary throughout the performance assessment. A permanent swap file is preferable to a temporary swap file not only in terms of stability and performance, but also because temporary swap files change dynamically in size. The size of this file can change from one session to another, depending on available disk space. To eliminate this source of variance, use a permanent swap file.

The size of the swap file is also very important. If the swap file is too large, more overhead is required, which will slow down the system. If, on the other hand, the file is too small, it will not be able to hold enough data and the system will be constantly swapping data, which is often called *thrashing*. This slows down the system drastically. Therefore, the size must be chosen carefully. In the case of performance analysis, the size of the swap file should not be changed from one performance analysis to another. This avoids introducing more instability into the system that can throw performance timings off.

NOTE: Be sure to keep the type and size of the swap file the same in order to ensure a more accurate timing analysis between two runs of an application. In the worst-case performance assessment, no swap file could be used, whereas the best-case performance assessment includes the use of a permanent swap file.

Disk Caching

In order to make the process of moving data to and from the hard drive faster and more efficient, Windows, in cooperation with DOS, commonly uses a technique called *drive caching*. A *hard drive cache* is a section of computer memory that holds data that normally goes on the hard drive. There are two main cache types: read and read/write caches. *Read caches* are used only for reading data. *Read/write caches*, on the other hand, can be read from and written to. The cache improves performance because instead of directly writing everything to the hard drive, the cache acts as a temporary data buffer. The cache holds the data that would normally go on the hard drive until the cache becomes full. When the cache fills up, it writes data out onto the hard drive. If the data is in the cache, it can be read much faster than from the hard drive because the cache uses memory.

Analogy: Accessing the Cache Versus the Hard Drive

Suppose that on some sunny afternoon you are stuck in your office doing some work. The work you are doing involves referencing a large number of books. Most of the books you need reside on your bookshelf. If every time you need a new book you have to walk over to the bookshelf, find the book, and bring it back to your desk, you could slow your work down considerably. A better solution would be to pull out several frequently required books and stick them on top of your desk. That way, when you need a new book, you will have a direct, fast way to get at it versus the slower approach of going over to the bookshelf. You won't have as many books on the top of the desk to access as you do at the bookshelf, however, so eventually you'll have to go back over to the bookshelf for more. The time you save by getting several books at once and having them close by, however, will make you more productive overall.

This simple analogy illustrates the benefit of using a disk cache versus exclusively using the hard drive. The books represent data, the bookshelf represents the hard drive, and the desktop represents the cache. When the operating system must access more data, it can save time by using the cache versus accessing the hard drive every time. True, you might run out of books on the desktop from time to time, but then you can grab a bunch more from the bookshelf when you need them. Similarly, the operating system might run out of data in the cache, but the caching program can go out to the hard drive to get more, when necessary, and save the time of continually having to access the hard drive.

Although this analogy paints a somewhat simplistic picture, it should convey to you the general idea of the practical use of a disk cache. Keep in mind that there are a variety of types of caches, and caching activity can vary widely based on the system configuration.

The size of a disk cache is very important. If the cache is too small, the management of getting data into and out of the cache can drown out the increase in performance from using it in the first place. Likewise, if the cache gets too big, the overhead required to manage it can decrease or even eliminate its positive effect. An optimal cache size should be determined based on the amount of available memory on the system. If the size of the cache is changed from one performance analysis to another, timings can be affected. In order to minimize the instability this would cause, the developer should make sure the size of the cache does not change from one timing to another.

The type of cache is also very important. A write cache has a much bigger impact on performance than does a read cache. A write cache must make sure its data is synchronized with the hard drive, and it must incur the additional penalty of writing data to the hard drive in order to maintain that synchronization. A read cache must also make sure its data is consistent with that of the hard drive, but it does not incur the time penalty of having to write to the hard drive. A write operation to the disk is much slower than a read operation.

Another issue for those using versions of Windows before Windows 95 is whether Windows uses 32-bit file and disk access. These options enable Windows to access data on the drive in a more efficient manner. The details of disk caching, 32-bit file and disk access, and memory management in general are beyond the scope of this book. Suffice it to say that if you are using 32-bit file or disk access, do not change the settings from one timing to another. Keep in mind that your users may have configurations that differ considerably from that of your own computer. You cannot predict what the user's settings will be, but you can make sure yours are consistent so that when you compare one timing to another, you can get more accurate results.

> **NOTE:** Keep the type and size of the cache consistent throughout performance assessment. For the worst-case scenario, do not even use a cache.

Multitasking Windows Applications

Another factor to consider when trying to make performance measurements as accurate as possible is *multitasking.* Multitasking is when the user runs more than one application at the same time. When several applications are run concurrently, those applications must share a finite amount of memory and hardware resources with each other. Under Windows 3.1 and 3.11, the applications must also actively cooperate with each other (with some help from the operating environment) to avoid causing the other programs to crash.

Because the operating environment must ensure that applications that run at the same time can live with each other, running multiple programs will almost always cause performance to drop. Taking timings in such a case can lead to a high degree of instability, because you cannot determine the state of the other applications running while your application is running, particularly from one instance to another. In order to better understand this, you must first understand how Windows multitasks applications.

When Microsoft Windows has more than one application running at the same time, it appears to the user that the computer is executing both applications at once. This, however, is an illusion. The computer is not capable of running more than one set of instructions at the same time. Either the computer runs program A or it runs program B. Windows creates the illusion that two programs are running at the same time by only running discrete parts of a program at any one time.

Windows 3.*x* and Windows for Workgroups rely on the individual programs to give control back to the Windows operating environment so that Windows can keep all the programs running along smoothly. Program A might run for 100 milliseconds and then relinquish control back to Windows. At that time, Windows might go ahead and run program B, which might run for 200 milliseconds. These programs can give control back to Windows so it can proceed to run each application, a little at a time. To the user, it appears that all the applications are running at the same time, albeit a bit slower than if just one were running. Figure 6.1 illustrates this concept.

Figure 6.1.
Non-preemptive multitasking Windows applications.

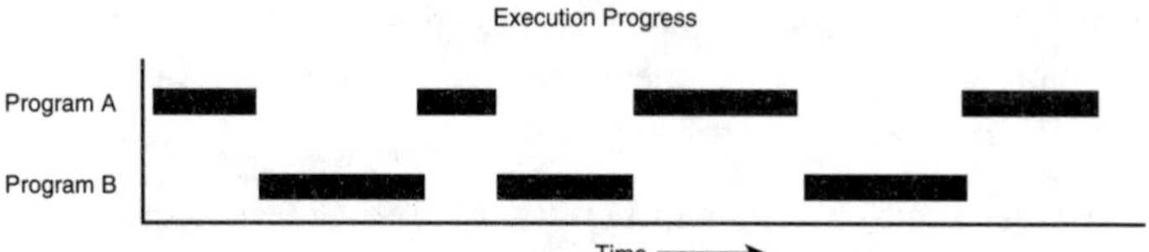

When users run Windows 3.*x* or Windows for Workgroups, if program A decides to run for 2 minutes before letting Windows run something else, there is nothing Windows can do about it. All the other programs simply have to wait for the program to finish and yield control. It is, therefore, the responsibility of the software developer to write a program that is well behaved and does not hog all the processing time for itself when running under these earlier versions of Windows. With the advent of Windows NT and Windows 95, however, Visual Basic programs can be targeted for true, preemptive multitasking operating systems.

When using a preemptive multitasking operating system such as Windows 95 or Windows NT, the operating system is the task manager. An operating system component called the *scheduler* enables processes to run a little at a time in fixed intervals in a fair manner. A simplified diagram of this is shown in Figure 6.2.

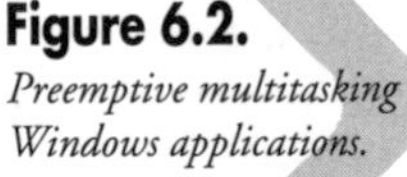

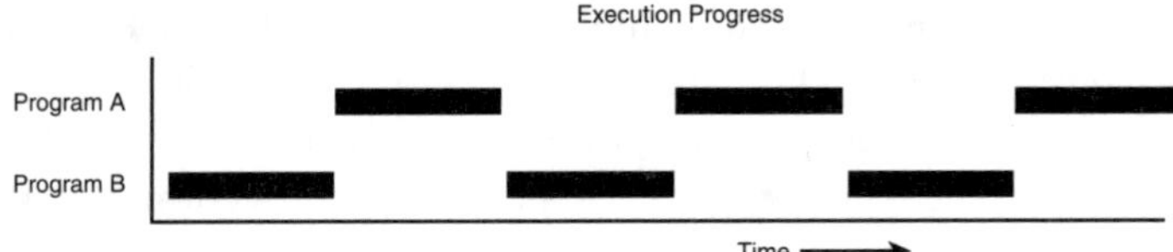

Figure 6.2.
Preemptive multitasking Windows applications.

Note that each slice of time given to a program is fixed and uniform. This assumes that the operating system is giving priority to every task equally. In most operating systems, tasks can be prioritized in such a way that certain applications get more computer than others. The picture presented in Figure 6.2 is quite simplistic, but it conveys the basic idea. The operating system, not each individual program, is in control. Thus, the operating system makes sure every program gets executed fairly (each in its own protected memory space).

Regardless of the nature of the operating system being used, the more programs you try to run simultaneously, the longer it takes for any one program to complete. As a result, the timings you take in an application can continue to increase as more applications are run simultaneously, because it takes longer for Windows to complete any one task.

Suppose you are trying to take a timing on an application and you have a spreadsheet and a word processor running as well. Assume that the spreadsheet is in the middle of a big calculation and the word processor is formatting a document for printing. If you execute your application at this point and take performance timings, the results you obtain might be considerably different than if it were the only program running. This is because the operating system has to run both programs, as shown in Figure 6.2, which makes any one program take longer to complete. Thus, the timing results would not be representative of the performance of any one program.

In order to minimize this instability, the most ideal solution is to have no other applications running at the time your application runs. If you must have other programs running in the background, the more consistent their usage of computer time and the better behaved they are, the better your readings will be. You should understand how those other applications demand computer time and how they affect your performance analysis. When doing performance comparisons, be aware of applications such as Microsoft Mail and Microsoft Exchange that run in the background and do background processing every so often. These types of applications introduce fluctuations in the system that can be avoided simply by not running them when doing performance analysis.

If possible, have only the application you are testing running in Windows when doing performance comparisons. Avoid whenever possible any type of multitasking activities. If you must run other applications, make sure they are being run in the same state and configuration every time you take timings. When assessing the performance expected on the user's computer (as opposed to doing comparison tests), run the application in an environment similar to what you anticipate the user will use, with the typical software he/she runs in order to get a fair picture of performance.

Network Loading and Drive Access

Another very important issue is network loading. *Network loading* refers to the amount of traffic on a network. As more users use the network at any given time, traffic increases on the system, and demands on the network servers increase as well. Network operations will, therefore, take more time to execute. When you're accessing any files, whether they are databases or anything else, the current load on the network will have an impact on the performance of your application. A perfect example of this is an application that uses a network database. If you were to run such an application, it might take much less time if you were to run it overnight when almost everyone in the company is off the network. If you were to run it during the morning, on the other hand, when peak network activity is taking place, you might see a totally different picture.

Thus, it is very important to understand how network loading issues affect performance. The more heavily your application draws from network resources, the greater the variability of timings when analyzing performance. The most sensible way to minimize this impact is to make sure the network has the same amount of loading for each trial run. The best case, of course, is to become the sole user of the network during the tests, but a more practical solution is simply to keep the number of users to a minimum. Beware of sudden surges in server activity, such as nightly server backups or other maintenance, that can drastically affect server loading.

In addition to network loading penalties, it takes more time to access a network drive than it does to access a local drive. This is because in order to access the network, your computer must communicate in a different way than it does with its own hard drive. The computer must retrieve the data through the use of network protocols and must read the data through the network's hard disk controller. These factors slow down the data-access process.

When you are running an application from a network versus from a local hard drive, performance will most certainly be affected in some way. Unless you have a very slow hard drive and the network server has a fast drive, the hard drive access on the network is likely to be slower and, as a result, your program will run more slowly as well. If you are taking timings on an application that runs on a local hard drive, and you then put the application on a network drive, your timings will not be consistent and you will not be able to make a valid comparison.

A more subtle but equally important issue is the use of floppy drives and CD-ROM drives versus hard drives. Floppy drives and CD-ROM drives are slower than hard drives, so here again, performance might be affected and timings would not be consistent enough for a valid comparison. A commercial application, for example, might make heavy use of a CD-ROM drive. If user A has a double-speed drive and user B has a triple-speed CD-ROM, performance could be drastically affected. Likewise, running an application from a floppy versus a hard drive would also be significant. Ultimately, the variance in speed depends on how much the application uses the floppy or CD-ROM drives for file I/O.

To minimize the impact of network drive speed, make sure you use the same drives and drive configurations when running multiple timings. If you take your first set of timings with the application on your hard drive, do not move the application to a networked drive and expect to get a comparable set of timings. Eliminate this problem simply by running the application in the same place. This applies not only to the executable file, but to data files and any associated files used to run the application.

Here are the important things to remember: When your application uses network resources, make sure the network load is as consistent across timings as possible. Run your application on the same drive with the same configuration. Avoid basing timing comparisons on applications that use networked drives whenever possible. Timings can fluctuate when using shared resources unless you're trying to specifically assess the network aspects of performance. Base network timings on typical network configurations—that is, the most common network card rather than the developer's newer and faster card. When assessing expected performance on the user's system, however, examine the application under expected typical loads.

Video Cards and Display Speed

A wide variety of graphics cards are on the market today. Most video cards are rated for their speed, essentially by how many pixels they can update per second. Many graphics cards accelerate their performance by making use of extra RAM on the video cards that is used as temporary buffer space to hold video information so that it can be manipulated faster. Other cards are faster because of the computer bus logic and communication that takes place between the monitor, the video card, and the video driver in the computer. Video display speed can have an impact on performance, particularly when it comes to loading and displaying Visual Basic forms. If your application makes use of animation, video speed becomes an even more important issue.

So to ensure accurate timings in an application, make sure the video card and its configuration are not changed from one run to another. Use a low-end video card to assess the worst-case performance scenario and a more standard video card for the typical case.

Factors Inside the Application That Limit Timing Accuracy

The issues discussed so far in this chapter have been issues *outside* the application that can cause performance measurements to be inaccurate. These issues are not inherent to the application, but are more specific to the way the computer hardware and operating system, and Windows in particular, are configured.

Also important are activities *inside* your application's source code that can cause timings to be inconsistent from one run to another. These activities occur as a *direct* result of some activity

in your application. Unfortunately, they are not as easy to eliminate as are the problems raised in the previous section because they are an inherent part of your application. In some cases, the impact can be minimized, but in most cases there is no way to eliminate the impact and the programmer must live with a particular amount of uncertainty. Here are some of the factors within an application that can make performance analysis unreliable:

- Database access
- DDE/OLE and interapplication communication
- Printing

Each of these issues is discussed, along with strategies for minimizing their impact on timing stability.

Database Access

If your application makes use of a database, whether it be private to the user or shared on a network, performance assessment can often be difficult. This is primarily due to the fact that databases are continuously changing in size. The performance of a database query, for instance, often depends to a great degree on the size of the database, causing results to vary greatly depending on that size.

Consider the following case. You are supporting an application that manages employee records in a company. You take a timing on Monday in which a query is performed and 100 records are retrieved from a table. After coming to the conclusion that performance is unacceptable, you apply one of the optimization techniques discussed in this book. You run the same application with the performance enhancements, only to find that the timing is worse. Is this because your performance method was ineffective? Not in this case. Since you last ran the application, the sales department placed 2,000 new entries into the database. The query might indeed be faster, but because it had to pull so many more records into memory, the application took longer to execute.

The same problem can apply to any database, whether on a network or stored locally. In order to minimize the impact of such instability, you must make sure the number of records in the database stays the same. If the number of records fluctuates, expect your timings to fluctuate as well if they are wrapped around any database activities.

Another potential problem occurs if the structure of the database changes. If tables are added or modified, it might take longer for your application to find and access what it needs to in the database. Again, in order to make your timings more accurate, you should avoid making any structural changes to the database. Other issues, such as database record locking and security, also have an impact on database performance.

OLE and Interapplication Communication

If your application communicates in any way with other applications, you have another potential source of timing instability. This is especially true if you use techniques such as *object linking and embedding* (OLE). When you rely on communication with another application, you are basing performance not only on the capability of Windows to establish communication in a timing-consistent manner, but also for the application you are communicating with to respond in a predictable, consistently timed manner. If you have experience with interapplication communication, you know you often cannot rely on consistency in communication timings between applications. Accurate, repeatable results are difficult to obtain for such communication.

This is one source of instability that is extremely difficult, if not impossible, to minimize. You usually have no way to control how quickly communication with another application is initiated, how quickly that communication proceeds, and how quickly the application you are calling has a chance to respond. Communication speed will also be affected by the current state of the application you are communicating with, which is often hard or impossible to predict. For example, OLE communication with Microsoft Word will occur more quickly if Word is already started prior to communication than if it is not currently loaded. For all these reasons, you must simply realize that any sections of your application where you communicate with other applications must be timed very cautiously. Expect to see inconsistent timings due to the variability in overhead required to establish and maintain the communication with another application.

Printing

Additional hardware devices that can affect performance, although usually to a lesser degree, are printing devices such as printers and plotters. These devices are usually very slow, but if your application takes advantage of printing and you rely on timings around these print operations, times can differ. If, for example, you print a document in your application, you might have to wait various amounts of time depending on how many print jobs are waiting to print, how many other users are printing if it is a network printer, and so on. There are hundreds of printers available on the market, with varying amounts of on-board memory. You have no practical way of knowing which printer your user will have, so you should not base performance decisions on your specific printer configuration.

The Elusive Nature of Stable and Reliable Timings

Throughout this chapter you have seen examples of how computer hardware, the operating system, and Microsoft Windows cause fluctuations and inaccuracy in performance-analysis timings. This chapter has proposed solutions that minimize the impact of these factors. Although many of the factors can be minimized, there is only so much the programmer can do to reduce variability. In reality, it is virtually impossible to eliminate all sources of variability simply because of the Windows environment and all of the behind-the-scenes activities that cannot be changed.

You can assume, however, that as long as you minimize uncertainty the same way when each timing is made, your values will be more stable and therefore more reliable. When you have eliminated from the system as many uncertainties as possible, the result will be a consistent baseline for performance analysis.

When all is said and done, it may simply not be possible to completely stabilize timing results. But take heart—timings that vary widely from one instance of an application to another are not necessarily useless. You should at least be able to ascertain the cause of the instability, which most likely involves one of the issues addressed in this chapter. Depending on the significance of the fluctuations and their impact on the user, you might want to redesign those areas in order to make timings more consistent. At the very least, it might point out areas where performance is apt to vary widely due to Windows or other aspects beyond your control. It is very important that you understand where these areas exist so that you will be better able to inform users if they have similar experiences.

Furthermore, areas of instability can be entirely system dependent. Just because the system you are testing yields unstable results does not necessarily mean that all systems will do so. For instance, one computer system might have a different video card than another, causing comparisons or configurations that perform poorly on one computer to appear normal on another. The programmer should be aware of these areas and be ready to inform users who experience these limitations. If your application relies heavily on graphics methods, the performance will be worse on a system with a slower video card or less memory. This underscores the importance of communicating to the user the minimum computer system and configuration necessary to run an application adequately. Users should then understand that if they run the application below that baseline, they should expect poor performance.

Summary

This chapter discussed a wide variety of factors that are of much concern to the programmer concerned with performance. These factors can cause a program to take a different amount of time to perform the same task each time it is run. When you are trying to assess the benefits of optimization techniques and use timing methods to do so, you are limited by these inherent variances of Windows. In order to ensure that you are getting as accurate a set of results as possible, you must reduce the impact of all the factors discussed in this chapter.

Many of the problems are discussed at length, pointing out that although some variances can be solved rather easily, others are very difficult to pin down and virtually impossible to totally eliminate. You must take steps to reduce these factors and ensure a consistent system state every time the application is tested for performance. Furthermore, this chapter underscores the importance of taking timings on the same system to view timings relative to each other, as well as taking absolute timings on the low-end system that is being targeted for the user. Making sure an application runs with an acceptable speed on the low-end system will help to ensure user satisfaction for those with more powerful systems.

As more and more of the factors that limit timing accuracy are eliminated, the timing results should become increasingly reliable. To determine the level of reliability, you can simply run the same test over and over again, examining the timing values. If they are increasingly more consistent, you can be sure you are getting closer to an acceptable level, as discussed in detail in Chapter 4, "Timing Methods." At that point you can make meaningful comparisons between timings as performance optimizations are applied.

Obey the Signs

Wrong Way: Factors that make timings of the same task come out differently every time can gradually be eliminated.

Although it certainly is true that many of these instabilities can be reduced and some might be eliminated, it is virtually impossible to completely eliminate all of them. You must get to a point where the timings of the same process are statistically close enough to each other to be satisfactory. When that point is reached, a meaningful analysis can be obtained.

Beware of Falling Rocks: Don't try to eliminate every possible source of uncertainty.

Because it is virtually impossible to eliminate every source of uncertainty, it is important not to spend too much time trying to do so. Decide on an acceptable level of uncertainty and stop your efforts there. If you spend too much time trying to make the numbers as stable as possible, your efforts might be counterproductive. After all, you are simply trying to establish a consistent measurement baseline. You have yet to implement the optimization technique and try to get a meaningful comparison.

Wrong Way: Performance timings are the same from one computer system to another.

Although this danger has been alluded to earlier in the book, it is stated again in this chapter. Computer systems, especially those that run in an environment such as Microsoft Windows, are simply too complex for you to expect consistent execution timings. Some concerted effort must be made to reduce instabilities on even one system, and far more when moving to different systems with different configurations. As you attempt to get meaningful timing data in your applications, avoid at all costs shifting from one computer to another. The uncertainty you introduce by doing so will significantly throw off your findings.

Wrong Way: Expect consistency when your application interacts with or on a network.

When you're running an application that interfaces with a network, there are so many unknown dependencies on the network state and configuration that it is difficult, if not impossible, to get meaningful, consistent data. For example, trying to take timings in a module that handles database accesses is very difficult. Timing results are simply not reliable, because the application is more bound by network issues than by its own performance on the network. Only when you can reduce network variances can results be more meaningful.

Q&A

Q How do you target a low-end system for the user?

A The best way to determine a low-end system is to find out, before you even start writing code, what type of computer system your users will most commonly use. When you identify the low-end configuration, you can design your application to perform satisfactorily on that system. In some cases, you might have no choice but to set some low-end target that is higher than many users can attain without upgrading. In some cases, this is appropriate, since this is often necessary to take advantage of new and emerging technologies. If, for example, your application relies heavily on multimedia, you might need to require that the user have a CD-ROM for loading many large graphics files.

Q What is the most appropriate system to use for testing?

A It is usually best to assess performance on a lower-end system, because this is where the impact of performance enhancements will be most heavily felt. If you can get your application to perform adequately on the low-end system, you can be confident that you will maximize user satisfaction in meeting performance requirements.

Workshop

1. If you work in a multiuser environment, take a survey of the average computer system configuration. Take into account the average hard drive size and controller speed, type of network card used, total memory, processor type and speed, and amount and type of peripheral devices. Formulate a low-end, average, and high-end computer configuration. Discuss this with the users and get their opinion on your configuration choices.
2. If you work on a computer network, do a survey on how the network load varies throughout the day by observing file-access performance. Find times where activity seems to peak, and when hardly any activity is observed. If you are designing an application that makes extensive use of the network, how would performance be affected during peak times? during quiet times?

CHAPTER 7

Supporting Utilities for Performance Analysis

Performance assessment can be difficult. An accurate assessment can involve inserting minutely detailed timings in source code, logging and analyzing the statistics related to those timings, launching programs under controlled conditions, profiling code, tracking system resources, monitoring DLL and OCX dependencies, watching the flow of Windows activity, and performing many other duties. Fortunately, there are utilities available to facilitate *almost* every aspect of the performance-tuning process. Of course, there's a well-known saying that "'Almost' only counts in horseshoes and hand grenades!" The best utilities in the world still require one very important element if they are to be of value in your optimization process: your creative skill in analyzing the results. Utilities can shine the spotlight on

characteristics and behaviors of your applications and the application environment that you could never deduce on your own, but then it's up to you to put the pieces of evidence together, mix them with your own insight and understanding, and arrive at final optimization decisions.

The available utilities for performance tuning should be considered the indispensable toolkit of a skilled craftsman. In many cases, a programmer would be at a disadvantage when optimizing his or her program without performance-monitoring tools, just as a carpenter would be if he were attempting to build a house without a hammer. Likewise, a novice carpenter who has a bag full of tools but doesn't know whether to pound with the hammer or screwdriver will get about as far as the programmer who isn't aware of the distinctions between some of the powerful performance-monitoring tools available.

That arena is the focus of this chapter. The first utilities outlined are those that are included with this book. These tools, which the authors have produced and found invaluable for their own performance-monitoring work, are accompanied by full source code on the CD-ROM so that you can understand their inner workings. Another class of tools described is those that are commercially available. Both the tools that come bundled with the Visual Basic Enterprise Edition and some of the top commercially available third-party performance-analysis products are examined. A specific emphasis is placed on several of the available code-profiling tools. All the tools share a common trait—they can't automatically optimize your code for you, but they can give you a detailed understanding of program and system behavior that will enable you to make the most informed optimization decisions.

Utilities Included with This Book

This book contains several tools that demonstrate performance concepts and aid you in your performance tuning. They include the following:

- *Strtr32*—A program loader that aids in assessing Visual Basic application load time
- *Timing32*—A performance log OLE server to save/analyze timings
- *Watchr16*—A resource monitor program
- *Common routines*—Common timing-task routines contained in a Visual Basic application source module

You can find the tools covered here on the CD-ROM that accompanies this book. As the owner of this book, you are free to use these utilities, but you may not redistribute them. All source code is provided so that you can have full insight into the programming techniques behind each of these utilities. Of course, the universal software disclaimer applies—use these applications at your own risk! With that out of the way, though, it is worth adding that these tools have been designed with an emphasis on convenience and ease of use. The authors firmly believe that an overly complicated utility is an underused utility. The utilities summarized here are easy to get started with and to incorporate, and can offer many types of beneficial insights into the performance-tuning process.

Startr32, the Program Launcher

The Startr32.exe program enables you to monitor the load time of a VB program when you launch it. You simply specify the name of the program to start (with the full path qualifier if the program is not in the current directory or path); or, alternatively, click the Browse button to browse the file tree and visually select the file and then click the Launch button. The Startr32 main window, shown after the program name has been specified but before it has been launched with the Launch button, appears in Figure 7.1. After the Launch button is clicked, the specified program is launched. The Startr32 program calls the `Common_PreLoadTime` routine immediately before launching the program. (`Common_PreLoadTime` is one of the timing routines available in the COMMON.BAS module that accompanies this book.) `Common_PreLoadTime` stores the start time of the program in an INI file; thus a prelaunch time is recorded before the specified program is started.

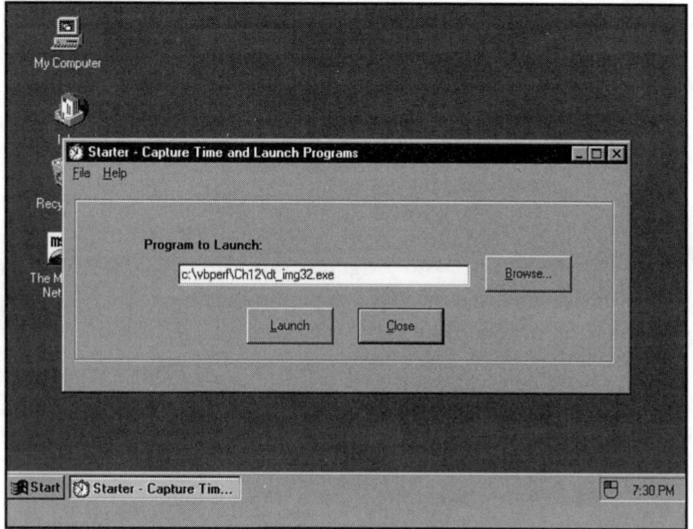

Figure 7.1.
Startr32, prior to program launch.

> **NOTE:** Startr32.exe also has a corresponding 16-bit version, Startr16.exe, which is included on the CD-ROM as well.

If the Visual Basic program to be launched has been correctly modified to work with Startr32 (a one-line source change), that Visual Basic program will be loaded and then call `Common_PostLoadTime` at the end of its `Form_Load` event. `Common_PostLoadTime` is another of the timing routines available in the COMMON.BAS module that accompanies this book. That routine captures postload time, retrieves startup time from an INI file, and prints the total load-time duration of the newly loaded form. See Figure 7.2 for an example of a VB program started by Startr32. Note that the total load time appears in the label on the bottom of the form.

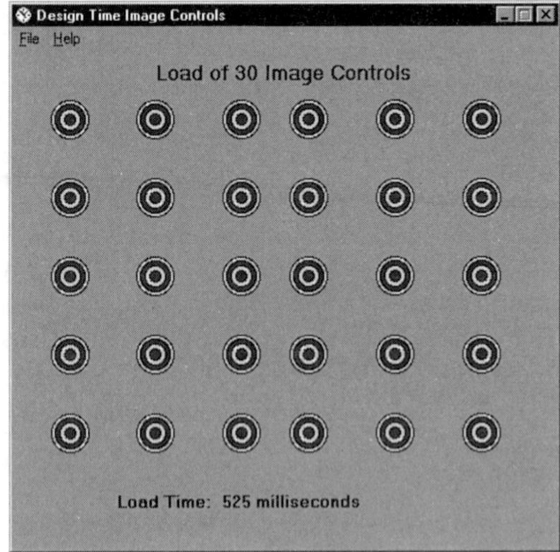

Figure 7.2.
A Visual Basic program loaded by Startr32 with load time displayed.

Startr32 uses an INI file to track the load time of programs it launches. When Startr32 first starts a program, it records the start time in file <WINDIR>VBPERF.INI. Then, when the program launched by Startr32 calls the `Common_PostLoadTime` routine, that routine uses the start time in the INI file and the postload time to calculate a total load duration. It is very easy to modify a Visual Basic program to work with Startr32 in this manner—you only have to add one line. The Visual Basic program to be launched should be modified to call subroutine `Common_PostLoadTime`, which is available in COMMON.BAS. This call should be made at the end of the main `Form_Load` event in the following format:

```
Call Common_PostLoadTime(lblResults)
```

where `lblResults` is the label on the Visual Basic program's main form. This label will be updated with the total load time. Listing 7.1 shows the modified `Form_Load` event for the dt_img32.exe program you'll read about in Chapter 12, "Control Loading." Note that the line in bold is the only code change that had to be made to incorporate load-time analysis into the program.

Listing 7.1. Modifying a program to work with Startr32.

```
Sub Form_Load ()

    ' Center form
    Call Common_CenterForm(Me)

    ' Analyze the amount of time it took to load - assumes
    '  that program was launched from STARTER32.EXE
    Call Common_PostLoadTime(lblResults)

End Sub
```

This single subroutine will take care of all activities relating to load-time analysis on the side of the Visual Basic program. That subroutine is shown in detail in the section on COMMON.BAS routines, later in this chapter.

Startr32, when used with a Visual Basic program that contains this one-line modification, provides an effective means to measure load performance. For accurate measurements, it is important to start load-time measurements *before* the target program is loaded because so much load-related activity must take place before your first line of code in a Visual Basic program even gets carried out. Load time of a Visual Basic program includes the overhead to move any non-loaded OCXs and DLLs into memory as well as to bring the program itself into memory, initialize custom controls, draw graphics, and perform any other `Form_Load` event initializations.

Without a utility like this, getting an accurate program load time is difficult. You cannot modify a program to monitor the start of its own load time, because you want to include in your measurement the work Windows does for the load before your program even gets control. Capturing load times by hand is very difficult and inaccurate, as it requires starting a stopwatch after clicking an icon or OK button to launch the target program. What seems like a short delay in reflexes between the click to start the program button and starting the stopwatch is usually subject to a wildly varying human reflex factor that can range from a split-second to as much as a few seconds. Likewise, stopping the stopwatch by visually observing the screen and waiting until the form appears to be drawn can introduce even greater inconsistency.

Startr32's automated load time calculation is much more reliable than the manual method, but even the Startr32 method is not perfect. Startr32 requires the Visual Basic runtime interpreter since it is a Visual Basic program itself. Therefore, as soon as Startr32 starts up, the Visual Basic runtime interpreter is loaded into memory. When Startr32 subsequently launches a program the system does not have to repeat the work of freshly loading the runtime interpreter into memory. However, the load time to load the interpreter into memory is relatively slight compared to overall load times. When Visual Basic applications are loaded, sometimes they require the runtime interpreter to be loaded and other times they don't if it is already in memory. The important factor in measuring load timings, then, is not so much to measure the absolute time of loading the runtime interpreter, but to ensure that all factors are *consistent* from one load timing to another. Startr32 ensures consistent timings because the load time for the runtime interpreter will never be a factor in loading the programs it calls.

Load times computed from the INI file entries stored by Startr32 will also include the overhead carried out between retrieving the original time, storing it in the INI file via the `Common` routine, and launching the Visual Basic program. The launched Visual Basic program itself adds even more overhead by use of the `Common_GetLoadTime` call. However, this overhead *is slight* and *consistent.* The overhead will likely be on the order of 10 milliseconds or fewer on most systems, which is a minimal impact in the face of load times measuring thousands of milliseconds.

Thus, load timings from Startr32 can serve as fairly good indicators of the absolute time it takes to load a program. Startr32 provides an even more accurate relative frame of reference when comparing code alternatives in load time of the same program, and gives a good relative frame of reference when comparing the load times of two different programs. Each program loaded with Startr32 will pay the same overhead penalty, so comparing the load-time patterns between two programs loaded with Startr32 is comparing apples to apples. As discussed in Chapter 6, "Factors That Affect Performance," system activity at any given moment can affect any single load-time reading, so multiple readings should be performed. Further load considerations for accurate timings are discussed in Chapter 12. Startr32.exe is used there and elsewhere throughout the book to capture load timings.

Timing32, the Performance Log OLE Server

One of the challenges of collecting timings is that, due to the wide system variability that has been previously discussed, one timing is never enough to form a conclusion. To truly interpret timings and compare timed alternatives, you must collect multiple timings. Typically, in the process of collecting repeated timings, you must factor out unusual "fluke" timings and repeatedly calculate and reconsider the average timing, median timing, and standard deviation timings. It's often a good idea to record all such timings taken during performance work so you have a means to revisit them later and add to them or re-analyze them.

An OLE Automation server is provided with this book for just such a purpose. You can invoke the server directly to sift through and analyze stored timings. In addition, services of the server can be directly accessed by any performance-testing program to automatically log timings and then invoke the server statistics viewer dialog box. Common routines included in the COMMON.BAS module on the sample CD-ROM make it painless to plug test programs into the server and easily take advantage of its statistics-gathering and analyzing capabilities. More detail on OLE servers in general can be found in Chapter 25, "OLE Automation Servers."

> **NOTE:** An identical server is also provided for 16-bit programs (Timing16.exe) that utilizes out-of-process OLE Automation server technology as opposed to the faster in-process OLE Automation server technology underlying Timing32.exe. A detailed discussion of the packaging and concepts behind these servers is provided in Chapter 25. The description here is restricted to just how to use the server and not the underlying OLE Automation server's implementation details.

The Startr32.exe program incorporates the server into its Timing Log feature. Figure 7.3 shows the Timing Log choice under the File menu. Selecting this option results in the display of the Log Timings dialog box shown in Figure 7.4.

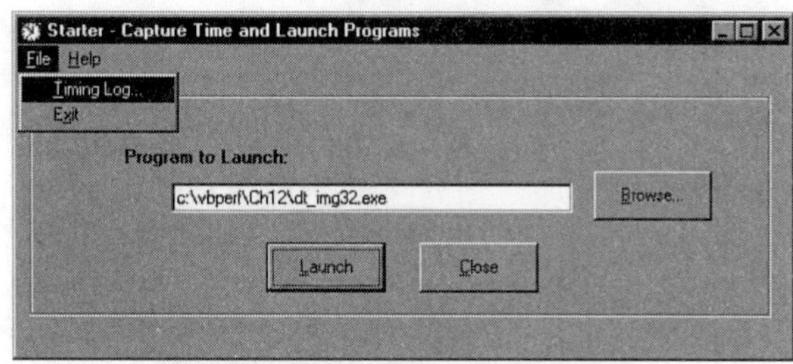

Figure 7.3.
The Timing Log menu option.

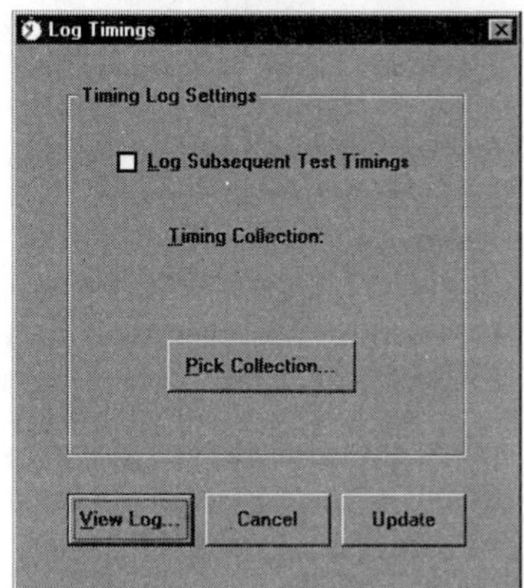

Figure 7.4.
The Log Timings dialog box.

> **NOTE:** The OLE server must be registered with your system for its objects to be exposed and available for use by other applications. If you go through the setup program on the CD-ROM that comes with this book, this should be taken care of automatically. However, if you move these files to another directory after installation, you will have to reregister them. In this case, you can manually register or unregister the DLL. To register the DLL, use the REGSVR32.EXE program in the CLISVR subdirectory installed with Visual Basic as follows:
>
> ```
> <VB\CLISVR PATH>\REGSVR32 <dll path>\perflog32.dll
> ```
>
> If you need to unregister the DLL to remove it from the list of available objects in the system registry, simply add the `/u` (uninstall) parameter:
>
> ```
> <VB\CLISVR PATH>\REGSVR32 /u <DLL path>\perflog32.dll
> ```
>
> Refer to Chapter 25 for full details on OLE server registration.

The Log Timings dialog box enables you to turn on automatic database logging of load times for any launched program. First, you must specify the name of a database collection under which to store the timings. To pick a collection to use, click the Pick Collection... button shown in

Figure 7.4, which results in the display of the Specify a Collection dialog box shown in Figure 7.5. From the list box on the left, which shows available collections, you can select a collection name that will be associated with any subsequent timings gathered.

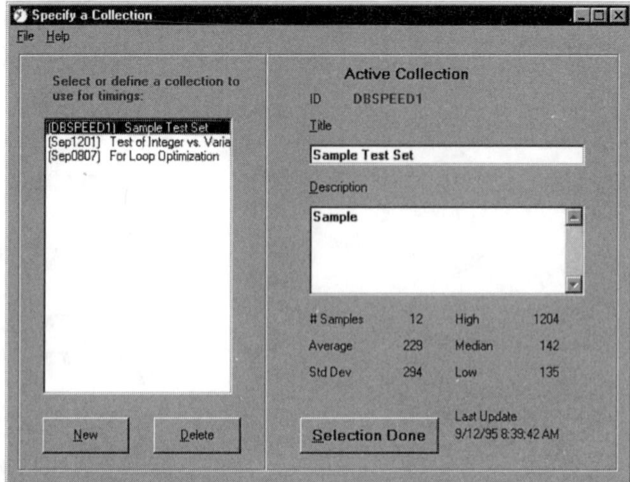

Figure 7.5.
The Specify a Collection dialog box.

Alternatively, you can click the New command button under the collections list box to define a new collection name. Figure 7.6 shows the resulting dialog box, which enables you to specify a new collection. You supply a collection ID that will be used as a key to store timings in the database, as well as an optional title and a description that can provide further details about this collection.

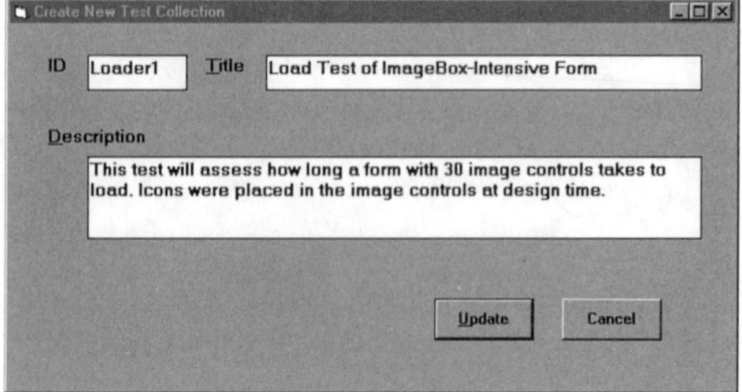

Figure 7.6.
Specifying a new test collection.

After selecting the Update command button to update the database with this new collection definition, you are returned to the Specify a Collection dialog box shown in Figure 7.7. At this point you simply have to select the newly created collection's ID from the list box and click the Selection Done command button.

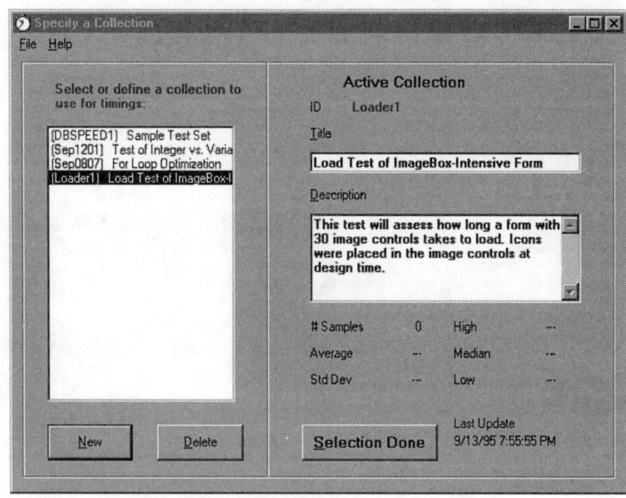

Figure 7.7.

Selecting the test collection.

You are then returned to the original Log Timings dialog box shown in Figure 7.8. Now the collection name appears on this dialog box, indicating the active collection ID that will be used for subsequent timings. To turn on the auto-timing storage capability for this set, simply click the check box labeled Log Subsequent Test Timings. After you make this selection and click Update to return to the main Startr32 application, any subsequent timings for the remainder of the session will be stored in the database.

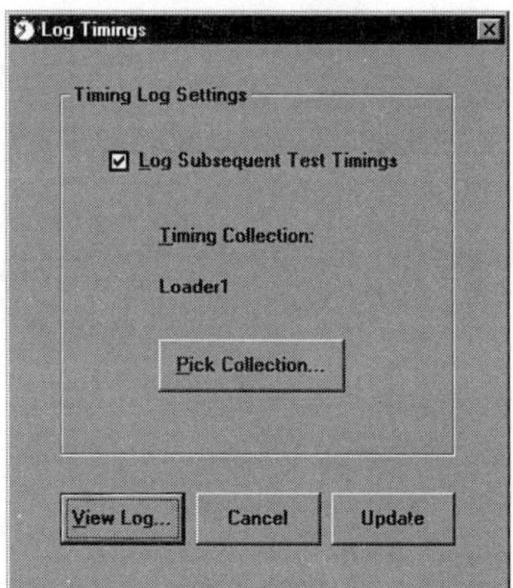

Figure 7.8.

Specifying that subsequent timings are to be logged.

Assume that you have carried out these steps so that Loader1 is the active collection and then logging has been turned on for Startr32. Next, you launch a program seven consecutive times, resulting in the called program displaying the following load times in milliseconds: 404, 421, 429, 436, 447, 481, and 602. Because logging is turned on, the `Common_PostLoadTime` routine in the launched program will use the services of the OLE Automation server to safely tuck these timings away in the database; this process is transparent to you when you use the application.

If you want to view these times after they are collected, you can do so through the Startr32.exe utility's menu. Select Timing Log from the File menu to redisplay the options form, as shown in Figure 7.8. From the Log Timings dialog box, clicking the View Log… command button invokes the OLE Automation server method to display full timing statistics. The resulting dialog box is shown in Figure 7.9.

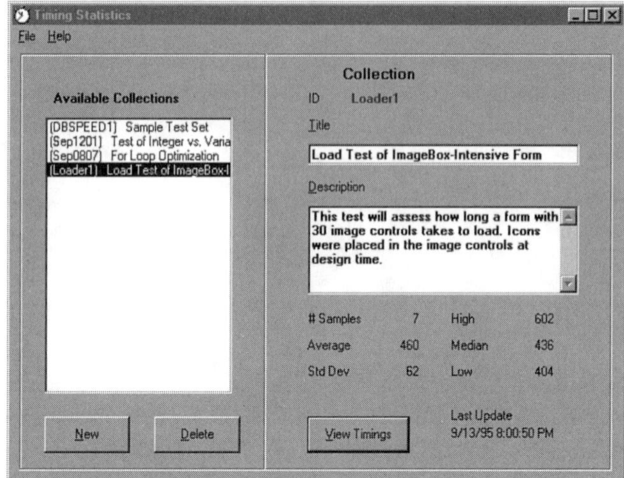

Figure 7.9.
The Timing Statistics dialog box.

Note that this figure, unlike the "pretiming" Figure 7.7, shows full statistics for the collection. The number of samples, average, standard deviation, high, median, and low are displayed based on all timings collected, as is the last update time. Select the View Timings command button to see individual timing information as well, as shown in Figure 7.10.

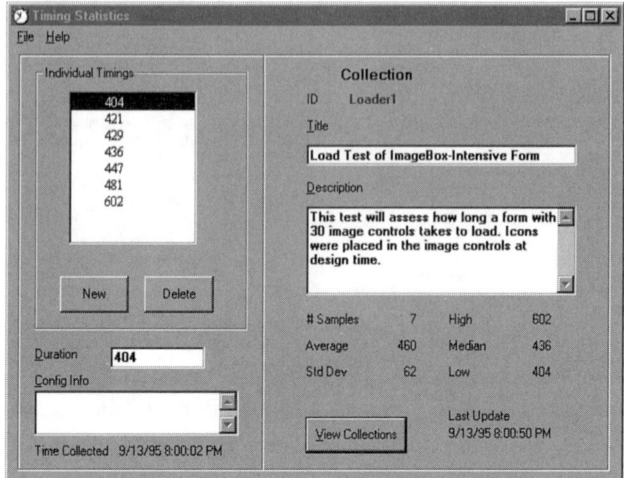

Figure 7.10.
Individual timings for the collection.

Now the list box on the left of the dialog box displays individual timing information. The duration and configuration for the currently highlighted timing are shown under the timing list box. Because you can delete timings or modify timing durations, you have the capability to throw out fluke timings or to play what-if scenarios by changing a timing value to observe what the effect would be on the average and standard deviation. For example, observe that in Figure 7.10 the current average for seven samples is 460. Likewise, the maximum timing, as shown in the list box and in the High label on the right of the dialog box is 602. If you decide that this timing was an aberration, perhaps postulating that it occurred during a period of mail polling that skewed the timing, you might want to remove that timing to see how much the average improves. To carry this out, all that is required is to highlight the suspect timing and click the Delete command button under the timings. The confirmation dialog box shown in Figure 7.11 will appear, to which you must respond affirmatively to cause the timing to be removed.

Figure 7.11.

The warning dialog box confirming the deletion of a timing.

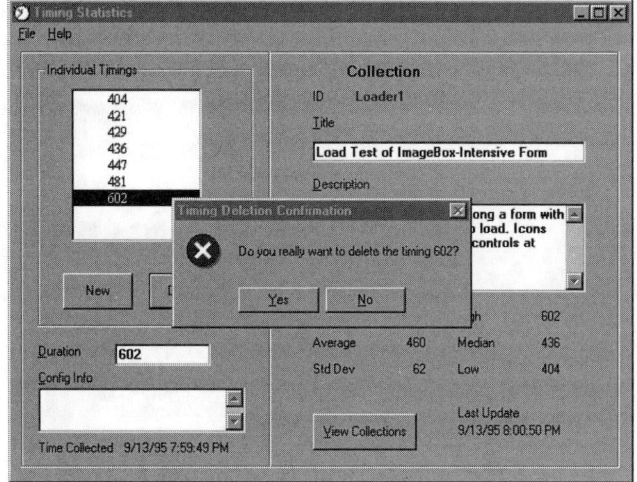

At this point, the deletion from the database takes place and the statistics display is updated immediately. (See Figure 7.12 for the new statistics.) The average has indeed shifted after you've eliminated the High timing, and now is 436, as shown in the dialog box. Even more significantly, the standard deviation has decreased from 62 to 24.

In this manner, you can carry out significant analysis and create several what-if scenarios. Of course, you must exercise discipline to not throw out or adjust so many timings that you permanently massage the data into whatever you want to see. If you decide that the 602 reading was a valid one after all and want to recover it, you can add it back by clicking the New command button. Then you must supply the duration and configuration information in the resulting Create a New Timing dialog box shown in Figure 7.13.

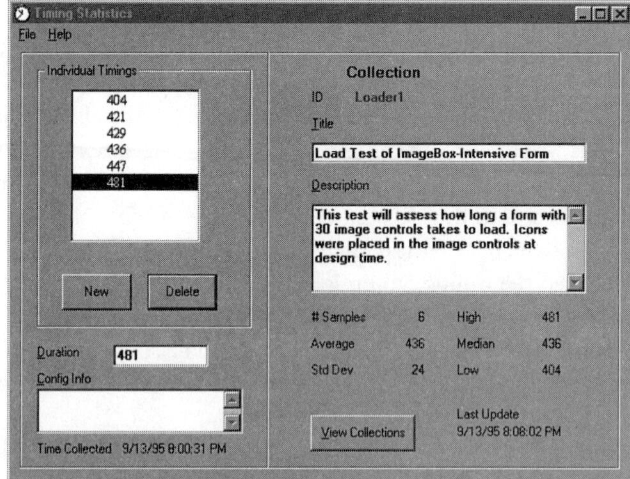

Figure 7.12.
Updated statistics after you delete the High timing.

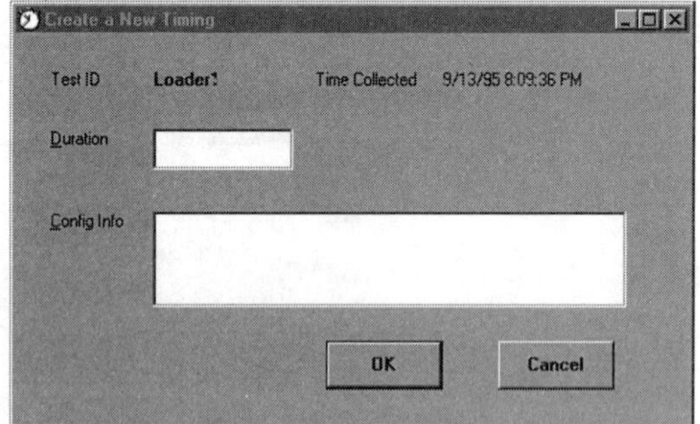

Figure 7.13.
The Create a New Timing dialog box.

The services of the Timing32 OLE Automation server utility are incorporated into most of the sample programs that come with this book. Most of these sample programs are built on the COMMON.BAS routines `Common_PreLoadTime`, `Common_PostLoadTime`, `Common_StartTimedTest`, and `Common_EndTimedTest`, and incorporate the common Log Timings dialog form. All of these components were designed to make seamless use of the Timing32 OLE Automation server's services. If you use these COMMON.BAS routines as building blocks for your own performance-analysis programs, as described later in this chapter, your programs too will automatically support the full range of logged timing features available from the Timing32 OLE Automation server utility.

Note that the display of timing log data doesn't have to occur only through the menu option of a test program. You also can start the Timing32 utility from the command line or from the executable files icon to directly view timing data. Simply click on the icon to start the

Timing32.exe utility, which provides a front end or starting point to the OLE server and displays as its main form the Timing Statistics dialog box shown in Figure 7.9. This is the same dialog box integrated under the View Log command button in the Log Timings dialog box.

The Timing32 OLE Automation server utility therefore serves several purposes. It enables the archiving of results and provides a statistical summary of those results, as well as enabling the hypothetical tweaking or modification of data to observe effects on statistics. If you've done extensive performance testing before, with the often-accompanying activities of scribbling results on notebook paper and punching numbers into the Windows calculator, you are likely to find Timing32 of considerable benefit!

Watchr16, the Resource Monitor Program

Those of you who can remember back to the days of Windows 3.1 probably recall the oft-viewed Program Manager About box that was available under the Program Manager Help|About menu option. This window displayed a summary of the percentage of free resources and memory, as shown in Figure 7.14. Watchr16 is a utility that provides similar information and also can generate low-resource warning messages.

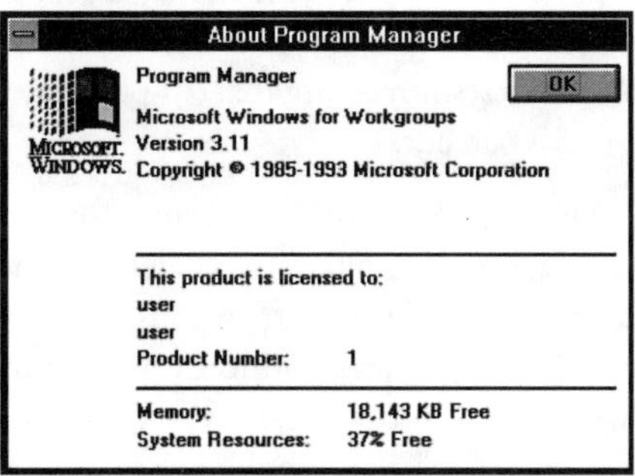

Figure 7.14.
The Windows 3.1 Program Manager About box.

The type of resource information displayed in the About box can be helpful during performance assessments. This is particularly true under Windows 3.1, which has less-robust and less-forgiving resource-management capabilities than does Windows 95. This section's discussion of resource monitoring pertains to applications in the 16-bit Windows 3.1 (and closely related Windows for Workgroups 3.11) environment because in such an environment, sluggish performance might be due to a low resource condition. An application might also cause a gradual memory leak, which can eventually place Windows 3.1 —as well as the application— in an unstable state. Viewing the Program Manager About box's settings is one way to check for these conditions.

The memory indicator under Windows 3.1 indicates available *virtual memory*; that is, it indicates how much memory Windows still has to work with in terms of both physical RAM and the space set aside on the hard disk for Windows to use as paging space. Paging space is information stored on disk that has been temporarily swapped out of memory by the operating system. The ability of the operating system to store some of its working information on disk rather than just in RAM in effect extends the amount of memory that Windows 3.1 can work with to support the running programs. This grand total is the *Virtual RAM* amount shown as the Memory setting in the About box.

The System Resources indicator in the About box provides the percentage of available system resources, but this term is a bit vague because there are several different types of system resources that are managed by Windows 3.1. One type is *GDI resources*, which includes management of items such as fonts, bitmaps, and low-level Windows API screen-generation constructs such as device context handles, brushes, and pens. Another type of resource is *User*, which includes management of items such as menu handles and window handles. The final category of system resources is *general system resources*, which, obviously, are used to carry out general system activity.

Each of these categories of resources can get low and itself be the cause of system instability. Thresholds for unstable performance vary greatly, but a general trouble area can usually be regarded to be anything under 20 percent, with some reason for concern even when resources dip below 30 percent. The Program Manager About box simply reports the *minimum* of all three categories. For example, if system resources stood at 35 percent, GDI resources stood at 40 percent, and user resources stood at 30 percent, the About box would show a System Resources value of 30 percent.

The Program Manager About box, therefore, provides a high-level gauge of resources, but it provides no *threshold detection*. It does not detect or notify you of the threshold or level at which the system becomes unstable. Resources constantly vary as you run programs. There is no built-in method to receive automatic notification when the system reaches a trouble area. This can be explicitly written into programs, however, so that a notification appears when resource levels dip below an undesirable threshold.

This can be very helpful to assess performance. You typically want to know where the system stands on resources to ensure consistent system behavior, and you want to know as soon as your system reaches a resource danger zone because that can have a significant impact on performance.

Watchr16 is a utility provided with this book to carry out such threshold-triggered performance monitoring and is pictured in Figure 7.15.

Watchr16 reports the level for each category of resource to provide the user with an accurate feel for what is really going on in the system. In addition, Watchr16 enables the user to provide a threshold level for each individual resource. Whenever the resources dip below the threshold specified by the user, Watchr16 displays a warning message. This occurs even if Watchr16 is minimized, which enables the utility to be run as an unobtrusive background task.

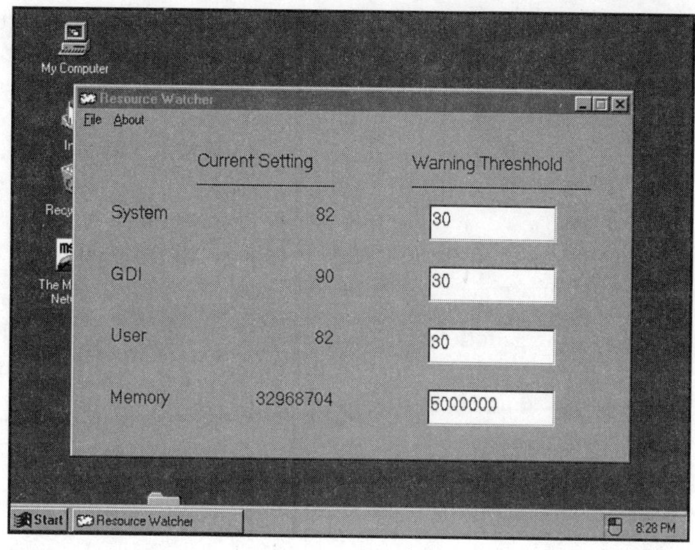

Figure 7.15.
The Watchr16 Resource Monitor Utility main window.

Watchr16 starts up in minimized mode. If the user selects it to reset the default low-resource warning thresholds, the screen shown in Figure 7.15 appears. When system resources dip below the specified threshold, the warning message shown in Figure 7.16 results, even if Watchr16 is not the currently active application. The user is automatically returned to the Watchr16 dialog box, even if the application was previously minimized. At this point the offending resource number is highlighted in red, accompanied by a storm cloud to indicate that it is a potential problem area.

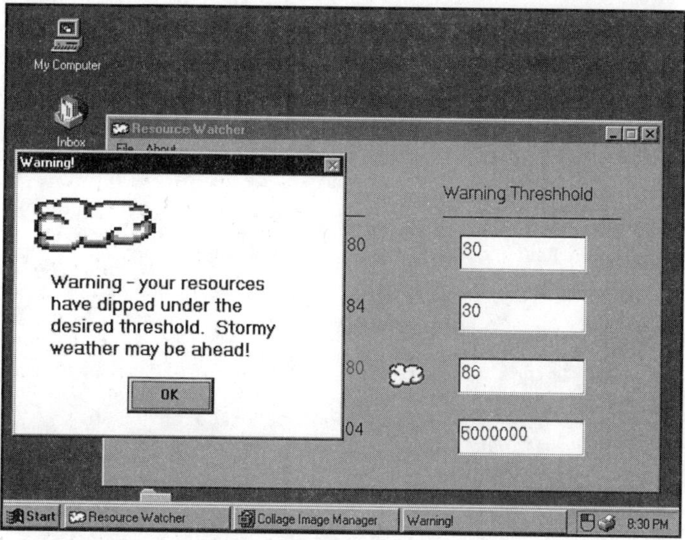

Figure 7.16.
The Watchr16 resource monitor warning message.

There is a minor performance consideration to note about this program that is also true of most other monitoring programs. This application runs on a timer, so a new assessment of the resources takes place every second. (This timer code is shown in Listing 7.2.) Therefore, running this program affects the amount of activity taking place in your system and could subtly influence the performance of programs it is intended to monitor. Thus you have affected performance simply by running an additional utility. In the case of Watchr16, the effect on other programs is so low that it is almost imperceptible. However, you should always carefully consider the impact of any tool you use and whether it affects the very performance you are attempting to measure.

Another way to gain the same functionality as that of Watcher16 is to build it right into your own program. Watchr16 source code is included on this book's CD-ROM for that purpose. This program simply builds on some key API calls to retrieve system values.

Listing 7.2. Watch16 resource-monitoring timer code.

```
Sub tmrWatch_Timer ()

Dim loopcount%
Dim intNewTroubleArea As Integer
Static intResourceLow(4) As Integer

'Get current resources
lblResource(0) = GetFreeSystemResources(GFSR_SYSTEMRESOURCES)   'System
lblResource(1) = GetFreeSystemResources(GFSR_GDIRESOURCES)      'GDI
lblResource(2) = GetFreeSystemResources(GFSR_USERRESOURCES)     'User
lblResource(3) = GetFreeSpace(0)                                'Memory

' Check each resource in the array
For loopcount% = 0 To 3

    ' Check if Resources are below threshhold
    If Val(txtResource(loopcount%)) < Val(lblResource(loopcount%)) Then

        ' OK now, but if res were previously low, restore regular color
        If intResourceLow(loopcount%) = True Then
            lblResource(loopcount%).ForeColor = BLACK
            imgWarning(loopcount%).Visible = False
        End If

        intResourceLow(loopcount%) = False


    ' Else resources are currently low
    Else
        ' Change label to red warning color if it wasn't already low
        If intResourceLow(loopcount%) = False Then
            lblResource(loopcount%).ForeColor = RED
            imgWarning(loopcount%).Visible = True
            intNewTroubleArea = True
        End If

        intResourceLow(loopcount%) = True
```

```
    End If

Next loopcount%

' Make sure user sees if a new area just dipped below the threshhold
If intNewTroubleArea Then
    ' Restore from icon if necessary, and bring window to foreground
    If Me.WindowState = 1 Then Me.WindowState = 0
    AppActivate Me.Caption
    frmCloud.Show 1
End If

End Sub
```

Watchr16 can be a helpful utility. Although it doesn't fix resource problems, it enables you to stay informed about what is happening to your system. Although it is targeted for the 16-bit Windows 3.1 environment and its corresponding resource-management issues, it can be useful in Windows 95 as well. Watchr16 is an excellent tool to inspect the state of the system and ensure that you have a roughly similar memory-management environment from one performance-tuning session to the next. Likewise, its threshold-detection warning can serve as a handy reminder that the state of the environment has changed significantly.

COMMON.BAS Routines

The intent of this book is to not only show you many performance-tuning examples, but more importantly to enable you to carry out performance tuning on your own code. Before you get very far with your own performance tuning, you will likely find it necessary to write your own test programs to compare methods or insert timings around key blocks of your own code. A common set of timing-related subroutines that you can use for this purpose is included in the COMMON.BAS module that comes on this book's CD-ROM. The sample programs throughout this book are also built on those same COMMON.BAS routines. The routines were designed with a clear structure and plenty of comments so that they would be easy to understand and incorporate into other programs.

In addition to serving as building blocks for your programs, the COMMON.BAS routines serve as a consolidated reference point for the use of various timing-based API calls and other techniques. Many of these routines are nothing more than *wrappers*—a few lines of code that simply call a system API that offers the real underlying function. Providing such wrappers makes the coding task easier and more convenient and provides ready examples of how to utilize these APIs. The performance-savvy reader might at this point wonder about the performance impact of having wrappers around API functions. There is, without doubt, more overhead needed when the interpreter calls these routines; more code paths must be traveled and more statements must be interpreted. However, the overhead penalty is minimal in the COMMON.BAS routines, and for most of the work the book's authors do, the convenience and good-programming-practice advantages of this modular collection of routines outweigh the millisecond-level penalties of additional calls. If you are optimizing a program to the hilt and you are making repeated calls to the routines within one block of code, however, you might consider the overhead of such wrappers and whether you should instead implement them as direct code statements.

COMMON.BAS can serve as an excellent starting point for taking the initial steps on the road to performance tuning. For extensive performance-tuning work, however, it is highly recommended that you use profiling tools, which are discussed later in this chapter. The key routines available in COMMON.BAS are as follows:

- Timing-related declarations
- `Public Function Common_SetOptimalTimer() As Long`
- `Public Function Common_FreeOptimalTimer() As Long`
- `Public Function Common_GetTimer() As Long`
- `Public Function Common_GetHighResTimer() As Long`
- `Public Function Common_GetHighResTimerFreq() As String`
- `Public Sub Common_PreloadTime()`
- `Public Sub Common_PostloadTime(ctlResultsControl As Control)`
- `Public Sub Common_StartTimedTest()`
- `Public Sub Common_EndTimedTest(ctlShowTime As Control)`
- `Function Common_FileExists(strFileName As String) As Boolean`
- `Public Sub Common_CenterForm(CurrentForm As Form)`

In the following sections you'll learn about these routines and get a look at the declarations used by this module. See Chapter 4, "Timing Methods," for a detailed explanation of the underlying API calls used in many of the timing routines.

Declarations

Many useful API functions appear in the Declarations section of COMMON.BAS. These are utilized by the COMMON.BAS routines in various ways to collect timings. The entire Declarations section is not repeated here due to space limitations, but a summary of some of the key timing-related APIs is shown in Listing 7.3.

Listing 7.3. API declarations.

```
' WIN APIs
#If Win32 Then ' 32-bit VB uses these Declares.
    ' GetTickCount has resolution that varies with Op Sys, Mode, PC
    Declare Function GetTickCount Lib "kernel32" () As Long
    ' timeGetTime has generally 1 millisecond or better resolution on Win95,
    '     5 milliseconds on NT.
```

```
    Declare Function timeGetTime Lib "winmm" () As Long
    ' Gives presence of high res timer, and current time in the high
    '      resolution timer, IF one exists on your system
    Declare Function QueryPerformanceCounter Lib "kernel32"
➥ (lpPerformanceCount As Long) As Boolean
    ' Tells how often per second your high resolution timer updates,
    '       IF one exists on system.
    Declare Function QueryPerformanceFrequency Lib "kernel32"
➥(lpFrequency As Long) As Boolean


    Declare Function timeGetDevCaps Lib "winmm.dll"
➥(lpTimeCaps As TIMECAPS, ByVal uSize As Long) As Long
    Declare Function timeBeginPeriod Lib "winmm.dll"
➥(ByVal uPeriod As Long) As Long
    Declare Function timeEndPeriod Lib "winmm.dll"
➥(ByVal uPeriod As Long) As Long

    '  ....more declarations appear in the actual file....
#Else   ' 16-bit VB uses these Declares.
    ' Windows API GetTickCount function is one method of extracting time, but
    '    is only accurate to roughly 55 milliseconds under Windows 3.1.
    '         See Chapter 4 of book for details!
    Declare Function GetTickCount Lib "User" () As Long
    ' Yank data in from an INI file in integer format
' Windows TOOLHELP DLL TimerCount function used for stopwatch purposes
    '    This function is accurate to roughly 1 millisecond.
    '    This function returns non-0 on success.
    '    Not supported in 32-bit API, use timeGetTime instead
    Declare Function TimerCount Lib "Toolhelp.dll" (typTimer As TIMERINFO)
➥As Integer
    '....more declarations appear in the actual file....

#End If
```

These declarations make use of a *conditional compile.* This feature ensures that if a 32-bit application is built, only 32-bit APIs are defined. Likewise, if a 16-bit application is built, only 16-bit APIs are used. A similar conditional compilation check is made within some of the COMMON.BAS routines that must differentiate between 16-bit and 32-bit so they can make the appropriate API call.

Look at the sample conditional compile illustrated here. The Win32 condition will be true whenever this code is compiled in the 32-bit environment, and only the code within the `#If...Then` branch of the conditional compilation will be generated as part of the 32-bit program. Likewise, if the compilation is carried out in the 16-bit environment, the Win32 condition will be false, and only code within the `#Else` branch of the conditional compilation will be generated as part of the resulting 16-bit program:

```
#If Win32 Then ' 32-bit VB uses these Declares.
Common_GetTimer = timeGetTime()
#Else ' 16- bit
Common_GetTimer = GetTickCount()
#End If
```

If you wanted to write the source code so that you could use the same function-call syntax regardless of which operating system mode you compiled for, you could define the declaration statements with the Visual Basic `Alias` declaration keyword. This allows you to specify your own name for any DLL function call. Using this technique, you could give the same name to a DLL function call from both a 16-bit and 32-bit DLL even if the original function names in each DLL are different. If both the 32-bit and 16-bit calls share the same alias, then code can be written to simply make a call to the alias name, rather than make a call to one name for 16-bit programs and a different name for 32-bit programs. For example, you could map your own name, `OurGetTime`, to the appropriate 16- or 32-bit API call by using `Alias` in the API declarations as follows:

```
#If Win32 Then ' 32-bit VB uses these Declares.
Declare Function OurGetTime() Lib "winmm" Alias timeGetTime As Long
#Else ' 16 bit
Declare Function OurGetTime() Lib "User" () Alias GetTickCount As Long
#End If
```

This technique enables you to simply call the `OurGetTime` function whenever you want to take a timing, rather than call a different function name depending on the operating-system environment. The `Alias` keyword approach was *not* taken when creating the COMMON.BAS routines so that it is explicitly clear which function call and corresponding timing technique is being used in all the samples. And because the COMMON.BAS routines explicitly use the `#If Win32` check to set up the correct declaration at compile time, the resulting code is completely portable. Any programs you build on the COMMON.BAS routines can be compiled to operate in either 16-bit or 32-bit mode with no modification or frustration required on your part (unless you introduce incompatibilities in your own code!).

Common_SetOptimalTimer

This routine serves as a wrapper to the API function, resetting the timer used with certain APIs to a more optimal timer resolution. Windows NT supports the setting of timers to use greater resolution than the default of 5 milliseconds or above. Timer resolution can be improved from 10 milliseconds to 1 millisecond with this call on some systems. This call is intended to be used in tandem with `Common_FreeOptimalTimer` to set and clear adjusted resolutions. (Refer to Chapter 4 for a detailed discussion of this function.) The `Common_SetOptimalTimer` function is shown in Listing 7.4.

Listing 7.4. The `Common_SetOptimalTimer` function.

```
Public Function Common_SetOptimalTimer() As Long
' Make sure app is using the lowest resolution timer
'   (most frequent updates) available for calls to Common_GetTiming
'
' Behavior: 16-bit app under Windows 3.1, Windows 95, or Windows NT  -
'    Not applicable, has no effect, returns standard default
'    32-bit app under Windows 95 - Relevant 32bit API to reset time is
```

```
'    supported, but has no effect
' 32-bit app under Windows NT -
'    Using relevant 32bit API, will reset default timer
'    resolution to the lowest available value.
'
'    NOTE on 32-bit usage: every Common_SetOptimalTimer call should
'       be paired with a Common_FreeOptimalTimer call. Refer to
'       timeBeginPeriod documentation for details.
'
'  Returns the current timing resolution that will be used with
'       Common_GetTiming, 0 if failure

#If Win32 Then

        Dim rc&

        ' This call retrieves minimum available timer value
        rc& = timeGetDevCaps(typTimeInfo, Len(typTimeInfo))

        ' This resets default timer resolution for Windows NT,
        '    has no effect for Windows 95
        rc& = timeBeginPeriod(typTimeInfo.wPeriodMin)
        If rc& <> 0 Then
            ' Something failed!
            Common_SetOptimalTimer = 0
        Else
            ' Note: Value is saved in module level variable
            '    typTimeInfo.wPeriodMin so that this resolution can be
            ' cleared later by Common_FreeOptimalTimer if needed
           Common_SetOptimalTimer = typTimeInfo.wPeriodMin
        End If
#Else

        '     The 16-bit API GetTickCount timer only has a resolution of 55
        '     milliseconds under Windows 3.1.
        '     Results vary slightly for 16-bit apps under Windows NT
        '     and Windows 95.

        '     Common_GetTimer uses 16bit Toolhelp.DLL TimerCount API if possible,
        '     which has a resolution of 1 millisec. under Windows 3.1, generally
        '     close to that for 16bit apps under 32bit Windows operating systems.
       Common_SetOptimalTimer = 1
#End If

End Function
```

Common_FreeOptimalTimer

This routine serves as a wrapper to the API function, clearing an adjusted timer resolution. Windows NT supports the setting of timers to use a different resolution, typically greater, than the default of 5 milliseconds or above. This call is intended to be used in tandem with `Common_SetOptimalTimer` to set and clear adjusted resolutions. Listing 7.5 shows the code for the `Common_FreeOptimalTimer` function.

Listing 7.5. The `Common_FreeOptimalTimer` function.

```
Public Function Common_FreeOptimalTimer() As Long
' Clear the lowest resolution timer (most frequent updates) that was being used.
' Behavior: 16-bit app under Windows 3.1, Windows 95, or Windows NT  -
'     Not applicable, has no effect
' 32-bit app under Windows 95 - Relevant 32bit API to clear time is supported,
'        but has no effect
' 32-bit app under Windows NT - Using relevant 32bit API, will clear last
'        setting for timer resolution
' NOTE on 32-bit usage: every Common_SetOptimalTimer call should be paired with
'        a Common_FreeOptimalTimer call. Refer to timeBeginPeriod
'       documentation for details.
'
' RETURNS 0 on success

#If Win32 Then
        ' This clears last timer setting for Windows NT, has no effect for
        '     Windows 95
        Common_FreeOptimalTimer = timeEndPeriod(typTimeInfo.wPeriodMin)
#Else
        ' Nothing to free under 16-bit apps, indicate success
        Common_FreeOptimalTimer = 0
 #End If

End Function
```

Common_GetTimer

This routine returns current time since system startup from the best available regular system timer API call and can be used to take general-purpose timings. Alternatively, the pair of routines `Common_StartTimedTest` and `Common_EndTimedTest` could be used to time a block of code. Those routines call `Common_GetTimer` to extract the time. Listing 7.6 shows the code for the `Common_GetTimer` function.

Listing 7.6. The `Common_GetTimer` function.

```
Public Function Common_GetTimer() As Long
' Return current time, to be used for benchmarking start or end of performance
'   test

#If Win32 Then
       ' The Win32 timeGetTime API is a high precision timer with a resolution of
       '    1 millisecond or better under Win95, default of 5 milliseconds or
       ' above under NT.
       ' Function Common_SetOptimalTimer can be used to get better resolution
       '   under NT.
       Common_GetTimer = timeGetTime()
#Else
```

```
        '     Timer API GetTimerCount under Win3.1 Toolhelp.DLL has a resolution
        '    of 1 millisecond, but that API is no longer available as a 32-bit
        '    API and is a not an upward compatible solution.
        '
        '     The 16-bit API GetTickCount timer only has a resolution of 55
        '     milliseconds under Windows 3.1.
        '     Results vary slightly for this API for 16-bit apps under Windows NT
        '     and Windows 95.

    If intTimerChoice = 1 Then

            ' Use optimal timer for Windows 3.1 - 1 millisec resolution
            intTimerCountRC% = TimerCount(typ16bitTiming)
            Common_GetTimer = typ16bitTiming.lngMillisec

    ElseIf intTimerChoice = 2 Then

            ' Use kernel function timing method -
            '    55 millseconds under Windows 95, Windows 3.1,
            '    resolution less on
            '    Windows NT, system specific
             Common_GetTimer = GetTickCount
    Else
        ' Initialization needed

            ' No timer selected yet, carry out first time nitializations
            '    so we avoid this overhead on future calls.
            '    Verify TOOLHELP.DLL TimerCount function, if not OK use
            '    standard kernel GetTickCount function for timings.
            '
            '    This approach is largely for educational purposes to document
            '    both timing methods here, in your own apps this not necessary.


            ' Standard timer structure size for our stopwatch purposes
            typ16bitTiming.lngSizeSetup = STANDARD_TIMER
            intTimerCountRC% = TimerCount(typ16bitTiming)
            ' If call fails, it will have 0 as current task time
            If typ16bitTiming.lngMillisec <> 0 Then
                Common_GetTimer = typ16bitTiming.lngMillisec
                ' Use TimerCount in future calls
                intTimerChoice = 1
            Else
                Common_GetTimer = GetTickCount
                ' Use GetTickCount in future calls since TimerCount has problem
                intTimerChoice = 2
            End If

    End If

 #End If

End Function
```

Common_GetHighResTimer

This routine returns a string that indicates the current time value in the high-resolution timer, or returns `0` if no high-resolution timer exists. High-resolution timers are only available on systems with corresponding specialized hardware. Listing 7.7 shows the code for the `Common_GetHighResTimer` function.

Listing 7.7. The `Common_GetHighResTimer` function.

```
Public Function Common_GetHighResTimer() As Long
' Return current time from high res timer, if one exists
'
#If Win16 Then
    ' High res API not supported!
    Common_GetHighResTimer = 0
#Else

    Dim lngCurtime As Long

    ' Return high res timer current time,  or 0 if none exists on this system

    If Not QueryPerformanceCounter(lngCurtime) Then
        ' There is no high res timer on this system
        Common_GetHighResTimer = 0
    Else
        ' Return the time
        Common_GetHighResTimer = lngCurtime
    End If
#End If

End Function
```

Common_GetHighResTimerFreq

This routine returns a string that indicates how frequently the high-resolution timer on a system is updated, or returns `0` if no high-resolution timer exists. Listing 7.8 shows the code for the `Common_GetHighResTimer` function.

Listing 7.8. The `Common_GetHighResTimer` function.

```
Public Function Common_GetHighResTimerFreq() As String
' Return string showing how often high res timer upates, or 0 if
'    none exists on this system

#If Win16 Then
    ' High res API not supported!
    Common_GetHighResTimerFreq = "0"
#Else
```

```
    Dim lngCurtime As Long

    ' Return the frequency of the high res timer on this system

    If Not QueryPerformanceFrequency(lngCurtime) Then
        ' There is no high res timer on this system
        Common_GetHighResTimerFreq = "0"
    Else
        ' Tells how often per sec. your high resolution timer updates,
        '     IF one exists on system.
         Common_GetHighResTimerFreq = Str(lngCurtime)
    End If

#End If

End Function
```

Common_PreLoadTime

This routine obtains a pre-form-load time for a program load analysis test. It is called with the Startr32.exe utility described earlier in this chapter. This call must be followed by a `Common_PreLoadTime` call at the end of the `Form_Load` event of the launched program to capture the total duration of the load time. The code for the `Common_PreLoadTime` subroutine is shown in Listing 7.9.

Listing 7.9. The `Common_PreLoadTime` subroutine.

```
Public Sub Common_PreloadTime()

    Dim rc&                           ' return code
    Dim strFileName As String         ' used to build ini file name
    Dim lngTime As Long               ' stores start time

    ' Get ini file location to use to store preload time
    strFileName$ = Common_GetIniFileName()

    ' Extract current time
    lngTime = Common_GetTimer()

    ' Save the Start Time to the ini file, so it can be retrieved later
    '    by the app being loaded
    rc& = WritePrivateProfileString(LOAD_TIME_APP, START_TIME_TOPIC,
    ➥Str(lngTime), strFileName)

    ' If a test collection is currently specified, store it for the launched
    '   app to use. Otherwise indicate none.

    If Common_bolRecordOn Then
        rc& = WritePrivateProfileString(LOAD_TIME_APP, TEST_COLLECTION_TOPIC,
        ➥Common_strTimingCollection, strFileName)
```

continues

Listing 7.9. continued

```
    Else
        rc& = WritePrivateProfileString(LOAD_TIME_APP, "NONE",
        ➥Common_strTimingCollection, strFileName)
    End If

End Sub
```

Common_PostLoadTime

This routine obtains a post-form-load time for a program load analysis test. It is intended to be used by a program that is launched with the Startr32.exe utility. This call must be preceded by a `Common_PreLoadTime` call (which Startr32.exe carries out) to correctly capture the load duration. `Common_PostLoadTime` should be the last call in the loaded program's `Form_Load` event. Listing 7.10 shows the code for the `Common_PostLoadTime` subroutine.

Listing 7.10. The `Common_PostLoadTime` subroutine.

```
Public Sub Common_PostLoadTime(cntResultsControl As Control)

    ' This function displays load time in the control passed as a parameter.
    ' The utility Starter.exe  should be used to launch the program whose
    '   load time you wish to evaulate.
    '    Starter calls Common_PreLoadTime to start the timed loading test.
    '    Then the loaded program should call this routine at the end of
    '    its Form_Load event to conclude the load time test.

    Dim rc&
    Dim strFileName As String
    Dim lngDuration As Long
    Dim lngEndTime As Long
    Dim lngStartTime As Long
    Dim strReturnString As String * 30

    ' Make sure form is showing already
     cntResultsControl.Parent.Show

    ' Extract current time
    lngEndTime = Common_GetTimer

    ' Get ini file location to use to retrieve preload time
    strFileName$ = Common_GetIniFileName

    ' Retrieve preload time
    rc& = GetPrivateProfileString(LOAD_TIME_APP, START_TIME_TOPIC,
➥  "0", strReturnString, Len(strReturnString), strFileName)

    ' Calculate duration and display on screen
    lngStartTime = Val(strReturnString)
```

```
    lngDuration = lngEndTime - lngStartTime

    If (lngStartTime = 0) Or (lngDuration <= 0) Then
        MsgBox "Load time cannot be calculated because " &
        ➥"the Starter.Exe utility was not used to launch this
        ➥application.", , "Warning!"
        cntResultsControl = "----"
        Exit Sub
    End If

    ' Show the duration
    cntResultsControl = lngDuration & " milliseconds"

    ' Retrieve test collection name to store time
      rc& = GetPrivateProfileString(LOAD_TIME_APP, TEST_COLLECTION_TOPIC,
➥ "NONE", strReturnString, Len(strReturnString), strFileName)

    ' If test collection name is none, bypass storage, otherwise store in db
    If Left(strReturnString, 4) <> "NONE" Then
            Call Update_Timings(Common_NullTrim(strReturnString),
      ➥ lngStartTime, lngEndTime, lngDuration)
    End If

    ' Clear out old entry for this now-completed load test
    rc& = WritePrivateProfileString(LOAD_TIME_APP,
   ➥ TEST_COLLECTION_TOPIC, "NONE", strFileName)
    rc& = WritePrivateProfileString(LOAD_TIME_APP,
➥ START_TIME_TOPIC, &O0, strFileName)

End Sub
```

Common_StartTimedTest

This routine obtains a starting time for a performance test, using the best available supported timing method. Typically `Common_StartTimedTest` and `Common_EndTimedTest` encase a block of code to be timed. Listing 7.11 shows the code for the `Common_StartTimedTest` subroutine.

Listing 7.11. The `Common_StartTimedTest` subroutine.

```
Public Sub Common_StartTimedTest()

    Dim rc%

    ' Store the current time
      typTestTime.lngStartTime = Common_GetTimer

    ' Indicate test has started by changing mouse pointer to an hourglass
     Screen.ActiveForm.MousePointer = HOURGLASS

End Sub
```

Common_EndTimedTest

This routine obtains an ending time for a performance test using the best available supported timing method. The duration of the timed activity is calculated and displayed in a label. The particular label used to display the duration will be the label that is supplied in the parameter to the routine. Therefore, this routine provides you with the flexibility to display the results wherever you wish on the form of your test application. If the Common Boolean variable indicates that the save mode is currently active, the timing is stored in the timing database through underlying utilization of the Timing OLE Automation server utility. Typically `Common_StartTimedTest` and `Common_EndTimedTest` are encased around a block of code to be timed. Listing 7.12 shows the code for the `Common_EndTimedTest` subroutine.

Listing 7.12. The `Common_EndTimedTest` subroutine.

```
Public Sub Common_EndTimedTest(ctlShowTime As Control)

    ' This routine performs the following functions based on input parameters:
    '
    ' (1) Collects time for the end of the test
    ' (2) Displays test duration in control passed in as ctlShowTime parameter.
    ' (3) If timing storage flag is on, updates test statistics in the timings
    '      database storing the entry under current test ID.
    ' (4) Redisplays the normal mouse pointer on the form since test is over

    Dim rc%                                  ' return code

    ' Store current msec time, the date/time test completed, and calc total
    '   time in module-level variable

    typTestTime.lngEndTime = Common_GetTimer()
    typTestTime.lngDuration = typTestTime.lngEndTime - typTestTime.lngStartTime

    ' Display the time result
     ctlShowTime.Caption = typTestTime.lngDuration & " ms"

    ' Update the results in the database if the user has requested this via
    '   selection of File-Timings menu option
    If Common_bolRecordOn Then
            Call Update_Timings(Common_strTimingCollection,
            ➥typTestTime.lngStartTime, typTestTime.lngEndTime,
            ➥typTestTime.lngDuration)
    End If

   Screen.ActiveForm.MousePointer = DEFAULT

End Sub
```

Common_FileExists

This routine indicates whether the specified file exists, returning the corresponding Boolean result. The code for this function is shown in Listing 7.13.

Listing 7.13. The `Common_FileExists` function.

```
Public Function Common_FileExists(strFileName As String) As Boolean

    Dim strFileCheckResult As String

    strFileCheckResult = Dir(strFileName)

    If Len(strFileCheckResult) = 0 Then
        Common_FileExists = False
    Else
        Common_FileExists = True
    End If

End Function
```

Common_CenterForm

The `Common_CenterForm` routine can be called to center a form in the middle of the screen. This routine simply readjusts the form's Top and Left properties. The corresponding code is shown in Listing 7.14.

Listing 7.14. The `Common_CenterForm` subroutine.

```
Public Sub Common_CenterForm(CurrentForm As Form)

    ' This routine screen-centers the form passed in the currentform parameter.
    '   It is suggested that a form call this routine in its load
    '   routine, passing the me keyword, to carry out centering.

    CurrentForm.Move (Screen.Width - CurrentForm.Width) / 2,
                   ➥(Screen.Height - CurrentForm.Height) / 2

End Sub
```

Commercially Available Performance Tools

The next category of tools addressed is commercially available tools to assess performance. Some are utilities that accompany the Visual Basic Enterprise Edition product. Others are separately available commercial products. All of these tools can be very helpful in monitoring system activity during performance tuning. Topics considered in this section are

- *WPS*—Monitors 16-bit tasks and modules loaded
- *PView95*—Monitors Windows processes and threads
- *General profiling concepts*
- *VBCP*—Visual Basic code-profiling tool
- *Avanti PinPoint*—Code profiling tool
- *Blue Lagoon JET Inspector*—Profiles database calls

You can carry out a great deal of effective performance analysis with the functions of the Visual Basic language, the Windows APIs, and the utilities provided with this book. With enough thought and elbow grease, you can achieve intelligent program assessments with the manual timer-insertion methods discussed in earlier chapters. However, there are some fine commercial products available, some included with Visual Basic and others that must be purchased as third-party packages, that can make this process much more effective and reduce the time spent on acquiring performance-analysis data.

For complex performance-analysis tasks, turning to these tools might be the only feasible alternative. Decisions to use any tool should be based on careful consideration of your own application-development needs and the benefits a tool might provide to your unique situation. Information on contact points for these products can be found in the Appendix B, "Sources of Information."

A type of tool not described here is the commercially available optimized routine. There are various packages on the market that provide libraries of routines you can use in Visual Basic source code to provide very efficient functionality for areas such as array management and sorting. However, categorizing these packages according to the payoffs and advantages of one tool over another is extremely dependent on the particular application under consideration.

The key issue in choosing any type of tool, from profilers to prepackaged routines, is to consider how much time it will save you in development and optimization and how much of an improved application speed it will provide to your end user. In many cases, if you perform this assessment you will find that the price of the tool is paid back many times by the advantages it provides.

WPS

You can find the WPS utility on the Visual Basic Enterprise Edition CD-ROM under the \tools\PPS subdirectory. WPS stands for *Windows Process Status.* This utility enables you to monitor the status of loaded programs (referred to in Windows 3.1 terminology as *tasks*) and

their support components such as VBXs, DLLs, and drivers (referred to in Windows 3.1 terminology as *modules*). This 16-bit utility does run under 32-bit operating systems but will not provide information on 32-bit components.

This information is helpful for a variety of reasons under Windows 3.1 and when viewing 16-bit programs under Windows 95. Windows 3.1 and Windows 95 load only one instance of a module when a 16-bit program requests it. For this reason, if your program requires a module already in memory and in use by a different program, another copy will not be loaded. The operating system will simply note that the module is now required by two programs rather than one.

Version problems can arise when sharing modules in this manner. WPS provides a way to ensure that the intended versions of your modules are loaded. Sometimes considerations of the location of the loaded file come into play as well. In these cases, you can verify the file location of the loaded module using information displayed in the WPS program window.

As you can see from the WPS window shown Figure 7.17, WPS provides a variety of information. The upper area of the window is devoted to *task information* that corresponds to a program. Columns of interest include those that show the task name (Name), task handle (hTask), instance handle (hInst), version number (Version), and file location (EXE). The lower area of the window is devoted to modules or supporting files such as DLLs, VBXs, OCXs, fonts, and drivers. Columns of information here include name (Name), module handle (hModule), the specific version number of a module (Version), how many programs are currently utilizing that component (Usage), and where it was loaded from (EXE). These pieces of information can be used to pinpoint version or load-path problems.

Figure 7.17.

The WPS process status window.

WPS

File Options Edit Update!

Name	hTask	hParent	nEvents	hInst	Version	Exe
Accstat	4516	0000	0000	2757	78.73.070	C:\WINDOWS\ACCSTAT.EXE
CAPTURE	405E	1E3E	0000	0B4E		C:\COLLWIN\CAPTURE.EXE
Explorer	1E3E	0000	0000	1D67	78.73.070	C:\WINDOWS\EXPLORER.EXE
Findfast	1B06	0000	0000	1B0F	78.73.070	C:\MSOFFICE\OFFICE\FINDFAST.EXE
KERNEL32	0097	0000	0000	010F	4.00.182	C:\WINDOWS\SYSTEM\KRNL386.EXE
MMTASK	12D6	14F6	0000	133E	4.00.182	C:\WINDOWS\SYSTEM\MMTASK.TSK
Mprexe	1EC6	0000	0000	1EA7	78.73.070	C:\WINDOWS\SYSTEM\MPREXE.EXE
MSGSRV32	14F6	0097	0000	14D6	4.00.182	C:\WINDOWS\SYSTEM\MSGSRV32.EXE
POINTEXE	1C1E	1E3E	0003	1B96	11.00.077	C:\MSINPUT\POINTER.EXE
Spool32	23C6	0000	0000	243F	78.73.070	C:\WINDOWS\SYSTEM\SPOOL32.EXE
TEMP16	2A86	1E3E	0004	2B06	1.00.000	C:\AAAA\TEMP16.EXE
Winword	3466	0000	0000	237F	78.73.070	C:\MSOFFICE\WINWORD\WINWORD.EXE

Name	hModule	Usage	Version	Exe
COMMDLG	1D7F	0009	4.00.182	C:\WINDOWS\SYSTEM\COMMDLG.DLL
COMPOBJ	367F	0005	2.20.040	C:\WINDOWS\SYSTEM\COMPOBJ.DLL
COURE	17F7	0001	4.00.182	C:\WINDOWS\FONTS\COURE.FON
CTL3D	2D7F	0001	2.00.000	C:\WINDOWS\SYSTEM\CTL3D.DLL
DBGRID16	37DF	0004	1.00.086	C:\WINDOWS\SYSTEM\DBGRID16.OCX
DDEML	181F	0061	4.00.182	C:\WINDOWS\SYSTEM\DDEML.DLL
DIALOG	0E8F	0001		C:\MSOFFICE\WINWORD\DIALOG.FON
DIBENG	030F	0004	4.00.182	C:\WINDOWS\SYSTEM\DIBENG.DLL
DISPLAY	01DF	0002	4.00.182	C:\WINDOWS\SYSTEM\FRAMEBUF.DRV
FIXFONTS	0707	0001	4.00.182	C:\WINDOWS\FONTS\VGAFIX.FON
FONTS	070F	0001	4.00.182	C:\WINDOWS\FONTS\VGASYS.FON
GALAXY	207F	0003	1.21.121	C:\WINDOWS\SYSTEM\MM16.DRV
GDI	0327	0066	4.00.182	C:\WINDOWS\SYSTEM\GDI.EXE
GRDKRN16	2C5F	0001	1.19.054	C:\WINDOWS\SYSTEM\GRDKRN16.DLL

WPS has other useful features in addition to the information it displays. There are options to load a specific module, save information to file, copy information to the Clipboard, and free a module or task. The capability to free a module under the Options | Free Module menu choice, however, should be used with care. For example, one experiment *not* to try under Windows 3.1 when running a Visual Basic 3.0 program is to unload VBRUN300.DLL (the Visual Basic 3.0 runtime interpreter). An impressive but expected general protection fault will result. If you try the same stunt under Windows 95 when running a 16-bit Visual Basic 4.0 program and unload the 16-bit runtime interpreter VB40016.DLL, you will get a less severe (but still critical) error message when the GPF is trapped: `This program has performed an illegal operation and will be shut down`. In either case, the lesson is the same. Unless you are very sure of a module's current dependencies, unload modules with care. Unloading a module while it is in use can have unexpected results!

> **WARNING:** Do not use WPS to unload the Visual Basic runtime interpreter program. An error message and potential corruption to unsaved data of any active Visual Basic program could result.

PView95

PView95, which also can be found on the Visual Basic Professional and Enterprise Edition CD-ROM in the \tools\PSS directory, is a tool that enables you to view 32-bit process information. (See Figure 7.18.) A Windows NT–specific version of this program, PView, is also available on the CD-ROM. A list of processes appears in the upper display area of the window; each process file's process ID, base priorities, number of threads, and file location also appears in the upper display area of the window. There is an option on the File menu to kill a process; select Process | Kill. Thread-specific information is displayed in the lower display area of the window. The threads displayed in this area correspond to whichever process is highlighted in the upper display area. Thread information includes the thread ID, the owning process's ID, and the thread's priority.

The process information in the figure shows a process that is of a higher priority, KERNEL32.DLL. This is the operating system itself, which is the reason for its high priority setting. The process priority and thread-specific information will not generally be of great relevance to your Visual Basic programs, however; a Visual Basic program will show up with a normal base priority, and Visual Basic does not provide for multithreaded programming. *Multithreaded programming* is the capability to write an application so that the operating system manages concurrent sequences of execution, or *threads*, all within the address space of the program, with potentially different priorities assigned to each thread. Although Visual Basic does not fully exploit these capabilities, other programs on your system will; thus the information in PView95 can give you a better general view of the overall performance environment.

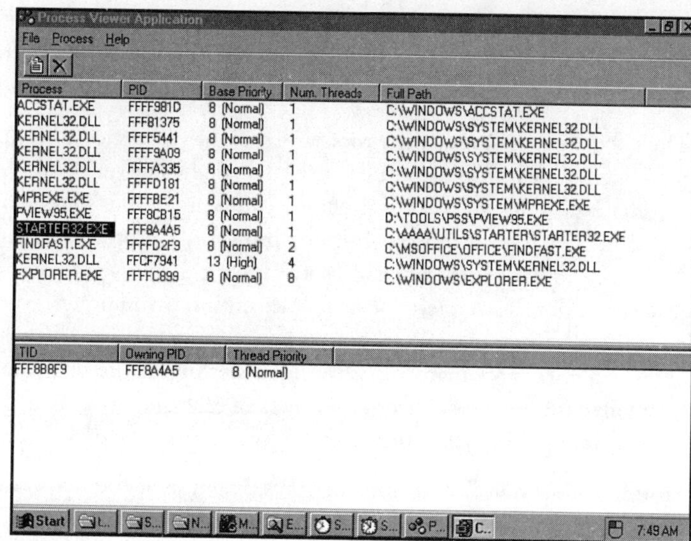

Figure 7.18.
The PView95 window.

General Profiling Concepts

One of the main methods of assessing the performance of an application and identifying bottlenecks is *profiling*. Profiling is much like the simple timed tests that have been presented in this chapter. However, instead of collecting just one timing to view the time spent on a specific block of code, timings are usually taken across many different application areas to characterize performance.

Profiling involves collecting timings for many different areas of the application, typically on a function-by-function basis, so you can evaluate how often each routine is called and how much time a function consumes when it is called. The collected timings are then used to characterize, or *profile*, application behavior to draw conclusions about overall application performance and relative performance between various areas of the application. This can highlight the areas of the code that consume the most execution time and are therefore the best candidates for subsequent optimization. Profiling-based performance assessment is perhaps one of the most effective and meaningful ways to understand what really goes on in an application.

There is good news and bad news when it comes to such profiling. The bad news is that manually modifying source code to put this type of profiling in place—using the timing methods discussed earlier in this chapter—is a time-consuming, potentially error-laden task. Likewise, after the timings have been gathered, it can be a very difficult task to collate them, sift through them and put them in order, and come away with meaningful conclusions. Timing data for a large application can easily consist of many thousands of data points that you must examine. After timings have been gathered, you must modify the code again or at least recompile it with conditional compilation `#If` definitions to remove the profiling statements before you release your product to your users, because you wouldn't want them to face the performance penalty of gathering timings every time they run the application.

The good news is that profiler tools are available that effectively automate every aspect of this task. A profiler tool is almost essential for analyzing very complex programs because it can automate so much of this information gathering. Code statements can be automatically inserted into each procedure to collect timings in a profiler-specific method of time measurement. The profiler data-collection software can then save the results when the program is run. After execution is complete (or during execution if you prefer), you can examine the results in a variety of formats to facilitate your interpretation of data. All aspects of profiling performance of an application are made dramatically easier by the use of a profiler tool. The alternative—manually inserting and collecting timings in each and every area of your code, and then collating and interpreting all of the results—would be very time-consuming.

Profiling your code offers several benefits. It can serve the purpose of tracing code paths. It can show you the flow of routines carried out in response to a specific action or series of actions, which can lead to important code insights. You can profile code to identify specific bottleneck areas that consume the most time when executing. Specific bottleneck areas are best assessed by looking at overall or cumulative time spent in each profiled block of code. There is another statistic that profiling can yield that is also helpful: the *hit count*, or frequency, with which each profiled block of code is called. This can be useful to identify "dead code" that is never used. It is also useful to couple two types of profiling information—cumulative time in a block of code and hit count of that block of code.

Because a profiler tool typically provides information on the frequency of calls to a block of code as well as the amount of time spent there, you can make a judgment about which area is the most important to optimize. If a routine `Inner_Loop_Calc` takes just 500 milliseconds and a routine `Clean_On_Exit` takes 2000 milliseconds, you might think your time would be better spent optimizing routine `Clean_On_Exit`. But when you look at the complete profiling statistics and see that `Inner_Loop_Calc` was called 1000 times during your profiling session and `Clean_On_Exit` was called just once, you might decide you'd be better off to optimize `Inner_Loop_Calc`. If you reduce the `Inner_Loop_Calc` time by 100 milliseconds, you've improved the session speed by 100 seconds (1000 hits×100ms), whereas if you reduce `Clean_On_Exit` by 100 milliseconds, you've improved the overall session time by just 100 milliseconds (1 hit×100ms). If `Clean_On_Exit` is a critical function that's highly visible to the user, it might still warrant optimization. However, for the best optimization decisions, you must consider the number of times a block of code is reached as well as the time spent in each block of code. Both factors determine the ultimate performance of your application.

Optimization decisions, then, are often based on the code paths traveled and on the number of hits on each of those code paths illuminated during profiling. It is critical, therefore, that profiling simulates expected usage patterns. After you have added profiling statements to your profiled code and you're ready to run your application to collected profiled timings, follow a specific test scenario that reflects the user behavior you want to model when using the application and generating results. If you profile your word-processing application but then when you run the profiling session to collect timings all you do is delete 1000 characters, your profiling results will show a high number of hits in the deletion-related functions and no hits in the insertion-related subroutines.

It would be wrong, however, to conclude that insertion-related subroutines are not worth optimizing because there were no hits! In this case, the usage test was not an accurate reflection of the real world, so hit rates are skewed and of little value in determining which optimization has the most payback for a user. Therefore, in profiling it is very important to use consistent, well-thought-out tests. There are many ways to approach profiling, but one truism that always applies is that you must carefully consider results and the context of the test before arriving at any optimization decision.

Profiling code, like the other timing techniques, carries with it its own overhead. When your program runs at the same time as an additional layer of software that is monitoring it and timing its operations, it takes the system more effort (and more time) to execute your application. This is to be expected during the profiling process and should not be viewed as a serious drawback. Some profilers take this overhead into account and factor it out of supplied timings. Most performance measurement consists of looking at relative, rather than absolute, timings. When profiling, you are comparing the relative overhead of one area of the application to the relative performance of others, so the consistent overhead of profiling does not skew the relative ranking of results. Also, profiling is typically a development-level step, and profiling statements are not normally part of the released product, so the overhead penalty is not one shouldered by the users.

Profiling is an important step in the performance-tuning methodology. Chapter 8, "The Brophy/Koets Optimization Methodology," presents a structured methodology for performance tuning and discusses where profiling activity would typically be carried out in the overall performance-tuning picture. Now let's look at some specific profiling tools.

The VBCP Profiler

The Visual Basic profiler, VBCP32.exe, is available on the Visual Basic Professional and Enterprise Edition CD-ROM in the \tools\vbcp directory in both a 16-bit version (VBCP16) and a 32-bit version (VBCP32). The VBCP tool enables you to profile code throughout your application. The profiler automates the process of modifying your programs with timing statements to collect this information and clearly summarizes and presents results. That information can then serve you in identifying performance-bottleneck areas and prime candidates for optimization.

The VBCP code profiler makes a backup copy of all your source code and inserts profiling statements in every routine. The profiler window you use to designate a project and its selected files for automatic profile-statement insertion is shown in Figure 7.19. Before adding profiling

statements, you can select the type of profiling you want. Available options include Line Timing, Line Hit Count, Function Timing, and Function Hit Count information. The line-based information shows you the time spent on each line and how many times a line was encountered by the interpreter during processing. Function-based information shows you the same statistics on a function level. Automatically modified source code is shown in Listing 7.15, with statements added by VBCP appearing in bold print. The source code is available in its premodified form on this book's CD-ROM (under the Sample project) so you can experiment with your own profiling. When the modified program is run, results are collected as each of the profiling statements is encountered.

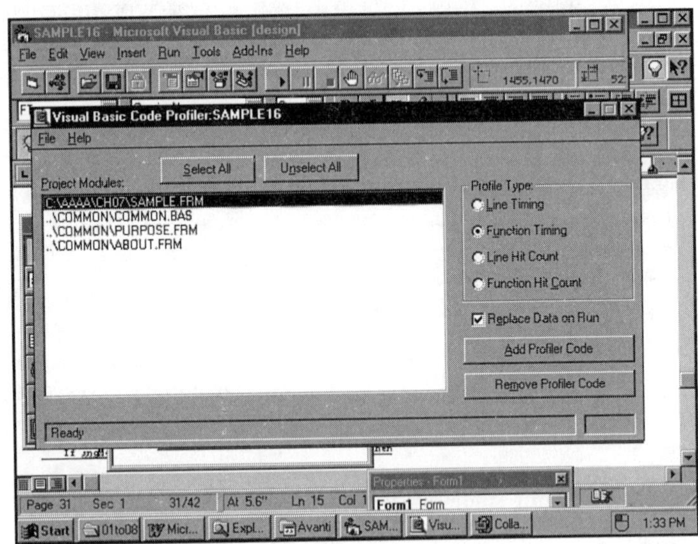

Figure 7.19.
The VBCP profiler's main window.

Listing 7.15. Source code with profiling statements added by VBCP.

```
Private Function BigCalc(salary As Long) As Long
  VBCP_Update 1, "BigCalc", 1

Dim lngMoney As Long


lngMoney = calc(salary)
  VBCP_Update 1, "BigCalc", 2


If lngMoney > 30000 And VBCP_UpdateIf(1, "BigCalc", 3) Then
    lngMoney = lngMoney - 2000
  VBCP_Update 1, "BigCalc", 4
End If

BigCalc = lngMoney
  VBCP_Update 1, "BigCalc", 5
```

```
End Function

Private Function calc(ByVal salary As Long) As Long
  VBCP_Update 1, "calc", 1

Dim sngMoney As Single
Dim strStatus As String

If salary > 20000 And VBCP_UpdateIf(1, "calc", 2) Then
    sngMoney = salary - (salary * 0.3)
  VBCP_Update 1, "calc", 3
    If sngMoney > 30000 And VBCP_UpdateIf(1, "calc", 4) Then
        sngMoney = (sngMoney * 0.3) + (salary * 0.2)
  VBCP_Update 1, "calc", 5
        sngMoney = sngMoney / 1.3
  VBCP_Update 1, "calc", 6
    End If
    strStatus = "Check 1:" & Date & time
  VBCP_Update 1, "calc", 7
    Me.BackColor = QBColor(4)
  VBCP_Update 1, "calc", 8
End If

If salary > 25000 And VBCP_UpdateIf(1, "calc", 9) Then
    sngMoney = salary - (salary * 0.3)
  VBCP_Update 1, "calc", 10
    If sngMoney > 27000 And VBCP_UpdateIf(1, "calc", 11) Then
        sngMoney = (sngMoney * 0.3) + (salary * 0.2)
  VBCP_Update 1, "calc", 12
        sngMoney = sngMoney / 1.3
  VBCP_Update 1, "calc", 13
    End If
    strStatus = strStatus & " Check 2:" & Date & time
  VBCP_Update 1, "calc", 14
    Me.BackColor = QBColor(2)
  VBCP_Update 1, "calc", 15
End If

If sngMoney > 40000 And VBCP_UpdateIf(1, "calc", 16) Then
    sngMoney = sngMoney - (salary * 0.04)
  VBCP_Update 1, "calc", 17
    strStatus = strStatus & " Check 3:" & Date & time
  VBCP_Update 1, "calc", 18
    Me.BackColor = QBColor(3)
  VBCP_Update 1, "calc", 19
End If

Me.Caption = strStatus
  VBCP_Update 1, "calc", 20

calc = Int(sngMoney)
  VBCP_Update 1, "calc", 21

End Function
```

Choosing Results from the View menu in the code profiler main window enables you to view profiled results after program execution. The VBCP results show individual total (cumulative) time and average time for each area's timed statistics, as well as a helpful percent-of-total-time indicator. Likewise, the actual hit count and the percentage of total hits for an area's hit count statistics are displayed. A results window from VBCP is shown in Figure 7.20.

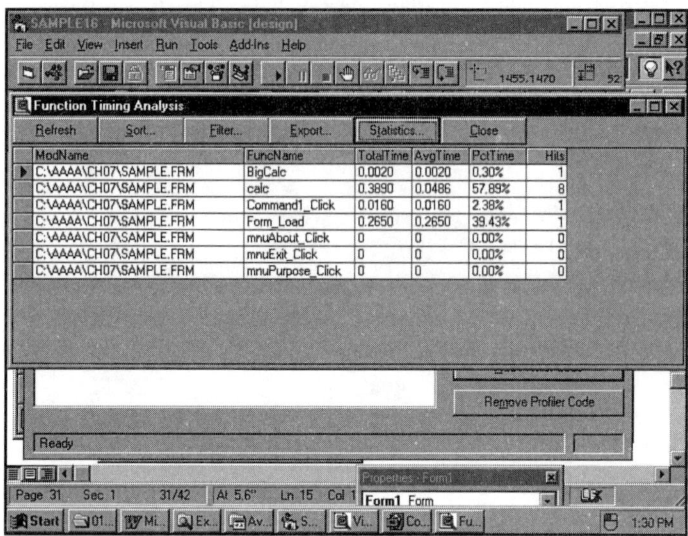

Figure 7.20.
VBCP profiler results.

VBCP provides a filtering capability that you can use to sift through results. This enables you to view, for example, only functions that were reached 100 or more times during execution rather than view the much larger data set with the hit counts for every function. A handy filter-selection box enables you to construct filters. You can export analysis results to a tab-delimited text file.

The VBCP profiler provides all the basic features needed to carry out effective profiling; only some of them are outlined here. It is a straightforward tool to use, and will enable you to gather profiling information that can help greatly in the process of program optimization. As with any tool, however, the most important part of the equation is the skill and judgment you apply in analyzing and interpreting results and in making subsequent optimization decisions.

The Avanti Software, Inc., PinPoint Profiler

PinPoint from Avanti Software, Inc., enables you to carry out the same basic profiling actions that VBCP does, with many additional features as well. Like VBCP, PinPoint can automatically insert procedure-based timing statements throughout an entire project. Then, when the program is executed, the procedure-by-procedure timings can be captured, displayed, graphically represented, and saved in a profiler application. They also can be logged directly to a file.

A helpful trace of program flow (the sequence of routines and lines called in carrying out the program) is available for viewing in the results window. All of these features combine for an effective analytical tool that can provide a quick and accurate application flow/performance trace.

> **NOTE:** Summaries that appear here are based on Windows 3.1 16-bit versions of products. Check with your vendor for 32-bit version information.

PinPoint consists of a few different executable files. The instrumentation program PPAutoVB.exe, pictured in Figure 7.21, provides a dialog box for the user to specify a project file and the specific files within that project that are to be profiled. After this information is specified, profiling code is inserted at the beginning and end of every function. Forms and modules must first be saved in Text format for this step to be carried out, however.

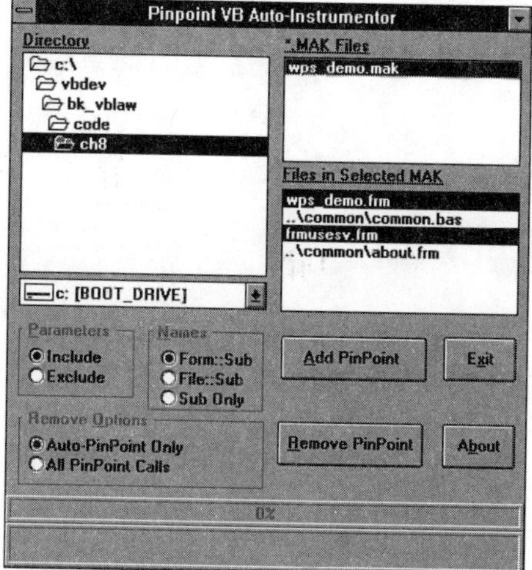

Figure 7.21.
PinPoint's PPAutoVB AutoInsertion.

Listing 7.16 shows a sample function that has been processed by the instrumentation program. The lines shown in bold type have been inserted automatically by PinPoint. These lines will handle the task of sending timing data to the separate Profiler program as the application is run.

Listing 7.16. A subroutine with automatically inserted PinPoint timing calls.

```
Public Function Calc (ByVal salary As Long) As Long
        Call ppBeginFunction("Form1", "Form1::calc", "  salary = " & salary)
                         ➥'#### AutoPinPointed ####

Dim sngMoney As Single
```

continues

Listing 7.16. continued

```
Dim strStatus As String

If salary > 20000 Then
    sngMoney = salary - (salary * .3)
    If sngMoney > 30000 Then
        sngMoney = (sngMoney * .3) + (salary * .2)
        sngMoney = sngMoney / 1.3
    End If
    strStatus = "Check 1:" & Date & Time
    Me.BackColor = QBColor(4)
End If

If salary > 25000 Then
    sngMoney = salary - (salary * .3)
    If sngMoney > 27000 Then
        sngMoney = (sngMoney * .3) + (salary * .2)
        sngMoney = sngMoney / 1.3
    End If
    strStatus = strStatus & " Check 2:" & Date & Time
    Me.BackColor = QBColor(2)
End If

If sngMoney > 40000 Then
    sngMoney = sngMoney - (salary * .04)
    strStatus = strStatus & " Check 3:" & Date & Time
    Me.BackColor = QBColor(3)
End If

Me.Caption = strStatus

calc = Int(sngMoney)

        Call ppEndFunction("")          '#### AutoPinPointed ####
End Function



Public Function BigCalc (salary As Long) As Long
        Call ppBeginFunction("Form1", "Form1::BigCalc", "  salary = " & salary)
                                  ➥'#### AutoPinPointed ####

Dim lngMoney As Long

lngMoney = calc(salary)

If lngMoney > 30000 Then
    lngMoney = lngMoney - 2000
End If

BigCalc = lngMoney

        Call ppEndFunction("")          '#### AutoPinPointed ####
End Function
```

After the program has been *instrumented*, or automatically modified to contain the profiling statements, it can be run either as an executable or directly from the Visual Basic development environment. The PinPoint Analyzer program (PinPoint.exe), which receives and displays timings from the Visual Basic application, is run concurrently. This program is pictured in Figure 7.22. The Analyzer program provides various options that aid in data analysis.

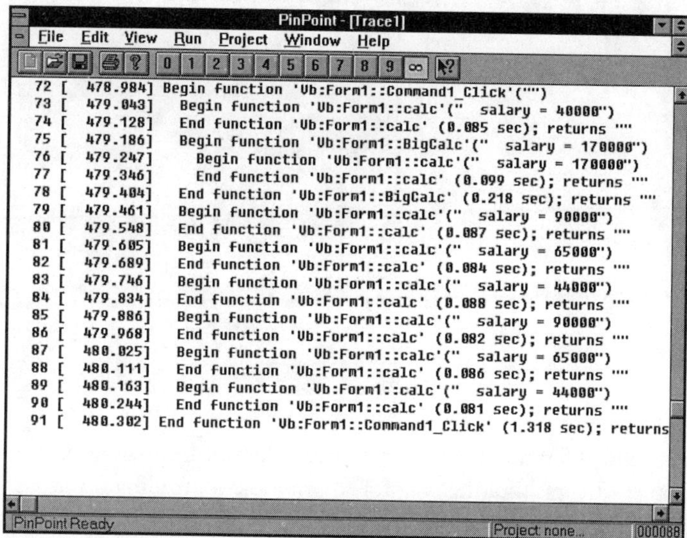

Figure 7.22.
The PinPoint Analyzer program.

Some of the useful information provided by these timings is evident in Figure 7.22. You can see that there is one function, `Calc`, that is frequently called and consumes a great deal of time. There is another function, `BigCalc`, that takes slightly more time but is not called nearly as frequently. This can be seen even more clearly when you save your trace data and load it into the PinPoint Visual Profile tool, Profile.exe. This resulting display tells you the total time consumed by each routine and displays this information in a graphical format, as shown in Figure 7.23. From this simple profiling exercise you could conclude that optimization efforts should focus first on the function `Calc` rather than `BigCalc` because it will likely provide more noticeable dividends to the end user.

PinPoint uses a message-based system to communicate between a profiled application and the PinPoint Analyzer program (PinPoint.exe) that collects results. The PinPoint DLL contains the code for the profiling API calls added to the Visual Basic application that result in the messages. These calls can also be used directly by a programmer to manually insert individual profiling calls into the Visual Basic source code for an application; a corresponding BAS module is supplied that makes such modifications an easy task. The PinPoint API calls are powerful, providing features such as the display of arguments with begin function messages (the messages generated in profiling results at the beginning of each profiled function) and the use of general trace messages. PinPoint uses this message-based approach to also offer support for running multiple profiled applications simultaneously. This capability is quite a benefit if you are assessing the performance of cooperating applications.

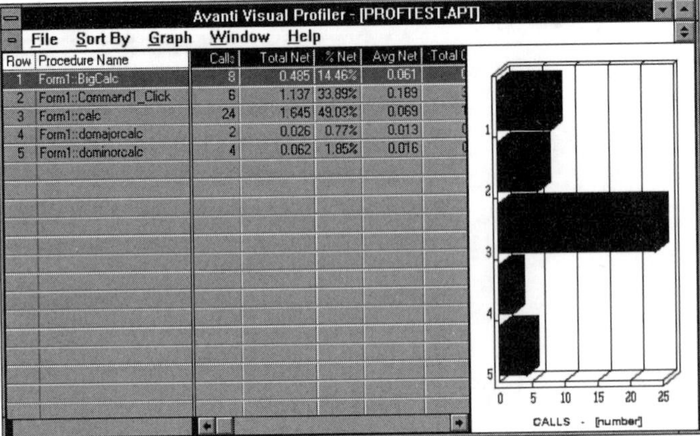

Figure 7.23.
The PinPoint Visual Profiler program with graphical results.

PinPoint offers a helpful filtering capability in the analyzer to select which trace messages are displayed. This filtering enables you to look at profiling information from just a subset of the functions in the application that is being profiled. PinPoint also contains various convenience features such as an indented display of results based on the nesting of called routines, and the capability to bookmark a specific spot in the results trace file for easy location later on. These features greatly enhance the process of analyzing data.

This has been a very high-level discussion of the PinPoint product but has not addressed all aspects of its feature set. The main benefits of the tool—increased efficiency in performance analysis and increased understanding of your application's behavior—is attractive to those who must do frequent profiling of applications. It can also serve as an effective debugging aid. This tool has high-end features that the Visual Basic VBCP profiler does not offer. For challenging performance-tuning tasks, PinPoint provides a robust profiling environment with many helpful features to facilitate the data-collection and analysis process. Even those whose performance-tuning tasks are not that complex might want to consider this tool for the convenience it offers in assessing performance data.

The Blue Lagoon JET Inspector

The JET Inspector from Blue Lagoon profiles the speed of the various operations of the Jet Engine database, which is the layer of software Visual Basic uses to carry out database operations. Because the low-level details of such operations are carried out by Visual Basic and the

Jet Engine to insulate the developer from those very details, many regard activities of the Jet Engine as out of their hands. All too often the Jet Engine is regarded as a black hole in terms of understanding performance impact.

The JET Inspector shines light into this black hole and puts some responsibility for database performance back into the hands of the developer. There are many database-implementation approaches that can be used for a specific series of database operations. Modifications to database code can often result in vastly improved performance if only you know which area to modify and where your expensive database operations are. JET Inspector profiles your database operations to tell you the expense of all database operations.

> **NOTE:** The summary for this tool that appears here is based on the Windows 3.1 16-bit version of products. Check with your vendor for 32-bit version information.

The JET Inspector is easy to use. Simply start up the application; a viewer program appears. Then, when a program that carries out JET-level operations is executed, timings for all operations appear in the window. Sample timings are shown in Figure 7.24.

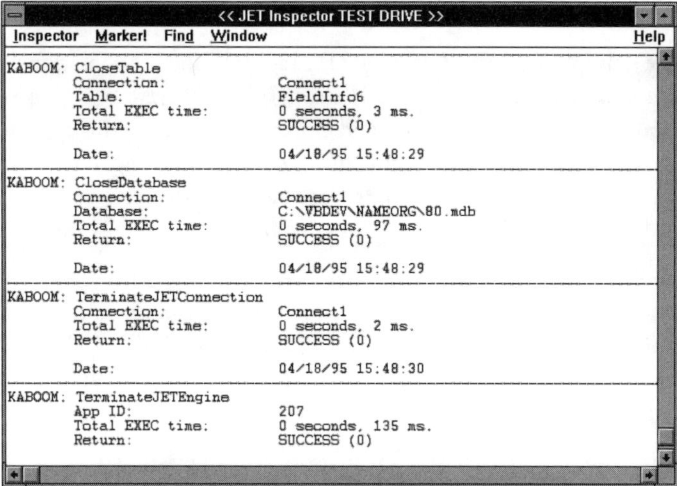

Figure 7.24.
The JET Inspector program after logging database operations.

Various options are available to view the data. A very convenient one is the capability to switch between viewing all JET operations, as shown in Figure 7.24, and viewing JET operations represented in a Visual Basic format. The format which allows you to view JET operations in a Visual Basic format maps JET operations to Visual Basic–level database operations, as exhibited in Figure 7.25. Note that timings of the form 000:000 (sec:millisec) accompany each line of Visual Basic–level operation information. This tool offers you the flexibility to view

low-level details to help you understand intricate performance issues of the multiple JET operations carried out for each Visual Basic database manipulation, or to take a higher-level view of performance by viewing timings simply in terms of Visual Basic–level operations.

Figure 7.25.
The JET Inspector program displaying data in Visual Basic mode.

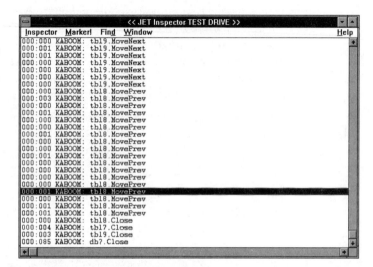

```
<< JET Inspector TEST DRIVE >>
Inspector  Marker!  Find  Window                    Help
000:000 KABOOM: tbl9.MoveNext
000:001 KABOOM: tbl9.MoveNext
000:001 KABOOM: tbl9.MoveNext
000:000 KABOOM: tbl9.MoveNext
000:000 KABOOM: tbl9.MoveNext
000:000 KABOOM: tbl9.MoveNext
000:000 KABOOM: tbl9.MoveNext
000:000 KABOOM: tbl8.MovePrev
000:003 KABOOM: tbl8.MovePrev
000:000 KABOOM: tbl8.MovePrev
000:001 KABOOM: tbl8.MovePrev
000:000 KABOOM: tbl8.MovePrev
000:000 KABOOM: tbl8.MovePrev
000:001 KABOOM: tbl8.MovePrev
000:000 KABOOM: tbl8.MovePrev
000:000 KABOOM: tbl8.MovePrev
000:001 KABOOM: tbl8.MovePrev
000:000 KABOOM: tbl8.MovePrev
000:000 KABOOM: tbl8.MovePrev
000:000 KABOOM: tbl8.MovePrev
000:000 KABOOM: tbl8.MovePrev
000:001 KABOOM: tbl8.MovePrev
000:000 KABOOM: tbl8.MovePrev
000:001 KABOOM: tbl8.MovePrev
000:001 KABOOM: tbl8.MovePrev
000:000 KABOOM: tbl8.Close
000:004 KABOOM: tbl7.Close
000:003 KABOOM: tbl9.Close
000:085 KABOOM: db?.Close
```

The example in Figure 7.25 shows that a close database operation is very expensive. It also shows that a close table operation is less expensive. Therefore, if you were considering a multiple-database approach that opens and closes database files, this type of optimization insight might lead you to focus on minimizing use of close database operations. Although this is a very simple example of the many extensive types of analysis that can be carried out with this tool, you can see how it opens the door to an understanding of database operations not easily available from manual timings.

Blue Lagoon sells similar ODBC and SQL Inspector products. Another very attractive feature of the JET Inspector is that it can work with the ODBC Inspector to show ODBC operations that result from JET operations. You can even view the split of execution time between JET and ODBC when you use the products in tandem.

Using the JET Analyzer for the first time on an existing database application can be a fascinating experience. The database performance bottlenecks that have typically just been speculated about are clearly spelled out. Using this tool would likely lead to better database programming for many just from the greatly increased exposure it provides to what is going on "under the hood."

One example of an interesting bit of performance analysis is to run the JET Inspector on an application that uses third-party bound data controls and view the low-level JET operations. The amount, and ordering, of JET operations might surprise you and explain why certain bound controls have sometimes less-than-ideal performance! As with any performance-optimization activity, it still takes considerable thought and analysis to use this information effectively. You must decide which paths of the application are significant.

Likewise, as Chapter 6 points out, you must keep in mind that many factors can influence the timings you are viewing, including network load, the size of the database, and even your network card's throughput speed if you are analyzing a networked database. The JET Inspector can only provide you with the facts for the given operations just carried out. The facts it provides you the next time you run it might be different if the environment or database differs. It is up to you as the user of the tool to determine the relevance of these facts. If you treat it in this regard, the ease of use of the JET Inspector, and the nature of the data it provides, can make it a key tool in your performance-assessment arsenal.

Tools in Perspective

All of these tools can aid in understanding application- or system-performance characteristics in one way or another. With some tools, it takes virtually no time to understand how they work and begin to apply them. With others, there can be a considerable learning curve to use the tools effectively.

The mix of tools appropriate to your particular needs depends entirely on your application, the target environment, and your application's own unique performance issues and customer expectations.

The point has been made in earlier chapters that informed decisions are critical to good optimization. In this respect, tools certainly lead to better optimization. At the same time, the best tool is careful research and analysis. There are no magic answers to escaping the need for careful performance assessment. Nothing can replace it, but in many cases the intelligent application of these tools can certainly ease the process.

Summary

This chapter presents an overview of some of the tools available that can save time and provide more accurate performance assessment during optimization. In addition, an overview of the types of tools available and why they are useful is provided to help raise your overall understanding of performance issues, regardless of whether you are going to use the specific tools discussed here.

The first category of utilities examined is those included on the CD-ROM that accompanies this book, including Watchr16, to monitor resources; Startr32, to assess program load time; Timing32, to store and analyze timing data from test programs; and COMMON.BAS routines, to incorporate into your programs for general timing purposes.

The second category, commercial tools, includes both those that come with the Visual Basic Professional and Enterprise Editions and those that are sold separately. For example, the chapter covers Visual Basic's WPS utility to monitor Windows 16-bit task and module status, as well as PView32 from Visual Basic. The latter is a tool that enables the user to view 32-bit process and thread status.

A definition of code profiling and some general profiling concepts includes a look at the various benefits derived from profiling—insight into code flow, into the execution time of blocks of code, and into number of times or "hits" various blocks of code are carried out during program execution. This is the kind of information you can analyze to determine which areas of an application are the best candidates for optimization.

A discussion of key profiling tools includes Visual Basic's VBCP and Avanti's PinPoint. Both tools automate insertion of profiling statements and collection of results and can serve as valuable profiling aids. PinPoint has some important additional functions that aid in performance assessment, such as an easy model to master for profiling multiple applications simultaneously and the capability to display results graphically. Blue Lagoon's JET Analyzer is an easy-to-use-tool for profiling database operations of the Jet Engine.

As you have learned, a wide variety of tools are available to assist in performance assessment. The real value of any individual tool depends on your specific application's performance-assessment needs. These tools can be a great aid in evaluating performance, but the ultimate performance-enhancement tool remains the judgment and analytical skill of the developer.

Obey the Signs

Wrong Way: Commercial tools factor out all system-behavior variability that can affect performance timings and yield timing analyses that prove conclusively which areas of code must be optimized.

This statement unfortunately is *not* the case. Currently, such a magical tool does not exist, but some of the commercial tools available today can provide extremely helpful information about your program's behavior and save you lots of time in the performance-tuning process. They do not, however, eliminate the work of performance assessment and do not automatically eliminate the many areas of variability in system behavior that can affect performance readings. You still must carefully consider which factors might be affecting your application's performance and try to eliminate as many of them as possible.

Likewise, when you get timings from the tools, you must think carefully about the ramifications. Perhaps the function or database call that consumes the most time is one that is used infrequently or would be extremely risky to optimize, but functions or series of

database operations in other places in the application that consume less time are executed frequently and are much easier to optimize. In that case, you would use your judgment as a developer to make the appropriate optimization decision. The tool points you in the right direction, but it doesn't make the decision for you.

Beware of Falling Rocks: When using a profiler to assess performance, be sure to save the results from each session.

This will be helpful if you need to go back and compare results later to gauge whether the program performance has improved during subsequent tuning efforts. You typically will want to clear results from old sessions before carrying out profiling, however, because you do not want old and new results to be intermingled. So, rather than simply discarding results, ensure that you have some form of backup, whether stored data on file or a printout. Most profiling tools provide such support.

Q&A

Q If I want to view the time my application spends in each different procedure, is there any way to do this short of editing every procedure and inserting timing code at the beginning and end of each one?

A Yes. One alternative is to use either the profiler that comes with Visual Basic Professional and Enterprise Editions or the commercially available Avanti PinPoint profiler tool. Both of these tools can automatically insert statements into every procedure in an entire product. You can then view timings through the accompanying profiler window or dump them to an output file for later inspection.

Another alternative is to write a Visual Basic routine that takes a starting timing and one that takes an ending timing. Then you can write your own program to process your Visual Basic source code and insert these modular calls into each routine. The time cost of this build-your-own-tool approach, however, is likely to be significantly higher than simply purchasing a profiling product.

Q How can I assess database performance?

A In addition to some of the source code–level timing approaches that have been identified in this chapter, you can receive profile timings at the Jet Engine (Visual Basic data access) level. Blue Lagoon's JET Inspector provides this level of analysis. Blue Lagoon also offers complementary products such as ODBC Inspector and SQL Inspector to provide even more detailed analysis, depending on your database needs. The timings and insight these tools provide enables you to make informed database-optimization decisions.

Workshop

1. Use the Startr32 utility to assess the load time of one of your Visual Basic programs. As described earlier in the chapter, you will have to add the COMMON.BAS module to your project and insert the following line at the end of your main form's `Form_Load` event:

   ```
   Call Common_GetLoadTime (labelname_on_form)
   ```

   Then, if you use Startr32 to launch your program, it will return the number of milliseconds it took to load. Load your program several times and see if the load times remain consistent.

   Next, use PPS or WPS as described earlier in the chapter to view the DLLs in memory both before and after your program is loaded. Based on this list, *preload* all the DLLs required for your program before it is launched. Then use Startr32.exe to again load your program. Check to see if the load time is perceptibly lower.

2. Profile the Sample.vbp project in the Chapter 7 subdirectory of the CD-ROM that accompanies this book. Use an automatic profiling tool if you have one available. If not, manually insert timings that display end-of-procedure total times in the debug window. Here's an example:

   ```
   Debug.Print "Total time for procedure A was " & total
   ```

   The command button on the main form causes procedures `Calc` and `Big_Calc` to be called. Determine which of the two procedures in the project takes more execution time.

CHAPTER

8

The Brophy/ Koets Optimization Methodology

Optimization is both an art and a science. Creativity and intuition are required to originate meaningful performance tests and performance assessments; a very disciplined, methodical approach is then necessary to smoothly implement such enhancements into your application. This chapter provides a specific structured methodology developed by the authors that provides for highly controlled, accurate, and efficient implementation of performance enhancements. This process, the Brophy/Koets Optimization Methodology, provides the framework for a series of sequential steps for code optimization. Without such a framework to follow, your performance tuning could easily degenerate into a series of undisciplined, bug-laden, "two steps forward, one step back" efforts. However, if you apply the methodology, all aspects of optimization—from creative identification of improvements to safe, widespread implementation of the improvements across the body of code—can be carried out in a controlled, effective manner.

Analogy: Pitching a Tent

Suppose that you have promised your spouse you will quickly put up a tent. If you have ever had the experience of putting up a pole tent, you know that your first goal is to simply get the tent standing, and then to adjust it. Adjusting the tent can consist of a series of steps of lengthening or shortening pole heights, moving stakes nearer or farther, and changing the slack on ropes that go from stakes to the poles. If you begin to adjust the tent by darting from one pole to another, considering only the closest pole with no regard to which pole is the shortest or longest from its desired size, you are likely to have to visit each pole repeatedly before the tent is straight. You may find that you fix one pole, only to make another go haywire. As a matter of fact, you may even make a poor adjustment that knocks down a pole or the entire tent! If your spouse demands an explanation of what you have been doing, you will be hard pressed to even remember the series of gyrations you have gone through. On the other hand, if you step back and observe the tent after it is first standing but *before* making any adjustments, you can see the overall picture and relation between the poles. By examining the overall situation and the relationship of the various pieces of the tent, you can then proceed to adjust poles, stakes, and ropes in a planned, methodical fashion, starting with the poles that look the worst. Not only will you be much less likely to knock the tent down, you may even have completed your work after adjusting just a couple of critical poles. And you will be able to provide a clear explanation of the steps you have carried out.

So it is with optimization. If you make adjustments without looking at the overall picture and proceeding without a plan, you may fix one problem area only to introduce new problems. You will likely have little understanding of the sequence of steps you have followed once you have spent some time in unorganized optimization. Your task will take considerably longer and carry with it considerably more risk than if you took the time to plan your approach in advance, and then proceeded with a clearly defined series of optimization steps.

This chapter provides you with all the details of this methodology. First, the appropriate point in the software-development process for applying the optimization methodology is identified. The methodology itself is then spelled out, including the recommended sequence of steps to follow when optimizing code, as well as related issues such as supporting these efforts through collections of reusable code.

When to Use the Brophy/Koets Optimization Methodology

You should keep optimization principles in mind during all phases of development. For example, loops built on integer indexes will be significantly faster than loops built on variant indexes. Therefore, you should select the integer type for loops where appropriate the first time you design or write that code. This type of optimization, choosing efficient design and code, is therefore a constant, ongoing development activity rather than a part of some distinct optimization phase.

Analogy: Pitching a Tent II

Consider again the case of pitching a tent. Even though you plan to readjust the stakes, ropes, and poles after the tent is up, you want to pitch the tent initially as close to correctly as possible. If you stand up an expandable pole and observe that it is just 2 feet tall while all other poles are between 4 and 5 feet, you will likely take the time to expand the 2-foot pole to a length between 4 and 5 feet like the other poles. You intuitively realize that making some simple, obvious adjustments now will help you get the tent standing faster and pave the way for making minor adjustments that will follow once the tent is up.

Similarly, it makes sense to carry out the obvious, intuitive performance-tuning steps when you design and write code. Even though you know that you will eventually have a focused optimization stage during your software development, if you are writing code and it occurs to you that it could benefit from a simple optimization, making the optimization on the spot will give you good initial code and make the ultimate optimization stage easier.

Such an approach, however, is usually not enough to produce fully optimized programs. Fully optimized programs require a separate focused period of optimization during which you concentrate *only* on assessing and improving performance, applying steps such as those of the Brophy/Koets Optimization Methodology. The ideal point in the software development cycle to enter this stage will vary from one project to another. Several factors can influence the decision of when to concentrate on performance tuning.

Analogy: Pitching a Tent III

Consider the case of the camper who loves to pitch tents but has never been taught the correct technique. The camper stops repeatedly while putting the tent up to tinker with the pole height, adjust the rope slack, and move stakes, even before all the poles are out of the box. The tinkering seems to point out the need for even more adjustments in the

continues

> mind of the camper, and one adjustment leads to another and another, without ever even raising the tent. The camper doesn't realize that you can never fully adjust all the pieces of the tent until the entire tent structure is in place. Eventually after an afternoon of work with little progress, the camper spends the night under the stars.
>
> The same fate can befall the untrained optimizer! If a programmer gives in to the temptation to constantly tinker and optimize even as the code is being written, the final program may never get done. And if it does get completed, many of the optimizations may have been done to no avail or might even have to be redone, since perspective on the entire program is often required to determine which optimizations are the key ones.

The overall software-development approach for a project is an important factor that influences when to go through the optimization methodology. The approach is likely to be different depending on whether you develop software in a waterfall fashion or spiral prototyping fashion. The *waterfall* approach consists of distinct design and implementation phases with an emphasis on identifying requirements at the start of the process, defining clear design plans, completely implementing and then testing them in a sequential fashion. The *spiral prototyping* approach incorporates continuous design, implementation, design touch-up, and more implementation throughout the software-development process, repeatedly revisiting and refining design requirements.

If you are developing software with the waterfall approach, rigidly laying out the design and then implementing at successive levels of detail, a good case can be made for scheduling performance tuning early in the feature-implementation process and again after development has been completed. If you carry out the first optimization cycle early in the feature-development process you can potentially catch bottleneck areas before the bulk of development is done. You will be better off finding problems that result in major architectural changes to the application early on than after more software has been completed. Likewise, you must carry out another optimization cycle at the end of the project because that will be the first chance to assess the completed state of the application. Performance issues when the code is complete can differ significantly from the state of the application during early feature development.

If you use spiral prototyping to develop the software, repeated applications of the performance-tuning methodology might be warranted from the start of the project to the finish. The best place to carry out the tuning phase is after each spiral, when the design and implementation have been significantly developed and have been solidified. When you incorporate an optimization cycle early on, you affirm the soundness of the evolving software architecture. Repeating the optimization cycles at successive spirals continues to ensure a solid product throughout the evolution of the product.

You should carry out the final round of the Brophy/Koets Optimization Methodology *after* preliminary testing and bug fixes in case you address a problem in early testing that has a major effect on the application architecture (and therefore on performance). Avoid undertaking performance assessment concurrently with regular testing or bug-fix activity; the intent of

optimization is to assess performance on a static, rather than dynamic, target and to enact changes for any trouble areas against that static target.

Your development schedule might be the most important factor in deciding when to do performance tuning. If the time required to release a product is short, performance tuning is an area that is frequently cut back on. Trade-offs can justifiably be made about the value of getting a slower product to customers sooner versus giving them a faster product later. However, you should always carry out at least a brief period of performance assessment to ensure that a product is not released with major performance bottlenecks that render it unusable.

Often you will need to incorporate the Brophy/Koets Optimization Methodology at more than one stage of the software development cycle to ensure that a program is fully optimized. You risk identifying problems late in the game that require extensive redesign to solve if you gamble on just one optimization methodology stage toward the end of development. As a result, the overall release dates could be delayed by a decision that was intended to accelerate them. If you plan on multiple optimization stages you create a safety net to deal with performance surprises. It comes at the cost, however, of a slower release time. Ultimately, the choice is likely to be dictated by the type of application, the required release time frame, and how much emphasis on performance is required to satisfy the product's users.

The Brophy/Koets Optimization Methodology Steps

The Brophy/Koets Optimization Methodology consists of a series of sequential activities that are carried out to assess, implement, and analyze controlled optimizations. Initially, you must get to know your application through interactive observation and detailed code profiling. This will enable you to identify bottleneck areas and establish a priority list of problem areas to tackle. With this information, you can implement the code changes needed to carry out the desired optimizations. You implement and test code changes by placing them in the application source code and verifying the results. Such source-code changes are introduced in an incremental manner one optimization at a time.

These steps make up the overall optimization methodology. You may need to cycle through this series of steps repeatedly if many performance problem areas are present. You address a particular performance bottleneck by carrying out all steps for that specific problem area; then you repeat the cycle to address the next bottleneck on the list. Such an approach is of potential benefit on any size of project, but it is generally true that the bigger the performance-tuning task, the more benefits there are from this disciplined approach. Larger performance-tuning efforts are much more prone to crumble under the weight of unexpected side effects, lost ability to regress and recover old code, and blurring of bottleneck priorities during performance assessment. The optimization methodology is intended to avoid exactly these problems. Steps for the Brophy/Koets Optimization Methodology are summarized here:

1. Identify the top-priority bottleneck.
2. Define the optimization objective or *quit satisfied*!
3. Identify target enhancement.
4. Implement the target enhancement in one place in the application.
5. Implement the target enhancement for the remaining instances in the application.
6. Assess results, and then repeat the cycle.

The flow of the steps of the methodology is illustrated in Figure 8.1. Each main optimization step entails its own sequential series of substeps.

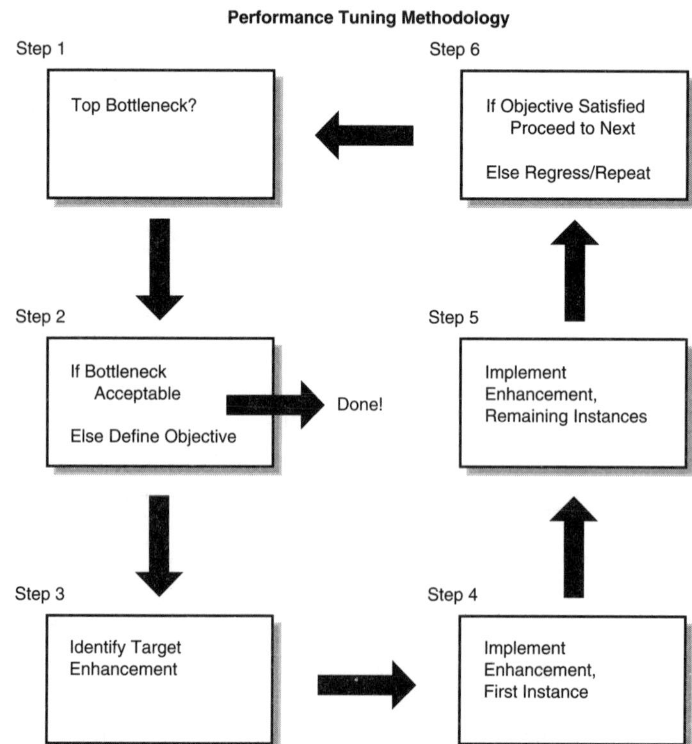

Figure 8.1.
The Brophy/Koets Optimization Methodology steps.

Step 1: Identify the Top-Priority Bottleneck

To identify the top-priority bottleneck you must measure the performance of the application and assess the results. Activity associated with the identification of performance bottlenecks is addressed in earlier chapters. Specifically, Chapter 5, "Collecting Performance Measurements," provides guidelines for measuring performance. Chapter 6, "Factors That Affect Performance," describes factors that can skew performance timings. Chapter 7, "Supporting Utilities for Performance Analysis," covers tools that can aid in measuring and assessing application performance, including code profilers.

Performance assessment, as described in those chapters, might involve a combination of getting feedback from actually using the application and subjectively gauging its performance, and objectively gauging performance by inserting timing statements into code or profiling the application using a profiling tool. From these assessments you can identify a prioritized list of potential optimization areas and select the top-priority bottleneck as the next one to attack.

In most applications, there are many areas of performance that could be optimized. Some optimizations can have a great payback and improve performance by a margin that is easily noticeable to the user; other potential optimizations have a minimal payback. You might invest considerable time to make a code change that speeds up some infrequently exercised operation by 3 milliseconds. Most likely, this improvement is too minimal to be perceived by a user unless it is encountered frequently or carried out in conjunction with a series of other improvements in the same area. On the other hand, perhaps you could devote the same amount of time to some other area of code and achieve an improvement of 150 milliseconds on a frequently exercised operation. Obviously, you would rather make the high-payback optimization than the one that will go virtually unnoticed.

Given that you are typically faced with more potential optimizations than time will allow to be carried out, you will want to focus your energy on the optimizations that will have the highest payback to the user. Therefore, the intent of Step 1 is to limit the current scope of the optimization effort to the most important bottleneck. If there are other bottlenecks worthy of being addressed, they can be considered on subsequent cycles through the Brophy/Koets Optimization Methodology. There are three main steps required to identify the top bottleneck:

1.1. Interactively assess the application for performance trouble spots.

1.2. Profile the application at the code level for performance trouble spots.

1.3. Rank areas to concentrate on from highest to lowest.

Step 1.1: Interactively Assess the Application for Performance Trouble Spots

This phase consists of observing the application from the subjective vantage point of the user. You should use the application as you believe a user would and take note of any areas of perceived slow performance. This interactive test, to be most valuable, should take place on the same performance class of PC that your users have. Testing on a top-speed Pentium is of little value if your user base will run your software on 33MHz 486s.

It is important when assessing the application in this manner to cover every area. A test script or written test plan can help ensure that no areas go untouched. Likewise, you should test from the perspective of users' data conditions. If you are assessing a recipe-management program, don't test its load speed with a database of 50 recipes if your real users will use databases with 20,000 recipes. It is helpful during this evaluation step to document in some type of performance log any areas that seem to have unsatisfactory performance. (A *performance log* is a document containing a chronological history of optimization steps.)

Step 1.2: Profile the Application at the Code Level for Performance Trouble Spots

The interactive assessment results from Step 1.1 identify potential performance trouble areas. The next step is to study more scientifically and objectively rather than subjectively what is happening in those areas. Profiling is the key to this more precise level of insight. *Profiling*, as you learned in Chapter 7, is the act of using slightly adjusted source code to trace code flow, measure frequency of usage of code areas, and measure execution time of segments of code. This can clearly highlight bottleneck areas.

Even if no major trouble spots were identified in the Step 1.1, there is still merit to profiling code to view the performance flow in a more detailed fashion. A clear understanding of code behavior is virtually guaranteed to lead to the best code-optimization decisions. Profilers provide the easiest way to get this level of understanding.

Profiling techniques typically modify your source code slightly by inserting statements around blocks of code to monitor the frequency with which those blocks of code are encountered and the time required to execute them. Generally, profiling takes place at a functional level, although it can take place at even an individual source-line level. Output is typically provided back to you through a results file or the debug window and details the speed and frequency of execution of code areas. The bigger the frequency and time hit, the more benefit your user will receive if you optimize that area. Likewise, if an operation is painstakingly slow but is exercised very infrequently under normal application use, your user will notice less benefit from an optimization to that area. Profiling helps you identify these areas. It doesn't fix the problems, but it shines a light on where the problems are occurring.

You can take several approaches to profiling. Most of these approaches are discussed elsewhere in this book, including a detailed look at profiling techniques and a couple of profiler products in Chapter 7. For small-scale profiling work, you can insert timing statements manually at the start and end of each block of code you want to test, as described in Chapter 4, "Timing Methods." Some of the routines included in the COMMON.BAS module on the CD-ROM that accompanies this book can serve as building blocks for this task. These statements can print out messages to a file or debug window to alert you to the time spent in a block of code and how frequently it is encountered in normal usage patterns. You can use such a manual profiling approach to focus on certain areas that the initial application assessment in Step 1.1 indicated might be problem spots.

Manual profiling works for small areas of activity, but quickly becomes impractical if you have large areas to cover. There are significant benefits to assessing the performance profile of an entire application. Often, an across-the-application profile can alert you to significant problem areas that you might not have been aware of had you just inserted a few of your own profiling statements. Fortunately, there are some powerful tools available to provide this level of profiling capability, including the Visual Basic profiler and the Avanti Software, Inc., PinPoint profiler described in Chapter 7.

There are some considerations to keep in mind when profiling code. Because profiling involves making temporary changes to your code, profiling is most safely applied to a backed-up version of your code, stored separately from your main source code. Then, after you assess your code's performance profile, you can easily discard the altered code and return to the original source code to make modifications.

Also, profilers themselves introduce performance skew into your applications. It takes time for the interpreter to process profiling statements, so a profiled application will perform more slowly than a non-profiled application. In most cases, this is not a problem because you are really comparing the relative performance of blocks of code at this stage and they all are subject to the same profiling overhead. In some cases of timing critical code, the additional artificial delay from the temporary timing statements could be a factor you have to take into account.

For this reason, it is generally preferable to treat profiling statements as temporary in your source code and discard the profiled code when you're finished rather than keep them as a permanent part of the application's code base. The profiling tools make it easy to add and remove profiling statements to code, so the time demands of repeated profiling are minimal. However, there might be some cases when you want to permanently leave profiling statements in code with the expectation that your user will not see the results (for example, if you use a flag to turn on profiling or it is routed to the debug window that the users will not have). That decision should be made carefully, because if you distribute your programs with profiling statements intact in source code, you have more lines of code that can potentially introduce errors as well as affect performance.

After you have inserted the profiling statements and are testing the code to collect the profiled results, it is very important to test a typical user pattern of activity. Test scripts or a detailed test plan are the best way to ensure that this is done fully and consistently each time profiling is carried out; otherwise, you might end up viewing as a major problem an area that is not really typical of a real usage pattern.

You should also be aware that proper profiling activity is not a one-time task; it must be carried out anew at each pass through the methodology cycle. This is because optimizations made to one area can affect other areas in subtle ways. A new set of statistics should be collected after each optimization, since you can never assume that results from earlier cycles are still relevant.

By taking advantage of any one of these profiling alternatives, you can take the *subjective* perceptions of interactive assessment and turn them into *objective* findings for the performance of specific code areas. The end result from this step should be a list of behaviors of various code areas.

Step 1.3: Rank Areas to Concentrate on from Highest to Lowest

After the profiling results are obtained, the next step is to evaluate them. Using the results from Step 1.2, you should give careful consideration to which areas have the biggest impact on the user. The best way to prioritize bottlenecks is to look at a blend of two factors: which segments of code take the longest to carry out and which are exercised the most frequently. A code segment that takes a long time but is hardly ever used is not a good optimization candidate, whereas a code segment that takes a moderate amount of time but is exercised repeatedly can provide much more perceived performance improvement to the user when optimized.

You create this ranking of priority areas by assessing the profiling results and subjectively ordering them based on your insights into how each area is used. You can also do this more objectively by looking at the cumulative time spent in each code segment during profiling. If your profiling-results collection was carried out while using a real-world script or test plan, the overall time spent on each code segment should serve as an accurate payback-for-optimization ranking method.

After you derive the ranked list, the next step is to select just the highest-priority area as the one to focus on for the remainder of the current optimization methodology cycle. If there are other significant bottleneck areas, they can be addressed on subsequent cycles of the methodology. But for maximum benefit, you should tackle the most significant bottleneck first.

To identify the biggest bottleneck, simply look at the top of the list and select the first problem area that is feasible to tackle. Some bottlenecks cannot be realistically addressed. For example, if the top bottleneck relates to a block of code that downloads data via modem and inserts it into a remote database, you might review this area and decide that the constraints are really the limits of technology and not the way the code is written. Some study and reflection might be needed to decide which bottlenecks are worth tackling. After such filtering, you should select the top bottleneck that you have determined to be under your control.

Step 2: Define Optimization Objective or Quit Satisfied!

After you have identified a specific bottleneck to address, the next step is to state a clear objective for that targeted enhancement, thus clarifying the task at hand. Often this step can seem so obvious that you might be tempted to skip it, but it can provide several benefits. The objective helps keep you focused on the specific enhancement you are working on and minimizes the likelihood that you will jump into tangential areas of source code when making the change. Jumping into tangential areas does, of course, carry with it the risk of introducing further problems outside the area being addressed.

When formulating the objective, you should also consider whether that top bottleneck is one that really adversely affects the user. If your biggest problem area has a small impact, the benefits to be gained by investing more time in optimization may be so minimal that you would be better off halting optimization activity and accepting current limitations. As you formulate the objective, you should ask "Is this application now optimized to an acceptable level?" If the answer is no, you can continue with the optimization objective clearly in mind. If the answer is yes, you are finished with the performance-tuning process. If you halt optimization in this manner, all lower-ranking bottlenecks can be ignored as well. If the methodology is carried out correctly, this will always be the case, because the top-priority bottleneck bubbles to the surface during the current optimization methodology cycle. Therefore, when you reach a point where even the highest bottleneck is considered not worth the time it would take to address, other bottlenecks should likewise not merit any further attention.

Stating a clear objective also helps with the process of documenting optimization methodology cycles. An *optimization methodology cycle* is considered to be one complete pass through all of the steps shown in Figure 8.1. Ideally, an optimization methodology document should be maintained for any application undergoing optimization. This document includes a record of every optimization cycle, including a specific objective for each cycle. The record should also document the results from the optimization attempts of each cycle, assessed with respect to whether the cycle's optimization objective was fulfilled. Clear objectives and a record of the implementation with the success or failure of each objective can aid immensely in the optimization process if trouble arises or complications result and steps must be revisited. Such a log is easily maintained on a notebook, in a database, or in a simple text file. Figure 8.2 is an example of a simple log. This file is also available on the CD-ROM that accompanies this book as PerfLog.doc and can be modified for your own projects.

Step 3: Identify Target Enhancement

After you have defined the area of code that is the optimization candidate, the next step is to identify the specific changes that can be made to improve that area and carry out the optimization. There may be several potential solutions to evaluate to decide which combination of changes results in the most improvement. Determining the best specific performance enhancement has been addressed from a philosophical standpoint in earlier chapters and is addressed from a detailed standpoint with many examples in the chapters to come. There are two primary steps to this phase:

3.1. Identify potential solutions.

3.2. Compare potential solutions in the test application.

Figure 8.2.
A sample optimization log.

Performance Tuning Log

Project: Stats
Date: 9/12/95
Programmer: Tim Shangle

Cycle	Step 1 Top Bottleneck	Step 2 Optimiz. Objective	Step 3 Target Enhance.	Step 4 First Instance	Step 5 Other Instances	Step 6 Checkpoint
Cycle 1	Functions use variant instead of integer math -A1:700ms, -B1:600ms, -C1:900ms	Improve math performance in functions A1,B1,C1	Change vars used in math to be of type integer	Fixed Function A1, 12 places. New time: 400 ms	Fixed B1, 11 places. 200ms. Fixed C1, 15 places, 500 ms.	Objective met. Overall 1100 ms better!
Cycle 2	Func StdDeviatn, 10 hits, 1100 ms	Reduce number of hits for StdDeviatn	Reorder logic, just call once per data set instead of 5 times	Fixed Func CalcSet, to just call StdDeviatn 2 times, 210 ms	N/A	Objective met! 890 ms better!
Cycle 3	Func Complex, 11 hits, 1700 ms	Reduce number of hits for Complex	Reorder call logic so Complex only called at data set initialization	Fixed Func MainInit to call Complex once instead of twice. Now 10 hits, 1500 ms	Fixed Func A1, B1, C1 to not call Complex at all. Now 7 hits, 900 ms.	Oops!! Testing showed Complex call needed prior to final calcs too! Objective failed, regress back from all changes in this phase.
Cycle 4	Func Complex, 11 hits, 1700 ms	Reduce time in Complex	Improve Complex search loop so exit occurs when neg number found	Fixed search loop in Complex. Now 11 hits, 1400 ms	N/A	Objective met! 300 ms better!
Cycle 5	Func StoreDB, 4 hits, 600 ms	Reduce time in StoreDB data save	Use transactions, commits, to buffer changes	Fixed Func StoreDB, now 4 hits, 130 ms	N/A	Objective met! 470 ms better!

Step 3.1: Identify Potential Solutions

The first step is to identify potential optimization alternatives. This involves both studying the current technique and considering related methods. This step is often closely intertwined with the next step: actually testing the alternatives. Often, the tendency is to intermingle these steps so that alternatives are tested and refined as they come to mind. The steps are listed separately here, however, because there is a distinct advantage to thinking through alternative solutions before turning yourself loose at the keyboard. If you take the time to reflect on the original code, and then seek alternatives and insights by referring to documentation, code samples, online forums, Microsoft's Knowledge Base, or many other resources before coding, you can be sure of making an informed decision from the body of knowledge available and will have a significantly greater chance of identifying "the best" optimization change on your first try.

On the other hand, if you plunge right into test coding without first identifying all the alternatives, you may spend a significant amount of time coding and re-coding optimization changes that turn out to be non-optimal or not the best from all available choices. Good research is often not as much "fun" as hacking away, but given the wealth of knowledge from the programming community about Visual Basic techniques, pre-coding research offers perhaps more productivity payback per hour invested than any other facet of performance tuning.

Step 3.2: Compare Potential Solutions in the Test Application

If you are evaluating a performance enhancement by comparing alternate code techniques, these comparisons should ideally *not* be made using the application itself. Rather, you should use small, specific test programs. You can move code from the application to the test program to produce a test program that focuses on the specific comparison under consideration. This has two advantages: It can make performance comparisons simpler by isolating them from application issues, and it removes the risk of introducing problems into the application itself when carrying out performance trade-offs.

Assessing performance by moving code to a test program is easy to accomplish when evaluating one or a few statements. It is more difficult to carry out when evaluating the effects of a major chunk of application code that depends on global variables and other facets of the application structure. However, carrying out comparisons in test applications should always be a goal. If you are evaluating performance alternatives and find that you cannot easily move your performance test to a test application, it is likely a sign that your application has not been developed in an ideally structured, modular fashion.

Performance comparisons and performance measurements in test applications delineate the target enhancement to be implemented in the application itself. The advantages of a specific improvement over other alternatives is identified through a test program or other means in this step. The end result is the identification of the designated target enhancement and the code techniques behind it. The final implementation in the application that follows in Step 4 is turned to only after this target enhancement has been clearly identified.

Step 4: Implement the Target Enhancement One Place in the Application

When you reach Step 4, you have a clearly defined target enhancement ready to implement, based on the research and analysis carried out in the preceding steps. In some cases, your target enhancement will clearly just apply to one area of code, in which case you can directly apply the implementation substeps 4.1 through 4.9 that follow. In other cases your target enhancement might be applicable to many areas of code rather than just one. If your target enhancement *does* apply to multiple areas of your source code, you should at this point narrow the initial scope to focus on just one particular source code area. After you choose one representative area where you will implement the target enhancement, you can carry out the implementation substeps 4.1 through 4.9 just as you would for any single change. Making related changes to other applicable areas occurs only after successful implementation and verification of the single change, and is dealt with in Step 5.

The following are the stages to implement a target enhancement to one area of code. These stages are summarized in Figure 8.3 as well:

4.1. Back up source code.
4.2. Measure the prechange performance of the area to change.
4.3. Measure the prechange performance across the entire application.
4.4. Insert the change.
4.5. Measure the postchange performance of the area changed.
4.6. Measure the postchange performance across the entire application.
4.7. Test the area changed.
4.8. Test the entire application.
4.9. If there are any problems, regress to Step 3.

Step 4.1: Back Up Source Code

The first step is to back up the application. All source code should be archived by whatever means are appropriate for the project. The key here is to back up *all* source code and not just the individual module that is the initial target for change. When you're carrying out performance enhancements, you may find that the source file you think will be the "only" file to change ends up becoming one of many files that must be modified after you dive into the code. Backing up all files ensures that there is an easy regression path to the original state of the software if your performance-enhancement technique is not successful or does not yield the desired changes.

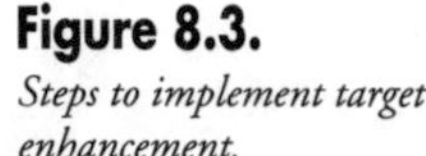

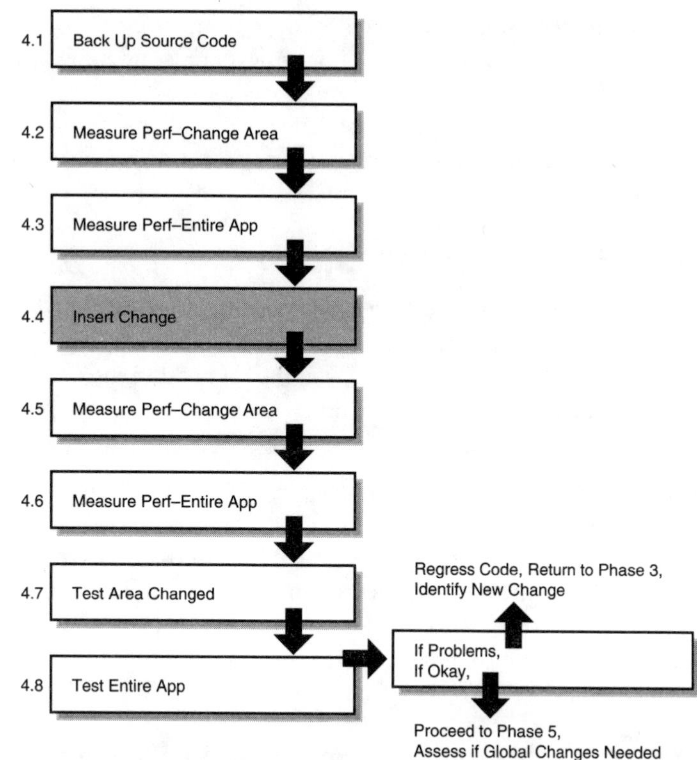

Figure 8.3.
Steps to implement target enhancement.

Step 4.2: Measure Prechange Performance of the Area to Change

The next step is to measure the performance of the specific area to be changed. Earlier measurements of the application will have been carried out during the process of assessing performance, identifying performance bottlenecks, and evaluating whether alternative approaches are necessary. Still, unless prior assessments were taken during this cycle on an identical code base and you have clear measurement statistics, you should take a new measurement at this point, using the guidelines presented in Chapter 5. This measurement should focus on the specific area of the application to be modified. The purpose of this measurement is to provide a metric to determine if the performance change is successful after the implementation is complete.

Step 4.3: Measure Prechange Performance Across the Entire Application

The next step is to take a comprehensive look at application performance. This involves looking not only at the specific spot to be changed, but at all areas of application performance. The purpose of this measurement is to provide a benchmark to determine that overall performance

does not regress from side effects after you improve one specific area of the application. This evaluation can range from a formal series of tests and measurements (as described in Chapter 5) to informal application-usage observations of performance, depending on the application and time constraints. Note that earlier profiling timings gathered on this cycle of the performance-tuning methodology can serve as the main reference point of overall application behavior.

Step 4.4: Insert the Change

After you have assessed prechange performance as described in Steps 4.3 and 4.4, the performance enhancement is inserted into the source code. It is very important that only the target change be inserted. In other words, you should not dive into the code to insert a performance-enhancement change and clean up three other minor bugs that you have recently noticed. *Only* the performance change should be included.

This ensures that the only factor you consider when assessing the results of this change is the change itself. Performance is affected by so many factors that it is very important that you not introduce any additional variables. Giving in to the urge to make additional changes adds uncertainty and increases the potential for errors. In addition to making only one specific change, log the details of that change into the optimization log that was discussed earlier. This will provide a detailed history of your optimization process in the log, and will be of value if you have to go back later to undo or reassess changes.

Step 4.5: Measure Postchange Performance of the Area Changed

After you have made the change, take another measurement on the specific area of the application affected by the change. Use exactly the same technique and test plan that you used for the prechange measurement for this postchange measurement. Depending on the type of change and the type of measurement you used, you might need to take multiple measurements to make an accurate assessment.

Step 4.6: Measure Postchange Performance Across the Entire Application

The next step is to measure comprehensive application performance in all areas of the application. Again, use the same technique and test plan as you used for the prechange applicationwide measurements. The purpose is to identify any unintended performance degradation in other areas of the application that is a side effect of improving performance in the specific area just addressed. The amount of time that must be devoted to this cross-application performance evaluation is very subjective, but in general the broader or more complex the change, the more applicationwide performance assessment is needed at this point. Profiling, and comparing before and after profiling results, is typically the best way to perform this assessment.

Step 4.7: Test the Area Changed

With performance assessment complete, you must then test the application from the user's standpoint to see if bugs have been introduced. The specific area of the application that is affected by the source code change should be tested in detail, and every directly related area of functionality should be exercised. For example, even if a change has to do with the handling list box items on the form, the entire form that contains the list box and results in updates to it should be retested in detail.

Step 4.8: Test the Entire Application

After you have verified that the area directly changed has no new bugs as described in Step 4.7, you should next examine the entire application. This testing should be carried out from the user's standpoint, interacting with the application in the manner a user would interact. The purpose here is to see if any unintended bugs (beyond just performance degradation) have been introduced into a completely different area of the application than where you applied the fix.

The ideal way to carry out this testing is through the use of test scripts if you are fortunate enough to have a library of automated test procedures to exercise your code. *Test scripts* are programs that can be written to take the place of the human tester: They automatically interact with the program and collect results. Correctly structured test scripts can detect new errors introduced into the code in the process of collecting results. There are specialized tools available to facilitate the creation of these scripts, such as Microsoft's MS Test and Segue's QA Partner. Test scripts can enable rapid and thorough replay of testing after each change, which is very helpful in optimization work where many cycles of changes are applied, each of which might inadvertently introduce bugs that affect the functionality of the original application.

Unfortunately, script tools cost money and it can take considerable time and talent to develop thorough test libraries; therefore, many software projects do not utilize them. If your project is in this category, you are forced to rely on a manual test plan or to come up with a subjective determination of how much interactive testing is necessary to verify that no side effects have been introduced into other areas of the application.

Step 4.9: If There Are Any Problems, Regress to Step 3

The final step is to evaluate the results of the postchange performance measurement and test to determine if an improvement has been achieved or if you are worse off than before because of additional bugs or unintended performance side effects.

If the change is acceptable, you should then decide whether the specific bottleneck under consideration has been fully addressed to your satisfaction, or if more fine-tuning is necessary. If the change is acceptable without further tuning, you can move on to Step 6. If fine-tuning is needed, keep your current changes in place (as opposed to regressing or removing the changes) and return to Step 3. Proceed to fine-tune the original changes, treating the fine-tuning as an

additional enhancement as you proceed through the optimization steps. This provides all the advantages of a controlled optimization process even at the fine-tuning stage.

On the other hand, if you reach the conclusion that you are worse off, the next step is to regress to the original version of source code before any changes were made. In this case you *do* want to truly regress, or remove any of the changes made. This can be accomplished simply by restoring your earlier backup. Then, based on the findings of this round of enhancements, you can proceed with Step 3 again to make another attempt at the enhancement, improving on the technique of the first go-around. As with all these steps, it is important to log the results and progression of each step in your optimization log.

Step 5: Implement the Target Enhancement Throughout the Application

As discussed in the section "Step 4: Implement the Target Enhancement One Place in the Application," many types of performance changes are not specific to just one area of an application's source code, but rather are enhancements that must be made at many different places throughout the application. For example, suppose you decide to use an integer in place of the variant type for most variables in order to benefit from the greater speed integer variables provide. This change might have to occur in 50 different places spread among 20 different procedures to update the entire application.

For this kind of across-the-board change, you first treat one specific instance of that change as an enhancement in and of itself in Step 4. By the time you reach Step 5, that change has been implemented successfully in one specific area and can now be propagated across the entire application.

The methodology of treating a global enhancement as if it is a single change first in Step 4 before making the global changes of Step 5, can save a lot of time in the long run. Many changes that appear clean and simple at first glance can actually introduce complications. Implementing the performance enhancement in one area in Step 4 gives you a safety net to conveniently catch any side effects or problems. A problem in just one area of the code can be more easily understood, addressed, and cleaned up. But if you originally made the change globally in many different areas, bypassing Step 4 before proceeding to Step 5, it would be more difficult to catch a problem and more complex to clear it up across many different procedures.

Ideally, with a change that has to occur in multiple places, each instance of the change should be treated as a separate performance enhancement. So if there are 6 different areas that need to have the same change made, the original implementation methodology should be applied 6 times, in 6 cycles: Change just the one area of code, test, and then repeat Step 4 for each instance of the change. However, if the change is required in 50 different places, it is not usually feasible to repeat Step 4 50 times to cover each individual area of code altered, due to the time this would entail.

In that case, the best approach is to address the first instance of the change individually in Step 4 of the cycle, and deal with the remaining changes as a group in Step 5, as described here. The substeps to implement optimization changes globally follow. The flow of these substeps is shown in Figure 8.4:

5.1. Evaluate whether global changes related to Step 4 optimization are required. If not, proceed to Step 6.

5.2. Back up source code.

5.3. Measure prechange performance across the entire application.

5.4. Insert the changes.

5.5. Measure postchange performance across the entire application.

5.6. Test the entire application.

5.7. If there are any problems, reexamine Step 4 results, and possible regress to Step 3.

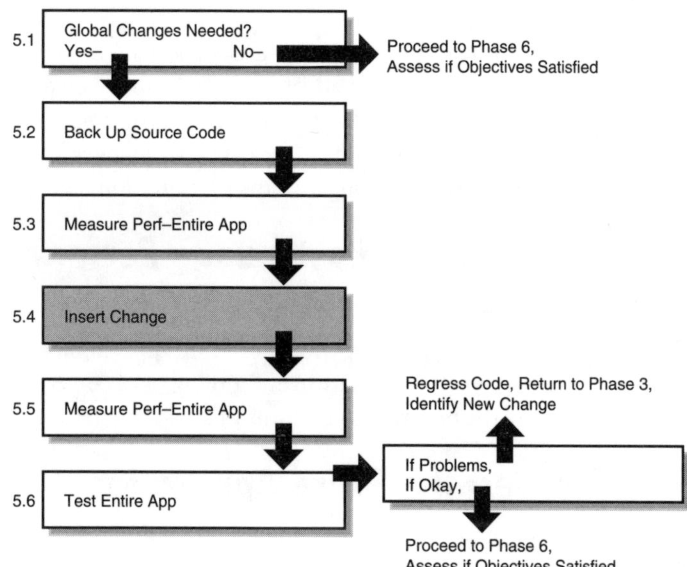

Figure 8.4.
Steps to implement target enhancement globally.

Step 5.1: Evaluate Whether Global Changes Related to Step 4 Optimization Are Required

Changes that affect many different areas require what could be a cost-prohibitive amount of time to take individual timings and carry out very focused testing on each of the many areas changed. Therefore, in applying global changes to implement performance enhancements there is a trade-off. Implementing all changes in a consolidated pass through Step 5 saves time, but with an increased risk of problems due to a lack of specific focus on each individual area of code changed.

Step 5.2: Back Up Source Code

This step is essentially the same as the back up step outlined in Step 4.1. However, when changes will be made globally across the application as opposed to in just one area, it is of even greater importance!

Step 5.3: Measure Prechange Performance Across the Entire Application

This step is essentially the same as the measurement step outlined in Step 4.3. Assess the performance of the entire application, utilizing the results from the earlier profiling phase on this cycle, if possible.

Step 5.4: Insert the Changes

Changes should be inserted in a controlled manner. Because these changes are global in nature, many lines of source code might change. There is great benefit in doing a follow-up search with the source code editor to reexamine each area changed after the global changes are made, even if many dozens of areas are affected. Because many changes are made, there are many chances for error in the process. It is also often helpful to record the number of occurrences changed in each module to document the extent of changes and to serve as a regression guide if needed. Carefully note the changes in the optimization log.

Step 5.5: Measure Postchange Performance Across the Entire Application

This is essentially the same as Step 4.6. The entire application's performance should be examined to ensure that results were positive. Profiling, and comparing before and after profiling results, is typically the best way to perform this assessment.

Step 5.6: Test the Entire Application

This step is the same as Step 4.8. The entire application should be tested to ensure that the global optimizations did not introduce any bugs and thereby break any functional behavior. The use of a test plan or test script is essential at this phase because without it there is no way to know if the original functionality has been fully covered again. If optimization did introduce a functional problem, you want to find out about it immediately while the optimization changes are fresh in your mind, rather than stumble across it later when the changes, and therefore your insights into side effects, are a fuzzy memory.

Step 5.7: If There Are Any Problems, Reexamine Step 4 Results, and Possibly Regress to Step 3

If you identify any problems during performance testing or functionality testing across the application, make an assessment of how serious they are. If they are minor, perhaps a few software changes can cure them and your optimization can stand as implemented. If they are major, use your backup to restore your code to the state it was in before applying any global optimizations thereby "regressing out" your changes; then return to Step 4 and reexamine the results of the single-instance change. If that change introduced fundamental problems that you did not detect earlier, you might have to use the backup carried out at the beginning of Step 4, unroll even the first single-instance change that was made, and back up to Step 3 to reexamine your target enhancement.

Most likely, the Step 4 single-instance change will have been adequate, and you must simply carry out Step 5 global changes again in a safer manner to avoid side effects. Global changes, or large-scale changes that affect many areas of an application, have a high propensity to "break code," or cause unintended side effect bugs. Perhaps you need to make each change individually in the editor to inspect each area of code. If a high degree of verification is needed because it's a high-risk change operation, it may be a sign that you should treat each change as a distinct optimization area dealt with in repeated cycles of Step 4.

Step 6: Assess the Results, and Then Repeat the Cycle

After you have implemented and verified the change, you should take a checkpoint to ensure that the original objective was met. A *checkpoint* is a subjective consideration, backed up by supporting documentation in the log, of whether the optimization objective was reached. If the objective was not met and you believe that further optimization could come closer to meeting the objective, the cycle should resume again at Step 3. If the objective has been met, the cycle should begin anew at Step 1 to proceed with the next performance problem, if more problems exist. In this manner, the Brophy/Koets Optimization Methodology is repeated for each round of enhancement changes, one bottleneck at a time, until all performance bottlenecks of concern have been covered. The outcome should be recorded in the optimization log to ensure that there is a full history of each cycle of the performance-tuning process. If you take the time to measure fulfillment of performance-tuning objectives, as well as to record them, you will find that they are not only of value in understanding and tracking the current tuning effort, but that a review of those records is often a beneficial reference point when you're working on other projects in the future.

The Brophy/Koets Optimization Methodology Outline

The Brophy/Koets Optimization Methodology cannot provide any magic answers for eliminating bottlenecks. That burden always rests on the shoulders of the programmer, and is dependent on creativity, experience, and insight. However, if this methodology is used as a road map to performance tuning, it will eliminate the risk of an uncontrolled optimization process that can ultimately hamper performance tuning, and instead provide the best possible controlled environment for facilitating optimization. The previous sections describe the individual steps for the Brophy/Koets Optimization Methodology. The fully detailed methodology, listing main steps as well as the specific substep activities, is summarized here to serve as a single, comprehensive reference point:

1. Identify the top-priority bottleneck.
   - 1.1. Interactively assess the application for performance trouble spots.
   - 1.2. Profile the application at the code level for performance trouble spots.
   - 1.3. Rank areas to concentrate on from highest to lowest. Take the highest-priority area.
2. Define optimization objective or *quit satisfied*!
3. Identify the target enhancement.
   - 3.1. Identify potential solutions.
   - 3.2. Compare potential solutions in the test application.
4. Implement the target enhancement in one place in the application.
   - 4.1. Back up source code.
   - 4.2. Measure prechange performance of the area to change.
   - 4.3. Measure prechange performance across the entire application.
   - 4.4. Insert the change.
   - 4.5. Measure postchange performance of the area changed.
   - 4.6. Measure postchange performance across the entire application.
   - 4.7. Test the area changed.
   - 4.8. Test the entire application.
   - 4.9. If there are any problems, regress to Step 3.
5. Implement the target enhancement for remaining instances in the application.
   - 5.1. Evaluate whether global changes related to Step 4 optimization are required across the application. If not, proceed to Step 6.
   - 5.2. Back up source code.
   - 5.3. Measure prechange performance across the entire application.

5.4. Insert the changes.

5.5. Measure postchange performance across the entire application.

5.6. Test the entire application.

5.7. If any problems, reexamine Step 4 results, and possibly regress to Step 3.

6. Assess results, and then repeat the cycle.

Modular Collections of Optimized Routines

Following a structured methodology when optimizing programs is one way to improve the quality and efficiency of the optimization. You can facilitate optimization efforts even further by building your own modular collection of optimized routines.

There are many advantages to building such a collection. It takes time and effort, and usually slows down the current project, but it can greatly speed development on future projects. It will take you longer to write a modular generic optimized routine than it would to write a non-generic optimized routine that has less potential for future reuse. Likewise, if you use commercial routines, it takes longer to build a useful collection for the future where they have been categorized and documented than it would take just to use them on the current project without worrying about future references.

For those cases when you can afford the time, attention to building up a repertoire of optimized routines can lay the groundwork for increasing the quality, efficiency, speed, and reliability of subsequent work. This is generally an effort well worth the cost. Unfortunately, however, software-development projects often tend to be behind schedule before they start and the development group that takes the time to build for the future is usually the exception rather than the rule.

If you are looking to pave a road for the future as well as the present, there is much you can do to facilitate future performance-enhancement work. This can be divided into two main categories: building collections of optimized in-house modules and building up collections of commercial modules.

Collections Developed In-House

After a routine has been optimized, in theory you should never again need to optimize the same type of routine. Even if future routines are not identical to this routine, the performance optimization assessment work and specific code changes that went into it might still be applicable to similar code.

Optimized routines that have any chance of being commonly applied in future projects should be moved to BAS modules. These modules can house a library of optimized routines for later reuse. In a typical collection of modules sorted by topic, each module contains generic routines optimized for performance for that specific topic. Typical areas might be database code, file I/O code, and animation code.

> **NOTE:** Another technique for packaging optimized routines is to store them in OLE Automation servers or other language dynamic link libraries. OLE Automation servers, addressed in detail in Chapter 25, "OLE Automation Servers," provide ease of packaging but offer slower performance than if the code were directly incorporated into the application through a BAS module. Other language DLLs, covered in detail in Chapter 22, "Moving code to DLLs," take considerably more effort to package, but offer generally faster performance than code directly incorporated into the application through a BAS module.

In building a modular collection of optimized routines, keep your ultimate purpose in sight. This effort is intended to provide samples of optimized code that could be used in their entirety, or simply studied and copied and pasted into other optimization work in the future. For this reason, it is important to comment code in the optimization step. Code that was changed to carry out a performance enhancement should be specifically noted. If you make the effort to do this, developers on future programming projects will have a convenient library from which to pull routines that are already efficient. They can also study and quickly learn about successful optimization techniques without having to repeat the same experiments.

An example of such code might be a complicated database-access sequence. If testing is carried out and a block of code is defined that improves the speed of data retrieval through enhanced SQL strings or the use of data-object methods, this code could be moved to a routine that accepts the data object as a parameter. Put your comments within the routine, noting the performance enhancements that were achieved with the final techniques used.

The same considerations apply to making use of optimized collections of code techniques stored in OLE Automation servers. OLE Automation servers provide a powerful vehicle for creating reusable components and leverage code on future projects, but they have more performance overhead than collections of routines placed within modules when incorporated into the calling application. Nevertheless, they are another option in packaging reusable optimized code. In addition, if your development team plans to build collections of OLE Automation servers to facilitate reuse, you should make a special effort to assess performance of these components and optimize them if needed when they are initially created. Not only do they have some of the implicit OLE overhead penalty, but because they are created as reusable components, they are likely to be used again and again, so time invested in performance tuning is paid back many times over on all the future products that stand to benefit from those efforts.

Commercial Collections of Routines

Many commercial packages are available that provide optimized routines. They cover a wide range of purposes, including sorts and array management. These packages are usually accompanied by ample documentation, but it often takes a lot of work with the packages to determine how they apply to your specific task, how successful the routines are, and any shortcomings they might have.

It can be very valuable to keep a log noting which commercial routines have been used and what performance speedups they are believed to provide. Then, in the future, developers have an easy way to see which areas of the packages you have already tried.

In addition, there can be significant advantages to creating your own module that contains examples of using the optimized routines. These customized examples can demonstrate specific ways that the routines were used to achieve real development solutions for your own problems. Some of the commercial packages come with demonstration programs and source code samples, but keeping a collection of routines that demonstrate your own real-world usage is much more helpful to the developer who must wrestle with the routines and find a starting point to apply them to future performance enhancements.

One of the key benefits of this activity is having documentation of representative enhancements gained by using the commercial routines, as well as of difficulties in applying them. This body of knowledge can have tremendous value in the future. This is true for even one-developer projects, because even a single developer won't be able to clearly remember key issues several months down the road. The benefits become even greater on multiple-developer projects.

Advantages of Building for the Future

There are many advantages to accumulating information on performance enhancements and putting together modular collections of optimized routines. One significant advantage is that there will be less need to test in the future. The collection of routines includes code that has already been tested and has been demonstrated to be solid and without side effects. Likewise, there will be less need to measure in the future. The libraries of code have already been measured, so they stand as ready representatives of the best optimization techniques available. Comparative timings can be included in the comments or documentation with the routines, so there is a frame of reference if future questions arise about how these conclusions were reached.

Perhaps most significantly, there will be less need to research. The collection of routines includes code that is the result of much research. The final answer to optimization questions for that type of code is already provided in the modular routine and the documentation that accompanies it. Future users will not have to carry on the same level of research and comparison of techniques if the findings are summarized and the best possible outcome is right there in front of them, ready to use.

One question you might ask when considering whether to build a modular collection of optimized routines is "Why not just let developers of future applications refer directly to the source code of the original application itself to view optimization techniques?" The disadvantage with this approach is that it can be time-consuming, confusing, or difficult to review a large application and scan through it for optimization areas. More often than not when you plan to use this approach, implementation areas that might be of significant interest are simply overlooked due to the difficulty of carrying out a full assessment of the original code. On the other hand, if you specifically build up a library of information on performance enhancements, it will be a central starting point for future projects and ensure that knowledge from performance enhancements today can be easily located in the future.

When all things are considered, the cost savings of this approach are significant. At a price of some additional time on current development projects, you can gain improved development time and better, faster programs on future projects.

Summary

This chapter looks at the Brophy/Koets Optimization Methodology for implementing performance enhancements. This optimization methodology provides controlled, stepwise, incremental changes to an application during optimization.

This approach is particularly necessary because of the subtle nature of performance, the many variables that affect optimization, and the great potential for performance tuning to affect code in ways not anticipated.

Optimizations carried out during this process involve doing things differently than your first instinct led you to do when you developed the application. This in itself makes these changes likely to be high risk or less completely understood. The optimizaton methodology outlined in this chapter helps to ensure that implementing such enhancements is a safe process through the use of backups, emphasis on inserting one change at a time, prechange measurements, postchange measurements and testing, and regressing to the earlier source-code baseline if necessary.

This chapter also examines the need to occasionally apply a performance enhancement in many places throughout the application. A technique is outlined for such situations; it consists of first implementing one case of the performance change in a controlled fashion using the regular methodology for implementing single-occurrence optimizations. If that is successful, the change is applied globally throughout the application, and the methodology is again applied with some slight refinements.

There are steps you can take during implementation to pave the way for future performance-enhancement implementation cycles. One way you can accomplish this is to build a modular collection of optimized routines. This can consist of building up a module of routines developed in-house that have been enhanced for performance and have ample documentation on those enhancements. Another strategy is to build collections of optimized code in OLE Automation servers, although this involves dealing with the overhead of OLE Automation. Still, such packaging offers maintenance advantages. Yet another way you can pave the way for future optimization is to simply build a document that describes the use of commercial packages and the performance enhancements achieved, and even build a module of routines that demonstrate the use of the commercial package functions. Although time is required to build up such a collection of optimized routines and documentation, it has many advantages down the road in terms of quicker time to develop optimized applications. If an OLE Automation server strategy is part of the development approach for the reuse benefits it can provide, special emphasis should be placed on initial performance tuning because the payback will be felt many times over in future projects.

If you use any or all of these techniques you can count on a more effective optimization process. Less time will be spent chasing performance side effects, looking for bugs introduced by optimization, and reinventing the wheel. You benefit by experiencing less frustration during your optimization efforts, and even more importantly, your end user benefits by receiving faster, more reliable applications.

Obey the Signs

Wrong Way: Apply all performance changes at one time to the source code to assess overall impact.

This technique can lead to disaster. Performance enhancements should be applied in an incremental fashion so that the impact and side effects of each one can be assessed individually. After all changes have been safely applied in this incremental fashion, you can assess the entire application. If the changes were introduced all at once, you might have to spend a great deal of time chasing performance and broken-code or new bug side effects.

Beware of Falling Rocks: It can take considerable time to correctly carry out and implement performance enhancements.

One of the keys to carrying out performance enhancements is to do it in a controlled fashion: logging activity at each step, carefully making backups, measuring before changes, and carefully verifying results. This level of control and discipline adds overhead to the development process that is not present if you are just "hacking in improvements and cranking out code."

If there is not time to carry out this process correctly, you should consider whether it is better to implement performance enhancements in a risky fashion, which could introduce further problems, or just skip the performance enhancements entirely. This is a subjective decision that differs from project to project. The best approach, and the correct one from a software-development perspective, is to follow the safe performance-implementation methodology and accept the time hit. This is the best way to guarantee the quality of the product the end user will receive.

Q&A

Q Is it necessary to make backups before carrying out performance enhancements because the code is being improved over its previous state?

A Yes, it *is* necessary. You should make backups before you apply a change. The change might introduce bugs as a side effect or cause performance degradation in other areas. It will often be desirable to get back to the clean slate before the change was ever introduced. Without a backup, you might think you have removed a bad change and returned to a previous state when you might have accidentally removed only part of the change and be even worse off than you were with the original source code.

Q What are the advantages of taking the time to build up a modular collection of performance-enhanced routines that might be used in the future?

A There are several advantages to this approach. It will mean that less time needs to be expended to test the blocks of code for bugs in the future, because the packaged routines should already be bug free. It will mean that less time is required to measure such optimized areas because the measurement has already been carried out and is documented in the routines, and the routines themselves can be considered to be a representative of optimized code. It will also mean that less time is required to research performance, because the routine that is already provided is the result of earlier research that would just be duplicated. In essence, the findings of the research are summarized in the routine itself and the documentation or comments that accompany the routine, and the research does not need to be repeated.

Q Is it true that *final* performance-tuning decisions should not be based on my performance-testing programs?

A Yes. Test programs you carry out to assess performance alternatives are helpful. However, the final conclusive test of your application's performance must come from running your application itself. Otherwise, you run the risk of overlooking factors or introducing complications. The ultimate test and proof of "is it good enough" should come from carefully reviewing the end-user application itself.

Workshop

Have you worked on projects where a collection of optimized routines was available? If not, how much might the existence of such a collection have aided your development and performance tuning?

Optimization Strategies: Programming

Now that the fundamental concepts of optimization have been presented, the remainder of the book discusses the actual strategies and techniques you can use to optimize your applications. Part III contains three chapters that specifically address the application's code.

Chapter 9, "Variables," introduces you to each of the fundamental Visual Basic 4.0 data types, explaining how they are used and how they are represented in memory. Simple variables of each data type are then compared to each other so that each data type can be evaluated based on its performance. While certain data types are specially geared for specific purposes, it is sometimes better to sacrifice the specificity of a data type in favor of a more general data type that performs faster. These and other considerations are discussed in this chapter through the use of test applications. Techniques and strategies are presented throughout.

Chapter 10, "Math," explores the most efficient way to apply variables in arithmetic operations. Each of the fundamental Visual Basic 4.0 arithmetic operators are compared to each other, and conclusions based on performance results are drawn from the test programs included in the chapter. These conclusions lead to practical techniques that you can use in your own applications.

Chapter 11, "Code Structure," explores the most efficient ways to structure code. Loops, conditional statements, functions versus subroutines, and other code structure topics are presented in this chapter as are code examples to support which technique is best.

After reading Part III, you will have a much clearer idea of the best data types to assign for variables, how best to use those variables along with arithmetic operators in mathematical calculations, and finally how best to structure your code in the applications you write. You will learn many practical techniques in this section that you can immediately apply to your projects.

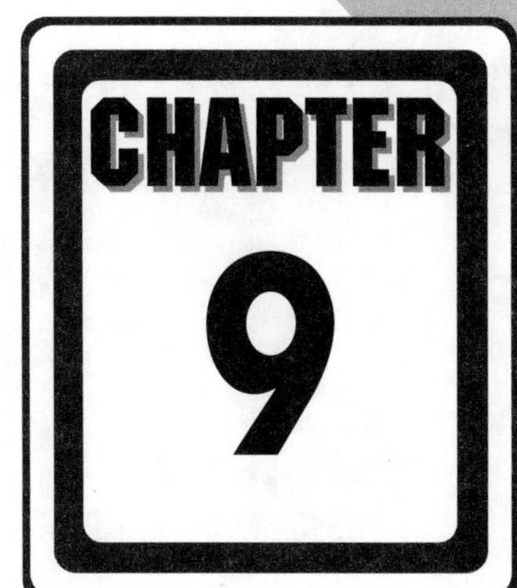

Variables

The first subject a programming student typically learns about a given language is how to use variables. In Visual Basic, variables can be created based on a variety of data types. As you might expect, some are more efficient than others. This chapter discusses the most efficient way to use variables in Visual Basic. In order to properly discuss the use of variables, an overview of the fundamental Visual Basic data types is presented first, followed by definitions of variable scope and lifetime, and then a discussion of data containers such as arrays and user-defined types. Having presented the necessary background for the chapter, several techniques are presented for optimizing variables. For each technique, background information is provided, followed by a sample application demonstrating the validity of the concept under discussion. An explanation of the application and relevant code listings are presented, as well as resultant timings showing the benefit of applying the technique.

Visual Basic Variables and Data Types

This section includes a discussion of the fundamental Visual Basic data types, a discussion of the scope and lifetime of the variables based on those data types, and the containers into which data can be placed. This overview of fundamental concepts prepares you for the performance techniques presented later in the chapter.

Data Types

Each of the following sections offers a brief description of each data type, including its size and its typical uses.

Integer

A variable that has been defined with the *integer* data type is a number that is 2 bytes in length. Because it is an integer, no fractional numbers or decimal places can be used. Integers can range from –32,768 to 32,767. The integer is the most commonly used data type in Visual Basic because it is the standard data type for representing both numbers for counting and those representing quantities. Because a great many quantities can be expressed without the need for a decimal point and can fit within the specified range, the integer is useful for many purposes.

Long

Variables of data type *long* are also integers, but they use 4 bytes of storage rather than 2. This gives them a much higher range: –2,147,483,648 to 2,147,483,647. Because this data type is also an integer, decimal points cannot be used. If the range of an integer is not suitably represented in 2 bytes, it can almost always be represented with 4 bytes. If the range exceeds even the *long* data type, you must use the floating-point data type.

Long integers are also quite common and are normally used in cases where the range of a variable might exceed that of a standard integer. If the programmer can ensure that an integer does not fall outside the range –32,768 to 32,767, the standard integer data type is preferable because the long integer would be overkill and would waste an extra 2 bytes.

Single

Some quantities or expressions cannot easily be represented without the use of a decimal point. Furthermore, sometimes programs require numbers with a much higher range than a long integer can provide. In either case, Visual Basic provides several floating-point data types. The first, the *single* data type, is a 4-byte value with a range of –1.4E-45 to –3.4E38 for negative numbers and 1.4E-45 to 3.4E38 for positive numbers. This data type is usually sufficient to represent most floating-point values. Although the single data type takes the same number of bytes as the long integer, additional computations are required by the computer to take the decimal place into account.

Double

When even larger floating-point values are required, you can use the *double* data type. A variable with this data type is 8 bytes in length and has a range from –4.9E-324 to –1.8E308 for negative numbers and 4.9E-324 to 1.8E308 for positive values. When you need to use floating-point numbers, you should use this data type only when this degree of precision or range is required. Because it takes 8 bytes to represent a variable, it requires more memory and takes longer in calculations.

Currency

The *currency* data type is an 8-byte data type that is stored in an integer-based format. The integer is scaled by 10,000, which simulates four decimal places. The currency data type has a fixed decimal point and a range of –922,337,203,685,477.5808 to 922,337,203,685,477.5808. This data type was designed for calculations requiring a higher degree of accuracy, such as currency mathematics. The currency data type is more accurate, due in part to the fact that its decimal point is fixed. It is also more accurate because its range is smaller than that of the double data type. This increased accuracy makes it less prone to the small rounding errors to which the other floating-point data types are more susceptible.

String

The *string* is a data type used to hold alphanumeric data. Strings are used extensively in most applications because they are required to store and represent textual information. The length of a string variable depends on whether the string is declared as fixed length or variable length. A *variable-length string* has 4 bytes of overhead along with the number of bytes it takes to represent the string (that is, the number of characters). In the case of a *fixed-length string*, the programmer specifies the number of bytes for the string when it is declared, and no overhead bytes are required. Visual Basic strings, whether fixed or variable, have a size limit of 65,400 bytes for Windows 3.*x* and approximately 2 billion bytes for Windows 95 and Windows NT.

Byte

The *byte* data type is intended for storing binary data. This data type is 1 byte in length and has a range of 0 to 255. The byte data type does not support negative numbers. Binary data can be preserved when stored in a variable of type byte, particularly during format conversions. This data type is new to Visual Basic 4.0. In earlier versions of Visual Basic, the integer is normally used to store values of one byte in length. The integer should be abandoned in favor of the byte data type in Visual Basic 4.0

Boolean

The *Boolean* data type is a 2-byte data type that represents a True/False or On/Off condition. The length of this data type is identical to that of the integer data type, but in this case it can only be set to `True` or `False`. (`True` and `False` are Visual Basic keywords that evaluate to –1 and

0, respectively.) This data type is extremely useful for functions that return success codes and when you're interfacing with DLLs in other languages that return Boolean values indicating the success or failure of a given function. This data type is new to Visual Basic 4.0. In earlier versions of Visual Basic, the integer is usually used to store Boolean values. The integer should be abandoned in Visual Basic 4.0 in favor of the Boolean data type.

Date

Both date and time values can be stored in the *date* data type. This data type consumes 8 bytes and can only store date and time information. Date and time information can also be stored in variants, but the variant consumes 8 additional bytes of memory. In earlier versions of Visual Basic, there was no date data type and programmers typically stored dates in the variant data type. Now that Visual Basic 4.0 provides the date data type, use it instead of the variant data type to store dates. The date data type will ensure that the value entered is a valid date, which means fewer errors for you, the programmer. While the variant may not be the best choice for storing dates, it is useful whenever you wish to represent data that may have to take on different data type formats.

Object

The *object* data type is a special Visual Basic data type used to reference objects within a Visual Basic application or another application. Because the data type holds an address to an object, and addresses in 32-bit Windows require 32 bits (4 bytes), this data type is 4 bytes in length. Variables declared with this type are usually assigned to an actual object via the `Set` command. The actual address is transparent to the programmer. To improve performance at runtime, Visual Basic resolves references to the properties and methods of objects assigned to variables of this data type before the application is run. This data type is new to Visual Basic 4.0 and is part of Visual Basic 4.0's powerful object capabilities.

Variant

The *variant* data type is a catch-all data type that can "represent" many other data types. A variant can, for instance, store date values from January 1, 0000, to December 31, 9999. It can also store numeric values up to the range of a double data type and string values with the same range as the string data type. The variant data type handles all types of fundamental data and converts between them automatically. Unfortunately, the variant adds a great deal of processing overhead and significantly increases the amount of time and memory used in an application. A variant used to represent a variable-length string, for example, takes 22 bytes plus 1 per character in the string. If a variant is used to represent a number, it requires 16 bytes of memory as opposed to 2 for an integer, 4 for a long or single, and 8 for a double.

Constants

Although the Visual Basic *constant* is not, strictly speaking, a data type, it is mentioned here because it is yet another way to represent data. Constants can be used to represent numeric values and strings. When a constant is declared, Visual Basic allocates space for it inside the program code itself. This means that Visual Basic does not need to dynamically allocate more memory for constants when applications execute. As the name implies, constants cannot be changed at runtime—they are specified at design time. In most programming languages, including Visual Basic, constants are faster than variables because they are easier to represent in code.

Variable Scope and Lifetime

Now that you have been introduced to the data types used to create variables, it's time to examine the scope and lifetime of those variables. Variable *scope* determines the rules that specify when, where, and for how long a variable exists in the application. In Visual Basic, variables can have two different levels of scope—procedure level and module level. You specify the scope of a variable when you declare that variable. You can assign a variable's scope based on where the variable is declared and whether the `Public`, `Private`, or `Dim` keywords are used. Each scope, as well as the manner in which variables are created with that scope, is discussed in the following sections.

Procedure-Level Variables

A *procedure-level* variable, also sometimes referred to as a local variable, exists only within the procedure in which it is declared. The variable is in existence only during the life of the procedure. Once the procedure ends, the variable is destroyed, although the `Static` keyword can be used to restore the value of the variable if the procedure is called again and the variable is recreated (the `Static` keyword is discussed in the next section). Procedure-level variables are declared using the `Dim` keyword in the procedure, as shown in Listing 9.1.

Listing 9.1. Declaring procedure-level variables.

```
Private Sub Procedure_1 ()

    ' Variable Declaration
    Dim bCheck as Boolean

    bCheck = optSelected.Value
    If bCheck Then
        End
    End If

End Sub
```

Visual Basic does not enable you to declare the variables inside a procedure as `Public`, because variables declared inside a procedure cannot be used outside that procedure.

Procedure-level variables are more common than module-level variables because variables often need to exist only within the confines of the procedure in which they are defined. Because the variable exists only within the "walls" of the procedure in which it was defined, different procedures can all use the same variable name without conflict; every procedure's collection of variables is private to that procedure and isolated from any other.

The `Dim` keyword creates a variable of local scope, and that variable is destroyed as soon as the procedure in which it is declared ends. The exception to this rule is when the programmer uses the `Static` keyword, which leaves the contents of a variable intact for the duration of the application even though it is still local to the procedure in which it was defined. This special keyword is discussed further in the next section. The `ReDim` keyword is also used to declare dynamic arrays within procedures where the array is dimensioned using another variable.

Module-Level Variables

Module-level variables can be declared in such a way that they are either private to the module in which they are declared or are public across the application. You use the keywords `Public` and `Private` when declaring variables to make this distinction. Module-level variables are declared in the declarations section of a module. A variable declared as `Public` is a global variable to which every part of the application has access. On the other hand, a variable declared in a module as `Private` can only be accessed by procedures within that module.

When you're working with class modules, variables that are declared as `Public` act as properties to objects created using these classes. These properties are available to all areas in the application where objects of this class have been created and can be referenced. Furthermore, if the application is an OLE server, they can also be visible and available to other applications. OLE servers are addressed in Chapter 25, "OLE Automation Servers."

Module-level variables declared as `Public`, commonly referred to as *global variables*, are shared across all code modules and forms in the application. The global variable, therefore, has the broadest scope possible within the application. Use global variables as seldom as possible because they take up memory during the entire life of the application, regardless of whether they are used. If they are not used throughout the application, they simply tie up memory that could be available for other programs. A program that uses global variables can also be more difficult to maintain. Since a global variable can be modified from anywhere in the code, bugs and unintended side effects can easily result in large programs. When data must be shared, however, they are often the most convenient method to store data that must be accessible to many different parts of the application.

Static Variables

As previously discussed, only procedure-level variables are created and destroyed as procedures begin and end during the lifetime of the application. Module-level variables remain in existence throughout the lifetime of the application in code modules, for the lifetime of a form in form modules, and the lifetime of an object in class modules. The `Static` keyword can, however, be used to preserve the contents of procedure-level variables. In this manner, if a variable is declared in a procedure and the procedure exits, the use of the `Static` keyword ensures that the next time the procedure is executed, the variable has the same data it had the last time it was used in that procedure.

Data Containers

Thus far you have examined the various data types and the scope and lifetime of variables in Visual Basic. You must also understand Visual Basic data containers in order to get a more complete picture of the way data can be represented in Visual Basic. The four fundamental data containers in Visual Basic are the class, the collection, the array, and the user-defined type, also known as a structure. Classes and objects are discussed in Chapter 23, "Objects," because they are unlike the simple data containers discussed in this chapter. Arrays and structures, however, are discussed later in this chapter.

Arrays

Arrays are used to store a series of variables of the same data type in a container that can easily be used to index the data inside the container. Each variable contained in the array is represented by a unique index value and is referenced using that index value. Arrays can aid greatly in making programs more structured and efficient, particularly when they are used in loops. (This topic is addressed in the section "Using Arrays to Represent Data Sets" later in this chapter.) All the elements in an array have the same data type, and arrays can be declared with the same level of scope as any standard variable. Arrays can be either fixed or variable size and can have up to 60 dimensions.

User-Defined Types

Visual Basic also supports the user-defined type, or *structure.* A structure is a container that enables you to store multiple variables or members in it, all of which are referenced by the structure name. Unlike an array, a structure can store variables of any data type—and they do not all have to be the same. When the programmer declares a variable as a specific structure type, that variable takes on all the characteristics of that structure.

Strings Versus Variants

The variant is perhaps the most flexible data type in Visual Basic, but that flexibility comes with a cost. Because variants can take on the form of any other fundamental data type, more overhead is required to process them. Variants, for instance, use 22 more bytes of memory to represent a string than fixed- or variable-length strings. No matter what type of data the variant stores, it usually takes the interpreter more time to manipulate a variant because of its flexible nature.

This section shows you, using a simple code example, the benefit of using the string data type versus the variant data type when storing data. To compare the use of fixed-length strings, variable-length strings, and variants, a sample application named StrVar32.exe has been constructed; you can find it on the CD-ROM that accompanies this book.

The StrVar application consists of three procedures that contain loops; each procedure assigns data to variables of each of the data types listed. You can control the number of times the assignment is repeated by adjusting the loop count. Three buttons are on the form, one for each data type, as shown in Figure 9.1.

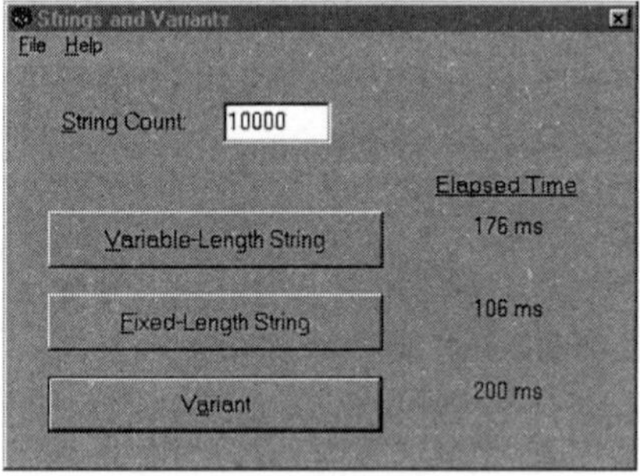

Figure 9.1.
Comparing strings and variants in the main form of the StrVar application.

The code that is executed when you click the Variant test command button is shown in Listing 9.2.

Listing 9.2. Making variant string assignments in code.

```
Private Sub cmdVariant_Click()

    ' Create long integer index
    Dim i&

    ' Start the timing
    Call Common_StartTimedTest

    ' Create an array of variable-length strings
    ReDim X(1 To txtStringCount) As Variant
```

```
    ' Loop through the calculations
    For i = 1 To txtStringCount
        X(i) = "123456789012345678901234567890"
    Next

    ' End the timing and display the results
    Call Common_EndTimedTest(lblElapsed(2))

End Sub
```

Note that an array gets created with a length of the value entered into the String Count text box. A loop is then executed that assigns string text to each variant in the array. In the similar test case for the variable-length string, which is executed using the command button labeled Variable-Length String, the code contains the declaration

```
' Create an array of variable-length strings
    ReDim X(1 To txtStringCount) As String
```

and the following declaration is for a fixed-length string:

```
' Create an array of fixed-length strings
ReDim X(1 To txtStringCount) As String * 30
```

You can see the results of a trial run of StrVar32.exe in Figure 9.1. The normalized times are shown in Table 9.1.

Table 9.1. Timing results of strings versus variants.

String Type	*Normalized Time*	*Memory Required for Array*
Fixed-length string	1.0	30×1000 = 30KB
Variable-length string	1.7	37×1000 = 37KB
Variant	1.9	54×1000 = 54KB

Note that the fixed-length string has the fastest execution time. This is to be expected because the use of the variable-length string and the variant require additional processing time in order to determine their size. The fixed-length string, however, has a predetermined size and therefore does not incur that overhead.

Not only is the fixed-length string the fastest, but it also requires the fewest bytes. Because the size is fixed at 30 bytes, and 1000 strings are created in the example shown, approximately 30KB of space is required. In the case of the variable-length string, 7 bytes of overhead is incurred for a string, for a total of 30 + 7 = 37 × 1000 ≈ 37KB of space required. Finally, in the case of the variant, 24 bytes of overhead is incurred for a string, for a total of 30 + 24 = 54 × 1000 ≈ 54KB of space required. The variant requires 80 percent more memory than the fixed-length string and 46 percent more memory than the variable-length string. Furthermore, the variant string assignments take approximately 90 percent longer to execute than those for the fixed-length strings, and approximately 15 percent more time than the variable-length string assignments.

Therefore, you not only improve execution time by using strings rather than variants, but you also use less memory. If you use a fixed-length string, you save even more execution time and memory. The fixed-length string certainly appears to be the best choice, particularly if you know the size of the string at design time and can therefore specify it as fixed. In reality, this is often difficult or impossible to do, especially in cases where a string of any possible size can be entered in the program. One way to get around this uncertainty is to create a fixed-length string of some maximum length and restrict the user to that length. This does, of course, require you to allocate more memory than you might need because the user might enter a string shorter than the maximum length and thus waste the allocated space.

In most cases, variable-length strings are the most practical data type for storing data, due in part to their dynamic nature. Fixed-length strings can and should be used where possible, although they are more memory efficient when declared at the module level rather than at the procedure level. They are certainly faster than the other alternatives and are generally preferable.

You can make one conclusion: The use of variants to represent strings at any level of scope should be avoided whenever possible. There are times when you must use a variant, usually when representing data whose data type cannot be determined beforehand or must be changed frequently in code. Their use, however, should be restricted—they should be used only when absolutely necessary.

> **TIP:** Use strings instead of variants whenever possible.

Integer-Based Data Types Versus Floating-Point Data Types

When examining the various data types available, you might wonder which numeric data type provides the best overall performance. This section presents an application that answers that question. You will soon see that the *integer* and *Boolean* data types perform better than any of the other numeric data types.

Consider the application IntAll32.exe, whose main form is shown in Figure 9.2. You can find this application on the CD-ROM that accompanies this book.

The application consists of nine command buttons, each of which executes code that assigns a value to the variable whose data type is represented by that command button. You can adjust the number of times this assignment is made by entering the loop count in the text box you see in the figure. The elapsed time then appears to the right of each command button as shown. The code for the Integer command button is shown in Listing 9.3.

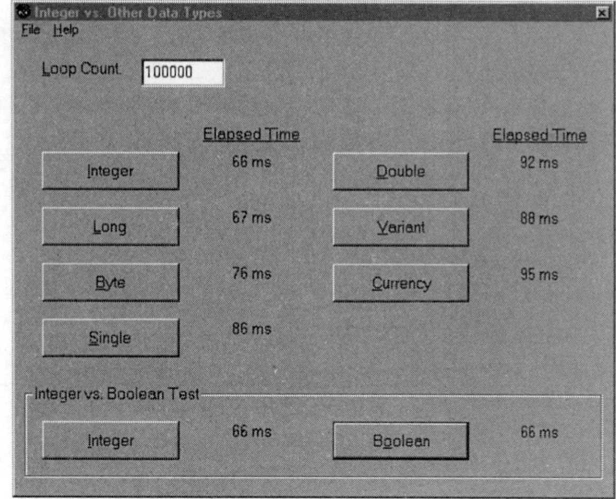

Figure 9.2.
Comparing the integer data type to all others in the IntAll32 application.

Listing 9.3. Making integer data assignments in code.

```
Private Sub cmdInteger_Click()

    ' Create long integer index
    Dim i&

    ' Create a variable of type Integer
    Dim x As Integer

    ' Get the starting time
    Call Common_StartTimedTest

    ' Loop through the calculations
    For i& = 1 To txtLoopCount
        x = 33   ' Simple assignment
    Next

    ' Get the ending time and display result
    Call Common_EndTimedTest(lblElapsed(0))

End Sub
```

Notice the loop that assigns the number 33 to the variable `x` whose data type is declared as `Integer`. Every other data type (except for the `Boolean` variable, which is tested separately with the integer data type) is assigned this value. The only line of code that changes for each data type is the variable declaration. For the Single command button, for example, the variable declaration is

```
' Create a variable of type Single
Dim X As Single
```

Every other procedure is modified the same way, based on the data type it represents. You can see the results in Figure 9.2; they are summarized in Table 9.2.

Table 9.2. Timing results of the IntAll32 application.

Data Type	*Normalized Time*
Integer	1.00
Long	1.02
Byte	1.15
Single	1.30
Double	1.40
Variant	1.33
Currency	1.44

The results show that the integer and long data types are approximately equivalent in terms of execution time. Minor variations show that it takes slightly longer to assign a value to the long data type than to the integer data type, but the integer data type is essentially identical to the long data type in terms of performance. Both of these data types are integer based; they simply differ in terms of their range and the number of bytes required to represent them. The byte data type requires 15 percent more time than the integer data type in this test, which is more considerable. One possible explanation is that Visual Basic must carry out some additional processing to work with just a single byte. It is easier for the computer to handle byte quantities in powers of 2 (that is, 2, 4, 8, 16, 32, 64) than a single byte. More processing is required to handle this special case.

The more interesting comparison is between the integer-based data types and the floating-point data types. Notice that the floating-point data types single and double require 30 percent and 39 percent more time to execute, respectively, than the integer-based data types integer and long. Note also that the single data type is slightly faster than the double data type, as you would expect. The floating-point data types are slower than the integer-based data types because of their larger size, their larger range, and the additional processing required to take into account the decimal-point arithmetic.

Notice that the variant requires 33 percent more time for simple variable assignments than do the integer-based data types. When the variant is assigned an integer value, Visual Basic *typecasts* the variable to an integer. This means that, although the data type of the variable is a variant, it is represented to the computer as an integer. Notice, however, that it takes much more time to process the variable due to the overhead required in working with a variant.

This again underscores the advantage of avoiding the use of the variant data type unless absolutely necessary. In this case, the penalty is not as severe as the string example discussed earlier in the chapter, but it is still significant. Keep in mind that, whereas the integer declaration only takes 2 bytes, the variant, which behaves as an integer in this case, takes 16 bytes. You will again save memory and execution time by using the integer rather than the variant. This savings can be seen not only in the case of the variant, but for the other floating-point data types as well.

The currency data type has the highest execution time—over 50 percent slower than the integer data type. Obviously, the currency data type adds quite a bit of overhead, even in simple data assignments. It should also be avoided when possible and practical to do so. The currency data type is discussed further in the next section.

Generally, it is preferable to use integer-based data types (the integer, long, and byte data types) rather than the floating-point data types (the single, double, variant, and currency), which represent decimal values. Whenever practical, stick with the simplest data type possible. If you only need to assign `True` or `False` to a variable, make it a Boolean. If you need an integer but don't need to exceed the range of the integer data type, use it. You will always have better performance with integers than with floating-point values.

Analogy: Using Efficient Versus Inefficient Data Types

It's time once again to go on your annual car-shopping spree. Since you already have a somewhat fancy car, you'd just like to buy one to go back and forth to work. Since you are a Visual Basic programmer, money is not a concern. You go to the dealer and decide you could either buy a huge luxury vehicle, complete with swimming pool and home theater, or you could buy a sleek, streamlined, high-performance sports car with excellent gas mileage. You give it some thought and decide that given your fear of future gas shortages, gas mileage is really your ultimate concern. You notice that the luxury vehicle has a miserable 12 miles to the gallon, but the sports car has 40 miles to the gallon. Both cars are the same price. Which should you buy?

Since your primary concern is efficiency, you should buy the sports car—it is more efficient because it has the better gas mileage of the two and has a higher-performance engine. The same principle applies to choosing the appropriate data type for a variable. Since efficiency is your primary concern, you should choose the simplest, fastest data type possible to accomplish the goal you intend for the variable you are creating.

> **TIP:** Use integer-based data types rather than floating-point data types whenever possible.

Now consider the comparison between the integer and Boolean data types. These are tested separately because the Boolean data type is assigned a value of `True` or `False` and cannot be assigned a number. The integer data type can also be assigned `True`. Before Visual Basic 4.0, you had to use the integer data type to represent Boolean information. Now that the Boolean data type is here, this test shows how they compare to each other. Based on Figure 9.2, the normalized results of the comparison between the integer and Boolean data types are shown in Table 9.3.

Table 9.3. Data type assignment results for Boolean versus integer.

Data Type	*Normalized Time*
Integer	1.00
Boolean	1.00

As you can see, there is no significant difference in execution times between the two data types. When performance is not a significant issue, it makes the most sense to use the data type that is best designed for the task and provides for more readable, maintainable code. Therefore, when working with Boolean data, use the Boolean data type. You will not incur any performance benefit by using the integer data type to represent Boolean data.

> **TIP:** The integer and Boolean data types offer almost identical performance. Use the Boolean data type rather than the integer data type when you only need to store a True/False or Yes/No condition.

Alternatives to the Currency Data Type

The case study shows that the currency data type requires the most execution time for a simple assignment. This section explores this data type in more detail. The currency data type manipulates data intended specifically to represent currency values. The principal benefit of using this data type is that it is an accurate, fixed-point data type that supports up to 4 digits to the right of the decimal point and 15 to the left, making it well suited for monetary calculations.

The primary disadvantage of the currency data type, however, is that it requires more execution time than its floating-point counterparts. It is often just as easy to use another data type for a calculation to obtain a faster execution time. Although you lose the convenience of the built-in rounding and formatting of the currency type, applications that make heavy use of the currency type can be sped up dramatically by using other alternatives.

Such alternatives are explored in the application examined in this section. You can find this application, CurAll32.exe, on the CD-ROM that accompanies this book. The goal of the application is to calculate the amount of taxes taken from your salary. The program takes the salary you supply as well as the percentage that must go for taxes, and then calculates the resultant tax. The main form is shown in Figure 9.3.

Note that the application has a default salary of $30,000 with a default tax rate of 25 percent. Because this simple multiplication executes very quickly, you can control how many times the multiplication is repeated. The default is set to 50,000 executions of the multiplication. You have the choice of using the currency, single, double, variant, or long data types. Each data type is represented by its own command button, as shown in Figure 9.3. The test case for the

currency data type, represented by the Currency command button, consists of the code shown in Listing 9.4.

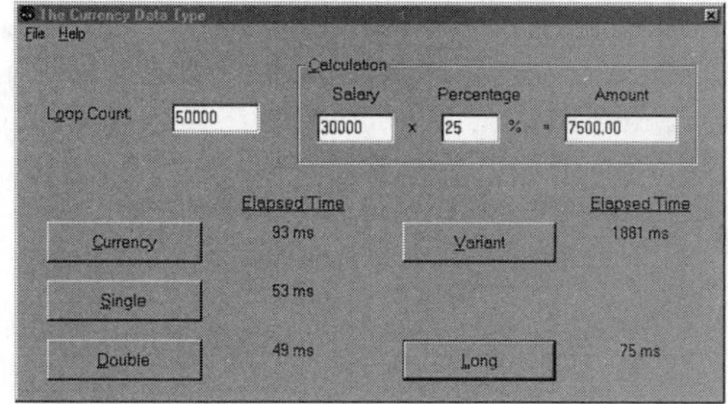

Figure 9.3.
Comparing the currency data type to all others in the main form of the CurAll32 application.

Listing 9.4. Tax computation using the currency data type.

```
Private Sub cmdCurrency_Click()

    ' Variable Definitions
    Dim i&                           ' Long index value
    Dim sngPercentage As Single      ' Create single percentage
    Dim curSalary As Currency        ' Create currency salary
    Dim curAmount As Currency        ' Create currency amount

    ' Set the currency variables
    curSalary = txtSalary
    sngPercentage = txtPercentage / 100

    ' Get the starting time
    Call Common_StartTimedTest

    ' Calculate the amount
    For i = 1 To txtLoopCount
        curAmount = curSalary * sngPercentage
    Next

    ' Get the ending time
    Call Common_EndTimedTest(lblElapsed(0))

    ' Display the amount
    txtAmount = Format(curAmount, "#####.00")

End Sub
```

The test cases for the single, double, and variant data types, each of which is executed using its respective command buttons, are identical to Listing 9.4 with one exception: The salary and currency variables are changed to reflect the data type of the test case. In the test case for the single data type, for instance, the variable definitions change from this:

```
    Dim curSalary As Currency        ' Create currency salary
    Dim curAmount As Currency        ' Create currency amount
```

to this:

```
Dim sngSalary As Single         ' Create single salary
Dim sngAmount As Single         ' Create single amount
```

The code listings for the currency, single, double, and variant data types are all identical except for the variable declarations for the amount and salary. The test case for the long data type, however, is different. In the previous four test cases, floating-point values and the currency data type are used. In the case of the long data type, however, a different technique must be employed. (See Listing 9.5.)

Listing 9.5. Tax computation using the long data type.

```
Private Sub cmdLong_Click()

    ' Variable Definitions
    Dim i&                          ' Long index value
    Dim sngResult As Single         ' Final result variable
    Dim intPercentage As Integer    ' Create INTEGER percentage
    Dim lngSalary As Long           ' Create long salary
    Dim lngAmount As Long           ' Create long amount

    ' Make sure the salary is within the valid range of the
    ' long data type.
    If txtSalary < 0 And txtSalary > 2147483647 Then
        MsgBox "The integer implementation requires a salary greater
➥       than 0 and less than 2,147,483,647.", , "Currency vs. Long"
        Exit Sub
    End If

    ' Set the currency variables
    lngSalary = txtSalary
    intPercentage = txtPercentage

    ' Get the starting time
    Call Common_StartTimedTest

    ' Calculate the amount
    For i& = 1 To txtLoopCount
        ' This calculation expresses the result in pennies
        lngAmount = lngSalary * intPercentage
    Next

    ' This calculation puts the amount in dollars
    sngResult = lngAmount / 100

    ' Get the ending time
    Call Common_EndTimedTest(lblElapsed(4))

    ' Display the amount
    txtAmount = Format(sngResult, "#####.00")

End Sub
```

First, notice that because the long data type is used, the range must not exceed 2 billion. Because the salary is represented using this data type, a 2-billion-dollar range is sufficient—except maybe for software developers. Notice also that the salary and amount variables are declared as long integers. Normally, the percent value entered by the user must be divided by 100 to put it in decimal form. That is not done here because it would require a floating-point value. In this case, the percentage is kept in its integer form so that an integer data type can be used. When the values are thus multiplied, all the data types are integer based.

Because the percentage is not scaled, the resulting salary is represented by pennies, not dollars. The value must be divided by 100 to obtain a dollar amount. This division is timed along with the multiplication loop to account for this extra step. Note, however, that the division is not placed *within* the loop. This is because the final conversion only needs to be performed when displaying the result to the end user.

The results of each test case are shown in Figure 9.3. They are summarized in Table 9.4.

Table 9.4. Timing results for the salary calculation.

Data Type	*Normalized Time*
Double	1.00
Single	1.08
Long	1.41
Currency	1.90
Variant	38.39

Notice that the currency method does indeed take longer to execute than the single, double, and long test cases. Notice also that the technique to use the long data type does not save more time than the single and double test cases. This illustrates the fact that no one data type is always the fastest for all operations.

You can make two primary conclusions from these results. First, the use of the variant data type should be avoided unless absolutely necessary! Note the much higher execution time compared to the others. The second conclusion is that the single, double, and long data types are faster than the currency data type. You should therefore avoid the currency data type unless you determine that the benefits of rounding and formatting inherent to it outweigh the decrease in performance caused by using it.

TIP: Avoid using the currency data type whenever possible. Use another floating-point data type instead.

Using Arrays to Represent Data Sets

This section examines three ways to store a set of data—using a multidimensional array, an array of user-defined types, or a simple set of variables—and compares them to determine the best approach. Keep in mind that data can be stored, collected, and interpreted in many different ways. This case study is intended to give you a general sense of which method to use.

The sample application in this section, Contnr32.exe, creates a collection of 25 employee records. Each employee record consists of 10 pieces of data: first name, last name, Social Security number, age, sex, job position, employee number, home phone, work phone, and office number. The application loads each employee record with these 10 pieces of data. Because you might be interested in performing the assignments more than once, a loop count text box is included on the form to set the number of times the assignments are performed. The application's form is shown in Figure 9.4. As always, the application can be found on the CD-ROM that accompanies the book.

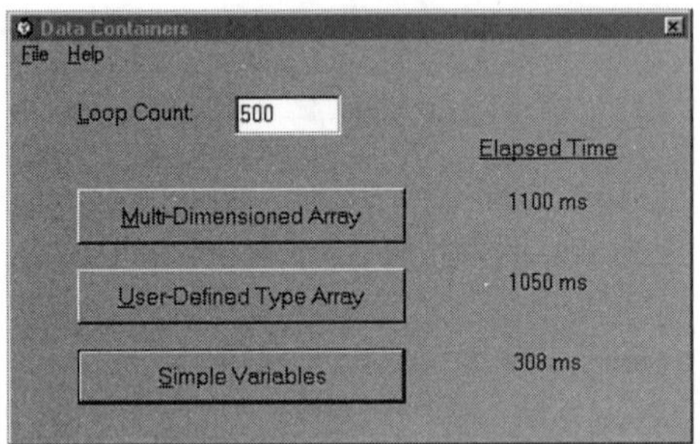

Figure 9.4.
Comparing variables, arrays, and user-defined types in the main form of the Contnr32 application.

Note that on the form you click on the button that represents the storage method. When you click the appropriate button, you are presented with the elapsed time it took that array type to create and fill each of the 25 employee records the number of times indicated by the user in the Loop Count text box.

If you click on the User-Defined Type command button, the following user-defined type is used in the code:

```
Private Type EMPLOYEE
    First_Name As String
    Last_Name As String
    SSN As String
    Age As String
    Sex As String
    Job_Position As String
    Employee_Number As String
    Home_Phone As String
    Work_Phone As String
    Office As String
End Type
```

An array of user-defined types is created and filled with data, as you can see in Listing 9.6. Note that the strings are of variable length. If they were fixed-length strings, performance would improve.

Listing 9.6. Creating employee records using the user-defined type.

```
Private Sub cmdType_Click()

    ' Create integer index values
    Dim i%, j%

    ' Start the timer
    Call Common_StartTimedTest

    ' Create an array of variable-length strings
    Dim DataSet(1 To 25) As EMPLOYEE

    ' Loop through the calculations
    For i% = 1 To txtLoopCount
        For j% = 1 To EMPLOYEE_COUNT
            DataSet(j%).First_Name = "FIRSTNAME"
            DataSet(j%).Last_Name = "LASTNAME"
            DataSet(j%).SSN = "123-45-6789"
            DataSet(j%).Age = "30"
            DataSet(j%).Sex = "M"
            DataSet(j%).Job_Position = "Engineer"
            DataSet(j%).Employee_Number = "123"
            DataSet(j%).Home_Phone = "123-4567"
            DataSet(j%).Work_Phone = "890-1234"
            DataSet(j%).Office = "#236"
        Next
    Next

    ' Stop the timer and display the elapsed time and memory used
    Call Common_EndTimedTest(lblElapsed(1))

End Sub
```

The next test case is similar, but uses arrays rather than structures. When the user clicks on the command button labeled Multi-Dimensioned Array, a multidimensional array is created:

```
' Create an array of variable-length strings
Dim DataSet(1 To 25, 1 To 10) As String
```

This array is dimensioned for 25 employees, with each employee having 10 data strings for storage. A loop similar to that of Listing 9.6 is used, except instead of using user-defined types, the array is filled, as shown in Listing 9.7.

Listing 9.7. Creating employee records using an array.

```
Private Sub cmdArray_Click()

    ' Define integer index values
    Dim i%, j%

    ' Set the timer
    Call Common_StartTimedTest

    ' Create an array of variable-length strings
    Dim DataSet(1 To 25, 1 To 10) As String

    ' Assign the array elements
    For i% = 1 To txtLoopCount
        For j% = 1 To EMPLOYEE_COUNT
            DataSet(j%, 1) = "FIRSTNAME"
            DataSet(j%, 2) = "LASTNAME"
            DataSet(j%, 3) = "123-45-6789"
            DataSet(j%, 4) = "30"
            DataSet(j%, 5) = "M"
            DataSet(j%, 6) = "Engineer"
            DataSet(j%, 7) = "123"
            DataSet(j%, 8) = "123-4567"
            DataSet(j%, 9) = "890-1234"
            DataSet(j%, 10) = "#236"
        Next
    Next

    ' Stop the timer and display the elapsed time and memory used
    Call Common_EndTimedTest(lblElapsed(0))

End Sub
```

When the user clicks on the Simple Variables command button, 10 variables are created for each of the 25 employees, for a total of 250 variables. Each of these variables is then assigned its data strings individually. This approach requires a great deal of code and is therefore not printed in this text. Refer to the CD-ROM for the complete code listing.

You can see the results for a loop count of 500 in Figure 9.4. They are listed in Table 9.5.

Table 9.5. Timing results of the Contnr32 application with loop count equal to 500.

Method	*Normalized Time*
Variables	1.0
Structure	3.4
Array	3.6

Notice that the individual variable assignments take the shortest amount of time to execute. If you examine the code, however, you will note that 250 variables must be declared and assigned

parameters individually. Obviously, this may not be an acceptable trade-off with maintainability of the program. The array and structure implementations are much shorter, more maintainable, and easier to manage. The structure is easier to work with because you do not have to keep track of how the employee data corresponds to the array values. For example, if you wanted to set the employee number of the fifth employee, you could simply enter

```
DataSet(5).Employee_Number = "236"
```

rather than having to look in the code and find the index number of the employee number within the array and have to enter

```
DataSet(5, 7) = "236"
```

Another option is to create a constant for every element in the array, which would require these statements:

```
Constant EMP_NUM = 7

DataSet(5, EMP_NUM) = "236"
```

Even so, the structure is easier to use. It is also faster than the multidimensional array. These factors combine to make the structure the best choice for this case study.

Again, even though the simple variable technique is the fastest, the amount of code is extremely large and very difficult to maintain. Unless the number of variables is small (certainly fewer than 250!), the use of a user-defined type still appears to be a better approach. Although the elapsed time is more even between the user-defined type and the array, the user-defined type is certainly easier to work with and maintain.

> **TIP:** Unless the set of data is very small, use user-defined types or arrays to store data sets rather than simple variables. While simple variables are faster, they are almost always not worth the trade-off in code maintenance.

Constants Versus Variables

When writing Visual Basic applications, programmers often use data that does not change in the program. Data of this nature is often referenced throughout the application for various purposes. This section explores the benefit of using constants to represent data that do not change versus using variables.

The application used to demonstrate this principle, GlbVar32.exe, is contained on the CD-ROM that accompanies this book. GlbVar32.exe uses the `Public` keyword to define an integer, long, single, double, and string constant in a module. This makes these variables global—that is, usable everywhere in the application code. In addition, constants are defined that also have global scope. The following excerpt of code from one of the application's modules shows these declarations:

```
' Global constant declarations
Public Const INTEGER_CONSTANT% = 1
Public Const LONG_CONSTANT& = 2000000
Public Const SINGLE_CONSTANT! = 1.24
Public Const DOUBLE_CONSTANT# = 5.67
Public Const STRING_CONSTANT$ = "This is a sample string"

' Global variable declarations
Public g_strGlobalString As String
Public g_intGlobalInteger As Integer
Public g_lngGlobalLong As Long
Public g_sngGlobalSingle As Single
Public g_dblGlobalDouble As Double
```

The application's form consists of two command buttons. The first command button, labeled Use Global Constants, executes code that assigns the global constants to local variables inside the `Click` procedure of the command button. The second command button, Use Global Variables, executes code that assigns the global variables declared in the code module to local variables in the procedure. To obtain useful timings, a loop counter is provided that allows you to adjust the number of times the assignments are made. The application's form is shown in Figure 9.5.

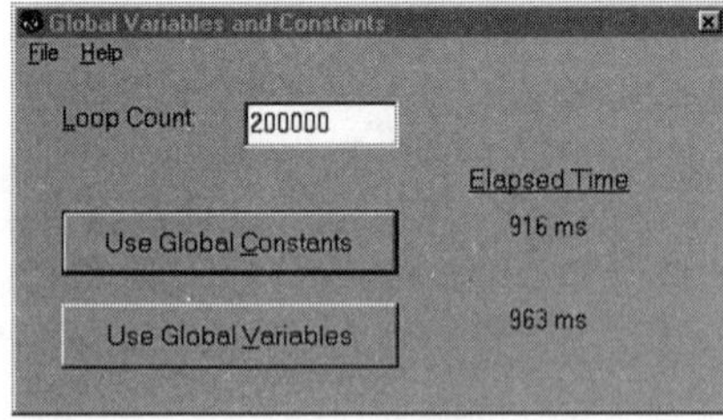

Figure 9.5.
Comparing global constants and global variables in the main form of the GlbVar32 application.

Note that the loop count is set to an initial value of 200,000. You can change this value to obtain meaningful timing data based on the platform being used. The procedure executed when the user clicks on the Use Global Constants command button is shown in Listing 9.8.

Listing 9.8. Using global constants to set local variables.

```
Private Sub cmdConstant_Click()

    ' Variable Definitions
    Dim i&                          ' Long index variable
    Dim strX As String
    Dim intX As Integer
    Dim lngX As Long
    Dim sngX As Single
    Dim dblX As Double
```

```
    ' Start the timer
    Call Common_StartTimedTest

    ' Assign the variables to the global constants
    For i& = 1 To txtLoopCount
        strX = STRING_CONSTANT$
        intX = INTEGER_CONSTANT%
        lngX = LONG_CONSTANT&
        sngX = SINGLE_CONSTANT!
        dblX = DOUBLE_CONSTANT#
    Next

    ' Stop the timer and report results
    Call Common_EndTimedTest(lblElapsed(0))

End Sub
```

Note that a local variable is created in the listing for each constant defined in the code module. In the loop, each variable is assigned its appropriate constant value. The second test case is executed when the user clicks on the command button labeled Use Global Variables. The approach is similar, but it uses variables instead of constants. The code for this second test case is shown in Listing 9.9.

Listing 9.9. Using global variables to set local variables.

```
Private Sub cmdVariable_Click()

    ' Variable Definitions
    Dim i&                          ' Long index value
    Dim strX As String
    Dim intX As Integer
    Dim lngX As Long
    Dim sngX As Single
    Dim dblX As Double

    ' Set the global variables outside the timing construct
    g_strGlobalString = "This is a sample string"
    g_intGlobalInteger = 1
    g_lngGlobalLong = 2000000
    g_sngGlobalSingle = 1.24
    g_dblGlobalDouble = 5.67

    ' Start the timer
    Call Common_StartTimedTest

    ' Assign the variables to the global constants
    For i& = 1 To txtLoopCount
        strX = g_strGlobalString
        intX = g_intGlobalInteger
        lngX = g_lngGlobalLong
        sngX = g_sngGlobalSingle
```

continues

Listing 9.9. continued

```
        dblX = g_dblGlobalDouble
    Next

    ' Stop the timer and report results
    Call Common_EndTimedTest(lblElapsed(1))

End Sub
```

In this case, the global variables must first be assigned, as they are at the beginning of the subroutine. Note that these variable assignments are made *outside* the timed portion of code. For an equivalent comparison, you must ensure that the global variables are assigned the same values as the constants before the timing and loop execute, because the constants are given values upon their declaration and prior to the timed test.

You can see the results of 200,000 iterations of the loop for these assignments in Figure 9.5. They are summarized in Table 9.6.

Table 9.6. Timing results of the GlbVar32 application with loop count equal to 200,000.

Method	*Normalized Time*
Global constants	1.000
Global variables	1.051

In 200,000 iterations of the loop, the global constant code is approximately 5 percent faster than the global variable code. Even though the performance improvement using global constants is modest in comparison to that using global variables, the use of constants versus variables has other advantages.

The primary benefit of using constants over variables is maintainability. A constant takes less code because it is only declared and assigned a value once, in the same statement. A variable, on the other hand, must first be declared and then assigned. And because it is a variable, it is subject to modification in the code. Using a constant ensures that the value will not change while the program executes. This benefit, along with the slight improvement in performance gained when using a constant versus a variable, makes using constants preferable whenever possible. Constants, therefore, should be used whenever data exists in the program that does not change and can be defined up front by the programmer.

> **TIP:** Use constants instead of variables for values that do not change.

Using the Correct Variable Scope

You have already learned in this chapter about the three levels of scope you can give to a Visual Basic variable, but here is a quick review. Procedure-level variables are created and destroyed when the procedure begins and exits. All memory used to store the variables is released when the procedure ends unless you want to preserve the data using the `Static` keyword. Module-level variables are defined in the declarations section of a form or code module. A module-level variable defined with the `Private` keyword is created when the module is loaded into memory at the start of the application. Module-level variables declared with the `Private` keyword exist throughout the lifetime of an application, but can only be referenced by procedures inside the module. Module-level variables declared with the `Public` keyword, often referred to as global variables, are also loaded into memory at the beginning of the application. Unlike private variables, public variables can be used anywhere at any time during the life of the application.

This section compares performance among these three levels of variable scope. The application used to make these comparisons, VarScp32.exe, is on the CD-ROM that accompanies this book. The application consists of a code module that contains public (global) variable declarations and a form that contains module-level and procedure-level variable declarations. Every Visual Basic data type is assigned its own variable in the test. The global variables are located in a separate code module as

```
' Public Module-Level (Global) variable declarations
Public g_Currency(1 To 25) As Currency
Public g_Double(1 To 25) As Double
Public g_Single(1 To 25) As Single
Public g_Integer(1 To 25) As Integer
Public g_Long(1 To 25) As Long
Public g_String(1 To 25) As String
Public g_Type(1 To 25) As UDTYPE
Public g_Variant(1 To 25) As Variant
```

where the user-defined type is represented as

```
' Sample user-defined type
Type UDTYPE
    intVar As Integer
    curVar As Currency
    dblVar As Double
    sngVar As Single
    strVar As String
End Type
```

The module-level private variables are identical, except that they are prefixed by `m_` to indicate module-level scope versus the `g_` prefix that identifies global scope. The main form is shown in Figure 9.6.

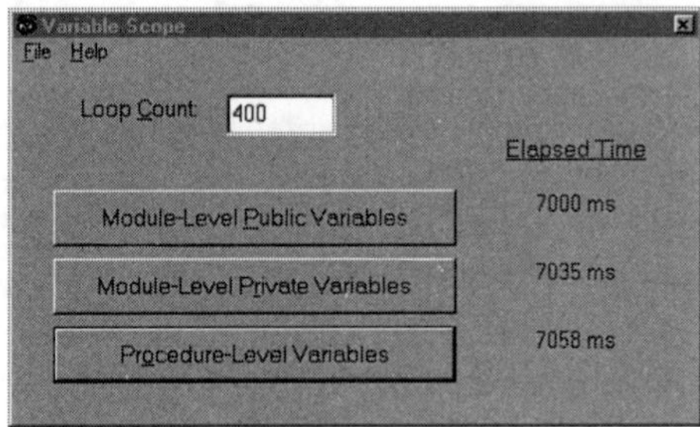

Figure 9.6.
Comparing variable scope in the main form of the VarScp32 application.

Each command button executes a subroutine that assigns data to each element and then assigns the variable to a local variable. Consider the test case for global variables. This test case is represented by the command button labeled Module-Level Public Variables. The code for this test case is shown in Listing 9.10.

Listing 9.10. Public (global) variable assignments.

```
Private Sub cmdPublic_Click ()

    ' Create long integer and integer indices
    Dim i&, j%

    ' Start the timer
    Call Common_StartTimedTest

    ' Define the variables
    Dim strX As String
    Dim intX As Integer
    Dim lngX As Long
    Dim sngX As Single
    Dim dblX As Double
    Dim curX As Currency
    Dim varX As Variant
    Dim typX As UDTYPE

    ' Assign data to the global variables and store them in local variables
    For i& = 1 To txtLoopCount
        For j% = 1 To 25

            g_String(j%) = "This is a test string"
            strX = g_String(j%)

            g_Integer(j%) = 123
            intX = g_Integer(j%)

            g_Long(j%) = 12345678
            lngX = g_Long(j%)

            g_Single(j%) = 1.2345
            sngX = g_Single(j%)
```

```
            g_Double(j%) = 124345.6789
            dblX = g_Double(j%)

            g_Variant(j%) = Date
            varX = g_Variant(j%)

            g_Currency(j%) = 32.495
            curX = g_Currency(j%)

            g_Type(j%).intVar = 123
            g_Type(j%).curVar = Date
            g_Type(j%).dblVar = 12345.6789
            g_Type(j%).sngVar = 1.2345
            g_Type(j%).strVar = "This is a test string"
            typX = g_Type(j%)

        Next
    Next

    ' Get the ending time
    Call Common_EndTimedTest(lblElapsed(0))

End Sub
```

Note that each global variable is an array that consists of 25 elements. A global variable is present for every data type.

The second test, represented by the command button labeled Module-Level Private Variables, uses module-level variables rather than global variables. The subroutine for the module variables is identical to that of the globals—except, of course, that the variables used are declared as `Private` rather than `Public`.

The third test case, represented by the command button labeled Procedure-Level Variables, uses local variables. Local variables are declared in the procedure using the `Dim` keyword. The code listing for the local variable test case is shown in Listing 9.11.

Listing 9.11. Making local variable assignments.

```
Private Sub cmdLocal_Click ()

    ' Create long integer and integer indices
    Dim i&, j%

    ' Local variable declarations
    Dim l_Currency(1 To 25) As Currency
    Dim l_Double(1 To 25) As Double
    Dim l_Single(1 To 25) As Single
    Dim l_Integer(1 To 25) As Integer
    Dim l_Long(1 To 25) As Long
    Dim l_String(1 To 25) As String
    Dim l_Type(1 To 25) As UDTYPE
    Dim l_Variant(1 To 25) As Variant
```

continues

Listing 9.11. continued

```
    ' Start the timer
    Call Common_StartTimedTest

    ' Define the variables
    Dim strX As String
    Dim intX As Integer
    Dim lngX As Long
    Dim sngX As Single
    Dim dblX As Double
    Dim curX As Currency
    Dim varX As Variant
    Dim typX As UDTYPE

    ' Assign data to the local variables and store them in local variables
    For i& = 1 To txtLoopCount
        For j% = 1 To 25

            l_String(j%) = "This is a test string"
            strX = l_String(j%)

            l_Integer(j%) = 123
            intX = l_Integer(j%)

            l_Long(j%) = 12345678
            lngX = l_Long(j%)

            l_Single(j%) = 1.2345
            sngX = l_Single(j%)

            l_Double(j%) = 124345.6789
            dblX = l_Double(j%)

            l_Variant(j%) = Date
            varX = l_Variant(j%)

            l_Currency(j%) = 32.495
            curX = l_Currency(j%)

            l_Type(j%).intVar = 123
            l_Type(j%).curVar = Date
            l_Type(j%).dblVar = 12345.6789
            l_Type(j%).sngVar = 1.2345
            l_Type(j%).strVar = "This is a test string"
            typX = l_Type(j%)

        Next
    Next

    ' Get the ending time
    Call Common_EndTimedTest(lblElapsed(2))

End Sub
```

In this case, the variables are declared locally and every element of each array is assigned data and stored in a local variable of the same data type. This gives a realistic picture of the cost of storing and retrieving variables of global, module, and local scope. Each data type was not timed separately; instead, all the variables were timed cumulatively. You can see the results of this timing in Figure 9.6. The normalized results are summarized in Table 9.7.

Table 9.7. Timing results of the VarScp32 application with count equal to 400.

Method	*Normalized Time*
Global variables	1.000
Module variables	1.005
Local variables	1.008

As you can see, local variables are 0.8 percent slower than global variables and 0.3 percent slower than module-level variables. This is because it takes more time to create the variables when the procedure is called than it takes to create the module and global variables when the application is loaded into memory. The additional time to create the local variables was, in this case study, not very significant. The percentages increase slightly when the loop count is increased, but still not significantly enough to arrive at a strong conclusion. As you can see, the difference in timing values is so slight that they can be considered identical in terms of execution time.

While the execution times are almost identical, the amount of memory required is not. Local variables free up the memory they use as soon as the procedure has finished executing. The global and module variables, on the other hand, claim memory for the duration of the application.

Therefore, when considering which level of scope to use for variables, you must be aware of how much memory will be consumed *as well as* the resultant execution time. Global variables might be slightly faster, but they consistently consume memory that could otherwise be free. If memory is a precious resource to the user, the use of local variables might be the better choice.

> **TIP:** To conserve memory, keep variable scope as tight as possible. Performance might be slightly worse as the scope tightens, but the overall maintainability and usability of the code is likely to be worth the small sacrifice in performance.

Summary

This chapter focuses on the best data types to use for variables in a Visual Basic application. Useful techniques are presented and demonstrated using sample applications. All the Visual Basic data types are presented and their common uses discussed. A discussion of variable containers such as arrays and structures, as well as a brief discussion of variable scope, is also presented. The discussion of these concepts provides you with the necessary background to understand the subsequent concepts.

Using the results of the sample applications, you have seen how the specific techniques relate to real-world examples. Both fixed-length and variable-length strings are compared to variants, and in both cases, the string is faster. Variants not only take more time to process, but they require more memory, as well. Therefore you should have come to the conclusion that you should always use strings rather than variants whenever possible.

The second technique focuses on using integer-based variables whenever possible. (This chapter does not delve into the use of integer variables versus other data types for mathematical applications, however, because that is covered in Chapter 10, "Math.") This technique focuses on the general usage of integer-based data types such as integer, long, and Boolean for data storage and simple manipulation. The sample application demonstrated that integer-based variables take less time to create and store data than do any other counterpart. This section also stresses once more the importance of avoiding variants whenever practical.

The third technique stresses the need to minimize the use of the currency data type. The currency data type is specialized for the use of monetary operations. The sample application for this section shows a simple multiplication of monetary values using currency versus the other data types. This section concludes that using the currency data type is slower than using its floating-point counterparts. You have seen that single and double data types are the best choice in this case, and that data types such as variants should, as always, be avoided.

The next section compares the use of arrays, user-defined types, and simple variables to store collections of data by using arrays or user-defined types to represent large sets of data rather than simple variables. Although simple variables are the fastest, you have seen that each variable must be distinctly defined in code at design time. The number of simple variables cannot be changed at runtime through user actions or data flow. Arrays, on the other hand, are dynamic and can easily be changed via the `ReDim` keyword at runtime. The sample application for this section uses a multidimensional array, an array of structures, and a collection of simple variables. Although the variables are the fastest, they are simply not practical to ensure maintainability. The array of structures is slightly faster than arrays and is easier to maintain; therefore, user-defined types are likely to be the best way to represent a collection of data unless the set is very simple.

The next section emphasizes the need to use constants instead of variables. The use of constants rather than variables is beneficial in terms of maintainability, because the constants are statically defined and cannot be changed in the code. When a value never changes in the application, it is desirable to use a constant to represent that value rather than a variable.

The last section in this chapter discusses the need to determine and use the most appropriate scope for variables. The sample application in this section creates and assigns data to module-level public, module-level private, and procedure-level variables, and then assigns each to procedure-level variables in subroutines. The purpose is to ascertain which data type provided the best performance.

The results demonstrate that there is relatively little performance difference between these types of variables. Public variables are slightly faster, followed by the module-level private variables, and finally the procedure-level, or local, variables. Although public variables offer the best performance, the gain in performance is rather small and not likely to be perceptible to the user. This is a case where the boost in performance might not be worth the cost. First, global variables consume more memory throughout the life of the application because they never release the memory that procedure-level variables do when the procedure ends. Furthermore, applications that rely heavily on global variables are more difficult to maintain and reuse. Local variables are usually preferred.

Chapter 10 further discusses variables in the context of mathematic operations to provide you with a well-rounded treatment of when to use which types of variables and how they are best used to perform mathematical operations. This chapter illustrates, in a more general sense, the performance of the various data types when compared to each other and how they compare under various scope and containment conditions.

Obey the Signs

Wrong Way: To make life easier, always use variants.

Variants are very flexible because they can represent numeric, date/time, or string data and because you don't have to convert between these types of data when assigning them to a variant—Visual Basic performs the conversion for you automatically. If, however, you are certain of the type of data you are storing in a variable, you should always use a variable whose data type is the same as the data you are storing. Even the Visual Basic Programmer's Reference indicates that, in order to handle data more efficiently, the variant data type should be used only when necessary.

Beware of Falling Rocks: Integers should be used whenever possible, but they cannot be used for everything.

This chapter stresses the performance advantages of using integers. The next chapter discusses math and once again explores the benefits of the integer data type versus its counterparts. Although integers certainly do save time and memory, they cannot always be substituted for other data types. In this chapter, when you looked at the currency data type, you discovered a way to use integers for decimal-point calculations. Although this is useful and saves time, it is actually slower than using floating-point variables, given the extra code required. You have seen that sometimes it isn't practical to spend great amounts of time converting all variables to integers, and other times it is simply impossible. As a general rule, however, using the integer-based data type versus the floating-point, variant, or currency data types improves the performance of your application. Whether the effort required to use integers in place of these other data types improves the performance of your application sufficiently to justify the extra development time is another matter.

Wrong Way: Always use individual variables rather than variable sets.

This chapter explores the various ways you can represent collections of data. An employee-record example is used in which each employee has 10 pieces of data associated with him. For 25 employees, you could simply create 25 × 10 = 250 variables to represent all the data, and this approach results in the fastest execution time. However, if you want to increase the number of employees from 25 to 30, you need to modify the code. On the other hand, the use of an array enables you to dynamically allocate space for employees, so that during runtime you can enlarge or shrink the number of employees and their data. Variable sets, whether grouped in arrays or structures, give you a modularity and dynamic capability that generally justifies the added time required to process them.

Q&A

Q When and why would I use a currency variable?

A Currency variables are useful whenever you want to avoid rounding errors in monetary calculations. They are also of a fixed-point data type tailored to represent dollar figures. Rounding errors are minimized in the currency type because it has a restricted range and has a fixed decimal point.

Q What kind of data can be declared "constant"?

A You can declare data as constant if you, as the programmer, know the value of the data and that the value never changes. Suppose, for example, you are a pet store owner. You have an inventory tracking application that you use to track how many pets of each type you sell. You may want to assign a variable to each pet in the database that indicates what type of pet they are. In such a case, you can create constants that can be used to represent each type of pet you sell. You might create the constants `BIRD`, `FISH`, `GERBIL`, and `GORILLA`, for example, in your code as

```
Public Const BIRD as Integer = 1
Public Const FISH As Integer = 2
Public Const GERBIL As Integer = 3
Public Const GORILLA As Integer = 4
```

which can be then assigned to your variables. Because you don't want to need to change these constants (you don't want to turn your inventory of a thousand fish into a thousand gorillas), it would be needless to use variables to represent them. Furthermore, you could be sure the values would not be inadvertently modified in the code, since Visual Basic does not allow a constant to be assigned any other value than what it was when defined.

Q How do I know what level of variable scope to use?

A When making a decision on what variable scope to use, you must first determine what the variable's use will be. If the variable must be shared among many procedures, and those procedures can be placed into one code module, declare the variable as `Private` in the declarations section of the code module. If you use the variable across many procedures, declare it as a public variable in the declarations section of the code module. If, on the other hand, you can restrict the use of a variable to a single procedure, you simply declare it in the procedure using the `Dim` keyword. Keep in mind that `Public` and `Private` are only applicable to variables created in the declarations section of a module. `Dim` or `Static` is used whenever a variable is declared within a procedure.

Quiz

1. Consider the following code example. Locate all the places in this subroutine where strings can be used rather than variants. Make the necessary conversions to the code. Refer to the 09Quiz32.exe application on the CD-ROM that accompanies this book for these subroutines:

```
Private Sub cmdProb1_Click ()

    ' This subroutine consists of a collection of variants
    ' that can be converted to strings.  Some variants cannot
    ' be easily converted, however, and must be left alone.

    ' Variable Declarations
    Dim i&                                   ' Long index value
    Dim j%                                   ' Integer index value
    Dim varName As Variant
    Dim varDate As Variant
    Dim varRace(1 To 10) As Variant
    Dim varPlace(1 To 10) As Variant

    ' Start the timer
    Call Common_StartTimedTest

    ' Assign data to the quiz variables
    For i& = 1 To txtLoopCount
        varName = "Tim Koets"
        varDate = Date
        For j% = 1 To 10
            varRace(j%) = Choose(j%, "Grand Rapids", "Boston",
             ➥"Boulder Springs", "San Fransisco",
             ➥ "Phoenix", "Battle Creek",
             ➥"Biloxi", "Kalamazoo", "Miami", "Houston")
            varPlace(j%) = Choose(j%, "1st", "3rd", "12th",
                ➥"25th", "3rd", "9th", "5th", "100th",
                ➥"7th", "1st")
        Next
    Next
```

```
    ' Stop the timer and display the results
    Call Common_EndTimedTest(lblElapsed(0))

End Sub
```

2. Consider the following code example. Locate all the places in this subroutine where integers can be used rather than the variables currently being used. Make the necessary conversions to the code. Refer to application 09Quiz32.exe on the CD-ROM that accompanies this book for the solutions:

```
Private Sub cmdProb2_Click ()

    ' This subroutine consists of a collection of variables
    ' that can be converted to integers.  Some variables cannot
    ' be easily converted, however, and must be left alone.

    ' Variable Declarations
    Dim i&                          ' Long index value
    Dim strName As String
    Dim sngAge As Single
    Dim varBirthDate As Variant
    Dim strSex As String

    ' Start the timer
    Call Common_StartTimedTest

    ' Assign data to the quiz variables
    For i& = 1 To txtLoopCount
        strName = "John Schmidt"
        sngAge = 23
        varBirthDate = CVDate("10/11/69")
        strSex = "M"
    Next

    ' Stop the timer and display the results
    Call Common_EndTimedTest(lblElapsed(2))
End Sub
```

3. Examine the following code listing. In every case where a variable is used to represent data that does not change, convert the code so that a constant is used instead. Refer to the application 09Quiz32.exe on the CD-ROM that accompanies this book for the solution:

```
Private Sub cmdProb3_Click ()

    ' This subroutine consists of a collection of variables
    ' that can be converted to constants.  Some variables cannot
    ' be easily converted, however, and must be left alone.

    ' Variable Declarations
    Dim i&                          ' Long index value
    Dim intBlack As Integer
    Dim intBlue As Integer
    Dim intGreen As Integer
    Dim intCyan As Integer
    Dim intRed As Integer
```

```
    Dim intMagenta As Integer
    Dim intYellow As Integer
    Dim intWhite As Integer
    Dim intGray As Integer
    Dim intLtBlue As Integer
    Dim intLtGreen As Integer
    Dim intLtCyan As Integer
    Dim intLtRed As Integer
    Dim intLtMag As Integer
    Dim intLtYel As Integer
    Dim intBrtWht As Integer

    ' Start the timer
    Call Common_StartTimedTest

    ' Assign the quiz variables
    intBlack = 0
    intBlue = 1
    intGreen = 2
    intCyan = 3
    intRed = 4
    intMagenta = 5
    intYellow = 6
    intWhite = 7
    intGray = 8
    intLtBlue = 9
    intLtGreen = 10
    intLtCyan = 11
    intLtRed = 12
    intLtMag = 13
    intLtYel = 14
    intBrtWht = 15

    ' Assign data to the quiz variables
    For i& = 1 To txtLoopCount
        Me.BackColor = QBColor(intBlack)
        Me.BackColor = QBColor(intBlue)
        Me.BackColor = QBColor(intGreen)
        Me.BackColor = QBColor(intCyan)
        Me.BackColor = QBColor(intRed)
        Me.BackColor = QBColor(intMagenta)
        Me.BackColor = QBColor(intYellow)
        Me.BackColor = QBColor(intGray)
        Me.BackColor = QBColor(intLtBlue)
        Me.BackColor = QBColor(intLtGreen)
        Me.BackColor = QBColor(intLtCyan)
        Me.BackColor = QBColor(intLtRed)
        Me.BackColor = QBColor(intLtMag)
        Me.BackColor = QBColor(intLtYel)
        Me.BackColor = QBColor(intBrtWht)
        Me.BackColor = QBColor(intWhite)
    Next

    ' Stop the timer and display the results
    Call Common_EndTimedTest(lblElapsed(4))

End Sub
```

Workshop

Look at an application that you have already written. As you examine the code, can you see areas in which you can apply the concepts discussed in this chapter? Take timings of each area you want to improve, make those improvements, and then take timings again. How much faster does your application run? Did you have to make trade-off decisions when you made your optimizations?

Math

In Chapter 9, "Variables," the primary Visual Basic data types are compared to one another in terms of performance. The focus in that chapter is the relative performance of variables whose data is assigned and retrieved, the performance of variables with different levels of scope, using constants versus variables, and using arrays versus structures. This chapter focuses on the most efficient mathematical operators as well as the most efficient way to apply them to the variables based on these data types. The following techniques are pointed out in this chapter:

- Integer math is generally faster than floating-point math.
- Do not use the floating-point division operator with integer-based data types.
- The exponent operator is faster using floating-point variables than using integer-based variables.
- Avoid mathematical operations using the variant data type.

- Avoid mathematical operations using the currency data type.
- Multiplication is faster than division.
- Multiplication can be faster than the exponent operator.
- Using the square root function is faster than using the exponent operator.

The validity of each technique is demonstrated with programming examples that show the benefit of applying the technique. Rather than consider every possible combination of mathematical functions, operations, and data types, this chapter addresses the most common cases you will encounter as a Visual Basic programmer. When you're finished with this chapter, you should have a clearer understanding of the best way to apply mathematical functions and operations in your code, as well as an understanding of which data types work best when performing those operations to maximize performance.

A Simple Program to Evaluate Arithmetic Operations

The first several techniques discussed in this chapter are demonstrated using the MthCmp32.exe application found on the CD-ROM that accompanies the book. A 16-bit version of this program, MthCmp16.exe, is also available on the CD-ROM. This program uses all the Visual Basic arithmetic operators—addition, subtraction, multiplication, and division, as well as the exponent and modulus operators—and lists resultant timings as applied to variables of each Visual Basic data type. The main form is shown in Figure 10.1.

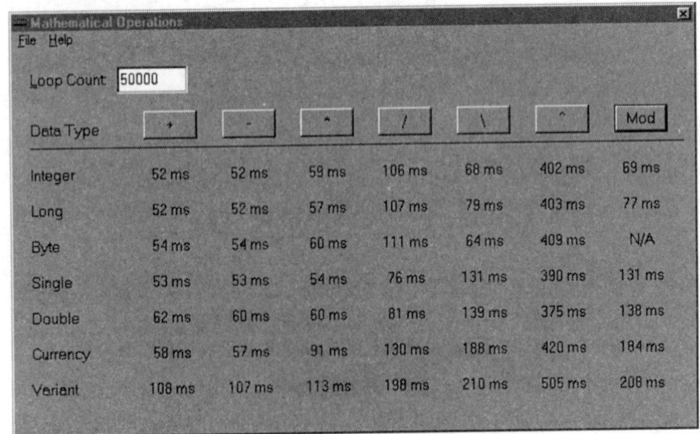

Data Type	+	-	*	/	\	^	Mod
Integer	52 ms	52 ms	59 ms	106 ms	68 ms	402 ms	69 ms
Long	52 ms	52 ms	57 ms	107 ms	79 ms	403 ms	77 ms
Byte	54 ms	54 ms	60 ms	111 ms	64 ms	409 ms	N/A
Single	53 ms	53 ms	54 ms	76 ms	131 ms	390 ms	131 ms
Double	62 ms	60 ms	60 ms	81 ms	139 ms	375 ms	138 ms
Currency	58 ms	57 ms	91 ms	130 ms	188 ms	420 ms	184 ms
Variant	108 ms	107 ms	113 ms	198 ms	210 ms	505 ms	208 ms

Figure 10.1.
The main form of the MthCmp32 application.

Note that each mathematical operation has an associated command button, and that the operation is applied to every data type. In order to ensure meaningful timings, you can adjust the number of times an operation takes place by changing the loop count. Each command button has an associated subroutine that performs the operation represented by the button. Consider the test case for addition, represented by the command button with the + on it. The code that is executed when you click on this button is shown in Listing 10.1.

Listing 10.1. The addition test case for the MthCmp32 application.

```
Private Sub cmdAdd_Click()

    Dim i&       ' Long index value

    ' Define the variables
    Dim intX1 As Integer, intX2 As Integer, intX3 As Integer
    Dim lngX1 As Long, lngX2 As Long, lngX3 As Long
    Dim sngX1 As Single, sngX2 As Single, sngX3 As Single
    Dim dblX1 As Double, dblX2 As Double, dblX3 As Double
    Dim curX1 As Currency, curX2 As Currency, curX3 As Currency
    Dim varX1 As Variant, varX2 As Variant, varX3 As Variant
    Dim bytX1 As Byte, bytX2 As Byte, bytX3 As Byte

    ' Assign values to the variables
    intX1 = 4: intX2 = 2: intX3 = 0
    lngX1 = 4: lngX2 = 2: lngX3 = 0
    sngX1 = 4: sngX2 = 2: sngX3 = 0
    dblX1 = 4: dblX2 = 2: dblX3 = 0
    curX1 = 4: curX2 = 2: curX3 = 0
    varX1 = 4: varX2 = 2: varX3 = 0
    bytX1 = 4: bytX2 = 2: bytX3 = 0


    ' Integer Calculation
    Call Common_StartTimedTest
    For i& = 1 To txtLoopCount                   ' Perform the integer calculation
        intX3 = intX1 + intX2
    Next
    Call Common_EndTimedTest(lblAdd(0))


    ' Long Calculation
    Call Common_StartTimedTest
    For i& = 1 To txtLoopCount                   ' Perform the long calculation
        lngX3 = lngX1 + lngX2
    Next
    Call Common_EndTimedTest(lblAdd(1))

    ' Byte Calculation
    Call Common_StartTimedTest
    For i& = 1 To txtLoopCount                   ' Perform the byte calculation
        bytX3 = bytX1 + bytX2
    Next
    Call Common_EndTimedTest(lblAdd(2))
```

continues

Listing 10.1. continued

```
    ' Single Calculation
    Call Common_StartTimedTest
    For i& = 1 To txtLoopCount                    ' Perform the single calculation
        sngX3 = sngX1 + sngX2
    Next
    Call Common_EndTimedTest(lblAdd(3))


    ' Double Calculation
    Call Common_StartTimedTest
    For i& = 1 To txtLoopCount                    ' Perform the double calculation
        dblX3 = dblX1 + dblX2
    Next
    Call Common_EndTimedTest(lblAdd(4))


    ' Currency Calculation
    Call Common_StartTimedTest
    For i& = 1 To txtLoopCount                    ' Perform the currency calculation
        curX3 = curX1 + curX2
    Next
    Call Common_EndTimedTest(lblAdd(5))


    ' Variant Calculation
    Call Common_StartTimedTest
    For i& = 1 To txtLoopCount                    ' Perform the variant calculation
        varX3 = varX1 + varX2
    Next
    Call Common_EndTimedTest(lblAdd(6))

End Sub
```

This subroutine calculates a simple addition the number of times you specify in the Loop Count text box. Timings are taken for each data type, and the elapsed time is displayed immediately after the calculation loop.

For every other test case, the only change in the code is the type of mathematical operation that is applied to the variables. The results of executing the application for each operation are shown in Figure 10.1, and the normalized times are summarized in Table 10.1.

Table 10.1. Normalized times for the MthCmp32.exe application.

Data Type	+	-	*	/	\	^	Mod
Integer	1.00	1.00	1.00	1.00	1.00	1.00	1.00
Long	1.00	1.00	0.97	1.01	1.16	1.00	1.12
Byte	1.03	1.04	1.02	1.05	0.94	1.02	N/A

Data Type	+	-	*	/	\	^	Mod
Single	1.02	1.02	0.92	0.72	1.93	0.97	1.90
Double	1.19	1.15	1.02	0.76	2.04	0.93	2.00
Currency	1.11	1.10	1.54	1.23	3.09	1.04	2.67
Variant	2.07	2.05	1.91	1.87	3.09	1.26	3.01

The test results of this application are used as a reference throughout the rest of the chapter to compare the various mathematical operations to each other with respect to each Visual Basic data type. The application demonstrates the validity of the techniques, which are discussed in the following sections.

Integer Math Versus Floating-Point Math

When thinking about whether integer math or floating-point math would be faster, most people would probably conclude that integer math is faster. This makes sense intuitively because the computer uses less memory when working with integers and does not have to perform the decimal-point manipulations required in floating-point math. You would expect, therefore, that a mathematical operation carried out on an integer would require less time than when carried out on a floating-point value. The MthCmp32.exe application introduced in the previous section demonstrates how the data types compare for every mathematical operation.

Refer to Table 10.1 for the timing results. In the case of addition, you see that the integer, long, and byte data types are all approximately equivalent. The single and double data types are not appreciably higher in execution time than the integer, long, or byte data types. The currency data type, which is integer based, performs similarly to the integer, long, and byte data types, and the variant takes the longest, as expected. In the case of subtraction, you can observe that the results are almost identical. For multiplication, note that all data types are approximately equivalent except for the currency and variant data types.

In Visual Basic 3.0, integer math is noticeably faster than floating-point math for these operations. In Visual Basic 4.0, however, integer math for addition, subtraction, and multiplication takes almost the same amount of time as floating-point math. This is due, most likely, to optimizations made to the Visual Basic 4.0 interpreter.

Differences in timings become more apparent when you consider the division operators and the exponent operator. Two types of division operators are tested in the application: integer division (represented by the / symbol) and floating-point division (represented by the \ symbol). In the case of the floating-point division operator, the floating-point data types are faster than the integer-based data types; similarly, with integer division operator, the integer-based data types are faster than the floating-point data types. These results and division in general are discussed in more detail in the next section, "Applying Floating-Point Division to Integer-Based Data Types."

In the case of the exponent operator test, the floating-point data types are somewhat faster than the integer-based data types. This result is discussed in the section "Simple Multiplication Versus the Exponent Operator." Finally, the modulus operator results show that integer data types work better with the modulus operator than do floating-point data types.

With the exception of the integer division and exponent operators, you can conclude that integer-based data types are preferable to floating-point data types. Most operations are faster, even if not significantly so, and integer-based variables use less memory. This makes them preferable in terms of performance. The exceptions to this rule are discussed in the sections that follow.

> **TIP:** Integer math is generally faster than floating-point math.

Applying Floating-Point Division to Integer-Based Data Types

Floating-point division (/) is different from integer division (\). *Floating-point division* returns a floating-point result regardless of the data type of the two numbers being divided. *Integer division,* on the other hand, rounds floating-point variables being divided into integers (unless they are already integers, in which case this is not necessary) and returns an integer result. If the numbers being divided do not divide evenly, the fractional portion of the result is truncated to ensure that the result is an integer. The integer result can be of data type integer or long, depending on the range of the result.

If you use integers in a floating-point division operation, the values are treated as floating-point values during the division. The result is a floating-point value (single or double, depending on which data type is better suited for the solution). If, however, the result is stored in an integer variable, it must be converted back into integer form. Converting the two integer variables to be divided into floating-point form for division and back into integer form for the result makes the cumulative time of the entire operation much slower than if you used floating-point variables.

Integer division, on the other hand, takes whatever variables are being divided and converts them into an integer-based format. The variables are essentially rounded to integer numbers and are cast with the integer or long data type, depending on the range of the value. If you use floating-point values with the integer division operator, the amount of time needed to round and convert the variables into integer form and then convert the result into a floating-point representation takes much more time than if you used floating-point division with floating-point variables.

Therefore, whenever you divide two integer values and want an integer result, use the integer division operator (`\`); *do not* use the floating-point division operator (`/`). If, on the other hand, you have two floating-point values and want a floating-point result, *do not* use the integer division operator. Table 10.2 shows the comparison between integer division using the integer data type and floating-point division using the floating-point data type.

Table 10.2. Normalized execution times for integer versus floating-point division.

Data Type	*Floating-Point Division*	*Integer Division*
Integer	1.56	1.00
Long	1.35	1.00
Byte	1.73	1.00
Single	1.00	1.72
Double	1.00	1.72
Currency	1.00	1.45
Variant	1.00	1.06

Notice that integer division using the integer, long, and byte data types is faster than floating-point division using the single, double, or variant data types, as well as the currency data type.

TIP: Do not use the floating-point division operator with integer-based data types.

The most common oversight of most programmers is to use the floating-point division operator with integer-based variables, as in the statement

```
intAnswer = intA / intB
```

This operation incurs a needless penalty of over 35 percent, 55 percent, and 73 percent for longs, integers, and bytes, respectively. The correct statement when dividing two integers is

```
intAnswer = intA \ intB
```

so that integer division is used. Likewise, the opposite is true for floating-point variables. The code statement

```
sngAnswer = sngA \ sngB
```

would not only exact a 75 percent performance penalty, but it would also provide an integer result and truncate the decimal point.

In circumstances when you want to convert between data types, using integer division with floating-point values or floating-point division with integer values might be appropriate. Such would be the case if, for example, you wanted to divide two integers and store them in a floating-point variable. In this case, you could use the floating-point division operator with the integers and set the result equal to a floating point value, as follows:

```
sngResult = intNumerator / intDenominator
```

Alternatively, you could create a temporary variable used to hold the integer result, which would enable you to use integer division. You would then set the floating point variable equal to the integer variable, as shown here:

```
intResult = intNumerator \ intDenominator
sngResult = intResult
```

This implementation would require the use of an additional variable, but would enable you to use integer division rather than floating-point division. You will compare these two approaches in an exercise at the end of the chapter.

You also might encounter situations in which you have two floating-point numbers that you want to divide, and then you want to store the result in an integer variable. In this case, you would use a statement such as

```
intResult = sngNumerator \ sngDenominator
```

to carry out the calculation. Alternatively, you might want to create a temporary floating-point variable that you could assign to the integer variable, as follows:

```
sngResult = sngNumerator / sngDenominator
intResult = sngResult
```

In this case, you could use the floating-point division operator, which makes the division much faster, and then simply assign the result to an integer variable. Again, you will compare these two approaches in an exercise at the end of the chapter.

Using Integers with the Exponent Operator

The other exception to the first tip, which states that integer math is faster than floating-point math, is in the use of the exponent (^) operator. The exponent operator calculates a result based on the following formula:

```
result = number ^ exponent
```

where *number* and *exponent* can be any numerical data type (except that *exponent* must be an integer if *number* is negative), and *result* is of type double or variant. It is very important to notice that the result defaults to the double data type. Even if *number* and *exponent* are both integers, the result is still converted into the floating-point, double data type.

The fact that the exponent operator always produces a floating-point result indicates that the operation is inherently a floating-point operation. Even if integer-based data types are used for the `number` and `exponent`, the processor still carries out floating-point math. This means that if the number and exponent are integer based, the interpreter must convert them into floating-point values before the calculation can be made. If `number` and `exponent` are already in floating-point form, the operation is faster because no conversions are necessary. The timing results are shown in Table 10.3.

Table 10.3. Exponent operator timings.

Data Type	*Exponent*	*Result*	*Normalized Time*
Integer	Integer	Double	1.07
Long	Long	Double	1.07
Single	Single	Double	1.04
Double	Double	Double	1.00
Currency	Currency	Double	1.12
Variant	Variant	Double	1.35

Note that the integer and long data types take approximately the same amount of time to execute, as do the single and double data types. From this data, you can conclude that when you're performing operations with the exponent operator, it is best to use floating-point variables for `number`, `exponent`, and the result in order to increase performance. Because the currency data type is integer-based, as described in Chapter 9, it is not surprising to see that its execution time is even greater than that of the integer and long data types. The variant is again, as always, the worst performer. The next sections discuss the currency and variant data types in light of mathematical operations applied to them.

TIP: The exponent operator is faster using floating-point variables than using integer-based variables.

Putting These Techniques to Work: Using Integer Math

You have now learned that, for arithmetic operators other than floating-point division and the `Mod` operator, integer math is faster than floating-point math. The floating-point data types include the single and double data types, as well as the currency and variant data types. At this point, it's time to examine several approaches to converting floating-point variables into integer variables so that integer math can be used instead, thus increasing performance.

First you must understand that, in some cases, it simply is not possible or practical to represent floating-point numbers as integers. This might be true because the amount of additional code and/or work required to do so might not be worth the improvements in performance or time required to make the modifications. On the other hand, there might be certain circumstances in which one simple conversion drastically improves performance and is worth every bit of the effort. You must decide how you will act on these trade-offs. This section simply presents techniques; you must take all competing factors into account when deciding how and whether to implement them.

One way to represent a floating-point number in integer format is to essentially drop the decimal point and keep track of where it would normally be. This strategy works fine so long as certain conditions are maintained. First, you must be able to determine where the decimal point is in any number during calculations. Second, an integer variable has a much lower range than its floating-point counterparts, so you might not always be able to represent a floating-point value with an integer or long data type. Take, for example, the floating-point value 2,456,230,235.1153. This value can be easily represented using the double data type. Neither the integer nor the long data type, however, is capable of storing the number without the decimal point; it would be 24,562,302,351,153. Therefore, the use of integers to store floating-point numbers is constrained somewhat by their range. Third, you must be aware that the solution of a particular calculation might exceed the range of the integer variables. In such a case, you must resort to the use of floating-point values, but you must have some idea of the anticipated solution ahead of time.

Therefore, you must know a significant amount of information about the calculations you want to represent with integers. These techniques are less useful when less is known about the data, its range, the arithmetic performed, and the range and format of the solution. From this point on, assume that these factors are known ahead of time so that the techniques used here will behave properly.

First, let's take a look at addition and subtraction. Suppose you have two floating-point numbers that you want to add: 32.95 and 15.30. The floating-point addition is carried out as

```
  32.95
+ 15.30
  48.25
```

You can apply the following rule for floating-point addition and subtraction: When any set of numbers is being added or subtracted, the resultant value contains the same number of digits to the right of the decimal point as the value with the highest number of digits to the right of the decimal point. You can carry out the addition using integers as

```
  3295
+ 1530
  4825
```

and, because you know ahead of time that the solution has two digits to the right of the decimal point, the solution can be represented using the integer by inserting the decimal point two places from the last digit, like this:

```
48.25
```

Here is an example of the code you might use if you were adding two floating-point numbers:

```
Dim sngX as Single, sngY as Single, sngZ as Single
sngX = 32.95
sngY = 15.30
sngZ = sngX + sngY
lblAnswer = "The result is" & sngZ
```

You could perform the same calculation using the following code:

```
Const DEC_POINT = 2
Dim intX As Integer, intY As Integer, intZ As Integer
Dim strZ As String
intX = 3295
intY = 1530
intZ = intX + intY
strZ = Format$(intZ)
lblAnswer = "Result = " &
    ➥Mid$(strZ, 1, Len(strZ) - DEC_POINT) & "." &
    ➥Mid$(strZ, Len(strZ) - (DEC_POINT - 1), DEC_POINT)
```

Note that when you're displaying the result to the user, the solution is treated as a string so that you can insert a decimal point in between the appropriate digits of the value. One way to do this is to treat the value as a string, move over to the correct digit, and insert the decimal point. The value can be represented properly by the statement

```
Mid$(strResult, 1, Len(strResult) - DEC_POINT) & "." &
Mid$(strResult, Len(strResult) - (DEC_POINT - 1), DEC_POINT)
```

where `strResult` is the result value converted into a string by the statement

```
strResult = Format$(intResult)
```

and the constant `DEC_POINT` represents the number of decimal places in the solution.

Another alternative is to simply divide the result by `10 ^ DEC_POINT` and display this result to the user as

```
lblAnswer = "Result = " & intZ / (10 ^ DEC_POINT)
```

The technique for multiplication and division can become more complicated, because the decimal place is not fixed as it is with addition and subtraction. Take, for example, the two floating-point values used in the previous example. If you were to multiply those two values, you would obtain the following solution:

```
   32.95
x  15.30
  504.1350
```

Similarly, if you were to multiply the two integers, you would obtain the solution

```
   3295
 x 1530
5041350
```

In this case, the floating-point solution now has four digits to the right of the decimal point. You can apply the following rule for floating-point multiplication: *When any set of numbers is being multiplied, the resultant value has a number of digits to the right of the decimal point equal to the sum of the number of digits to the right of the decimal point for each value being multiplied.* The solution, in this case, has four digits to the right of the decimal point because each number being multiplied has two digits to the right of the decimal. When carrying out the program to handle the numbers using integers, you could write code as

```
Const DEC_POINT = 4
Dim lngX As Long, lngY As Long, lngZ As Long
Dim strZ As String
lngX = 3295
lngY = 1530
lngZ = lngX * lngY
strZ = Format$(lngZ)
lblAnswer = "Result = " &
    ➥Mid$(strZ, 1, Len(strZ) - DEC_POINT) & "." &
    ➥Mid$(strZ, Len(strZ) - (DEC_POINT - 1), DEC_POINT)
```

To write this code, you must know beforehand how many decimal places are in the two numbers being multiplied.

Division is the most complicated case of all. If you were to divide these floating-point values using floating-point division, you would obtain the solution

```
   32.95
÷  15.30
    2.154
```

but you would obtain the following solution using integers and integer division:

```
  3295
÷ 1530
     2
```

Because integer division does not allow for decimal points, you lose the information that would normally go to the right of the decimal point. In cases when you must divide two floating-point numbers, you can instead multiply the numerator by the inverse of the denominator. You could calculate 1/15.30 as 0.06536 and multiply the two values, like this:

```
  32.95
x  0.06536
   2.1536120
```

If you were to do integer multiplication here, you would have

```
    3295
  x 6536
21536120
```

Because the first floating-point value has two values to the right of the decimal point and the second value has five digits to the right of the decimal point, you must represent the value with seven digits to the right of the decimal point, or 2.1536120. This can be performed using code as

```
Const DP = 7
Dim lngX As Long, lngY As Long, lngZ As Long
Dim strZ As String
lngX = 3295
lngY = 6536
lngZ = lngX * lngY
strZ = Format$(lngZ)
lblAnswer = "Result = " & Mid$(strZ, 1, Len(strZ) - DP) &
            ➥"." & Mid$(strZ, Len(strZ) - (DP - 1), DP)
```

in order to properly represent the result.

Another technique for using integers to represent floating-point data is to temporarily ignore the decimal point and use integer math until the value must be stored. At that point, the value can be divided and stored in a floating-point form. Consider, for example, a case in which you wanted to take 45 percent of 60. Using floating-point math, you could multiply 0.45 by 60. Using this integer technique, however, you could simply multiply 45 by 60 and store the result in an integer. When you want to store the result, you can simply divide by 100 and store the result in a floating-point variable. The following is an example of doing this in code:

```
Dim intBase as Integer
Dim intPercent as Integer
Dim intResult as Integer
Dim sngResult as Single

intBase = 60
intPercent = 45
intResult = intBase * intPercent

sngResult = intResult / 100
```

If you need this calculation to be performed only once, it might be easier to use floating-point variables. If, on the other hand, you will use the result in other calculations, the integer form of the result could be used for further integer math and the final result could be stored as a floating-point value later.

Using Variants for Mathematical Operations

In the MthCmp32.exe application introduced earlier, the variant was one of the data types compared. The variants were assigned the following integer values:

```
varX1 = 4: varX2 = 2: varX3 = 0
```

and the solution for the addition subroutine was calculated as

```
For lngLoop = 1 To lngLoopCount
    varX3 = varX1 + varX2
Next
```

As described in Chapter 9, variants can represent data in various data types. The interpreter variant takes the values assigned to a variant and converts and stores them in the variant variable in the format that makes the most sense for the data at hand. Note that in this case, the variants `varX1` and `varX2` represent the data to which they are assigned in the most efficient manner available, by converting the values to integers. This can be verified by using the Visual Basic `VarType` function after the original assignment statements. In doing so, it is reasonable to expect that the addition that gets carried out with these variants is a simple integer addition. You would expect, therefore, that the execution time to carry out this addition would be roughly equivalent to addition with the integer data type. Likewise, you would expect the result to be stored as an integer in the result variant type. Table 10.4 shows which data type the interpreter uses to represent each variant result, based on the data type of its originally assigned operands. The type of the variant result can be verified with the `VarType` function.

Table 10.4. The interpreter's conversions of the variant data type when integer values are assigned to operands in arithmetic operations.

Operation	`varX1`		`varX2`		`varX3`
Addition	Int	+	Int	=	Int
Subtraction	Int	-	Int	=	Int
Multiplication	Int	*	Int	=	Int
FP Division	Int	/	Int	=	Double
Int Division	Int	\	Int	=	Long
Exponent	Int	^	Int	=	Double
Modulo	Int	Mod	Int	=	Long

As you can see, the two variables being added and the result variable, even though they are variants, are all treated as though they have integer-based data types, with the exception of the floating-point division and the exponent operators. As you may recall, it was pointed out earlier in the chapter that both of these operations always return floating-point results. You would expect, therefore, the timings for each of the operations that use variants but return integer-based data to be roughly equivalent to the timings where the native data types are used. Look at Table 10.5, however, and notice that the execution times are significantly greater for variants than they are for the native integer-based data types.

Table 10.5. Normalized execution times for variant integer-based arithmetic operations versus other types.

Data Type	+	-	*	/	\	^	Mod
Variant	1.00	1.00	1.00	1.00	1.00	1.00	1.00
Integer	0.48	0.49	0.52	0.53	0.32	0.80	0.33
Long	0.48	0.49	0.50	0.54	0.38	0.80	0.37
Byte	0.50	0.50	0.53	0.56	0.30	0.81	N/A
Single	0.49	0.50	0.48	0.38	0.62	0.77	0.63
Double	0.57	0.56	0.53	0.41	0.66	0.74	0.66
Currency	0.54	0.53	0.80	0.66	0.90	0.83	0.88

As you can see from Table 10.5, in *every* case where you'd expect the performance of the variant to be close to the integer, the execution time for the integer is significantly less than the variant. For addition, subtraction, and multiplication there is almost 108 percent more time required for the variant than for the integer. But for integer division and the `mod` operators, the percentages jump way up to 208 percent and 201 percent, respectively. You saw in Chapter 9 the importance of avoiding the general use of the variant data type; when applying mathematical operations to variants, you again see the benefit of avoiding them whenever possible.

TIP: Avoid using the variant data type in mathematical operations whenever possible.

Using Currency for Mathematical Operations

We will now take a look at currency math. In Chapter 9, you observed the increase in execution time that results from the use of the currency data type. This chapter applies arithmetic operators to the currency type, highlights its execution time, and compares it to the other data types. The results presented in Figure 10.1 are summarized with respect to the currency data type in Table 10.6.

Table 10.6. Normalized execution times for currency versus other data types.

Data Type	+	-	*	/	\	^	Mod
Currency	1.00	1.00	1.00	1.00	1.00	1.00	1.00
Integer	0.90	0.91	0.65	0.81	0.36	0.96	0.96

continues

Table 10.6. continued

Data Type	+	-	*	/	\	^	Mod
Long	0.90	0.91	0.63	0.82	0.42	0.96	0.96
Byte	0.93	0.95	0.66	0.85	0.34	0.97	0.97
Single	0.91	0.93	0.59	0.58	0.70	0.93	0.93
Double	1.07	1.05	0.66	0.62	0.74	0.89	0.89
Variant	1.86	1.88	1.24	1.52	1.12	1.20	1.20

The results show that, when adding or subtracting, the currency data type is slower than any other data type except the variant and double. The results again illustrate the benefit of avoiding the currency data type whenever possible. Of particular interest, however, is the amount of additional time it takes to perform a math operation on the integer data type. Notice, for example, that it takes about 51 percent longer to perform a multiplication between two currency variables than it does between two integer variables. Thus, if you can use the integer, long, or byte data type in place of the currency data type, you will avoid a significant increase in execution time.

TIP: Avoid using the currency data type in mathematical operations whenever possible.

Multiplication Versus Division

Now that you've seen how to use variables with the math operators, it's time to focus on the arithmetic operators and mathematical functions themselves. This section compares multiplication to division, regardless of data type. Consider the MthCmp32.exe application introduced at the beginning of the chapter. Table 10.7 summarizes the results of the multiplication and division operations for each data type.

Table 10.7. Normalized times for multiplication versus division.

Data Type	*Multiplication*	*Floating-Point Division*	*Integer Division*
Integer	1.00	1.80	1.15
Long	1.00	1.88	1.39
Byte	1.00	1.85	1.07
Single	1.00	1.41	2.43
Double	1.00	1.35	2.32

Data Type	Multiplication	Floating-Point Division	Integer Division
Currency	1.00	1.43	2.07
Variant	1.00	1.75	1.86

Note that in every case, multiplication is faster than either floating-point or integer division. Because multiplication is faster than division, it is obviously preferable to multiply rather than divide whenever possible. Notice also that integer division using variables of the integer data type can actually be faster than floating-point division using floating-point variables. If the two values being divided are of the integer data type, and the result is to be an integer, integer division will be faster than floating-point division. In most cases, however, when dividing two quantities, you need to use floating-point math because a decimal number can result. Therefore, use integer division only when you don't need or won't get a remainder (that is, a decimal value).

In this section, assume that you cannot accept an integer result and that you must take decimal numbers into account. In such a case, you should consider multiplying by the reciprocal of the divisor rather than simply dividing the two values. Consider the application whose main form is shown in Figure 10.2. The application, MltDiv32.exe, is on the CD-ROM that accompanies this book.

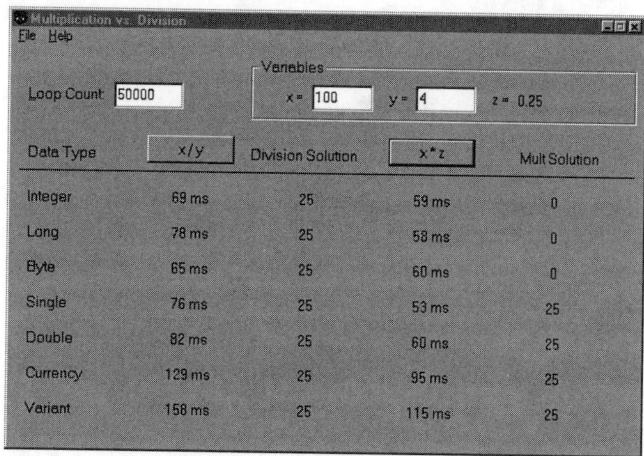

Figure 10.2.
The main form of the MltDiv32 application comparing multiplication and division.

This application takes, for each data type shown, the value x and divides it by the variable y in the first test. The second test multiplies x by z, the inverse of y. The code used to accomplish these operations is shown in the following code examples. First, see Listing 10.2 for the subroutine that performs the division operations.

Listing 10.2. Simple division.

```
Private Sub cmdDivide_Click()

    Dim i&      ' Long integer index

    ' Define the variables
    Dim intX As Integer, intY As Integer, intAns As Integer
    Dim lngX As Long, lngY As Long, lngAns As Long
    Dim bytX As Byte, bytY As Byte, bytAns As Byte
    Dim sngX As Single, sngY As Single, sngAns As Single
    Dim dblX As Double, dblY As Double, dblAns As Double
    Dim curX As Currency, curY As Currency, curAns As Currency
    Dim varX As Variant, VarY As Variant, varAns As Variant

    ' Assign values to the variables
    intX = txtX
    lngX = txtX
    bytX = txtX
    sngX = txtX
    dblX = txtX
    curX = txtX
    varX = txtX
    intY = txtY
    lngY = txtY
    bytY = txtY
    sngY = txtY
    dblY = txtY
    curY = txtY
    VarY = txtY

    lblZ = "N/A"

    ' Integer Division
    Call Common_StartTimedTest
    For i& = 1 To txtLoopCount                  ' Perform the integer calculation
        intAns = intX \ intY
    Next
    Call Common_EndTimedTest(lblDiv(0))
    lblAns(0) = intAns                              ' Display the result

    ' Long Division
    Call Common_StartTimedTest
    For i& = 1 To txtLoopCount                  ' Perform the long calculation
        lngAns = lngX \ lngY
    Next
    Call Common_EndTimedTest(lblDiv(1))
    lblAns(1) = lngAns                              ' Display the result


    ' Byte Division
    Call Common_StartTimedTest
    For i& = 1 To txtLoopCount                  ' Perform the byte calculation
        bytAns = bytX \ bytY
    Next
    Call Common_EndTimedTest(lblDiv(2))
    lblAns(2) = lngAns                              ' Display the result
```

```
    ' Single Division
    Call Common_StartTimedTest
    For i& = 1 To txtLoopCount                          ' Perform the single calculation
        sngAns = sngX / sngY
    Next
    Call Common_EndTimedTest(lblDiv(3))
    lblAns(3) = sngAns                                      ' Display the result

    ' Double Division
    Call Common_StartTimedTest
    For i& = 1 To txtLoopCount                          ' Perform the double calculation
        dblAns = dblX / dblY
    Next
    Call Common_EndTimedTest(lblDiv(4))
    lblAns(4) = dblAns                                      ' Display the result

    ' Currency Division
    Call Common_StartTimedTest
    For i& = 1 To txtLoopCount                          ' Perform the currency calculation
        curAns = curX / curY
    Next
    Call Common_EndTimedTest(lblDiv(5))
    lblAns(5) = curAns                                      ' Display the result

    ' Variant Division
    Call Common_StartTimedTest
    For i& = 1 To txtLoopCount                          ' Perform the variant calculation
        varAns = varX / varY
    Next
    Call Common_EndTimedTest(lblDiv(6))
    lblAns(6) = varAns                                      ' Display the result

End Sub
```

Notice that, in the case of the integer, long, and byte data types, the integer division operator is used. For all other data types, the floating-point division operator is used. The two division operators are used with the appropriate data types to make the divisions as efficient as possible. Because you are comparing multiplication to division, this makes each arithmetic operation as efficient as possible for each data type. Now look at Listing 10.3 for the inverse multiplication.

Listing 10.3. Inverse multiplication.

```
Private Sub cmdMultiply_Click()

    Dim i&       ' Long integer index

    ' Define the variables
    Dim intX As Integer, intZ As Integer, intAns As Integer
    Dim lngX As Long, lngZ As Long, lngAns As Long
    Dim sngX As Single, sngZ As Single, sngAns As Single
```

continues

Listing 10.3. continued

```
    Dim dblX As Double, dblZ As Double, dblAns As Double
    Dim bytX As Byte, bytZ As Byte, bytAns As Byte
    Dim curX As Currency, curZ As Currency, curAns As Currency
    Dim varX As Variant, varZ As Variant, varAns As Variant

lblZ = 1 / txtY

    ' Assign values to the variables
    intX = txtX
    lngX = txtX
    bytX = txtX
    sngX = txtX
    dblX = txtX
    curX = txtX
    varX = txtX
    intZ = lblZ
    lngZ = lblZ
    bytZ = lblZ
    sngZ = lblZ
    dblZ = lblZ
    curZ = lblZ
    varZ = lblZ

    ' Integer Reciprocal Multiplication
    Call Common_StartTimedTest
    For i& = 1 To txtLoopCount                    ' Perform the integer calculation
        intAns = intX * intZ
    Next
    Call Common_EndTimedTest(lblMul(0))
    lblAns(7) = intAns                                ' Display the result


    ' Long Reciprocal Multiplication
    Call Common_StartTimedTest
    For i& = 1 To txtLoopCount                    ' Perform the long calculation
        lngAns = lngX * lngZ
    Next
    Call Common_EndTimedTest(lblMul(1))
    lblAns(8) = lngAns                                ' Display the result


    ' Byte Reciprocal Multiplication
    Call Common_StartTimedTest
    For i& = 1 To txtLoopCount                    ' Perform the byte calculation
        bytAns = bytX * bytZ
    Next
    Call Common_EndTimedTest(lblMul(2))
    lblAns(9) = sngAns                                ' Display the result


    ' Single Reciprocal Multiplication
    Call Common_StartTimedTest
    For i& = 1 To txtLoopCount                    ' Perform the single calculation
        sngAns = sngX * sngZ
    Next
```

```
    Call Common_EndTimedTest(lblMul(3))
    lblAns(10) = sngAns                              ' Display the result


    ' Double Reciprocal Multiplication
    Call Common_StartTimedTest
    For i& = 1 To txtLoopCount                    ' Perform the double calculation
        dblAns = dblX * dblZ
    Next
    Call Common_EndTimedTest(lblMul(4))
    lblAns(11) = dblAns                              ' Display the result


    ' Currency Reciprocal Multiplication
    Call Common_StartTimedTest
    For i& = 1 To txtLoopCount                    ' Perform the currency calculation
        curAns = curX * curZ
    Next
    Call Common_EndTimedTest(lblMul(5))
    lblAns(12) = curAns                              ' Display the result


    ' Variant Reciprocal Multiplication
    Call Common_StartTimedTest
    For i& = 1 To txtLoopCount                    ' Perform the variant calculation
        varAns = varX * varZ
    Next
    Call Common_EndTimedTest(lblMul(6))
    lblAns(13) = varAns                              ' Display the result

End Sub
```

The normalized results of this application are shown in Table 10.8. As you can see from the table, inverse multiplication is faster than division for every data type tested.

Table 10.8. Normalized times for inverse multiplication versus division.

Data Type	*Multiplication of Inverse*	*Division*
Integer	1.00	1.16
Long	1.00	1.34
Byte	1.00	1.08
Single	1.00	1.43
Double	1.00	1.37
Currency	1.00	1.36
Variant	1.00	1.37

In the inverse multiplication subroutine, notice that the inverse of variable y is calculated only once outside the loop. This is because the program was written assuming that you will know ahead of time what number to use as the divisor. Suppose, for example, that this division procedure is part of an application that calculates a fraction of a salary to compute taxes. In this case, suppose you wanted to calculate 25 percent of the worker's salary. You could do this either by multiplying by 0.25 or by dividing by 4. You cannot predict ahead of time what the salary, or x, will be, but you do know the value of y.

If the value of either variable is not known at design time, you would have no choice but to divide y into 1 to obtain the inverse value. In such a case, you are no further ahead. If, on the other hand, you know y ahead of time, you can put the inverse directly into code without having to calculate it. In this case, the values of the variables can be changed by the user, so you do have to take the inverse of y.

Also keep in mind that if your program is going to repeatedly divide by the same number, it might be worthwhile to take the reciprocal of the number once in code and use that value from then on to multiply instead of divide. If you only multiply by the inverse once, you are no better off, but if you can multiply by the inverse of the same number many times in an application rather than divide the two values several times, you should come out ahead. Consider, for example, the subroutine in Listing 10.4, where repeated divisions of the same two numbers take place.

Listing 10.4. Performing several divisions in a subroutine.

```
Sub GetResults()

    Dim A as Single
    Dim B as Single
    Dim C as Single
    Dim D as Single

    Dim Y as Single

    Dim sngResultA as Single
    Dim sngResultB as Single
    Dim sngResultC as Single
    Dim sngResultD as Single

    ' Get the values from text boxes on a form
    A = txtA
    B = txtB
    C = txtC
    D = txtD
    Y = txtY

    ' Calculate A/Y
    sngResult = A/Y
    txtResult = sngResult

    ' Calculate B/Y
```

```
    sngResult = B/Y
    txtResult = sngResult

    ' Calculate C/Y
    sngResult = C/Y
    txtResult = sngResult

    ' Calculate D/Y
    sngResult = D/Y
    txtResult = sngResult

End Sub
```

Notice that the four values must be divided by the same number. In this case, it would be preferable to take the inverse of Y and multiply it in all four cases. This method is shown in Listing 10.5.

Listing 10.5. Performing several inverse multiplications in a subroutine.

```
Sub GetResults()

    Dim A as Single
    Dim B as Single
    Dim C as Single
    Dim D as Single

    Dim Y as Single

    ' Define a new variable to store the inverse
    Dim Z as Single

    Dim sngResultA as Single
    Dim sngResultB as Single
    Dim sngResultC as Single
    Dim sngResultD as Single

    ' Get the values from text boxes on a form
    A = txtA
    B = txtB
    C = txtC
    D = txtD
    Y = txtY

    ' This time, calculate the inverse of Y
    Z = 1/Y

    ' Calculate A*Z
    sngResult = A*Z
    txtResult = sngResult

    ' Calculate B*Z
    sngResult = B*Z
    txtResult = sngResult
```

continues

Listing 10.5. continued

```
    ' Calculate C*Z
    sngResult = C*Z
    txtResult = sngResult

    ' Calculate D*Z
    sngResult = D*Z
    txtResult = sngResult

End Sub
```

All the changes are shown in boldface type. In this case, you are substituting four floating-point divisions with one floating-point division and four integer multiplications. You will compare the performance in an exercise at the end of the chapter.

As you have seen, it is faster to multiply by the inverse of a value than to divide by it. Whenever you must perform multiple divisions with the same divisor, take the inverse of the divisor and multiply by it instead. The more divisions you carry out, the greater savings you will obtain.

> **TIP:** Use multiplication instead of division whenever possible.

Performance and the Exponent Operator

The next two sections both investigate the most efficient use of the exponent operator. The first section explores the use of the exponent operator versus simply multiplying the same value by itself in a loop when possible. The second section explores the use of the exponent versus the square root, or `Sqr` function.

Simple Multiplication Versus the Exponent Operator

This section considers using the exponent operator as opposed to performing repeat multiplications in a loop. The applicability of using multiplication in a loop is restricted to the case in which the exponent is a positive integer. In such cases, rather than using the expression

```
y = x^n
```

you can use the expression

```
y = x*x*x*x ... *x
```

where you multiply the variable `x` a total of `n` times. This can also be performed in a loop, as follows:

```
y = 1
For counter = 1 to n
    y = y * x
Next counter
```

The application in this section, MltExp32.exe, enables you to set the value n and specify the value of x, comparing the multiplication loop versus the exponent for every data type. MltExp32.exe is on the CD-ROM that accompanies this book. A 16-bit version of the program, MltExp16.exe, is also available on the CD-ROM. The main form is shown in Figure 10.3.

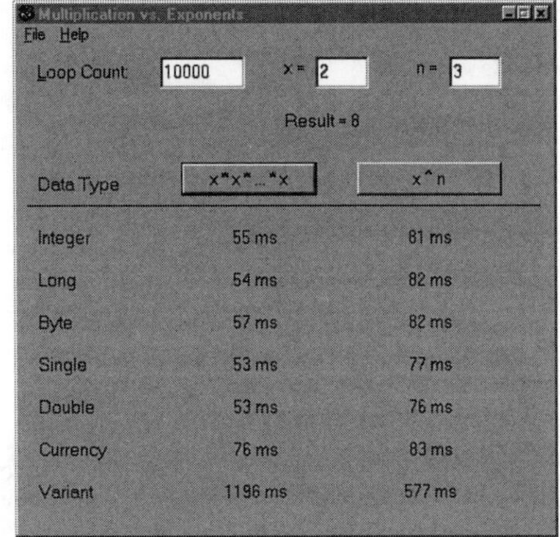

Figure 10.3.
The main form of the MltExp32 application, which compares the exponent operator to repeated multiplications.

The two command buttons carry out the operations indicated in their captions. First, the loop multiplication case is shown in Listing 10.6.

Listing 10.6. Repeat multiplication of variable x.

```
Private Sub cmdMultiply_Click()

    Dim i&       ' Long Index
    Dim j%       ' Integer Index

    ' Define the variables
    Dim intN As Integer
    Dim intX As Integer, intAns As Integer
    Dim lngX As Long, lngAns As Long
    Dim bytX As Byte, bytAns As Byte
    Dim sngX As Single, sngAns As Single
    Dim dblX As Double, dblAns As Double
    Dim curX As Currency, curAns As Currency
    Dim varX As Variant, varAns As Variant

    ' Assign the exponent variable
    intN = txtN
```

continues

Listing 10.6. continued

```
    ' Assign the base variables
    intX = txtX
    lngX = txtX
    bytX = txtX
    sngX = txtX
    dblX = txtX
    curX = txtX
    varX = txtX

    ' First, make sure that the result is not larger than the
    ' integer data type.  If the solution is greater than
    ' 32,767, the integer operation is skipped.
If intX ^ intN > 32767 Then
        lblMult(0) = "N/A"
    Else
        ' Integer Multiplication
        Call Common_StartTimedTest
        For i& = 1 To txtLoopCount           ' integer calculation
            intAns = 1
            For j% = 1 To intN
                intAns = intAns * intX
            Next
        Next
        Call Common_EndTimedTest(lblMult(0))
    End If


    ' First, make sure that the result is not larger than
    ' the long data type.  If the solution is greater than
    ' 2,147,483,647, the long operation is skipped.
    If lngX ^ intN > 2147483647 Then
        lblMult(1) = "N/A"
    Else
        ' Long Multiplication
        Call Common_StartTimedTest
        For i& = 1 To txtLoopCount            ' long calculation
            lngAns = 1
            For j% = 1 To intN
                lngAns = lngAns * lngX
            Next
        Next
        Call Common_EndTimedTest(lblMult(1))
    End If

    ' First, make sure that the result is not larger than
    ' the byte data type.  If the solution is greater than
    ' 255, the byte operation is skipped.
    If bytX ^ intN > 255 Then
        lblMult(2) = "N/A"
    Else
        ' Byte Multiplication
        Call Common_StartTimedTest
        For i& = 1 To txtLoopCount            ' byte calculation
            bytAns = 1
            For j% = 1 To intN
                bytAns = bytAns * bytX
```

```
            Next
        Next
        Call Common_EndTimedTest(lblMult(2))
    End If


    ' Single Multiplication
    Call Common_StartTimedTest
    For i& = 1 To txtLoopCount                  ' single calculation
        sngAns = 1
        For j% = 1 To intN
            sngAns = sngAns * sngX
        Next
    Next
    Call Common_EndTimedTest(lblMult(3))


    ' Double multiplication
    Call Common_StartTimedTest
    For i& = 1 To txtLoopCount                  ' double calculation
        dblAns = 1
        For j% = 1 To intN
            dblAns = dblAns * dblX
        Next
    Next
    Call Common_EndTimedTest(lblMult(4))


    ' Currency multiplication
    Call Common_StartTimedTest
    For i& = 1 To txtLoopCount                  ' currency calculation
        curAns = 1
        For j% = 1 To intN
            curAns = curAns * curX
        Next
    Next
    Call Common_EndTimedTest(lblMult(5))


    ' Variant multiplication
    Call Common_StartTimedTest
    For i& = 1 To txtLoopCount                  ' variant calculation
        varAns = 1
        For j% = 1 To intN
            varAns = varAns * varX
        Next
    Next
    Call Common_EndTimedTest(lblMult(6))

    lblAns = "Result = " & dblAns               ' Display the result

End Sub
```

In Listing 10.6, the repeat multiplication is applied to each data type. Now consider the exponent case, shown in Listing 10.7.

Listing 10.7. Exponent operator on variable X.

```
Private Sub cmdExponent_Click()

    Dim i&        ' Long index

    ' Define the exponent variable
    Dim intN As Integer

    ' Define the variables
    Dim intAns As Integer, intX As Integer
    Dim lngAns As Long, lngX As Long
    Dim bytAns As Byte, bytX As Byte
    Dim sngAns As Single, sngX As Single
    Dim dblAns As Double, dblX As Double
    Dim curAns As Currency, curX As Currency
    Dim varAns As Variant, varX As Variant

    ' Set the exponent value
    intN = txtN

    ' Assign values to the variables
    intX = txtX
    lngX = txtX
    bytX = txtX
    sngX = txtX
    dblX = txtX
    curX = txtX
    varX = txtX

    ' First, make sure that the result is not larger than
    ' the integer data type.  If the solution is greater than
    ' 32,767, the integer operation is skipped.
    If intX ^ intN > 32767 Then
        lblExp(0) = "N/A"
    Else
        ' Integer Exponent Calculation
        Call Common_StartTimedTest
        For i& = 1 To txtLoopCount          ' integer calculation
            intAns = intX ^ intN
        Next
        Call Common_EndTimedTest(lblExp(0))
    End If

    ' First, make sure that the result is not larger than
    ' the long data type.  If the solution is greater than
    ' 2,147,483,647, the long operation is skipped.
    If lngX ^ intN > 2147483647 Then
        lblExp(1) = "N/A"
    Else
        ' Long Exponent Calculation
        Call Common_StartTimedTest
        For i& = 1 To txtLoopCount          ' long calculation
            lngAns = lngX ^ intN
        Next
        Call Common_EndTimedTest(lblExp(1))
    End If
```

```
    ' First, make sure that the result is not larger than
    ' the byte data type. If the solution is greater than
    ' 255, the byte operation is skipped.
    If bytX ^ intN > 255 Then
        lblExp(2) = "N/A"
    Else
        ' Byte Exponent Calculation
        Call Common_StartTimedTest
        For i& = 1 To txtLoopCount          ' byte calculation
            bytAns = bytX ^ intN
        Next
        Call Common_EndTimedTest(lblExp(2))
    End If


    ' Single Exponent Calculation
    Call Common_StartTimedTest
    For i& = 1 To txtLoopCount              ' single calculation
        sngAns = sngX ^ intN
    Next
    Call Common_EndTimedTest(lblExp(3))


    ' Double Exponent Calculation
    Call Common_StartTimedTest
    For i& = 1 To txtLoopCount              ' double calculation
        dblAns = dblX ^ intN
    Next
    Call Common_EndTimedTest(lblExp(4))


    ' Currency Exponent Calculation
    Call Common_StartTimedTest
    For i& = 1 To txtLoopCount              ' currency calculation
        curAns = curX ^ intN
    Next
    Call Common_EndTimedTest(lblExp(5))


    ' Variant Exponent Calculation
    Call Common_StartTimedTest
    For i& = 1 To txtLoopCount              ' variant calculation
        varAns = varX ^ intN
    Next
    Call Common_EndTimedTest(lblExp(6))

    lblAns = "Result = " & dblAns           ' Display the result
End Sub
```

Notice that in the case of the integer data types, the result is first checked to see if the range of the integer, long, or byte data types is exceeded. If so, the applicable calculations are skipped. In such a manner, the floating-point data types can still be tested. A run of this application with x = 2 and n = 3 yields the results shown in Figure 10.3. The normalized execution times are summarized in Table 10.9.

Table 10.9. Normalized times for multiplication versus exponents, n = 3.

Data Type	*Multiplication*	*Exponent Operator*
Integer	1.03	1.53
Long	1.02	1.55
Byte	1.08	1.55
Single	1.00	1.43
Double	1.00	1.43
Currency	1.43	1.57
Variant	22.57	10.89

Notice that simple multiplication seems to be faster than the exponent operator (with the exception of the variant data type). Watch what happens, however, as the exponent value is increased from 3 to 10. The normalized results are shown in Table 10.10.

Table 10.10. Normalized times for multiplication versus exponents, n = 10.

Data Type	*Multiplication*	*Exponent Operator*
Integer	1.81	1.07
Long	1.76	1.07
Byte	N/A*	N/A*
Single	1.71	1.01
Double	1.71	1.00
Currency	2.57	1.09
Variant	52.36	8.15

*The resultant value is beyond the range for this data type.

This time, the results are quite different. In every case, the exponent operator is faster. As the value of n increases, so does this trend. Note, for example, the normalized execution times for the application when n = 20, which are shown in Table 10.11.

Table 10.11. Normalized times for multiplication versus exponents, n = 20.

Data Type	*Multiplication*	*Exponent Operator*
Integer	N/A*	N/A*
Long	3.27	1.01
Byte	N/A*	N/A*

Data Type	*Multiplication*	*Exponent Operator*
Single	3.11	1.00
Double	3.01	1.01
Currency	4.90	1.11
Variant	104.51	8.16

*The resultant value is beyond the range for this data type.

In this case, the results are even more dramatic. Notice the tremendously large decrease in execution time for the variant—over 1,207 percent! As you have seen throughout this and the previous chapter, the variant adds a great deal of overhead to the operation and should be avoided for mathematical operations unless absolutely necessary.

The results demonstrate that simple multiplication is only beneficial when you're multiplying two or three times. If you do have a situation in which you simply have to multiply a few times, you could potentially code each multiplication in the same statement, avoiding the need for a loop and improving the performance time of this technique even further. After a few multiplications, however, the exponent operator is faster than multiplication. Fortunately, it is also easier to use and implement, because it does not require a loop like multiplication does for multiplications of more than a few powers. As a general rule, you should use the exponent operator unless you are multiplying a value just two or three times in your code.

> **TIP:** The exponent operator becomes increasingly better than multiplication in a loop as the exponent value increases.

The *Sqr()* Function Versus the Exponent Operator

The last section in this chapter compares the `Sqr` function to the exponent operator. The `Sqr` function is written in the form `Sqr(x)`, where Visual Basic takes the square root of the value represented by `x`. The alternative approach is to use the exponent 0.5, that is, `x^0.5`, which is equivalent to taking the square root. In this section, an application is presented that takes both approaches and shows the timing results of each approach. The application, SqrExp32.exe, is on the CD-ROM that accompanies this book. The 16-bit version of this program, SqrExp32.exe, is also available on the CD-ROM. The application's main form is shown in Figure 10.4.

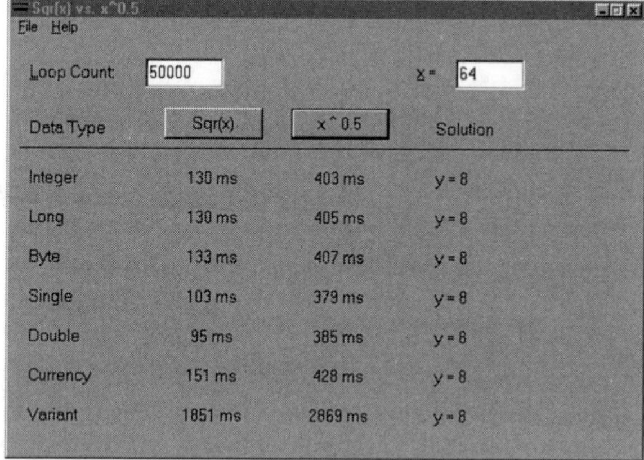

Figure 10.4.
The main form of the SqrExp32 application, which compares the performance of using the square root function to using the exponent operator.

The subroutine for the square root function is shown in Listing 10.8.

Listing 10.8. Using the square root function.

```
Private Sub cmdSqrt_Click()

    Dim i&      ' Long integer index

    ' Define the variables
    Dim intX1 As Integer, intX2 As Integer
    Dim lngX1 As Long, lngX2 As Long
    Dim bytX1 As Byte, bytX2 As Byte
    Dim sngX1 As Single, sngX2 As Single
    Dim dblX1 As Double, dblX2 As Double
    Dim curX1 As Currency, curX2 As Currency
    Dim varX1 As Variant, varX2 As Variant

    ' Assign values to the variables
    intX1 = txtX
    lngX1 = txtX
    bytX1 = txtX
    sngX1 = txtX
    dblX1 = txtX
    curX1 = txtX
    varX1 = txtX


    ' Integer Square Root Calculation
    Call Common_StartTimedTest
    For i& = 1 To txtLoopCount            ' Integer calculation
        intX2 = Sqr(intX1)
    Next
    Call Common_EndTimedTest(lblSqr(0))
    lblX(0) = "y = " & intX2              ' Display the result


    ' Long Square Root Calculation
    Call Common_StartTimedTest
```

```
    For i& = 1 To txtLoopCount                  ' Long calculation
        lngX2 = Sqr(lngX1)
    Next
    Call Common_EndTimedTest(lblSqr(1))
    lblX(1) = "y = " & lngX2                    ' Display the result

    ' Byte Square Root Calculation
    Call Common_StartTimedTest
    For i& = 1 To txtLoopCount                  ' Long calculation
        bytX2 = Sqr(bytX1)
    Next
    Call Common_EndTimedTest(lblSqr(2))
    lblX(2) = "y = " & lngX2                    ' Display the result

    ' Single Square Root Calculation
    Call Common_StartTimedTest
    For i& = 1 To txtLoopCount                  ' Single calculation
        sngX2 = Sqr(sngX1)
    Next
    Call Common_EndTimedTest(lblSqr(3))
    lblX(3) = "y = " & sngX2                    ' Display the result

    ' Double Square Root Calculation
    Call Common_StartTimedTest
    For i& = 1 To txtLoopCount                  ' Double calculation
        dblX2 = Sqr(dblX1)
    Next
    Call Common_EndTimedTest(lblSqr(4))
    lblX(4) = "y = " & dblX2                    ' Display the result

    ' Currency Square Root Calculation
    Call Common_StartTimedTest
    For i& = 1 To txtLoopCount                  ' Currency calculation
        curX2 = Sqr(curX1)
    Next
    Call Common_EndTimedTest(lblSqr(5))
    lblX(5) = "y = " & curX2                    ' Display the result

    ' Variant Square Root Calculation
    Call Common_StartTimedTest
    For i& = 1 To txtLoopCount                  ' Variant calculation
        varX2 = Sqr(varX1)
    Next
    Call Common_EndTimedTest(lblSqr(6))
    lblX(6) = "y = " & varX2                    ' Display the result

End Sub
```

As with all the programs presented in this chapter, you can change the loop count in order to obtain meaningful timing results. The exponent code is presented in Listing 10.9.

Listing 10.9. Using the exponent operator.

```
Private Sub cmdExponent_Click()

    Dim i&      ' Long integer index

    ' Define the variables
    Dim intX1 As Integer, intX2 As Integer
    Dim lngX1 As Long, lngX2 As Long
    Dim bytX1 As Byte, bytX2 As Byte
    Dim sngX1 As Single, sngX2 As Single
    Dim dblX1 As Double, dblX2 As Double
    Dim curX1 As Currency, curX2 As Currency
    Dim varX1 As Variant, varX2 As Variant

    ' Assign values to the variables
    intX1 = txtX
    lngX1 = txtX
    bytX1 = txtX
    sngX1 = txtX
    dblX1 = txtX
    curX1 = txtX
    varX1 = txtX


    ' Integer Exponent Calculation
    Call Common_StartTimedTest
    For i& = 1 To txtLoopCount          ' Integer calculation
        intX2 = intX1 ^ 0.5
    Next
    Call Common_EndTimedTest(lblExp(0))
    lblX(0) = "y = " & intX2            ' Display the result


    ' Long Exponent Calculation
    Call Common_StartTimedTest
    For i& = 1 To txtLoopCount          ' Long calculation
        lngX2 = lngX1 ^ 0.5
    Next
    Call Common_EndTimedTest(lblExp(1))
    lblX(1) = "y = " & lngX2            ' Display the result


    ' Byte Exponent Calculation
    Call Common_StartTimedTest
    For i& = 1 To txtLoopCount          ' Byte calculation
        bytX2 = bytX1 ^ 0.5
    Next
    Call Common_EndTimedTest(lblExp(2))
    lblX(2) = "y = " & bytX2            ' Display the result


    ' Single Exponent Calculation
    Call Common_StartTimedTest
    For i& = 1 To txtLoopCount          ' Single calculation
        sngX2 = sngX1 ^ 0.5
    Next
    Call Common_EndTimedTest(lblExp(3))
    lblX(3) = "y = " & sngX2            ' Display the result
```

```
    ' Double Exponent Calculation
    Call Common_StartTimedTest
    For i& = 1 To txtLoopCount              ' Double calculation
        dblX2 = dblX1 ^ 0.5
    Next
    Call Common_EndTimedTest(lblExp(4))
    lblX(4) = "y = " & dblX2                ' Display the result

    ' Currency Exponent Calculation
    Call Common_StartTimedTest
    For i& = 1 To txtLoopCount              ' Currency calculation
        curX2 = curX1 ^ 0.5
    Next
    Call Common_EndTimedTest(lblExp(5))
    lblX(5) = "y = " & curX2                ' Display the result

    ' Variant Exponent Calculation
    Call Common_StartTimedTest
    For i& = 1 To txtLoopCount              ' Variant calculation
        varX2 = varX1 ^ 0.5
    Next
    Call Common_EndTimedTest(lblExp(6))
    lblX(6) = "y = " & varX2                ' Display the result

End Sub
```

See Table 10.12 for the normalized results of executing the program.

Table 10.12. Normalized times for `Sqr()` versus the exponent operator.

Data Type	`Sqr(x)`	`x^0.5`
Integer	1.37	4.24
Long	1.37	4.26
Byte	1.40	4.28
Single	1.08	4.00
Double	1.00	4.05
Currency	1.59	4.50
Variant	19.48	30.20

As you can see from the table, the execution times for the exponent operator are significantly higher than when using the square root function. Therefore, whenever you need to take the square root of a number or have an exponent of 0.5, use the `Sqr()` function to improve performance.

TIP: Use the `Sqr()` function rather than the `x^0.5` exponent operator when taking the square root of a number.

Summary

This chapter looks at the various mathematical operations that can be applied to the data types introduced in Chapter 9. First, floating-point math and integer math are compared in an application that performs each basic arithmetic operation on every data type. The results show that, in most cases, the integer data types are faster than the floating-point data types. The two exceptions, floating-point division and the exponent operator, can be explained by the nature of how they perform their calculations and the data types they use; these exceptions are discussed. The chapter concludes that, whenever possible, integer math is preferable to floating-point math. You have also learned that math using the variant and currency data types is not as efficient as using the standard integer or floating-point data types.

These conclusions lead to a few techniques that enable you to use integer variables instead of floating-point variables for floating-point arithmetic. Although it is not always possible to use integers to handle floating-point math, the methods presented have the potential to dramatically improve performance. You have seen when it is or is not practical to apply the techniques presented.

This chapter also compares the multiplication operation to division and shows that multiplication is, in general, faster. As an alternative to division, the chapter presents a technique that enables you to multiply by the inverse of a value rather than perform a standard division. The technique presented can, in most cases, improve performance, but it does require that the inverse be known up front or calculated in code, which might or might not improve performance, depending on the context in which it is being applied. Again, you have seen when it is appropriate to apply the technique.

Finally, you have learned about alternatives to the exponent operator, specifically using multiplication and using the square root function versus the 0.5 exponent value. You now know that repeated multiplication of the same value to itself is usually not preferable to the exponent operator unless the variant data type is being used or the exponent—that is, the number of multiplications—is less than three. The chapter also showed a clear performance improvement when you use the `Sqr()` function in place of the exponent 0.5 when you want to take the square root of a result.

This chapter, in conjunction with Chapter 9, should give you a better idea of which data types and mathematical operators perform better and which combinations perform best. You also have several techniques to circumvent performance bottlenecks and improve the efficiency of your code.

Obey the Signs

Wrong Way: You can always replace floating-point math with integer math.

Although it is generally beneficial to replace floating-point math with integer math because dramatic improvements in execution time can result, it is not always practical or even possible to do so. In every technique presented in this chapter, there are certain limitations to consider. For example, using long integers to simulate floating-point multiplication works fine until the answer exceeds the range of the long data type. In such a case, floating-point values *must* be used. Therefore, with every method for improving performance comes a set of accompanying limitations. You must understand and be able to accept those limitations before incorporating the method into the application. If you can satisfy the constraints those limitations impose and at the same time satisfy the users, the techniques can be very beneficial.

Beware of Falling Rocks: Do not use variants where you can use specific data types instead.

The variant data type is very convenient because it enables you to ignore what type of data is being stored in it. When you're using a variant, the interpreter takes care of how to best represent the data type internally and automatically converts it when necessary. This is great for the programmer, but often not so great for the user who has to wait longer for Visual Basic to deal with the variants.

Beware of Falling Rocks: Don't automatically use the currency data type whenever you're performing financial calculations.

The currency data type has the advantage of a fixed decimal point and special rounding for monetary values. This improved functionality, however, comes at the cost of performance. In certain circumstances, it might be worth the drop in performance to use the currency operator. You must decide if the trade-off is worth it in your particular situation. What is cautioned against here, however, is the blind use of data types without recognizing and dealing with the trade-offs. You might, for instance, declare a variable with type currency merely because you want to store a salary value in that variable. This might not be necessary because you might be able to use a variable of type long to do the same thing. When performing math using the salary, you might needlessly cause a drop in performance from using the currency data type when the long would have been sufficient. The point is that you must be very careful which data types you choose. Always know why you are choosing a particular data type and how you intend to use the variable. If you don't plan to use the special features of a data type, use another data type if that type can represent the value in a more simple and efficient manner. Your users will thank you for it.

Q&A

Q Why does floating-point math take so much longer than integer math?

A Floating-point values take longer to process than integer values because of the way the computer stores floating-point numbers. Integer values are inherently natural to the computer, because the binary number system that the computer is based on is an integer number system. The binary number 0011, for example, represents the integer value 3. There is no concept of a decimal point in a binary value. Computers must simulate floating-point data by storing it and handling it in a special way. This special handling takes much more time and is another reason for a longer execution time.

Q What limitations do I have to worry about when using integer math to simulate floating-point math?

A You have seen two primary limitations in this chapter. The first limitation is the range. Floating-point values have an incredibly high range as compared to the integer, simply because they have so many more bits. If the result of a mathematical operation exceeds 32,768, the integer data type cannot be used. If the result exceeds 2,147,483,647, the long data type cannot be used. Keep in mind that if you "simulate" floating-point math using integer data types, you simply eliminate the decimal point in the calculations and keep track of the decimal point location manually. Therefore, a floating-point value of 56.230 cannot be represented by the integer data type, because the integer equivalent (removing the decimal point) is 56,230. The long data type could represent the value, but what if the floating-point value were 23,385.45535? That value, less the decimal point, would be 2,338,545,535 in integer form, which is beyond the range of the long data type. Therefore, in this case you would have to resort to floating-point values. Therefore, you must have some idea of the range of the values involved in the calculation. You must make sure the two numbers being multiplied will never be such that the solution exceeds the range of the long or integer data types, depending on which you use. Depending on the type of calculations you are performing, this restriction may be too severe and may rule out this technique.

The second limitation involves situations in which floating-point math cannot be avoided. If, for example, you must calculate an exponent using an expression such as `23^0.3`, there is no straightforward way to do so using the integer-based data types. You must resort to using the floating-point data type in such a case.

Quiz

1. Consider a case where you have two integer values that you would like to divide and assign the result to a floating-point variable. One approach would be to use the integer division operator to divide two integer values and assign the result to a single variable:

```
intZ = intX \ intY
sngZ = intZ
```

The other approach would be to divide the two integer values using the floating-point division operator and assigning the result directly to a floating-point value:

```
sngZ = intX / intY
```

Write a simple application with two command buttons, each button performing each method above, respectively. Put the operations in a loop and display the resultant timings. Which approach is faster?

(Refer to the application 1001Qz32.exe on the CD-ROM that accompanies this book for the executable and source code.)

2. Write a simple application to multiply the following two decimal values *using integer variables only.*

```
2.34 x -3.7
```

Include in your application another procedure that performs the multiplication using floating-point values. Put both operations in a loop and take timings for each. Which is faster?

(Refer to the application 10402Qz32.exe on the CD-ROM that accompanies this book for the executable and source code.)

Workshop

If you have written any applications in Visual Basic that use math, apply the techniques introduced in this chapter to improve performance. Take incremental timings of each optimization step and see which of them are more useful and practical than others.

Code Structure

As a programmer, you are faced with a steady stream of code-structure and syntax alternatives when assembling a program. In many cases, a seemingly similar group of approaches can have drastically different performance impacts. Therefore, you should carefully evaluate your code structure and syntax choices during program implementation.

Code structure is the way a program is put together, using modules, forms, procedures, and functions as building blocks. Code syntax is the specific language keywords that are used in the program. Structural decisions—such as when to use functions or subroutines, where to declare such procedures, and even the development-time considerations of running a program inside or outside the Visual Basic environment to assess performance—are often difficult to make. Likewise, Visual Basic often presents you with many equivalent syntactical choices to carry out the same task, such as using Do...While loops or For...Next loops. Choosing from among the available alternatives often comes down to a style preference, because performance insights might not seem readily apparent. However, there are times when the considerations for structured code based on good programming practice might not be the same as for structuring for maximum speed.

This chapter provides background information to help you make sound decisions in such areas. Several code structure- and syntax-related performance trade-offs are examined, including

- *Routine types*—Functions versus subroutines
- *Parameter declaration*—`ByVal` or no `ByVal`
- *Looping constructs*—`Do While` versus `For Next`
- *Selection methods*—`Select` versus `If Then ElseIf`
- *Miscellaneous topics*—Various topics such as spreading statements across multiple lines and running in (versus out of) Visual Basic

The test programs and discussions in this chapter provide you with insight into performance considerations that pertain to some of the decisions you frequently face. In addition, you can use the framework and test approach here to carry out your own, more detailed tests in virtually any area of Visual Basic structure and syntax.

Call Technique Alternatives: In-Line, Subroutines, or Functions?

The first issue to consider is one that every programmer frequently faces. When you have a block of code that is a candidate for bundling up in a separate routine, what is the cost of calling the code in that routine? Which type of procedure definition is the fastest—a subroutine, or a function? The answers to these questions can be discovered using the simple test case presented in this chapter.

A simple test program, callty32.exe, is provided on the CD-ROM that accompanies this book. The main window of this test program is shown in Figure 11.1. This program has buttons that trigger a timed test for in-line calls, function calls defined in the same module, subroutine calls defined in the same module, and subroutine calls packaged in a different module.

The code for the first button, the in-line module test, appears in Listing 11.1. You specify the number of loop iterations that will be carried out for the test. For this test, the algorithm is placed directly in the calling code, or *in line*, as opposed to packaged in a separate routine. As with all the testing methods in this book, a start time is collected in the line of code prior to the code lines we wish to assess, and an end time is collected immediately after those lines. The start time is then subtracted from the end time to derive the total time that was required to execute the loop lines of code and the algorithm within the loop.

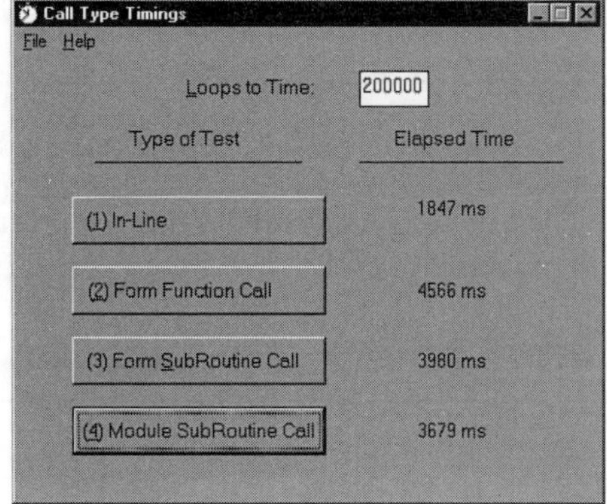

Figure 11.1.
The call technique test program.

Listing 11.1. The in-line module test button.

```
Sub cmdInLine_Click ()


Dim dblInput1 As Double        ' Contains num to use in calculations
Dim dblInput2 As Double        ' Contains num to use in calculations

Dim i&                         ' Loop counter

Call Common_StartTimedTest

For i& = 1 To txtLoops

' The sample algorithim below serves as a simple
'   example of an algorithm which takes two initial values,
'   performs calculations on them, and modifies a global variable
'   with the product of the results.

    dblInput1 = START_VALUE1

    dblInput2 = START_VALUE2

    dblInput1 = dblInput1 * 2

    dblInput2 = dblInput2 * 3

    g_dblAnswer = dblInput1 * dblInput2
```

continues

Listing 11.1. continued

```
Next i&

Call Common_EndTimedTest(Me.lblInLine)


End Sub
```

The code for the second button appears in Listing 11.2. It consists of a loop that carries out a function call for the number of iterations that you specify. The called function is defined within the same form as the button click event routine that calls it rather than in a separate module.

Listing 11.2. A call to a same-form function.

```
Sub cmdFunc_Click ()


Dim dblInput1 As Double         ' Contains num for function calculations
Dim dblInput2 As Double         ' Contains num for function calculations

Dim i&                          ' Loop counter

Call Common_StartTimedTest

For i& = 1 To txtLoops

' The sample algorithim below serves as a simple
'   example of an algorithim which takes two initial values,
'   then calls a function to perform calculations on them
'   and return the updated value into a global variable

    dblInput1 = START_VALUE1

    dblInput2 = START_VALUE2


    g_dblAnswer = FuncCallTest(dblInput1, dblInput2)


Next i&

Call Common_EndTimedTest(Me.lblFunc)


End Sub
```

Listing 11.3 is the function definition for the same-form function `FuncCallTest`.

Listing 11.3. The definition for the same-form function `FuncCallTest`.

```
Function FuncCallTest (ByVal dblNum1 As Double, ByVal dblNum2 As Double)
             ➥ As Double
' This function is defined in the same form module as
'   the code which calls it.

' The sample algorithim below serves as a simple
'   example of a routine which takes two input arguments,
'   performs calculations on them, and returns a function value
'   which is the product of the results.

    dblNum1 = dblNum1 * 2

    dblNum2 = dblNum2 * 3

    FuncCallTest = dblNum1 * dblNum2

End Function
```

The code for the third button appears in Listing 11.4. It consists of a loop that carries out a subroutine call for the number of iterations that you have specified in the Loops to Time text box. The only difference from the previous test code is that a subroutine call, rather than a function call, is inserted within the `For` loop. This subroutine, like the function just reviewed, is defined within the same form as the button click event that calls it, rather than in a separate module.

Listing 11.4. A call to the same-form subroutine.

```
Private Sub cmdSubCall_Click()


Dim dblInput1 As Double        ' Contains num to use in subroutine calculations
Dim dblInput2 As Double        ' Contains num to use in subroutine calculations

Dim i&                         ' Loop counter

Call Common_StartTimedTest

For i& = 1 To txtLoops

' The sample algorithim below serves as a simple
'   example of an algorithim which takes two initial values,
'   then calls a subroutine to perform calculations on them
'   and return the updated value through the modified third parameter

    dblInput1 = START_VALUE1

    dblInput2 = START_VALUE2
```

continues

Listing 11.4. continued

```
    Call SubCallTest(dblInput1, dblInput2, g_dblAnswer)


Next i&

Call Common_EndTimedTest(lblSubCall)


End Sub
```

The subroutine that is called again performs the same algorithm that was previously described. However, to comply with the format of subroutine calls rather than functions, this subroutine returns the result through a parameter rather than through a return code. This is shown in Listing 11.5.

Listing 11.5. The definition for the same-form subroutine `SubCallTest`.

```
Sub SubCallTest (ByVal dblNum1 As Double, ByVal dblNum2 As Double,
                ➥dblResult As Double)
' This subroutine is defined in the same form module as
'   the code which calls it.

' The sample algorithim below simply serves as a simple
'   example of a routine that takes two input arguments,
'   performs calculations on them, and modifies a third argument
'   with the product of the results.

    dblNum1 = dblNum1 * 2

    dblNum2 = dblNum2 * 3

    dblResult = dblNum1 * dblNum2

End Sub
```

The alternative to the same-form subroutine call is a call to a subroutine when that subroutine is defined in another module. The code for the command button that carries out this test looks very similar to prior tests, with simply a new call inserted in the `For` loop, as shown in Listing 11.6.

Listing 11.6. A call to different-form subroutine.

```
Private Sub cmdModSub_Click()


Dim dblInput1 As Double        ' Contains num to use in subroutine calculations
Dim dblInput2 As Double        ' Contains num to use in subroutine calculations
```

```
Dim i&                          ' Loop counter

Call Common_StartTimedTest

For i& = 1 To txtLoops

' The sample algorithim below serves as a simple
'   example of an algorithim that takes two initial values,
'   then calls a subroutine defined within a different module
'   to perform calculations on the values and
'   return the updated value through the modified third parameter

    dblInput1 = START_VALUE1

    dblInput2 = START_VALUE2


    Call Utils_ModuleSubCallTest(dblInput1, dblInput2, g_dblAnswer)


Next i&

Call Common_EndTimedTest(lblModSub)


End Sub
```

The subroutine definition for the subroutine called here is identical to the previous test, shown in Listing 11.5, except this definition is declared in a separate module rather than the same form. To distinguish it from the same-form subroutine definition `SubCallTest`, the different-form subroutine definition declares the subroutine with the name `Utils_ModuleSubCallTest`. In all other respects the subroutines are the same.

Call Type Results

Figure 11.1 shows the results of one run of each of the test cases. The normalized results, gathered over multiple runs, are shown in Table 11.1.

Table 11.1. Call technique comparisons.

Type of Test	*Normalized Time Ratio*
In-line code	1.00
Same form function call	2.47
Same form subroutine call	2.15
Other module subroutine call	1.99

One very obvious finding emerges from a look at the results in Figure 11.1: *In-line code is much faster than procedure calls.* In-line code refers to placing statements that must be carried out directly in the code path rather than packaging them in a subroutine or function call. The reason for the speed is apparent—if statements are simply part of the current logic flow, no extra call overhead is incurred when the statements are carried out.

If those statements are placed in a separate procedure and must be reached by a call, more low-level machine instructions must be executed simply to change the flow of code from the current sequence of statements to the procedure's statements, which are at a different address in memory. Accordingly, additional overhead is expended at the end of the procedure call to return to the original flow of statements and return results back to the calling code.

It stands to reason that it takes more work on the part of the CPU, and therefore more time, to branch *to* and return *from* another location to carry out statements than to simply include them in the current flow or make them in-line code. The performance payoff for the in-line code technique is significant—code will execute up to twice as quickly when it's in line, so the procedure calling overhead penalty is considerable. However, anyone who has much experience programming has a pretty good feel for the advantages inherent in packaging routines into a procedure call. The modular maintenance benefits and clarity provided from packaging code into routines are regarded as the most basic of good, standard programming practices. The value of in-line code, then, must be considered with respect to the trade-off with procedure maintainability. If a block of in-line code is inserted 20 different places in the program and a bug is found in that block, a change must be made in those 20 places. By contrast, if a procedure had been used instead of separate blocks of in-line code, the change would only need to be made once in the procedure it is contained in. The 20 calls to the procedure would remain unchanged. If you are willing to sacrifice the maintenance advantages of using routines in some areas, you may want to use in-line routines, but this decision should be made after careful consideration.

> **TIP:** In-line code performs significantly faster than calls to the same code packaged in subroutines or function calls. However, in-line code has inherent maintenance disadvantages. Therefore, use of in-line code is a good optimization approach for just those areas of a program that have particular speed demands.

The same-form subroutine test shows some particularly interesting results. It does run somewhat faster than the same-form function call test. A function call incurs the overhead of assigning its return value to the calling argument, whereas the subroutine call simply assigns the value to the parameter passed by reference. Of course, the exact comparison depends on the type of data returned and whether the subroutine data is passed by reference or by value, which is discussed later in the section "Argument Alternatives: `ByVal` or No `ByVal`?"

> **TIP:** Subroutines are generally slightly faster than function calls because of efficiencies in returning data.

The different-form subroutine call result is slightly ahead of the same-form subroutine call in normalized time ratios. However, the duration is of little difference from the same-form subroutine time. Even though the module containing the called subroutine must be loaded into memory at the first call, whereas the form-defined subroutine was already in memory, the time impact difference is small. A procedure in a module is loaded on demand if that module has not already been loaded, so the code for the module must be pulled into memory when the call is made. The form, however, is already in memory along with its code, so it does not incur the same penalty. Because the procedure is defined in the form, however, the form and its code take up more memory as soon as the form is loaded.

With small programs, or programs on memory-constrained systems, the impact of where the code is declared is not likely to be significant. However, because a module is loaded only when a subroutine from that module is called, you can improve the efficiency of your programs by grouping similar routines likely to be used together into one module rather than in many. For example, calls to 10 different routines defined in 10 different modules would cause 10 modules to be loaded to memory. Calls to 10 different routines defined in 1 module would only cause 1 module to be loaded to memory.

> **TIP:** Performance will be roughly the same to call a subroutine in either a form or a module. However, modules are loaded on demand, so you can minimize module load time by defining related routines that are likely to be called together into the same modules.

Argument Alternatives: *ByVal* or No *ByVal*?

So far this chapter has focused on different types of procedure-call alternatives. However, even within one type of call, many factors can affect performance. Of course, the amount of data passed to a procedure has an effect on performance—the more data passed as parameters, the greater the performance impact. However, it is not just the type and quantity of data that is passed that affects speed. Another often-overlooked factor is the issue of *how* the data is passed into parameters.

Data can be passed by reference or by value. If you do not provide the `ByVal` keyword in the declaration, the data will be passed by reference for a given parameter. That means that variables passed into the procedure and changed within the procedure *will* reflect the updated values back in the flow of statements that made the procedure call after the call is complete. Even though Visual Basic hides pointers, this by-reference technique is essentially carried out by the Visual Basic runtime interpreter with pointers at an internal level not visible in your source code. A by-reference parameter is passed to the procedure as a memory location of where the data resides. If there is any change made to a variable that results in changing that master memory location, the rest of the program will see that changed value.

On the other hand, if you specify the `ByVal` keyword on a parameter declaration, that parameter will be passed simply by value. In effect, when the procedure is called, Visual Basic looks at the master memory location and provides a copy of it to the called procedure. Then, when a parameter is updated in that called procedure, only the local copy is altered; the original variable supplied as the parameter will be left untouched when the original flow of statements resumes after the call completes. Using `ByVal` when you do not intend for a parameter to result in a changed variable outside of the local procedure scope is very good programming practice and can prevent many unintended side effects.

> **NOTE:** There is an exception to almost every rule, and that is true for the `ByVal` parameter. Strings are not handled using the normal `ByVal` convention in Visual Basic—they are always passed by reference. Using `ByVal` with a string indicates that it will be passed as a C-style string.

A simple test program can demonstrate this difference. The program, callar32.exe, is available on the CD-ROM that accompanies this book. The interface for the program is shown in Figure 11.2. This program has command buttons that carry out, when clicked, a timed function call that passes parameters with `ByVal`, an identical function call without `ByVal`, a timed subroutine call that passes parameters with `ByVal`, and the identical subroutine call without `ByVal`.

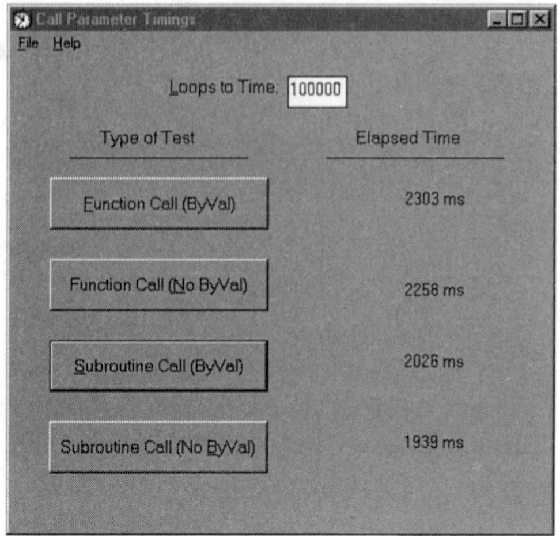

Figure 11.2.
The main form of the call arguments test program.

The code for the `ByVal` function call test that is executed in response to a click on the button labeled Function Call (ByVal) appears in Listing 11.7.

Listing 11.7. The `ByVal` function call.

```
Sub cmdFuncByVal_Click ()


Dim dblInput1 As Double        ' Contains num for function calculations
Dim dblInput2 As Double        ' Contains num for function calculations

Dim i&                         ' Loop counter

Call Common_StartTimedTest

For i& = 1 To txtLoops

' The sample algorithim below serves as a simple
'   example of an algorithim that takes two initial values,
'   then calls a function to perform calculations on them
'   and return the updated value into a global variable
'   The parameters are passed by value rather than by reference,
'   via the ByVal used in the function declaration.

    dblInput1 = START_VALUE1

    dblInput2 = START_VALUE2


    g_dblAnswer = FuncCallTest(dblInput1, dblInput2)


Next i&

Call Common_EndTimedTest(Me.lblFuncByVal)


End Sub
```

The test code simply loops the number of iterations that you specify in the Loops to Time text box, making a call to `FuncCallTest`, with two passed parameters, on each loop. `FuncCallTest` is a function that has been defined with `ByVal` parameters and performs a simple calculation. (See Listing 11.8.)

Listing 11.8. The `FuncCallTest` function definition with `ByVal` parameters.

```
Function FuncCallTest (ByVal dblNum1 As Double, ByVal dblNum2 As Double)
                     ➥ As Double
' This function is defined in the same form module as
'   the code which calls it.

' The sample algorithim below serves as a simple
'   example of a routine which takes two input arguments,
```

continues

Listing 11.8. continued

```
'   performs calculations on them, and returns a function value
'   which is the product of the results.

    dblNum1 = dblNum1 * 2

    dblNum2 = dblNum2 * 3

    FuncCallTest = dblNum1 * dblNum2

End Function
```

The next step is to run an identical test using the same function call declared without `ByVal`. The test code that is carried out in response to a click on the button labeled Function Call (No ByVal) is the same as that of the click on the Function Call (ByVal) button, as shown in Listing 11.7, except that a different function is called in this test. The single different source code line is shown in bold type. Rather than a call to `FuncCallTest`, a call is made to function `FuncCallTest_NoByVal`. (See Listing 11.9.) `FuncCallTest_NoByVal`, as the name implies, does not use any `ByVal` parameters, but rather is declared to accept all parameters by reference.

Listing 11.9. A modified test to call a function with no `ByVal`.

```
Sub cmdFuncNoByVal_Click ()



Dim dblInput1 As Double       ' Contains num for function calculations
Dim dblInput2 As Double       ' Contains num for function calculations

Dim i&                        ' Loop counter

Call Common_StartTimedTest

For i& = 1 To txtLoops

' The sample algorithim below serves as a simple
'   example of an algorithim that takes two initial values,
'   then calls a function to perform calculations on them
'   and return the updated value into a global variable
'   The parameters are passed by reference rather than by value,
'   since no ByVal was used in the function declaration.

    dblInput1 = START_VALUE1

    dblInput2 = START_VALUE2


    g_dblAnswer = FuncCallTest_NoByVal(dblInput1, dblInput2)


Next i&
```

```
Call Common_EndTimedTest(Me.lblFuncNoByVal)

End Sub
```

The declaration and contents of `FuncCallTest_NoByVal` are identical to those of `FuncCallTest`, which you saw in Listing 11.8, except in this case the function declaration does *not* include the `ByVal` keyword. The revised function-declaration line is shown in Listing 11.10. This function call passes parameters by reference, without taking the time to make a copy of the data. The rest of the function is identical to that of `FuncCallTest`.

Listing 11.10. The `FuncCallTest_NoByVal` declaration.

```
Function FuncCallTest_NoByVal (dblNum1 As Double, dblNum2 As Double) As Double
```

The next step in the analysis is to carry out the same test on subroutine calls to see if the results are consistent across both types of procedure calls. Listing 11.11 shows the code that is carried out for the subroutine `ByVal` test. This is the test that is carried out in response to a click on the Subroutine Call (ByVal) button. The code is essentially the same as the earlier function-call tests, except in this case the `ByVal` subroutine `SubCallTest` is called.

Listing 11.11. The `ByVal` subroutine call.

```
Sub cmdSubCallByVal_Click ()


Dim dblInput1 As Double       ' Contains num for subroutine calculations
Dim dblInput2 As Double       ' Contains num for subroutine calculations

Dim i&                        ' Loop counter

Call Common_StartTimedTest

For i& = 1 To txtLoops

' The sample algorithim below serves as a simple
'   example of an algorithim that takes two initial values,
'   then calls a subroutine to perform calculations on them
'   and return the updated value through the modified third parameter
'   The parameters are passed by value rather than by reference,
'   via the ByVal used in the function declaration.

    dblInput1 = START_VALUE1

    dblInput2 = START_VALUE2


    Call SubCallTest(dblInput1, dblInput2, g_dblAnswer)
```

continues

Listing 11.11. continued

```
Next i&

Call Common_EndTimedTest(Me.lblSubCallByVal)

End Sub
```

Like the function-call test case, this subroutine test simply loops the number of iterations you specify in the Loops to Time text box, making a call to `SubCallTest` with three passed parameters on each loop. The function-call test only passed two parameters because a return value was provided directly by the function. In this case, to do an equivalent test and have the subroutine provide a result, you must pass in a third parameter. This third parameter, however, *cannot* be declared with `ByVal`, because that parameter must receive an updated value whose changed value (the result) is visible to the calling code. Therefore, that third parameter is passed by reference. `SubCallTest` is a function that has been defined with two `ByVal` parameters used in the simple calculation it performs. Then it provides the result in the third parameter. (See Listing 11.12.)

Listing 11.12. The `SubCallTest` subroutine with `ByVal` parameters.

```
Sub SubCallTest (ByVal dblNum1 As Double, ByVal dblNum2 As Double,
                ➥ dblResult As Double)
' This subroutine is defined in the same form module as
'   the code which calls it.

' The sample algorithim below simply serves as a simple
'   example of a routine that takes two input arguments,
'   performs calculations on them, and modifies a third argument
'   with the product of the results.

    dblNum1 = dblNum1 * 2

    dblNum2 = dblNum2 * 3

    dblResult = dblNum1 * dblNum2

End Sub
```

The next step is to run an identical test using the same subroutine call declared without `ByVal`. The test code that's carried out in response to a click on the button labeled Subroutine Call (No ByVal) is the same as that of the click the Subroutine Call (ByVal) button, which is shown in Listing 11.10, except that a different subroutine with no `ByVal` parameters is called in this

test. The single line that is different between the two test cases appears in bold. Rather than a call to SubCallTest, a call is made to a function SibCallTest_NoByVal. (See Listing 11.13.)

Listing 11.13. A modified test to a call subroutine with no ByVal.

```
Sub cmdSubCallNoByVal_Click ()


Dim dblInput1 As Double        ' Contains num for subroutine calculations
Dim dblInput2 As Double        ' Contains num for subroutine calculations

Dim i&                         ' Loop counter

Call Common_StartTimedTest

For i& = 1 To txtLoops

' The sample algorithim below serves as a simple
'   example of an algorithim which takes two initial values,
'   then calls a subroutine to perform calculations on them
'   and return the updated value through the modified third parameter
'   The parameters are passed by reference rather than by value,
'   since no ByVal was used in the function declaration.

    dblInput1 = START_VALUE1

    dblInput2 = START_VALUE2


    Call SubCallTest_NoByVal(dblInput1, dblInput2, g_dblAnswer)


Next i&

Call Common_EndTimedTest(Me.lblSubCallNoByVal)


End Sub
```

As in the previous pair of function tests, the declaration and contents of SubCallTest_NoByVal are identical to those of the SubCallTest subroutine shown in Listing 11.12, except that in this case the subroutine declaration does *not* include the ByVal keyword. The revised subroutine-declaration line is shown in Listing 11.14; the rest of the subroutine definition is identical to that of Listing 11.12. Calls to this subroutine, due to this declaration, will pass all parameters by reference without taking the time to make a copy of the data.

Listing 11.14. The SubCallTest_NoByVal declaration.

```
Sub SubCallTest_NoByVal (dblNum1 As Double,
                       ➥ dblNum2 As Double, dblResult As Double)
```

Call Argument Results

You can see the results for one run of these tests in Figure 11.2. The normalized results gathered over multiple runs of these tests are shown in Table 11.2.

Table 11.2. Call argument technique comparison.

Type of Test	*Normalized Time Ratio*
Function call (`ByVal`)	1.19
Function call (no `ByVal`)	1.16
Subroutine call (`ByVal`)	1.04
Subroutine call (no `ByVal`)	1.00

The results show, as they did in previous test cases, that subroutines are generally faster than function calls. The results also show that `ByVal` parameter handling is a little slower than no `ByVal` parameter handling.

So, like many good programming practices, `ByVal` comes at the cost of a slight performance penalty. Calls made with the `ByVal` keyword, whether function or subroutine calls, will be measurably slower. More work takes place when a `ByVal` is encountered: A special, local copy of the variable must be made. This overhead is not present when a parameter is passed by reference.

Still, you should carefully consider the impact of this before carrying out any optimizations based on this finding. `ByVal` is slower, but 4 percent or less signifies a minimal performance penalty. The cumulative effect is not likely to be large enough to be noticeable to a user even if the application makes many repetitive procedure calls. However, if procedure calls use more than the two parameters used for this test, you would expect the potential savings to be greater. Like most performance decisions, this one is not cut and dried, and will depend very much on the nature of your specific application.

> **TIP:** Calls with `ByVal` parameters take longer than calls without `ByVal` parameters, but the difference is very slight.

Looping Methods

The next area to consider is *looping*. Two well-known standard approaches to looping exist—using the `While` loop and using the `For` loop. Some programmers may use a particular looping method simply out of habit. Other programmers might choose a looping method because it is perceived to be a better programming style. The pertinent question is "Are there non-trivial

performance differences between these approaches?" You can use the loop32.exe program, found on the CD-ROM that accompanies this book, to find the answer to this question. (See Figure 11.3.)

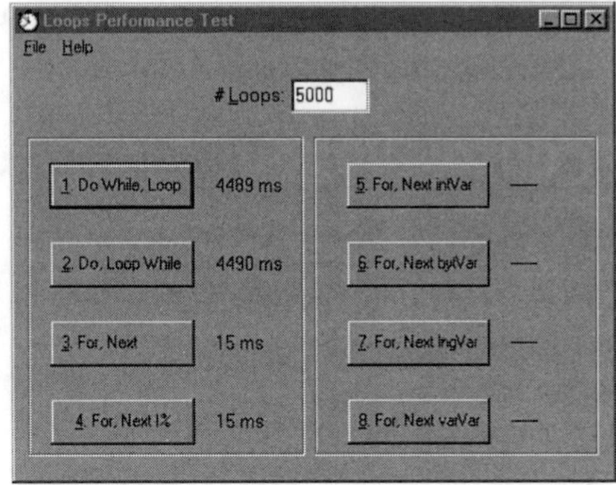

Figure 11.3.
The main form of the loop timings comparison program with test results from 5000 loops.

This program provides tests for various looping approaches. The listing for the first test, which contains the code carried out when you click on command button 1. Do While, Loop appears in Listing 11.15. This test case uses a `Do…While` looping construct to carry out the number of loops that you specify.

Listing 11.15. Test case 1: The `Do While...Loop` structure.

```
Private Sub cmdWhile_Loop_Click()
' This routine tests speed of While / Loop structure

' loop counter, locally defined var starts with value of 0 at each call
Dim i%
' used for assignments within loop
Dim intDummyAssign As Integer


If txtMaxLoops > 32767 Then
    MsgBox "The max value an integer variable can contain is 32767.
    ➥ The number of requested loops cannot exceed this maximum
    ➥ value of the data type. Test is cancelled!", , "Data Type Limitation"
    lblWhile_Loop = "——"
    Exit Sub
End If

Call Common_StartTimedTest

Do While i% < txtMaxLoops
    intDummyAssign = i%
    i% = i% + 1
Loop

Call Common_EndTimedTest(lblWhile_Loop)

End Sub
```

The listing for the second test, which contains the code carried out if you click on command button 2. Do, Loop While, appears in Listing 11.16. This test case uses a `Do...loop While` looping construct to carry out the number of loops you specify. This construct is very similar to the `Do While...Loop` construct, except that the `Do...loop While` format syntax will cause the loop to be entered at least once, regardless of condition settings. By contrast, the `While` condition is not evaluated until the end of the loop.

Listing 11.16. Test case 2: The `Do...Loop While` structure.

```
Private Sub cmdLoop_While_Click()
' This routine tests speed of While / Loop structure

' loop counter, locally defined var starts with value of 0 at each call
Dim i%
' used for assignments within loop
Dim intDummyAssign As Integer


If txtMaxLoops > 32767 Then
    MsgBox "The max value an integer variable can contain is 32767.
    ➥ The number of requested loops cannot exceed this maximum value of
    ➥ the data type. Test is cancelled!", , "Data Type Limitation"
    lblWhile_Loop = "——"
    Exit Sub
End If

Call Common_StartTimedTest

Do
    intDummyAssign = i%
    i% = i% + 1
Loop While i% < txtMaxLoops

Call Common_EndTimedTest(lblLoop_While)

End Sub
```

The listing for the third test, which contains the code carried out when you click on the command button labeled 3. For, Next, appears in Listing 11.17. This test case uses a `For...Next` looping construct to carry out the number of loops specified by the user.

Listing 11.17. Test case 3: The `For...Next` structure.

```
Private Sub cmdForNext_Click()
' This routine tests speed of integer-based For Loop index with
' "i%" loop var syntax and no "i%" on Next

' for loop counter
Dim i%
' used for assignments within loop
Dim intDummyAssign As Integer
```

```
' make sure user is not requesting more loops than this data type can support
If txtMaxLoops > 32767 Then
    MsgBox "The max value an integer variable can contain is 32767.
    ➥The number of requested loops cannot exceed this maximum value
    ➥of the data type. Test is cancelled!", , "Data Type Limitation"
    lblForNextI_Int = "——"
    Exit Sub
End If

Call Common_StartTimedTest

For i% = 0 To txtMaxLoops - 1
    intDummyAssign = i%
Next

Call Common_EndTimedTest(lblForNext)

End Sub
```

The listing for the fourth test, which contains the code carried out when you click on the command button labeled 4. For, Next I%, appears in Listing 11.18. This test case uses the same `For...Next` construct as the previous test, except this test also includes the optional loop index variable indicator on the `Next` statement. In other words, a `Next I%` statement occurs at the end of the `For` loop rather than a `Next` statement.

Listing 11.18. Test case 4: The `For...Next I%` structure.

```
Private Sub cmdForNextI_Click()
' This routine tests speed of integer-based For Loop index with
'"i%" loop var syntax
' for loop counter
Dim i%
' used for assignments within loop
Dim intDummyAssign As Integer

' make sure user is not requesting more loops than this data type can support
If txtMaxLoops > 32767 Then
    MsgBox "The max value an integer variable can contain is 32767.
   ➥ The number of requested loops cannot exceed this maximum value
   ➥ of the data type. Test is cancelled!", , "Data Type Limitation"
    lblForNextI_Int = "——"
    Exit Sub
End If

Call Common_StartTimedTest

For i% = 0 To txtMaxLoops - 1
    intDummyAssign = i%
Next i%

Call Common_EndTimedTest(lblForNextI)

End Sub
```

Results of *While* Versus *For*

Figure 11.3 shows the application with the results from one run of the loop comparison tests, using a loop value of `5000`. The normalized results of repeated runs of the first four tests that compare the `While` and `For` loops are shown in Table 11.3.

Table 11.3. Loop technique comparisons.

Type of Test	*Normalized Time Ratio*
`Do While, Loop`	299.50
`Do, Loop While`	299.00
`For, Next`	1.00
`For, Next I%`	1.00

It is clear from these results that the `For` loop offers very significant performance advantages over the `While` loop. Differences between looping approaches such as placement of the `While` before or after the loop and whether to use the `Next` index indicator appear to have little overall impact on performance.

> **TIP:** Use `For...Next` rather than `While` loops to reap significant performance benefits.

Comparing Various Index Types in the *For* Loop

Since the `For` loop is the fastest looping alternative, the next question is how to optimize the `For` loop itself. Every `For` loop requires an index that is incremented each time through the loop. This index can be any of several possible types including integer, byte, long, or variable. The next series of tests is aimed at determining if there are some types of variables that make for faster indexes than others.

The first test case used is shown in Listing 11.19. This code is carried out when you click on the command button labeled 5. For, Next intVar and uses an integer-based index variable within the `For` loop.

Listing 11.19. Test case 5: The `For...Next` loop with an integer index.

```
Private Sub cmdForNextI_Int_Click()
' This routine tests speed of integer-based For Loop index
'   with "intCounter" loop var syntax

' for loop counter
Dim intCounter As Integer
```

```
' used for assignments within loop
Dim lngDummyAssign As Long

' make sure user is not requesting more loops than this data type can support
If txtMaxLoops > 32767 Then
    MsgBox "The max value an integer variable can contain is 32767.
   ➥ The number of requested loops cannot exceed this maximum value
   ➥ of the data type. Test is cancelled!", , "Data Type Limitation"
    lblForNextI_Int = " — — "
    Exit Sub
End If

Call Common_StartTimedTest

For intCounter = 0 To txtMaxLoops - 1
    lngDummyAssign = intCounter
Next intCounter

Call Common_EndTimedTest(lblForNextI_Int)

End Sub
```

The second test case used to test `For` index handling is shown in Listing 11.20. This code is carried out when you click on the command button labeled 6. For, Next bytVar. It uses a byte-based index variable within the `For` loop.

Listing 11.20. Test case 6: The `For...Next` loop with a byte index.

```
Private Sub cmdForNextI_Byte_Click()
' This routine tests speed of byte-based For Loop index

' for loop counter
Dim bytCounter As Byte
' used for assignments within loop
Dim lngDummyAssign As Long

' make sure user is not requesting more loops than this data type can support
If txtMaxLoops > 255 Then
    MsgBox "The max value a byte variable can contain is 255.
   ➥ The number of request loops cannot exceed this maximum value
   ➥ of the data type. Test is cancelled!", , "Data Type Limitation"
    lblForNextI_Byte = " — — "
    Exit Sub
End If

Call Common_StartTimedTest

For bytCounter = 0 To txtMaxLoops - 1
    lngDummyAssign = bytCounter
Next bytCounter

Call Common_EndTimedTest(lblForNextI_Byte)

End Sub
```

The third test case used to test For loop index speed is shown in Listing 11.21. This code is carried out when you click on the button labeled 7. For, Next lngVar. It uses a long index variable within the For loop.

Listing 11.21. Test case 7: The For…Next loop with a long index.

```
Private Sub cmdForNextI_Long_Click()
' This routine tests speed of long-based For Loop index

' for loop counter
Dim lngCounter As Long
' used for assignments within loop
Dim intDummyAssign As Integer

' make sure user is not requesting more loops than this data type can support
If txtMaxLoops > 2147483647 Then
    MsgBox "The max value a long variable can contain is 2,147,483,647.
   ➥ The number of requested loops cannot exceed this maximum value
   ➥ of the data type. Test is cancelled!", , "Data Type Limitation"
    lblForNextI_Long = "— — "
    Exit Sub
End If

Call Common_StartTimedTest

For lngCounter = 0 To txtMaxLoops - 1
    intDummyAssign = lngCounter
Next lngCounter

Call Common_EndTimedTest(lblForNextI_Long)

End Sub
```

The fourth test case used to test the For loop index approach is shown below in Listing 11.22. This code is carried out when you click on the button labeled 8. For, Next varVar. It uses a variant-based index variable within the For loop.

Listing 11.22. Test case 8: The For…Next loop with a variant index.

```
Private Sub cmdForNextI_Var_Click()
' This routine tests speed of variant-based For Loop index

' for loop counter
Dim varCounter As Variant
' used for assignments within loop
Dim intDummyAssign As Integer

Call Common_StartTimedTest
```

```
For varCounter = 0 To txtMaxLoops - 1
    intDummyAssign = varCounter
Next varCounter

Call Common_EndTimedTest(lblForNextI_Var)

End Sub
```

For Loop Index Type Test Results

The test cases with the four different index types were carried out with the specified loops for each test set at 255. The value 255 was selected because it is the maximum number of loops that can be supported by a byte-type index variable. You can see the results from one run of this test in Figure 11.4. The normalized results for multiple timings are shown in Table 11.4.

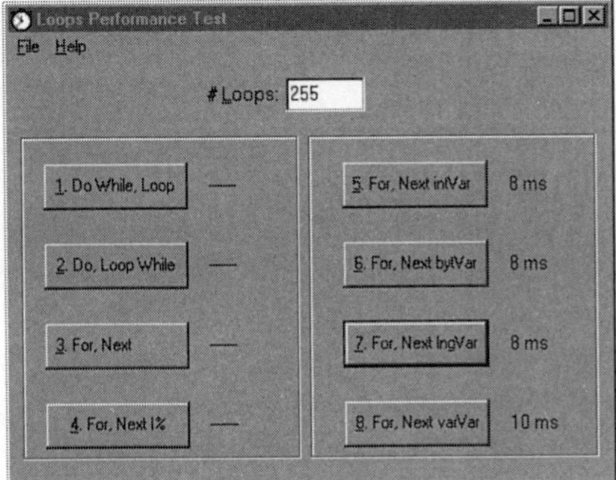

Figure 11.4.
The loop index test main form results for a test with 255 loops.

Table 11.4. Loop index technique comparisons for 255 loops.

Type of Test	*Normalized Time Ratio*
`For, Next Integer`	1.00
`For, Next Byte`	1.00
`For, Next Long`	1.00
`For, Next Variant`	1.28

The results show that there is no appreciable difference between the integer, byte, and long data type–based index variables when the variable only has to store a small integer number of 255 or less. The variant data type, however, is significantly slower.

The next test carried out is similar, but with a greater number of loops for each `For` loop index. The tests were repeated with a specified loop count of 32,000 (almost the limit of what an integer data type can hold). You can see the results for one test run in Figure 11.5. The normalized results for multiple test runs are shown in Table 11.5.

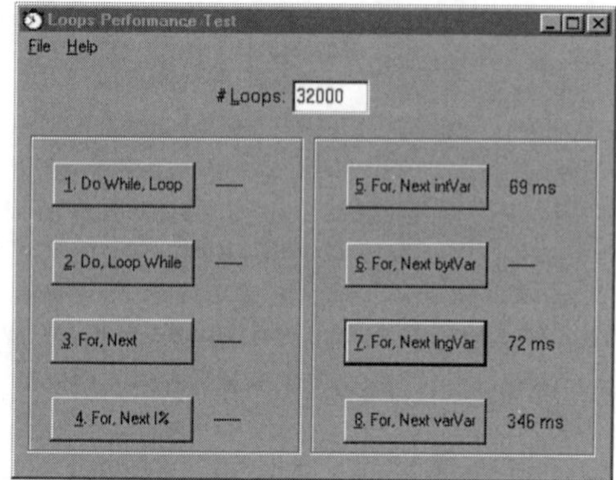

Figure 11.5.
Loop index test results for a test with 32,000 loops.

Table 11.5. Loop index technique comparisons for 32,000 loops.

Type of Test	*Normalized Time Ratio*
`For, Next Integer`	1.00
`For, Next Byte`	(N/A; byte type can't store 32,000)
`For, Next Long`	1.06
`For, Next Variant`	5.01

Once again, the results show that the variant type is clearly one to avoid for the purposes of `For` loop indexes. In addition, the long data type has a slight performance disadvantage over the integer data type.

The final looping test carries out a head-to-head comparison of the long and the variant data types. The tests were repeated with a specified loop count of 1,000,000, which is beyond the capacity of an integer or a byte variable to contain. You can see the test results in Figure 11.6. The normalized results for multiple test runs are shown in Table 11.6.

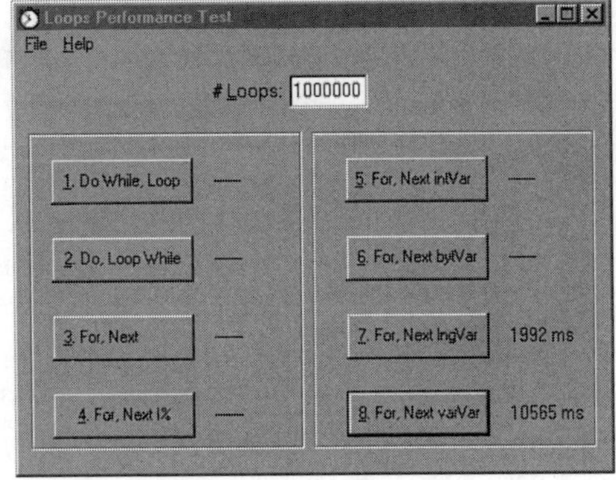

Figure 11.6.
Loop index test results for a test with 1,000,000 loops.

Table 11.6. Loop index technique comparison for 1,000,000 loops.

Type of Test	*Normalized Time Ratio*
`For, Next Integer Byte`	(N/A; integer type can't store large numbers)
`For, Next Byte`	(N/A; byte type can't store large numbers)
`For, Next Long`	1.00
`For, Next Variant`	5.30

The variant type again makes out very poorly in the timed tests. It is clear that the variant should be avoided as an index for any looping operation.

TIP: Do not use any variables of variant data type as index types in your `For` loops.

Integers, bytes, and longs have generally the same performance, with the drawback that integers and bytes are quite restricted in the maximum value they can contain.

Selection Methods

The next area to be tested is another of the most commonly encountered during programming—selection methods. There are several alternatives available when writing code, including the `Select` statement and a series of nested `If…Then…Else` statements. The nesting can be avoided if you use `If…Then…ElseIf` statements in their place. And finally, another variation of these same methods is to encompass the conditional part of the expression in parentheses, such as `if (A = B)`, rather than `if A = B`.

These alternatives are the focus of the next series of tests. The program select32.exe, which you can find on the CD-ROM that accompanies this book, demonstrates such tests. Figure 11.7 shows this test program. The test program enables the you to specify the number of loops the test should carry out, as have the other test programs. In addition, it prompts you for the test condition to make true. The test cases used can match any of seven conditions. For example, in the `Select Case` statement test case, there are seven cases that can be satisfied. Likewise, in the `If...Then...ElseIf` test case, seven `Then...ElseIf` branches can be reached. Performance conditions will be different for these constructs depending on whether the first or last condition is the condition to be tested, so this test program was designed with the flexibility to let the user indicate which condition is the `True` condition. The test condition indicator box enables the user to specify a `True` condition ranging from the first possible to the seventh (and last) possible.

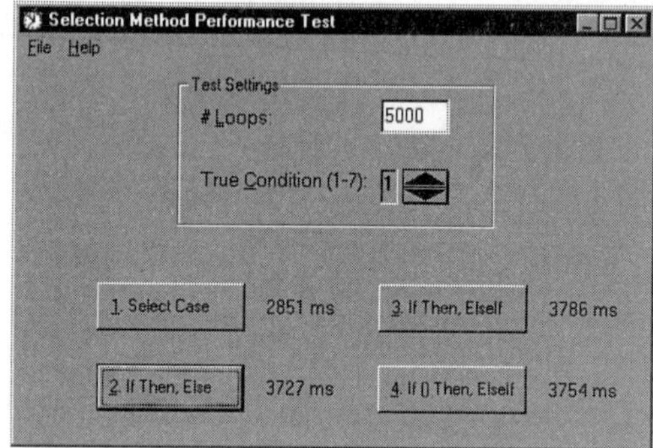

Figure 11.7.
The selection test program with Condition 1 `True`.

The first test case is the `Select Case` construct. The code associated with this test case, which is carried out when the command button labeled 1. Select Case is clicked, is shown in Listing 11.23.

Listing 11.23. Test case 1: The `Select Case` statement.

```
Private Sub cmdSelectCase_Click()
' This routine tests speed of Select Case structure

' for loop counter
Dim lngLoopCount As Long
' used for assignments within loop
Dim strDummyAssign As String

Call Common_StartTimedTest

For lngLoopCount = 0 To txtMaxLoops - 1
    Select Case lblCondition
    Case 1:
        strDummyAssign = "One"
    Case 2:
        strDummyAssign = "Two"
```

```
    Case 3:
        strDummyAssign = "Three"
    Case 4:
        strDummyAssign = "Four"
    Case 5:
        strDummyAssign = "Five"
    Case 6:
        strDummyAssign = "Six"
    Case 7:
        strDummyAssign = "Seven"
    Case Else
        strDummyAssign = "Error"
    End Select
Next lngLoopCount

Call Common_EndTimedTest(lblSelectCase)

End Sub
```

Code for the next test case is based on a series of nested `If...Then...Else` statements. These statements carry out essentially the same logic as the `Select Case` test case. The code associated with this test case, which is carried out when the command button labeled 2. If Then, Else is clicked, is shown in Listing 11.24.

Listing 11.24. Test case 2: The `If...Then...Else` statement.

```
Private Sub cmdIfElse_Click()
' This routine tests speed of If Then, Else structure

' for loop counter
Dim lngLoopCount As Long
' used for assignments within loop
Dim strDummyAssign As String

 Call Common_StartTimedTest

For lngLoopCount = 0 To txtMaxLoops - 1
    If lblCondition = 1 Then
        strDummyAssign = "One"
    Else
        If lblCondition = 2 Then
            strDummyAssign = "Two"
        Else
            If lblCondition = 3 Then
                strDummyAssign = "Three"
            Else
                If lblCondition = 4 Then
                    strDummyAssign = "Four"
                Else
                    If lblCondition = 5 Then
                        strDummyAssign = "Five"
                    Else
                        If lblCondition = 6 Then
                            strDummyAssign = "Six"
```

continues

Listing 11.24. continued

```
                        Else
                            If lblCondition = 7 Then
                                strDummyAssign = "Seven"
                            Else
                                strDummyAssign = "Error"
                            End If ' = 7
                        End If ' = 6
                    End If ' = 5
                End If ' = 4
            End If ' = 3
        End If ' = 2
    End If ' = 1
Next lngLoopCount

Call Common_EndTimedTest(lblIfElse)

End Sub
```

Code for the third test case of this series is based on the `If...Then...ElseIf` statements rather than the many nested `If...Then...Else` statements of the previous test case. These statements carry out essentially the same logic as that test case. The code associated with this test case, which is carried out when the command button labeled 3. If Then, ElseIf is clicked, is shown in Listing 11.25.

Listing 11.25. Test case 3: The `If...Then...ElseIf` statement.

```
Private Sub cmdIfElseif_Click()
' This routine tests speed of If Then, ElseIf structure

' for loop counter
Dim lngLoopCount As Long
' used for assignments within loop
Dim strDummyAssign As String

Call Common_StartTimedTest

For lngLoopCount = 0 To txtMaxLoops - 1
    If lblCondition = 1 Then
        strDummyAssign = "One"
    ElseIf lblCondition = 2 Then
        strDummyAssign = "Two"
    ElseIf lblCondition = 3 Then
        strDummyAssign = "Three"
    ElseIf lblCondition = 4 Then
        strDummyAssign = "Four"
    ElseIf lblCondition = 5 Then
        strDummyAssign = "Five"
    ElseIf lblCondition = 6 Then
        strDummyAssign = "Six"
    ElseIf lblCondition = 7 Then
        strDummyAssign = "Seven"
    Else
        strDummyAssign = "Error"
    End If
```

```
Next lngLoopCount

Call Common_EndTimedTest(lblIfElseIf)

End Sub
```

The final test case in this series is a test case that is the same as the previous `If...Then...ElseIf` test cases except that this test case has the conditional expression enclosed in parentheses. Visual Basic enables you to optionally specify parentheses around expressions, including conditional expressions. Many programmers rarely use this feature; others use it routinely. Some would state that it is good programming practice because the clearly delimited expression makes programs more readable and lessens the chance for unintended errors by explicitly grouping the expression to be evaluated. This test case, then, is identical to the prior one except for these parentheses, so that you can determine whether they enhance or hinder performance in a selection. The code associated with this test case, which is carried out when the command button labeled 4. If() Then, ElseIf is clicked, is shown in Listing 11.26.

Listing 11.26. Test case 4: The `If` with the conditional expression in parentheses.

```
Private Sub cmdIfParen_Click()
' This routine tests speed of If (conditional with parens)
'     Then, ElseIf structure

' for loop counter
Dim lngLoopCount As Long
' used for assignments within loop
Dim strDummyAssign As String

Call Common_StartTimedTest

For lngLoopCount = 0 To txtMaxLoops - 1
    If (lblCondition = 1) Then
        strDummyAssign = "One"
    ElseIf (lblCondition = 2) Then
        strDummyAssign = "Two"
    ElseIf (lblCondition = 3) Then
        strDummyAssign = "Three"
    ElseIf (lblCondition = 4) Then
        strDummyAssign = "Four"
    ElseIf (lblCondition = 5) Then
        strDummyAssign = "Five"
    ElseIf (lblCondition = 6) Then
        strDummyAssign = "Six"
    ElseIf (lblCondition = 7) Then
        strDummyAssign = "Seven"
    Else
        strDummyAssign = "Error"
    End If
```

continues

Listing 11.26. continued

```
Next lngLoopCount

Call Common_EndTimedTest(lblIfParen)

End Sub
```

Results of Selection Tests

Evaluating selection performance adequately consists of several steps. You must evaluate performance for each method when the first condition is true, when the middle condition is true, and again when the last condition is true. You might assume that whichever selection method is fastest for the case in which the first condition is true will also be the fastest when the middle or last conditions are true. However, this would be just an *assumption*, and a very important aspect of performance tuning is to check all your assumptions at the door. Assumptions in performance tuning are likely to lead you astray far more often than they will help you. Therefore, for this type of test case, you should set up your test to cover all the bases, and check all aspects of the alternate methods under comparison.

The first test was to examine each method when the first condition of the selection was satisfied, with 5000 loops used in the test. You can see the results of one run of this test in Figure 11.7. The normalized results for multiple timings are shown in Table 11.7.

Table 11.7. Test scenario: Condition 1 of 7 `True`, 5000 loops.

Type of Test	*Normalized Time Ratio*
`Select Case`	1.00
`If Then, Else`	1.32
`If Then, ElseIf`	1.33
`If () Then, ElseIf`	1.31

In this test round, only one clear result emerges: The `Select Case` statement is significantly faster than the other methods. The differentiation between the remaining methods is very small, with very close averages. Additionally, standard deviations are large for these methods, which indicates a variance in timings and an average that is likely to fluctuate as more timings are gathered.

The next step is to see if the same findings hold true when the `True` condition for the selection approaches is the fourth of seven rather than the first of seven. The tests are rerun with 5000 loops and the fourth condition is set to `True` on the test program main form. You can see the

results of one run of this test in Figure 11.8. The normalized results for multiple timings are shown in Table 11.8.

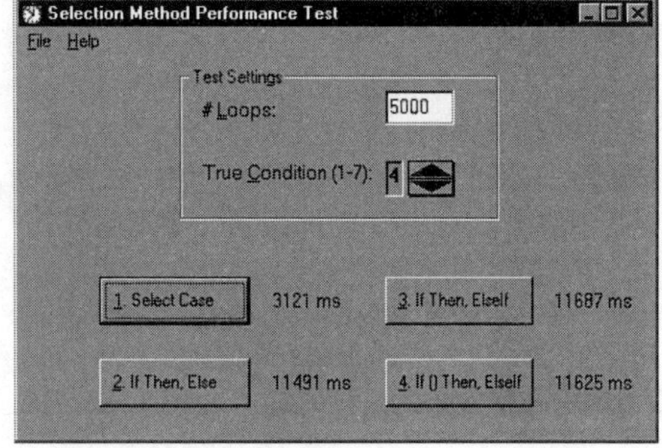

Figure 11.8.
A selection test program with condition 4 `True`.

Table 11.8. Test scenario: Condition 4 of 7 `True`, 5000 loops.

Type of Test	*Normalized Time Ratio*
`Select Case`	1.00
`If Then, Else`	3.68
`If Then, ElseIf`	3.74
`If () Then, ElseIf`	3.72

In this test round, again one clear result emerges: The `Select Case` statement is still significantly faster than the other methods. In fact, the `Select Case` method has a much larger performance advantage over the other methods when the `True` condition is the fourth rather than the first, as shown by the normalized data for both test runs. If the testing had been stopped after the first test round, you might have mistakenly assumed that `Select Case` provides performance boosts on the range of 30 percent, whereas now you can see that the potential boosts can be much greater than that. The differentiation between the other methods remains very small. Interestingly enough, though, the relative order of the `If()` approach compared to the other approaches remains the same, giving you slightly more confidence in the data.

Next, the third round of testing is carried out with the seventh condition satisfied to see if the results still hold true. The tests are rerun with 5000 loops and the seventh condition set to `True` from the test program main form. You can see the results from one run of this test in Figure 11.9. The normalized results for multiple timings are shown in Table 11.9.

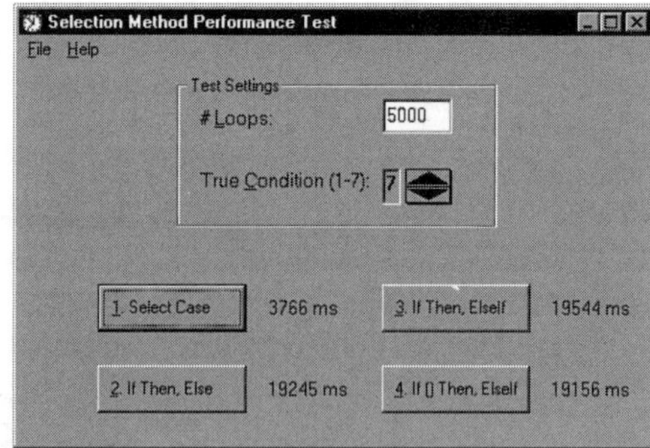

Figure 11.9.
A selection test program with condition 7 `True`.

Table 11.9. Test scenario: Condition 7 of 7 `True`, 5000 loops.

Type of Test	*Normalized Time Ratio*
`Select Case`	1.00
`If Then, Else`	5.12
`If Then, ElseIf`	5.19
`If () Then, ElseIf`	5.09

Once again, the `Select Case` statement remains the clear winner. And in this case, its margin of victory over the other methods is the largest yet. A clear optimization advantage is evident: `Select Case` should be used over the other methods because it offers significant performance advantages. Another clear trend is apparent: The greater the number of conditions there are to evaluate, the larger the performance benefit of `Select Case` over alternative methods. This implies that it might even be worth restructuring code if a series of disjointed `If...Then` statements can be reordered into the significantly faster `Select Case` selection method. Performance paybacks can be very significant.

> **TIP:** Use the `Select Case` selection method whenever possible. It offers significant performance benefits over alternative methods such as `If...Then...ElseIf`. The farther down in the selection levels that you place the `True` condition within the selection evaluation, the greater the performance benefit.

The data comparing the other methods doesn't enable you to reach any sweeping conclusions. The methods remain very close. However, sometimes in performance tuning the absence of a dramatic difference between approaches can itself be a valuable finding. The `If` parentheses method has turned out to be slightly faster than alternative `If` methods in each test round. Its

degree of advantage over other methods is too slight to list it as a significant performance advantage, but it does demonstrate that there is no performance penalty for using `If()`. Those who like to use this method for the good programming practice benefits it provides can, with this test data, breathe easy and continue the practice, comforted by the thought that in this case at least, their good programming practice is not adversely affecting performance.

> **TIP:** Use of the parentheses expression qualifier in conditional statements makes no significant difference in performance.

There is yet another performance judgment you can make from the data gathered so far. You have already looked at data separately depending on which condition is satisfied; there is also a benefit to looking at this data together. It can be quite interesting to evaluate the comparative performance between a match on the first, fourth, and seventh conditions. The following normalized-result table pulls together data from the first three test rounds. Absolute average times for each test carried out are compared for all methods and converted into normalized results, as shown in Table 11.10.

Table 11.10. Test scenario: Comparison of conditions 1, 4, and 7 of 7 `True`, 5000 loops.

	Normalized Time Ratio		
Type of Test	*1 of 7* `True`	*4 of 7* `True`	*7 of 7* `True`
`Select Case`	1.00	1.10	1.32
`If Then, Else`	1.32	4.03	6.75
`If Then, ElseIf`	1.33	4.10	6.86
`If () Then, ElseIf`	1.31	4.08	6.72

A clear trend is evident from this data. Regardless of which selection method you use, the deeper the `True` condition, the longer Visual Basic takes to process the selection. Any selection method will perform much more quickly if the satisfied criterion is the first choice rather than the last. This offers you another significant area of optimization when designing your selections. If you can group the conditions that are most likely to be satisfied at the start of your selection method, and those that are least likely to be satisfied at the bottom of the selection method, you will enhance performance. For example, if you must set up a selection statement to handle orders for product A, B, C, or D, and 80 percent of your sales are for product B, make sure that B appears as your first `Case` statement. You will have more first-case optimal matches and fewer last-case, least optimal matches.

TIP: Ensure that your most frequently matched conditions appear at the front of your selection case structure and that your least frequently matched conditions appear at the end of the choices. Likewise, put the conditions that are most likely to be true conditions first in `If` statements. This can result in significant performance gains.

Miscellaneous Syntax

The final series of tests in this chapter consists of a look at a variety of miscellaneous code issues. The focus in this round of tests is to study issues of perhaps less importance or visibility, but nevertheless issues that you are likely to encounter frequently when entering code. If you have ever thought "I wonder if the interpreter is slow to process this…" but considered the issue too trivial to pursue at the time, perhaps you will find your answer in this round of tests! The sample program for this round of tests, Misc32.exe, is available on the CD-ROM, and its main form is shown in Figure 11.10.

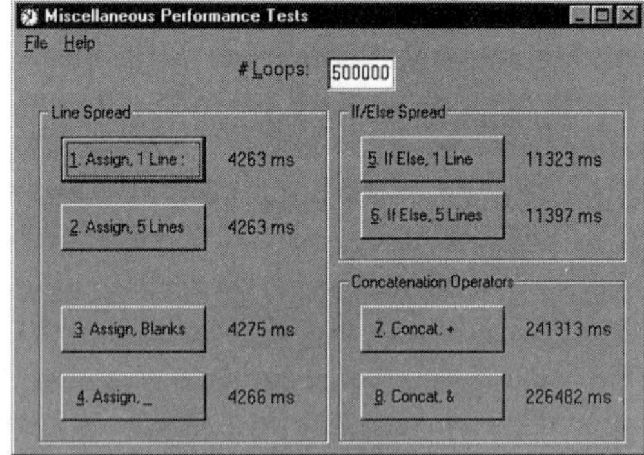

Figure 11.10.
Miscellaneous tests.

One-Line Versus Multiline Assignments

The first test is a look at the performance comparison of carrying out multiple assignments on one line or each on a separate line. You can merge statements on one line with the : separator. This technique is used in the test code associated with the command button labeled 1. Assign, 1 Line that appears in Listing 11.27.

Listing 11.27. Test case 1: Assignments on one line.

```
Private Sub cmdAssign1_Click(Index As Integer)

' This routine tests speed of 5 assignments on 1 line

' for loop counter
Dim lngLoopCount As Long
```

```
' used for assignments within loop
Dim lngDummyAssignA As Long
Dim lngDummyAssignB As Long
Dim lngDummyAssignC As Long
Dim lngDummyAssignD As Long
Dim lngDummyAssignE As Long

Call Common_StartTimedTest

For lngLoopCount = 0 To txtMaxLoops - 1
    lngDummyAssignA = lngLoopCount + 1: lngDummyAssignB = lngLoopCount + 2:
   ➥ lngDummyAssignC = lngLoopCount + 3:
   ➥  lngDummyAssignD = lngLoopCount + 4:
   ➥ lngDummyAssignE = lngLoopCount + 5
Next lngLoopCount

Call Common_EndTimedTest(lblAssign1)

End Sub
```

The alternative is to carry out each assignment on a separate line. This technique would generally be regarded as better programming practice because it provides programs that are more readable and maintainable. The test case is carried out when you click the command button labeled 2. Assign, 5 Lines and is shown in Listing 11.28.

Listing 11.28. Test case 2: Assignments on five lines.

```
Private Sub cmdAssign5_Click()
' This routine tests speed of 5 assignments over 5 lines

' for loop counter
Dim lngLoopCount As Long
' used for assignments within loop
Dim lngDummyAssignA As Long
Dim lngDummyAssignB As Long
Dim lngDummyAssignC As Long
Dim lngDummyAssignD As Long
Dim lngDummyAssignE As Long

Call Common_StartTimedTest

For lngLoopCount = 0 To txtMaxLoops - 1
    lngDummyAssignA = lngLoopCount + 1
    lngDummyAssignB = lngLoopCount + 2
    lngDummyAssignC = lngLoopCount + 3
    lngDummyAssignD = lngLoopCount + 4
    lngDummyAssignE = lngLoopCount + 5
Next lngLoopCount

Call Common_EndTimedTest(lblAssign5)

End Sub
```

One-Line Versus Multiline Assignment Results

You can see the results for one run of this test in Figure 11.10. Normalized results collected over multiple runs yield essentially the same findings. There is little significant performance difference between dividing a statement over multiple lines or merging it on one line with the : separator.

> **TIP:** There is little performance difference between statements on multiple lines and statements merged onto one line with the : separator. Therefore, it is recommended that you use separate lines for statements to enhance program readability and maintainability.

Blank Lines and Line-Continuation Symbols

The next test is similar to the previous one but focuses on the impact of blank lines and statements spread across multiple lines with the underscore (_) statement separator. The code associated with the command button labeled 3. Assign, Blanks will carry out the same multiline assignments as the previous test, except that the test has now been modified so that it is interspersed with many blanks lines. You can see the code in Listing 11.29. This test is conducted to see if the act of processing blank lines slows down the interpreter. Because blank lines are supposedly not generated in the Visual Basic–produced executable, you would expect the answer to be no. This test is conducted outside of the development environment. In the Exercises section you will conduct the test within the development environment.

Listing 11.29. Test case 3: Blanks separating assignment lines.

```
Private Sub cmdAssignBlanks_Click()
' This routine tests speed of blank lines interspersed with assignments

' for loop counter
Dim lngLoopCount As Long
' used for assignments within loop
Dim lngDummyAssignA As Long
Dim lngDummyAssignB As Long
Dim lngDummyAssignC As Long
Dim lngDummyAssignD As Long
Dim lngDummyAssignE As Long

Call Common_StartTimedTest

For lngLoopCount = 0 To txtMaxLoops - 1
```

```
    lngDummyAssignA = lngLoopCount + 1


    lngDummyAssignB = lngLoopCount + 2



    lngDummyAssignC = lngLoopCount + 3


    lngDummyAssignD = lngLoopCount + 4



    lngDummyAssignE = lngLoopCount + 5




Next lngLoopCount

Call Common_EndTimedTest(lblAssignBlanks)

End Sub
```

The other related test is to carry out the same assignment statements, spreading them over multiple lines by using the _ line-continuation symbol. As with the previous test case, no slow-down is expected here because the Visual Basic executable contains the nontextual p-code rather than direct source code lines, and this test is conducted with the executable outside of the development environment. In the Exercises section at the end of the chapter you will conduct the test within the development environment. The code for this test is associated with the command button labeled 4. Assign, _ and appears in Listing 11.30.

Listing 11.30. Test case 4: Line continuation spreading assignment lines.

```
Private Sub cmdAssignSeperators_Click()
' This routine tests speed of assignments spread across
' multiple lines with line continuation

' for loop counter
Dim lngLoopCount As Long
' used for assignments within loop
Dim lngDummyAssignA As Long
Dim lngDummyAssignB As Long
Dim lngDummyAssignC As Long
```

continues

Listing 11.30. continued

```
Dim lngDummyAssignD As Long
Dim lngDummyAssignE As Long

Call Common_StartTimedTest

For lngLoopCount = 0 To txtMaxLoops - 1
    lngDummyAssignA _
    = _
    lngLoopCount _
    + _
    1
    lngDummyAssignB _
    = _
    lngLoopCount _
    + _
    2
    lngDummyAssignC _
    = _
    lngLoopCount _
    + _
    3
    lngDummyAssignD _
    = _
    lngLoopCount _
    + _
    4
    lngDummyAssignE _
    = _
    lngLoopCount _
    + _
    5
Next lngLoopCount

Call Common_EndTimedTest(lblAssignSeperators)

End Sub
```

Blank Line, Continuation Line Results

You can see the results for one run of this test in Figure 11.10. Although you can observe a slight difference, normalized results collected over multiple runs indicate that the performance of test cases 2, 3, and 4 on the test program have no significant performance difference. There is no measurable impact of a regular series of assignment statements as demonstrated in test case 2, a series of statements interspersed with blanks as in test case 3, or the same statements divided with line-continuation symbols as in test case 4.

One-Line or Five-Line *If...Then...Else*

The next test case looks at performance differences between an `If...Then...Else` statement on one line, and the same statement spread over five lines. Note that an `End If` is required if the `If`

statement is spread over multiple lines, but is not allowed if it is on just one line. You can see the code associated with the command button labeled If 5. Else, 1 Line in Listing 11.31.

Listing 11.31. Test case 5: One-line `If...Then...Else`.

```
Private Sub cmdIfElse1_Click()

' This routine tests speed of an If then, else contained all on one line

' for loop counter
Dim lngLoopCount As Long
' used for assignments within loop
Dim lngDummyAssign As Long

Call Common_StartTimedTest

For lngLoopCount = 0 To txtMaxLoops - 1
    If lngLoopCount Mod 2 = 0 Then lngDummyAssign = lngLoopCount + 1 Else
➥ lngDummyAssign = ((lngLoopCount + 2) / 100) ^ 2
Next lngLoopCount

Call Common_EndTimedTest(lblIfElse1)

End Sub
```

The code associated with the command button labeled 6. If Else, 5 Lines is shown in Listing 11.32.

Listing 11.32. Test case 6: Five-line `If...Then...Else...EndIf`.

```
Private Sub cmdIfElse5_Click()

' This routine tests speed of an If then, else spread across 5 lines

' for loop counter
Dim lngLoopCount As Long
' used for assignments within loop
Dim lngDummyAssign As Long

Call Common_StartTimedTest

For lngLoopCount = 0 To txtMaxLoops - 1
    If lngLoopCount Mod 2 = 0 Then
        lngDummyAssign = lngLoopCount + 1
    Else
        lngDummyAssign = ((lngLoopCount + 2) / 100) ^ 2
    End If
Next lngLoopCount

Call Common_EndTimedTest(lblIfElse5)

End Sub
```

One-Line or Five-Line *If...Then...Else* Results

You can see the results for one run of this test in Figure 11.10. Multiple runs show a similar result: The one-line `If...Then...Else` seems to have a slight performance advantage, but over repeated test runs the difference is negligible. There seems to be no significant benefit to one-line `If` statements. Some would say that one-line `If` statements are bad programming practice because they are less readable. In any event, there seems to be no major performance advantage to such an approach.

String Concatenation

Visual Basic provides two operators for concatenating strings: Both the + operator and the & operator will merge strings. Arguments have been made by various industry experts for each operator to become the standard. The next test compares the speed of these two methods. The first test case is carried out by the code in Listing 11.33. This code is associated with the command button labeled 7. Concat, +.

Listing 11.33. Test case 7: Plus-sign concatenation.

```
Private Sub cmdConcatPlus_Click()
' This routine tests speed of assignments using + concatenation

' for loop counter
Dim lngLoopCount As Long
' used for assignments within loop
Dim strDummyAssign As String

Call Common_StartTimedTest

For lngLoopCount = 0 To txtMaxLoops - 1
    strDummyAssign = "Your program load time should be optimized " + "
    ➥ if you have time during the load period to recite three times: "
    strDummyAssign = strDummyAssign + "Sly " + "Sally " + "sickly " +
    ➥"slurped " + "the " + "purple " + "slop!"
Next lngLoopCount

Call Common_EndTimedTest(lblConcatPlus)

End Sub
```

The next test case is carried out by the code in Listing 11.34. This code is associated with the command button labeled 8. Concat, &.

Listing 11.34. Test case 8: Ampersand concatenation.

```
Private Sub cmdConcatAmpersand_Click()
' This routine tests speed of assignments using & concatenation

' for loop counter
Dim lngLoopCount As Long
' used for assignments within loop
Dim strDummyAssign As String

Call Common_StartTimedTest

For lngLoopCount = 0 To txtMaxLoops - 1
    strDummyAssign = "Your program load time should be optimized " & "
    ➥if you have time during the load period to recite three times: "
    strDummyAssign = strDummyAssign & "Sly " & "Sally " & "sickly " &
    ➥"slurped " & "the " & "purple " & "slop!"
Next lngLoopCount

Call Common_EndTimedTest(lblConcatAmpersand)

End Sub
```

String Concatenation Results

The results from one test run appear in Figure 11.10. Repeated runs showed normalized values of

Ampersand operator (&): 1.00
Plus sign operator (+): 1.06

The ampersand offers a slight performance advantage over the plus sign. Using the ampersand is better programming practice in a sense, because when you're viewing source code it is clear that the operator will work with string data. When you're viewing source-code statements that use the plus sign, on the other hand, that operator could be adding numbers or concatenating strings. Therefore, there is greater risk of coding errors and readability errors with the plus-sign approach. The performance benefits are small, but experience has shown that the use of such operators is often highly subjective among programmers. If you are embroiled in an office debate over whether + or & is a preferable standard and your heart lies with & for its good programming practice advantages, the performance-benefits ammunition should be enough for you to emerge victorious!

> **TIP:** The ampersand offers a negligible or very slight performance advantage over the plus sign.

Execution Time Inside and Outside the Development Environment

So far, the timings you have examined have come from outside the Visual Basic development environment. What if you were to carry out the same tests within the development environment? This is the mode in which many developers carry out performance testing because it is more convenient to modify source code and run a quick trial right in the environment than to generate an executable and execute it. However, this is *not* the correct way to assess Visual Basic performance.

Users will not be running their programs in this environment, so if performance analysis is performed here, results will be skewed and not representative of the performance issues facing the user who simply runs his executable file. The purpose of the next test is to determine how big of a skew the Visual Basic development environment introduces to performance assessments.

To carry out this test, you simply go into the Visual Basic development environment and load the callar32.vbp project, which is on the CD-ROM that accompanies this book. This enables you to repeat the same test program that was used to evaluate `ByVal` versus no `ByVal` timings earlier in this chapter. Figure 11.2 shows the timings produced by running the callar32.exe independently of the Visual Basic environment. These timings were then reproduced by running the source code from within the development environment. Those normalized results are shown in Table 11.11.

Table 11. 11. Comparison of call argument technique test outside and inside the Visual Basic environment.

Test	*From EXE File*	*From Within Visual Basic*
Function call (`ByVal`)	1.19	2.21
Function call (no `ByVal`)	1.16	2.29
Subroutine call (`ByVal`)	1.04	1.88
Subroutine call (no `ByVal`)	1.00	1.91

The execution times for these particular tests increase significantly in the Visual Basic environment, with test-case duration nearly double in some cases. In addition, notice that the relative order of the test-case performance changes whether the tests are run within Visual Basic or outside of it! This is because different actions are taken to handle the interpreted code at runtime than at development time. The effect is particularly noticeable with `ByVal` parameters. The development versus runtime skew is less noticeable in many other areas. Nevertheless, it is an important factor of which you should be aware.

With a little thought it is easy to deduce at least one reason for the additional slowness. When you have the VB environment running, the environment itself is another program loaded by Windows that takes up memory and resources and can have memory-swapping ramifications that can translate into performance impact. Some insight into the memory layout of Visual Basic provides further understanding. Visual Basic maintains symbol tables in data segments in the development environment that are not present in the final executable. When your program runs in the development environment, VB has stored the text-name representations of your variables and constants in this symbol table. This is, in effect, optimized out when you produce your executable, because the executable does not contain the textual representations for them. The Visual Basic environment also provides support when your program runs under it for a robust range of debug capabilities, which adds further overhead to the processing going on. The Visual Basic development environment, in conjunction with Windows, is doing more work to make your program run than would be carried out by the system if your program were interpreted by the runtime interpreter outside Visual Basic. On the other hand, in certain cases a program can load faster when run from the Visual Basic development environment. One example of this is if you are in the 16-bit environment running a program that utilizes VBXs. When you're in the development environment, the VBXs required by your project are likely already loaded and do not have to be freshly loaded from disk when you start your program.

All these considerations add up to one important bottom line—don't gauge the performance your users will be faced with based on testing carried out in the Visual Basic environment. Even though performance assessments can always be skewed by a myriad of system factors, that is no need to introduce a large skew that can be easily avoided. Simply generate EXE files and carry out your timings outside Visual Basic. Likewise, if you are running programs in the Visual Basic environment as a user rather than as a developer to accomplish tasks with those applications, you can enjoy performance benefits simply by running your user-level applications from executables instead.

TIP: Always run applications in their executable (EXE) format rather than from within the Visual Basic environment when assessing performance. Running programs from within the Visual Basic environment can not only cause programs to run slower, it can also provide different relative performance results than you would observe outside the environment.

Summary

This chapter focuses on the structure of code, the selection of specific syntactical constructs, and the impact they have on performance. Sample programs highlight various aspects of performance.

The first focus is on the packaging of routines. In-line code is demonstrated to be significantly faster than procedures. The use of in-line code offers significant performance advantages, at the cost of program maintainability. Subroutines are faster than functions. Functions incur slightly more overhead in passing back return values.

The speed difference between calling procedures in the same form and those in another module is negligible. Decisions on the approach to use in this area should probably be based as much on desired program standards and conventions as on performance considerations.

`For` loops are significantly faster than `Do...While` loops. Variants should be avoided as loop indexes. `Select` statements are much faster than `If...Then...ElseIfs`, and placing frequently matched conditions at the top of such selections is an important optimization tactic.

The execution times are slower in the Visual Basic development environment than outside it. Therefore, you should assess performance outside the Visual Basic development environment to get the most accurate and user-relevant data, because that is the expected user configuration for most applications.

These tips provide some insight into code structuring that can result in measurable performance improvements. Some of these come at the cost of code maintainability. The value of such tradeoffs will be unique to each application and programming situation. If you're armed with performance knowledge, you are at least in a position to understand these trade-offs and to optimize where appropriate.

Obey the Signs

Wrong Way: You should attempt to optimize procedure calls that are infrequently executed.

This chapter demonstrates that you can perform significant optimization on procedures by using in-line code as opposed to procedure calls. Additionally, subroutine calls can be more efficient than function calls. However, the sample programs presented in this chapter that make those points clear consist of code that calls procedures or in-line statements hundreds or thousands of times. Most program flows will not execute a procedure or in-line code candidate block repeatedly in that fashion. Therefore, before optimizing procedure calls, you should give careful consideration to how frequently the calls are exercised. If a call is made just occasionally in a program flow, there will be little benefit to focusing optimization attention on that call.

Beware of Falling Rocks: Don't gauge performance for your user within the Visual Basic development environment.

Programs perform differently in the Visual Basic development environment than when run as an executable with a runtime interpreter outside Visual Basic. A common mistake in gauging performance is considering performance inside the development environment because that is where you are typically working with your source code.

However, the performance impact felt by your user will occur outside of the development environment. Because the timings will differ, performance analysis should be carried out on an executable outside the environment.

Q&A

Q Will a program run faster inside the Visual Basic development environment or outside the Visual Basic development environment?

A Programs execute more quickly outside the Visual Basic development environment because, among other reasons, symbol names have been optimized into intermediate pseudo code or p-code. However, in certain cases programs can load more quickly within the Visual Basic development environment.

Q Which has faster performance when a return value is required—a function call or a subroutine call?

A A subroutine call will generally have faster performance, as shown by the examples in this chapter.

Q Are there significant performance differences between a call made within the same form module or a call made from form code to a subroutine defined in a different BAS module?

A The actual performance difference will be slight, particularly with small programs that are not run under memory-constrained conditions. However, there are some memory considerations that come into play. Code defined in forms will always be loaded with the form and thus take up more memory, whereas if it's defined in the module it will be loaded the first time a call for that module is required. Therefore, in some cases the module approach can offer memory advantages that can result in performance benefits. However, in most cases the difference between these two approaches will likely be slight.

Workshop

1. Write a program that passes many parameters to a function. The function should perform a calculation and build a complex return string. Then implement the same program with a subroutine, passing the return value calculated by the subroutine in a parameter of the subroutine. Compare the performance of the function call and the subroutine call. What percentage of speedup does the subroutine call yield for you over the function call?
2. Return to the test cases in misc32.vbp. Rerun the tests to assess performance with blank lines and line-continuation characters inside the Visual Basic environment rather than from the EXE file. Are the results the same as or different from within the Visual Basic environment?

Optimization Strategies: Controls

Controls provide the Visual Basic programmer with the ability to extend the capabilities of Visual Basic. When it comes to performance considerations, however, the programmer must use controls responsibly. The chapters in this section present information about how to maximize performance when using custom and built-in Visual Basic controls.

Chapter 12, "Control Loading," focuses on how long it takes controls to load into memory. Specifically, the chapter addresses controls that are "lightweight" and "heavyweight," comparing their loading times. The chapter also discusses other memory and loading concerns, such as dynamically creating controls at runtime.

Chapter 13, "Control Properties," takes a look at controls in general and how best to use them in code. The chapter focuses on the pros and cons of using the default property value on controls versus using explicit property value references, the direct use of control properties versus placing them in variables, and other control behavior issues such as referencing properties with the `With` keyword.

Chapter 14, "Custom Controls," discusses the benefits and drawbacks of using custom controls versus using standard Visual Basic controls. A comparison between using a custom control versus implementing the same functionality using a little ingenuity and a standard Visual Basic control is presented, along with an analysis of which performs better.

At the end of Part IV, you should have a much clearer picture of how controls operate, how to maximize efficiency in your applications when using controls, and the trade-offs you'll always face when trying to balance maintainability with program speed.

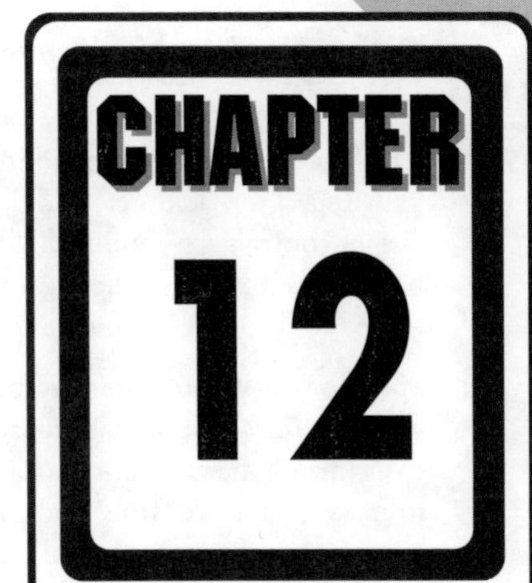

Control Loading

One of the performance problems many Visual Basic programmers are all too familiar with is the load time of custom controls. Perhaps you have had the experience of turning to your boss or your users after they have watched the 15-second load time of their program with dismay and said, "There's nothing I can do about that, that's just how fast the controls load!" This chapter examines those issues. Are you really helpless to do anything about the speed of custom control loads? And for that matter, how much of a performance penalty is inherent in the loading of custom controls? Is it really as severe as everyone says?

The first thing this chapter addresses is the question of whether all controls are created equal with respect to load time. Load time differences between various types of lightweight and heavyweight controls are examined. Then the chapter moves on to consider whether load time can be enhanced by the judicious use of control types and multiple instances of a control. The related topic of the advantages of dynamically creating controls is also examined.

Specific sample programs are provided both to illustrate the load times of programs with various control configurations and to demonstrate the improvements that can be gained by reorganizing the custom-control approach. This chapter does not provide any magic answers to make custom controls load instantly. However, it *can* enable you to understand—and in some cases enhance—control load time rather than simply use control loading as a generic scapegoat for any program that is slow to load.

Comparing Control Loading Between 16-Bit VBXs, 16-Bit OLE Controls, and 32-Bit OLE Controls

32-bit Visual Basic 4.0 supports 32-bit OLE controls (sometimes referred to as OCXs). Thus, the control-load activity it carries out is different than that of 16-bit Visual Basic 4.0, which supports both 16-bit OLE controls and VBXs (all 16-bit). Visual Basic 3.0, of course, supports only VBX controls. For test purposes, a series of conversions was carried out by the authors between different Visual Basic environments and configurations. A series of programs was converted from a Visual Basic 3.0 VBX implementation to a Visual Basic 4.0 16-bit VBX implementation to a Visual Basic 4.0 16-bit OLE control implementation to a 32-bit OLE control implementation by simply changing the controls, with no code changes.

As for load times, general findings held consistent between all versions. It was always true that dynamically created picture controls outperformed design-time picture controls with respect to loading, that picture controls loaded faster than image controls, and that custom controls, whether VBXs or OLE controls, introduced noticeable load delay with each additional control included.

In the test applications that were examined, 16-bit VBX programs loaded in roughly the same amount of time as similar programs based on 16-bit OLE controls programs. In most cases, 16-bit OLE control programs did load significantly faster than the same programs using 32-bit OLE controls, particularly in cases in which a very large number and variety of controls were used. Load-time considerations are therefore likely to remain a serious concern to the Visual Basic 4.0 developer. They do not disappear with the transition of an application to a 32-bit application based on OLE controls. In some cases, load-time performance will be significantly slower. The results will be different for every application, so the information summarized here should be viewed as just one set of test data and not a sweeping statement about all control load times. The key guide to control-loading issues remains the same for both the 16-bit and 32-bit Visual Basic application world: The fewer controls you have, the faster your programs will load. The more controls you have, the more overhead that takes place at load time, and the slower the performance for your end user.

Influence of Controls on Load Time

The focus of this chapter is on the load time of controls. Program *load time* is the time required to complete all load activity, from when a program is first invoked to when the startup window is fully displayed and the user gains control. To assess such activity, it is important to accurately measure starting at the point when Windows is requested to load the program and concluding on the last statement of the `Form_Load` event. Program *initialization* includes the load phase when Windows loads your executable and all supporting DLL files into memory.

Taking a measurement that encompasses this program-load activity can pose somewhat of a problem for traditional timing methods because it is hard to have a program time itself, so to speak, when the measurement of time should start before the launched program ever has control. Therefore, a special load utility is used to gather the timings discussed in this chapter.

That utility, Startr32.exe, measures program load time of Visual Basic programs and is supplied on the CD-ROM that accompanies this book. This program is also available in a 16-bit version, startr16.exe, on the CD-ROM. The starter utility launches the program specified in the Launch text box. If that program was built with the `Common_PostLoadTime` routine as the last statement of its `Form_Load` event, after that program loads, the total load-time duration is displayed. The starter program's main form is pictured in Figure 12.1. Refer to Chapter 7, "Supporting Utilities for Performance Analysis," for a detailed discussion of this utility.

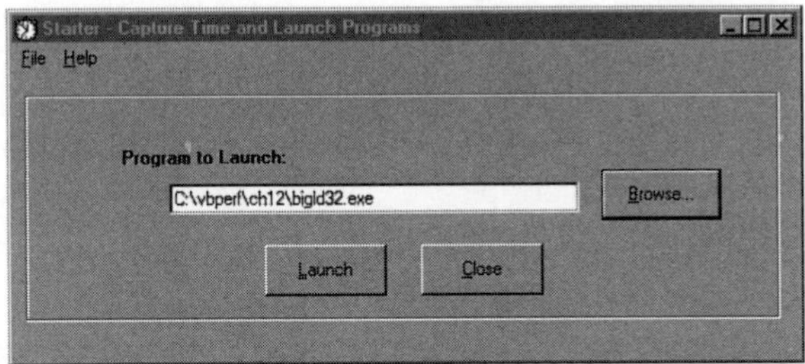

Figure 12.1.
The main form of the starter utility.

The need to use such a utility brings up a couple important considerations about control load time. Much of the load time is a burden carried by Windows before your program ever gets to its first line of code. The controls you use affect load time as much as or more than the lines of code in your startup `Sub Main` or `Form_Load` events. Programs can use both custom controls and standard controls. *Custom controls* are controls stored in separate files, such as 32-bit OLE controls, 16-bit OLE controls, and the inherently 16-bit VBX control for 16-bit applications.

Standard controls are the built-in Visual Basic controls, such as the text box and label controls, that are part of Visual Basic, as opposed to stored in a separate control file. Each custom control must be copied into memory from its file on disk before it can be used, and even standard controls must be initialized into memory for the same reason. Therefore, the more total custom controls you use, the more time is spent loading. The ramifications are clear. The fewer controls in your application, the faster it will load.

> **TIP:** If you can reduce the total number of custom controls your application uses, you will reduce load time.

Another way to reduce control-constrained load time is to redesign your application so that fewer controls must be generated at program load and are instead defined as they are needed. Only certain types of applications lend themselves to this approach, because this design is best suited for a program that has to display graphics on demand or in response to user events than for one that must display all graphics at startup. For those types of applications, however, the create-on-demand approach can greatly improve startup time.

There are several ways to carry out on-demand control creation for graphics images such as bitmap displays, which are addressed in Chapter 16, "Displaying Pictures." Briefly, these methods of deferred loading are

- Create a new control using a control array `Load` statement and copy the picture from another image or picture box control to load the image.
- Create a new control using a control array `Load` statement and load the image with `LoadResPicture` from a resource file.
- Create a new control using a control array `Load` statement and use the `LoadPicture` technique to load the image.

Of these methods, the third will be the slowest because it must read the control from a file. Nevertheless, all these approaches can enhance initial form load time by reducing the number of controls loaded at startup.

> **TIP:** To improve startup load time, only load controls that are initially required. If other controls might be required later but are not required initially, they can be created when needed using a control array `Load` statement. Graphics controls that display bitmap images are the most likely candidates for deferred creation. These controls can be created on demand with a control array `Load` statement, with their corresponding bitmap images loaded from a resource file, from a bitmap file, or assigned from another image control.

TIP: If you are loading a picture or image control on demand, assign the picture from a resource file compiled into your project EXE with the `LoadResPicture` statement, or just reassign from the `Picture` property of an existing picture or image control when possible. This offers faster performance than loading the image directly from a bitmap file with the `LoadPicture` statement, and it eliminates the need to distribute that file with your application.

Another technique that offers the same type of advantages is to simply move controls from the main startup form to secondary forms that the program can load when required. You can use a sample application with many custom controls, BigLd32.exe, to look at this type of deferred control loading. This program is available on the CD-ROM that comes with this book in a 16-bit version, BigLd16.exe, as well as the 32-bit version, BigLd32.exe. The main window of this program is shown in Figure 12.2. The program has no code, but is simply a container for controls. Despite the fact that you have done no real code work, the required load is significant. This program takes more than 4 seconds to load on a 50MHz 486, but simply eliminating controls drastically speeds up the application. An immediate benefit is gained for each control eliminated; if several are eliminated the cumulative savings are very significant. You will go through this process in the Exercises section at the end of the chapter. After completing the exercise, you will have a clear incentive to minimize the number of controls in any of your applications about which you have performance concerns!

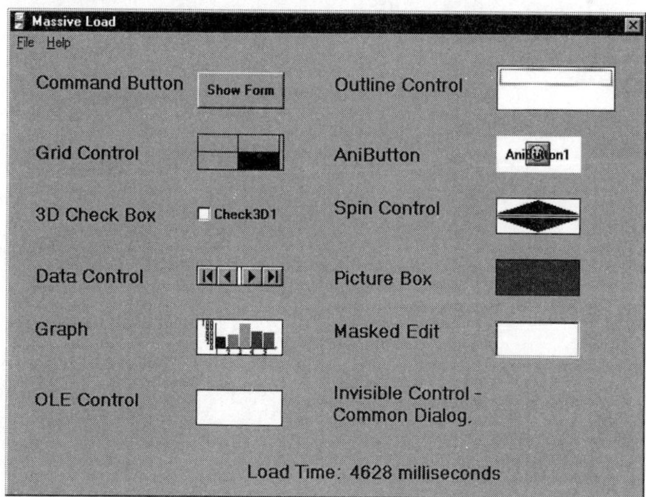

Figure 12.2.
The main form of the control-intensive load test program.

Another sample application provides an interesting contrast to the BigLd32.exe program. The startup form of this second application, LoadCt32.exe, is pictured in Figure 12.3. This program is available on the CD-ROM that comes with this book in a 16-bit version, LoadCt6.exe, as well as the 32-bit version LoadCt32.exe. This form has only two controls, both of which are command buttons. Each command button loads the same form that was used as the main form for program BigLd32.exe. Although it is a much larger program, containing two other forms as well as the main form, it loads more quickly than the BigLd32.exe program because there are fewer controls on the main form. LoadCt32.exe took just under 1 second to load, as opposed to the 4.6 seconds required by BigLd32.exe. (See Figure 12.3.)

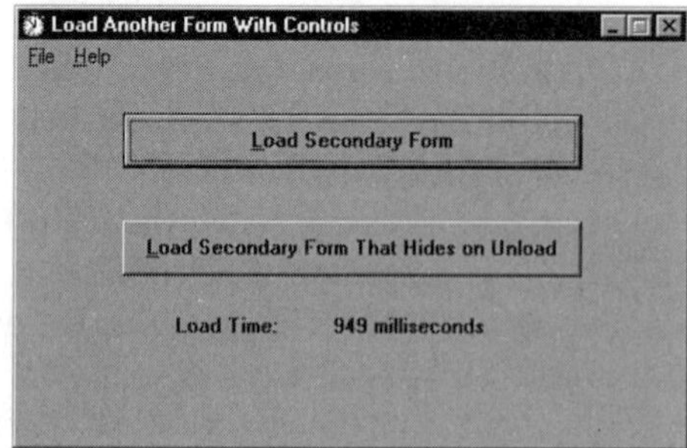

Figure 12.3.
The main window of the deferred control load program.

After the main form is displayed, you can use the command button labeled Load Secondary Form to initiate a second form load of the same form used by BigLd32.exe. You can see the resulting secondary form and its load time in Figure 12.4. The very same form that took over 4.6 seconds to load as a main form in the other program now loads in 3.9 seconds when loaded as a secondary form. In addition, if you were to close the secondary form and then select the command button to display it again, you would see that the redisplay time is in the area of 1.5 seconds.

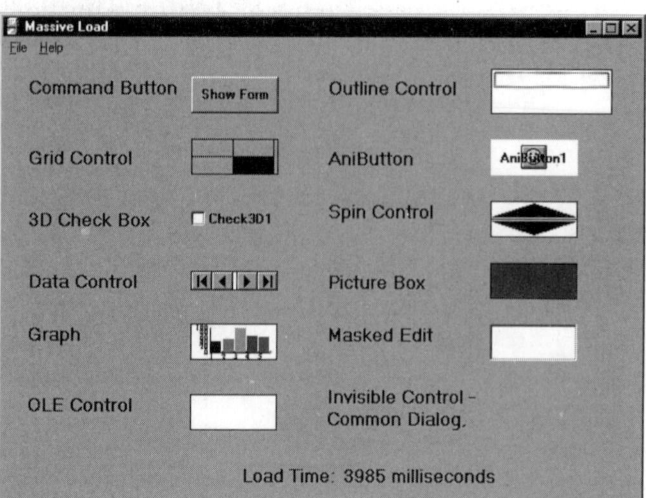

Figure 12.4.
The second form of the two-stage load test program.

Several observations can be made from these comparisons. One is that by deferring the controls to a secondary form, you have greatly reduced the user's perceived startup time, from 4.6 seconds to 1 second. This is a bit of user trickery in some respects, because the controls haven't been loaded yet when the user sees the main form. But from the user's perspective he has a program that is faster to start. Splash-screen tactics to show the user a preliminary form that diverts his attention while another form load is occurring (as discussed in Chapter 2, "When to Optimize") provide much the same benefit.

When feasible, you can design applications that put controls on a form other than the startup form to improve perceived load time. The performance bottlenecks are separated into pieces rather than delivered as one big hit. The startup time the user initially sees is reduced, because the main startup can essentially serve as a preloader for forms to follow. This delivers at least a perceived performance improvement to the user, although it certainly has design implications that might not be practical in every case.

> **TIP:** Move controls to secondary forms rather than the main form to improve the user's perceived load time.

With this sample program, you will still experience a delay when you start the second form, but it takes just 3.9 seconds to display the form when it is a secondary form rather than the 4.6 seconds required to display it as the initial form. This shows that some of the initial load time is devoted to program-initialization activity. The two-form approach has actually increased the user's overall time spent to get to the secondary form (0.9 seconds at startup plus user mouse-click time plus the 3.9 seconds to view the second form). However, the user's overall perception of his longest wait on the program has been reduced (3.9 seconds is now the longest wait he experiences, rather than the 4.6 seconds of the single-form method). The benefits of such trade-offs is sometimes difficult to assess because they are so subjective, but should be considered if you encounter a serious form load–time problem.

> **NOTE:** While the 0.7 second savings here may not seem that substantial, it is enough time to be perceptible to the user. For many short-duration operations, performance savings of a half second or more can make a tangible difference on the user's perception of the program. More important, this relatively small savings could be much more significant in other such scenarios, based on the number and type of controls deferred to the second form.

Another interesting aspect of the two-form program is that the first time the control-intensive secondary form is loaded by a click on the command button, it takes 3.9 seconds. Subsequent selections of the command button to reload the form will be in the area of 1.5 seconds. This illustrates that there are economies in reloading a control that has been previously loaded in an application. With 16-bit applications and 16-bit tools such as the WPS tool mentioned in Chapter 7, you can monitor the loading of components and observe that after a control is loaded into memory it stays loaded until the application terminates, speeding subsequent form loads that might reuse the control. With 32-bit applications the same behavior is not as easily tracked because there is no 32-bit equivalent of WPS with which to monitor it, and the ground rules are a bit different with 32-bit applications. Nevertheless, the sample program clearly illustrates that reloading a control-intensive form after its controls have been previously loaded offers a faster load operation than the original.

> **TIP:** Be aware when assessing load time of forms that reloads of control-intensive secondary forms will be quicker than the original load. Consider the time of the first load of a form to evaluate worst-case performance.

> **NOTE:** It is very important to not have other programs running when assessing load times to ensure the most accurate performance assessments. Other programs might load components into memory that affect the load time of your program under test, in effect preloading certain DLLs, VBXs, or OLE controls..

There is a method, however, that can speed up form reloads even more. If you know a given form will be frequently selected for redisplay, simply hide it rather than unload it. It will then redisplay itself very quickly when the program must redisplay it at some later point. A form can make itself visible much more quickly than it can reload itself. It is safe to assume that there is less form load/control re-initialization that must be carried out. A hidden form still has everything in its original loaded state; it simply has to repaint itself.

The command button labeled Load Secondary Form That Hides on Unload, shown in Figure 12.3, demonstrates this technique. Clicking this button loads a special version of the control-intensive form being used (as shown in Figure 12.4). This form still has just as many controls. It still is loaded initially in about the same amount of time as the other secondary form: just under 4 seconds. The difference between this form and the other secondary form is the way it unloads itself. Whenever an attempt is made to unload this form, code in the `Unload` event will instead hide the form by modifying the form's `Visible` property. Then, to keep the Visual Basic interpreter from proceeding with the unload, the `Unload Cancel` property supplied by Visual Basic is set to `True` to cause cancellation of the `Unload` event. This code appears in Listing 12.1.

Listing 12.1. The `Unload` event code to hide instead of unload.

```
Private Sub Form_Unload(Cancel As Integer)

' Hide the form, so when user causes program to request it again,
'  it can be rapidly redisplayed. Subsequent Form.Show statements
```

```
'  will cause a fast reactivate/repaint rather than a slower reload.
Me.Hide

' Set this variable which will flag Visual Basic interpreter to
'    abandon the unload.
'   The form will remain loaded in memory.
Cancel = True

End Sub
```

From the user's perspective, it will appear that the form has unloaded. It is actually just hidden from view and continues to take up memory. Then, when the user clicks on the Load Secondary Form That Hides on Unload button to view the form again, the `Show` method is carried out. In response to the Show method, Visual Basic detects that the form is loaded and hidden, and just makes it visible. The form redisplays itself in a lightning-fast 0.4 second! The other secondary form takes in the area of 1.5 seconds for each redisplay, because a reload is carried out again for each redisplay.

One other minor change is needed for this approach. The call that is used to collect postload timings, `Common_PostLoadTime`, must be moved from the `Form_Load` event to the `Form_Activate` event. Because the form is no longer reloaded with each request, the `Load` event is only called once. Because you still want to measure user-perceived redisplay time, you can move this call to the `Form_Activate` event, which will be called every time the form is redisplayed. This code is shown in Listing 12.2.

Listing 12.2. The `Activate` event called at form redisplay.

```
Private Sub Form_Activate()

' Postload call must appear here rather than load event since the technique
'   to remove the form is a hide, when form is redisplayed
'   it will not be reloaded.
Call Common_PostloadTime(lblResults)

End Sub
```

The hide technique to pave the way for rapid redisplay of forms is commonly used during optimization. The extent of the benefit of this technique depends on the type of application to which it is applied. If your application has one main form with many controls that the user spends most of his time with, and then a few supporting forms that have few controls and are infrequently utilized, the user will not realize a great difference if you implement the hide technique. On the other hand, if your application consists of many control-rich forms that a user must frequently navigate, the hide technique could substantially improve program speed and therefore the user's perception of the program's speed.

TIP: If you have a secondary form that is frequently accessed by the user and contains many controls, you can substantially improve the redisplay speed of that form by hiding it rather than unloading it when the user closes the form. It remains in memory, and subsequent `Form.Show` statements will quickly reactivate/repaint it rather than carry out the more time-consuming reload. Time savings of 1 second or more can result, depending on the type of form displayed.

Standard Control Loading

Although all controls affect load time, all controls are *not* created equal. Unlike custom controls, standard controls do not have to be loaded from a separate OLE control or VBX file because they are along for the ride with Visual Basic. In this sense, standard controls have an innate load-time performance advantage over custom controls. You can easily determine which controls are standard controls. Simply uncheck every custom control selection on the dialog box that appears when you choose Custom from the Tools menu in the Visual Basic development environment. When you view the toolbox with no custom controls defined, all the remaining controls you see are standard controls. In some cases a standard control can be used to carry out the same task for which you might turn to a custom control. For example, you could use a regular standard control check box to provide the same selection capabilities to your user as would the 3D custom control. In many cases it might not be possible or perhaps not desirable to use a standard control alternative for a custom control. Custom controls provide many rich features and functional advantages. But if your motivation is sheer performance, you might be wise to consider a standard control rather than its three-dimensional, multimedia, fireworks-color-generating alternative!

TIP: Use standard controls in lieu of custom controls, where possible, to enhance performance. Standard controls load faster due to reduced disk access at load time.

Although a standard control does not have to be loaded from a file or incur all the OLE overhead of an OLE control, it nevertheless must still be initialized and generated on the form, just as a control loaded from an OLE control file is. This is the other load penalty of controls: Not only must they be moved into memory, but they must also be initialized and painted on the form.

Because the initialization work for a control varies from one control to another, you can't predict performance of control load time without taking the time to assess and measure each individual custom control. Therefore, optimization of control loading requires considerable familiarity with your custom controls. Each has unique performance constraints, not to mention functional advantages and disadvantages.

You should expect that some controls will load faster than others; after all, each control is based on different underlying code with different resource requirements. One of the challenges of evaluating the performance of your applications, then, becomes determining which controls load faster than others.

Although this must often be considered on a case-by-case basis, one generalization can be made. Lightweight controls load faster than heavyweight controls. A *lightweight control* is one that carries less baggage than a heavyweight control. Specifically, a lightweight control does not have a window handle or associated `hwnd` property because it is not created as a window in the system as many controls are. Therefore, there is less overhead in creating it and it requires fewer resources. Lightweight controls include the align, shape, label, and image controls. The image control is perhaps the most significant in this group because it can be used in place of the picture control to contain bitmaps. An easy way to determine if a control you are considering using is a lightweight control is to check in the help file. In the help file you can search for the control you are interested in and then view the Help File control topic's property list. Next inspect the property list help file information to see if the control has an `hWnd` property. If no `hWnd` property is listed in the help file, you can consider the control to be a lightweight control. Don't just inspect the property window of the design environment, because the `hwnd` property is never listed in that property sheet for any control.

Design-Time–Created Picture Controls

A sample program to focus on showing the advantages of the lightweight image control over the heavyweight picture control is provided on the CD-ROM that accompanies this book. The program, Dt_Pic32.exe, consists of a form that loads 30 picture controls. This program is available on this book's CD, as is its 16-bit equivalent, Dt_Pic16.exe.

The picture controls loaded by this program are defined at design time. In other words, they are placed on the form in design mode and are automatically loaded when the form loads itself. The starter utility discussed earlier, Startr32.exe, is used to launch the picture-control program after capturing a start-of-load time. You can see the main window of the launched program Dt_Img32.exe in Figure 12.5. Load-time results are displayed at the bottom of that window.

Because this program consists simply of loading a form full of controls, little source code is required to create it. The only source code in the program is in the `Form_Load` event to center the form and to record the postload time. As you can see from the results displayed in Figure 12.3, the picture control program loads in slightly over 2.2 seconds. The next step is to compare this load time with that of an equivalent program based on the lightweight image controls.

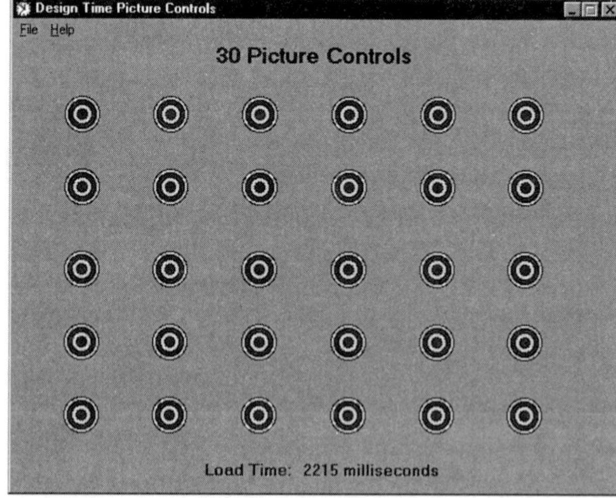

Figure 12.5.
Loading many design-time picture controls.

Design-Time–Created Image Controls

This comparison program Dt_Img32.exe is also available on the CD-ROM that accompanies this book, as is its 16-bit equivalent. This program is essentially identical to the picture control load program, except that the controls used here are image controls. This program consists of a form that has the image controls placed on it at design time just as the picture control program does. The method for timing this program is the same: The Startr32.exe utility is used to launch the program and record the time. You can see the results of launching Dt_Img32.exe in Figure 12.6. The main window looks similar to that in Figure 12.5, but image controls rather than picture controls are displayed in this window.

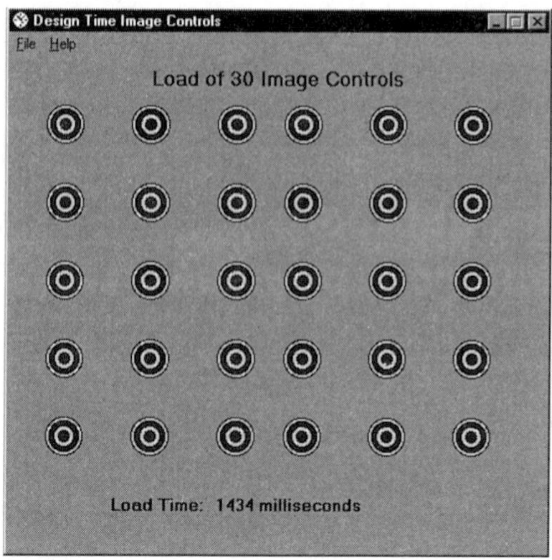

Figure 12.6.
Loading many design-time image controls.

The results show that the image-control program loads in just over 1.4 seconds. The picture control–based program takes nearly 60 percent longer to load on the PC used for the test. Windows and the Visual Basic interpreter carry out less work to create the non-window image control than they do to create the picture control, which has a window handle and other resource requirements that the lightweight image control does not have. A clear law emerges: Image controls offer faster load performance than do picture controls. If there is no reason to use a picture control, you should use an image control instead to take advantage of its faster performance.

> **TIP:** Lightweight controls are faster to load than heavyweight controls, which is a significant performance benefit.

Runtime Control Array–Created Controls: The Elegant Approach

You have seen that lightweight controls load faster than heavyweight controls. You might think that the best you can do to optimize form loading is to simply use lightweight controls when you lay out your form. There is, however, yet another related optimization step you can use if the situation warrants: You can dynamically create multiple instances of an image control during the form-load stage rather than create them at design time and pay the performance price for loading those predefined controls when the program loads.

For example, the previous sample program consists of a form with 30 image controls that were laid out at design time. Another approach can be taken to generate the same form. Only one image control needs to be created at design time, and that must be indicated as a control array by setting the image control `Index` property to `0`. Its `Visible` property is also set to `0` because it will serve as a template for the creation of other controls rather than as a control for the user.

Code can be written based on this form declaration with its one control to dynamically create more controls. This code is added to the `Form_Load` event to create additional instances of that control in a control array as the program starts, rather than explicitly creating them at design time. This code is shown in Listing 12.3.

Listing 12.3. `Form_Load` code to create a control array of 30 additional image controls at runtime.

```
Private Sub Form_Load()


Dim i%                          ' loop counter
Dim intRow As Integer           ' Current row position
Dim intCol As Integer           ' Current column position
```

continues

Listing 12.3. continued

```
Dim intCols_Desired As Integer    ' Number of columns required
Dim intRow_Spacer As Integer        ' Filler between rows
Dim intRow_Offset As Integer        ' Space between rows
Dim intRow_First As Integer         ' Position of first row
Dim intRow_Last As Integer          ' Position of last row
Dim intCol_Offset As Integer        ' Spacing between columns
Dim intCol_Spacer As Integer        ' Filler between columns


' Define the row/column positioning desired
'    Note: You only have to change two parameters to generate a
'          new layout - CONTROLS_DESIRED and ROWS_DESIRED.
'          The rest of the positioning info can be calculated
'          based on this.


' How many total controls should appear?
Const CONTROLS_DESIRED = 30

' How many rows should these controls be spread across?
Const ROWS_DESIRED = 5

' Spread total controls over given number of rows to determine number
'   of columns needed.
intCols_Desired = Fix(CONTROLS_DESIRED / ROWS_DESIRED)

' Calculate the space between each row, and between form border top/bottom
'    Allow for extra spacing above top row and below bottom row.
intRow_Spacer = (Me.Height - (ROWS_DESIRED * imgArray(0).Height))
                ➥ \ (ROWS_DESIRED + 3)
intRow_Offset = intRow_Spacer + imgArray(0).Height

' Calculate where the top and bottom row will be
intRow_First = (intRow_Spacer * 3) \ 2
intRow_Last = intRow_First + (imgArray(0).Height * ROWS_DESIRED)
                             ➥ + (intRow_Spacer * ROWS_DESIRED - 1)

' Calculate the space between each column, and between form border left/right
intCol_Spacer = (Me.Width - (intCols_Desired * imgArray(0).Width))
                            ➥ \ (intCols_Desired + 1)
intCol_Offset = intCol_Spacer + imgArray(0).Width

' Center the form on screen
Call Common_CenterForm(Me)


' Create more controls based on the one created at design time

    ' Set starting position of first control
    intRow = intRow_First
    intCol = intCol_Spacer

    ' Create each of the new controls, calculate its position, and show it
    For i% = 1 To CONTROLS_DESIRED
        ' Create and show the new control
        Load imgArray(i%)
        imgArray(i%).Visible = True
```

```
        ' Calculate the row/column position of this control.
        '    Controls are placed a column at a time before advancing
        '    to next column.
        If intRow > intRow_Last Then
            ' Need to start a new column
            intRow = intRow_First
            intCol = intCol + intCol_Offset
        End If

        ' Update the position of this new control
        imgArray(i).Left = intCol
        imgArray(i).Top = intRow

        ' Advance to next row for next time through loop
        intRow = intRow + intRow_Offset

    Next i%

' Determine the time it took the form to load
Call Common_PostloadTime(lblLoadTimeResults)

End Sub
```

This code creates additional instances of the image control by using the `Load` statement to load a new control from that first control. When creating controls in this manner, you must set the `Visible` property to `True` for the control to be visible. Likewise, you must specify the correct `Top` and `Left` properties for this newly created control. Normally they would be specified on the controls directly at design time, but with a dynamically created control they must be defined after the control is created.

Some rather extensive calculations take place to determine the correct top and left position of each control. These calculations are based on the total number of controls that should be displayed and the total number of rows to be displayed, which are both constants you can specify in the source code. With that starting point, the code displayed here will correctly handle all placement and spacing tasks. It does take considerably more development effort to implement this solution than to just lay out controls at design time. However, utilizing sample code like that in this example drastically reduces the time demand and difficulty of the development task. Using the generic code in the sample, you could quickly create your own runtime control creation and have all the spacing issues addressed in this manner. The question nevertheless remains: If you have to pay the price of some level of additional programming for this technique, do the performance paybacks merit that effort?

The answer is *perhaps*. Even with the additional code overhead to loop through the control array, carry out the load statements, and perform the left and top initializations and calculations, the program with a runtime dynamic load of controls performs faster than its counterpart that had all the image controls laid out at design time. This program, Rt_img32.exe, is available on the CD-ROM that accompanies this book, as is the 16-bit version, Rt_img16. You can see the main window of the runtime creation program and the results from one run when the program was launched with Startr32.exe in Figure 12.7. This program looks much like the design-time image-control and picture-control programs. The difference is that the controls you see on this form are image controls that were created at runtime rather than design time.

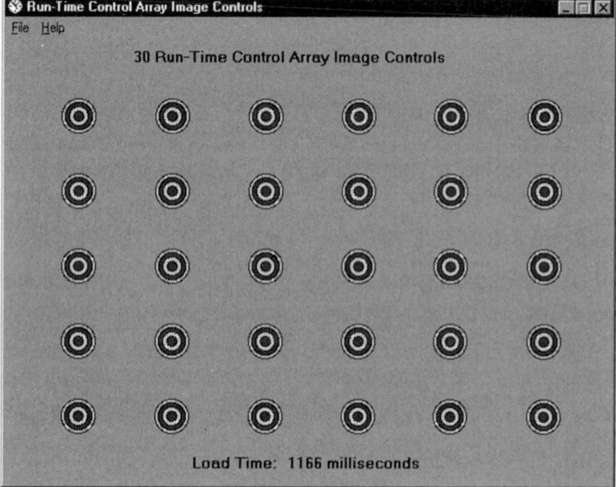

Figure 12.7.
Loading many runtime control array image controls.

As you can see from the results, this program loaded in just over 1.1 seconds. Repeated tests indicated that the program based on the design-time image control took around 27 percent longer to load than the program based on the image controls created at runtime. This is a significant savings. Whether it warrants the extra programming work to implement it, along with the maintenance penalties that go with the generation of more lines of code, depends on the degree to which the load speed of your application is perceived to be a problem. This technique is one to keep in mind when considering ways to speed up your program if you use many instances of the same type of control. The greater the number of image controls on your form with the same image, the more speedup you stand to gain from this approach. If you have many image controls but all contain different images, the speedup will not be as substantial and will be application dependent. In some cases, the dynamic load could even be slower. The best way to gauge the potential speedup is with the same type of test program used here.

It has been stated that every control has different performance considerations because every control is based on different code and has different resource demands. The dynamic load versus design-time load trade-offs are another example of these control differences. If you carry out the same type of trade-off for the picture controls (using the design-time picture controls program Dt_Pic32.exe and another program supplied on the CD-ROM, runtime picture controls Rt_Pic32.exe), you will see that creating identical picture controls dynamically offers even more of a time savings. However, if you try the same test with shape controls, you will find that shape controls load faster from design-time creation than from dynamic loading. This is because the low-level graphics activity required to generate a shape region can be handled much more quickly than that required to map all the individual pixels of a bitmap-oriented control.

> **TIP:** If a form requires many identical image and picture controls, runtime control array–created controls provide faster program loads than design-time–created controls. The more identical image or picture controls you have, the greater the speedup you stand to gain from this technique. If you have shape controls, it will be faster to lay them out at design time than to dynamically create them.

There is yet another efficiency introduced by the use of dynamically loaded image or picture box controls through a control array. These controls can also be removed if they're no longer needed through the `Unload` statement. In certain cases, this allows for more efficient programs that can reduce their memory consumption even when a form is still loaded by unloading particular controls.

Runtime Control Array–Created Controls: The Inelegant Approach

The code technique just discussed for implementing controls was a rather elegant one. The code was very maintainable and modifiable. All the developer needed do to increase the number of controls or change the row/column layout on the form is simply change a constant at the top of the `Form_Load` event. A looping construct makes it easy to follow the code. The sophisticated offset calculation approach frees the programmer from having to enter hard-coded, or exact, `Top`/`Left` property information for every control.

As elegant as this code is, however, it is not the most efficient possible. If you could eliminate the offset calculations and even eliminate the overhead of your loop you could speed up the calculations even more. The inelegant approach in Listing 12.4 accomplishes this.

Listing 12.4. The inelegant but optimal approach to dynamic control creation.

```
Private Sub Form_Load()

' Center the form on screen
Call Common_CenterForm(Me)

' Load each control, make it visible, and set right/left properties.
'   For maximum speed, no looping or variables used.
Load imgArray(1)
imgArray(1).Visible = True
imgArray(1).Left = 814
imgArray(1).Top = 810
```

continues

Listing 12.4. continued

```
Load imgArray(2)
imgArray(2).Visible = True
imgArray(2).Left = 814
imgArray(2).Top = 1830

Load imgArray(3)
imgArray(3).Visible = True
imgArray(3).Left = 814
imgArray(3).Top = 2850

Load imgArray(4)
imgArray(4).Visible = True
imgArray(4).Left = 814
imgArray(4).Top = 3870

Load imgArray(5)
imgArray(5).Visible = True
imgArray(5).Left = 814
imgArray(5).Top = 4890

Load imgArray(6)
imgArray(6).Visible = True
imgArray(6).Left = 2108
imgArray(6).Top = 810

Load imgArray(7)
imgArray(7).Visible = True
imgArray(7).Left = 2108
imgArray(7).Top = 1830

Load imgArray(8)
imgArray(8).Visible = True
imgArray(8).Left = 2108
imgArray(8).Top = 2850

Load imgArray(9)
imgArray(9).Visible = True
imgArray(9).Left = 2108
imgArray(9).Top = 3870

Load imgArray(10)
imgArray(10).Visible = True
imgArray(10).Left = 2108
imgArray(10).Top = 4890

.
.
' Middle lines ommitted in the interest of space.
'  in actual listing all index values are handled
.
.


Load imgArray(26)
imgArray(26).Visible = True
imgArray(26).Left = 7284
imgArray(26).Top = 810
```

```
Load imgArray(27)
imgArray(27).Visible = True
imgArray(27).Left = 7284
imgArray(27).Top = 1830

Load imgArray(28)
imgArray(28).Visible = True
imgArray(28).Left = 7284
imgArray(28).Top = 2850

Load imgArray(29)
imgArray(29).Visible = True
imgArray(29).Left = 7284
imgArray(29).Top = 3870

Load imgArray(30)
imgArray(30).Visible = True
imgArray(30).Left = 7284
imgArray(30).Top = 4890


' Determine the time it took the form to load
Call Common_PostloadTime(lblLoadTimeResults)

End Sub
```

The sample program with this implementation is program Rt_Img32.exe, which is on the CD-ROM. Its 16-bit equivalent, Rt_Img16.exe, is also available. The code for this approach is much uglier. It is not as easy to maintain because now there are many more lines to cover. There is a high likelihood of error because every `Top` and `Left` property was explicitly specified and might have had typing errors during data entry. And if you want to change the number of controls, rows, or columns, you have a logistical nightmare. You would have to manually recalculate the entire spacing and adjust all the index entries accordingly.

You have now eliminated work that the Visual Basic interpreter was carrying out before. It no longer has to do conditional checks and calculations inside each loop. It no longer even has to loop, eliminating the `For` overhead as well. Although the number of source-code lines is longer, when you consider the loop that was eliminated, the number of statements for the server to act on is considerably smaller with this approach.

Because the interpreter has less to cover, it can do it more quickly. However, the time consumed by the interpreter to process statements is minimal compared to the time spent on Windows initialization and paint operations during form load. Eliminating a few statements doesn't speed up the real bottleneck, which is waiting for the controls to be generated. The results confirm this. Even with the eliminated statements, performance of the elegant code approach and the inelegant approach is so close as to not be statistically significant. Each approach takes about 1.1 seconds for total load time. Given the maintenance disadvantages of the inelegant approach, it is likely not one that should be applied except in the most desperate of situations. In theory, the changes in the inelegant approach should provide some speedup, but in practice the difference is not noticeable and the code-maintenance disadvantages *are* noticeable.

Summary of Approaches

Of the approaches considered in this chapter, design-time picture boxes are the slowest, with design-time image boxes offering significantly better performance, and then runtime dynamic control creation offering the best performance. The normalized results of the timings are shown in Table 12.1.

Table 12.1. Comparison of load techniques.

Test Case	*Normalized Result*
PictureBox, design time	2.0
Image, design time	1.3
Image, runtime elegant	1.0
Image, runtime inelegant	1.0

For projects with severe load problems and many controls on the main form, a runtime dynamic creation load approach should be considered.

Summary

This chapter looks at control-loading issues and discusses the need for a careful approach to timing load duration. Consideration is given to tips that relate to control loading. One important guideline is that *if you can reduce the total number of custom controls your application uses, you will reduce load time.* The benefits of reducing the overall number of program controls to enhance load time are discussed. Techniques for reducing controls include just loading them on demand rather than initially or moving them to a secondary form rather than the startup form. Hiding a form for future redisplay is one way to enhance the speed of secondary forms; this chapter gives an example.

Another important guideline is to *use standard controls in lieu of custom controls where possible to enhance performance.* Standard controls load faster due to reduced disk access, memory load, and initialization overhead at load time. Among the standard controls, *lightweight controls are faster than heavyweight controls.* A sample program is used in this chapter to demonstrate that lightweight image controls load significantly faster than heavyweight picture controls. These same advantages are inherent in other lightweight controls.

An important load-tuning technique for many situations is to use dynamic control creation. *Runtime control array–created images and picture-box controls load faster than design-time–created controls.* The dynamic creation of such controls and the performance advantages this offers are covered in detail. You can see in the sample program that measurable improvement could be obtained by this technique and an example of going too far to optimize dynamic control creation. The dynamic load time improvements do not, however, apply to other types of controls such as shape controls.

These guidelines highlight some of the major factors that affect control performance. However, the biggest factors, particularly for custom controls, are very likely out of your hands and in some cases perhaps not easily understood. This is because there are significant code-specific performance factors for each unique custom control. You typically have no insight into the code behind commercially purchased controls because they have their own initialization techniques, resource considerations, and related performance impacts. The best you can do to understand all the load implications of such controls is to use techniques outlined in this chapter to perform your own load-time analysis. Armed with this information, you can make decisions on the merits of avoiding controls to improve form load time and performance, at the cost of the rich functionality such controls provide. The answer you settle on will be one that is unique to your own applications and circumstances.

Obey the Signs

Wrong Way: Always use dynamic control creation when multiple image controls of identical appearance are on a form.

That should not be an absolute approach, because you can overdo a good thing! It is true that dynamic control creation is faster than design-time loading of controls, but the code needed to implement this comes at the cost of additional development effort and potential for bugs. Consider each form on a case-by-case basis. If it is one that has or is likely to have performance problems, evaluate the dynamic control-creation approach. If you blindly apply it to every form, you will hamper development time and be expending effort coming up with an optimal solution in areas where your user might not perceive any difference from a less optimal approach.

Beware of Falling Rocks: When using the form-hiding technique for rapid redisplay of forms, implement the hide technique in the `Unload` event. Resist the urge to implement it elsewhere.

If you decide to hide secondary forms rather than unload them so they can be rapidly redisplayed, make sure that you code accordingly. You will have to modify the form's `Unload` event to intercept the unload and carry out the hide. Do not simply put the `Hide` statement in your own `Close` button event, because there are ways a user can cause your form to be unloaded, such as using the system Alt+F4 key combination (predefined systemwide Windows keystrokes to close a window). The only way to ensure that a form is hidden is to implement it at the `Unload` level.

Beware of Falling Rocks: Do not use a heavyweight control if a lightweight control will suffice.

There is no need to use a picture control unless you need some of its special properties. Otherwise, use an image control for the enhanced performance it provides. Likewise, do not use a text box to display non–user-supplied information if a label control will do the job, because the lightweight label control also offers efficiencies. Although the use of one lightweight control by itself might not make a big performance difference, if you use this approach whenever possible, the cumulative effect might be enough for the user to perceive.

Q&A

Q Does a picture control or an image control load faster?

A An image control loads faster because it is a lightweight control and does not have a Windows handle.

Q What statement is required to dynamically load controls through a control array?

A The `Load` statement will load and create an additional instance of a control based on the control supplied in the parameter.

Quiz

Write a program that starts with one text box on a single form and then propagates this to five total text boxes at form load time.

The answer is provided in Listing 12.5. and also as project Quiz1_32.mak in the Chapter 12 directory of the CD-ROM that accompanies this book.

Listing 12.5. The `Form_Load` event that dynamically creates four text boxes.

```
Private Sub Form_Load()
' NOTE: For this routine to work, you must have
'   added one textbox to your form in design time.
'   The name used below for this textbox is txtArray.
'   Its index property must have been set to 0 at
'   design time to make this a control array.


Dim i%  ' loop counter


Call Common_CenterForm(Me)

' Create more controls based on the one created at design time
For i% = 1 To 4
    Load txtArray(i%)
```

```
    txtArray(i%).Visible = True
Next i%

' Position the new controls on the form
txtArray(1).Left = 1080
txtArray(1).Top = 2040
txtArray(2).Left = 1080
txtArray(2).Top = 3000
txtArray(3).Left = 1080
txtArray(3).Top = 3960
txtArray(4).Left = 1080
txtArray(4).Top = 4920

End Sub
```

Workshop

1. Take the sample application from the quiz and modify it so it gathers a load time. To do this you must add the `Common_PostLoadTime` call at the end of the `Form_Load` event. Then you must start the program from the Startr32 program launcher to capture the load time. After carrying this out and recording a few load times, modify the program. Remove the code that creates the controls dynamically through a control array in the `Form_Load` event. Instead of relying on the dynamic creation, simply add the additional text boxes at design time. Then repeat the timing and notice the difference in load duration.
2. A sample application with many custom controls, BigLd32.exe, is presented in the chapter. The program has no code that was carried out at all, but is simply a container for controls. Use the Chapter 7 utility for collecting load times, Startr32.exe, to time this program on your system. Then reduce the number of controls on the main form one control at a time, collecting a new load time after each control is removed. See how many controls must be removed to shrink the load time in half. Note the savings from each control removed, and observe which types of controls seem to cost the most load time.

Control Properties

Nearly every Visual Basic program is built on controls in one way or another. Therefore, nearly every Visual Basic application is affected by the performance considerations imposed by controls. Now that you have learned the basic concepts of what controls are and how they work, this chapter discusses the use of control properties in Visual Basic code. As you know, the Visual Basic programmer cannot typically see inside a custom control to determine how it operates. This chapter analyzes some of the control behavior not readily apparent to the developer.

Although every control is a different collection of code with unique characteristics and performance considerations, you can make some very important performance generalizations. Such guidelines for control use are presented in this chapter. Using the default values of controls is compared to explicitly referencing the property whether it is the default or not. The chapter also compares the direct use of control properties in code versus the use of variables to store properties for controls.

After reading this chapter, you should be able to write more efficient code to handle properties for the controls you are using. This chapter, along with the others in Part IV, "Optimization Strategies: Controls," should give you a well-rounded insight into performance considerations of standard and third-party controls.

Control Behavior

Control behavior, whether of standard controls or of custom controls, is a result of code built into the control. This is not something that you can review or inspect when incorporating the control, however. As the control integrator, you are at the mercy of the control's documentation and must place a great deal of faith in the custom control vendor, hoping that the control will work as advertised with no bugs or negative performance consequences.

Unfortunately, controls often do introduce bugs or performance surprises. The best way to guard against these is to thoroughly test any control you will be using from a performance perspective. This includes stretching it to its limits. If your control is a tree list box control that can handle graphics, for example, you should create a test that fills it with thousands of records and then observe the performance that results. You must poke into the nooks and crannies of the custom control to determine if performance is adequate. Don't leave it up to your user!

If you do find a problem or a performance bottleneck, your choices are limited. The control implementation, including its code that deals with the properties and methods your code must interact with, is hidden from you. You can't modify it or even inspect it to help you track down what is causing a problem. You can report problems to the vendor, ask the vendor for advice about performance bottlenecks, or simply abandon the control and write the needed functionality yourself.

Often, however, developers are too quick to fault a custom control's performance or ease of implementation. Many times what seem to be shortcomings can be overcome with a better understanding of the control's attributes and characteristics, particularly for complex controls. Sometimes using the right combination of properties, as intended by the vendor, can get you past what seem to be insurmountable problems.

So there are several important considerations to keep in mind regarding controls and their impact on performance. Most importantly, realize that you are at the mercy of the control code. Of course, your users won't care much when you explain to them that the poor performance of your application isn't your fault and is due to a dog of a control. Therefore, thoroughly test and analyze the performance of any control you are thinking about incorporating. If you can't easily implement it in a simple test application, there is little reason to expect you'll fare better incorporating it into your product itself. Know your controls well. Study the documentation on available methods and properties. And finally, if you hit a road block, don't hesitate to turn to vendors or fellow programmers in forums such as those on CompuServe for a further consultation before abandoning a poor performer. Sometimes there's nothing you can do, but other times a change in technique can improve the situation.

Control Default Properties

Even though custom controls can be markedly different from one another, there are some general rules that pertain to them all. In particular, you can make some safe assumptions, backed by research, about the trade-off of speed in using control default values versus properties. Likewise, with some research we can identify performance trade-offs that pertain to the use of variables versus properties.

Working with controls involves using control methods and setting control properties. Most Visual Basic developers are aware of that. However, many new Visual Basic developers are not aware that controls can have default settings. And even those developers who are aware that these settings exist often think of them as little more than a coding convenience.

It is easy to see why many who have an awareness of the default property capability assume that using the default value for a control or specifying the property explicitly are truly equivalent. The following two lines, the first using the label's default property and the second explicitly referencing the label's caption property, have the same end result:

```
Label = "This is a test"

Label.Caption = "This is a test"
```

However, performance does seem to be different for the two methods. A simple test program can help you delineate this difference. The test program used for this purpose is shown in Figure 13.1. The program, PropDf32.exe, is available on the CD-ROM that accompanies this book. The 16-bit version, PropDf16.exe, is also available on the CD-ROM.

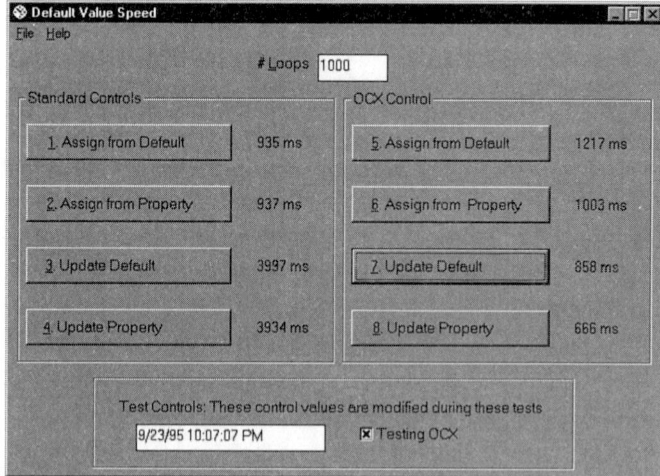

Figure 13.1.
The main window of the property assignment program.

Assigning Values from Standard Control Properties

This test program carries out a separate, default-related comparison for each command button. The top two command buttons carry out tests that compare variable assignments from a control property. The first test assigns text to a variable by using the default value of the text box standard control. (See Listing 13.1.)

Listing 13.1. Variable assignment from a default control property.

```
Private Sub cmdVal_Click()
' Test speed of standard controls in assignments by default value


Dim i% ' loop counter
Dim strTextBox As String        ' gets textbox contents

Call Common_StartTimedTest

' Carry out test algorithim repeatedly
For i% = 1 To txtLoops

    strTextBox = txtTester

Next i%


Call Common_EndTimedTest(lblValTime)

End Sub
```

This event routine, which is executed when the user clicks the top command button (labeled Assign from Default), carries out the assignment of the text box default control property to a variable. You specify the number of times this assignment is to be carried out in the # Loops text box, and the entire sequence of assignments is timed.

Then, to see the performance trade-offs of default property assignments versus explicit property assignments, you simply have to modify the program slightly as shown in Listing 13.2. This code, executed when the second button (labeled Assignment from Property) is clicked, carries out the same test except for one small difference. Here the variables are assigned from the explicit Text property of the control rather than default value. The difference between this second test case and the first is highlighted in the listing in bold.

Listing 13.2. Variable assignments from control properties.

```
Private Sub cmdProp_Click()
' Test speed of standard controls in assignments by property value


Dim i% ' loop counter
Dim strTextBox As String        ' gets textbox contents


Call Common_StartTimedTest


' Carry out test algorithim repeatedly
For i% = 1 To txtLoops

    strTextBox = txtTester.Text

Next i%


Call Common_EndTimedTest(lblPropTime)

End Sub
```

These two tests enable you to do a head-to-head comparison of the assignment speed of defaults versus property values. You can see the results from one run of this test in Figure 13.1. When repeated tests were carried out with this Visual Basic 4.0 test program, the performance of these approaches was virtually identical. However, carrying out a similar test on a program made with Visual Basic 3.0 using the Visual Basic runtime interpreter showed that the test using the Text property assignment took approximately 25 percent longer than the default property assignment method! Visual Basic 3.0 provides a clear speed advantage when the default property is referenced. Visual Basic 4.0, on the other hand, seems to provide no speed advantage at all in this area. A frequently repeated performance tip regarding Visual Basic 3.0 is to refer to controls by their default properties. This is valid advice for Visual Basic 3.0, but in light of the performance observations mentioned, seems far less pertinent for Visual Basic 4.0.

TIP: Behavior and performance of Visual Basic 4.0 programs are significantly different from Visual Basic 3.0 programs in some areas. Some optimization steps that were relevant for Visual Basic 3.0 are not relevant for Visual Basic 4.0. For instance, using the default property when assigning the value of a standard control property does not offer significant time savings in Visual Basic 4.0.

Updating Values of Standard Control Properties

Now that you have examined the effects of assigning the value of a standard control, the next question you might ask is "Is performance of the two techniques also similar when updating a control property?" In other words, when the control is on the left side of the assignment statement as opposed to the right, is using the default property faster? To test this, code was defined to update control default properties. This code is associated with the third command button from the top in Figure 13.1, labeled Update Default Values. See Listing 13.3 for the code for this button's `Click` event.

Listing 13.3. Control default value updates.

```
Private Sub cmdValUpdate_Click()
' Test speed of standard control updates with default value

Dim i% ' loop counter

' Hide the control to be updated, so our test measures just
'   update speed, and not drawing time
    txtTester.Visible = False

Call Common_StartTimedTest



' Carry out test algorithim repeatedly
For i% = 1 To txtLoops

    ' Assign the control default value to the variable
    txtTester = Now

Next i%


Call Common_EndTimedTest(lblDefUpdate)

' Show the control
txtTester.Visible = True

End Sub
```

This code simply performs updates to the default property of a standard text box control inside a loop. Timings are captured for the entire series of updates.

To compare this approach to an assignment to an explicit property, the same update is carried out to the explicitly named control's `Text` property. This code is associated with the fourth button from the top in Figure 13.1, labeled Update Properties. The code for the `Click` event of this button is shown in Listing 13.4. The only difference between this test and the last, the use of the `Text` property, is indicated in bold.

Listing 13.4. Control property updates.

```
Private Sub cmdDefUpdate_Click()
' Test speed of standard control updates with property


Dim i% ' loop counter
' Hide the control to be updated, so our test measures just
'   update speed, and not drawing time
txtTester.Visible = False

Call Common_StartTimedTest


' Carry out test algorithim repeatedly
For i% = 1 To txtLoops

    ' Assign the control default values to the variables
    txtTester.Text = Now

Next i%


Call Common_EndTimedTest(lblPropUpdate)

' Show the controls
txtTester.Visible = True

End Sub
```

The code is identical to the default property test except that the `Text` property is explicitly called out (as indicated by bold type in Listing 13.4). So you have identical assignments, except the first test updates the default value and the second updates the explicit `Text` property. You can see the results from one run of these tests in Figure 13.1. Repeated timings showed the two methods to be virtually identical, just as in the case of the assignment of control properties in the first test case. These results generally apply to all standard controls. (You will verify this in a Workshop exercise at the end of the chapter.) Therefore, you can reach the conclusion that using the default property for standard controls does not produce any significant performance savings. Once again, this finding differs slightly from Visual Basic 3.0, in which the explicit property reference method was approximately 10 percent slower than the default property reference approach.

> **TIP:** Using the default property of a standard control offers no significant performance advantages over explicitly referencing the property.

Assigning Values from OLE Control Properties

The first set of tests focused on the standard controls that are built into Visual Basic. However, all controls are not created equal. While standard controls are built in to Visual Basic, OLE custom controls are stored in separate OCX files. Likewise, it is reasonable to expect that they are implemented differently. Therefore, it is not surprising that OLE controls have different performance considerations than do standard controls. The next step, then, is to determine whether there is a measurable performance difference between property reference methods with OLE controls.

The code associated with the command button labeled Assign from Default in Figure 13.1 assigns an OLE three dimensional check box control `Value` property to a variable by simply referencing the default property of the OLE control. That code appears in Listing 13.5. (The particular OLE control used comes with Visual Basic in file THREED23.OCX.)

Listing 13.5. Assigning an OLE three-dimensional check box control default value.

```
Private Sub Command1_Click()
' Test speed of OLE control in assignments by default value


Dim i% ' loop counter
Dim intCheck box As String        ' gets check box contents


Call Common_StartTimedTest

' Carry out test algorithim repeatedly
For i% = 1 To txtLoops

    intCheck box = sschkOCX

Next i%


Call Common_EndTimedTest(lblOCXVal)

End Sub
```

To compare methods, you must next carry out the same assignment using an explicit reference to the OLE check box control's `Value` property. That test case is carried out when the command button labeled Assign from Property in Figure 13.1 is clicked. The code for that test appears in Listing 13.6.

Listing 13.6. Assigning an OLE check box explicit property value.

```
Private Sub Command2_Click()
' Test speed of OLE control in assignments by property value

Dim i% ' loop counter
Dim intCheck box As String        ' gets check box contents


Call Common_StartTimedTest

' Carry out test algorithim repeatedly
For i% = 1 To txtLoops

    intCheck box = sschkOCX.Value

Next i%


Call Common_EndTimedTest(lblOCXProp)


End Sub
```

The results here differ from those of the standard control comparison. You can see the results from one test run in Figure 13.1. Over repeated runs, the default method proved to be 21 percent slower than the explicit property reference method!

Updating Values of OLE Control Properties

The same type of test was next carried on an OLE control. The check box labeled OLE custom control was the item to be updated. Listing 13.7 is the code for the default property reference method.

Listing 13.7. Assigning an OLE check box control default property.

```
Private Sub cmdUpdateOCXDef_Click()

' Test speed of OCX updates with default value

Dim i% ' loop counter
```

continues

Listing 13.7. continued

```
' Hide the control to be updated, so our test measures just
'   update speed, and not drawing time

sschkOCX.Visible = False

Call Common_StartTimedTest


' Carry out test algorithim repeatedly
For i% = 1 To txtLoops

    ' Assign the control default values to the variable
    sschkOCX = (i% Mod 3)


Next i%


Call Common_EndTimedTest(lblOCXDefUp)

' Show the control
sschkOCX.Visible = True


End Sub
```

The code for updating a comparable explicit property reference method is shown in Listing 13.8. The only difference from the previous test, the explicit property reference, is shown in bold.

Listing 13.8. Assigning an OLE check box control explicit property.

```
Private Sub cmdOCXPropUp_Click()
' Test speed of OCX updates with default value

Dim i% ' loop counter

' Hide the control to be updated, so our test measures just
'   update speed, and not drawing time

sschkOCX.Visible = False

Call Common_StartTimedTest

' Carry out test algorithim repeatedly
For i% = 1 To txtLoops

    ' Assign the control default values to the variable
    sschkOCX.Value = (i% Mod 3)

Next i%

Call Common_EndTimedTest(lblOCXPropUp)
```

```
' Show the control
sschkOCX.Visible = True

End Sub
```

The results of this test also favor the explicit property approach. Results from one run are shown in Figure 13.1. Normalized results from repeated timings show that the default method takes 29 percent longer than explicitly calling out the property to be updated for the check box control. Of course, performance behavior is specific to each control since each control is based on different code. However, the results noted here do seem to generally apply to all OLE controls to one extent or another. You will verify this in a Workshop exercise at the end of this chapter. You can conclude from this test that you should avoid using the default property when working with custom controls, because performance will be slower.

> **TIP:** Using the default property of an OLE custom control results in slower performance than explicitly referencing the property. Avoid using default properties when working with OLE controls.

Storing Property Values in Variables

Control properties are, like variables, essentially a named location in memory to store data. Likewise, property values can be used in assignments much the same way as variables. A control property behaves in some sense like a special variable that is always associated with a given control. A control property, then, is much like a variable with special overhead associated with it. The natural question that follows is "Can variables that cache property values offer better performance because they are not encumbered by control overhead?" The test that follows shows that this is indeed the case. Sample program PropVr32.exe, which is on the CD-ROM that accompanies this book, provides a ready comparison of variable versus control property update speeds. A 16-bit version of this program, PropVr16.exe, is also provided on the CD-ROM. The main window of this program is shown in Figure 13.2.

The top button of this form carries out a test that analyzes the speed of code that stores control property values in variables and then updates those variables in subsequent calculations. This technique of temporarily storing data where it may be retrieved more quickly is sometimes referred to as *caching*. The next button on the form carries out the corresponding test that analyzes control property updates. In the test all updates are carried out directly on controls, without the use of intermediate variable storage or cache. The elapsed time is displayed on the form for each test after its completion. The code associated with the first test, which is executed when the button labeled Variable Update is clicked, is shown in Listing 13.9.

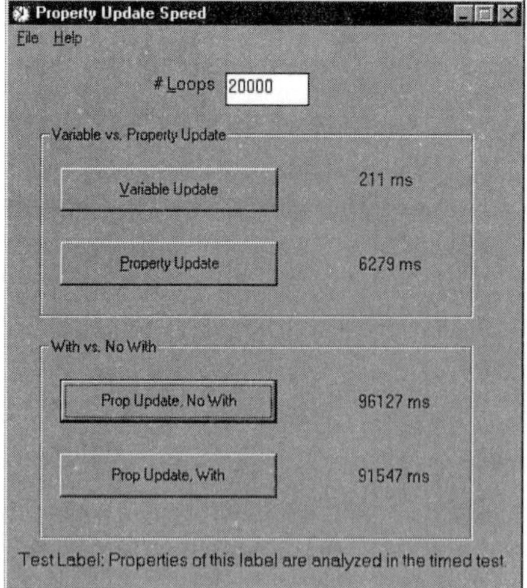

Figure 13.2.
The variable versus control property updates program.

Listing 13.9. Variable storage of property values.

```
Private Sub cmdVar_Click ()
' Use variables to speed up an algorithim based on Control properties


Call Common_StartTimedTest

Dim i% ' loop counter


Dim intRightBoundary As Integer   ' calculated right boundary of label
Dim intBottomBoundary As Integer   ' calculated bottom boundary of label

Dim lngNumberofLoops As Long ' number of times to loop
Dim intFontSize As Integer   ' stores control font size for use in test
Dim intFontBold As Integer   ' stores control bold setting for use in test
Dim intLeft As Integer       ' stores control left setting for use in test
Dim intTop As Integer        ' stores control top setting for use in test
Dim intWidth As Integer      ' stores control width setting for use in test
Dim intHeight As Integer     ' stores control height setting for use in test

' Assign intial values for test alogirithim
lngNumberofLoops = txtLoops
intFontSize = lblTester.FontSize
intFontBold = lblTester.FontBold
intLeft = lblTester.Left
intTop = lblTester.Top
intWidth = lblTester.Width
intHeight = lblTester.Height

' Carry out test algorithim repeatedly
For i% = 1 To lngNumberofLoops

    intRightBoundary = intLeft + intWidth
```

```
    intBottomBoundary = intTop + intHeight

    If (intFontSize > 8) And (intFontBold = False) Then
        intRightBoundary = intLeft + 1000
        intBottomBoundary = intTop + 100
    End If

Next i%


Call Common_EndTimedTest(lblVarTime)

End Sub
```

This code carries out the number of loops that you specify in the # Loops text box. The assignment lines immediately prior to the loop statements will cache the control's properties in variables. Variable values are initialized to contain several different label control properties. Within the loop, the variables are manipulated. Because the variables contain property settings, the properties themselves are not modified during the algorithm. The variables are directly updated during the calculations.

A similar test is carried out when you click the button labeled Property Update. The difference here is that no property caching takes place. Variables are not set up for manipulation within the loop. Rather, the properties themselves are directly referenced. The code for this test is shown in Listing 13.10.

Listing 13.10. Directly accessing property values.

```
Private Sub cmdProp_Click ()

' An algorithim based on Control properties


Call Common_StartTimedTest

Dim i% ' loop counter


Dim intRightBoundary As Integer   ' calculated right boundary of label
Dim intBottomBoundary As Integer   ' calculated bottom boundary of label


' Carry out test algorithim repeatedly
For i% = 1 To txtLoops

    intRightBoundary = lblTester.Left + lblTester.Width
    intBottomBoundary = lblTester.Top + lblTester.Height

    If (lblTester.FontSize > 8) And (lblTester.FontBold = False) Then
        intRightBoundary = lblTester.Left + 1000
```

continues

Listing 13.10. continued

```
        intBottomBoundary = lblTester.Top + 100
    End If

Next i%


Call Common_EndTimedTest(lblPropTime)

End Sub
```

The results for one trial of clicking each button to successively carry out each test are shown in Figure 13.2. The normalized results based on the average of repeated timings show that those results are consistent across multiple tests. (See Table 13.1.)

Table 13.1. Comparison of updates to variables versus control properties.

Test	*Normalized Results*
Variable update test	1.00
Property update test	30.00

The variable update test takes 1/30 the time required by the property update test! This test shows the value of storing control property values in variables whenever they will have to be repeatedly referenced. This has slight maintenance drawbacks of requiring additional development time and introducing more code to debug and maintain. On the other hand, it includes a great performance payback to any program that has to frequently reuse the same property value.

> **TIP:** Store control properties in variables if you will reference those properties frequently in code. Substantial performance savings can result.

With Statements for Property References

Visual Basic 4.0 provides the capability to use `With` *`control_name...`* `End With` to indicate that a given control is the subject of a series of statements. Within the encasing `With` statements, code can then reference properties by just the property name preceded by the period reference symbol (*`.property_name`*), without spelling out the control name. Few would disagree that this is a coding convenience. It allows for easier-to-read code, and code that is quicker to enter. But does it come at the price of performance?

Two tests, one that uses `With` and another that doesn't, are defined to test this aspect of performance. These two tests are associated with the bottom two buttons in Figure 13.2. Code for the first test, associated with the command button labeled Prop Update, No With, is shown in Listing 13.11. This test simply updates various property values using a full control-name reference.

Listing 13.11. Referencing property values by full control name.

```
Private Sub cmdNoWith_Click()
Dim i&                            ' Loop counter

Call Common_StartTimedTest

For i& = 1 To txtLoops

 lblTester.AutoSize = False
 lblTester.AutoSize = True
 lblTester.Enabled = False
 lblTester.Enabled = True
 lblTester.Tag = lblTester.Caption

Next i&

Call Common_EndTimedTest(lblNoWith)

End Sub
```

Code for the second test, associated with the command button labeled Prop Update, With, is shown in Listing 13.12. This test uses a `With` statement to indicate the subject control name, and then performs the same property-value updates of the previous method using only a property-name reference within the context of that `With` statement.

Listing 13.12. Referencing property values by `With` context.

```
Private Sub cmdWith_Click()
Dim i&                            ' Loop counter

Call Common_StartTimedTest

With lblTester
For i& = 1 To txtLoops

   .AutoSize = False
   .AutoSize = True
   .Enabled = False
   .Enabled = True
   .Tag = .Caption
```

continues

Listing 13.12. continued

```
Next i&
End With

Call Common_EndTimedTest(lblWith)


End Sub
```

Results from one run of these test cases are shown in Figure 13.2. The normalized results for repeated tests show similar results. (See Table 13.2.)

Table 13.2. Comparison of control property references using explicit reference and `With` reference.

Test	*Normalized Results*
No `With`	1.05
`With`	1.00

The time difference between the two methods is slight. Referencing the control properties via `With` is only 5 percent faster. However, this finding can at least ensure those who want to take advantage of the convenient referencing capabilities of `With` that they can do so without fearing that they are paying a performance price for this convenience.

> **TIP:** There is no performance penalty for referencing control properties via the `With` construct. `With` even seems to be marginally faster than referencing controls via the full control name and property.

Comparing Specific Properties of Different Controls

Controls are essentially libraries of code written by programmers that provide you with a convenient interface to utilize the underlying services of the control. Every control has unique design and code. There is code underlying the property updates as well as the methods of the controls. Most of the controls you use likely had different developers. And likewise, most fulfill different functions. Therefore, it is natural that each has its own performance considerations.

Do not make the mistake of assuming that control properties will have similar performance characteristics just because the function of properties seems similar. For example, the text box `Text` property and label `Caption` property can both display text to the user, and both deal with storing string data. However, a timed test that recorded the amount of time required to update the string displayed by each of these controls shows the normalized results shown in Table 13.3.

Table 13.3. Comparison of text box `Text` property updates versus label caption updates.

Test Case	*Normalized Results*
`Label.Caption`	1.00
`Textbox.Text`	19.00

There is likely more overhead involved in updating the text box `Text` property because it offers a richer variety of capabilities. Even if you are utilizing a text box just to display text, and thereby what might seem to be a simulation of the label control, it took approximately 19 times as long to update the text box `Text` property as it did to update the label `Caption` property in the test that was carried out. (You will see this test program in an exercise at the end of the chapter.) The striking difference between these two property updates illustrates that every control and property has unique performance considerations. A seeming similarity of function is no guarantee of a similarity of performance. The only way to fully gauge performance of two different properties is to carry out a comparison test like those in this chapter.

Summary

This chapter focuses on the use of control properties. Every control brings with it unique performance considerations based on the unique code behind that particular control. Each control has its own performance bottlenecks and resource and memory constraints awaiting your discovery.

If you discover through experimentation that a control has performance problems, your choices are somewhat limited. You have no insight into the particular implementation details of the control code, and even if you did, you would not be able to modify the code. Some custom-control performance issues are insurmountable, putting you in a take-it-or-leave-it situation.

On the other hand, you can realize some significant performance savings through an informed use of control properties. Under Visual Basic 3.0, savings could be realized if you *used default values of controls*. However, under Visual Basic 4.0 the use of default values is slower than the explicit reference of properties for OLE custom controls, and of about the same performance for standard controls.

The most significant way to enhance control property–related performance is to *store control properties in variables if you will reference those properties frequently in code.* Variable access that is 30 times faster than property access is demonstrated in the corresponding sample program in this chapter. A little more coding effort is required, but the performance payback is substantial.

This chapter also examines the use of the `With` control reference construct. There is no performance penalty for referencing properties within the context of a `With` statement, and it even appears to be marginally faster. Therefore, it is a valuable construct to use for the coding convenience and added source code readability it provides. Finally, the label `Caption` and text box `Text` properties are compared. The label `Caption` property updates dramatically faster than does the text box `Text` property. This highlights the important point that every control and its properties have different performance considerations.

Obey the Signs

Wrong Way: If two controls have similar properties, assume that performance relating to those properties is similar.

This would be an incorrect assumption. The update speed of the label `Caption` and text box `Text` properties was given as one example. The text box `Text` property took 19 times as long to update as did the label `Caption` property in the test that was discussed. The only way to truly understand performance of two alternatives is to carry out comparison testing like that of this chapter.

Beware of Falling Rocks: Visual Basic 4.0 has different performance from Visual Basic 3.0 in some areas.

Performance is different in various ways between these two versions of Visual Basic. This is not surprising, considering that Visual Basic 4.0 has a new underlying *engine* or implementation (called the VBA engine, this is the same code used to support the latest Visual Basic for Applications; VBA is available as a macro language in various Microsoft applications). Some techniques that were optimizing steps in Visual Basic 3.0, such as referring to controls by default properties, might now be non-optimal (for example, explicit property reference is slightly faster under Visual Basic 4.0).

Q&A

Q Which is faster—assigning a variable to a control property, or assigning a variable to a control default?

A Assignment to a control default is significantly faster under Visual Basic 3.0, but under Visual Basic 4.0, using the explicit control property is marginally faster for standard controls, and clearly faster for OLE controls, as demonstrated by the sample programs in this chapter.

Q Assume you have a program that carries out a lengthy calculation that repeatedly uses a control property. Is it worth the overhead of an extra `Dim` statement to declare an additional variable to hold the property value, in order to reference that variable within the calculation instead of the property value?

A Yes, despite the added overhead of `Dim`, the variable-based approach generally is significantly faster.

Quiz

Take the code sample in Listing 13.13 and change all default property references to explicit references. Note how this change affects the performance of the code. This code is available in the Quiz1_32.vbp project file on the CD-ROM that accompanies this book.

Listing 13.13. The code you need to optimize.

```
Sub Command1_Click ()


Call Common_StartTimedTest

' Set up initial values

' Assign values to text boxes
Text1 = "VB Rules."
Text1.Visible = True     ' Note - visible is not a default property!
Text2 = "C++ is powerful."
Text2.Visible = False    ' Note - visible is not a default property!
Text3 = "So are active volcanoes."
Text4 = "And rapid dogs."
Text5 = "And agitated skunks."

Check1 = 1
Check2 = 1
Check3 = 2

label1 = "Mastering performance issues takes experimentation, knowledge, and common
➥sense."

Option1 = True


Call Common_EndTimedTest(label1)

End Sub
```

The altered code, with explicit properties replaced by default references to the control, is shown in Listing 13.14.

Listing 13.14. An optimized version of the code in Listing 13.13.

```
Sub Command1_Click ()


Call Common_StartTimedTest

' Set up initial values

' Assign values to text boxes
Text1.Text = "VB Rules."
Text1.Visible = True
Text2.Text = "C++ is powerful."
Text2.Visible = False
Text3.Text = "So are active volcanoes."
Text4.Text = "And rapid dogs."
Text5.Text = "And agitated skunks."

Check1.Value = 1
Check2.Value = 1
Check3.Value = 2

label1.Caption = "Mastering performance issues takes experimentation, knowledge,
➥and common sense."

Option1.Value = True


Call Common_EndTimedTest(label1)

End Sub
```

If you carry out this test, you will have to look carefully to see a performance difference. The duration of the test is so short that differences between the two methods will appear slight. A better way to compare the methods is to put these updates in a `For` loop and compare multiple iterations of each technique. Do this as an exercise and see if the difference between the two methods becomes clearer.

Workshop

Make a test program similar to the ones used in this chapter to compare the update performance of text box control `Text` property to label control `Caption` updates. Use this program to verify that the label control updates are faster. This is a good example of the fact that different controls and different properties all have different performance levels.

Compare the update time of default property references to explicit property references for various standard controls such as the text box, check box, and label controls. Are performance comparison results of the default and explicit property references consistent across the standard controls?

Next carry out the same test on some of the OLE custom controls that come with Visual Basic. Compare assignments and updates to default and explicit property references. As discussed in this chapter, you should notice that the relative performance of explicit versus default property usage is significantly different for OLE controls than for standard controls.

Custom Controls

Visual Basic is a powerful programming tool largely due to the ability to extend its capabilities with custom controls. The rich suite of custom controls available today are a testament to the power they give to Visual Basic. Microsoft never fully expected such a large number of companies to market these third-party controls, but their existence has shaped and continues to shape the role of Visual Basic. A great many custom controls have been established in the Visual Basic programming community and are widely used.

When considering the performance of an application, the programmer must be concerned about custom controls. As this chapter points out, the Visual Basic programmer usually has no easy way to get "under the hood" of these custom controls and therefore must rely on the control itself to behave properly and efficiently. As a result, you are somewhat limited in making controls perform faster.

This chapter compares built-in Visual Basic controls to custom controls to see just what kind of impact custom controls have on performance. Because every control is different, and many exist, it is impossible to discuss and compare them all. This chapter examines a few specific controls and shows you how to determine the length of time it takes to load them into memory when the application starts. The built-in Visual Basic controls, coupled with some supporting code, are then used to simulate the functionality of a custom control. A comparison of load time and performance is made for both VBX and OLE controls, contained in OCX files, along with discussions on functionality and the trade-offs involved. The result of these comparisons will lead you to the following conclusion: There are viable alternatives to custom controls that often can eliminate many of the negative side effects custom controls impose.

As a result of reading this chapter, you should have a better sense of how custom controls operate and perform, as well as the ways you can use standard Visual Basic controls instead of custom controls to speed up your applications.

What Are Standard Controls?

Visual Basic has a collection of *standard controls* that are readily available to the programmer and appear in the Visual Basic toolbox. Standard controls are built into the Visual Basic environment and are different from custom controls, which can be added or removed. Standard controls are a permanent part of the Visual Basic environment. Here is a list of the commonly used standard controls available to you:

Picture Box	Directory ListBox
Timer	Drive ListBox
Label	File ListBox
Text Box	Shape
Frame	Line
Command Button	Image
Check Box	Data Control
Option Button	Vertical Scroll Bar
ComboBox	Horizontal Scroll Bar
ListBox	OLE

You are probably already familiar with many of these standard controls. As with any control, you can select a standard control from the tool palette and place that control on the form. In most cases, you place the control on the form and set the various properties of the control. For example, you may want to place a label next to a text box so that you can indicate the purpose of the text box. In such a case, you select the label control from the palette, place the label on the form, and select the Caption property of the label, entering the text for the caption. An example of this process is shown in Figure 14.1. Note that the programmer is in the Visual Basic programming environment and is setting the Caption property of the label control on the form.

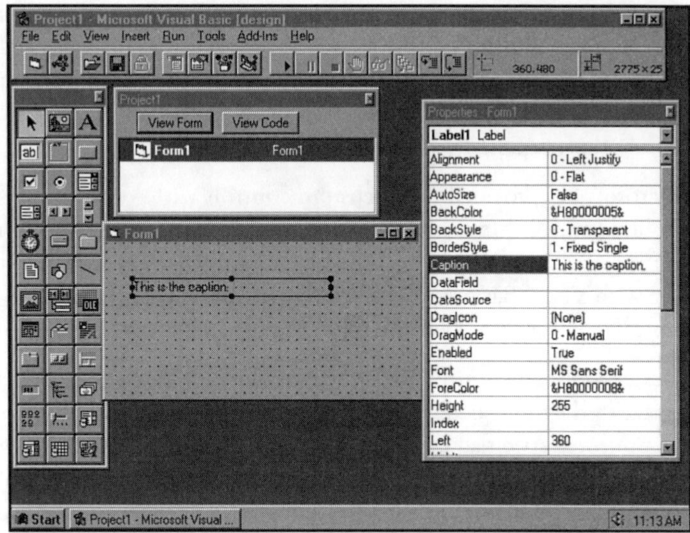

Figure 14.1.
Using the label control on a Visual Basic form.

> **NOTE:** The use of controls is not covered in this book, but you can learn it easily by consulting either the *Visual Basic Programmer's Guide* or Sams Publishing's *Teach Yourself Visual Basic 4 in 21 Days.*

What is significant about standard controls in terms of performance is that no VBX or OLE controls are required. In the case of custom controls, each must exist as either a VBX or an OLE control. The inclusion of the VBX or OLE control causes the control to appear in the tool palette. For standard controls, no additional files are needed. That means that no additional files must be loaded when the application starts, the significance of which is examined later in this chapter.

What Are Custom Controls?

Custom controls are specialized controls not automatically built into the Visual Basic language. Custom controls include specialized controls such as common dialog boxes and third-party controls, as well as enhanced versions of standard controls. These controls come in two varieties: VBXs and OLE controls. *VBXs* are 16-bit custom controls that can be used with the 16-bit version of Visual Basic 4.0 and Visual Basic 3.0. The VBX is not a 32-bit control (nor does it use OLE technology) and therefore cannot be used in the 32-bit version of Visual Basic 4.0. An *OLE control*, or *OCX*, takes advantage of OLE technology, as the name implies. OLE controls can be designed for 16-bit and 32-bit operating systems, which can be used in 16-bit or 32-bit Visual Basic 4.0, respectively. Although most component manufacturers build equivalent OLE controls for 16-bit and 32-bit systems, some OLE controls are only available for one or the other, depending on their function.

Microsoft has provided many custom controls with Visual Basic 4.0, such as the data bound list box control, the common dialog control, the gauge control, the graph, the masked edit control, the rich text edit control, and many others. In addition to the custom controls that ship with Visual Basic 4.0, a great many additional controls can be purchased from third-party control vendors. You have the option to include these controls in your project.

Because standard controls are inherent to Visual Basic, they are always available and always appear in the tool palette. Custom controls, on the other hand, only appear when loaded into the project as specified in the Visual Basic project (VBP) file. Both standard and custom controls have a collection of *properties* and *methods* that can be used to perform actions and otherwise manipulate the control. This gives every control a standard interface that you can use consistently for all controls.

Figure 14.2 shows an example of a custom control. The control pictured is the Pinnacle-BPS graph control. Note that the control is represented by an additional icon at the bottom of the tool palette. When you click the graph control icon and place the control on the form, a property sheet appears, as shown in the figure. This enables you to set the various properties of the control while in design mode.

When an application executes, the custom controls specified for the application are loaded into memory when the application starts. The presence of the control on the tool palette simply means that the control is available for placement on a form and use in an application. The control is not loaded into memory when the application runs unless it is used in the application. As you will see, the larger the variety of custom controls you place on a form, the more memory and, consequently, more time required to load those controls. Because custom controls typically require more resources than do standard controls, the impact on system resources becomes greater as different kinds of custom controls are used.

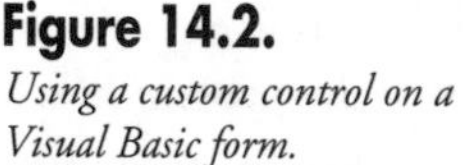

Figure 14.2.
Using a custom control on a Visual Basic form.

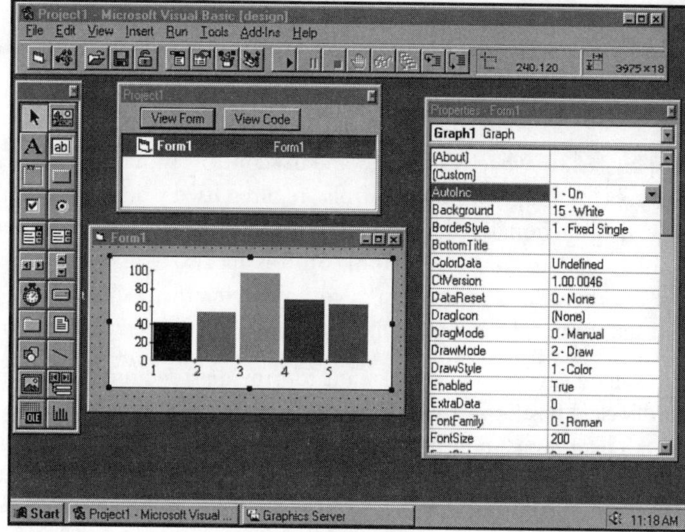

Standard Controls Versus Custom Controls

First, consider the advantages of using standard controls over custom controls. You have learned that standard controls are built into Visual Basic. This means that the controls are integrated into the Visual Basic development environment and do not need to be "included." Because they are already built into Visual Basic, there is no need to load additional code into memory or consume additional resources that a custom control would require. As a result, standard controls can make for a faster application through lower memory demands and, therefore, lower amounts of system memory-management activity. One of the benefits of using a custom control, as stated previously, is that custom controls provide greater functionality. This additional functionality usually comes with a price, however, and that price most often is speed and memory usage. The standard controls, although simple in comparison to some of the complex, third-party controls, usually have the edge in terms of performance.

Standard controls are also advantageous in terms of their reliability. Because Microsoft has designed them and placed them into Visual Basic, you can be reasonably sure that they have been well tested and are reliable. Although this certainly does not imply that custom controls are unreliable, many vendors simply do not have the resources to perform the type of

high-intensity testing that Microsoft must put into a programming tool with as wide an audience as Visual Basic. Because standard controls are such an essential part of the programming tool, it is a reasonable expectation that Microsoft would spend a great amount of effort ensuring that they behave properly.

The biggest drawback in using standard controls is that the functionality they provide can, at times, be limiting. Custom controls are often used when there are no standard controls to perform the functionality desired. The custom control therefore enhances the existing functionality of a standard control. Custom controls are also used when there is functionality you would like to provide that, even though you could manually implement, is already done for you in a custom control. In any case, the desired benefit is increased functionality.

Consider a case in which you want to provide some functionality you can't get using a standard Visual Basic control. Suppose, for example, that you want to send messages to the Windows operating system from a form. There is no standard control or Visual Basic code that enables you to do this, but there are custom controls you can purchase that do. Therefore, often a custom control can or must be used to provide functionality that neither the Visual Basic language nor its suite of standard controls can provide.

The second case is when you would like to enhance the capabilities of an existing standard control. Take, for example, the Visual Basic ComboBox control. Suppose you wanted to bind the ComboBox control to a database table and update a different database table based on the combo box selection. The standard ComboBox can be bound to a database table but cannot update another based on the user's selection. You can, however, use the DBComboBox custom control that *does* give you this functionality. In such a case, you are using a custom control to extend the capabilities of a standard control.

The last case is when you can use a custom control to carry out some function more easily than you could by manually coding it in Visual Basic. Consider, for example, a case in which you want the user to enter a telephone number into a text box in the format `(xxx) yyy-zzzz`. One way to do this would be to take the text out of a standard text box and force the 10-digit number into the format `(xxx) yyy-zzzz` regardless of the way the user entered the number. A simpler way, however, would be to use the masked-edit custom control. This custom control can be configured to automatically handle this task for you. When you set the mask of the control to `(###) ###-####`, the edit control automatically formats the user's text and ensures that the format is correct.

In each case, the advantage of using the custom control is its increased functionality or ease of implementation. There is no need to figure out how to carry out the functionality; the control provides it for you. Again, this added functionality often comes at the cost of increased memory and resource usage. Increased memory usage means that the forms in which those controls are contained will take longer to load and the application might run more slowly. Furthermore, less free memory will be available to other programs running concurrently in Windows, so that every program could be slowed down, and each OLE control has a certain amount of overhead that increases the load time of the control at startup.

As stated earlier, another drawback to using custom controls is that you must depend on the inner workings of a custom control to be correct. In a sense, you are trusting that the custom control is bug free and will not cause your application to become unstable or crash. Because you cannot examine or change the control's code (unless you built it or have access to the source code), you must place your trust in its developers. This can be frightening to you as the developer, and potentially to the user. There is nothing more frustrating to a user than a program that locks up, especially when that user hasn't saved the data in that program that he or she happened to be working on when it crashed. If you've ever had this happen to you, you know the feeling of frustration that results.

Alternatives to Using Custom Controls

Now that the standard controls and custom controls have been explained and the pros and cons of using each have been addressed, it's time to look at a case study that helps to reinforce these concepts. This case study demonstrates that standard controls can sometimes be used to emulate custom controls, often resulting in a substantial performance savings. The case study does *not* imply that the necessity of a custom control can always be easily worked around, nor that it should be. After all, the availability of a rich set of custom controls is one of the great strengths of Visual Basic that allows for rapid application development. This chapter does, however, show the benefit of avoiding them, whenever possible and practical, for the sake of efficiency.

This simple case study considers a case in which a custom control exists that gives you the functionality that (and, in fact, even *more* functionality than) you need. In this case study, no Visual Basic standard controls exist that automatically provide you with the functionality you desire. Therefore, you must either use a custom control or write code and work with the standard controls to get the functionality you want. Both approaches are considered in this study.

The case study is presented this way because this is a quite typical situation you might encounter. Often, a programmer doesn't need or use the entire set of features a custom control provides. Unfortunately, when the programmer proceeds to use the control, the user must often pay the performance price for a set of features that the application never uses. Therefore, it is often advantageous to use an alternative approach devoid of the extra functionality that never gets used. This case study assumes such conditions and provides an alternative implementation. The performance of the alternative versus the custom control is then considered.

Custom Control Case Study: Bill's Ongoing Adventure

By now, Bill, who was the subject of the timer method case study in Chapter 4, "Timing Methods," is a pretty good Visual Basic programmer. He wants to include in one of his stellar applications a simple progress indicator for a task that will take a significant amount of time to execute. He wants to implement the indicator as a simple bar that moves from left to right as the task is completed. (Perhaps you have seen such indicators in Windows applications you have used.) Bill could not find a standard Visual Basic control that provides this functionality. After looking through the Visual Basic help file, however, he did run across an interesting control that appeared to meet his needs—the MicroHelp Gauge Control that comes with Visual Basic.

Bill is excited about his newly discovered gauge control because it automatically does everything he wants. All he has to do is set a property on the control that increments the progress indicator for him. Bill has used custom controls in the past, however, and has observed many times that custom controls can slow down his application. Bill wants to impress his friends and relatives, so he decides to try a little experiment. He wants to know if his application could be more efficient if he were to design his own progress indicator using nothing but standard controls and some code.

Bill must keep in mind that just because one method is faster or slower than another does not always make it the best choice. As discussed in earlier chapters, performance must be weighed against ease of use, maintainability, resource investment, and a host of other factors. It is also important for Bill to realize that gauge controls are typically used as progress indicators for lengthy activities that constrain performance. Therefore, the performance of the gauge control itself is not likely to be a major performance concern because of the duration of the activity being gauged. In such a case, the performance of a gauge control is not necessarily a discriminating factor in deciding whether to use that control.

Bill realizes, however, that he might want to use the progress indicator for many different operations. If he can use as efficient a solution as possible, he will be helping to maximize the efficiency of his application. He also wants to verify the principle that manual solutions are often faster than custom-control solutions. With these thoughts in mind, he proceeds to perform his experiment.

Bill's task is to compare the gauge control to a manual implementation using standard controls. Bill decides to write two applications, both of which accomplish his goal. He writes the first application, MhGage32.exe, using the custom gauge control. For the second application, MyGage32.exe, he uses both standard controls and his own code. Both applications are contained on the CD-ROM that accompanies this book.

> **NOTE:** The MicroHelp gauge control (GAUGE16.OCX and GAUGE32.OCX for 16-bit and 32-bit, respectively) is an OLE control that ships with Visual Basic 4.0. The OCX must be installed on your computer for the MhGage32.exe application to execute.

Bill not only wants to know which application *performs* better, but he also wants to know which application *loads* faster. Therefore, he will use the Startr32.exe utility that comes on the CD-ROM that accompanies this book. The MhGage32.exe main form is shown in Figure 14.3.

Figure 14.3.
The main form of MhGage32, showing the gauge control demo.

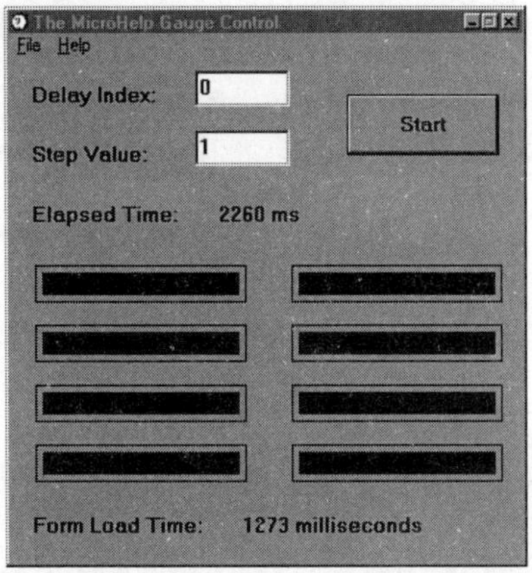

As you can see, the application consists of a control array of eight gauge controls that are incremented from 0 to 100. You can set the step value so that the count from 0 to 100 can be incremented faster. If, for example, the step value is set to 1, the counter increments 0,1,2,3,…,100. If the step value is set to 10, the counter increments 0,10,20,30,…,100, arriving at the 100-percent mark more quickly. You can also specify a delay index, which sets a loop counter that performs a mathematical operation simply to delay the program. Use this delay index if you want to slow the program down to observe its behavior or adjust the elapsed time so that it is more meaningful.

When you click on the Start command button, each custom control is incremented from 0 to 100. The subroutine that gets executed when you click on this command button is shown in Listing 14.1.

Listing 14.1. The gauge control subroutine.

```
Private Sub cmdStart_Click()

    Dim i&, j%, k&                       ' Index Variables
    Dim lngDummy As Long
    Dim intStep as Integer
    Dim intDelay as Integer

    intStep = txtStep                    ' Set the step & delay values
    intDelay = txtDelay

    Call Common_StartTimedTest
    For i = 0 To 100 Step intStep     ' Increment gauge counter
        For j = 0 To 7                   ' Do every gauge on the form
            For k = 1 To intDelay
                lngDummy = j * k         ' Dummy calculation for delay
            Next
            Gauge(j).Value = i           ' Increment gauge position
            Gauge(j).Refresh             ' Refresh gauge control
        Next
    Next
    Call Common_EndTimedTest(lblTime)

End Sub
```

In the code listing, notice that the `Value` property of the gauge control is used. The control has `Min` and `Max` properties that specify the starting and ending values. The `Min` property is set by default to `0` and the `Max` property is set to `100`. The `Value` property simply tells the gauge control how much of the status bar to draw. The `Refresh` method is also very important. This control method updates the display to reflect the change of the gauge. If this method were not invoked, the control would not update on the screen and the user would not see the bar progress across the control from left to right. This line of code ensures that each control is displayed properly to the user.

In order for Bill to determine how long it takes for the application to load, he simply calls the `Commmon_PostLoadTime` function in the `Load` event of the main form, as shown in Listing 14.2.

Listing 14.2. The Visual Basic gauge control `Form_Load` event.

```
Private Sub Form_Load()

    Common_CenterForm Me

    Call Common_PostloadTime(lblLoadTime)

End Sub
```

Bill then uses the Startr32 utility to time how long the application takes to load. That time is displayed on the main form, as shown in Figure 14.3. Now Bill knows how long it takes to load the custom-control application and how long it takes to increment each gauge control. His next task is to create the second application using standard controls and his own code to create progress indicators.

This application, called MyGage32.exe, contains eight image controls that are used to represent the gauges. The application also draws a box (using the standard shape control) around each image control to give each gauge a border. The indicator bar, which is drawn inside the image control, is implemented using the `Line` method in the code. This method is used to draw a solid rectangle within the image control, the width of which is specified by the user. The main form for MyGauge32.exe is shown in Figure 14.4.

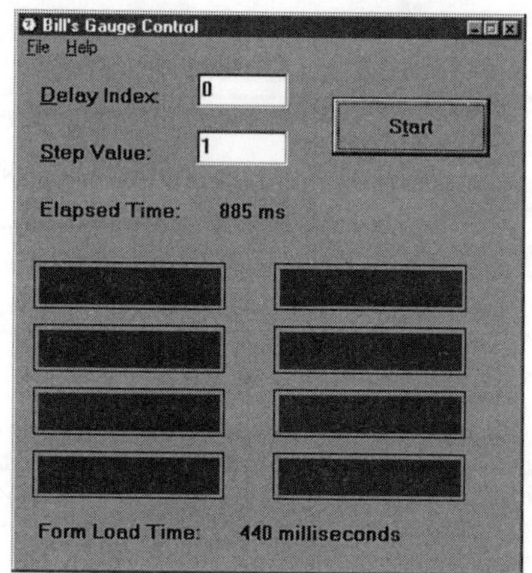

Figure 14.4.
The main form of Bill's gauge-control demo.

The subroutine for the `Click` event of the "Start" command button of MyGauge is shown in Listing 14.3.

Listing 14.3. Bill's gauge subroutine.

```
Private Sub cmdStart_Click()

    Dim i%, j%, k&                      ' Index variables
    Dim lngDummy As Long

    Dim intStep as Integer
    Dim intDelay as Integer

    intStep = txtStep                   ' Set the step & delay values
    intDelay = txtDelay

    Call Common_StartTimedTest
    For i = 0 To 100 Step intStep     ' Counter for gauge
        For j = 0 To 7                  ' Do every control in index
            For k = 1 To intDelay
                lngDummy = i * j        ' Dummy calculation for delay
```

continues

Listing 14.3. continued

```
            Next
            Call SetGauge(j, i)          ' Increment gauge position
        Next
    Next
    Call Common_EndTimedTest(lblTime)

End Sub
```

As you can see, this procedure calls another subroutine named `SetGauge`. The `SetGauge` function is called to update the progress indicator and is shown in Listing 14.4.

Listing 14.4. Bill's gauge implementation.

```
Sub SetGauge (intIndex As Integer, intPercent As Integer)

    ' Consider an image control with the coordinates
    ' (X1, Y1) at the upper left corner and (X2, Y2)
    ' at the lower right corner.

    Dim lngTop As Long              ' Y1
    Dim lngHeight As Long           ' Y2 - Y1
    Dim lngLeft As Long             ' X1
    Dim lngWidth As Long            ' X2 - X1

    ' This is the Y1 and Y2 coordinate of the box that
    ' represents the progress indicator. This box is
    ' drawn dynamically, as shown below
    Dim lngRight As Long

    ' Store the image properties in the variables
    ' that were defined above
    lngTop = imgGauge(intIndex).Top
    lngHeight = imgGauge(intIndex).Height
    lngLeft = imgGauge(intIndex).Left
    lngWidth = imgGauge(intIndex).Width

    ' If the percentage is zero, the gauge is being reset.
    ' In this case, erase the red box.
    If intPercent = 0 Then
        Line (lngLeft, lngTop)-(lngLeft + lngWidth,
        ➥lngTop + lngHeight),
        Me.BackColor, BF

    ' If the percentage is between 1 and 100, draw the
    ' box inside the image conrol.
    ElseIf intPercent >= 1 And intPercent <= 100 Then
        lngRight = lngLeft + (lngWidth * intPercent) \ 100
        Line (lngLeft, lngTop)-(lngRight, lngTop + lngHeight),
        ➥RGB(255, 0, 0), BF
    Else
        Exit Sub
    End If
```

The first thing this subroutine does is calculate the coordinates of the image control for the progress indicator. The index of the control array for the image is passed in as a parameter to the subroutine, along with the percentage to completion desired. The box is simply drawn using the line method, and the width of the box is calculated using integer math to set the percentage of the total width as you specify on the form. Unlike the custom control, there are no gauge objects with simple properties that can be set. In this case, the functionality is handled completely in code. This is one of the disadvantages of using a manual implementation. Additional features must be coded and do not simply appear as properties and methods as they do in a control.

Notice the difference in times between the gauge control application in Figure 14.3 and Bill's solution in Figure 14.4. Bill's implementation not only loads faster, but it also executes faster. The gauge control solution requires 1,273ms to load, but Bill's only requires 440ms! Furthermore, the gauge control solution requires 2,260ms to complete, whereas Bill's takes only 885ms. Even though Bill's implementation requires more code and manual intervention, and restricts almost all flexibility, it does the job Bill wants it to in the fastest amount of time.

These results are not presented to imply that the manual solution is necessarily better than the gauge control, only that it is *faster*. The MicroHelp gauge control that comes with Visual Basic offers a rich suite of features, including

- A `Caption` property that enables you to display text in the progress bar
- An optional 3D appearance, including the font used in the caption
- Control of all the colors used in the control
- The capability to align the caption
- The capability to use two different pictures to indicate the percentage complete on the status bar
- The capability to fill the inner area from left to right or top to bottom with a semi-needle, full needle, horizontal bitmap, vertical bitmap, or horizontal or vertical bars.

As you can see, the gauge control provides a great deal of functionality. Depending on how and where it is used, those features might be worth the increase in execution and loading time in using the control. The manual approach, on the other hand, has a very specific set of features that are very limited. Several controls are required, and the only feature you can control as a programmer is the length of the indicator. It is possible to make the manual implementation behave more like the custom control solution, but at some point the amount of work required to do so may not justify the savings in performance. Furthermore, as more functionality is added to Bill's solution, performance might drop to a point at which the custom control is the better choice. So, in terms of functionality, the gauge control is the clear winner. But in terms of performance, Bill's solution is more desirable for his specific needs.

> **TIP:** There are viable alternatives to custom controls that often can eliminate many of the negative side effects imposed by custom controls.

In this case study, the alternative to using the custom control is to implement the functionality manually. The manual implementation considerably reduces the two factors that make the custom controls a drawback: load time and execution time. The load time is improved primarily because the standard controls do not require the amount of memory and resources that the custom controls do. The execution time is also better because the code required to set the standard controls in the manual implementation is faster than the complex custom controls with their OLE overhead. A great deal of functionality is sacrificed in the manual implementation, but it was determined up front that the additional functionality the custom control provides was not to be used. In such a case, you can conclude that the manual-implementation approach is the most efficient choice when only a subset of functionality is required that can be implemented in code.

As a general rule, this same philosophy applies to any custom control. Typically, you do not need all the functionality of the control. It might be possible to implement the solution manually to obtain a significant increase in performance, particularly if the user will use the custom control a great deal in the application. You must make the judgment call as to whether the boost in performance is worth the work of producing the manual implementation and accepting the decreased functionality. If you want to enhance the manual solution in the future when the custom control already provides the functionality, using the manual solution might become counterproductive. Once again, note the trade-off between functionality and performance. As is usually the case, functionality and flexibility must usually be sacrificed in order to improve performance.

Summary

The chapter begins by stating the difference between a standard control and a custom control. A *standard control* is built into the Visual Basic environment, whereas a *custom control* is a separate file that must be included in the project as a standalone component, much like a DLL. This means that a standard control does not require a separate file as a custom control does. Custom controls are contained either in VBX files for 16-bit development or OCX files for 16-bit and 32-bit development.

Then, the chapter points out the primary advantages and disadvantages of both custom controls and standard controls. Standard controls are usually more limited than custom controls,

whereas custom controls offer a richer suite of functionality or provide functionality otherwise unavailable in the Visual Basic environment. The increased functionality of a custom control often comes at the cost, however, of reduced performance and increased memory usage. Standard controls are usually more limited in functionality than custom controls, but have the benefit of taking less memory and performing better because they are inherent to Visual Basic.

The three primary uses of a custom control are

- To provide functionality that is not possible in Visual Basic using a standard control
- To enhance or otherwise extend the functionality of an existing standard control
- To provide functionality more easily through the use of a custom control than with Visual Basic code

In any of these cases, the trade-off between performance and functionality must be considered.

Often you will want to use only a subset of a control that provides a wealth of functionality. It is often unnecessary to use a custom control that slows down the application and requires a great deal of memory if, for example, only 25 percent of the control's functionality is ever used. You can often use existing standard controls and code techniques to simulate the custom control to the extent of functionality you need. This comes at the cost, however, of development, maintenance, and debugging time. This chapter presents a simple case study using the gauge control, as well as a manual implementation using the Visual Basic image control, shape control, and line method.

The results demonstrate that the manual implementation is faster than the custom control implementation. In fact, the more complex and feature rich the control, the longer it typically takes to manipulate and exercise the control. As controls become simpler and have less functionality, the execution time typically improves, as well. Furthermore, the time required to load controls into memory improves. The manual approach requires the least amount of time because all its controls are inherent to Visual Basic and are set using code.

The use of code and standard controls is often advantageous. This does not mean that custom controls should not be used, but that the best tool should be chosen for the task at hand. Often, the solution does not have to involve custom controls. The performance of one custom control versus another is not just related to its feature set and complexity. Custom control performance also depends, of course, on how well the control was written and how efficient its underlying code is. It is wise to experiment with all the control options at your disposal, comparing each in terms of performance and functionality to arrive at the best decision. Often, that decision might involve doing the work manually, as in the case study in this chapter.

Obey the Signs

Wrong Way: If you see a feature in a custom control that's not in a standard control, just go ahead and use the custom control.

While this is very tempting to the programmer, this is not always necessarily the wisest choice. The custom control you want to use may be a heavyweight control laden with performance penalties. You should test the control and see if it detracts performance significantly enough to consider another alternative. Never use a control without first seeing what kind of a performer you're dealing with.

Beware of Falling Rocks: Manual solutions to work around a custom control are not always the best choice.

This chapter shows an example of implementing a solution using a group of standard controls instead of a custom control. This solution provides a rather dramatic performance boost. Keep in mind, however, that the results of every case will vary. Sometimes, manually implementing a custom control solution can backfire down the road. If you wish to take advantage of many features you could have obtained using the custom control, you may wish you had simply used it in the first place. On the other hand, you can simply plug it in and use it after the manual solution, but you may wind up throwing away all of your manual implementation code. In any case, you must be aware of the trade-offs and be practical and wise when making the decision of which approach to take.

Q&A

Q When I want to provide functionality in an application, how do I know which control to use, or whether I should implement the solution manually?

A The best way to make this determination is, first of all, to understand exactly what kind of functionality you want to provide to the user. Write down what you want the control to do and how you want it to do it. Then, search for a control appropriate for the task. When you have a collection of controls that approximate the functionality you desire, compare them to see how many extra features you get that you won't necessarily need. Perform a simple test for each control, much like what was done in this chapter, to see which control seems to perform better. You must then determine the best trade-off between performance and functionality. You should also consider what it would take to implement a manual solution, particularly if performance seems problematic or a control appears unreliable or has other negative side effects. You might want to build a manual solution, as done in this chapter, and compare all the controls you could possibly use with the manual solution. Ultimately, you will have to make the decision and think about all the trade-offs involved in each option.

Q Why does it take an application more time to load when custom controls are used?

A Custom controls make an application take longer to load for several reasons. First, an OLE control is a custom control stored in a special file called an OCX (in Visual Basic 3.0, custom controls were called VBXs and did not use OLE technology). If the control is placed on a form, that control must be loaded into memory when the application starts, even if the form or forms it is used in are not yet loaded. Depending on the size and complexity of the control, this requires extra time. If the control is an OLE control, the OLE overhead required to initialize the control adds even more time to the load operation. Furthermore, when the form loads, the control might execute some initialization code and/or might have to be painted on the screen. If the control is bound to a database or waits for some other action to take place, the form might take longer to load. All of these factors contribute to a longer load time.

Q Is a manual solution always faster than a custom control?

A Not necessarily. A manual solution is only as good as the way it was designed. The same is true of a custom control. Both custom controls and manual solutions that use a combination of standard controls and code techniques are only as good as the implementation behind them. They both essentially consist of code, except that the code of the control is *compiled* whereas the VB code is *interpreted*. The control also shields you from the VB code and presents you with a standardized interface. Some controls are more efficient than others because of the way they have been written, and it is certainly possible to write a manual solution that is slower than the custom control. In fact, the more you try to get the manual solution to duplicate the control, the greater the chances are that the manual solution will not be as efficient. Ultimately, if you aim for a manual solution that behaves *exactly* the way a control does, you might go through a great deal of work and not come out ahead at all. Furthermore, you might spend more development time than the custom control package would have cost in the first place. Therefore, you should typically only consider a manual implementation of a control when you want to provide some subset of the control's functionality suite.

Q How do I know how reliable a commercial custom control is before using it in my application?

A The reliability of a control can be ascertained from magazine or electronic-forum reviews of the control, but the only real test is to integrate it into your application. Control behavior can be very specifically related to certain aspects of your application, so you simply cannot tell how reliable it will be ahead of time. You can get the general sense of the reliability from reviews and others who have used the control, but ultimately you must simply give it a try to get a more complete picture.

Workshop

This chapter points out the benefits that can come from imitating certain functions of a custom control in code. Consider one of your applications that uses one or more custom controls. Determine the range of functionality each control provides and how much functionality the application actually uses. Ask yourself if it is possible to implement a manual solution using standard controls instead of using the custom control. If this is possible, construct a manual implementation. Compare the performance of the two approaches. Did you have to make any trade-offs in terms of the appearance of your solution versus the control? How easy will it be to extend the capabilities of the custom solution in the future? Are the trade-offs you have to make worth the increase in performance?

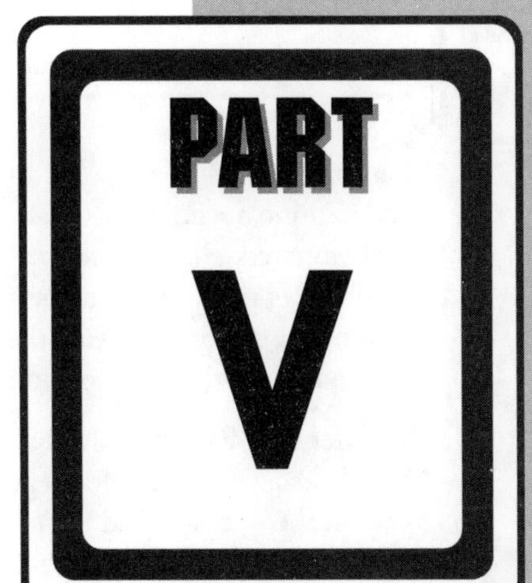

Optimization Strategies: Graphics

This section introduces the reader to Visual Basic graphics and the most efficient way to create and manipulate various forms of graphics in Visual Basic 4.0.

Chapter 15, "Graphics Controls, Methods, and the API," introduces you to three ways you can use Visual Basic to display graphics. Controls, methods, and the API each have pros and cons for practical use in applications, many of which are discussed in this chapter. The main goal of this chapter, however, is to compare them in terms of performance. Sample applications step you through the use of controls, methods, and the API, comparing the performance of each step along the way.

Chapter 16, "Displaying Pictures," introduces you to another powerful way you can display and manipulate graphics—using bitmaps through image and picture controls. Image controls are compared to picture controls, and the pros and cons of each are taken into account in light of which control performs better. Other techniques are discussed which reduce the time of loading those controls with the graphics they display, as well as the most efficient means of displaying multiple image and picture controls within an application.

Chapter 17, "Painting and Redrawing," ties graphical concepts together by showing you how Windows paints and redraws graphics within a Visual Basic application. Various properties of graphical containers and forms that govern the way graphics paint and redraw are examined, and techniques and suggestions are given for the most optimal approach.

Part V will provide you with comprehensive coverage of all the important performance issues that revolve around Visual Basic graphics. You will not only have a better understanding of how graphics can be used in Visual Basic, but you will see how best to take advantage of the techniques presented in these chapters to make those graphics display to the user as efficiently as possible.

CHAPTER 15

Graphics Controls, Methods, and the API

Most programmers who have used Visual Basic appreciate the ease with which it enables them to design programs with sophisticated user interfaces and effectively presented graphics. You can easily build an application that contains bitmaps, command buttons with pictures, toolbars, custom controls, and animation. These, taken together, present a very attractive interface to the user. Such tasks can be more difficult using a language such as C or C++. Due to the complexity of those languages, programmers who work with them can require more time to design what could otherwise be a very appealing graphical user interface for their application. Although it might be possible to build an application with an appealing graphical user interface using a more complex language, the programmer often simply may not have the time or skill required to do so.

Visual Basic makes it very easy to display graphics in applications. In order to make it so easy, however, certain types of graphics and methods for producing those graphics in an application are very expensive in terms of memory, resources, and, ultimately, performance. As is typically the case, you must handle the power at your fingertips responsibly and make sure that your use of graphics in your application does not bring performance or memory demands down to an unacceptable level for the user.

In this chapter, several methods are explored for producing graphics in Visual Basic: Visual Basic graphics controls, Visual Basic graphics methods, and Windows API function calls. Each approach has advantages and disadvantages in terms of performance, ease of programming, and maintainability. This chapter compares and contrasts the approaches in light of these criteria. This chapter should provide you with a good understanding of each technique, including the knowledge of which approach is typically faster under what conditions. Then, you should be better able to decide which technique is preferable to use for every situation you encounter when programming.

The chapter begins by presenting each of the three techniques used to display graphics and pointing out some of their primary strengths and weaknesses. Along the way, applications are introduced that demonstrate the use of each technique. The techniques are then compared in light of the criteria just mentioned. Finally, the chapter specifically introduces such concepts as coding effort versus performance gains, printer speed versus display speed, and the proper use and manipulation of bitmaps.

Creating Graphics Using Graphics Controls

Visual Basic has the following three standard *graphics controls* designed for creating graphics:

- The image control
- The line control
- The shape control

Each of these controls is represented on the Visual Basic toolbar. They are *standard controls*, meaning that they are built into the Visual Basic environment. As discussed in Part IV of the book, "Optimization Strategies: Controls," standard controls usually require less memory and resources than do heavyweight controls. As you would expect, they are usually better performers as well. The following sections discuss each of these controls individually.

The Image Control

The *image control* is essentially a control that takes up a rectangular piece of real estate on a form. Inside this rectangular box you can load *picture files*, which are files such as bitmaps (BMP

files), GIF files, PCX files, TIF files, and other types and formats of graphics files. Image controls can also show icons and *metafiles*, which are special graphics files that require less space because they have a more efficient storage mechanism. As the programmer, you can size image controls, and the image inside the image control shrinks or stretches to use all the real estate of the image control.

The Line Control

The Visual Basic *line control* is a simple control you use to draw lines on the screen. The line drawn with this control can start and end at any point on the screen and has several properties that can be changed, including its thickness, color, length, and style. This simple control can be very useful when used for drawing graphs or separating sections of a form.

The Shape Control

The *shape control* assumes a predefined shape that is determined by the control's `Shape` property. The set of possible shapes includes a rectangle with square or rounded corners, a square with square or rounded corners, an oval, and a circle. Again, the thickness, size, position, color, and style of the shape can be set, using the appropriate properties, both at design time and at runtime. For more information regarding each of these controls, refer to the *Visual Basic Programmer's Guide.*

Using Graphics Controls in Code

A graphics control must be placed on a form at design time before it can be used. You can create a control array and dynamically create controls at runtime, but you still must create the first, or *parent* control, on the form at design time. To see how graphics controls can be used in an application, examine the Ctl32.exe program contained on the CD-ROM included with this book. This application consists of a shape control array, each element of which is defined and placed on the form at design time. When the main form loads, no code is necessary to show the controls. The main form of the application is shown in Figure 15.1.

Because the controls are created at design time, Visual Basic displays them as the application's main form is loaded. As a result, the time it takes to display these controls is included in the time it takes for the form to load, since they are displayed as the form loads. If the load time of the form is measured, that time includes the time required to load and display the controls. Since we want to know the time required for the controls to load and display, this program is written to do exactly that. In order to measure the time required to load the form, the form's `Load` event must include the common function call to post the load time. The `Load` event procedure is shown in Listing 15.1.

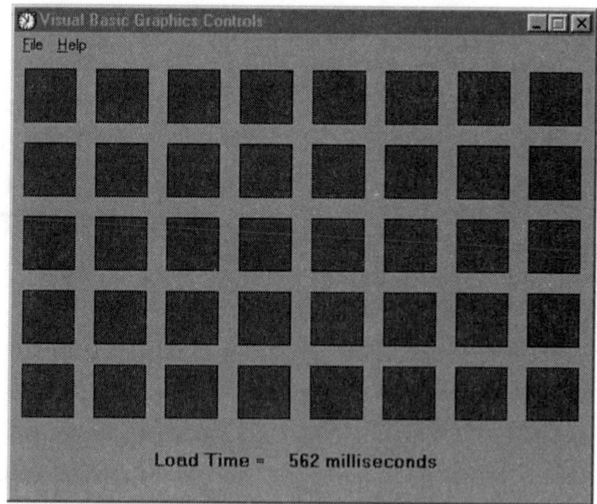

Figure 15.1.
Running the Ctl32.exe application.

Listing 15.1. Using controls at design time.

```
Private Sub Form_Load ()
      Call Common_CenterForm(Me)
      Call Common_PostLoadTime(lblLoadTime)
End Sub
```

This code listing is pretty boring! As you can see, no code to handle any graphics is required or used. The form's `Load` event simply centers the form and calls the subroutine to post the load time of the form. The Startr32 utility is used to get the loading time of the application, which is displayed in Figure 15.1. The time required to display the controls is compared with other techniques later in the chapter.

Graphics controls have several benefits, some of which have already been discussed. Less code is typically needed when you're using graphics controls, because much of the work can be done visually at design time. In the case of the Ctl32.exe application, no code whatsoever was needed to display the graphics. Although some code usually must be used to manipulate graphics controls, the amount of code is much less than when using other techniques such as graphics methods and the Windows API, both of which are discussed later in this chapter. The fact that the controls can be placed on forms at design time makes it much easier for you to lay out the form the way you want, because you can then experiment visually with the graphics.

The Ctl32.exe application consists of an array of graphics controls that were constructed completely in the design environment of Visual Basic. Another approach is to create one control at design time and then programmatically create clones of the control and put them on the form using code. This way you can compare the performance of creating all the controls at design time versus creating them dynamically using code. An application, called CtlArr32.exe, has been written for this purpose; it is included on the CD-ROM that accompanies this book. The main form of the application in the Visual Basic design environment is shown in Figure 15.2.

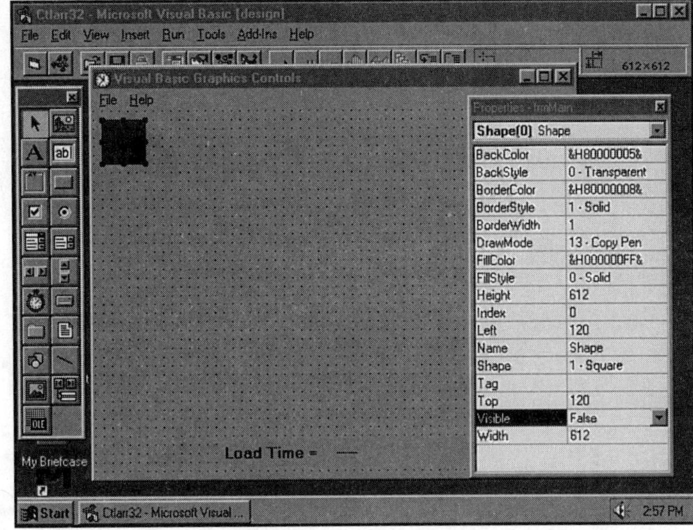

Figure 15.2.
The CtlArr32.exe main form in Visual Basic 4.0's design mode.

Note that only one control is on the form. The property sheet of the graphics control indicates that the `Visible` property of the control is set to `False` and the `Index` property of the control is set to `0`. This establishes the control as part of an array of controls that can be created. In the Ctl32.exe application, no code is required to show the controls because they were all created at design time. In the case of CtlArr32.exe, however, you must create the controls using code. The most appropriate place to do so is in the `Load` event of the main form. The code for the `Load` event is shown in Listing 15.2.

Listing 15.2. Using control arrays at runtime.

```
Private Sub Form_Load()

    Dim X As Integer, Y As Integer
    Dim iRows As Integer, iCols As Integer
    Dim iCount As Integer

    Call Common_CenterForm(Me)

    iRows = 5
    iCols = 8

    For X = 120 To 840 * iCols Step 840
        For Y = 120 To 840 * iRows Step 840
            iCount = iCount + 1
            Load Shape(iCount)
            Shape(iCount).Left = X
            Shape(iCount).Top = Y
            Shape(iCount).Visible = True
```

continues

Listing 15.2. continued

```
        Next
    Next

    Call Common_PostloadTime(lblLoadTime)

End Sub
```

Note that each control must not only be made visible when created, but it must also be positioned in the right place. Position logic must therefore be built into the application for each row and for the columns within the rows to display the controls properly. You can see that logic in Listing 15.2. The amount of time it takes for this application to load is shown in Figure 15.3, which shows the application's display when executed.

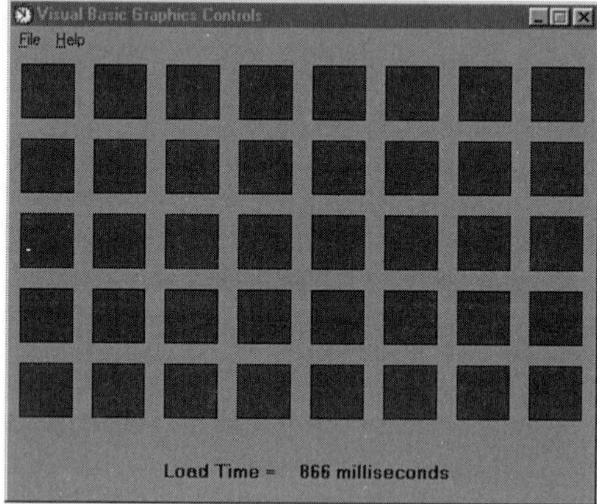

Figure 15.3.
Running the CtlArr32.exe application.

As you can see from the results, it is slightly faster to explicitly create and position each shape control on the form at design time than it is to create them dynamically in code. If you think about what Visual Basic must do, the reasoning behind this is clear. When all the controls are defined up front, they become a part of the form's design. As such, they are simply generated along with the form when the application starts. Because it is a quick operation for Windows and the underlying display driver to fill a region with the same color to generate a shape, little overhead is incurred at load time for these operations.

On the other hand, with the dynamic load approach, in which controls are generated at runtime rather than at design time, more overhead is present. The CtlArr32 application might load into memory slightly more quickly because it has fewer controls on the form initially, but then the interpreter must step in and intervene, creating the controls that automatically appear in the

Ctl32 application. The interpreter's intervention slows down the application's load time slightly, as you can see by the results. It appears, then, that the interpreter uses more time to create the shape controls using code than the application takes to load when the controls are predefined.

This is in contrast to the behavior of image and picture box controls demonstrated in Chapter 12, "Control Loading." There it is shown that if many instances of the same image and picture box controls are required, it is measurably faster to generate them dynamically through control array `Load` statements than to lay them all out at design time and have them predefined when the form loads. Performance considerations are different for each type of control. For picture box and image controls with identical images (that is, with identical per-pixel memory-map requirements), loading an image dynamically from a control already in memory is faster than individually loading each file from the design-time definition during the form-load process. There are some "economies of scale" in loading from the template already in memory when the design-time approach must load each image control as if it contains a separate image. Shape controls are drawn using much simpler region-fill operations than the per-pixel mapping of image and picture box controls offer and do not have this load penalty. Likewise, line controls are really specialized shape controls, and therefore also load more quickly from a design-time definition than with the overhead of the interpreter generating them.

TIP: Shape and line controls cause form loading to be slightly faster if they are explicitly defined at design time rather than dynamically created at runtime. By contrast, if many identical image and picture box controls are required, the form will load more slowly if all are predefined at design time rather than dynamically created from the first instance of a form load at runtime.

Graphics controls are a very effective way to display graphics. They are not always preferable, however, and they do have drawbacks. Graphics controls can sometimes limit your flexibility because you are often limited to working within the context of the control's definition in determining how the graphics appear. Consider, for example, the shape control. The `Shape` property of the shape control can be set to rectangle, oval, circle, rounded rectangle, or rounded square. If you want to create a triangle or a polygon, however, you're out of luck. The shape control does not provide you with that flexibility.

If you want to manipulate the control in a way that is not possible using properties or methods of the control, you must often use some other technique, such as graphics methods or the Windows API. As you will soon see, graphics *methods* can be used in addition to or in place of graphics controls, often providing additional levels of functionality and operations not possible to perform with graphics controls. Often, graphics controls are simply not flexible enough to meet the programmer's needs.

Creating Graphics Using Graphics Methods

The typical Visual Basic programmer finds that graphics controls are often inadequate to meet all of his or her needs. In addition to using graphics controls, you can also use graphics methods. Often times, graphics methods are used *with* graphics controls so that they complement each other. The purpose of this section is to see how graphics methods compare to graphics controls as an *alternative* technique. This section sets out to determine whether a task can be accomplished faster with a graphics control or with graphics methods.

Visual Basic provides the following graphics methods:

- `Cls`—Clears all graphics drawn on a form
- `PSet`—Sets the color of a single pixel
- `Point`—Returns the color of a pixel
- `Line`—Draws a line or box on a form
- `Circle`—Draws a circle, an ellipse, or an arc on a form

This chapter does not discuss in detail the graphics methods and all the ways they can be used. Although a brief introduction is presented, the authors suggest the *Visual Basic Programmer's Guide,* as well as Sams Publishing's *Teach Yourself Visual Basic 4 in 21 Days* for more detailed information.

The *Cls* Method

The `Cls` method can be used whenever you want to clear the drawing area of a form or object. The object or form is painted with the background color. The syntax for the method is

```
[object].Cls
```

where the `object parameter` is optional. If the object is not supplied, the active form is cleared. This method is very simple to use and is most often used to clear the existing graphics on the form or object and start a fresh drawing.

The *PSet* Method

You use the `PSet` method to place individual points, or *pixels,* on a form. The syntax for this method is

```
[object].PSet [Step](x,y)[, color]
```

where the `object` and `color` parameters are optional. If the object is omitted, the points are plotted to the active form. If the color is omitted, the `ForeColor` property of the object or form is used as the color. The `x` and `y` values are the coordinates of the container, whether it is an object or the form. If the optional `Step` keyword is used, those coordinates are relative to the `CurrentX` and `CurrentY` properties of the object. This method is useful whenever you want to plot a point, such as when you are drawing a graph.

The *Point* Method

The `Point` method is related to the `PSet` method. This method simply returns the color of a pixel represented by the coordinates passed to the method. The syntax for the method is

```
Point(x,y)
```

where `(x,y)` is the coordinate on which to evaluate the color. This method is useful to evaluate the color of a point, possibly to make some sort of program decision based on that color.

The *Line* Method

The `Line` method is one of the more useful of the available methods. When used in its basic form, it simply connects two coordinates with a line. You can set the thickness and style of the line using the container's `FillStyle` and `FillThickness` properties, respectively. The syntax of this command is

```
[object].Line[[Step](x1,y1)]-[Step](x2,y2)[,color], [BF]
```

As with the other controls, the line is drawn to the form if the object is omitted. The `(x1,y1)` parameter is optional and, if omitted, starts drawing from the endpoint of the last line drawn. This is useful if you are using several line-method commands to draw a shape. The `Step` keyword is optional and, if included, specifies that the endpoints of the line are not absolute but instead relative to the beginning points of the line. The *`color`* parameter is also optional and, if omitted, takes on the color of the object or form's `ForeColor` property. The `F` parameter can be used with `B` to draw a box between the two points, and `F` fills the box with the color provided or the `FillColor` of the container. There are many ways you can use the line method to draw all kinds of shapes. Such techniques are presented in the *Visual Basic Programmer's Guide,* as well as Sams Publishing's *Teach Yourself Visual Basic 4 in 21 Days.* Although specific methodologies for drawing shapes are beyond the scope of this book, this and the other methods are used to teach you how methods relate to other techniques in terms of performance.

The *Circle* Method

The `Circle` method can be used to draw circles, ellipses, and arcs. The syntax of the method is

```
[object].Circle [Step](x,y), radius[, color],[start],[end],[aspect]
```

This method draws a circle, an ellipse, or an arc whose radius is at the coordinate `(x,y)` and whose radius value is specified by the *`radius`* parameter. You can also specify the color. To draw an ellipse, you can simply adjust the *aspect ratio,* which adjusts the ratio of the vertical and

horizontal dimensions. Using this ratio, you can elongate the circle or flatten it, making it elliptical. You can also draw an arc by specifying start and end values, which represent radial degrees in which to start and end the arc that is patterned after the circle that would be drawn if the arc were completed from 0 to 360 degrees.

Comparing Graphics Methods to Graphics Controls

Graphics methods draw graphics directly to the form, whereas controls reside on their own layer on the form (this is discussed further in Chapter 17, "Painting and Redrawing"). Therefore, methods produce graphics that cannot be moved around or manipulated as controls can. For example, after you use a method to draw a line, that line is painted to the form like graffiti is painted on a wall. After the graffiti is painted on the wall, the only way to remove it is to clean the wall's surface. Likewise, when you use methods to draw graphics on a form, you can use the `Cls` method to clear the surface of the form; but remember that *all* the painting on the form gets erased.

A control, on the other hand, is like a picture that gets taped *on* the wall and does not become part *of* the wall. Therefore, if you want to move the control, you simply change its coordinate properties. If you want to remove the control, you simply turn its `Visible` property off or unload the control from memory. In this case, controls are more flexible in that they do not become a permanent part of the form after they're drawn.

Each of the graphics methods described in this section can be used to create graphics effects in applications. An application is now presented that uses some of the graphics methods discussed as an alternative to the graphics controls of the Ctl32 and CtlArr32 applications. This application, Method32.exe, is also on the CD-ROM that accompanies this book. In this application, no controls are used to display or generate the graphics. The main form is shown in Figure 15.4.

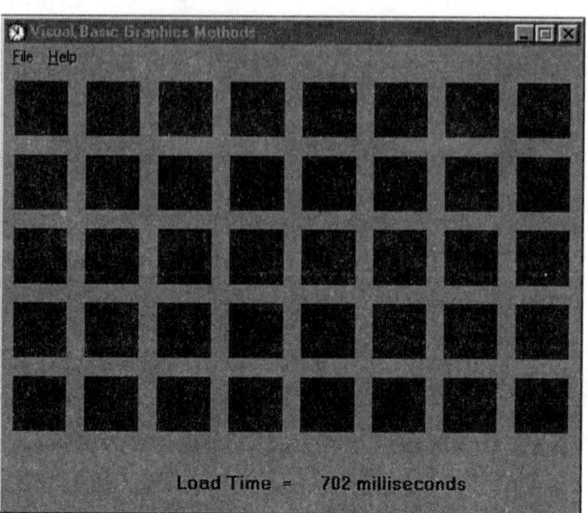

Figure 15.4.
The Method32.exe application at runtime.

As you can see, the main form at runtime looks identical to the Ctl32 main form. There is a significant difference, however. When in design mode, the Ctl32 main form has all the controls on it and looks just like it does at runtime. When the Method32 main form is viewed in design mode, it is totally blank except for the menu bar. Rather than placing all the graphics on the form at design time, the graphics are created in code and drawn at runtime. The CtlArr32 application takes a similar approach, but it already has a template to work with and simply creates more instances of the control that was placed on the form in design mode. The code used to draw the boxes for the Method32 application is shown in Listing 15.3.

Listing 15.3. Using methods at runtime.

```
Private Sub Form_Load()

    Dim X As Integer, Y As Integer
    Dim iRows As Integer, iCols As Integer

    Call Common_CenterForm(Me)

    iRows = 5
    iCols = 8

    For X = 120 To 840 * iCols Step 840
        For Y = 120 To 840 * iRows Step 840
            Line (X, Y)-Step(612, 612), RGB(255, 0, 0), BF
        Next
    Next

    Call Common_PostloadTime(lblLoadTime)

End Sub
```

In Listing 15.3, a code loop is used to draw 5 rows of 8 boxes each for a total of 40. The positioning logic is similar to that of the control array created at runtime, except that in this case, the `Line` method is used to create the boxes instead of using a graphics control. The width and height of the box are specified in the `Step` portion of the `Line` method statement. It would be very easy to change the shape of the square into a rectangle by simply adjusting the step values.

You can easily see in the code that you have to do more work (and thinking) to implement graphics methods than to implement graphics controls. You must calculate the position of each control rather than place them all visually on the form at design time. Even though this is also true of the control array of CtlArr32, here you must go a step further and use the method to create a line whose width and height must be determined in code to create the box.

Note the total load time of the Method32 application shown in Figure 15.4. As you can see from the timing, when shape graphics controls are defined explicitly at design time, they are faster than graphics methods used at runtime. Shape graphics *methods,* however, are faster than shape graphics *controls* when created dynamically at runtime—the graphics methods approach is 10 percent faster than the graphics control array approach. Keep in mind, however, that these timings depend a great deal on the type of graphics adapter and system display speed.

> **TIP:** Creating graphics at design time using shape and line controls is faster than using graphics methods at runtime.

> **TIP:** Graphics created at runtime using methods are typically faster than graphics dynamically created at runtime using shape and line controls.

The total time required to use graphics controls as opposed to graphics methods depends on the number and type of graphics being displayed. As a rule, the results favor the use of lightweight graphics controls, particularly when those graphics controls are created at design time. Keep in mind that, although the load time of an application that uses controls is faster than that of one that uses methods, the former has a larger executable file size and requires more memory and resources. This is so because the controls must be stored as a part of the form rather than created on the fly at runtime. The time it takes for the interpreter to implement the methods takes more cumulative time than when the graphics are predefined with a graphics control.

The results of these comparisons do not automatically mean that you should rule out the use of graphics methods in every instance. You must also consider the pros and cons of each approach in light of the way it is used. One primary benefit of graphics methods is that some of them can produce graphics that are impossible to create using the standard graphics controls, as you have already seen in the case of a triangle or polygon. Furthermore, graphics methods do not consume the memory and resources that controls do.

Often, you can quickly generate a great number of graphics using code when using controls might be otherwise cumbersome or impractical. For example, suppose you need to draw 100 grid lines for a graph. Rather than constructing 100 controls, it might be easier to write a simple code loop that plots the 100 lines on the form using graphics methods. The 100 graphics controls would also take up space in memory, because they are controls that must be addressable until they are destroyed. Graphics methods, however, are simply painted on the form and cannot be addressed as graphical entities. Thus, they take up fewer resources and memory than do the graphics methods. If memory is limited, the benefits of using methods might outweigh the speed benefits of using controls.

As expected, graphics methods also have disadvantages compared to controls. Although they often paint and redisplay faster on forms (which is discussed in Chapter 17), they take more processing time to create and place on the form. Furthermore, they often require more programming effort to implement, as illustrated in the applications presented thus far in this chapter.

The first application is very easy to implement; in fact, no code whatsoever is required. You simply have to create a shape visually, and then duplicate it using a control array on the form. The second application requires some code, but still makes use of a master control to create replicas in a control array. When working with the graphics methods, however, you have to write code to perform simple drawing and positioning of graphics on the form. As the programmer, you not only have the responsibility of calculating the size and position of each graphic drawn; you must also define the shape and its dimensions.

Controls, on the other hand, have a shape that is specified at design time, but you can change the shape at runtime. Also, when using methods, you cannot see the graphics on the form at design time, which is a big disadvantage when you're trying to put graphics together quickly. Fortunately, the Visual Basic environment enables you to step through each line of code, make changes, and determine the next line of code to be implemented. This very powerful aspect of Visual Basic, which languages such as C/C++ lack, considerably eases the burden of incremental development and debugging. For all these reasons, graphics controls are often easier to use and faster to display than graphics created using methods. This ease comes at the cost, however, of additional memory consumption, which can often be a significant issue when memory and resources are scarce.

Creating Graphics Using the Windows API

Now that you have examined the ways to create graphics within the Visual Basic environment, you have the background to discuss an alternative approach outside of the Visual Basic native environment: the Windows API. When creating graphics in Visual Basic, you are shielded from the underlying Windows API. The cost of this shielding is paid, in part, by you. You do not have easy access to the underlying graphics functionality of the Windows API, which is more extensive than that of Visual Basic.

The cost of using the Windows API is that you, the programmer, must learn more about how Windows handles graphics and must do more work to get those graphics on the screen. This section of the chapter introduces you to a subset of the Windows API graphics functions and how they work. Keep in mind that this presentation only skims the surface of the information required to use the API to create graphics. It is not the purpose of this book to make you an expert in Windows API graphics programming, but simply to show you the benefit of learning the API to produce high-performance graphics when necessary.

hWnd and *hDC*

Before any specific API functions are discussed, you need to know a few important items regarding the Windows system. Two variables are important when working with the API, particularly if you are working with graphics. The first is called a *window handle* and is often represented by the variable `hWnd`. This long integer variable is a unique ID that gets assigned to any window and most of the Visual Basic controls. Another important handle is a *device context handle*, or hDC. A *device* is anything that can receive graphics input, such as a form, a printer page, or a control. A *device context* determines all the aspects of the surface that is being drawn to, including the coordinate system used and other drawing attributes. The device context handle, therefore, is a unique ID that gets assigned to a device context to represent it when referred to by other graphics functions.

Drawing Attributes

When preparing to draw graphics, you must first select an object on which to draw. When the object is selected, a device context for that object is created. You set the drawing attributes of that object, such as the thickness of lines to be drawn and the pattern used to fill images on the object, by creating and setting *drawing attribute objects,* which are then assigned to the object you are drawing on. Here are two common drawing objects used when working with simple shapes:

- `Pen`. A *pen* is an object that defines the way lines and borders are drawn. Because a pen is used to draw lines, it has three specific properties: `color`, `width`, and `style`. The color of a pen represents the color of the line drawn. The width is self-explanatory. The style represents the pattern of the line, whether it be `solid`, `dashed`, `dotted`, or a combination of these.
- `Brush`. A *brush* is another important graphics object that determines the way in which drawing areas are filled. Brushes define what color and pattern are placed into 8×8-pixel areas, which are used to fill in graphics. The boxes that have been drawn on the forms in this chapter, for example, are filled with a solid red pattern. The brush can be defined in such a way. Brush properties include the color of the brush as well as its pattern. For instance, you might want to fill a box with blue diagonal lines. The brush could be defined to do so and selected into the appropriate device context.

Later in this section, you will see how these two attribute objects can be used to draw simple boxes on a form like the other applications you have already seen in this chapter. There are many more important concepts you need to understand when dealing with graphics and the API, including coordinate systems, clipping regions, and color palettes. It is beyond the scope of this book, however, to introduce and fully explain them. The intent here is to provide you with a few of the basics so you can compare the performance benefits of using the API to draw simple graphics against the other alternatives.

Essentially, the most important steps to creating graphics on a form are as follows:

1. Get a device context handle for the area upon which you want to draw. Most often, Visual Basic windows and controls have device context handle properties that you can access directly.

2. Select pens, brushes, and other graphics objects into that device context as needed. These can be selected into the device context using the API function `SelectObject`.
3. Invoke the appropriate graphics functions to produce the desired effects on the object selected.

Graphics Functions

Here are the graphics functions in the API that can be used to draw shapes:

- `Arc`—Draws an arc
- `Chord`—Draws a chord
- `DrawFocusRect`—Draws a rectangle with a dotted line; often used to show that a control has focus
- `Ellipse`—Draws an ellipse
- `ExtFloodFill`—Fills an area on the screen with a brush pattern
- `FillRect`—Fills a rectangle with a specific brush pattern
- `FillRgn`—Fills a graphics region with a specific brush pattern
- `FloodFill`—Fills an area on the screen with a specific brush pattern
- `FrameRect`—Draws a frame around a rectangle
- `FrameRgn`—Draws a frame around a graphics region
- `GetPixel`—Gets the color of a specified pixel
- `LineDDA`—Retrieves a list of all pixels that will be set by a specified line
- `LineTo`—Draws a line
- `PaintRgn`—Fills a region based on the current brush
- `Pie`—Draws a pie-shaped graphic
- `Polygon`—Draws a polygon shape
- `Polyline`—Draws a sequence of lines that are connected to each other
- `PolyPolygon`—Draws a sequence of polygons
- `Rectangle`—Draws a rectangle
- `RoundRect`—Draws a rectangle with rounded corners
- `SetPixel`—Sets the color of an individual pixel

As you can see, you can use a wide variety of useful functions to create graphics. Some of these functions are not directly supported in Visual Basic. In such cases, you can use the Windows API to achieve the results you want.

Comparing API Graphics to Graphics Methods and Graphics Controls

Now that you've learned the basics about using the Windows API to create graphics, this section presents an application that uses the Windows API to produce the same graphics as the other applications in this chapter. This application, called Api32.exe, is on the CD-ROM that accompanies this book. The main form is blank in design mode, just like the main form in the Method32 application. All the code used to create the boxes is in the `Load` event of the main form as shown in Listing 15.4.

Listing 15.4. Using the Windows API to create graphics.

```
Private Sub Form_Load()

#If Win16 Then
    Dim hdc As Integer
    Dim hBrush, hOldBrush As Integer
    Dim bOK As Integer
#Else
    Dim hdc As Long
    Dim hBrush, hOldBrush As Long
    Dim bOK As Long
#End If

    Dim iCols As Integer, iRows As Integer
    Dim PX As Integer, PY As Integer
    Dim DX As Integer, DY As Integer

    Call Common_CenterForm(Me)

    ' Get the device context for the form to be drawn on
    hdc = Me.hdc

    ' Get and select a solid red brush into the device context
    hBrush = CreateSolidBrush(RGB(255, 0, 0))
    hOldBrush = SelectObject(hdc, hBrush)

    ' Set initial position of first control
    PX = 120 / Screen.TwipsPerPixelX
    PY = 120 / Screen.TwipsPerPixelY

    ' Set increments
    DX = 840 / Screen.TwipsPerPixelX
    DY = 840 / Screen.TwipsPerPixelY

    For iRows = 1 To 5
        For iCols = 1 To 8
            ' Draw a rectangle on form to coordinates specified
            bOK = Rectangle(hdc, PX, PY, PX + 40, PY + 40)
            PX = PX + DX
        Next
        PY = PY + DY
        PX = 120 / Screen.TwipsPerPixelX
```

```
    Next

    ' Restore the original brush and delete the solid red brush
    If hOldBrush <> 0 Then
        hBrush = SelectObject(hdc, hOldBrush)
        bOK = DeleteObject(hBrush)
    End If

    Call Common_PostloadTime(lblLoadTime)

End Sub
```

Notice the conditional compile statements at the beginning of the procedure. The reason for defining the variables differently depending on the operating system is the API: The 16-bit API requires integer parameters, whereas the 32-bit API requires long integer parameters.

Since each API uses different parameters, a conditional compile must also be used when declaring the API functions. These declarations are in the COMMON.BAS module used by all of the applications in this book. The conditional compile takes care of declaring the values properly:

```
#If Win32 Then
Declare Function CreateSolidBrush& Lib "GDI" (ByVal crColor&)
    Declare Function GetStockObject& Lib "GDI" (ByVal nIndex&)
    Declare Function Rectangle& Lib "GDI" (ByVal hdc&, ByVal X1&,
    ➥ByVal Y1&, ByVal X2&, ByVal Y2&)
    Declare Function SelectObject& Lib "GDI" (ByVal hdc&,
    ➥ByVal hObject&)
#else
    Declare Function CreateSolidBrush% Lib "GDI" (ByVal crColor%)
    Declare Function GetStockObject% Lib "GDI" (ByVal nIndex%)
    Declare Function Rectangle% Lib "GDI" (ByVal hdc%, ByVal X1%,
    ➥ByVal Y1%, ByVal X2%, ByVal Y2%)
    Declare Function SelectObject% Lib "GDI" (ByVal hdc%,
    ➥ByVal hObject%)
#end if
```

The first task when creating the graphics is to select the device context into which the graphics will be placed. In this case, that device context belongs to the form within which you want to display the graphics. It is not necessary to select a pen into the device context, because no lines are being drawn in this example. In order to fill the box with the red color, however, you must select a red brush into the device context. The default solid pattern can be used. At that point, the rectangle is ready to be drawn.

The Windows API `Rectangle` function requires a device context handle and four coordinate values. The coordinates used by the API functions are *pixel units*. In all the other applications in this chapter, the default coordinate system is the Visual Basic twip unit. The *twip* is defined as $^1/_{1440}$ *logical inch*, where a logical inch is a fixed distance of one inch across the surface for which it is being measured. It follows, therefore, that 1,440 twips extend out to 1 logical inch horizontally. Pixel units depend on the screen resolution of the monitor being used, whereas twips are independent of resolution.

Both the screen object and printer object have two useful properties for determining how many pixels are in a twip for the resolution under consideration. You can use the `TwipsPerPixelX` and `TwipsPerPixelY` properties for this purpose. You obtain the number by dividing the number of twips by the `TwipsPerPixelX` and `TwipsPerPixelY` values. The number of pixels can then be used for any function that requires such a value. As you can see in Listing 15.4, this technique is used to calculate the starting position of the first rectangle as well as the increments required to display the remaining 39 rectangles on the form.

Having determined the equivalent positioning of the boxes using pixels rather than twips, the Windows API `Rectangle` function is then used to draw the box. The loop used to create the boxes in this program is very similar to those of the previous applications studied in this chapter. When the program is executed, the main form, shown in Figure 15.5, looks identical to the other forms.

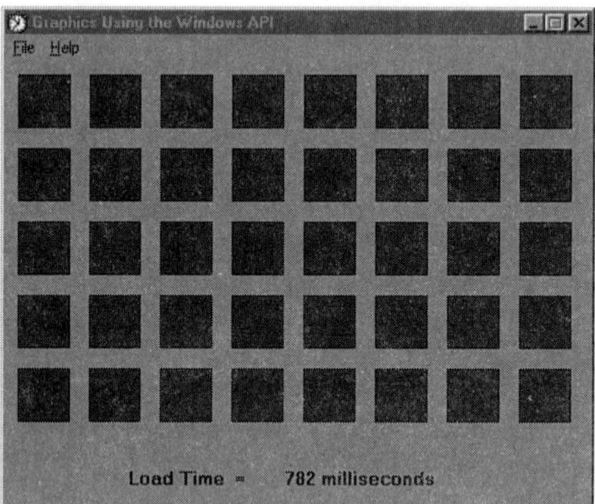

Figure 15.5.
The Api32.exe application at runtime.

The load time of the application, produced by Startr32, is shown at the bottom of the form. As you can see from the load time, this approach takes approximately the same amount of time as the Method32.exe application, differing by approximately 10 percent. It appears from these results that the direct use of the Windows API does not provide a significant performance improvement over the use of graphics methods. You must keep several factors in mind, however.

First, the graphics being drawn in these applications are very simple. More complex graphics, as well as complex interaction such as animation, often require techniques that Visual Basic either cannot provide or cannot provide efficiently. Often, we can turn to the Windows API to provide that functionality. In such cases where Visual Basic cannot provide the functionality, the use of the Windows API is indispensable. This is not a performance issue, but is instead an issue of functionality that the Windows API can provide and Visual Basic cannot. In cases in which the solution cannot be easily implemented in Visual Basic, the API can often be used instead of Visual Basic to provide the same functionality. In most cases, Visual Basic controls and methods offer similar performance to the Windows API functions in providing the same graphical functionality.

> **TIP:** Standard Windows API graphics functions do not provide significant performance advantages over graphics controls and graphics methods implementations that provide the same functionality.

Certainly, no general conclusions can be made across the board regarding whether Visual Basic or the Windows API is faster in *every* possible situation. The results simply point out that, although the Windows API can provide the same functionality as Visual Basic to produce graphics, it is usually practical to avoid using the API unless you need it to do something Visual Basic simply cannot do. The effort it takes to learn the Windows API, coupled with its complexity in maintenance and debugging, make it a less preferable choice than the other alternatives in most cases.

Printer Speed Versus Display Speed

In the discussion thus far, it has been assumed that the graphics are printed to the screen. In reality, those graphics might be output to a file or, more commonly, sent to a printer. A word about printer performance is therefore in order, because the difference in performance between a printer and a video display can be significant and should be acknowledged.

It is important to note that the time it takes to prepare and send graphics images to the printer is not the same as the time it takes to print to the screen. The type of printer being used, the amount of memory the printer uses to store graphics, whether the printer can display color images, and the technology used to print (that is, laser printer, dot matrix, ink jet) are all factors in determining how fast data can be sent to the printer as well as how fast something actually prints.

Color

One thing you should consider when you want to print graphics to a printer is whether the printer can print in color. If the printer is not a color printer, its performance can be improved by sending monochrome images to it. Otherwise, you must send a great deal of extra color information to the printer, which only gets translated into a black-and-white shading scheme anyway. If you send the image with no color information, but only shades of black and white (pictures can be created without color), the printer does not have to make these conversions and can print the graphics faster.

Resolution

Another consideration when printing graphics to a printer is the resolution of the graphics being sent. Some printers, particularly laser printers, have a very high resolution. The higher the resolution of the graphics being sent to the printer, the more time it will take to print because more information is being sent. If, on the other hand, the resolution of the graphics being sent is lower, the image will print faster. If you are printing a form which contains a picture box or image control, you can control the color and resolution of the graphics in that control by setting the format of the graphics file when it is assigned to the control.

> **TIP:** Printing graphics to a printer takes longer than displaying those graphics on the screen.

You should expect that sending graphics to the printer and printing those graphics will, in almost all cases, take considerably longer than displaying graphics on the screen. Video-display resolutions have, over the years, been more standardized than the various printers and printer drivers out on the market. Because the printer is a mechanical device, whereas the video display is essentially an electronic device, you should always favor providing graphics output to the screen when possible, and not just to the printer.

Print Preview

It is wise, for example, to provide the user with a print-preview screen in a word processing application to show what the document will look like when it comes out of the printer before it is actually sent there. Because it takes so much longer to print the document than to view it, you as a user can make changes and see on the monitor what the document will look like on the printed page. In this manner, you can refine the document until you get it just the way you want it, and then you can send it to the printer. You might become very frustrated if you have to wait 3 minutes every time you want to print the document and make a change, and you will waste a lot of paper in the process.

Therefore, when you're considering printing speed versus display speed, keep in mind that display speed is almost always much faster and that your application should always enable the user to see what he is about to print before it gets printed. In this manner, you can only print when you need to and are not dependent on a slow printer for making changes to something you could do much faster by seeing it on the screen. Furthermore, by keeping the resolution of graphics higher and using monochrome if a printer does not support color, you can dramatically improve the performance of the printing process.

Summary

This chapter examines the three fundamental techniques you can use to create graphics: Visual Basic graphics controls, Visual Basic graphics methods, and the Windows API. Each technique has its advantages and disadvantages, and each performs differently. Applications are examined for each of the three techniques to evaluate their performance. The results indicate that placing shape and line controls on forms at design time is faster than creating them dynamically at runtime using code. The results also show that design-time shape controls are faster than graphics methods but that graphics methods are faster than dynamically created shape controls. The Windows API is also compared to methods and controls, and the performance is comparable to that of graphics methods.

The evaluation of performance in this chapter is based primarily on the load time of the form on which the graphics are drawn. (See Chapter 17 for a discussion about the time it takes to repaint and reposition those graphics on forms and controls.) When you're simply considering the amount of time it takes to display graphics on a form initially, however, remember that static lightweight controls perform better than dynamic controls or methods. When you're dealing with the API, methods and controls can be faster in some cases and comparable in others.

This does not mean that you should always use static controls. Often, graphics must be loaded dynamically because different numbers and types of graphics might be required based on user actions. In such cases, it might not be practical to design every type of graphics control up front that might need to be used. In such cases, you can often use graphics methods to create those graphics. Because they are not controls, they do not require the level of memory that controls need to be stored and manipulated. Thus, although graphics methods are not always as fast as controls, they are often preferable in terms of practicality.

The Windows API can provide any level of functionality Visual Basic provides and much more. Although this chapter does not delve into the great flexibility and functionality of the API, you should note that the API can often be used to extend graphics capabilities far beyond what Visual Basic is capable of performing. This might come at the cost of performance, but the benefits of the API can outweigh such considerations in the appropriate situation.

Finally, the chapter briefly examines the issue of display speed versus printer speed. Outputting graphics to a printer is almost always much slower than to a video screen, so you should always provide graphical display output as well as printed output. The user might consider the performance of an application to be very poor if he must always print graphics to the printer instead of being able to see them and change them in the application first. Furthermore, you can use techniques to make the printing process faster, such as using lower-resolution graphics and avoiding the use of color when possible to make it easier for the printer to process the graphics.

Obey the Signs

Wrong Way: Turning to Windows API calls is always faster than Visual Basic.

In some cases, this might be true, but certainly not all the time. Depending on how the API is used, a great deal of knowledge must be amassed on the Windows internals to make effective use of the API. Depending on how the user implements his solution, Visual Basic might use techniques that are faster than yours. Therefore, you cannot always come to this conclusion.

Beware of Falling Rocks: Using graphics controls or methods exclusively is not *the best way to create graphics.*

As the chapter points out, graphics controls and methods are different and have their respective strengths and weaknesses. You must be careful to use each appropriately. Whereas shape graphics controls created at design time seem to yield the fastest load-time performance, they might not always be the best choice, particularly when memory and resources are limited. Five hundred line controls on a form used to draw a grid might cripple a system with limited memory or exceed VB control limitations, whereas the use of a method to draw directly to a form might have very small resource demands.

Wrong Way: The user won't care if you force him/her to print graphics data from an application without being able to see that data on the screen first.

Have you ever used an application that did not provide a way to preview something you wanted to print? If so, you are probably very familiar with the fact that printing graphics takes longer than displaying them. The user will become very frustrated and unhappy with the performance of an application if he has to print every time he makes a change to a record or document. Even if the application performs very well, the time it takes to print will make it seem to run slowly. The printer he is using might be terribly slow, but the user might take it out, in part, on your application. So be sure to provide a way to look at the information before it gets printed.

Q&A

Q If shape controls are faster than methods, why should I even consider using the methods?

A Graphics methods and controls both have their strengths and weaknesses. The wise programmer will use whichever technique is appropriate for the situation, and will likely use both together in applications where appropriate. Often, the use of methods versus controls is not so much a performance issue as a functionality issue.

Q I thought that using the Windows API was always faster because it works directly with Windows and doesn't have to filter through Visual Basic. Isn't that true?

A It is true, but in some cases, the ways Visual Basic displays graphics can be better than the particular API solution on which you might settle. You are shielded from how Visual Basic works with the API, but in some cases Visual Basic might use the API more efficiently than the programmer does. In certain cases, you must use the API to get the functionality you want in the application. This again is a functionality issue rather than a performance issue. The bottom line is that, in most cases, the API can and should be avoided unless some special type of graphics functionality must be provided that you can't get from Visual Basic.

Quiz

Consider the application 15Quiz32.exe on the CD-ROM that accompanies this book. This application uses controls and methods to draw various lines and shapes on a form. The main form is shown in Figure 15.6.

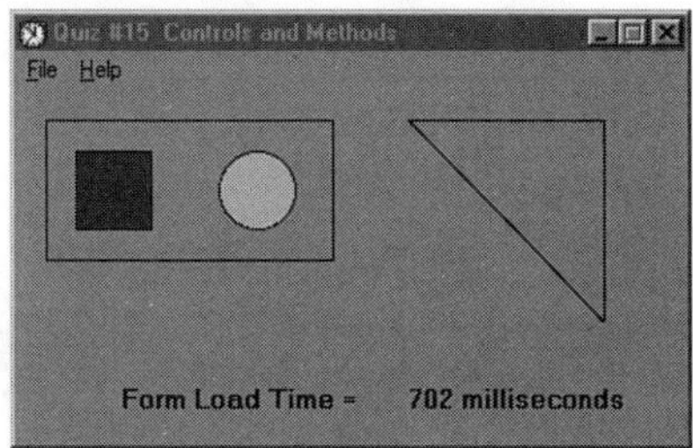

Figure 15.6.
The 15Quiz32.exe application at runtime.

The graphics contained within the box on the left of the form are drawn using controls at runtime. The triangle on the right side of the form is drawn using graphics methods at runtime. The graphics methods used to draw the triangle are implemented in the application's main `Form_Load` event. (See Listing 15.5.)

Listing 15.5. Drawing a triangle using graphics methods.

```
Private Sub Form_Load()

    Call Common_CenterForm(Me)

    ' This section of code uses methods to draw a triangle
    ' on the screen
    Line (3120, 240)-(4680, 240)
    Line (4680, 240)-(4680, 1800)
    Line (3120, 240)-(4680, 1800)

    Call Common_PostloadTime(lblLoadTime)

End Sub
```

Note the load time of the 15Quiz32 application in Figure 15.6. The application load time was obtained using Startr32.

Here are some questions you should be able to answer after looking at the code and reading this chapter:

1. Rewrite the application to use controls, rather than methods, exclusively. Compare the performance of the resultant application to that of the original. Which performs better?

   Answer: In order to convert the graphics that use methods to controls, the code used in the form's `LOAD` event to implement the methods is replaced by simply drawing the controls on the form at design time. In order to produce a triangle using graphics controls, you must use three line controls to form the triangle. The resultant application, 15AnsA32.exe, is on the CD-ROM that accompanies this book. All the code that was originally used for methods can be eliminated, as shown in Listing 15.6.

Listing 15.6. Graphics controls used exclusively.

```
Sub Form_Load ()

    Common_CenterForm Me

    Common_PostLoadTime Me

End Sub
```

   When Startr32 is used to execute the application, the load time of the application is displayed, as in Figure 15.7.

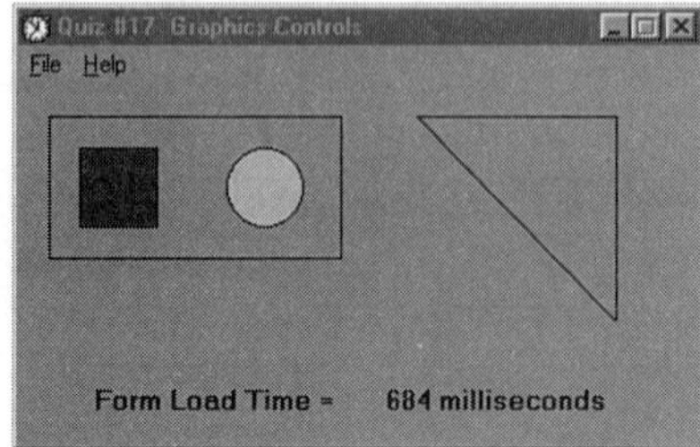

Figure 15.7.
Executing 15AnsA32.exe using Startr32.

2. Now rewrite the application to use methods exclusively. Again, which is the better performer?

   Answer: In order to convert the graphics that use controls to methods, you must write code that was originally not necessary because you were using controls. This application, 15AnsB32.exe, is on the CD-ROM that accompanies the book. The additional

code should be placed in the main `Form_Load` event. The complete code is shown in Listing 15.7.

Listing 15.7. Graphics methods used exclusively.

```
Private Sub Form_Load()

    Call Common_CenterForm(Me)

    ' This section of code uses methods to draw a triangle
    ' on the screen
    Line (3120, 240)-(4680, 240)
    Line (4680, 240)-(4680, 1800)
    Line (3120, 240)-(4680, 1800)

    ' This section uses a method to draw a red box on
    ' the screen
    Line (480, 480)-Step(612, 612), RGB(255, 0, 0), BF


    ' This section uses a method to draw a black box around
    ' the circle and square on the form
    Line (240, 240)-Step(2292, 1092), , B

    ' This section uses methods to draw a yellow circle on
    ' the screen
    Me.FillColor = RGB(255, 255, 0)      ' Set fill color to yellow
    Me.FillStyle = 0                     ' Set fill style to solid
    Circle (1926, 776), 306              ' Draw the circle

    Call Common_PostloadTime(lblLoadTime)

End Sub
```

You can use the Startr32 utility to run the application so that the load time is displayed. The results are shown in Figure 15.8.

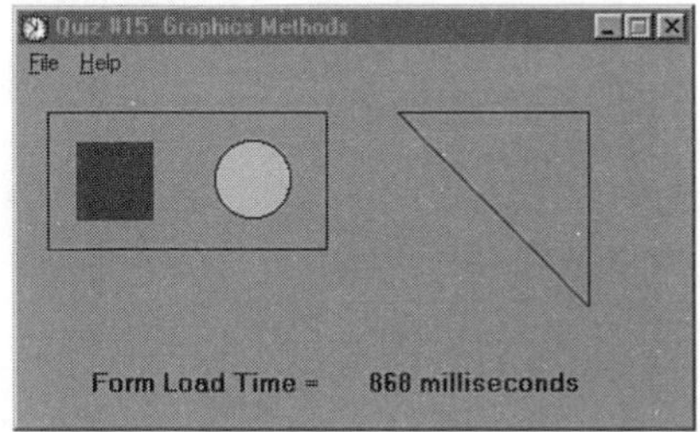

Figure 15.8.
Executing 15AnsB32.exe using Startr32.

As you can see from the results, the implementation using graphics controls exclusively at design time is faster than using methods exclusively or using a mixture of methods and controls. This supports the conclusions made throughout the chapter.

Workshop

Applications that rely heavily on graphics can often be optimized. If you have an application that makes heavy use of graphics controls and methods, try using controls in place of the methods. Does the performance of the application improve? How much more memory and resources does the application require, and how is the size of the executable file affected? Now use methods exclusively, if possible, instead of controls. What are the effects on the application? What conclusions can you draw?

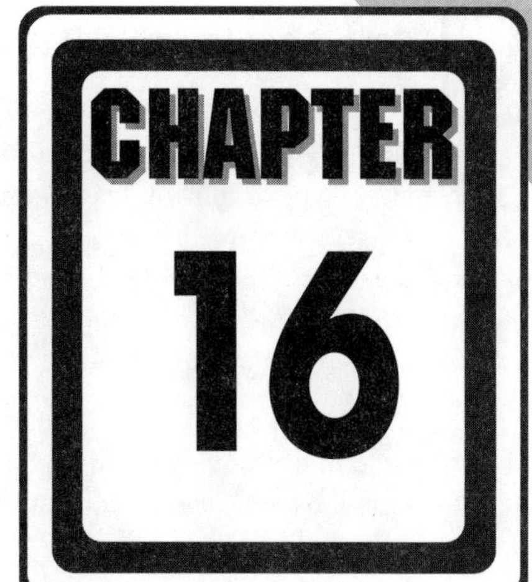

Displaying Pictures

In addition to displaying lines and shapes, you often want to incorporate pictures into your applications for animation and other visual effects. Visual Basic displays pictures in a variety of ways: every form has a `Picture` property that can be set to a graphics file, and both picture box and image controls are designed to display pictures inside forms.

The picture box and image controls differ somewhat in functionality and performance. Some programmers do not understand the fundamental differences between these controls and might use a picture box control where an image control could provide the same functionality but with better performance. This chapter compares the picture box and image controls in terms of their functionality and performance.

The chapter begins by describing the various types of graphics files that can be loaded into either type of control. Having discussed those files and the way they are constructed, the chapter describes the picture box control, pointing out its features and uses. The image control is then presented, again with its primary features highlighted. In both cases, applications are presented that display bitmaps using each control on a form. Having presented the two controls, the two applications are then compared in terms of performance.

This chapter also explores techniques for using both controls more efficiently in applications, including various techniques for loading pictures into controls. Having read this chapter, you should have a clearer understanding of how each control works, what types of graphics can be displayed in each, which control performs better, and what is the best way to load pictures into these controls.

Graphics File Formats

Before this chapter discusses how to display graphics files in picture box controls, image controls, or forms, you need to be familiar with the graphics files themselves. A wide variety of file formats exist for representing graphics. The most commonly used formats are discussed briefly in the following list:

- *BMP files.* This file format is one of the most common. Bitmap files store data on a point-for-point basis. The higher the resolution of the image, the larger the bitmap file. As a result, a bitmap file can be of such a high resolution on a monitor or printer as to look photographic in quality.
- *DIB files.* DIB stands for *device-independent bitmap.* Data is stored in a DIB file so that the image will look the same regardless of the device on which it is displayed or printed. In contrast, the BMP file image can appear differently depending on the device on which it is being displayed. Like the BMP file, the DIB file structure consists of information about the size and other characteristics of the image, definitions of the colors used by the image, and the values of the pixels that make up the image.
- *WMF files.* WMF stands for *Windows metafile.* There are two types of metafiles—standard metafiles, or WMF files; and enhanced metafiles, or EMF files. Metafiles are not stored point-for-point as BMP and DIB files are; rather, these images are stored using vector graphics and mathematical constructs that signify color, fills, and shapes to create the image. Metafiles behave much like PostScript files do when sent to a printer. Rather than sending a dot-by-dot map to the printer, a PostScript file sends a series of commands to the printer to draw lines and produce text. Using these commands cuts down on the size of the PostScript file, although certainly not on its complexity. Metafiles are typically smaller than BMP files because less information

must be stored using vector math versus a point-by-point map of the image. Metafiles are not only smaller, but they typically display faster than BMP files. The drawback of WMF files is that you don't get the same resolution as you do with a BMP file. Therefore, metafiles load and display faster, but they don't give you the photographic quality that bitmaps can provide.

- *ICO files.* These files are commonly referred to as *icons.* You are already familiar with icons, because every file that can be run within Windows can have an icon defined for it. If, for example, you have installed Visual Basic within Windows, you can double-click on the Visual Basic icon to start the program. In Visual Basic, forms and applications can have their own icons. Icon files can also be loaded into picture box and image controls. Icons are much smaller than the other graphics files discussed in this chapter. Whereas BMP, DIB, and WMF file images can vary in size, icons are fixed in size. This makes them very fast to display, because they don't take up very much memory compared to the other formats.
- *RLE files.* One common way of saving bitmaps is in the *run-length encoded,* or RLE, format. This format compresses bitmap files in a way that cuts down significantly on the size of a bitmap image. They are slightly slower to paint and display, however, because they first must be uncompressed. Furthermore, they take considerably longer to display than a bitmap if they are scaled to something other than their original size. The savings in size, however, can be over 10 times that of a bitmap, which can be significant when users run applications on memory-constrained systems.
- *Other formats.* There are a variety of other file formats, including PCX, TIF, JPG, GIF, and JIF files, just to name a few. *PCX files* can be created using Microsoft Paint and other paint programs. *TIF files* are commonly used with scanner software. *GIF files,* which are commonly seen on bulletin board systems, are a common file format used to store bitmaps, although the JPG file format is quickly replacing the GIF format. All these file formats differ in how they structure and represent graphic information. The differences between every file format are not discussed here because there is such a wide variety. You have been introduced, however, to the primary graphics file formats you use when developing Windows applications.

The main difference between these file formats is the way the images are represented. Formats that store images point-by-point are typically larger and require more memory, and the images look more photographic in quality. Other file formats are very small and efficient, but lack the high resolution quality of the BMP and DIB formats. This trade-off between resolution and display speed and storage requirements is typical. When deciding which graphics file format to use, determine what the acceptable resolution is for the image you want to display. Then you can determine the most appropriate file type to use in the application you are creating.

After you have decided which file format to use, you must determine the type of container into which you want to place the graphic. This is the subject of the remainder of this chapter.

Picture Box Controls

Picture box controls are very powerful and are useful for displaying pictures. You select the picture box control from the Visual Basic tool palette and then place the control on the form. You can set the `Picture` property of the picture box control at design time or runtime to store a graphics file to the control. When you place a picture box control on a form, you have control over the dimensions of the control, in particular the width and height. When a picture is loaded into the control, the picture consumes as much space as when created. In other words, if you have a bitmap that is 2 inches wide by 2 inches high, and you create a picture box control 4 inches by 4 inches, the bitmap will fit into the picture box control and there will be 12 square inches of space remaining in the picture box control. Figure 16.1 illustrates how this picture box control would appear on the form in design time.

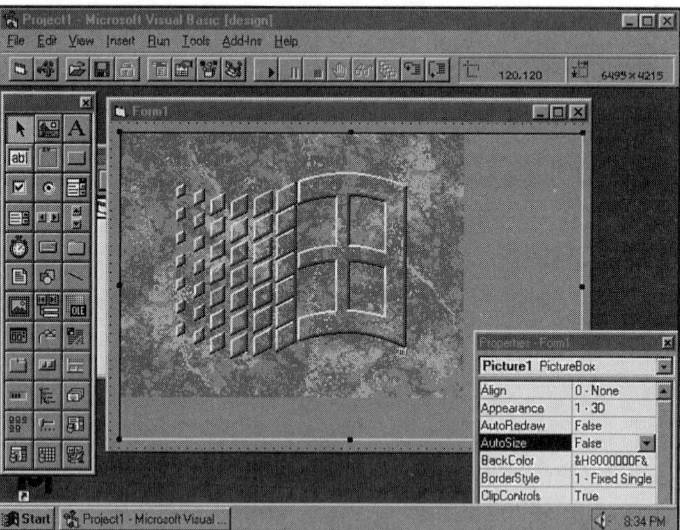

Figure 16.1.
A picture box control that is larger than its picture.

In order to resize the picture box control so that there is no extra space, you can set the `AutoSize` property to `True`, which resizes the control to fit around the bitmap image, as shown in Figure 16.2.

Controls such as labels and command buttons can be placed inside picture box controls and, in essence, become "child controls" of the parent picture box control. This makes the picture box control not only a powerful mechanism for displaying pictures, but also for containing and manipulating groups of controls in addition to pictures.

In order to see how picture box controls operate and perform, consider the Bmp32.exe application included on the CD-ROM that accompanies the book. This is a simple application that consists of four picture box controls. Each picture box control is assigned its own graphics file—the WINLOGO.BMP file—at design time. As a result, no code is required to initialize the bitmaps. The code listing for the `Load` event for the application is shown in Listing 16.1.

Figure 16.2.

A picture box control that is autosized to its picture.

Listing 16.1. The `Form_Load` event code for Bmp32.exe.

```
Private Sub Form_Load ()

    Call Common_CenterForm(Me)
    Call Common_PostLoadTime(lblLoadTime)

End Sub
```

As you can see, no code is required for the bitmaps. The form is simply centered and the load time is posted. Note that the `AutoSize` property was set to `True` for each of the bitmaps so that they size correctly regardless of the resolution of the user's computer. When the application is run, the four identical bitmaps appear cascaded across the form, as shown in Figure 16.3.

Note the load time of the main form, which is displayed in the figure. This load time will be compared to the load time using image controls, which are discussed in the next section.

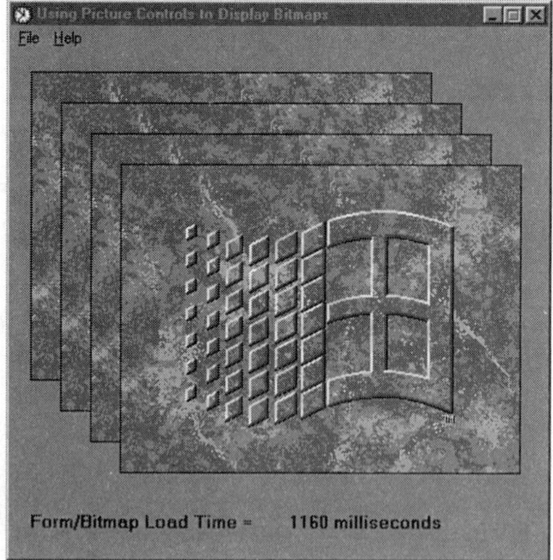

Figure 16.3.
The Bmp32.exe application at runtime.

Image Controls

An *image control* is another one of the three ways to display a picture in a Visual Basic application. In the *Visual Basic Programmer's Guide*, an image control is defined as "a rectangular area into which you can load picture files." Image controls, unlike picture box controls, enable you to "stretch," or resize, pictures so that they utilize the entire rectangular area of the image control. When you use a picture box control, the size of the picture being loaded into the control cannot change. With image controls, however, the `Stretch` property can be set to `True`, which automatically resizes the picture to take up the entire region of space defined by the image control.

Figure 16.4 shows a form in design mode with an image control that has a bitmap loaded into it.

As was true with the picture box control, the bitmap is smaller than the actual control that stores the picture. The image control does not have an `AutoSize` property as the picture box control does; therefore, you cannot automatically size the control to fit the bitmap. In the case of the image control, you have to go the other way around. By setting the `Stretch` property to `True`, you can increase or decrease the size of the picture to fill up all the space in the image. In Figure 16.5, the picture is stretched to fill the image control.

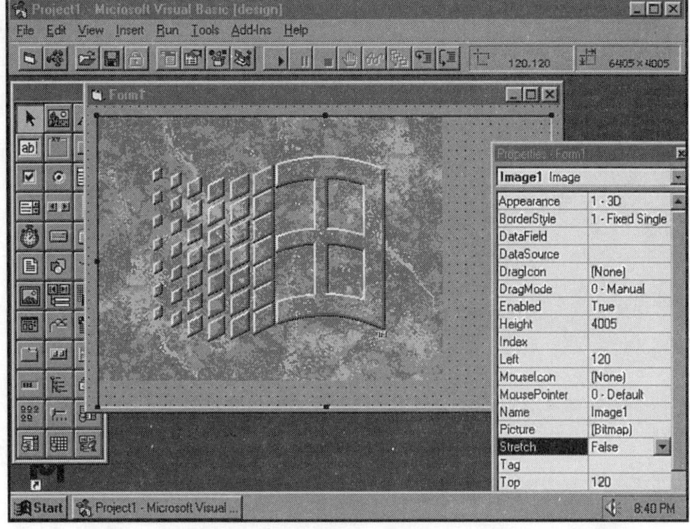

Figure 16.4.
An image control with a smaller picture and `Stretch` *set to* `False`.

Figure 16.5.
An image control with the same picture and `Stretch` *set to* `True`.

As you can see, the image appears elongated so that it fits in the image control. Conversely, the image control might be smaller than the picture. If the `Stretch` property is set to `True`, the picture will shrink to fit the size of the image control, as shown in Figure 16.6.

Figure 16.6.
An image control with the same picture, but "scrunched."

As you can see, the "scrunched" picture does not necessarily retain its proportions, since the user controls them via the size of the image control. Image controls are also different from picture box controls in that you cannot place child controls inside them. Nothing can be placed inside an image control other than an image, which must be set using the `Picture` property or loaded into the control at runtime.

In order to demonstrate the use of the image control, the authors constructed another application that essentially performs the same task as the Bmp32.exe application. This application, Img32.exe, is on the CD-ROM that accompanies this book. Four image controls are created at design time; each of these controls is loaded with the WINLOGO.BMP graphics file. The Stretch property of the image control is used to automatically size the bitmap to the image control. The resultant form looks identical to the Bmp32.exe application's main form. The Img32.exe main form is shown in Figure 16.7.

The code for the Img32.exe application is identical to that of the previous application; that is, no code is required to display the images because they were configured at design time. When the application is run using Startr32, the load time of the application is again displayed as shown in Figure 16.7. As you can see from the results, the image controls load faster than the picture box controls. In the applications compared, the image controls are faster than the picture box controls by 115 percent!

> **TIP:** Image controls are faster than picture box controls.

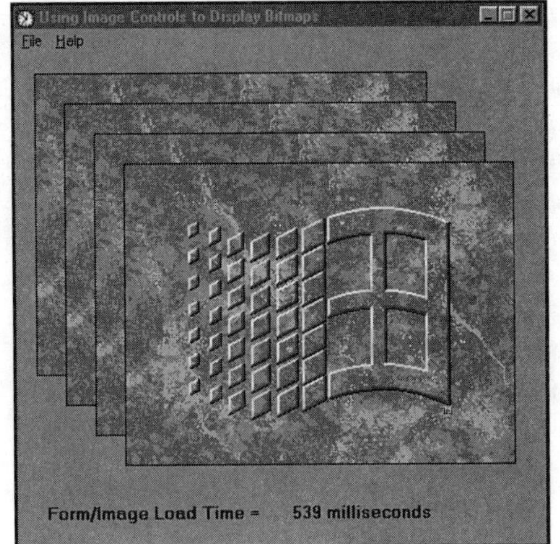

Figure 16.7.
The Img32.exe application at runtime.

Image Controls Versus Picture Box Controls

One of the reasons that image controls are faster is that the underlying structure of the image control is simpler than that of the picture box control. A picture box control is essentially a window of the type similar to a Visual Basic form. First, it can contain child controls like a form can. This means that the picture box control must keep track of all of its child controls and pass Windows messages to them. This requires additional complexity and processing time that are not required of the image control. Furthermore, the picture box control has more properties, events, and methods than the image control. These are the events for an image control:

```
Click
Double-Click
DragDrop
DragOver
MouseDown
MouseUp
MouseMove
```

Compare this to the list of events for a picture box control:

```
Click
Double-Click
DragDrop
DragOver
```

```
MouseDown
MouseUp
MouseMove
Change
GotFocus
KeyDown
KeyUp
KeyPress
LinkClose
LinkError
LinkNotify
LinkOpen
LostFocus
Paint
Re-size
```

Having examined the much larger list of properties for the picture box control, you now recognize that the picture box control has several capabilities that the image control does not have. Picture box controls can recognize keyboard input, can initiate OLE links, can recognize when focus is lost, and are notified by Visual Basic when they are painted and resized. This means that Visual Basic must perform additional processing with picture box controls than it must with image controls due to the increased functionality of the picture box control.

This additional processing takes more time, which is the primary reason for the decrease in performance of the picture box control versus the image control. Unlike the image control, the picture box control is an actual window, which means that it consumes a greater amount of resources. In some cases, it might be clearly desirable to take advantage of the picture box control's additional functionality at the cost of decreased performance. In many other cases, however, this added functionality is not needed or used and it is therefore preferable to use an image control rather than a picture box control. If the only thing you have the user do with a picture box control is click it or drag and drop it, you are needlessly wasting resources and degrading performance. The image control would be sufficient—and would be faster. If, as in the examples presented in this chapter, you are simply displaying a picture and do not need to worry about keyboard input, OLE, and resizing and painting of the control, then the image control is clearly more desirable.

The image control might also be preferred, in certain cases, for its functionality. Although it is not as complex as the picture box control, developers often take advantage of the powerful stretch feature of the image control, which might make it the ideal candidate apart from performance considerations. The stretch feature is often used when programmers want to change the dimensions of a graphic image to fit the needs of their application.

Although the performance increase is not dramatic in the example shown in this chapter, it might become more dramatic as the number of controls, resolution of the pictures in those controls, and interaction between controls and the forms used to contain them increases. Now that you have seen the performance benefits of using the image control rather than the picture box control, the following section discusses strategies for increasing the performance of applications using either control.

Using Picture Box and Image Controls Efficiently

The first optimization technique for both the picture box control and the image control deals with when and how to load the picture being used into the control. This chapter has already discussed how to load a picture into a control at design time: You can select the Picture property from the control's Properties list and select the graphics file to be loaded from the list. You can also paste a graphic from the Clipboard into the control. Therefore, if you created a graphic using PaintBrush, you could copy the graphic to the Clipboard, switch to Visual Basic, and paste the image into a control. Both of these techniques are design-time techniques.

You can also load pictures into the picture box and image controls at runtime. By loading the pictures at runtime, you might be able to increase the performance of your application. How? Suppose, for example, you are writing a poker game using Visual Basic. You obviously need a separate picture for the face of each unique card in a standard card deck. One way to implement this is to create a picture box or image control for each card, loading them into memory when the application starts. You could keep the controls invisible until needed, and then turn on the Visible property of the required card when needed.

This approach does not require the user to wait for every card to load at the beginning of the application. It is conceivable that every card in the deck might not be required for display. By only loading the controls you need at runtime, the user might not have to wait as long. Even if all the graphics are required throughout the life of the application, the user still has less initial time to wait for the application to load. As discussed earlier in the book, the initial loading time of an application is very important to the user. If it takes forever for an application to load, the user might reject it as too slow even if it runs like lightning after it is loaded. Therefore, you increase the perceived speed of the application by reducing the load time of the application.

Graphics-Loading Techniques

Pictures can be loaded, traded, and removed at runtime using the following techniques in Visual Basic:

- The `LoadPicture` function—Load from a file
- The `LoadResPicture` function—Load from resources built into the application's executable file
- Copy a picture from the Picture property of an existing control

You have already seen during a series of tests with the test program BmpLd32.exe that the copy technique is the fastest. The `LoadResPicture` technique—loading from a resource that has been built into the executable—takes nearly three times as long. And the `LoadPicture` technique—which loads a bitmap directly from a file—takes nearly six times as long.

The BmpLd32.exe program, which is included on the CD-ROM, simply loads four picture controls repeatedly with a bitmap. There are three command buttons, each of which supports a different bitmap loading technique: `LoadPicture`, `LoadResPicture`, and the copy technique, respectively. See Listing 16.2 for the code for the `LoadPicture` technique.

Listing 16.2. The `LoadPicture` external file test.

```
Private Sub cmdStart_Click()
Dim i As Integer
    Dim j As Integer

    Call Common_StartTimedTest

    For j = 1 To txtLoops
        For i = 0 To 3
            'Note that an external file must be distributed with the app !
            Picture1(i).Picture = LoadPicture(App.Path & "\winlogo.bmp")
        Next
    Next j

    Call Common_EndTimedTest(lblElapsedTime)
end sub
```

Code for the `LoadResPicture` technique appears in Listing 16.3.

Listing 16.3. The `LoadResPicture` resource test.

```
Private Sub Command1_Click()
Dim i As Integer
Dim j As Integer


    Call Common_StartTimedTest

    For j = 1 To txtLoops
       For i = 0 To 3
```

```
            ' Note that this resource ID=1 was built into the
            ' VB executable file (.exe) from a resource .res file
            Picture1(i).Picture = LoadResPicture(16, vbResBitmap)
        Next
    Next j

    Me.Refresh
    Call Common_EndTimedTest(lblElapsedTime)

End Sub
```

Code for the copy technique appears in Listing 16.4.

Listing 16.4. Copying from picture to picture.

```
Private Sub Command2_Click()
    Dim i As Integer
    Dim j As Integer

    Call Common_StartTimedTest

     For j = 1 To txtLoops
        For i = 0 To 3
            Picture1(i).Picture = Picture1(4)
        Next i
    Next j

    Call Common_EndTimedTest(lblElapsedTime)

End Sub
```

The normalized timings for each of these methods tested from a series of tests are shown in Table 16.1.

Table 16.1. Normalized execution times of bitmap loading techniques.

Method	*Normalized Results*
`LoadPicture`	6.0
`LoadResPicture`	3.0
Copying	1.0

The copy method offers clear savings, but requires that a picture box control containing the graphic is predefined on the form, which has a slight adverse affect on load time and has some maintenance drawbacks. If, for these reasons, the copy method is not feasible in your program, the `LoadResPicture` approach is clearly superior to the `LoadPicture` approach and eliminates the need to distribute the separate BMP files that are required with `LoadPicture`. Each of these alternatives is discussed in more detail in the following sections.

TIP: Copying a picture to the picture box to be updated from an existing picture box is by far the fastest approach to loading a picture box with a bitmap at runtime. This approach requires that a picture box control already exists with the desired picture. The slower method is to load a bitmap from a resource that has been built into the Visual Basic executable file with the `LoadResPicture` function. This technique has the advantages of requiring neither a preexisting control nor a distributable file. A much slower alternative is to load the bitmap from a file with the `LoadPicture` function. However, this technique requires an external file to be distributed with the application in addition to the performance penalty paid.

The *LoadPicture* Function

This function has one argument: the filename of the graphics file to be loaded. The syntax of the function is

```
Object.Picture = LoadPicture(filename)
```

where `Object` is either an image control, a picture box control, or the form itself. Loading a new picture into a form, an image control, or a picture box control completely replaces the picture previously contained in the object. In order to remove a picture from a control or a form, you can simply use an empty string for the `LoadPicture` function's argument.

It is important to realize one big drawback of using the `LoadPicture` function versus including the graphics in the form at design time. If you use the `LoadPicture` function, the bitmap files must also be provided to the user outside of the executable file. If, on the other hand, you define all the graphics inside the executable—that is, specify them in controls at design time—those picture files do not have to be provided because they are contained inside the executable. Again, you must consider the trade-off between these two approaches. This usually can only be done by trying both techniques to see which is more practical and efficient. The next technique presented in this chapter can help to minimize the impact of storing all the pictures in the executable at design time.

You can clear the contents of a picture control with the `Cls` method, and memory can be reclaimed in picture and image controls by using the `LoadPicture` function. Rather than simply hiding a control when it is no longer needed, it is much better to use `LoadPicture` and hide the control, as follows:

```
Picture1.Hide
Picture1.LoadPicture()
```

In this manner, you not only hide the control from view, but you also free up the memory it was using to display the picture.

Comparing Performance

In order to compare the performance of using the `LoadPicture` function versus placing pictures in the application at design time, two applications are now presented for performance comparisons. In the first application, BmpLd32.exe, the same four cascaded picture box controls are placed on the main form, but this time they are not loaded with pictures initially. The main form of the application at runtime is shown in Figure 16.8.

Figure 16.8.
The BmpLd32.exe application at runtime.

Notice that two times are recorded in the application: the time it takes to load the form and the time it takes to load the bitmaps controls. When the application is executed, only the form-load time is displayed. Then, when the user clicks the command button labeled Load, the picture controls are loaded with the WINLOGO bitmap and the time required to load the bitmaps is shown on the screen. With these two times, the total elapsed time can then be calculated. The event code for the `Click` event of the Load command button is shown in Listing 16.5.

Listing 16.5. Loading bitmaps using the `LoadPicture` function.

```
Private Sub cmdStart_Click()

    Dim i As Integer

    Call Common_StartTimedTest

    For i = 0 To 3
        Picture1(i).Picture = LoadPicture(App.Path & "\winlogo.bmp")
    Next

    Call Common_EndTimedTest(lblElapsedTime)

End Sub
```

As you can see from Listing 16.5, a simple loop that loads each picture box control with the same picture is executed, and the entire procedure is timed. The results of clicking on the Load command button are shown in Figure 16.9.

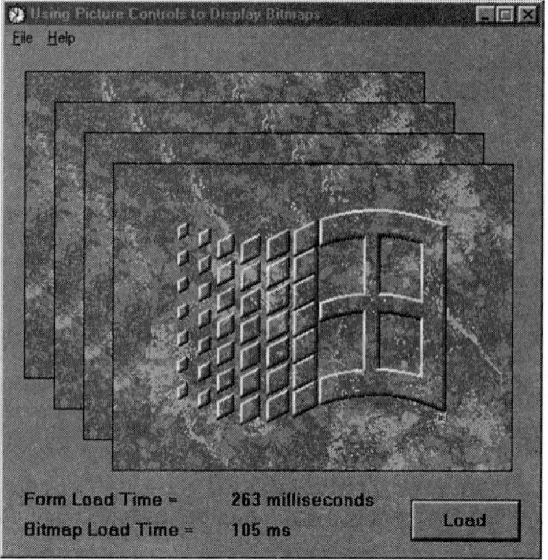

Figure 16.9.
Elapsed time to load bitmaps in BmpLd32.exe.

Note that now you have the total form load time and the total time to load the individual picture controls with the bitmaps. You can now compare the performance of BmpLd32 with that of Bmp32. Because the BmpLd32 application does not load the bitmaps in the `Form_Load` procedure, you would expect that the form-load time would be less than that of Bmp32, which *does* load the bitmaps during the `Form_Load` event. Therefore, a fair comparison is to compare the form-load time of Bmp32 with the form-load time plus the control-load time of BmpLd32. This comparison is made in Table 16.2.

Table 16.2. Comparing Bmp32.exe to BmpLd32.exe.

Application	*Form Load*	*Bitmap Loads*	*Total Time*
Bmp32	1160ms	N/A	1092ms
BmpLd32	263ms	105ms	386ms

As you can see from the results, it is considerably faster to load the bitmaps at runtime than to preload them at design time. This is partially due to the fact that the size of the executable file to be loaded into memory is considerably smaller. Furthermore, the same bitmap must be stored into each picture box control separately, which wastes space and increases time. The BmpLd32 application, however, loads the bitmap from a file, making the load time of the form considerably faster. Furthermore, the time required to display the bitmaps is also faster. This shows

that, when loading the same bitmap multiple times in an application, it is best to do so dynamically using the `LoadPicture` function.

Comparing Image Controls and Picture Box Controls

To compare the dynamic loading performance of image controls to the picture box control application just examined, the same application has been written using image controls instead of picture box controls. The application, ImgLd32.exe, is also on the CD-ROM that accompanies this book. The application is identical to BmpLd32.exe, except that the code statement

```
Picture1(i).Picture = LoadPicture(App.Path & "\winlogo.bmp")
```

is replaced with the statement

```
Image1(i).Picture = LoadPicture(App.Path & "\winlogo.bmp")
```

signifying the use of the image control rather than the bitmap. When the application is executed and the Load button is clicked, the results shown in Figure 16.10 are obtained.

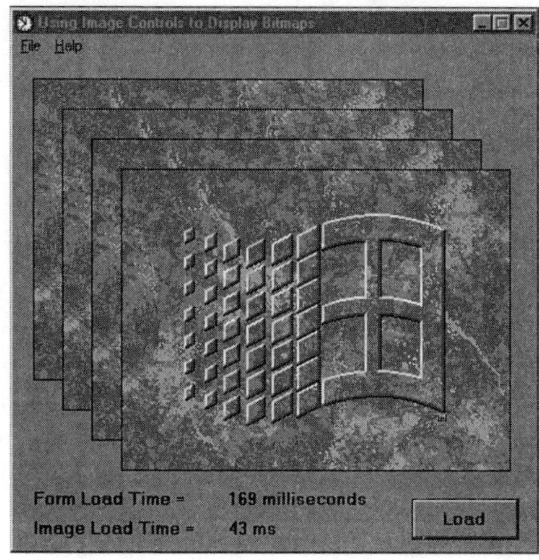

Figure 16.10.
The ImgLd32.exe application with bitmaps loaded.

This comparison results in the normalized execution times as shown in Table 16.3.

Table 16.3. Comparing Img32.exe to ImgLd32.exe.

Application	*Form Load*	*Bitmap Loads*	*Total Time*
Img32	539ms	N/A	539ms
ImgLd32	169ms	43ms	212ms

As you can see from the results, the load times for the application that loads the image control at design time requires 218 percent more time to load. Again, the savings in loading the image controls dynamically at runtime makes the load time of the form considerably shorter. The total time, which includes the time required to load the image controls dynamically, shows a savings of 154 percent when the image controls are loaded dynamically versus being set statically at design time. This shows again, even for the case of the image controls, that it is better to use dynamic loading.

Conclusion

You have already seen that the Img32.exe application is faster than the Bmp32.exe application. How do the dynamic loading applications compare? The picture box control application requires 368ms to execute, whereas the image control application requires 212ms. The image controls again provide a savings, in this case of almost 75 percent. The savings is not as significant seen with Bmp32 and Img32, where the bitmaps are loaded at design time. It is reasonable to conclude that the savings in the application load time combined with the savings in the control load times is greater with static loads than dynamic loads simply because of the overhead required in loading the applications. In both cases, image controls are faster, and, based on the results, the best technique is dynamic loading using image controls.

Furthermore, with judicious use of loading and unloading picture box and image controls during the life of an application, the amount of memory consumption can be reduced and reclaimed rather than be used up the entire time the application runs. `LoadPicture` can be used with an empty string (`""`) argument to erase the contents of a picture box or image control, thereby deallocating the memory previously required.

The *LoadResPicture* Function

The `LoadResPicture` function loads a picture into a picture box or image control. `LoadResPicture` extracts the picture from a resource area of the Visual Basic executable, which offers a much higher-speed load than does accessing an external file through `LoadPicture`. Loading from the resource area of the executable also provides a significant advantage of being able to manage resources in a resource file at design time and then distribute them all as part of the executable.

This approach is the same as the approach traditionally used by C and C++ applications to distribute and access resources. The first step to defining a resource is to specify it in a *resource definition file*, which has an .rc extension. Resource definition files can be defined and automatically generated in their text format through interactive resource editors available with products such as the Microsoft or Borland compilers and the Microsoft SDK. For simple definitions such as bitmap references, you can also directly generate the files in text format, as illustrated in Listing 16.6.

Listing 16.6. The resource-definition file Resource.rc.

```
//////////////////////////////////////////////////////////////////////////////
//
// Bitmap
//

16                      BITMAP  MOVEABLE PURE   "WINLOGO.BMP"
```

This defines one bitmap file to be built into the resource. That resource will be assigned an ID of 16 with which it can be referenced within the program.

> **NOTE:** A resource compiler and minimal documentation on building a resource definition file is redistributed with the Enterprise Edition of Visual Basic in the \Tools\Resource directory. Different compilers, each with the name rc.exe, are provided for 16-bit and 32-bit applications under the rc16 and rc32 bit subdirectories, respectively.

The next step is to compile the resource-definition file into an intermediate resource format, which has the file extension .res. You can do this by using the rc.exe resource compiler (that comes with many development tools, including the Visual Basic Enterprise Edition) as follows:

```
rc resour32.res
```

The `rc` command results in the generation of the intermediate-format resour32.res resource file. You can then add this file to a Visual Basic project by choosing Add File from the File menu, after which it appears in the project window. The contents of the res file will not be viewable from Visual Basic, but the resource definitions can be accessed by source code, and when a Visual Basic executable is generated, the resource definitions from the .res file are built directly into the executable. This provides for fast retrieval of the resource. Resources can be retrieved by referencing the resource ID in conjunction with the appropriate resource function, such as `LoadResPicture`:

```
Picture1(i).Picture = LoadResPicture(1, vbResBitmap)
```

Such resources load up to twice as fast as retrieving the same information from an external file with the `LoadPicture` command. Resources provide similar advantages for handling strings and data and likewise enable you to build this information into the executable for fast retrieval. Programs that will be translated into foreign languages are likely candidates for using resource strings because the translated strings are easily maintained in a resource file. Resource strings also offer faster retrieval than storing them externally, and better maintenance than having the translations intermingled with source code.

> **TIP:** Bitmaps, strings, and data can all be stored as resources that are built into the executable file for fast retrieval. All of them load faster when they're retrieved with `LoadResPicture`, `LoadResData`, or `LoadResString`, respectively, than they would if loaded from external files. Resources also provide significant maintenance advantages. For example, they eliminate the need to distribute external data or bitmap files. Likewise, it is easier to maintain translated strings in a separate .rc file for each language and build them into the final executable than to have translations spread throughout the source code.

Copying Pictures from One Object to Another

Another useful technique is to copy pictures from one control to another. Rather than use the `LoadPicture` or `LoadResPicture` function for every control, it is faster to copy pictures from one control to another. Suppose, for example, that you want to load the same picture into an image control that currently exists in a picture box control. You could use the command

```
Image1.Picture = Picture1.Picture
```

where `Image1` and `Picture1` are the names of the image and picture box controls, respectively. You can use this technique if the same graphics must be duplicated across forms or controls in the same form. If you decide to load all the pictures into the application in design mode, there should be no need to load two pictures into all the controls. Instead, the picture could be loaded once into a control and then just copied from one control to all the others. The performance benefit of doing so is great.

Using the Clipboard

A fourth (but not recommended) technique is to copy a picture from the Clipboard using the Visual Basic `Clipboard` object. If your application uses the Clipboard to transfer information from one application to another, or even within the same application, a picture can be copied to the Clipboard and then pasted into a control. In such a manner, a bitmap could be transferred from one control to another. This is somewhat risky, however, because another application could potentially interfere with your application or vice versa. Likewise, it is slower than the direct picture-copying method mentioned previously, and thus offers no benefits.

Using the Windows API and the WinG API

In addition to the techniques described so far, you can use the Windows API to transfer graphics. Microsoft has created a new API set, the WinG API, which is a special API that enables you to use a device-independent bitmap (DIB) as the drawing surface. This special WinG bitmap can then be transferred to the screen more quickly than when you're using the standard API. The WinG API is very useful for animation and provides much faster results than Visual Basic controls, methods, and the standard Windows API. The standard API performs at identical or even slightly lower levels than methods that use Visual Basic picture or image controls. The WinG, however, is claimed to deliver a much greater punch that speeds up the process considerably.

Because the WinG API requires a considerable amount of background knowledge, it is not covered extensively in this book. If your application relies heavily on animation, you might want to consider learning how the API works. Refer to Microsoft documentation on the WinG API, which is contained in WING.DLL for Microsoft's 16-bit operating systems and WING32.DLL for 32-bit operating systems.

Summary

The chapter begins by introducing you to the standard graphics files and their formats. These graphics files are used to load and store pictures into pictures into Visual Basic applications. The five primary graphics files—BMP, DIB, WMF, RLE, and ICO—are introduced. Other file formats, such as PCX, TIF, and GIF, are also discussed briefly. The chapter points out that the lower the resolution of the graphics being used and loaded into a control, the faster the resulting performance. Furthermore, certain types of graphics file formats are inherently faster than others. The Windows metafile (WMF), for example, is faster than the bitmap (BMP), yet the resolution of a metafile cannot be as high as a bitmap file's resolution.

Having discussed the various graphics file formats and their optimal use, the chapter introduces the controls used to display pictures, namely the image and picture box controls. Their strengths and weaknesses are discussed, and sample applications are presented that compare the amount of time it takes to load each control, respectively, with a picture. The chapter shows that a picture can be loaded into the image control faster than into the picture box control.

Although the image control is faster, it should not necessarily always be your control of choice. The picture control has additional functionality that the image control does not have, such as the capability to store child controls in a picture box, OLE support, and other events about which the image control is not notified. The added features of the picture box control might make up for the loss in performance that result from using the control. On the other hand, you might not need to use the added functionality of the picture box control and are just as well off using the image control. In such a case, performance improves and application overhead drops. As the pattern has been throughout this book, each control has its own disadvantages and advantages. The balance between functionality, ease of use, and performance must be carefully determined to arrive at the best compromise.

Having discussed and compared the two controls, the chapter goes on to present strategies for maximizing the performance of both the image and picture box controls. The `LoadPicture` function, which is used to load graphics into a control at runtime rather than at design time, is introduced. This function enables the application to load much faster and results in a smaller executable file, since the pictures do not have to be saved inside the executable file. Unfortunately, those picture files must be provided with the executable because they are outside of it, whereas if they are included inside the executable, they do not have to be supplied. You can transfer pictures from one control to another, however, which is a very useful technique to reduce time and can result in considerable performance gains. Similarly, using a resource file can also increase performance.

The case studies in this chapter show that an application loads much faster if the graphics are loaded dynamically. This is important for optimization when you want to cut down on the amount of time an application takes to load initially. Often, if the perceived speed of an application can be reduced, the user is much more impressed with the application.

In the next chapter, all of the graphics techniques discussed in this and the previous chapter are discussed in the context of painting and redrawing those graphics on the screen. Thus far, the focus has been primarily that of time in loading and initially displaying the graphics in the application. Another very important aspect is yet to be covered—redrawing and repainting those graphics after they are on the form for the lifetime of the application.

Obey the Signs

Beware of Falling Rocks: Don't blindly use a picture box control without evaluating the application to see if an image control is sufficient.

Without knowing the differences between a picture box control and an image control or the performance ramifications of using one or the other, you might be tempted to use the picture box control exclusively. This often leads to applications that are more "bloated" than they need to be. Not only do they run slower, but they also consume more memory. The biggest culprits are applications with too many picture box controls that are very large and have a very high resolution. Too much of any of these factors slows the application down considerably. Before using a picture box control or an image control, think carefully about how the control will be used in the application. If the added functionality of the picture box control is not needed, you should opt for the image control.

Beware of Falling Rocks: Don't load picture box or image controls with pictures at design time without checking to see if performance is better by loading them dynamically at runtime.

Another common programming mistake is to load every control with its picture in design mode. Often, this is not necessary, and it can dramatically affect the load time of the application, particularly if a large number of controls is used with large, high-resolution graphics. Depending on the application and the users' expectations, you should only load graphics into applications when necessary. If you store all the graphics in controls at design time, make the controls invisible until they are needed. Try to avoid overloading the startup form with a large number of controls, particularly those that display graphics. Your users will likely thank you for it, because the application will load much faster.

Wrong Way: If one or more controls use the same picture, store the picture in each control at design time.

This is another programming oversight that is easy to make. Suppose, for example, you are writing a game that shows seven quarters on the screen. If every control shows a quarter, seven of the same graphics images are required if the coins are all facing the same direction. Rather than loading the same bitmap into all seven controls, it would be best to only load the picture into one of the controls, whether at runtime or design time, and then copy the picture from one control to another. The performance benefit of doing so is determined in the Quiz section.

Q&A

Q Why is the image control faster than the picture box control?

A The image control is faster than the picture box control for several reasons. First, the image control has reduced functionality compared to the picture box control. It is not capable of directly using OLE, has no event structure for intercepting keystrokes from the keyboard, cannot receive notification by Windows when it is repainted or resized, and cannot be used to place controls inside itself. Consequently, Windows does not have to do as much housekeeping with an image control as it does with a picture box control.

Q Why is it faster to load pictures into controls at design time than to load them from a file at runtime?

A As this chapter points out, the amount of time it takes to load an application with predefined pictures in picture box and image controls is less than it takes to load each control with a picture at runtime. One reason for this is that the Visual Basic interpreter is not required when the controls are set at design time. Loading the pictures at runtime requires the interpreter to go out to the disk, open a graphics file, and load it into the control. If the controls are loaded at design time, they are already in memory and no files need to be accessed outside the executable. This makes the overall process faster. The only drawback to this approach is that more memory is required to load the executable. In memory-constrained systems, this could be a potential problem when large amounts of high-resolution graphics are used in an application. In such cases, it is easier on memory if they are loaded and unloaded only when needed versus all loaded when the application starts.

Q How can I change the resolution and color of a picture file so that, when it's loaded into Visual Basic, performance is improved?

A Most graphics files can be changed using utilities such as Microsoft Paintbrush and other commercial programs. You can often save the graphics file in a lower-resolution format and restrict the number of colors used. Although it is sometimes impractical or not beneficial to modify graphics files, doing so can often speed up applications considerably.

Quiz

In this chapter, the picture box control is used to display graphics. In the applications presented, the picture files are loaded at design time using the `Picture` property and at runtime using the `LoadPicture` function. Another technique, loading the picture into one control and then copying the image from one control to another, is also introduced. Write an application that behaves similarly to the Bmp32.exe application with the following exceptions: Load the WINLOGO.BMP file into the first picture box control only. Then, in the main form's `Load` event, write code that copies the picture from the first control to all the others. What is the difference in load time and execution time of the application compared to the BMP.EXE application?

Quiz Solution

The easiest way to implement the solution is to use the BmpLd32.exe application, removing the Load command button and label and the associated code. Then you can set the `Picture` property of the first control to display the WINLOGO bitmap file. The application's main form at design time is shown in Figure 16.11.

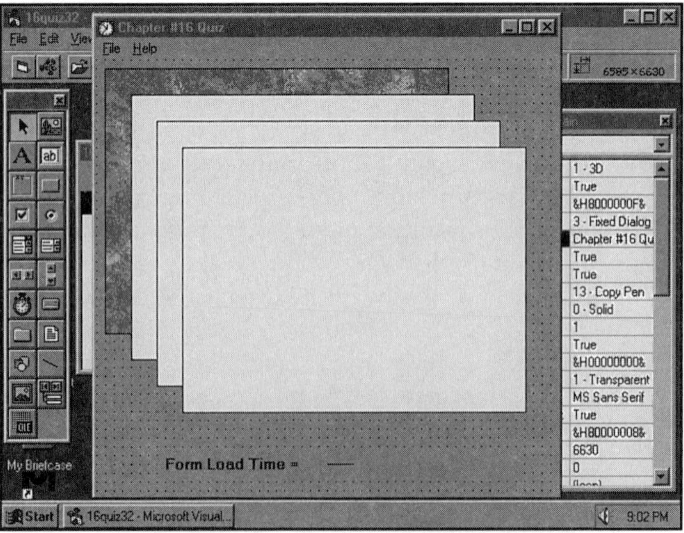

Figure 16.11.
The main form of the 16Quiz32 application in design mode.

Note that only one control has been loaded with the bitmap. Because the bitmap image is stored in the picture box control, it is not necessary to provide the WINLOGO.BMP file to the user. The code in the main form's `Load` event is shown in Listing 16.7.

Listing 16.7. Copying pictures from control to control.

```
Private Sub Form_Load ()

    Dim i As Integer

    Call Common_CenterForm(Me)

    For i = 1 To 3
        Picture1(i).Picture = Picture1(0).Picture
    Next

    Call Common_PostLoadTime(lblLoadTime)

End Sub
```

As you can see, the picture stored in the first picture box control is copied into all the other controls. The total load time is obtained using Startr32, and the code that assigns the pictures to the remaining controls is included in the `Load` event of the application's startup form. The load time of the application can be taken using the Startr32 utility; the results are shown in Figure 16.12.

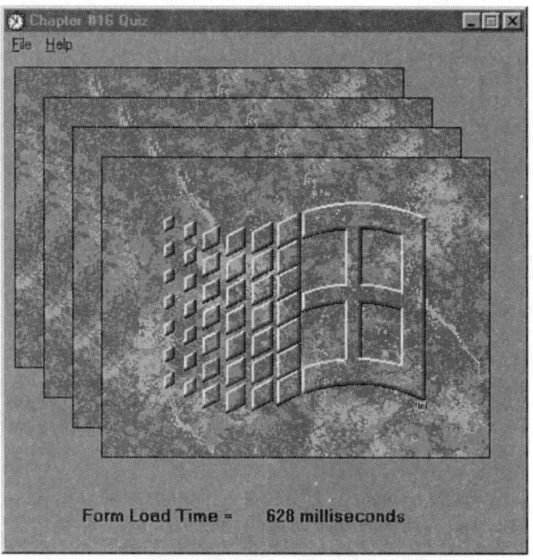

Figure 16.12.
The 16Quiz32 application at runtime.

The resulting load time is considerably faster than the load time of the Bmp32.exe application. This verifies that it is faster to load only one image and then copy that image to the other controls in the application whose picture files are the same. In reality, this is not a common practice, because picture box and image controls typically are each assigned unique pictures. Still, when you're designing an application that uses the same picture in many places throughout the application, this can be a useful technique.

Workshop

In this chapter, both the image and picture box controls are presented and pros and cons for using each control are discussed. If you already have an application that uses picture box and/or image controls, experiment with converting all the picture box controls to image controls. Assess the resulting performance of the application. Is it possible to convert the picture box controls to image controls, or does your application take advantage of the additional functionality a picture box control provides, making it impossible to convert? Now experiment with loading the pictures into the controls. Load them all into memory in design mode and then try loading them dynamically with the `LoadPicture` function. What difference is there in performance? How about memory consumption? What conclusions can you make based on these experiments?

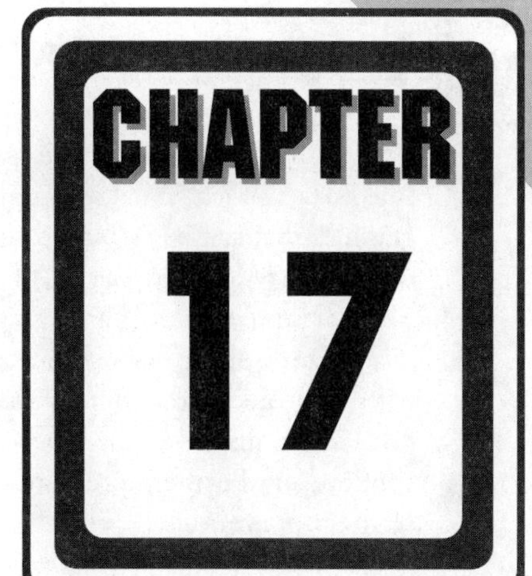

Painting and Redrawing

Thus far, you have examined techniques for using graphics methods, controls, and the Windows API, as well as using the picture box and image controls to display graphics. Before completing this discussion of graphics, however, it is very important to understand the way Windows draws those graphics on the screen, and how to make that process as fast and efficient as possible. As this chapter points out, Visual Basic provides you with various properties and techniques that cause forms and controls to paint and redisplay differently. These properties and techniques are discussed in this chapter, along with the most appropriate ways to use them together to optimize the performance of an application.

This chapter begins by describing the structure of a graphics container such as a form or picture box. You learn that a container has three layers, each of which is assigned a subset of all graphics that can be displayed. Having presented the graphics layers, the chapter proceeds to discuss the relevant properties of graphics containers that affect how graphics are placed in their layers. Those properties are described and discussed, and strategies for using them together to maximize display efficiency are examined at length. Several new guidelines are presented, along with applications that demonstrate their validity. This chapter helps you to understand how graphics are displayed and behave in the Windows environment and specifically in Visual Basic applications. Furthermore, it teaches you to use graphics effectively to maximize the efficiency of your applications.

Graphical Layering

In Chapter 15, "Graphics Controls, Methods, and the API," you learned that graphics can be produced in a Visual Basic application using *graphics methods* and *graphics controls*. These graphics must be created inside *containers*, which consist of *forms* and *picture boxes*. In this chapter, the form is used as the container because it is the most widely used. Keep in mind, however, that the concepts discussed in this chapter apply equally to picture box controls.

Visual Basic divides a container into three distinct *layers* for displaying graphics. The topmost layer contains any nongraphical controls, such as command buttons, option buttons, check boxes, and list boxes. The middle layer contains all the graphical controls such as the line, shape, image, and label controls, as discussed in Chapter 15. The bottom layer contains graphics produced using graphics methods such as the `Line`, `Circle`, and `PSet` methods, each of which is also discussed in Chapter 15. The layers and what they can contain are summarized in Table 17.1.

Table 17.1. Visual Basic form layers.

Layer	*Contents*
Top	Nongraphical controls such as command buttons, option buttons, check boxes, and list boxes.
Middle	Graphics controls and labels.
Bottom	Drawing space for the container. Graphics methods appear in this layer.

Any graphics produced in the top layer of a container obscure the graphics contained in the middle and bottom layers. Furthermore, graphics in the middle layer of a container obscure the graphics found in the bottom layer of the container. Thus, nongraphical controls are displayed over the top of any other graphics on a form, and graphics created using controls are displayed over the top of graphics created using methods. Layering is important when considering performance because, depending on the type of graphics being used, the type of layering used can have a direct impact on performance.

You can use the `AutoRedraw` and `ClipControls` properties, together with the `Paint` event, to change the default behavior of layering and the display of graphics in each layer. After these properties and events are introduced in this chapter, their impact within the graphics layers is discussed. As you would expect, the settings of these various properties have a direct impact on performance. Typically, you must consider these two properties and the `Paint` event together when discussing performance impacts. Therefore, these variables are examined together as a coherent set after an introductory discussion of each.

The *AutoRedraw* Property

Consider a Visual Basic application that contains graphics on a form. Suppose you are running the application and then switch to another application. The application you switch to consists of a window that you proceed to drag on top of the Visual Basic application, thereby overlapping the Visual Basic form. When you move that window back off the Visual Basic form, you would expect Windows to repaint the Visual Basic form as it appeared before the overlapping occurred. This, however, might not necessarily happen. It depends, in part, on the `AutoRedraw` property.

`AutoRedraw` is a Boolean property that determines whether graphics drawn in a container using methods (specifically `Circle`, `Line`, and `PSet`) are automatically redrawn after they get covered up by other, overlapping windows or get hidden when the container is minimized. If this property is set to `True`, the graphics are automatically redrawn after those windows are moved out of the way or the container is restored. If the property is set to `False`, the methods are not redrawn automatically and the graphics that once existed on the form but were overlapped are destroyed.

Consider, for example, the form shown in Figure 17.1. It contains a command button, which is a nongraphical control, and a circle produced using a graphics method in the form's `Load` event.

Now consider what happens when another window is dragged over the form and partially overlaps it, as shown in Figure 17.2.

At this point, part of the circle is obscured by the other window. If the `AutoRedraw` property of the form is set to `False` when the circle is drawn, you see the result shown in Figure 17.3 when you move the window back off the form.

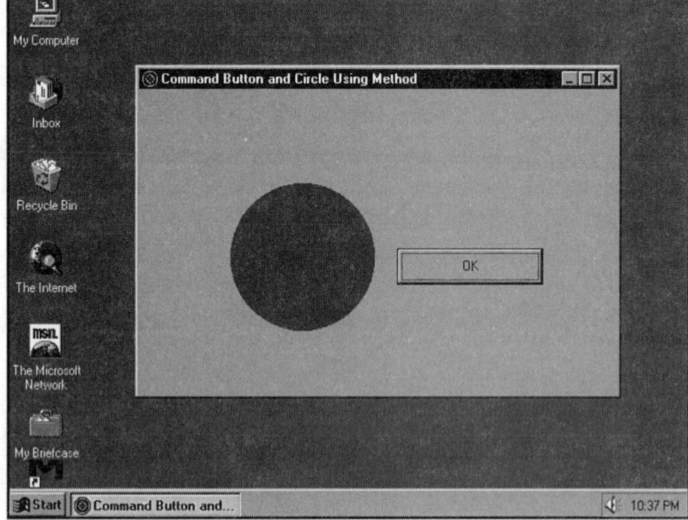

Figure 17.1.
A form with a command button and a circle using a graphics method.

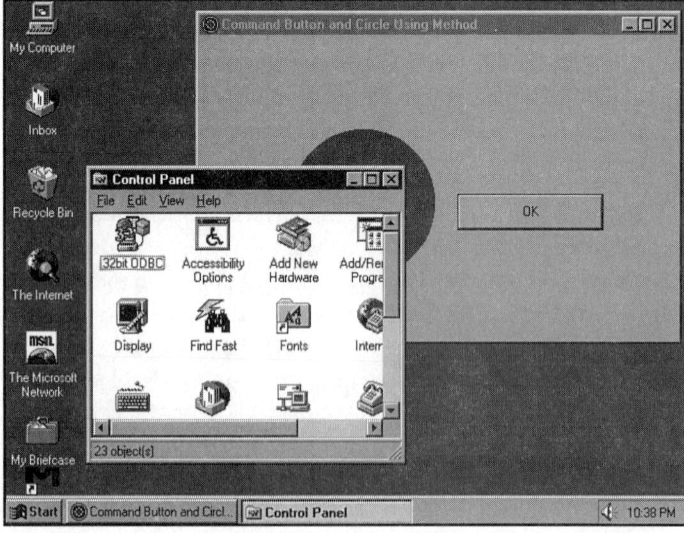

Figure 17.2.
A form with a command button and a circle obscured by an overlapping window.

If, on the other hand, the `AutoRedraw` property of the form is set to `True` when the circle is drawn, the result shown in Figure 17.4 appears when you move the window away from the form.

As you can see, the image is fully restored when the `AutoRedraw` property is set to `True`. This property essentially determines whether the bottom layer of graphics is stored in memory. When `AutoRedraw` is set to `True`, Windows stores the bottom layer of graphics as a bitmap in memory. Thus the original image can be restored on the form exactly as it appeared before the window was minimized and then restored, or when a window that obscures it is moved away.

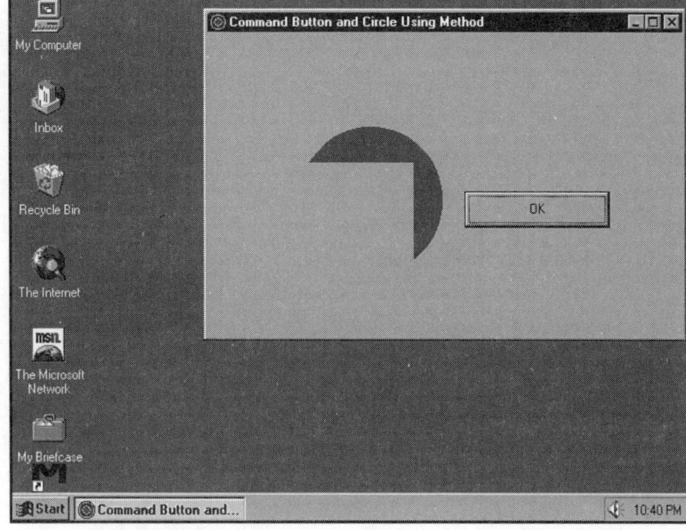

Figure 17.3.
A form with a command button and a circle obscured by an overlapping window with `AutoRedraw` *set to* `False`.

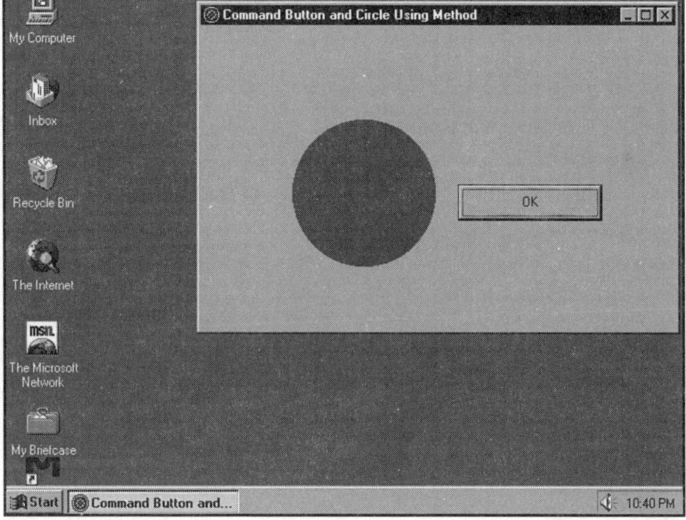

Figure 17.4.
A form with a command button and circle obscured by an overlapping window with `AutoRedraw` *set to* `True`.

When the `AutoRedraw` property is set to `False` (which is the default setting when you create a new form), no such image is stored in memory. It is then up to the user to redraw the graphics in the bottom layer whenever the form needs to be refreshed. Windows lets Visual Basic know when that refresh needs to take place by sending Visual Basic a `WM_PAINT` message, causing Visual Basic to execute the `Paint` event for the form. In this situation, you would have to place the code used to draw the graphics on the bottom layer in the `Paint` event. When `AutoRedraw` is set to `True`, on the other hand, there is no need to bother with the `Paint` event because Visual Basic takes care of refreshing the bottom layer for you.

Depending on the size of the form and the resolution of the system, the bitmap used to store the bottom layer of graphics varies in size. Regardless of its size, however, it takes time and memory to create and store the bitmap, not to mention the additional time needed to load and display the bitmap again on the form whenever it needs to be redisplayed.

You can avoid the creation and storage of this bitmap by simply setting `AutoRedraw` to `False`, but then you must be responsible for using code to display the graphics. This, too, can be prohibitive if the code used to create the graphics is very time-consuming. In such a case, it might actually take longer to redisplay the form than when using a bitmap image. So the winner in terms of performance essentially depends on the complexity of the graphics and the amount of time and memory needed to store them.

So when is it best to use (and not to use) `AutoRedraw`? The main purpose of the `AutoRedraw` property is to store graphics created in the bottom layer—that is, graphics created using methods—into memory to make redrawing possible with no direct intervention by the program. If you don't use any methods to create graphics in your form, and therefore do not use the bottom layer, it makes no sense to incur the overhead of copying an empty bitmap to memory.

> **TIP:** Set `AutoRedraw` to `False` if you have not used graphics methods to create graphics in a container.

To illustrate this principle, consider the sample application NoMeth32.exe, available on the CD-ROM that accompanies this book. A 16-bit version of this application, NoMeth16.exe, is also available on the CD-ROM. The main form of the application is shown in Figure 17.5.

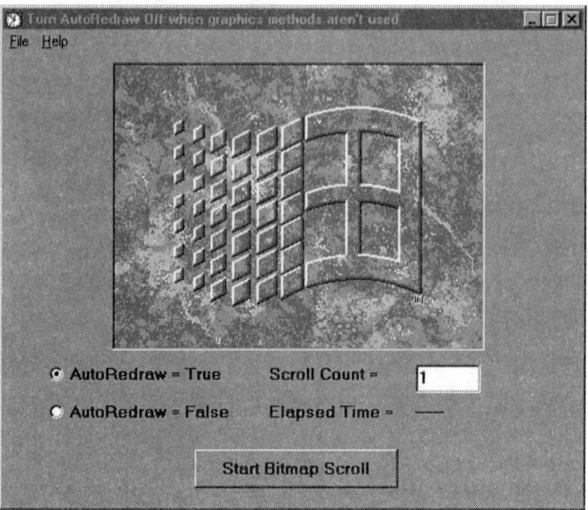

Figure 17.5.
The NoMeth32.exe application at runtime.

The application consists of a form with a picture box control that is scrolled across the form from left to right in small increments. The application contains another form, called a *cover form*, that is displayed *over* the main form every time the picture box changes position. This forces Visual Basic to store the bitmap image of the bitmap form's lower layer of graphics every time the position of the bitmap is changed. The code required to scroll the bitmap is found in the `Click` event of the command button labeled Start Bitmap Scroll and is shown in Listing 17.1.

Listing 17.1. The bitmap scroll procedure for NoMeth32.exe.

```
Private Sub cmdScroll_Click()

    Dim i%, j%       ' Index values

    ' Begin testing
    Call Common_StartTimedTest

    For i = 1 To txtRefresh
        ' Scroll the bitmap across the screen in 50 twip increments
        For j = 0 To Me.Width Step 50
            picBitmap.Left = j
            frmCover.Show       ' This forces VB to re-create the form image
            frmCover.Hide
            DoEvents
        Next
    Next

    ' End the test
    Call Common_EndTimedTest(lblElapsedTime)

    ' Get rid of the cover form
    Unload frmCover
    picBitmap.Left = 1440

End Sub
```

In the loop that resets the position of the bitmap, the bitmap is shifted and then the cover form is shown, which obscures the main form. The cover form is then hidden and a `DoEvents` statement is executed. The `DoEvents` statement enables Windows to send the `WM_PAINT` message to the Visual Basic form, which in turn triggers the `Paint` event *if* `AutoRedraw` *is set to* `True`. Otherwise, the `Paint` event is simply ignored.

As shown in Figure 17.5, the user has the option of setting `AutoRedraw` to `True` or `False` via the set of option buttons at the bottom of the form. When it is set to `True`, Visual Basic must go through the overhead of creating the background bitmap. Because no methods are used, the background bitmap is always the same, but there is no need to create it each time. When `AutoRedraw` is set to `False`, this background bitmap is not set and, because no methods are used, the overhead is reclaimed. When `AutoRedraw` is set to `True`, the results shown in Figure 17.6 are obtained.

When, on the other hand, the user sets `AutoRedraw` to `False`, the results in Figure 17.7 are obtained.

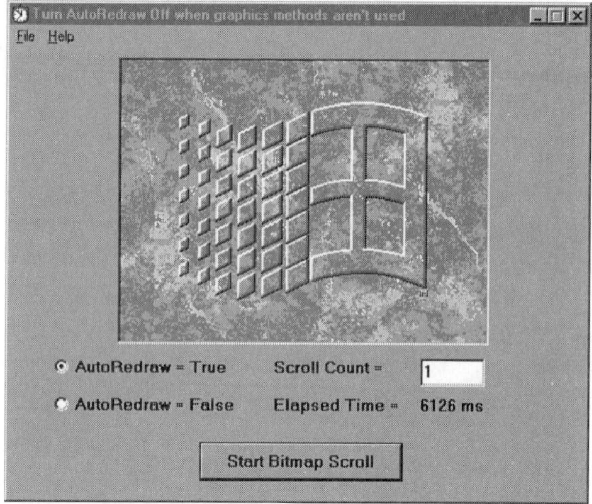

Figure 17.6.
The NoMeth32.exe application at runtime with `AutoRedraw` *set to* `True`.

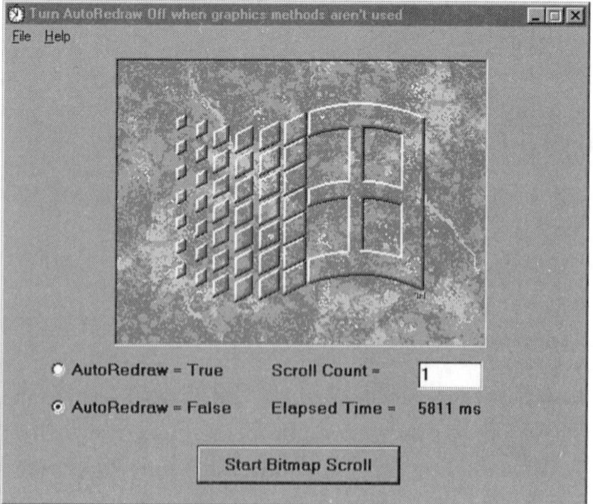

Figure 17.7.
The NoMeth32.exe application at runtime with `AutoRedraw` *set to* `False`.

Note from the results that the solution that does not use `AutoRedraw` is slightly faster simply because the extra time and memory needed to store the bottom-layer graphics are not required.

There might be times when you want to turn off `AutoRedraw` even if you use graphics methods in your application. This means, of course, that you must write code that exercises the methods to draw the graphics within the `Paint` event of the form in question. If you have a limited number of graphics created using methods, it might be faster to simply place the code that draws them into the `Paint` event rather than storing the entire layer into memory. If, for

example, the graphics in the bottom layer are changing a great deal throughout the lifetime of the application, Visual Basic has to constantly re-create the bitmap image and store it, which can reduce the speed of the application.

> **TIP:** Set `AutoRedraw` to `False` whenever you can quickly re-create the graphics using graphics methods in the `Paint` event, and/or when the graphics change often.

If, on the other hand, the graphics methods used are complex and/or require a great deal of code to implement, the opposite might be true. In this case, it might be better to set `AutoRedraw` to `True` rather than incur the performance penalty of executing the method code every time the form has to be repainted. Furthermore, if those graphics rarely change within the application, the bitmap does not have to be created very often—perhaps only once. In such a case, it is preferable to set `AutoRedraw` to `True`.

Consider the sample application, Meth32.exe, on the CD-ROM that accompanies this book. The main form of the application enables the user to turn `AutoRedraw` on or off, as well as set the number of times the screen is to be refreshed. When the form loads, the `Load` event consists of the code shown in Listing 17.2.

Listing 17.2. The `Load` event for the Meth32.exe application.

```
Private Sub Form_Load()

    Call Common_CenterForm(Me)

    Call InitializeGraphics

End Sub
```

The `InitializeGraphics` subroutine sets several arrays that determine where to place the graphics on the screen. This code is shown in Listing 17.3.

Listing 17.3. The `InitializeGraphics` subroutine for the Meth32.exe application.

```
Public Sub InitializeGraphics()

    Dim i&

    Randomize

    For i = 1 To 100

        ' Select a set of random coordinates
        x(i) = Int((Me.Width * Rnd) + 1)
        y(i) = Int((Me.Height / 2 * Rnd) + 1)
```

continues

Listing 17.3. continued

```
        ' Select a random shape
        j(i) = Int((4 * Rnd) + 1)

    Next

    Call DrawGraphics

End Sub
```

As you can see, this subroutine creates 100 sets of coordinates and chooses 100 shapes at random. The shapes that get generated are then drawn at the coordinates specified. The subroutine calls the `DrawGraphics` subroutine, which then draws the graphics on the form. The code for `DrawGraphics` is shown in Listing 17.4.

Listing 17.4. The `DrawGraphics` subroutine for the Meth32.exe application.

```
Public Sub DrawGraphics()

    Dim i%

    Me.Cls

    For i = 1 To 100

        Select Case j(i)
            Case 1:
                Circle (x(i), y(i)), 300, RGB(0, 255, 0)
            Case 2:
                Line (x(i) - 500, y(i) - 500)-(x(i) + 500, y(i) + 500),
                ➥RGB(0, 0, 255), BF
            Case 3:
                Line (x(i), y(i))-(x(i) + 500, y(i) - 500), RGB(255, 0, 0)
            Case 4:
            Case DEFAULT:
                PSet (x(i), y(i))
        End Select
    Next

End Sub
```

As you can see, the `DrawGraphics` subroutine actually places the graphics on the form. This procedure is called once when the form loads to place the graphics on the screen. If the user turns `AutoRedraw` on, the image is stored and used throughout the life of the application. If, on the other hand, the user turns `AutoRedraw` off, the `Paint` event of the main form is called. In the `Paint` event, the `DrawGraphics` subroutine is called, thereby refreshing the form every time it gets painted.

The command button labeled Start Redraws is used to force the form to repaint. The code is shown in Listing 17.5.

Listing 17.5. The `Redraw` subroutine for the Meth32.exe application.

```
Private Sub cmdRefresh_Click()

    Dim i&      ' Index value

    Call Common_StartTimedTest

    For i = 1 To txtRefresh
        frmCover.Show
        frmCover.Hide    ' This forces the main form to repaint
        DoEvents
    Next

    Call Common_EndTimedTest(lblElapsedTime)

    ' Unload the cover form
    Unload frmCover

End Sub
```

In the loop that shows and hides the cover form, the `DoEvents` statement enables Windows to send the `WM_PAINT` message to the Visual Basic form, which in turn triggers the `Paint` event if AutoRedraw is set to `True`. Otherwise, the `Paint` event is simply ignored. When the `Paint` event executes, the `DrawGraphics` procedure is called, which refreshes the screen.

First, the test case is tried with `AutoRedraw` set to `True`. The results are shown in Figure 17.8.

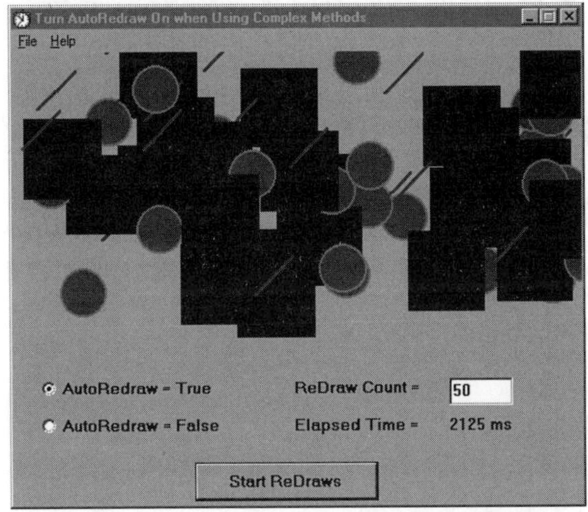

Figure 17.8.
The Mth32 application with `AutoRedraw` set to `True`.

Then the test is tried with `AutoRedraw` set to `False`. Notice the results shown in Figure 17.9.

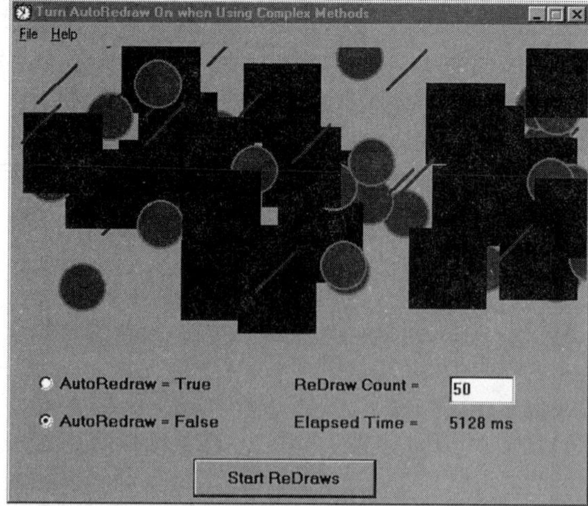

Figure 17.9.
The Mth32 application with `AutoRedraw` *set to* `False`.

The results clearly indicate that it takes considerably more time to redraw the graphics using code when `AutoRedraw` is `False` than when simply storing the image in memory and setting `AutoRedraw` to `True`. Therefore, as a general rule, it is best to avoid placing code in the `Paint` event to draw graphics methods when they can be more efficiently stored in memory.

> **TIP:** Set `AutoRedraw` to `True` if the container has many complex graphics that are difficult to reproduce in code and/or if the form doesn't change very often.

The ClipControls Property

An equally important property involved with drawing graphics on a form is the `ClipControls` property. Every form, picture box control, and frame control has this property. When `ClipControls` is set to `True (the default when you create a new form)`, the container (form, picture box, or frame) creates a "clipping region" around all the controls inside the container except for the following:

- The shape control
- The line control
- The image control
- Labels
- Custom controls that display graphics on the screen

The clipping region surrounds these controls but does not include the "real estate" on the form behind them. This real estate is not included in the clipping region because it cannot be seen

anyway—the controls cover it up. Thus, the *clipping region* is the area inside the container that gets painted whenever the container must be repainted. This region is created before the `Paint` event occurs, thus ensuring that only the necessary parts of the form are painted.

Consider the example presented in the *Visual Basic Programmer's Guide*. Figure 17.10 shows a box drawn on a form using the `Line` method. A command button and text box control are also on the form and overlap the box. Finally, a label and shape control are on the form, and they also overlap the box that was drawn using a method.

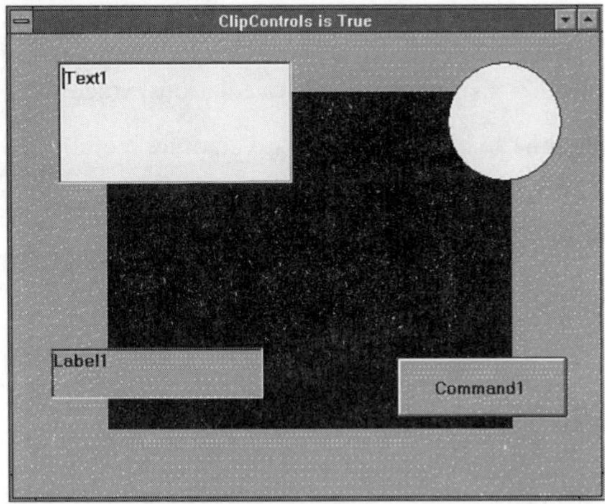

Figure 17.10.
Controls and methods on a form.

If `ClipControls` is set to `True`, a clipping region is created that includes the entire form except for the text box control and the command button. Thus, when it comes time to repaint the form and redisplay the box, only the portion of the box that is *not* underneath the command button and text box control is painted. The resultant clipping area is shown in Figure 17.11.

Figure 17.11.
The clipping region for the application.

The clipping region can speed up the painting process because less surface area must be painted when the form must be refreshed. After this area is painted (automatically, if `AutoRedraw` is set to `True`; otherwise implemented manually in the `Paint` event), Windows redraws the command buttons and other controls on the form. The areas underneath nongraphical controls that do not need to be painted are not, thus saving time.

Although the clipping region *can* save time, it does not always do so. Suppose, for instance, that the form contains a large number of controls. The more controls there are on the form, the more complex the clipping region, and therefore the more time it requires to repaint. This is because the clipping region must clip around those controls, which can result in a clipping region that looks like a piece of Swiss cheese. The process of creating these holes in the clipping region requires a large number of calculations which requires more time.

The situation can be even worse if no graphics methods are used on the form. The whole purpose of the clipping region is to avoid painting areas on the lower layer of the form that are covered up anyway by higher layers. If nothing is put *into* the lower layer, the clipping region is never used. If the lower layer is not used, it is simply a waste of time to create the clipping region.

To demonstrate this principle, consider two more test applications, ClipT32.exe and ClipF32.exe, which are both on the CD-ROM that accompanies this book. The main form of the ClipT32.exe application is shown in Figure 17.12.

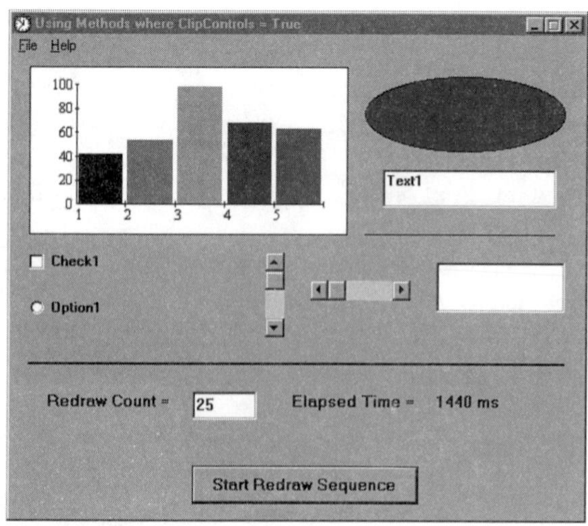

Figure 17.12.
The main form of the ClipT32.exe application.

As you can see, the form is laden with several controls. No graphics methods are used on the form. The same cover form used in the previous applications in this chapter is used again here to force the form to repaint. Once again the user can specify how many repaints to use in the test. When the user clicks the Start Redraw Sequence command button, the code in Listing 17.6 is executed.

Listing 17.6. The redraw procedure for ClipT32.exe.

```
Private Sub cmdRefresh_Click()

    Dim i&       ' Index value

    Call Common_StartTimedTest

    For i = 1 To txtRefresh
        frmCover.Show
        frmCover.Hide    ' This forces the main form to repaint
        DoEvents
    Next

    Call Common_EndTimedTest(lblElapsedTime)

    ' Unload the cover form
    Unload frmCover

End Sub
```

Note that this code is identical to that of the Meth32.exe application. The `ClipControls` property of the main form is set to `True` in the ClipT32.exe application and to `False` in the ClipF32.exe application in order to determine the difference between the two property settings. Two separate applications have been constructed for this test because this property cannot be set at runtime. Other than the change of the `ClipControls` property's value, however, the applications are identical. The results for ClipT32.exe are shown in Figure 17.12; those for ClipF32.exe are shown in Figure 17.13.

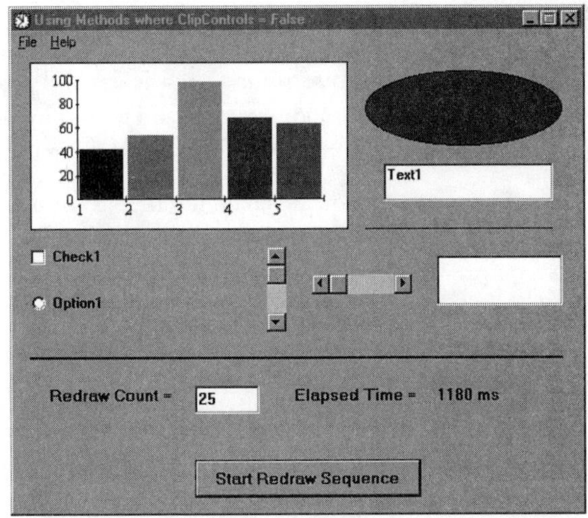

Figure 17.13.
The main form of the ClipF32.exe application.

Notice that turning off `ClipControls` results in a considerable performance improvement in this test case. As a rule, when a number of controls are on a form and no graphics methods are used, it is better to set the `ClipControls` property to `False` to avoid the creation of the clipping region that isn't used anyway. Even if methods *are* used, it might still be advantageous to turn `ClipControls` off. This is particularly true if many controls are on the form.

> **TIP:** Set `ClipControls` to `False` if the form has many controls on it and graphics methods are not used. If graphics methods are used, it might still be beneficial to turn `ClipControls` off, but this must be determined on a case-by-case basis.

Minimizing the Number of Repaints

Thus far in the chapter, a great deal of discussion has focused on the fastest way to repaint graphics on a form when Windows must do it. What has not been discussed is how to actually minimize the number of times this repainting has to occur. The techniques presented thus far are designed to minimize the amount of time it takes to repaint a window. If, however, the *entire* repaint can be avoided, no time is required whatsoever—clearly this is an even better solution. This section presents a technique to minimize the number of times a form must be repainted in an application.

> **TIP:** You can improve performance by making controls invisible while manipulating them. This minimizes the number of repaints and makes the graphics display faster.

Making controls invisible while manipulating them is very useful, particularly when you have to move or resize controls on a form. Remember that Windows must repaint the form any time a control changes display attributes such as size and position. If you can hide one or more controls, make the necessary modifications, and then show them, you minimize the number of repaints. This is particularly effective if you are making changes to several controls at once.

Suppose, for instance, that you are changing the position of five image controls. You can hide all the image controls, move them all while they are hidden, and then make them visible again. Doing so requires just one repaint when you hide the controls and another repaint when you make them visible again. If you manipulated the controls without hiding them, your form would have to be repainted five times, once for each control you move. In this case, you can reduce the number of repaints from five to two.

While this technique is very effective, it is not always appropriate. If you are only moving a single image control, for example, you do not increase performance by first hiding the control. You need one repaint when hiding the control and another for making it visible, for a total of two. If you simply move the control without first hiding it, you need only one repaint, which is faster.

If, on the other hand, you change not only the position of the control but also its height and width, you are better off making the control invisible. Making the control invisible uses two repaints—one to hide it and one to redisplay it. If, on the other hand, you leave the control visible, you need at least one repaint for moving the control and at least one for changing its dimensions. If you change the `Top`, `Bottom`, `Height`, and `Width` properties, four repaints take place versus the two by hiding the control.

It is fairly easy to count the number of repaints necessary. Any change you make to the control that changes the way it appears on the form requires a repaint. If you can save repaints by hiding the control, do so; otherwise, for situations when only one or two repaints are required, this might not be necessary.

Consider the application RePnt32.exe, which demonstrates the use of this technique. RePnt32.exe is found on the CD-ROM that accompanies this book. A 16-bit version of this program, RePnt16.exe, is also available on the CD-ROM. The application consists of four picture controls that are moved and resized on the form. One implementation makes the changes without hiding the controls; the other hides the controls first and then makes the changes. The main form of the application is shown in Figure 17.14.

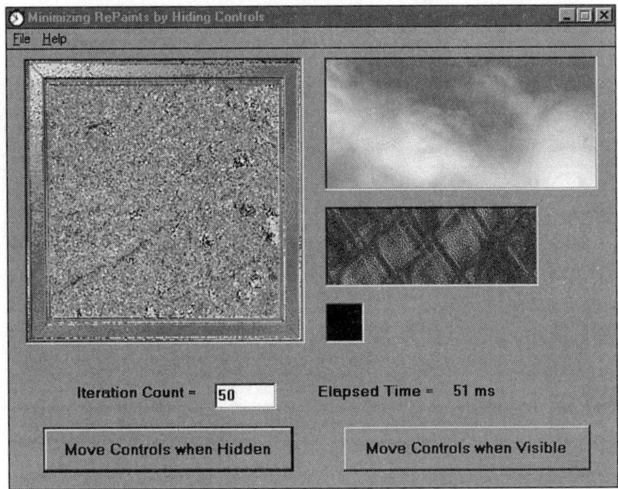

Figure 17.14.
The RePnt32.exe application at runtime, hiding the controls.

As you can see, the application has two command buttons: one to hide the controls and then manipulate them and the other to simply manipulate them without hiding them. The first test case manipulates the group of controls while hiding them. The code for this case is shown in Listing 17.7.

Listing 17.7. A control-manipulation subroutine with controls hidden.

```
Private Sub cmdMoveHidden_Click()

    Dim i%, j%          ' Index values
    Dim x%              ' Temporary position holder

    ' First, hide the controls
    For i = 0 To 3
        picControl(i).Visible = False
    Next

    ' Time the moving operation
    Call Common_StartTimedTest

    For i = 1 To txtIterations
        x = picControl(1).Left
        picControl(1).Left = picControl(0).Left
        picControl(2).Left = picControl(0).Left
        picControl(3).Left = picControl(0).Left
        picControl(0).Left = x
    Next

    ' End the timing
    Call Common_EndTimedTest(lblElapsedTime)

    ' Then, show the controls
    For i = 0 To 3
        picControl(i).Visible = True
    Next

End Sub
```

The second test case leaves the controls visible. This procedure is identical to that of Listing 17.7 except that no code is included to make the controls invisible and then visible. The code is shown in Listing 17.8.

Listing 17.8. A control-manipulation subroutine with controls visible.

```
Private Sub cmdMoveRevealed_Click()

    Dim i%, j%          ' Index values
    Dim x%              ' Temporary position holder

    ' Time the moving operation
    Call Common_StartTimedTest

    For i = 1 To txtIterations
        x = picControl(1).Left
        picControl(1).Left = picControl(0).Left
        picControl(2).Left = picControl(0).Left
        picControl(3).Left = picControl(0).Left
        picControl(0).Left = x
    Next
```

```
    ' End the timing
    Call Common_EndTimedTest(lblElapsedTime)

End Sub
```

Keep in mind that `AutoRedraw` is set to the default of `False` in the form because no graphics methods are used. This forces the forms to repaint every time the control positions change. Four repaints must be made per iteration when the controls are revealed, whereas only two repaints are needed when the controls are hidden. The elapsed time required to manipulate the controls when they are hidden is shown in Figure 17.14. Compare that to the time required to manipulate the controls when they are left visible, which is shown in Figure 17.15.

Figure 17.15.
The RePnt32.exe application at runtime, leaving the controls visible.

Notice the rather striking results. It takes considerably longer to repaint the forms if the controls are visible. This illustrates the validity and importance of making controls invisible while manipulating them in order to minimize the number of repaints. Your results will vary depending on the controls being manipulated and the way they are changed, but the fundamental principles will certainly apply.

Summary

This chapter discusses several practical techniques for maximizing the efficiency of a Visual Basic application when painting and redrawing graphics in an application. The two properties critical to optimizing painting and redrawing, `AutoRedraw` and `ClipControls`, are both described and techniques are presented that relate to each property.

The AutoRedraw property determines whether the lowest graphics layer of a form or picture box control is saved in memory so that when the form or picture box control needs to be repainted, Windows can simply use a predefined bitmap. When this property is set to True, Visual Basic stores the image in memory and redisplays it as necessary. Although this frees you from worrying about redisplaying graphics generated using methods, the process consumes memory and can ultimately degrade performance. If, however, the property is set to False, the extra memory is freed up at the expense of your redrawing the graphics in the Paint event of the form or picture box control. Again, whether this improves performance depends on certain conditions as discussed in this chapter, such as the complexity of code required to generate your graphics and how often those graphics change on the form.

Two techniques are presented that clarify how to determine the most appropriate setting for this property in your application as summarized below.

> **TIP:** Set AutoRedraw to False if you have not used graphics methods to create graphics in a container.

This tip states that the AutoRedraw property should be set to False when graphics methods are not used in a form. In such a case, nothing is stored in the lower layer and there is no point in generating the background image.

> **TIP:** Set AutoRedraw to True if the container has many complex graphics that are difficult to reproduce using code and/or if the form doesn't change very often.

This tip states that it is best to set AutoRedraw to True whenever a significant number of graphics methods are used that take longer to execute in code than to simply store in memory. It is quite common for Visual Basic to require more time to execute that code than to simply retrieve the image from memory.

The chapter also discusses the ClipControls property, which determines whether a clipping region is created for the back layer of the form that is used for graphics methods. A clipping region is created by determining the area on a container which must be painted when the form repaints. If controls such as command buttons reside on the form, there is no point in bothering with painting anything in the layers below the button, because the command button is always displayed over top of them. Therefore, if a form has a great number of controls on it, and very few graphics methods are used, it is best to set the ClipControls property to False. If, on the other hand, many graphics methods are used, it might be desirable to set ClipControls to True. Defining a clipping area in this case means that the graphics produced by those methods get drawn more efficiently and time is not wasted drawing to the form where graphics at higher layers overwrite what gets drawn at the lowest layer. Again, the decision on whether to set the property to `True` depends on the situation. These guidelines are presented in general terms; you must experiment on your own to make the right decision based on your specific situation.

Finally, the chapter presents a technique to minimize the number of repaints necessary in Visual Basic applications: Hide controls that are changed in ways that affect their display. Often, if many changes must be made to a single control or the same change is to be made across many controls, it is desirable to hide the control or controls while those manipulations are taking place. Thus you can potentially save a repaint for every modification and only require one repaint to hide the control(s) and one repaint to redisplay the control(s). A sample application is presented to illustrate the benefits of doing so.

This chapter provides you with the techniques and strategies necessary to create applications that paint and redraw graphics in the most optimal way—that is, using the best compromise between functionality and performance that is acceptable to the user.

Obey the Signs

Beware of Falling Rocks: Use graphics methods outside the `Paint` *event of a form or container when* `AutoRedraw` *is set to* `False`.

Using graphics methods any place other than the `Paint` event of a container can cause problems when `AutoRedraw` and `ClipControls` are both set to `False`. Any graphics method that is drawn on a form or container in this situation might cover any controls or graphics methods already there, because no clipping region has been defined to clip around. This can make results very unpredictable and should be avoided. If `AutoRedraw` is set to `True`, this problem does not apply.

Wrong Way: Always set `AutoRedraw` *and* `ClipControls` *to* `False` *in your applications to maximize efficiency.*

Although setting both of these properties to `False` does result in maximum efficiency, it can also cause problems if you use graphics methods to put graphics on the screen in any place other than the `Paint` event. For some programs, this can be a problem. Consider, for instance, the case when you want to draw a circle on the screen as a response to clicking a command button. In this case, the code to draw the circle is not inside the `Paint` event. If `AutoRedraw` is `True`, you will always observe proper behavior when windows are moved across the application or the application is minimized. If, however, `AutoRedraw` is `False`, unpredictable results can occur depending on the `ClipControls` property. (You can consult the *Visual Basic Programmer's Guide* for more information on the interaction between these properties.) But keep in mind that maximum efficiency might not always provide satisfactory results in your application.

Q&A

Q This chapter has shown optimal settings for the `AutoRedraw` and `ClipControls` properties. Are there any possible conflicts between these properties?

A The *Visual Basic Programmer's Guide* discusses the effects on layering when using these properties. As long as code that draws graphics methods in a container is placed in the `Paint` event of that container, normal layering will occur, which means that each layer will behave as expected. If, however, `AutoRedraw` is set to `False` and the code to display graphics is written outside the `Paint` event, graphics methods and controls can appear mixed in the three layers. This can cause unpredictable results and is not recommended.

Q I need to conserve memory as much as possible! Is there any way I can use `AutoRedraw` for parts of my form without having to store the entire form bitmap into memory?

A Yes, there is. All you have to do is create a picture box on the form and put all of your graphics in that control. You can set the `AutoRedraw` property of the form to `False`, but the `AutoRedraw` property of the picture box control to `True`. That way, you can conserve memory by storing only the picture box background into memory.

Q How do I check to see if the `Paint` event is being called when testing my application?

A Often, when you're trying to optimize painting and redrawing graphics on a form, you will experiment with these properties to make the application as efficient as possible. During that process, you might want to make sure the `Paint` event is being called and your code is responding properly to it. By placing a breakpoint in the `Paint` event, you can watch for entry into that event procedure and ensure your code is executing properly.

Quiz

Write an application that uses a picture box control to store graphics that would otherwise be placed on a form. Compare the case of putting the graphics on the form with `AutoRedraw` set to `True` for the form to the case of placing the graphics in the picture box and setting `AutoRedraw` to `True` for the picture box control but to `False` for the form. Use a cover form to hide and reveal the main form as is done with the applications in this chapter. Compare the performance of the two approaches.

Quiz Answer

The solution can be found in the 17Quiz32.exe application that's on the CD-ROM that accompanies this book. As always, there is an accompanying 16-bit version (17Quiz16.exe). The main form of this application is shown in Figure 17.16.

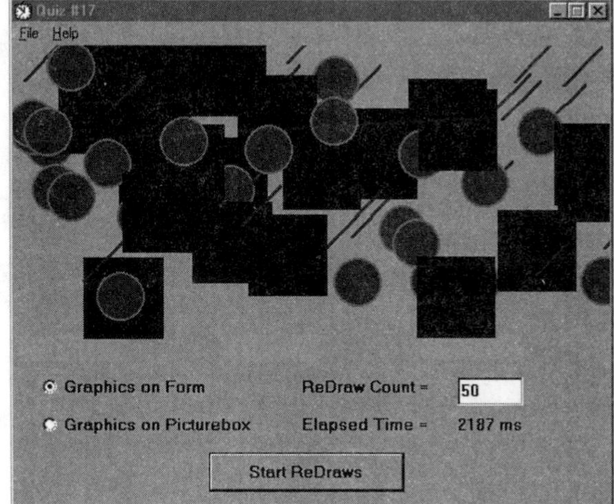

Figure 17.16.
The 17Quiz32.exe application at runtime, using the form to display graphics methods.

The application contains two option buttons: one to place the graphics on the form and the other to place them on a picture box on the form. The code for the two option buttons is shown in Listing 17.9.

Listing 17.9. Option buttons for setting method destination.

```
Private Sub optUseForm_Click()
    Me.AutoRedraw = True
    picPicturebox.Visible = False
    Call DrawGraphics
End Sub

Private Sub optUsePicture_Click()
    Me.AutoRedraw = False
    picPicturebox.Visible = True
    Call DrawGraphics
End Sub
```

Notice that `AutoRedraw` is toggled for the form and that the picture box is either made visible or invisible, depending on which button the user clicks. Each function then calls `DrawGraphics`, which is shown in Listing 17.10.

Listing 17.10. The `DrawGraphics` function.

```
Public Sub DrawGraphics()

    Dim i%

    If optUsePicture.Value = True Then

        picPicturebox.Cls

        For i = 1 To 100

            Select Case j(i)
                Case 1:
                    picPicturebox.Circle (x(i), y(i)), 300, RGB(0, 255, 0)
                Case 2:
                    picPicturebox.Line (x(i) - 500, y(i) - 500)-(x(i) + 500,
                    ➥ y(i) + 500), RGB(0, 0, 255), BF
                Case 3:
                    picPicturebox.Line (x(i), y(i))-(x(i) + 500, y(i) - 500),
                    ➥ RGB(255, 0, 0)
                Case 4:
                Case DEFAULT:
                    picPicturebox.PSet (x(i), y(i))
            End Select
        Next

    Else

        Me.Cls

        For i = 1 To 100

            Select Case j(i)
                Case 1:
                    Me.Circle (x(i), y(i)), 300, RGB(0, 255, 0)
                Case 2:
                    Me.Line (x(i) - 500, y(i) - 500)-(x(i) + 500, y(i) + 500),
                    ➥ RGB(0, 0, 255), BF
                Case 3:
                    Me.Line (x(i), y(i))-(x(i) + 500, y(i) - 500),
                    ➥ RGB(255, 0, 0)
                Case 4:
                Case Else:
                    Me.PSet (x(i), y(i))
            End Select

        Next

    End If

End Sub
```

This is the same function as in the Mth32.exe application except that an `If...Then` conditional statement is placed in the code to indicate the location to which the graphics are being drawn.

The application also contains the `InitializeGraphics` subroutine, which is in the `Load` event of the main form. That code is shown in Listing 17.3.

The results using the picture box control are shown in Figure 17.17.

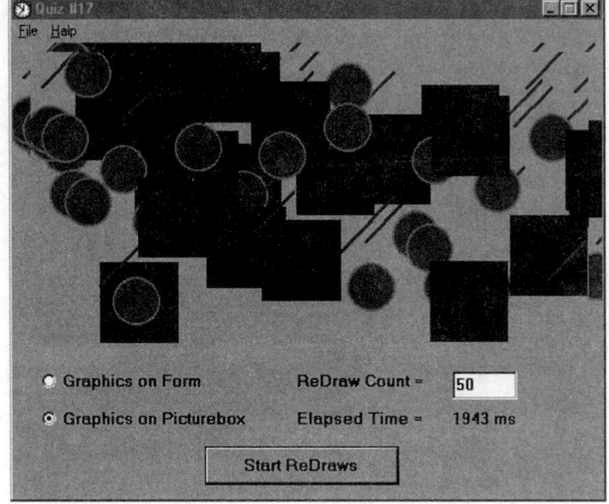

Figure 17.17.
The 17Quiz32.exe application at runtime, using the picture box control to display graphics methods.

As you can see by the results, using the picture box control takes less time than using the form. The application is more memory efficient because Visual Basic only stores into memory the picture box image, not the form image, which usually consists of the entire screen. Therefore, it takes less time to store the image, and performance is improved.

Optimization Strategies: System Environment and Interaction

There are many ways that your Visual Basic programs can interact with the system and are affected by the nature of the operating environment. To understand this interaction, we must look above and beyond the standard constructs of the Visual Basic language and have some understanding of the system itself. Such considerations include the use of memory, the nature of a multitasking system, file generation, the differences between a 16-bit and 32-bit operating system environment, Jet Engine database capabilities, and the incorporation of other-language DLLs into an application.

Chapter 18, "Multitasking and Memory," addresses the benefits of the `Nothing` keyword to free object memory. It also examines multitasking and the impact of the `DoEvents` statement in applications.

Chapter 19, "File I/O," looks at specific techniques for generating and reading files. The merits of various file I/O types are compared. Specific techniques, such as the `Write` and `Print` alternatives for writing to a file, are compared.

Chapter 20, "16-Bit Versus 32-Bit Code," considers differences between the 16-bit Windows 3.1 environment and the 32-bit Windows 95 environment. The ramifications of running Visual Basic applications in these environments are addressed. A summary of some key environmental differences is also provided. This includes a discussion of services available to 32-bit programs which are not available to 16-bit programs. Although performance trade-offs between the environments are very application specific, some relative performance differences of selected sample applications are provided to illustrate the performance differences an application may experience between the two environments.

Chapter 21, "Jet Engine/Access," looks at Jet Engine database optimization techniques from the perspective of Access database operations. Performance tuning methods such as the use of transactions and optimal field referencing are outlined. In addition, an examination is provided of techniques such as the `Seek` method, `DELETE` updates from SQL, and stored queries.

Chapter 22, "Moving Code to DLLs," focuses on the incorporation of DLL function calls into a Visual Basic program when that DLL is produced by another language such as C++ or Delphi. Reasons for turning to DLL calls are discussed. In addition, specific examples are provided of the same code in Visual Basic, C++, and Delphi, to provide a feel for the type of performance trade-off available in one application.

By the end of this section, you should have a clearer picture of how a Visual Basic application interacts with the system. Furthermore, you will better understand the performance impacts on Visual Basic applications due to system interaction. In addition, you will have gained insight into optimization techniques for some of the system interaction areas under the control of the Visual Basic application developer.

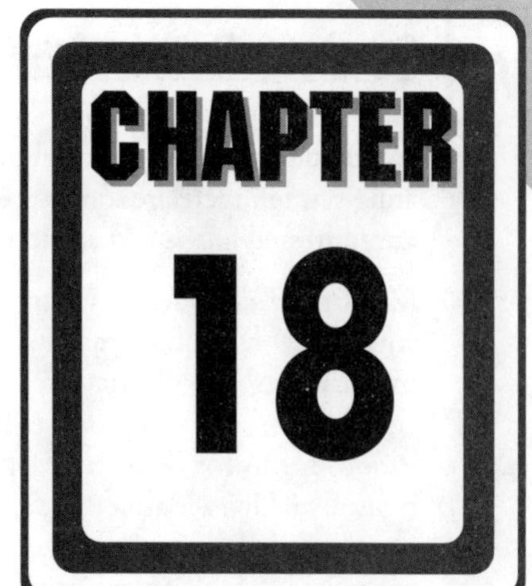

Multitasking and Memory

This chapter examines some of the issues at the heart of the Windows environment: multitasking and memory. Visual Basic largely shields you from much direct insight into these areas—until, that is, an out-of-memory error occurs or an event is not responded to in a timely manner! A little understanding can go a long way to help avoid such situations.

The first topic addressed in this chapter is multitasking. Multitasking refers to the operating system's balancing act of letting applications coexist and appear to the user to be running concurrently. Likewise, even within your specific program, multitasking is important. You may want your user to be able to click on a command button and immediately get a response (for example, at the same time an animation sequence is carried out). While much of this activity is out of your hands and under control of the operating system, there are some steps you can take to facilitate efficient multitasking. These steps are addressed in the first section of this chapter.

Memory management is as important an issue as multitasking to applications in a Windows environment. Memory management is a very big area. The second section of this chapter narrows the scope to illustrate key concepts through a specific focus on form removal. You can choose from several approaches for an application that must repeatedly show and then remove various forms for the user. Each approach has different memory and performance ramifications. By taking a look at these approaches, you can gain some insight into Visual Basic memory management in general and get a better idea of what is the highest-performance technique for potential use in your own applications.

By the conclusion of this chapter you'll have a better understanding of these important areas of system interaction. You'll know some tricks for efficiently conserving memory. You'll have a technique for having some control over multitasking. These approaches can then be added to the arsenal of knowledge you're accumulating throughout the book. The end result will be more highly optimized programs in the future.

Multitasking and *DoEvents*

The capability of the 32-bit Windows 95 operating system to carry out priority-based, preemptive multitasking is very significant to performance measurement. First of all, it makes assessing performance much harder. In a cooperative multitasking environment such as Windows 3.1, programs have, generally speaking, full control of the processor when they execute. Once a process gains control, no other process gets a turn until the process underway completes or explicitly yields control of the CPU. The process itself is in charge of deciding how long its particular turn in the CPU will be. This is what is termed *cooperative multitasking,* because applications must be designed to cooperate for effective sharing of the CPU. This means that programs under Windows 3.1 can potentially "hog" the CPU, locking out other applications until their own turn is complete. The only alternative is programs sprinkled with `DoEvents` statements that cause Visual Basic to temporarily give up or share the CPU.

From a performance-assessment standpoint, obtaining meaningful timings can be somewhat easier under this type of cooperative multitasking. If you look at a piece of code that doesn't yield control of the CPU and then time that code segment, you might find that system activity has affected the timing somewhat. However, you can be confident that no other application was given a slice of the processor time during the time slice you measured if no `DoEvents` statements appear in that code.

With Windows 95, however, the ground rules are different. No longer must an application explicitly turn over control of the CPU to be a good neighbor and give other processes a turn during lengthy calculations. The operating system takes care of that itself if needed, temporarily cutting off one process to give another a turn. The operating system makes these decisions based on scheduling algorithms that take many factors into account. The processes or applications that are managed are no longer in the driver's seat for juggling their own CPU time after they begin to execute. Therefore, when you time a given piece of code, even if that code does not yield control of the CPU, the operating system might give other processes turns before every instruction in your timed piece of code completes. This can certainly affect the duration of your timing.

When your application is running in the Windows 95 environment, you have no guarantee that it will run from start to finish without the operating system intervening to give another application a turn. For many interactive applications, user events are serviced with code running at equivalent priorities and there is relatively little priority-based bumping. (You can verify with the PSS priority-monitoring utility described in Chapter 7, "Supporting Utilities for Performance Analysis.") However, the potential exists for the operating system to suspend processing of the current process and give another process a turn. In Windows 3.1 an application is in control of its own destiny after it gets control. In Windows 95, as well as Windows NT, this is not the case.

Windows 3.1 does not provide true preemptive multitasking. Therefore, one of the challenges of developing programs in the Windows 3.1 environment is to provide programs that peacefully coexist with other applications that might be running at the same time. This can involve not only sharing memory and resources correctly, but also allowing other applications their turn with the CPU. An application requires processing time to carry out its actions, but it is also easy for the Windows 3.1 application developer who does not plan ahead to end up with an application that hogs the CPU. Such an application will carry out its own code for a considerable block of time without giving other applications a turn, effectively locking out other applications in the system while such a block of code is running.

Likewise, even in a Visual Basic 4.0 program under Windows 95, a similar type of contention can occur. The multitasking, priority-based operating system generally gives each application attention when it's requested. However, within a single application event contention can still occur, depending on how that application is written. A process can be cranking through one block of code, which in effect temporarily locks out another event handler in the same application from responding until that first area of code completes.

Windows 3.1, Windows 95, and Windows NT are all event-driven, message-based systems. The system generates a message in response to any user event such as a mouse click or keyboard entry. The messages are then placed by the system in a queue to be processed by the appropriate application. If there is a lag between the time a message is generated and the time an application completes the required processing for that message, the user will have the perception of waiting. With 16-bit applications, contention can occur between applications that delays message processing. When messages are queued, the application they are intended for may not be given an immediate chance to run if another application is still processing an event. With 32-bit applications, contention between applications is generally avoided by the operating system, but contention *within* an application itself can occur. A 32-bit application may be written in such a way that it does not immediately suspend the processing of its current event to give a turn to other, more recently introduced events.

To circumvent this problem, programming languages typically provide function calls that enable an application to give other applications a turn and thus avoid CPU contention. In the C/C++ programming world, this can consist of API calls such as `Yield`, `GetMessage`, and `PeekMessage`. However, using these API calls can pose some problems in a Visual Basic application. Fortunately, Visual Basic provides an easy-to-use counterpart native to the Visual Basic language: the `DoEvents` statement. `DoEvents`, when called, allows applications to process any waiting messages before control returns back to the area of the application that made the `DoEvents` call.

`DoEvents` solves one problem but introduces another. A very useful place to use the `DoEvents` statement is within a loop, because it is in such code areas that an application could lock out other applications for long periods of time. On the other hand, the `DoEvents` statement imposes a performance penalty as well.

This sample program DoEvnt32.exe from the CD-ROM is shown in Figure 18.1. This program is also available on the CD-ROM in a 16-bit version, DoEvnt16.exe. The program provides a means to look at the penalty imposed by using the `DoEvents` statement. Various techniques for using `DoEvents` are also presented. These include using `DoEvents` every time through a loop, using `DoEvents` only periodically within a loop, and using the Windows API to determine if the use of `DoEvents` is necessary. The performance trade-off of each approach is outlined as well. After considering these techniques, you will be able to write programs that function as good neighbors to other applications by sharing the CPU. Your programs will also function as good neighbors to users who must live with the ramifications of their performance.

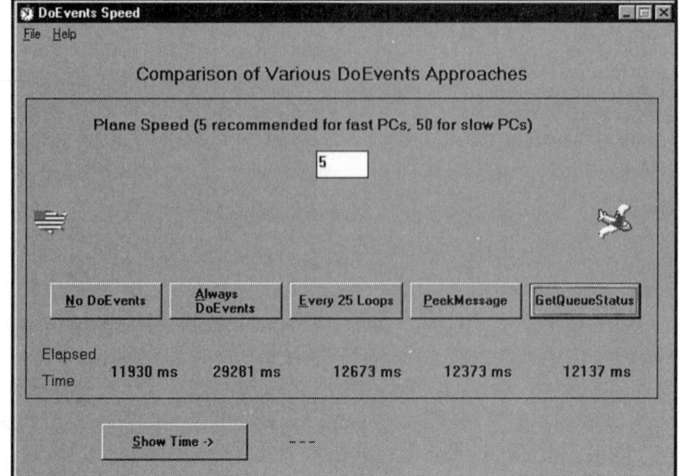

Figure 18.1.
`DoEvents` tests.

A Loop with No *DoEvents*

The sample program is used to illustrate various aspects of using `DoEvents` within loops. The performance characteristics highlighted in this section refer to Windows 95 unless noted otherwise. Keep in mind that because of the difference in multitasking capabilities, Windows 3.1 behavior will differ. This program consists of a command button that covers each aspect of `DoEvents`. The first aspect to be considered here is a loop with no `DoEvents` statements at all. The code for such an approach is shown in Listing 18.1. This code is carried out whenever the No DoEvents button is clicked. As Listing 18.1 shows, this code loop simply takes an image control containing a plane icon and "flies" it across the form, moving from left to right. Each time through, the loop statements increment the Left property of the image to move it farther across the screen.

Listing 18.1. The No DoEvents button's `Click` event.

```
Sub cmdNoDoEvents_Click ()


Call Common_StartTimedTest

'Ensure plane takes of from USA
imgPlane.Left = imgUSA.Left

Do While imgPlane.Left < imgJapan.Left
    imgPlane.Left = imgPlane.Left + txtMovement
Loop


Call Common_EndTimedTest(lblNoDoEvents)


End Sub
```

Notice also that there is another command button at the bottom of the form labeled Show Time. This command button enables you to see whether multitasking is taking place during a test. When you click the command button, the current time will be displayed if the test program gives the system a chance to respond to other events. Listing 18.2 shows the code associated with the Show Time command button. This code results in the current time being displayed in a label to the right of the Show Time command button.

Listing 18.2. The Show Time button's `Click` event.

```
Sub cmdMultiTask_Click ()

' This button updates time, it is intended to demonstrate
'    system multitasking performance...i.e. click button
'    when plane is moving, to see if event gets carried out
'    before plane reaches destination.
```

continues

Listing 18.2. continued

```
lblTimeofDay = Time


End Sub
```

Using these two command buttons together illustrates the advantages of the `DoEvents` statement. First, start the DoEvnt32.EXE program and observe that the plane image begins moving from left to right. As the plane continues to move, click the hourglass cursor several times on the Show Time command button. Notice that even though you have clicked the command button, no update takes place on the screen. Only after the plane reaches the right side of the form and the No DoEvents command button code has completed does the Show Time command button code run. In other words, the *application* locked out response to all other events it generated while carrying out the `No DoEvents` loop. If you rerun the test however, but then click anywhere on a different application window as the plane moves, you'll see it move to the foreground. This shows that the *system* does respond to external events, but the application itself does not respond to its own application-generated events.

Even though Windows 95 supports preemptive multitasking, it doesn't guarantee immediate response to events from within the same application, depending on how that application was written. Visual Basic applications will not respond to other application events when application code is currently executing unless you have used the `DoEvents` statement. However, as the above test showed when you clicked on another application in the system when the test application was running, Windows 95 *does* provide generally immediate response to system events external to the application.

Windows 3.1 Behavior

Under Windows 3.1, neither internal application events nor external system events will be responded to as long as application code is currently running.

Just as the test program does not allow other events within the test application to be processed, it likewise does not allow system events for other applications to be processed when run under the cooperative multitasking Windows 3.1 environment. You can observe this by repeating the test and trying to click anywhere on another application in the background, such as the clock. When you click the clock it does not move to the foreground until the plane has completed its journey. This is because, unlike Windows 95, Windows 3.1 provides no system-enforced multitasking between applications.

A Loop with *DoEvents*

For the next example the code is slightly modified from the `No DoEvents` test. This modified code is shown in Listing 18.3. The code is essentially the same except that the Visual Basic `DoEvents` statement has been added, as indicated in bold. Wherever this statement is encountered it tells the system to immediately check the message queue and give applications a chance to respond to any messages awaiting them. Thus, on each loop the `DoEvents` is encountered and the system passes on waiting messages for processing at that time instead of holding on to them.

Listing 18.3. The DoEvents button's `Click` event.

```
Sub cmdDoEvents_Click ()


Call Common_StartTimedTest

'Ensure plane takes of from USA
imgPlane.Left = imgUSA.Left


Do While imgPlane.Left < imgJapan.Left
    imgPlane.Left = imgPlane.Left + txtMovement
    DoEvents
Loop


Call Common_EndTimedTest(lblDoEvents)


End Sub
```

To check this out, simply click the DoEvents command button. The plane begins to move from left to right. Now click the Show Time command button several times while the plane continues to move. Notice that the current time updates to the left of the Show Time command button even before the plane's journey is complete. Other events are given a turn in addition to the event whose code first started executing.

`DoEvents` thus provides an effective and easy-to-use solution to the problem of code that locks out other events in the application (or even those outside the application, in the case of Windows 3.1). The drawback is that this code executes more slowly because it does the additional work of processing `DoEvents` each time through the loop. The Visual Basic interpreter processes an additional instruction each time through the loop, and this instruction takes a nontrivial amount of processing time.

You can observe the time impact from a `DoEvents` statement by running the no `DoEvents` test and comparing it to the always `DoEvents` test. It is important for comparison's sake to look at time durations for these two code samples when no other activity is going on in the system. Do not click the Show Time command button when gathering these two timings to limit system activity and ensure a fair comparison of the two techniques.

The results are shown in Figure 18.1. Code with the `DoEvents` statement takes nearly twice as long as code without that statement. The `DoEvents` statement in this case does not case any events to be processed because you did not introduce any additional events during the plane's journey. However, as this test shows, just the overhead of calling `DoEvents` still consumes significant amounts of time. Developers new to the `DoEvents` statement often mistakenly assume that `DoEvents` consumes little (if any) time unless system activity is occurring. To the contrary, it is an expensive operation under any circumstances.

> **TIP:** The `DoEvents` statement consumes significant amounts of time even if there are no events to which it needs to respond.

DoEvents at Specified Loop Intervals

Given that `DoEvents` is clearly an expensive operation, the next question is "Are there ways to achieve the functionality of `DoEvents` without the expense?" The typical use of `DoEvents` is in repeated loop situations where the time spent on any one specific loop iteration is not likely to be significant in and of itself. Therefore, you can develop a workaround based on the fact that it is the cumulative spent in loops and not the time of individual loops that produces a noticeable wait.

If your loops execute very quickly, you can likely get away with carrying out `DoEvents` only on some selected loops rather than on each and every iteration. For example, you can set up a counter that is incremented within the loop, and only when the counter reaches a specified number of loops is `DoEvents` carried out. Then the counter can be reset, and the process starts over. In this manner, you can control how frequently `DoEvents` takes place, choosing whether to carry it out every 5th loop, every 25th loop, or any other increment you choose.

Listing 18.4 is an example of such code. This code, which is carried out when the Every 25th Loop button is clicked, is very much like earlier examples. The only difference is that now the test code counts the number of loops and just carries out the `DoEvents` once every 25 loops.

Listing 18.4. Every 25th Loop button's `Click` event.

```
Sub cmdEvery25_Click ()

Dim i%                          ' loop counter

Call Common_StartTimedTest

'Ensure plane takes off from USA
imgPlane.Left = imgUSA.Left
```

```
Do While imgPlane.Left < imgJapan.Left
    imgPlane.Left = imgPlane.Left + txtMovement

    i% = i% + 1
    If i% = 25 Then
     DoEvents
     i% = 0
    End If
Loop

Call Common_EndTimedTest(lblEvery25)

End Sub
```

This approach works well if you make a good decision about how often to allow `DoEvents`. If you allow `DoEvents` too often, you won't achieve a significant performance speedup over simply having `DoEvents` occur every time through the loop. On the other hand, if you don't allow `DoEvents` often enough, then when the user interacts with the system during the looping, the `DoEvents` may not take place immediately. The user is still likely to experience a temporary delay before the specific `DoEvents` loop is reached and the computer responds to his keystroke or mouse interaction.

The only good way to derive the number of loops that should pass between `DoEvents` is through experimentation. Try different increments until you find one that enables smooth system response with no noticeable time lag. Of course, the number of loops required to give a smooth response depends very much on the time that each loop takes. If a loop takes a great deal of time to complete due to a particular algorithm or processing need, `DoEvents` must occur more frequently to provide the perception of smooth response.

In the case of the sample program with its relatively simple loop processing, allowing `DoEvents` to take place once every 25 loops seems to provide for smooth system response and provides performance that is measurably better than carrying out `DoEvents` each time through. Those results are shown in Figure 18.1 as well.

DoEvents After Checking for Messages with *PeekMessage*

There is still a significant problem with carrying out `DoEvents` at specific loop increments, however. The decision to carry out `DoEvents` only every 25th loop was based on the performance of one given system; other systems might have different performance considerations. For example, the results displayed in Figure 18.1 are from a 50MHz 486DX2. If the same program runs on a 25MHz 386, each loop will take longer to complete. Therefore, the time gap between every

25th loop will be larger, and response time to a keystroke may be very poor indeed and give the impression of lockout, even though no lockout perception would occur on the faster system.

> **NOTE:** The user perception of waiting for the system to respond to keystroke or mouse interactions is sometimes referred to as *lockout.* If an event caused by a user interaction is not immediately responded to by the system, it is a sign that the CPU is currently occupied with running other code. That code that is currently running is preventing, or locking out, an application from receiving the event message, which will cause it to respond to that most recent user event.

There is a method which avoids having to call `DoEvents` every loop but is considerably more reliable than the platform-performance-sensitive "every *x* number of loops" approach just discussed. The original poor-performance problem occurred because you were attempting to carry out `DoEvents` every time through the loop, even when it was not needed. Then you shifted to a method that just carries out `DoEvents` every 25th time through the loop, *whether it was needed or not.*

The remaining performance problem lies in the fact that you were still carrying out `DoEvents` statements when they were not needed. A far better method is to carry out `DoEvents` only if there is some processing waiting to be carried out. To implement such an approach requires knowledge of the way Windows works. User interactions with programs cause a steady stream of messages to be generated that are managed by Windows and passed on to the appropriate application. Each application is given its turn by Windows to respond to messages that have been placed in that application's message queue. Therefore, if you could tell whether your application had a message waiting for it, you could then allow `DoEvents` to be carried out only at those times.

If you have access to the Microsoft Developers Network CD-ROM or Microsoft Software Development Kit and browse through the Windows API documentation, you will soon find the `PeekMessage` API. As the documentation indicates, this enables you to peek into the message queue to see if any messages are waiting for your application. You can even request which type of messages you want to look for—for example, whether you want to look for mouse or keyboard messages. The declarations required to use the `PeekMessage` API, which are declared in the COMMON.BAS module used by the sample program, are shown in Listing 18.5.

Listing 18.5. The `PeekMessage` API declaration in COMMON.BAS.

```
' WIN APIs
#If Win32 Then' 32-bit VB uses this Declare.
   'Required for MSG type, which is required to use PeekMessage API
    Type POINTAPI
           x As Long
           y As Long
```

```
    End Type

'Required to use PeekMessage API
    Type MSG
       hwnd As Long
       message As Long
       wParam As Long
       lParam As Long
       time As Long
       pt As POINTAPI
     End Type


       ' Peek into the message queue to see if window has any waiting messages
       Declare Function PeekMessage Lib "user32" Alias "PeekMessageA"
       ➥ (lpMsg As MSG, ByVal hwnd As Long, ByVal wMsgFilterMin As Long,
       ➥ ByVal wMsgFilterMax As Long, ByVal wremoveMsg As Long) As Long

#Else '16-bit VB uses this Declare.

       'Required for MSG type, which is required to use PeekMessage API
     Type POINTAPI
        x As Integer
        y As Integer
      End Type

     'Required for PeekMessage API
     Type MSG
        hwnd As Integer
        message As Integer
        wParam As Integer
        lParam As Long
        time As Long
        pt As POINTAPI
      End Type

      'Peek into the message queue to see if window has any waiting messages
       Declare Function PeekMessage Lib "User" (lpMsg As MSG, ByVal
      ➥ hwnd As Integer, ByVal wMsgFilterMin As Integer, ByVal
      ➥ wMsgFilterMax As Integer, ByVal wRemoveMsg As Integer)
      ➥ As Integer
#End If

'Constants that can be used with PeekMessage API
Global Const WM_KEYFIRST = &H100
Global Consr WM_KEYLAST = &H108
Global Const WM_MOUSEFIRST = &H200
Global Const WM_MOUSELAST = &H209

'Tell windows not to remove message from queue after we peek with PeekMessage
Global Const PM_NOREMOVE =&H0
```

You can use this API declaration within the loop to check for the presence of a message. If the `PeekMessage` call indicates that a message is waiting, `DoEvents` can be carried out. If no message is waiting, there is no need to waste time on a `DoEvents` statement and it is bypassed. The code for this modified loop, which is much the same as the loops of previous examples but with the added `If…Then` check, is shown in Listing 18.6. This code is carried out in response to a click on the PeekMessage command button.

Listing 18.6. `DoEvents` after a `PeekMessage` check.

```
Sub cmdPeek_Click ()


Dim msgCheck As MSG

Call Common_StartTimedTest

'Ensure plane takes of from USA
imgPlane.Left = imgUSA.Left


Do While imgPlane.Left < imgJapan.Left
    imgPlane.Left = imgPlane.Left + txtMovement
    If PeekMessage(msgCheck, Me.hWnd, WM_KEYFIRST, WM_KEYLAST,PM_NOREMOVE) or
     ➥ PeekMessage(msgcheck,me.hwnd,WM_MOUSEFIRST,
     ➥ WM_MOUSELAST, PR_NOREMOVE) Then
     DoEvents
    End If
Loop


Call Common_EndTimedTest(lblPeek)


End Sub
```

This approach does work well in the sample program. Notice that `PeekMessage` has been instructed through the parameters to look only for keystroke and mouse responses. After the PeekMessage command button is clicked and the plane begins to move, a check is made on every loop to see if keyboard or mouse requests are waiting to be processed. If so, they are processed immediately.

Try out the program: Select the PeekMessage command button; and then as the plane is traveling, click the Show Time command button or press Alt+S. Notice that the time appears immediately! This implementation enables the snappy response of a `DoEvents` in every loop, but without the performance penalty. In fact, examine the timing for this test that is shown in Figure 18.1. Notice that performance of this test is significantly faster than the test with a `DoEvents` in every loop, and not that much slower than the test that uses no `DoEvents` at all!

So performance is very good, and responsiveness is fully adequate. Have you found the ideal solution? Well…almost, but not quite. This solution is close to being a robust solution, but it's not perfect. There are still a couple drawbacks to the `PeekMessage` approach, and they center on the nature of that API call itself.

Visual Basic is a language that is intended to shield you from concerns about low-level Windows processing, and in particular, the constant stream of messages flowing about the system that make an application work. `PeekMessage` is an API call intended to let you get at the heart of messaging. Depending on the parameters supplied, `PeekMessage` can even remove messages from the application's message queue before Visual Basic gets a chance to respond to them! `PeekMessage`, therefore, is not recommended for use in Visual Basic programs unless you have a great deal of Windows API knowledge.

Notice in the call to `PeekMessage`, as shown in the following code, that `PM_NOREMOVE` is used (this tells `PeekMessage` not to disturb the message queue; obviously this API has the potential to inflict pain and suffering if misused):

```
If PeekMessage(msgCheck, Me.hWnd, WM_KEYFIRST, WM_KEYLAST, PM_NOREMOVE) Then
```

Given the potential for misuse, including the API call in your code is not generally recommended. Maybe you know how to use it safely, but how about the new programmer who takes over your code six months from now and likes to experiment? It is a foolish programmer who tempts fate by including this API call if alternatives are available.

There are additional reasons to avoid the API call as well. Notice the first parameter to the call. A type variable `msgCheck`, of type MSG, is supplied. The API documentation indicates that this structure is filled by the API at each call with the message information. Intuition should tell you that this built-in message retrieval carries with it some overhead. Another minor drawback is that two type definitions required to define the required parameter types. Therefore, this API call is somewhat confusing at first glance. A simpler API call would eliminate these problems; that API call is discussed next.

DoEvents After Checking for Messages with *GetQueueStatus*

There is another API call that can serve our purpose. An inspection of the API calls in the Windows API documentation will lead you to `GetQueueStatus`. The documentation for `GetQueueStatus` explains that this API checks the queue for an application *without* modifying the contents of the queue.

So already you have an improvement over `PeekMessage`. `GetQueueStatus` is still a call that goes beyond the boundaries of the Visual Basic language, and you still must carefully consider its use because you do not have insight into the inner workings of Visual Basic. However, at least this API call doesn't carry with it the queue-altering risk of `PeekMessage`.

Likewise, another advantage is immediately apparent. This API call is much simpler to use than `PeekMessage`. It has fewer parameters, and requires fewer supporting types. Although this may not seem like a major consideration from the vantage point of an experienced Windows API programmer, if your code must be developed in a manner that is to be easily maintained by nonexpert programmers, it is wise to keep it as simple as possible. The declaration for

GetQueueStatus, which is made in COMMON.BAS for the sample program, is shown in Listing 18.7. Compare it to the complexity of the declaration for PeekMessage shown in Listing 18.5 to see the difference between the two approaches.

Listing 18.7. The GetQueueStatus API declaration in COMMON.BAS.

```
'WIN APIs
#If Win32 Then ' 32-bit VB uses this Declare.
   'Get status of queue
   Declare Function GetQueueStatus Lib "user32" (ByVal fuFlags As Long) As Long
#Else   ' 16-bit VB uses this Declare.
   'Get status of queue
   Declare Function GetQueueStatus Lib "User" (ByVal fuFlags As Integer) As Long
#End If

'Constants that can be used with GetQueueStatus API
Global Const QS_KEY = &H1           'A key was pressed
Global Const ZS_MOUSEBUTTON = &H4   'A mousebutton was pressed
```

The code that uses the GetQueueStatus call looks much the same as the earlier code that used PeekMessage, except that the simpler API is used. This code, which is carried out in response to a click on the GetQueueStatus command button, is shown in Listing 18.8. Notice that the only parameters specified for GetQueueStatus are the QS_KEY and QS_MOUSEBUTTON constants. These constants instruct GetQueueStatus to indicate if keystroke or mouse button messages await the calling thread. Essentially this means the check is carried out just for messages intended for this application. As with PeekMessage, you could also have instructed GetQueueStatus to inform you of other types of messages, such as mouse movement, by using other constant indicators.

Listing 18.8. The GetQueueStatus command button's Click event in COMMON.BAS.

```
Sub cmdCheck_Click ()


Call Common_StartTimedTest

'Ensure plane takes of from USA
imgPlane.Left = imgUSA.Left


Do While imgPlane.Left < imgJapan.Left
    imgPlane.Left = imgPlane.Left + txtMovement
    If GetQueueStatus(QS_KEY) or GetQueueStatus(QS_MOUSEBUTTON)Then
     DoEvents
    End If
Loop


Call Common_EndTimedTest(lblGetQueue)


End Sub
```

The next step is to test the code and see whether response is adequate. Click the GetQueueStatus command button and observe the plane's flight. While the plane is still flying, click the Show Time command button or press Alt+S to select it. In response, the current time field is immediately updated. Event response, therefore, is just as immediate as it was for always using `DoEvents` in every loop and for using `PeekMessage` in every loop.

The final step is to assess performance and compare results to the other test cases. As with all these test cases, you must take care to compare apples to apples. You must let the code run without introducing additional events for `DoEvents` to process. Do not interact with the system during the plane's flight. Each approach should be timed from start to finish without interference to ensure accurate comparisons. One resulting time for the `GetQueueStatus` approach is shown in Figure 18.1.

Normalized results for the tests discussed are shown in Table 18.1.

Table 18.1. Comparison of multitasking techniques.

Test	*Normalized Results*
`No DoEvents`	1.00
`Always DoEvents`	2.40
Every 25 loops	1.06
`PeekMessage`	1.04
`GetQueueStatus`	1.02

As the results show, the `GetQueueStatus` API is slightly faster than the `PeekMessage` API. In fact, the `GetQueueStatus` approach is not only faster than all the other approaches that permit `DoEvents`—it only lags slightly behind the test case that uses no `DoEvents` at all! The `GetQueueStatus` method of checking for messages and then handling `DoEvents` is the best approach of those discussed. It offers performance almost on par with that of not doing this check, but provides the event-response time users expect in a multitasking (or simulated multitasking, in the case of Windows 3.1) system. Of course, any API should be used with care and only if you have a firm understanding of what the API does. The approach shown here only checks for certain types of messages, and is not as all inclusive as simply carrying out a `DoEvents` every time through.

> **TIP:** The `GetQueuedStatus` API is a safe and quick method to enable response to other events when coupled with `DoEvents`. A `GetQueueStatus` with `DoEvents` is faster than using `DoEvents` alone.

Memory Considerations

Memory issues are, from a certain perspective, less of an issue in Windows 95 than they were in Windows 3.1. Under Windows 3.1, an application can allocate memory resources and neglect to free them up before the program completes. This can be true even with a Visual Basic application where the Visual Basic interpreter allocates and deallocates memory resources on behalf of your Visual Basic application. If an application does not properly free resources, the result can be that those resources are simply unavailable for the rest of that Windows session. In this manner resources can gradually leak away, causing eventual memory errors.

Windows 95 provides a much more robust memory cleanup. Under Windows 95 when an application (called a *process* in Windows 95 terminology) terminates, resources that were in use by any of the one or more concurrently executing sequences of code for that application (called *threads*) are automatically released. This to a large extent avoids the insidious memory-leakage problem prevalent under Windows 3.1. Likewise, 32-bit Windows applications can access what is called a "flat" memory space without having to live with the hoop jumping inherent in the old memory-management approach of Windows. For these reasons, memory is perhaps less of a problem in Windows 95. But unfortunately for you as a programmer, it is not a dead issue. It doesn't take much effort to generate an out-of-memory error if you use certain programming approaches. For example, write a program to simultaneously display a large number of forms; odds are you will see this grim reaper of the error-message family!

One of the best ways to gain insight into some of the intricacies of Visual Basic memory management is to consider the case of form removal. Each of the various techniques available has different memory trade-offs. The first approach consists of removing an unneeded form from the user's view by simply hiding it. The second approach is to remove the form by carrying out the Visual Basic `Unload` statement. The final approach is to not only unload the form, but also to set the object variable containing the form to the Visual Basic keyword `Nothing`. Through the process of examining these approaches, you will uncloak some of normally hidden layers of Visual Basic memory management.

Form Hiding

The first technique to be examined is hiding forms. The form `Hide` method is commonly used to remove a form from the user's view. This section examines the memory ramifications of this approach. The form `Hide` method leaves the form loaded in memory but sets its `Visible` property to `False`. Chapter 12, "Control Loading," demonstrates that it is much quicker to show a form by *redisplaying* a hidden form than by reloading a previously unloaded form. Correspondingly, it might seem that it would be quicker to remove a form from view by hiding it rather than unloading it. However, as the examples in this chapter show, this is not necessarily true.

The sample program, forms32.exe (which is included on the CD-ROM that accompanies this book), illustrates this approach. This program is also available in a 16-bit version, forms16.exe,

on the CD-ROM. The main form of the program is shown in Figure 18.2. The program consists of a form with three command button choices. Each of the buttons demonstrates a different form-removal technique. The first command button is Make Forms, Hide. When this command button is clicked, code is carried out that loads the specified number of forms into memory and then immediately hides all the forms. A before-and-after check is done to derive the total time used for this operation and the amount of memory consumed.

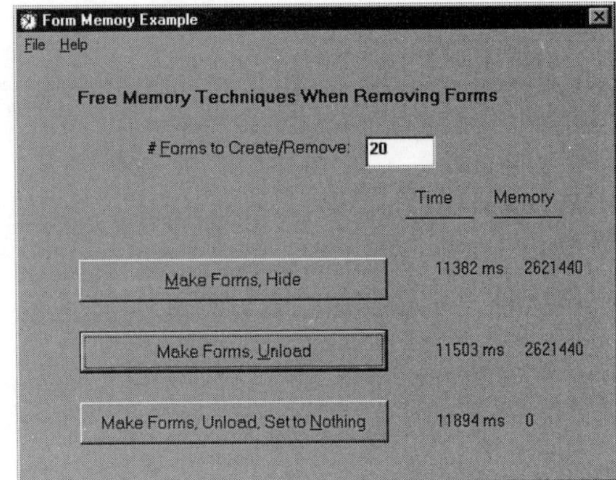

Figure 18.2.
A form-removal test.

First the forms must be created. An array is used to store all the forms as they are created. This array is declared as a local-level variable in the event procedure. The event procedure for the form hide technique is shown in Listing 18.9.

Listing 18.9. The Make Forms-Hide Forms program.

```
Sub cmdMakeHide_Click ()

Dim i%

Call Common_SaveStartingMemory
Call Common_StartTimedTest

' Create the forms
For i% = 0 To val(txtForms.text) - 1
    Set arrForms(i%) = New frmClone
    arrForms(i%).Caption = i%
    arrForms(i%).Show
Next i%

' Hide the forms
For i% = val(txtForms.text) - 1 To 0 Step -1
    arrForms(i%).Hide
Next i%
```

continues

Listing 18.9. continued

```
Call Common_EndTimedTest(lblMakeHide)
Call Common_ShowEndingMemory(lblMakeHide2)

' Get rid of the forms so next test starts out clean
For i% = val(txtForms.text) - 1 To 0 Step -1
    Unload arrForms(i%)
Next i%

End Sub
```

The code consists of two loops. The first loop creates the specified number of forms. Note that around 75 to 80 forms is the maximum that can be created before you'll encounter an out-of-memory error. The exact number of forms that can be generated before causing this error will depend on the state of your system.

> **NOTE:** The number of forms you can generate before running into the out-of-memory limitation depends on how much memory each form requires. This limitation is encountered only for concurrently loaded forms. You can have approximately 260 forms defined in a Visual Basic project if they are not all concurrently loaded.

You create forms by making additional form instances using the `Set New` command. This command creates a new instance of a form from an existing form with the following statement:

```
Set arrForms(i%) = New frmClone
```

For the test program the form that is cloned to produce additional forms is a simple form with nothing but a label on it. (See Figure 18.3.) If a more complex form is used as the basis of generating further forms, the memory constraints are even greater. For example, if the form to be cloned has many image or picture controls full of graphics on it, those memory demands are multiplied with each form created and you could run out of memory well before creating 80 forms.

Each time the `Set…New` command is carried out, another form is created and its code and data are loaded into memory. For a more complete discussion of form data segments and how Visual Basic represents these in a memory layout, refer to the *Visual Basic Programmer's Guide.* For purposes of this discussion it is sufficient to realize that when a form is created, its code and data are moved to memory and consume space there. It is easy to comprehend that the more forms created the more memory consumed. That is what is accomplished by the first loop in the sample listing. When new form instances are created from an existing form with `Set…New`, the new form is initially invisible. Therefore, the sample code sets the `Visible` property for each new form to `True`. Likewise, the `Caption` property for each new form is set to display the form number.

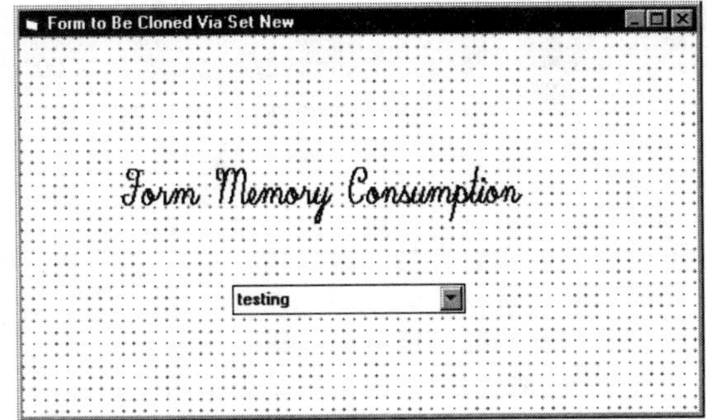

Figure 18.3.
A form that is repeatedly cloned and loaded.

When the forms are created, they are stored as elements of an array of forms. The array index provides a means to reference individual forms. This is essential because since these forms are part of an array of forms, there is not a unique form name available with which to reference each form. This technique is commonly used with Visual Basic *MDI* (multiple-document interface) applications, but can be used with any non-MDI applications as well.

The second loop of the listing hides all the forms. This loop cycles through every form referenced by the array and applies the Hide method for each form. Again, specific form instances are referenced by using the appropriate array index. At the conclusion of this loop all forms are still loaded in memory, but now are hidden so they are not visible to the user.

The last loop in this routine that follows the collection of time and memory results is simply used to unload all forms after the test is completed. This allows the test to be carried out repeatedly without exhausting memory resources, but does not affect the timing or memory measurement for this test.

The results from running this test are shown in Figure 18.2. Not surprisingly, a significant amount of memory is consumed because forms are still loaded in memory at the conclusion of this test. Why would anyone want to hide a form, then? The main advantage comes if you need to quickly display the form again later in the program. Simply showing a hidden form (which changes the `Visible` property to `True`) is much faster than loading a form from scratch. The speed advantages to this approach are demonstrated in Chapter 12. This form redisplay speed comes at the cost of the memory that the loaded but invisible form consumes.

> **TIP:** Loading then hiding forms is a memory-expensive operation and should be utilized only if later speedy retrieval of forms is desired.

Form Unloading

Unlike the form `Hide` method, which leaves forms loaded in memory, the form `Unload` statement removes forms from memory as well as removing them from the user's view. However, a common misperception is that the `Unload` statement unloads all form data and code. Actually, the `Unload` statement does not unload *everything* associated with the form. The Visual Basic help information for the `Unload` statement states that when a form is unloaded, only the displayed component will be unloaded. Code associated with the form module will still be present in memory.

Therefore, the code behind the form is not purged from memory when the form is unloaded. The next step is to compare the memory and timing characteristics of this approach. The corresponding test case uses `Unload` to unload every form that has been previously loaded into memory. The code for this test case is executed when the Form Unload command button is clicked, as shown in Listing 18.10.

Listing 18.10. The Form Unload command button's `Click` event.

```
Sub cmdMakeUnload_Click ()

Dim i%

Call Common_SaveStartingMemory
Call Common_StartTimedTest

' Create the forms
For i% = 0 To val(txtForms.text) - 1
    Set arrForms(i%) = New frmClone
    arrForms(i%).Caption = i%
    arrForms(i%).Show
Next i%

' Get rid of the forms
For i% = val(txtForms.text) - 1 To 0 Step -1
    Unload arrForms(i%)
Next i%


Call Common_EndTimedTest(lblMakeUnloadTime)
Call Common_ShowEndingMemory(lblMakeUnloadMemory)


End Sub
```

This code sample is very much like the previous sample that used the `Hide` method. The difference is that after creating all forms in the first loop, the second loop goes through and unloads every form rather than hides it. Forms are again referenced through a control array.

See Figure 18.2 for representative results of repeated trials of this test. As you can see from the results, the time required to unload every form is just slightly greater than the time required to hide every form! The unload statement itself is not an inherently slow operation. You can also see the memory consumption in the results. The amount of memory consumed after all forms are unloaded under Visual Basic 4.0 and Windows 95 is the same as if the forms had simply been hidden. This result differs from Visual Basic 3.0 and Windows 3.1, where the same approach would have resulted in much more free memory at the end of the test. In either case, there is some memory that has not been recovered by the `Unload` statement. This is because although Visual Basic has unloaded the form, it has not deallocated all of the memory originally set aside for the form object when it was created. In particular, as mentioned previously, code memory has not been released after the `Unload`. The form `Unload` statement for a form object is therefore by itself not a complete memory-recovery step.

It is important to consider in context the finding that the performance of unloading a form is on par with the performance of hiding a form. In an overall performance-tuning effort you are trying to optimize user-discernible bottlenecks. In this context, speed of removing any one form is unlikely to be a major concern. Both available approaches are fast enough in an absolute sense that a user is not likely to perceive any major wait when a single form is removed. This focus on form-removal speeds is largely an academic exercise to illustrate memory concepts. However, there are some practical applications. It is in cases when multiple forms must be cleared at one time that the cumulative form-removal time is more likely to be noticeable to the user.

It's also important to realize that removing a form from view may be only half the picture. If a form is going to have to be displayed again, a form that has been hidden shows itself much more quickly than a form that has been unloaded and must be reloaded into memory. Therefore, the real performance bottleneck in removing forms from view and then showing them again is on the other side of the operation—the form `Show` method.

Despite causing a longer redisplay time, there are clearly some advantages to the form `Unload` method. The unload is no slower, and much less memory is consumed than with the hide technique. It is also not perfect in this respect, however, as evidenced by the fact that some memory is not recovered.

Setting the Unloaded Form Object to *Nothing*

The next quest in the search for optimum memory management and performance is to come up with a technique to recover the lost space after all forms are unloaded. You might think it's a good idea to resort to Windows memory management API calls at this point. However, using Windows API calls for memory management to override Visual Basic's actions is a risky venture because Visual Basic hides the memory-management layers from you. You don't have a clear vision of what you must do to reclaim the space, so any attempts to use the Windows API for this purpose would be guess work. Likewise, the Visual Basic language does not provide you with any memory-management techniques...or does it?

Fortunately, if you are using object variables there is a way to indicate to Visual Basic that you want a certain level of memory-management cleanup to take place. An *object variable* is a variable that refers to an object such as a form, control, or specific control type like command button or text box. You can build arrays of objects, as done with form objects in this chapter's test program. Each element of the array contains a form object. After these form objects have been allocated in the array and then later unloaded, you can tell Visual Basic to free the resources associated with the unloaded objects. You accomplish this by using the `Set` command to set that object reference to `Nothing`. An example of this technique is

```
Set arrForms(i%) = Nothing
```

> **NOTE:** You can group objects into *collections* of objects as well as arrays of objects. Collections are similar in concept to arrays but provide some advanced collection management capabilities. Collections are discussed in Chapter 23, "Objects."

Because you can assign `Set…Nothing` to *any* object, you can apply this technique to objects such as databases and recordsets as well. These database objects are discussed in detail in Chapter 21, "Jet Engine/Access." Since the applicability of `Set…Nothing` is so great, there might be many areas in your code where you can set objects to `Nothing` to recover resources associated with those objects when you are through using them.

Two key questions then arise: How much memory reclamation do you gain by using `Set…Nothing`? How much of a performance penalty do you pay for using `Set…Nothing`? Precise answers to these questions, as with most performance questions, are application specific, but the sample program can give you some general guidance.

Of course, the performance-penalty question is a tricky one typical of performance assessment. If you add extra statements to the code to set objects to `Nothing`, it is a fair guess that they will slow the program down because the interpreter has more work to do. In this sense, this technique would slow performance. On the other hand, setting objects to `Nothing` is essentially a memory-recovery/conservation strategy. In this regard, the extra statements serve to make more memory available and keep the system from reaching a low memory state. Low memory states can bring with them their own performance penalties, so setting objects to `Nothing` can be viewed as a potential performance-enhancing strategy. The performance gained is just difficult to accurately gauge, since the performance benefit can be situation dependent.

The next step is to use the sample program to find some general answers to these question areas. The sample program is shown in Listing 18.11. The program is essentially the same as the prior sample code that loaded and then immediately unloaded all forms. The only difference is that there is now one additional source line, which is the line that sets each form object element to `Nothing` after the unload operation has taken place for that form.

Listing 18.11. Setting the unloaded form object to `Nothing`.

```
Sub cmdNothing_Click ()


Dim i%
```

```
Call Common_SaveStartingMemory
Call Common_StartTimedTest


' Create the forms
For i% = 0 To val(txtForms.text) - 1
    Set arrForms(i%) = New frmClone
    arrForms(i%).Caption = i%
    arrForms(i%).Show
Next i%


' Get rid of the forms
For i% = val(txtForms.text) - 1 To 0 Step -1
    Unload arrForms(i%)
    Set arrForms(i%) = Nothing
Next i%



Call Common_EndTimedTest(lblMakeNothing)
Call Common_ShowEndingMemory(lblMakeNothing2)

End Sub
```

The results from running this sample code (by clicking on the Make Forms, Unload, Set to Nothing button) are shown in Figure 18.2. First, examine the performance statistics. This technique results in a time barely over the time of the unload technique that did not have the extra `Set...Nothing` statement! Statistically speaking, `Set...Nothing` imposes little performance penalty. The slight slowdown in the face of the overall execution time is of little significance. So if there is a benefit to be gained by setting an object to `Nothing`, you should certainly not avoid this assignment out of an unfounded fear of greatly increased interpreter/memory-management time.

The next issue, then, is to determine if the use of `Set...Nothing` provides you with any benefit. This answer can be found by comparing the memory consumption of simply unloading the forms versus unloading the forms and then setting them to `Nothing`. In the `Set...Nothing` test, no bytes were lost from when the first form was created to when the last was deallocated. By contrast, the earlier test case where forms were unloaded *without* setting the object to `Nothing` `(as described in the section "Form Unloading")` resulted in substantial memory loss at the end of the test.

This advantage to using `Set...Nothing` applies to other objects as well, including data-access objects. Clearly, the use of `Set...Nothing` yields memory savings. The lost memory would be reclaimed when your program exits under Windows 95, but would not be available as long as your program continues to run. The amount of the savings is very application specific—or more correctly, object specific—and depends on the amount of form code and other factors. In a small application that does little object creation, there may be little perceptible benefit to using `Set...Nothing`. But as demonstrated by the visible savings in this example, the cumulative effect of using `Set...Nothing` and the compounded memory savings it can provide can be significant for some programs.

The fact that the penalty for using `Set...Nothing` is very slight, and the cumulative memory savings can be significant, indicate that you should routinely use the `Set...Nothing` approach when disposing of objects. As for the original quest, to determine how best to remove multiple forms, the results remain inconclusive. The best choice for form removal is application specific. If an application requires frequent and speedy redisplay of forms, the hiding forms with the corresponding memory penalty of that approach may be best. On the other hand, if an application runs into out-of-memory errors, then it may be necessary to unload the forms and set them to Nothing when they must be removed from view, at the subsequent price of decreased form redisplay speed.

TIP: When dealing with arrays or collections of form objects, hide forms to enhance redisplay speed at the cost of increased memory consumption. Alternatively, unload the forms and set the form object to `Nothing` to optimize memory use at the cost of form redisplay speed. The best approach is application specific.

TIP: Object variables should be set to `Nothing` after object use is complete. The potential memory conservation benefits normally outweigh the negligible cost of extra processing time.

Considerations When Assessing Memory

If you run the sample programs when several other programs are running, you might see some interesting results. This is particularly true if you interact with other programs while carrying out tests in form32.exe. For example, run a test case, then task out to a different program with Alt+Tab. Carry out some work in that other application then return to form32.exe to start another test case. You might observe that considerably more space is now consumed when you run the next test case than it would if you ran all test cases immediately after starting the test program.

The explanation for this is the nature of memory management. The sample program techniques all cause system memory-management actions to be applied at low levels. Memory management is not application specific, but is carried out by Windows as kind of a juggling act to service all applications. The state of this memory management, as discussed in earlier Chapter 6, "Factors That Affect Performance," can vary greatly at certain times depending on the system state and recent and current system activity.

This can be seen when you leave the application in between test cases. In particular, you may notice that the amount of memory consumed on the test case associated with the Make Forms-Unload command button is not be consistent if you have forced other activity in the system prior to the test. You might expect that because the same number of forms is created and unloaded in every test, the number of lost bytes is always the same. This is generally true if you stay in the application and run the test repeatedly. But if you get adventurous and leave and return to the program between test cases you will have a good chance to observe some of the variance in a complex operating system. Under Windows 3.1, the degree of fluctuation will be great (in one system that was tested, from 2.5KB all the way up to over 40KB). Under Windows 95 it will be minimal, reflecting its improved memory management.

Likewise, setting forms to `Nothing` after they are unloaded can show similar behavior depending on system activity. If you stay within the application, the memory loss should generally be 0. But if you stray outside the application and return, particularly under Windows 3.1, you might observe strange numbers, and in some cases even see that the test returns a number like -2KB. In this case, the results would seem to indicate that memory was actually claimed during the test. More memory was available by the end of the test than was available at the start of the test!

The amount of memory left after hiding forms can also vary, but generally by a much smaller range. The reason for the smaller variance with this technique is that this test does not involve deallocation or freeing of memory.

The important lesson from such observations is that Windows memory management is complex, and your Windows application's performance will be affected by other activity of your system. The more multitasking your user carries out, working with other applications concurrently with your application, the less predictable the performance of your application, particularly with respect to what is happening with system memory management. The good news is that if you use proper programming techniques in your application and take advantage of advanced techniques such as `Set…Nothing`, you are likely doing all the self-defense possible. Your application can then at least be counted on to serve your users' needs well under normal circumstances.

Out-of-Memory Errors

On some systems an out-of-memory error can occur when running this chapter's sample program, or when running other programs that generate many forms. This can occur under Windows 95 as well as Windows 3.1. The error occurs when there is not enough available memory to generate all the new forms. The sample program from this chapter should run successfully on a system with at least 8MB of memory up to around 80 forms if there are no other "memory hog" applications also running at the time.

If you experience problems running the sample program, you should first check to see if any other applications are open. Shut down those applications to free up memory and then run the program again. If you still experience problems, simply rerun the test with a smaller number of forms requested in the text box field.

The more serious problem you might be faced with is how to handle this problem if it occurs with your own applications that create many forms. Of course, you should not leave your user stranded when this error occurs. The first important action to take is to detect the error and continue. This can be accomplished with a simple error handler like the sample shown in Listing 18.12.

Listing 18.12. A sample error handler to detect low memory on form creation.

```
Sub cmdMakeUnload_Click ()


On Error GoTo cmdMakeUnload_Click_Err

' This array will hold the forms we create, so that we can
'    reference a new forms properties and methods through this array.
ReDim arrForms(200) As Form

Dim i%


Call Common_StartTimedTest

' Create the forms
For i% = 0 To 200
    Set arrForms(i%) = New frmClone
    arrForms(i%).Caption = i%
    arrForms(i%).Show
Next i%

' Get rid of the forms
For i% = 200 To 0 Step -1
    Unload arrForms(i%)
Next i%


Call Common_EndTimedTest(lblMakeUnload)


Exit Sub

cmdMakeUnload_Click_Err:

    ' Out of Memory Error is 7
    If Err = 7 Then

        MsgBox "Out of Memory Error in creating forms!"

        ' Take appropriate recovery steps unique to your app here

        i% = i% - 1
        Do While i% >= 0
            Unload arrForms(i%)
```

```
            i% = i% - 1
        Loop
        Call Common_EndTimedTest(lblMakeUnload)

    End If

    Exit Sub

End Sub
```

When an out-of-memory error occurs, the event procedure's error handler can detect it by checking for the out-of-memory error code 7. Then the application can perform whatever cleanup is needed to allow it to continue without coming to a crashing halt. Of course the best approach is to design your application so that it has a high likelihood of staying out of trouble on your average user's system. Suppose you have a pool of users that includes many on low memory systems with 8MB of memory or less. Many of these users are also expected to be heavy users of applications and have several applications open at any one time. In this case, you would not want to write an application that attempts to have 80 forms loaded at once. Your likelihood of memory failure, and disgruntled users, would be high indeed! When you are armed with a good understanding of the memory ramifications of your program, you are in a much better position to assess such trade-offs. This chapter focuses just on the impact of form removal on memory. However, you can apply the same type of approach to examine any area of your application.

Summary

One focus of this chapter is the rationale for using the `DoEvents` statement and the performance ramifications of that statement. An example highlights the necessity of `DoEvents`. Without this statement, program code that carries out repeated loops may temporarily lock out processing of other events within the same application. Under Windows 3.1, the processing of events in other applications can be locked out as well. One solution to this problem is to simply place a `DoEvents` statement inside the loop. Then each time through the loop the `DoEvents` statement gives other events a chance to be processed. The sample program in the chapter shows, however, that such an approach carries with it a nontrivial performance penalty. The use of a `DoEvents` statement can nearly double the execution time of a simple loop.

A tactical workaround to this approach is illustrated that consists of keeping track of the number of loop iterations and, at some set number of iterations, carrying out `DoEvents`. For example, every 25th loop could call `DoEvents` and reset the iterations counter so that 25 loops later another `DoEvents` takes place. This approach significantly improves performance over using `DoEvents` in every loop. However it can be difficult to determine the optimum number of loops that should occur between `DoEvents` calls to provide for the smooth handling of events. Even if an optimal number is determined, the optimum for smooth response time is likely to vary from system to system.

To remedy this problem, alternative approaches are examined. The first alternative consists of using the `PeekMessages` Windows API to determine when messages are waiting. `PeekMessages` is used to check for any keyboard or mouse button events that have occurred. If a keyboard event is detected, `DoEvents` takes place during the loop. If no keyboard events are detected, no `DoEvents` takes place within the loop. This approach provides much better performance than using a `DoEvents` statement in every single loop. However, `PeekMessages` fills a message structure at each call that you never use, so intuitively it would seem that there should be a better method to carry out this check. Likewise, the `PeekMessage` API has the potential to alter the contents of the message queue. Because Visual Basic normally masks the messaging level this technique is potentially dangerous and not recommended.

Finally, an improved approach for checking the queue within the loop is presented. This approach uses the `GetQueueStatus` API call. If the `GetQueueStatus` API call indicates that a message is present for the application, `DoEvents` is called to deal with that message. If `GetQueueStatus` indicates that no messages are present, `DoEvents` is not called within the loop. `GetQueueStatus`, like `PeekMessage`, checks for certain types of messages. However, unlike `PeekMessages`, `GetQueueStatus` does not fill up a message structure. `GetQueueStatus` also carries with it no risk of perturbing the message queue and changing its contents. The sample program in this chapter illustrates that this technique is faster than any of the other techniques that enable event processing, and is not even that far behind the simple loop that carries out no `DoEvents` processing. Therefore, `GetQueueStatus` is both a faster and safer approach to use.

Your use of `DoEvents` will be unique based on unique application needs. If you heed the principles in this chapter, you can leverage `DoEvents` to enhance the multitasking behavior of your application without sacrificing adequate performance.

This chapter also looks at memory considerations related to form removal. Three techniques are examined to remove forms that have been loaded through an array of form objects. The first technique is to hide forms. This is shown to be an expensive memory operation compared to the alternatives. Loading then hiding forms is a memory-expensive operation and should be utilized only if later speedy retrieval of forms is desired.

The next technique examined is to unload the loaded forms rather than hide them. The form `Unload` method does not unload a form's code from memory but simply clears out the visible form data. Therefore some memory loss should normally be expected after unloading a form. The unload technique shows similar execution time to the hiding forms, offers no memory savings, and results in slower redisplay of the form. Form unload operations are not significantly slower than form hide operations, but they do not free up any more memory and would result in slower redisplay of forms.

The final technique illustrated is to unload forms and set the form object variables to the `Nothing` keyword. This approach is shown to be almost as quick as the plain unload approach and to provide significant memory savings. Object variables should be set to Nothing after object use is complete. The potential memory conservation benefits easily outweigh the negligible cost of extra processing time. The best overall approach to remove arrays of form objects is application dependent. Hiding the forms is best for applications that must maximize form redisplay speed. Unloading forms and then setting them to Nothing is best for applications that must minimize memory consumption.

The discussion of these techniques is followed by a general look at memory issues. Memory management can be heavily influenced by system activity levels and concurrent use of programs. Such activity can affect test results for these sample programs, as well as affect user programs. In addition, the out-of-memory error that can occur on form loading is addressed. A technique to trap this error and allow a program to recover is provided.

All of these techniques provide important background for dealing with memory-related Visual Basic issues in general. Every application has unique performance considerations for which the best approach is simply to have a well-rounded understanding of the complexities of the memory-management aspects of Visual Basic and Windows.

Obey the Signs

Wrong Way: You should insert a `DoEvents` statement into every loop.

Many programmers feel the temptation to blindly insert a `DoEvents` statement into every loop to guarantee that the program always shares the CPU and never locks out user interactions with other programs. However, as this chapter demonstrates, `DoEvents` can have negative performance implications. There are viable alternatives to having a `DoEvents` carried out every time through a loop that offer better performance and provide just as good of multitasking service through Windows. These approaches include checking the message queue before calling `DoEvents` using the `GetQueueStatus` API, or alternatively only carrying out the `DoEvents` periodically rather than every time through the loop. In some cases, if the duration of the looping activity is very small, using a `DoEvents` might not even be merited in the first place.

Beware of Falling Rocks: Avoid using consecutive `DoEvents` statements.

Many programs address timing problems by inserting multiple `DoEvents` statements to slow down a piece of code. For example, some sample programs available use five `DoEvents` statements in a row in a timing-critical area of the code where a pause is necessary before the next action. This practice, although common to some programs, should generally be avoided. It is questionable programming practice to use a statement repeatedly when the need for the statement is other than its documented purpose. Using a `DoEvents` statement to enact a program pause could be confusing to those who must maintain the program in the future. `DoEvents` statements also slow down program performance in an unpredictable fashion. On a faster system the pause might not be long enough and on a slower system, the pause might be much longer than needed. It is better to package a pause routine that can be used to pause for an explicit number of milliseconds built on techniques outlined in Chapter 4, "Timing Methods." Alternatively, you should reexamine areas that have timing dependencies requiring a pause to see if they can be redesigned to utilize timers or avoid such dependencies.

Beware of Falling Rocks: Hiding a form is of little value if your program is not likely to display it again.

The advantage of the hide technique is quick redisplay if the form must be shown again later. If it is unlikely to be needed again, consider unloading it to recover memory.

Wrong Way: You should steer clear of `Set objectvar = Nothing` *to avoid having extra statements for the interpreter.*

This is not a valid guideline! The time consumed by such a `Set…Nothing` statement is negligible compared to the benefits it can provide. Unless there is a clear, project-specific reason not to, using `Set objectvar = Nothing` after an object variable is no longer needed should be standard practice.

Q&A

Q Is the `PeekMessage` or the `GetQueueStatus` API faster?

A As the sample program in this chapter demonstrates, the `GetQueueStatus` API is slightly faster. This is explained, among other reasons, by the fact that the `PeekMessage` API fills up a message structure with information on each call. In general, the use of `PeekMessage` is not recommended with Visual Basic. The `GetQueueStatus` message is a faster and safer alternative. When using any API that deals with message flow, proceed with caution because Visual Basic is intended by design to hide the messaging layer from you, and the use of such APIs circumvents that to a certain degree.

Q If you are implementing a periodic `DoEvents` after every set number of loops, how can you decide how many loop iterations to allow between `DoEvents`?

A The decision of how many iterations to allow before doing the `DoEvents` within a loop should be based on experimentation. Through experimentation you can identify the acceptable number of iterations to allow smooth processing. If you run the program, start the loop, and then face a wait as you interact with other areas of the application, too many iterations are passing between `DoEvents`. The optimum number of iterations provides virtually instantaneous response to user interactions. In some loops this can be accomplished by doing a `DoEvents` once every 200 iterations; with other loops this might need to be accomplished by doing a `DoEvents` once every 5 iterations. However, keep in mind that the optimal number will vary depending on the speed of the PC where the program is run. That is why the `GetQueueStatus` technique described in the chapter are preferable to simply using `DoEvents`.

Q Will the `Unload` statement remove a form and all its controls and code from memory?

A No! `Unload` unloads the form from memory, but the code associated with the form remains in memory. In fact, the test program shows that no more memory is freed with the `Unload` statement than by hiding a form under Visual Basic 4.0 and Windows 95.

Q Does the test program show that it's faster to hide a form or to unload it?

A Both approaches take approximately the same amount of time.

Q Therefore, should I never hide a form?

A No, if a form is to be displayed again, it will redisplay much more quickly if still loaded. However, you will pay a memory penalty for keeping it loaded. Therefore, the hide-versus-unload issue is very much dependent on your application's unique performance needs.

Quiz

Design a main form and a secondary form named frmClone. Add 30 picture controls filled with bitmaps to form frmClone. On the main form, provide a command button with the `Click` event code shown below. Collect timing and memory data for that code, which will load and unload copies of frmClone. Then optimize this click event code to free more memory and re-collect the timings:

```
Sub cmdTestUnload_Click ()

Dim i%


Call Common_SaveStartingMemory
Call Common_StartTimedTest


' Create the forms
For i% = 0 To 30
    Set arrForms(i%) = New frmClone
    arrForms(i%).Caption = i%
    arrForms(i%).Show
Next i%


' Get rid of the forms
For i% = val(txtForms.text) - 1 To 0 Step -1
    Unload arrForms(i%)
Next i%
```

Quiz Answer

```
Sub cmdTestUnload_Click ()

Dim i%


Call Common_SaveStartingMemory
Call Common_StartTimedTest


' Create the forms
For i% = 0 To 30
    Set arrForms(i%) = New frmClone
    arrForms(i%).Caption = i%
    arrForms(i%).Show
Next i%


' Get rid of the forms
For i% = val(txtForms.text) - 1 To 0 Step -1
    Unload arrForms(i%)
    Set arrForms(i%) = Nothing

Next i%


Call Common_EndTimedTest(lblMakeNothing)
Call Common_ShowEndingMemory(lblMakeNothing2)


End Sub
```

Workshop

> **NOTE:** Save any relevant work and close all open applications prior to attempting this workshop. The system might be in an unstable state if you receive an "out-of-memory" error.

1. Write a program that loops from 1 to 1,000,000 and adds the sum of every loop index (that is, add every number in the set 1 to 1,000,000). Add a command button named Msg to pop up a message box. Time the calculation loop and verify that no other application events are addressed while this loop is processing. (Click on the Msg command button to verify this.) Next, insert a `DoEvents` statement within the loop and compare the new time to the old time. It will be significantly slower. Verify that other application events now are addressed during the loop. (Again, click on the Msg command button to verify this.) Finally, modify the `DoEvents` statement within the loop so that a check is first performed to see if queued messages are available using the

`GetQueueStatus` API, and if that value if `True` the `DoEvents` is carried out. Time this third implementation and notice the difference. The new time should be much closer to that of the no `DoEvents` loop than to that of the loop with a `DoEvents` every time through.

2. Write a program that generates as many forms as possible on your system until an error occurs. Your program should trap the resulting error, using the techniques outlined in this chapter. Can you exceed the 80 forms used in the sample program? What is the system memory amount when you hit a limit? Are you constrained by available memory or Visual Basic implementation?

File I/O

Many applications must preserve data between sessions. Files provide a means for this permanent data storage. They also bring with them some of the biggest areas of performance bottlenecks. Moving information to and from permanent storage is an inherently slow operation given the mechanics of disk access. A simple disk-storage operation can take longer to complete than storing many times that amount of memory to faster *random access memory* (RAM) storage. Likewise, one disk-storage operation can absorb more time than a complex series of mathematical calculations. The calculations simply involve RAM and do not entail the underlying electromechanical manipulations that must be carried out to permanently store information on disk. One of the best optimization techniques for file I/O is therefore to simply minimize the amount of I/O that must take place within an application. However, there often are reasons for file-based storage that cannot be avoided. When this is the case, you can still enhance the speed of those operations by keeping in mind the guidelines in this chapter.

Why Optimize File I/O?

If you are carrying a mouse and an elephant on your back, the mouse's weight is not likely to have much impact on the extent of your effort. The mass of the elephant, on the other hand, is guaranteed to be noticed. Likewise, if you must frequently move such cargo, you would soon notice that some elephants weigh more than others! And so it is with file I/O. File I/O speed typically takes up a much larger percentage of application time than do other activities because it is such an expensive operation. However, different file I/O techniques can have drastic performance impacts. You can't turn an elephant into a mouse. File I/O, even after optimization, will remain one of the more expensive operations in your application. But with some optimization effort, you can transform file I/O from a heavier elephant to a lighter one. When you can work this magic, the performance rewards can be significant.

File I/O is also one of the performance areas about which it's difficult to make generalizations. This is due to several different factors. You can use many different types of storage for file I/O, including binary file I/O, random file I/O, sequential file I/O, Windows API-based file storage, resources in the executable file, and database file storage. Even for a given type of file I/O, the required storage implementation can be extremely application-specific. Some applications might need to write data, others to read it, and others to intermix read and write operations nonsequentially. Various file I/O approaches also have different maintainability advantages and disadvantages. Some approaches may be better from a performance standpoint at the cost of code that is difficult to understand and maintain. So there are no one-size-fits-all file I/O guidelines. Still, some insights into the nature of file I/O can lead you to your own best application-specific optimizations.

Such insights, and the evidence that backs them up, are the focus of this chapter. Two of the most frequently used file I/O types—sequential and binary—are discussed in detail. Then, two different data-storage scenarios are tested for each file I/O type; these tests consist of ordered reads and ordered writes. After all these approaches are presented, a cross-comparison of results is provided. You can derive some important insights into file I/O from these results and identify corresponding guidelines.

Non-Program Factors That Affect File I/O Speed

The speed of the code that interacts with files depends on both the techniques and efficiency with which that code was written and the horsepower of the CPU that processes that code. The most significant area of performance impact when utilizing file I/O, however, is disk speed itself. The speed of the physical disk and disk control constrains programs that must repeatedly read or write information to a file. Faster hardware makes for faster disk interaction. Slower hardware means slower performance.

This is typically not an area that a developer is free to optimize, for several reasons. There is often no way to easily change hardware speed short of replacing the hardware itself. Requiring users to use the application only with a specified disk configuration incurs expense to end users and limits the pool of users who can use an application. Neither of these outcomes is normally received well by end users, nor really feasible to you as the developer of the product. The same situation applies with strengthening the CPU requirements for a slow program. You typically cannot mandate that your users replace their CPUs to upgrade the speed of their PCs. And even if you could, a CPU upgrade might offer less speed relief than upgrading the disk or disk controller! That leaves you with one choice when you need to speed up file I/O code: Ensure that you are using the best method of file I/O for the task at hand. This is addressed through the series of tests in this chapter.

Minimize File I/O

Since file I/O is such an expensive operation, there are clear advantages to simply reducing the number of times an application must read or write to a file. You must pay careful attention when designing your application to minimizing file access. If an application constantly stores and retrieves data, the application probably carries out a steady stream of file operations in response to user actions. However, this can often be avoided by taking care when designing the application. If the application does not have to deal with large volumes of data, the application could be designed to simply store and retrieve information from memory. At the start of the application, it could initially retrieve all stored data from a file and move it to an array in memory. As the application manipulates data in response to user interactions, it could update the array in memory rather than in the hard disk file. Then, at the termination of the application, all the array data in memory could be stored back to the file. This provides all the advantages of persistent file storage, but reduces the number of times the application must turn to slow disk storage operations. With this approach, only two instances of file I/O occur, as opposed to potentially many hundreds as the user interacts with the program.

There are several disadvantages with this approach. If volumes of data are large, there may not be enough memory for this technique. All data entered during a session could be lost while the application is running if power is lost before the user has exited the application. By contrast, it would be safely stored on the file if it were immediately saved to file after entry. And the user would experience a considerable wait at application startup and termination as the application reads and then writes every single record. In light of these problems, the best approach is often to design the application to buffer some of the data, rather than all of it, in memory. In any case, if you make a conscious effort to minimize file I/O when you design an application, you can avoid paying some file I/O penalties in the first place.

File I/O Comparisons

The following comparison concentrates on sequential and binary file I/O, comparing performance for various write and read operations. The sample program file IO32.exe, on the CD-ROM that accompanies this book, is used for this test. This program is also available on the CD-ROM in a 16-bit version, FileIO16.exe. The main form of the program is shown in Figure 19.1.

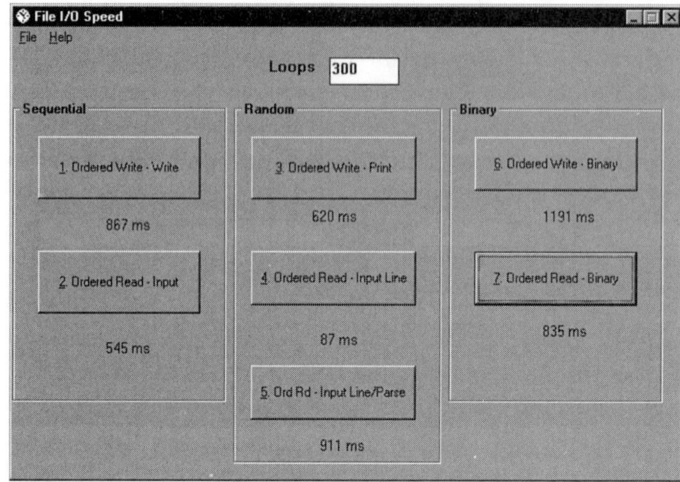

Figure 19.1.
A file I/O test program.

A look at a sample program that carries out tests of each type enables you to make some general comparisons. For example, you can see which type of file I/O is the fastest for the sample program for an ordered write of records. However, it is important to realize that a variety of options and approaches can be used even for a specific type of file I/O such as binary or sequential access. The best file I/O for a given application depends on the unique blend of application characteristics and the type of data being manipulated. This chapter focuses on information that can be stored and retrieved sequentially. If you have a problem that focuses on storing a large quantity of image information that requires a record-oriented, nonsequential byte access, the examples in the chapter are not directly relevant. They do, however, provide the background to enable you to devise your own test. If you model the approach used in the test here, you can come up with your own assessment of the strength of a particular file I/O method for your own needs.

Sequential File I/O Test Cases

The first test is carried out when you click the button labeled 1. Ordered Write. This test uses a sequential write technique. The code is shown in Listing 19.1. This test sequentially writes a

file using the `Write` statement. This statement enables you to pass individual variables to be written.

Listing 19.1. A test using sequential file I/O and the `Write` statement.

```
Private Sub cmdSeqSeqW_Click()

Dim i% ' loop counter
Dim strFileName As String
Dim intFileID As Integer

strFileName = App.Path & "\SeqOrd1.dat"

' Delete file if left over from previous run
If Common_FileExists(strFileName) Then Kill strFileName


Call Common_StartTimedTest

intFileID = FreeFile


Open strFileName For Output As intFileID

' Carry out test algorithm repeatedly
For i% = 1 To txtLoops

    ' Write LastName, Serial Number, TeamName, Avg Score, HiScore, and LowScore
    Write #intFileID, Str(i%), Str(i%), Str(i%), i%, i%, i%
Next i%

Close intFileID


Call Common_EndTimedTest(lblResults(1))


End Sub
```

The next test is carried out when you click the button labeled 2. Ordered Read. This test is a sequential read that can be used to read back the data file generated in the first test. The code for this test is shown in Listing 19.2. This test uses the `Input` statement to read records back in from the file. This statement, like the `Write` statement, can read variables on an individual basis into the multiple variables specified on the statement line.

Note that all tests should be carried out with the value specified in the `Loops` text box remaining constant. The code uses this value to determine how many records to read or write.

Listing 19.2. A test using sequential file I/O and the `Input` statement.

```
Private Sub cmdSeqSeqR_Click()

Dim i% ' loop counter
Dim strFileName As String
Dim intFileID As Integer
Dim strName As String
Dim strSN As String
Dim strTeam As String
Dim intAvg As Integer
Dim intHiScore As Integer
Dim intLowScore As Integer


strFileName = App.Path & "\SeqOrd1.dat"


' Abort if file does not exist
If Not Common_FileExists(strFileName) Then
    MsgBox "Warning, the expected data file does not exist.
    ➥ Run the WRITE test first!", , "Test Error"
    Exit Sub
End If


Call Common_StartTimedTest

intFileID = FreeFile


Open strFileName For Input As intFileID

' Carry out test algorithm repeatedly
For i% = 1 To txtLoops

        ' Read in the file data
        Input #intFileID, strName, strSN, strTeam, intAvg,
      ➥ intHiScore, intLowScore

Next i%

Close intFileID


Call Common_EndTimedTest(lblResults(2))


End Sub
```

The next test cases covered are virtually the same except that they use different commands to carry out the read and the write. The alternative write test is carried out when you click the button labeled 3. Ordered Write—Print. The code for this test is shown in Listing 19.3. Like the first test, this test also uses sequential output to write the file, but it uses the `Print` statement instead of the `Write` statement. The `Print` statement requires one string as a parameter

rather than individual variables. As you can see from the results in Figure 19.1, this statement is substantially faster than the `Write` statement of the first test. The `Write` statement takes nearly 30 percent longer on the system tested.

TIP: The `Print` statement generally offers significantly faster file I/O speed than does the `Write` statement.

Listing 19.3. A test using sequential file I/O and the `Print` statement.

```
Private Sub cmdSeqRndRW_Click()


Dim i% ' loop counter
Dim strFileName As String
Dim intFileID As Integer

strFileName = App.Path & "\SeqOrd.dat"

' Delete file if left over from previous run
If Common_FileExists(strFileName) Then Kill strFileName


Call Common_StartTimedTest

intFileID = FreeFile


Open strFileName For Output As intFileID

' Carry out test algorithm repeatedly
For i% = 1 To txtLoops

    ' Write LastName, Serial Number, TeamName, Avg Score, HiScore, and LowScore
    Print #intFileID, Str(i%) & Str(i%) & Str(i%) & Str(i%) & Str(i%)
     ➥ & Str(i%)
Next i%

Close intFileID


Call Common_EndTimedTest(lblResults(3))

End Sub
```

You can click the command button labeled 4. Ordered Read—Line Input to carry out the code that will read in the file generated in the previous test case. This test case also uses sequential I/O, as have the other test cases. But rather than using the `Input` statement of the second test to read data back in, the `Line Input` statement is used. `Line Input` reads a line at a time rather than the variable orientation of the `Input` statement. The code for this test is shown in Listing 19.4.

The results in Figure 19.1, representative of a series of tests, show that the `Line Input` method takes approximately one-seventh the time of the variable-based `Input` method! `Line Input` is clearly faster for line-oriented file I/O.

> **TIP:** Use `Line Input` rather than `Input` for line-oriented file I/O. The line-at-a-time retrieval of `Line Input` is much faster than the variable-based `Input` retrieval approach.

Listing 19.4. A test using sequential file I/O and the `Line Input` statement.

```
Private Sub cmdReadInputLn_Click()



Dim i% ' loop counter
Dim strFileName As String
Dim strLine As String
Dim intFileID As Integer
Dim strName As String
Dim strSN As String
Dim strTeam As String
Dim intAvg As Integer
Dim intHiScore As Integer
Dim intLowScore As Integer
Dim intNextBlank As Integer


strFileName = App.Path & "\SeqOrd.dat"


' Abort if file does not exist
If Not Common_FileExists(strFileName) Then
    MsgBox "Warning, the expected data file does not exist.
     ➥ Run the WRITE test first!", , "Test Error"
    Exit Sub
End If


Call Common_StartTimedTest

intFileID = FreeFile


Open strFileName For Input As intFileID

' Carry out test algorithm repeatedly
For i% = 1 To txtLoops

        ' Read in the file data
        Line Input #intFileID, strLine
Next i%
```

```
Close intFileID

Call Common_EndTimedTest(lblResults(4))

End Sub
```

This is a tremendous speedup. However, if you evaluate the test carefully, it is clear that for certain kinds of data retrieval this is not really a fair test of the `Input` and `Line Input` statements. `Input` can be used to separate a series of values into the appropriate variables. `Line Input` just leaves you with one long string that represents all the individual values about which you want information. `Line Input` is fine if you just need to read in strings a line at a time, which is sometimes the case, but if you need more than just the string, you still have to do the work to massage the lines into variables. For a fair comparison of variable I/O, that should be included in your tests. The next test takes this into account.

This next test, then, uses the same sequential I/O `Line Input` technique to provide a comparison to the `Input` technique. The test also must parse out individual values from the string that is retrieved using `Line Input`, to ensure a fair comparison to the `Input` technique. The code for this test is shown in Listing 19.5. This test is carried out when you select the command button labeled 5. Ord. Rd—Input Line/Parse.

Listing 19.5. A test using sequential file I/O and the `Line Input` statement with parsed results.

```
Private Sub cmdRead_Click()


Dim i% ' loop counter
Dim strFileName As String
Dim strLine As String
Dim intFileID As Integer
Dim strName As String
Dim strSN As String
Dim strTeam As String
Dim intAvg As Integer
Dim intHiScore As Integer
Dim intLowScore As Integer
Dim intNextBlank As Integer


strFileName = App.Path & "\SeqOrd.dat"


' Abort if file does not exist
If Not Common_FileExists(strFileName) Then
    MsgBox "Warning, the expected data file does not exist.
     ➥ Run the WRITE test first!", , "Test Error"
    Exit Sub
```

continues

Listing 19.5. continued

```
End If


Call Common_StartTimedTest

intFileID = FreeFile


Open strFileName For Input As intFileID

' Carry out test algorithm repeatedly
For i% = 1 To txtLoops

        ' Read in the file data
        Line Input #intFileID, strLine
        strName , strSN, strTeam, intAvg, intHiScore, intLowScore

        ' Parse out values
        strLine = Trim(strLine)
        intNextBlank = InStr(1, strLine, " ")
        strName = Left$(strLine, intNextBlank - 1)

        strLine = Right$(strLine, Len(strLine) - intNextBlank)
        strSN = Left$(strLine, intNextBlank - 1)

        strLine = Right$(strLine, Len(strLine) - intNextBlank)
        strTeam = Left$(strLine, intNextBlank - 1)

        strLine = Right$(strLine, Len(strLine) - intNextBlank)
        intAvg = Val(Left$(strLine, intNextBlank - 1))

        strLine = Right$(strLine, Len(strLine) - intNextBlank)
        intHiScore = Val(Left$(strLine, intNextBlank - 1))

        strLine = Right$(strLine, Len(strLine) - intNextBlank)
        intLowScore = Val(Left$(strLine, intNextBlank - 1))


Next i%

Close intFileID


Call Common_EndTimedTest(lblResults(5))

End Sub
```

The results in Figure 19.1 show that this test takes significantly longer than the second test, which uses the `Input` statement. This tells you that the `Input` statement is more efficient at assigning values to its parameters than your code is at parsing our string into the variables. Performance of the `Line Input` test could be improved by optimizing the parsing technique. However, performance would still not reach that of the `Input` statement. In general, the more variables retrieved from a file line, the better the performance of `Input` over `Line Input`.

> **TIP:** If you need to read a series of values from a line into variables, `Input` offers similar or better performance than does `Line Input` to read the whole line, if you take into account the extra time you must spend parsing the string with that approach. `Input` also makes for more maintainable code with its clearer, code-eliminating approach.

Binary File I/O Test Cases

The next test turns to binary I/O instead of sequential I/O. *Binary I/O* consists of writing a series of bytes. *Sequential I/O*, on the other hand, uses an end-of-line marker to mark each line. The sequential I/O statements such as `Write` and `Input` take care of this for you, taking it into account when reading and writing. Binary I/O has no such record separators. It is up to you to build your own logic to keep track of records or the structure of storage with binary file I/O. Binary file I/O commands use a byte offset supplied as a parameter to determine where to read from or write to, with no regard to record layout.

The binary write test is carried out with the `Put` statement. This test is launched when you click on the command button labeled 6. Ordered Write—Binary. The code for this test is shown in Listing 19.6.

Listing 19.6. A test using binary file I/O and the `Put` statement.

```
Private Sub cmdBinSeqW_Click()
Dim i% ' loop counter
Dim Recordsize As Long
Dim intFileID As Integer
Dim typPerson As Person
Dim strFileName As String


strFileName = App.Path & "\BinOrd.dat"

' Delete file if left over from previous run
If Common_FileExists(strFileName) Then Kill strFileName


Call Common_StartTimedTest

Recordsize = Len(typPerson)

intFileID = FreeFile


Open strFileName For Binary As intFileID
```

continues

Listing 19.6. continued

```
' Carry out test algorithm repeatedly
For i% = 1 To txtLoops
    typPerson.LastName = Str(i%)
    typPerson.SerialNumber = Str(i%)
    typPerson.TeamName = Str(i%)

    typPerson.AvgScore = i%
    typPerson.HiScore = i%
    typPerson.LowScore = i%

    Put intFileID, , typPerson
Next i%

Close intFileID

Call Common_EndTimedTest(lblResults(6))

End Sub
```

The representative results in Figure 19.1 show that the binary method takes longer than the first test using the sequential `Write` approach. Sequential file I/O offers a better approach for sequential writes. Binary file I/O, however, can provide very flexible file-write services if you have to write nonsequentially. If you had to write a record at the end of the file, then at the top, then in the middle, and then at the top, with the `Put` statement you would have no problem—you would simply supply the appropriate offset. With the sequential `Write` or `Print` statements, however, you would have to close and reopen the file over and over again.

Furthermore, sequential data handling techniques can't be used to replace existing data in a file as binary data can. If you used sequential techniques for such an operation, you would have to regenerate the entire file to modify data in an existing file. For an application which required such operations, sequential file I/O would be much slower than binary file I/O, if it could be used at all.

The next test determines if the same performance insight holds true for reading files. The binary file I/O `Get` command is used to retrieve the values just written by the previous test. Like the binary `Put` command, the `Get` command simply deals with a block of bytes, reading however many bytes you specify. The code for this test is shown in Listing 19.7. The test is launched by clicking the command button labeled 7. Ordered Read—Binary.

Listing 19.7. A test using binary file I/O and the `Get` statement.

```
Private Sub cmdBinSeqR_Click()
Dim i% ' loop counter
Dim Recordsize As Long
Dim intFileID As Integer
Dim strFileName As String
ReDim ArrTypPerson(txtLoops) As Person
```

```
strFileName = App.Path & "\BinOrd.dat"

' Abort if file does not exist
If Not Common_FileExists(strFileName) Then
    MsgBox "Warning, the expected data file does not exist.
     ➥ Run the WRITE test first!", , "Test Error"
    Exit Sub
End If


Call Common_StartTimedTest

Recordsize = Len(ArrTypPerson(0))

intFileID = FreeFile

Open strFileName For Binary As intFileID

' Carry out test algorithm repeatedly
For i% = 1 To txtLoops
    Get intFileID, , ArrTypPerson(i%)
Next i%

Close intFileID


Call Common_EndTimedTest(lblResults(7))

End Sub
```

The results in Figure 19.1 show that the binary read, like the binary write, is slower than sequential techniques when used for sequential operations. For binary operations where different nonsequential portions of a file must be accessed, binary or the similar random file I/O techniques are required. Using sequential file I/O for nonsequential tasks would be cumbersome. As the name implies, sequential I/O is best for reading in sequential series of bytes, where the simple line-oriented record format is handled more efficiently than other types of file I/O for sequential operations.

> **TIP:** Sequential I/O is faster than binary I/O when reading or writing a line at a time sequentially. If you need to write or read from varying locations, binary or random file I/O is the only feasible approach.

Summary of File I/O Approaches

Comparing the various approaches to file I/O can be a challenging task because there are so many different approaches you can take. Those you have looked at in the sample program are binary file I/O and sequential file I/O. Binary file I/O is appropriate for handling a sequence of bytes while sequential I/O is most appropriate for reading and writing text or other line-oriented records that will be accessed in order. In addition to these traditional methods, there are many other approaches you can use. Each method has advantages and disadvantages depending of the type of information storage and retrieval that must be carried out.

Sequential File I/O

Sequential file I/O consists of reading or writing lines in sequence. It is typically used for text files. Lines are separated by end-of-line markers. For nonsequential data access needs, the performance of this approach pales in comparison to alternatives such as random and byte I/O without the overhead of line separators and sequential addressing. The sequential approach is easy to program and offers maintenance advantages.

Binary File I/O

Binary file I/O involves simply writing a byte stream to the file. No specific record ordering is required, and there is no implicit record-retrieval capability built into this method. Any retrieval that takes place must be managed by the program's byte-manipulation code. Therefore, if data is to be treated as a collection of records, it is up to the program to store and retrieve the bytes to those records in some meaningful format.

One way to do this is to simply use binary file I/O much like random file I/O. This consists of writing a fixed number of bytes to represent each record using the byte-oriented I/O. Then the bytes representing a given record can easily be retrieved by calculating the virtual record based on the byte counts of each record. This method works, but is essentially implementing record-oriented file I/O with extra work, when the random-access method handles it implicitly.

Binary file I/O differs from random file I/O in that any size information can be written at a time to the file, as opposed to the one-record-at-a-time approach of random file I/O. Therefore, byte I/O provides the flexibility for shorter records to be written when record-oriented file I/O is needed and fast, same-size record retrieval isn't mandatory. For example, rather than writing fixed-size records where each field is a set size (setting aside, say, 20 characters for every last name even if the names are sometimes smaller), you can first write a size indicator for variable-length fields to the file and then write the appropriate bytes. When the record is read back in using binary file I/O, there will be an indicator of how many bytes to read in for the non-fixed field. Such variable-size records reduce storage needs, but require more code and potentially more time to retrieve.

Random Access File I/O

Random access file I/O enables you to specify a record to read from a file. All records must be a consistent size. This approach makes it possible to read random locations throughout a file without reopening and closing the file. Its performance is therefore best for record-oriented files, particularly if the records must be read in a nonsequential manner.

Random access is a record-oriented file I/O method. When you open a file for random-access writes, Visual Basic expects record-oriented information to be supplied in parameters to the function calls. For example, the `Get` and `Put` statements that work with random file I/O take a record number as a parameter to calculate the position of the data. This flexibility enables a program to insert records—even out of order, if necessary—simply by supplying the appropriate record number. Therefore, random file I/O is tailored for a record-based approach.

Random I/O is sensitive to the type of record information that is supplied, because it must maintain the appropriate data type representation when it lays it out and retrieves the information later. If you will be using random I/O, refer to the type rules described under the `Get` command for random file I/O in the Visual Basic help file.

Private Profile and Registry I/O

Another method of moving information to a file is through the Windows API private profile calls, which are typically used to write to INI files. Because they are relatively easy to program for the developer who is familiar with dynamic link libraries, they are often used to store program data. Some programs make extensive use of these to store much data in the INI file, above and beyond program-configuration data. Profile techniques are slower than regular file I/O.

Windows 95 provides another approach for storing such data that is intended to replace the older, private profile storage. This 32-bit operating system alternative consists of using the system registry to store a program's settings. The Visual Basic language provides the `SaveSetting` and `GetSetting` statements for this purpose. These techniques do provide a controlled storage mechanism, but other methods would be more optimal for storing large quantities of data.

Resource Information

Another alternative for information that only needs to be read in, and not written, is to build that information directly into the program's executable file as an available resource. Strings, data, and bitmaps can be defined in resource definition files. These resource definition files can then be compiled into resource files. Visual Basic can then directly build the compiled resource files into the program executable file it generates.

At runtime, then, the data is accessible directly from the Visual Basic program already loaded into memory rather than available in an external program file. This offers significant savings over file I/O approaches. However, since you cannot write back to the resources stored with the application's executable file, this technique can only be used with read-only data.

Database File I/O

Database storage has largely displaced file I/O over the last few years. Databases provide sophisticated storage management and are often easier to implement than file I/O. It is much easier to use a data control to lay out a simple database to store address information than to write a file-management program to do the same. Database performance depends very much on the specific database and database implementation used. Likewise, file I/O is extremely dependent on the application and implementation. Therefore, no blanket statement can be made as to whether database or file I/O is faster. Results will vary.

Database storage does bring with it significant layers of overhead that file I/O does not. For many applications, using a database will indeed be much slower than using a carefully crafted file I/O approach. On the other hand, database storage also brings to bear database engines that have been highly optimized and tuned for data-storage tasks for years by large teams of professional programmers. There are cases when a database program can easily outperform a complex file I/O program. Even if performance is slower than with a carefully crafted binary file I/O approach, the ease of programming and maintenance with a database is far greater. Database file I/O is the topic of a separate chapter later in this book, Chapter 21, "Jet Engine/Access."

> **TIP:** Consider using database storage as an alternative to file storage because it provides a much easier implementation path. Database performance, depending on the application, the database, and the implementation, might be slower but is generally not an impediment except for a timing-critical application.

Summary

This chapter looks at the performance of various file I/O techniques, which have advantages for different types of data storage and retrieval. The sample program in this chapter demonstrates performance of the file-access methods with various types of storage and retrieval models. In any implementation, choosing the best file I/O technique is extremely application and data dependent. Nevertheless, the examples in this program demonstrate some general performance trade-offs.

This chapter illustrates that the degree of performance advantages of different file I/O techniques depends on the application. Random file I/O is especially strong for unordered, record-based file manipulations. Binary file I/O is speedy, but requires more implementation work and might be particularly suited to managing large amounts of data. Sequential file I/O is, in

some respects, the easiest to use but does not provide the random data-access capabilities of random or even binary file I/O.

Likewise, the Windows API profile function calls do not execute as quickly as some of the other techniques. Their advantage is in ease of use at the programming level. They also enable data to be retrieved quite easily with no concern for file layout or the order of data in the file, but this comes at the expense of performance. If an application has simple file I/O needs, these functions can provide an easy programming solution. If your data needs are more complex, these functions are not the most optimal solution.

Database performance is examined in more detail in Chapter 21. The additional overhead of a particular database approach is likely to be slower than file I/O. It does, however, provide advantages in data management. If quantities of data are vast, the programming and data-management effort can be greatly simplified by using a database technique. A database is an additional layer laid on top of file I/O, and that in and of itself imposes an overhead performance penalty that doesn't exist if you use file I/O directly. However, today's databases come highly optimized, so this penalty is not necessarily a big enough barrier to justify file I/O.

Obey the Signs

Beware of Falling Rocks: Do not expend considerable energy trying to use a sophisticated file I/O method when a simple approach will do.

Beware of the temptation to utilize a speedier but less maintainable file I/O approach when you are not forced to do so for performance reasons. If you are simply storing a single name and address in your program, the performance penalty of using the easy-to-understand Windows API profile function when compared to more complex record-management techniques of binary or random-access methods will have virtually no perceptible performance difference to the user. In such a case, do not go to extra work to save a couple milliseconds that your end user will never notice. The disadvantage you pay for tuning and going with the more complex methods in such cases is additional debug time, and perhaps significantly greater maintenance expense in the future when others work with the program.

Wrong Way: Use the Windows API profile functions `GetPrivateProfile` and `WritePrivateProfile` to store massive quantities of data.

The Windows API profile functions are nice because they provide a very friendly programming interface and they also place the burden of file I/O on the Windows layer. However, these function calls introduce some overhead not present in the VB file I/O methods and take up additional disk storage space as well because they store text strings and topic indicators. Because the profile functions are so easy to use, some programmers fall prey to the temptation to use them to store vast quantities of data.

Q&A

Q Is random file I/O the only file technique that lets you write anywhere within the file?

A No. Binary file I/O also lets you write anywhere if you supply the correct byte offset. The current byte offset when using binary file I/O can be determined using the `Loc` function so you always have an easy means to move backward and forward in the file. Also, the profile and database techniques enable you to move back and forth, in a sense, at the virtual level, because they free you from any concerns about file order or layout.

Q Is it faster to read a file or write a file?

A Reading a file is significantly faster than file-write operations. This is easy to understand when you consider that the electromechanical action of the disk drive is significantly more involved during a write operation. If disk caching comes into play, the software management needed to ensure reliable writes is also more involved at than at reads. Although file read time can certainly be a source of bottlenecks in an application, this is usually because vast quantities of data are read at any one time. File-write techniques are much more likely to be bottleneck areas than are file-read operations due to the slower performance of writes.

Workshop

Write a program that stores finishing times, names, ages, and states for every runner in a marathon. This program should also allow for retrieval of all the information into a list box. Implement this program four different ways: using database storage, using the `GetSetting` and `SaveSetting` Visual Basic functions, using binary file I/O, and using sequential file I/O. Compare the performance of these alternatives in the final program. Also keep track of the programming bugs that are chased down during the development of each of these programs. Which technique seemed to be the most difficult to debug and introduces the highest risk of error during development? Which technique seems to be the simplest and best for future maintenance?

16-Bit Versus 32-Bit Code

Visual Basic 4.0 consists of both a 32-bit and a 16-bit integrated development environment. The resulting 32-bit programs can only run in 32-bit Windows environments, such as Windows 95 and Windows NT, while 16-bit programs can run in either 32-bit environments or 16-bit environments, such as Windows 3.1 or Windows for Workgroups 3.11. While the 16-bit programs can run on the widest range of systems, they cannot exploit all the features that a 32-bit program can. In addition, the performance of 16-bit and 32-bit programs may differ, in some cases quite significantly.

There are many reasons performance can differ. Visual Basic uses a runtime interpreter that is 16-bit or 32-bit depending on the type of compilation used for the program. Only the 32-bit interpreter used for 32-bit programs can fully exploit the features of the 32-bit environment. Thus, the choice of 16-bit or 32-bit format for programs determines whether the runtime interpreter used to interpret the code will take full advantage of the operating system and underlying processor capabilities. Even if source code is the same for 16-bit and 32-bit programs, performance will differ for this reason.

Another clear area of difference between 16- and 32-bit programs is the source code that can be used when writing the programs. There are some technologies and language constructs that can only be leveraged from 32-bit programs. Source code that is tailored to take advantage of such items, such as the use of 32-bit Application Program Interface (API) calls, is not legal in 16-bit programs. Likewise, there are some OLE controls that are only available in 32-bit versions. Thus, another important difference between 16-bit and 32-bit programs, in addition to the interpreter used to carry out that code, is source code that allows the leveraging of certain advanced features not supported in both platforms.

Both of these differences—underlying operating-system ramifications and visible source code differences—is addressed in this chapter.

The Underlying 32-Bit Operating System

This chapter first considers performance variations from a different angle: the ability of 32-bit programs to fully exploit the operating system capabilities of a 32-bit environment. A 32-bit program has inherent performance advantages because it can use the 32-bit operating system environment and APIs to the fullest extent. There are many complex reasons for the superiority of the 32-bit environment based on its ability to more fully exploit the underlying microprocessor. Windows 95 provides a significant break from Windows 3.1 in its capacity for preemptive multitasking and the fact that programs are freed from the shackles of the 16-bit segmented memory architecture. Memory addressing is much more flexible in Windows 95, allowing an application to easily address memory space without the constraints of dealing with memory in separate, limited-size segments. This reduces the overhead—and therefore the number of instructions carried out by the CPU. And fewer instructions translates into faster programs.

Also, with Windows 95, the ground rules for multitasking are different than for the cooperative multitasking of Windows 3.1. As discussed in Chapter 18, "Multitasking and Memory," no longer must an application use the `DoEvents` statement to be a good neighbor and give other processes a turn during lengthy calculations. The Windows 95 operating system takes care of that itself, temporarily cutting one process off to give another a turn. The operating system makes these decisions based on scheduling algorithms that take many factors into account. This, by itself, doesn't provide faster programs, since now a program's performance can be affected by other programs and forced by the operating system to share time with other processes in the system.

This priority-based, preemptive multitasking does allow the operating system to support both processes and threads. A process can loosely be thought of as a program or application. Each process can have one or more threads concurrently executing. A thread can be loosely viewed as a flow of instructions that is carried out. Threads belong to their parent process and have the same shared address space as their parent process and as other threads that belong to that parent. The 32-bit operating system implementation of Windows 95 and Windows NT can juggle threads very efficiently to allow multiple strains of processing.

A 32-bit operating system itself does not necessarily provide for faster execution of 16-bit programs. A 16-bit operating system such as Windows may be more efficient in executing a 16-bit program than a 32-bit program such as Windows 95 or Windows NT. The non-preemptive multitasking may actually work to its advantage. Rather than incurring the overhead of attempting to juggle many balls in the air as do Windows 95 and Windows NT, Windows can focus its attention on the program currently occupying the processor. However, a program that is a 16-bit program under Windows may operate more efficiently when converted to a 32-bit program to run under Windows NT or Windows 95 if it takes full advantage of the improved capabilities of the 32-bit operating system.

By now you may be wondering how any of these performance considerations may really benefit or even influence your own 32-bit Visual Basic applications. You know that you don't (and can't) set the priorities of tasks, or create threads, or supply direct memory addresses anywhere in your source code. But you must also keep in mind that even though you don't use these techniques, the code your program utilizes may.

While Visual Basic 4.0 does not allow your programs to take direct advantage of threads or nonsegmented memory addressing, 32-bit Visual Basic programs can still benefit indirectly from the presence of these features. Flexible memory management or threaded processing implementations in other components can provide advantages when you incorporate their services. The use of mail packages or database engines is one example where you might benefit from such technology. If those components have code written in a more powerful, elegant method by taking advantage of threads and your Visual Basic program interacts with them, then your programs will benefit as well. 32-bit programs can directly benefit from incorporating such components. 16-bit Visual Basic programs can only utilize 16-bit components that cannot directly take advantage of these techniques since they are targeted for a 16-bit operating system environment.

And every 32-bit Visual Basic application uses at least one very important 32-bit program: the Visual Basic runtime interpreter. The interpreter is written as a 32-bit application and therefore you can be sure that it exploits many of the advantages of the 32-bit operating system as it carries out execution of your program. Even when your program is exactly the same for 32-bit and 16-bit versions, the interpreter will be different. It will either exploit the 32-bit capabilities on behalf of your application when running a 32-bit program or be unable to take advantage of them when running a 16-bit program.

Source-Code Level Differences

Source code for the two environments is largely the same. For many non-complex programs or programs with few external dependencies, there might be no changes at all between the 32-bit and 16-bit versions of a program. For other programs, source-code differences may be minor enough that they can be easily dealt with in one body of source code, using conditional compilation to process one set of statements when the 32-bit compilation into runtime code takes place and another when the 16-bit compilation takes place. Programs can automatically be compiled with one set of declarations when targeted for the 16-bit environment, and another set of declarations when targeted for the 32-bit environment. This technique, illustrated in Listing 20.1, shows how you can bring enhanced performance to your high-end users without abandoning your 16-bit holdouts.

Listing 20.1. Conditional compilation for 32-bit or 16-bit programs.

```
#If Win32 Then ' 32-bit VB uses this Declare.
     Declare Function GetTickCount Lib "kernel32" () As Long
     Declare Function GetWindowsDirectory Lib "kernel32" Alias
     ➥ "GetWindowsDirectoryA" (ByVal lpBuffer As String,
     ➥ ByVal nSize As Long) As Long

#Else   ' 16-bit VB uses this Declare.
     Declare Function GetTickCount Lib "User" () As Long
     Declare Function GetWindowsDirectory Lib "Kernel"
     ➥ (ByVal lpBuffer As String, ByVal nSize As Integer) As Integer


#End If
```

Different rules that exist between 32-bit and 16-bit programs can affect your source code approach. In most cases, these differences involve the use of components or calls. Some key services that are available only for 32-bit are

- The use of in-process OLE Automation servers
- The generation of in-process OLE Automation servers
- The generation of remote automation objects
- The use of remote data objects
- The use of remote data controls
- The data access object layer 3.0
- Jet Engine 3.0
- 32-bit Windows API calls
- 32-bit OLE controls

In-process OLE Automation servers provide a DLL-based packaging of OLE Automation server services. Calling applications can utilize the methods and properties of the server. An out-of-process server is an executable file-based packaging that offers the same function. However, the in-process server, when called, will be in the same address space as the calling program. The out-of-process server will be in a separate address space. Sharing the same address space offers significant performance advantages by eliminating much overhead. Only 32-bit programs can use these faster in-process servers, and the in-process servers themselves can only be created as 32-bit DLLs.

Remote automation objects, or RAOs, are automation servers that can be called across a network. This powerful capability allows you to launch a program on a different PC than the one where your program is running and to receive results notification when that program completes. Furthermore, this is an asynchronous operation, meaning that your program does not have to stop and wait for results but can continue processing at the same time that the called program across the network is working. RAOs can only be created as 32-bit applications. They can be called by both 16-bit and 32-bit client applications that use their services. A layer of code provided in a DLL, called an *automation proxy,* serves as an interface layer on the side of the client PC making the RAO call. This automation proxy exists in both 16-bit and 32-bit versions, so 32-bit programs will take advantage of the 32-bit version and any performance benefits that it provides.

Remote data objects, or RDOs, provide the capability to access server data across the network through the appropriate object reference. They eliminate some of the overhead of the Jet Engine and therefore can offer improved performance. A similar capability is that of the *remote data control*, which packages RDO-type network data access capability inside a control. These capabilities exist only in 32-bit programs. Other potentially slower approaches would have to be used to access the same data in 16-bit applications.

The most advanced version of the data access object layer, DAO 3.0, is available only to 32-bit applications. This layer of references, like DAO 2.5 which is available to 16-bit programs, provides objects for data access. Various properties and methods of the objects can be used for database related operations. DAO 3.0 provides more objects than DAO 2.5 and can provide further flexibility in certain operations. More flexible alternatives can lead to better implementation, which may provide better performance than alternative home-grown techniques. It is also able to take advantage of the Jet Engine 3.0.The highly optimized Jet Engine 3.0 is also only available to 32-bit applications.

The 32-bit engine exploits threads to carry out database operations, offering significant performance benefits.

32-bit applications can likewise use 32-bit system API calls. 16-bit Visual Basic applications cannot directly take advantage of this capability. 32-bit API routines are likely to perform better than their 16-bit counterparts because of the operating system architecture. Likewise, many API calls for advanced techniques are only available as 32-bit APIs.

Comparing Control Loading of 16-Bit and 32-Bit Visual Basic Applications

There are significant performance differences between the control loading of 16-bit and 32-bit programs. 32-bit Visual Basic load performance is dependent on the 32-bit OLE controls (contained in OCX files) that it supports. 16-bit Visual Basic 4.0 applications can make use of 16-bit OLE controls as well as 16-bit VBXs, but cannot incorporate 32-bit OLE controls.

32-bit Visual Basic 4.0 supports 32-bit OLE controls only, and not 16-bit OLE controls or 16-bit VBXs. Thus, its control-load activity is different from that of 16-bit Visual Basic 4.0. Visual Basic 3.0, of course, supports only 16-bit VBX controls.

One other difference between applications produced in these different versions is that the application executable size differs. For comparison purposes, a series of programs was converted from a Visual Basic 3.0 VBX implementation, to a Visual Basic 4.0 16-bit VBX implementation, to a Visual Basic 4.0 16-bit OLE control implementation, to a 32-bit OLE control implementation. This was done by simply changing the controls, making no code changes. The size of the executables generally changed as documented in Table 20.1.

Table 20.1. Comparison of executable size when using VBXs, 16-bit OLE controls, and 32-bit OLE controls.

Environment	*Normalized Sizes*
Visual Basic 3.0 VBX	1.00
Visual Basic 4.0 VBX	1.15
Visual Basic 4.0 16-bit OLE control	1.15
Visual Basic 4.0 32-bit OLE control	1.20

The difference in the size of Visual Basic 4.0 executables is simply attributable to the switch between versions of Visual Basic. The Visual Basic 3.0 program executable became larger when generated as a Visual Basic 4.0 16-bit program. The different controls would not by themselves be expected to have a direct impact on size since the control code is contained in a separate VBX or OCX file. In keeping with this expectation, there is no significant difference between VBX and 16-bit OLE controls in terms of their impact on Visual Basic 4.0 16-bit executable size. There is another slight overhead factor evident in the move from a 16-bit Visual Basic 4.0 program to a 32-bit Visual Basic 4.0 program.

The size of the runtime interpreter itself varies between Visual Basic 3.0, 16-bit Visual Basic 4.0, and 32-bit Visual Basic 4.0. Table 20.2 summarizes the names of the runtime files in each environment.

Table 20.2. Runtime interpreters for various versions of Visual Basic.

Version	*Runtime Interpreter*
Visual Basic 3.0	VBRUN300.DLL
Visual Basic 4.0	VB40016.DLL
Visual Basic 4.0	VB40032.DLL

However, Visual Basic 4.0 programs require additional OLE support files that Visual Basic 3.0 programs do not, so looking at the differences in runtime interpreter size is also not a meaningful comparison. A full comparison would have to take into account all other required dependency files for each program. This will vary depending on the application. However, the amount of files required can be substantial. A simple program that presents a "Hello world!" message when a button is clicked takes 9KB for the executable file under 32-bit Visual Basic 4.0. The setup wizard, however, indicated that seven program and program support files were required for the application, bumping the total amount of required files to over 1.4MB. Often times, many of the required files, which are commonly used by other programs, may already be in memory when a program starts. Obviously the number of support files required for a program will have some impact on load speed. Comparing the size of program files for the same 16-bit and 32-bit program is presented as a Workshop exercise at the end of this chapter. Program size, of course, is one factor that affects load speed, but it is not necessarily the most significant factor.

In the test applications that were examined, 16-bit Visual Basic 4.0 VBX programs loaded in roughly the same amount of time as similar 16-bit Visual Basic 4.0 programs based on 16-bit OLE controls. In most cases, 16-bit Visual Basic 4.0 OLE control programs did load significantly faster than the same programs compiled as 32-bit Visual Basic 4.0 programs using 32-bit OLE controls. This was particularly true in cases where a very large number and variety of controls were used. Standard controls showed a slight trend to load faster in 16-bit versions than in 32-bit applications, but the difference was not statistically significant. Load times will be extremely application specific. However, in general, 32-bit Visual Basic programs did not seem to offer improved load speed over 16-bit Visual Basic 4.0 versions in the tests conducted, and often took noticeably longer to load when 32-bit OLE controls were used. This is likely a function of OLE support files as well as OLE controls rather than a Visual Basic 4.0 limitation, and it may improve with future OLE releases.

The results will be different for every application and control combination, so the information summarized here should be viewed as one set of test data and not a sweeping statement about all control-load times. However, it does point out that load-time considerations are very much present on Visual Basic 4.0 and not eliminated by any means in the 32-bit world. The fewer controls you have, the faster your programs will load. The more controls you have, the more overhead that takes place at load time and the slower the performance will be for your end user.

Performance Differences of the Same Application in 16-Bit Versus 32-Bit Executable Formats

Performance is a consideration when you're deciding whether to develop a 32-bit or 16-bit application if the answer is not dictated by your user base. While the control load time performance of 32-bit applications when compared to 16-bit applications may be bad news, there is good news on overall performance. You can generally count on the fact that users with 32-bit operating systems will enjoy better performance if you can provide them with 32-bit applications rather than 16-bit applications. The exact degree of speed increase that you will see in an application when it is moved from the 16-bit world to the 32-bit world is extremely application specific. However, with this disclaimer in mind, tests on a variety of small applications show that performance improvements of 50 percent are commonly achieved when code is migrated from 16-bit to 32-bit VB programs. This is a significant performance improvement since it pertains to overall program performance. The reasons for this improved performance are the factors mentioned earlier in this chapter in the sections "The Underlying 32-Bit Operating System" and "Source Code Level Differences." This overall performance improvement is likely to be more important to your user than the potential added OLE control initialization overhead at program startup. While the load time performance is a one-time occurrence at program startup for the user, the overall application performance affects them as long as they use the application.

This is enough of a performance gain to offer considerable incentive to developers to move their applications to 32-bit format. Fortunately, the 16-bit user base does not have to be abandoned to make this a reality. The previously mentioned conditional compilation capability of VB 4.0 makes it feasible to maintain the same program in both 32-bit and 16-bit versions from the very same source files.

Performance Data

Every application has different performance characteristics because each uses a different blend of internal language constructs and external components. You have already seen in the examples in this book that each individual area of Visual Basic represents a trade-off. When you multiply the unique performance considerations of each area times the thousands of elements that might appear in a complex program, you begin to get a feel for how hard it is to make a generalization about performance.

Most 32-bit programs will be faster than their 16-bit counterparts when both are compared on Windows 95. However, some areas of 32-bit Visual Basic programs are no faster in their 32-bit form than the equivalent 16-bit program. The information that follows will demonstrate how variable this effect is. This material is intended to highlight the fact that you really must do your own application-specific comparison before making any blanket statement about the amount of performance improvement you will get in moving to 32-bit programming.

The statistics that follow are all from Visual Basic 4.0 programs that were run under Windows 95. The numbers provide you with a head-to-head comparison of two similar programs, one 32 bit and the other 16 bit.

The first unusual area is the Graph OCX. The Graph test program is discussed in detail in Chapter 26, "Know Your Objects: The OLE Graph Control Sample," and makes use of the Graph OCX. The 16-bit OCX version of this test program is shown in Figure 20.1. The corresponding 32-bit OCX test program is shown in Figure 20.2. The 32-bit program was no faster than its 16-bit counterpart. As a matter of fact, it took measurably longer to perform various runtime operations than the 16-bit program in our series of tests as shown in the figures. The corresponding 16-bit program based on the old 16-bit VBX rather than OCX is displayed in Figure 20.3. The VBX test case was much quicker than the 32-bit OCX and slightly quicker than the identical 16-bit OCX test case. The OCX approach took around 16 percent more time than its Visual Basic cousin. It was stated earlier in this chapter in the section "Comparing 16-Bit and 32-bit Visual Basic Program Load Times" that the load time of 32-bit OLE controls could be measurably slower than that of 16-bit OLE controls and VBXs. While this is true, keep in mind this is not load behavior that we are measuring with our graph program. It is behavior that results when updating and working with the control at runtime. In such a case, depending very much on the specific control, the performance of the sophisticated OLE approach may be slightly slower than the old-fashioned VBX.

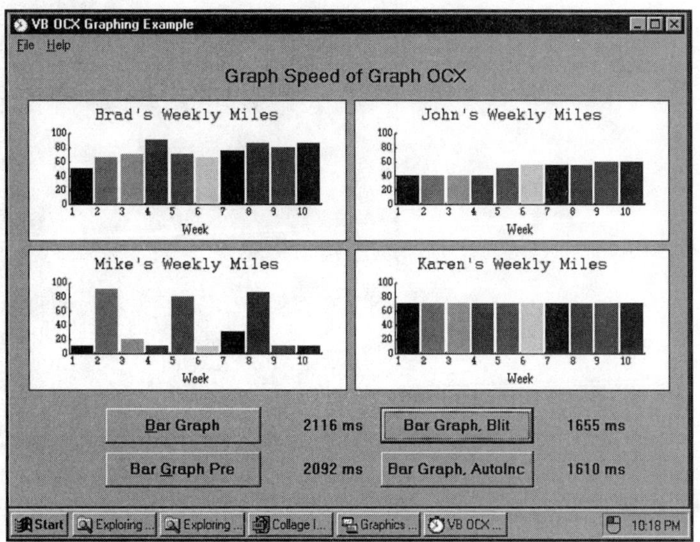

Figure 20.1.
16-bit OCX graph-generation performance.

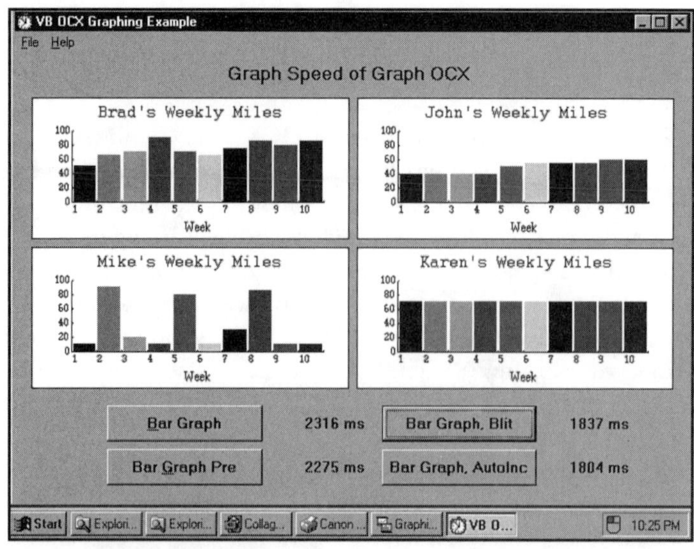

Figure 20.2.
32-bit OCX graph-generation performance.

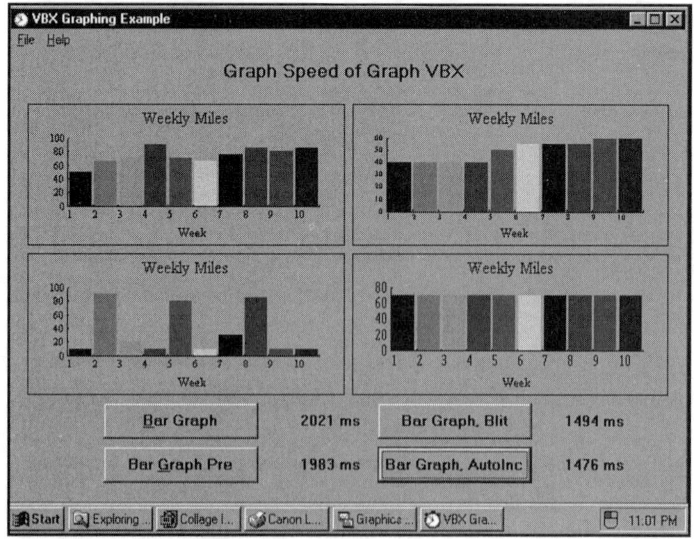

Figure 20.3.
16-bit VBX graph-generation performance.

No normalized times are supplied here because this finding is so control dependent and even usage dependent. Nevertheless, it is important to realize that 32-bit OCX usage can be slower than the same approach in 16 bit. It is a mistake to think that 32-bit programs automatically improve every area of performance in every application. Here are the rankings of the Graph OCX runtime data setting and graph-generation test results:

16-bit VBX: Fastest

16-bit OCX: Slightly slower than 16-bit VBX

32-bit OCX: Slightly slower than 16-bit OCX

Another interesting area to examine is procedure-call performance. The callty program from Chapter 11, "Code Structure," provided an easy comparison of this aspect of 32-bit and 16-bit behavior. The results are shown in Figure 20.4 for a 32-bit program. Figure 20.5 shows the results from the same program compiled as a 16-bit application. These results show a significant advantage for the 32-bit version. 32-bit call-related code seems to execute anywhere from 20 to 50 percent faster depending on the type of call technique that is compared.

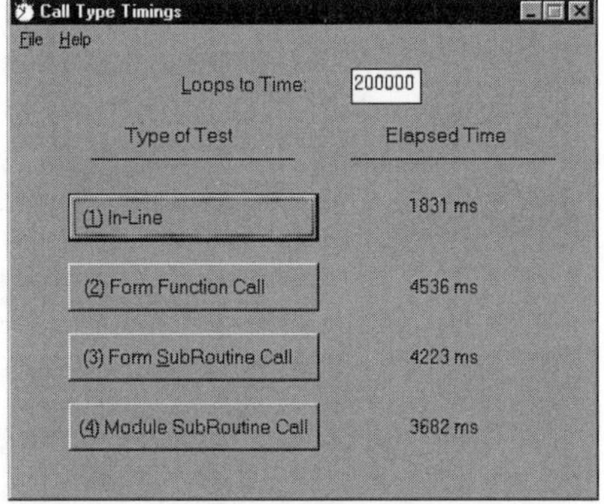

Figure 20.4.
A 32-bit callty performance test.

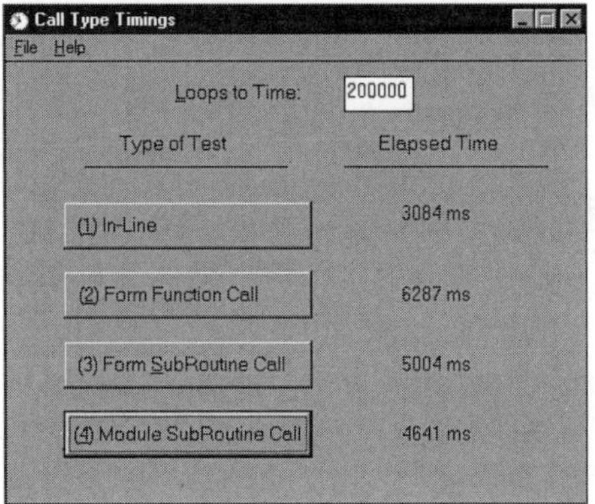

Figure 20.5.
A 16-bit callty performance test.

The Loop program from Chapter 11 also shows that the 32-bit version is faster, but by a much smaller amount than in the callty test. Figure 20.6 shows the 32-bit version of the Loop program with results, and Figure 20.7 shows the 16-bit version.

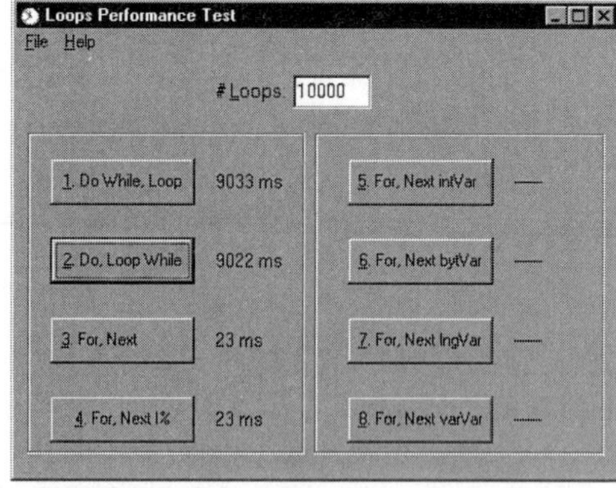

Figure 20.6.
A 32-bit loop performance test.

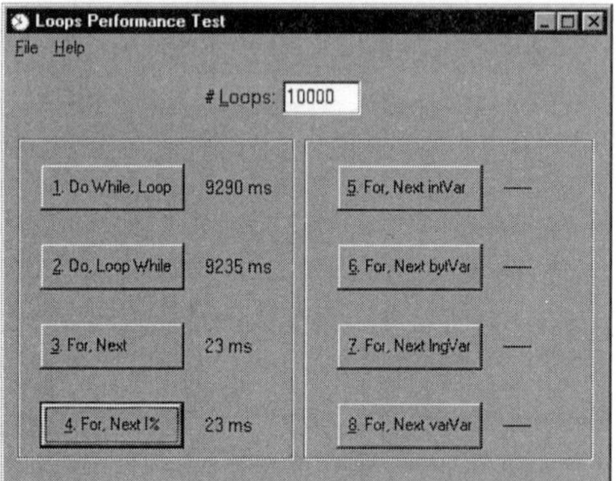

Figure 20.7.
A 16-bit loop performance test.

> **NOTE:** Comparing the speed of Visual Basic 3.0 16-bit programs and Visual Basic 4.0 16-bit programs when both are run under the same environment is similar to comparing Visual Basic 4.0 16-bit and 32-bit programs. Speed trade-offs will be application specific, and there may be some aberrations where differences are slight. In general, however, Visual Basic 4.0 offers major performance advantages over its predecessor. The Visual Basic runtime interpreter is substantially improved.
>
> In addition, repeated timings taken for Visual Basic 3.0 programs typically yield a drastically higher standard deviation than what can be observed with Visual Basic 4.0 programs. Visual Basic 3.0 programs seem to have a lot more flux and sensitivity to the system. Visual Basic 4.0 programs, by contrast, seem to exhibit considerable consistency of results.

Just to remind you to be ever vigilant and never assume generalities about performance, we next consider another program where the 32-bit versus 16-bit trade-off is different than you might expect. The program used here is the DoEvents sample application. The DoEvents test

program involves a high degree of system interaction, because it makes calls which affect system control of message handling. The 32-bit version results can be seen in Figure 20.8, and the 16-bit results appear in Figure 20.9.

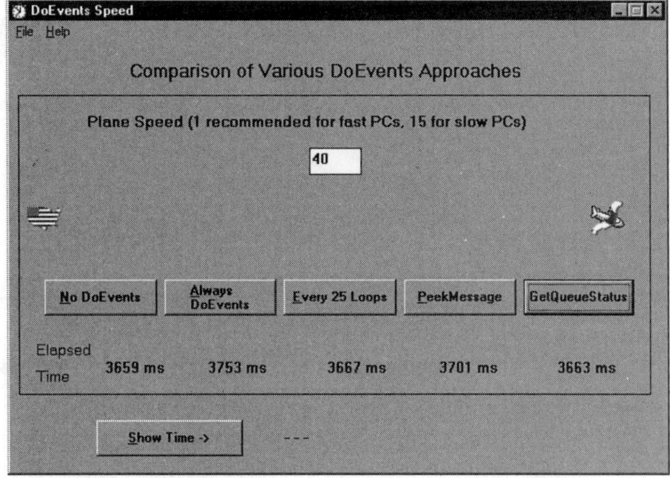

Figure 20.8.
A 32-bit DoEvents performance test.

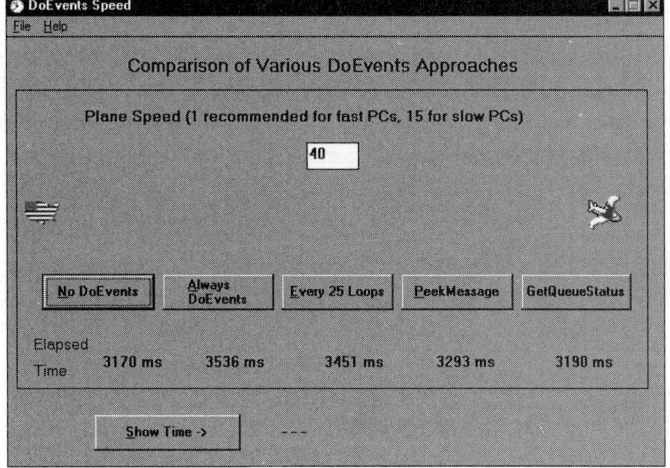

Figure 20.9.
A 16-bit DoEvents performance test.

As you can see, the 32-bit program takes longer to complete the test cases than the 16-bit program in the series of tests conducted. In some cases, the 32-bit program takes nearly 15 percent longer. Part of this difference may be explained by system variability, which points out the need for more extensive, detailed testing. However, you can also surmise that this particular test is highly related to operating-system handling of our programs (which indeed it is, since it is DoEvents centered). 16-bit programs are handled differently by the Windows 95 scheduler than 32-bit programs are. For example, they share a cooperative multitasking space with other 16-bit applications, as opposed to the preemptive multitasking of Windows 95.

It is important to note that for most programs, overall performance will improve when you generate them as 32-bit applications. If you use databases in your code, you can take advantage of the faster Jet Engine 3.0 if your application is 32 bit. Doing so will garner considerable speedup. The examples just shown were admittedly selected to emphasize that performance speedup is very application dependent. You should benchmark the particular application you are interested in to determine what the bottom line is on speed rather than relying on anyone else's numbers.

Summary

This chapter presents some of the key points and strategies concerning 16-bit versus 32-bit applications. Differences between 16-bit and 32-bit Visual Basic applications fall into two categories: those you can't see reflected in your source code and those you can. Differences that you can't see are related to the fact that a 32-bit Visual Basic application will exploit the underlying 32-bit operating system, regardless of your program structure. This has some architectural advantages over the less-sophisticated 16-bit operating system. And even 16-bit programs that run under the 32-bit system will still use an interpreter whose code is targeted for the less sophisticated 16-bit environment.

The differences that you *can* see involve source code and programming capabilities that are unique to 32-bit Visual Basic programs. These areas include the ability to create and use in-process OLE automation server DLLs, to use the more optimal Jet Engine 3.0 layer based on threads, and to create and use remote data objects which bypass the Jet layer, among others. Some capabilities offered by 32-bit programs, however, do not provide tangible improvement in performance. The load and initialization time of 32-bit OLE custom controls is one such area. Overall, 32-bit programs can be expected to perform noticeably faster than equivalent 16-bit programs if both are run on a 32-bit environment. As with all performance testing, though, results can be expected to vary by application.

Obey the Signs

Wrong Way: Throw out old 16-bit code when starting a similar 32-bit program.

This would not be a productivity-enhancing move. Most of your code will be directly usable as a 32-bit program. API calls will be one main area of difference. With the conditional compile capability, many programs can easily be maintained as both 32-bit and 16-bit programs from the same body of source code.

Beware of Falling Rocks: Do not assume that the ability to produce 32-bit programs drastically reduces the need for performance optimization procedures.

32-bit programs will generally be faster than equivalent 16-bit programs. However, the speed improvement is generally in the form of a steady evolution rather than a dramatic revolution. The same type of performance bottlenecks can still creep up. Don't assume that the burden of performance tuning has gone away simply because you can produce a 32-bit program.

Q&A

Q Because my program is interpreted, does it really benefit from being generated as a 32-bit application?

A Yes. Don't forget that your application is interpreted by the 32-bit Visual Basic interpreter rather than the 16-bit interpreter if you generate it with the 32-bit compiler. This is where the real leverage of the 32-bit environment comes into play, because the 32-bit interpreter can in many cases exploit capabilities in ways it could not as a 16-bit program.

Q Why is the 32-bit-specific in-process OLE Automation server (available in a DLL file) faster than an out-of-process OLE Automation server (available in an EXE file)?

A The in-process server shares the same address space as the calling program, while the out-of-process server does not.

Workshop

1. Build an application that loops 100,000 times, performing a math operation within the loop. Build another application that loops 100,000 times, making an image control with a bitmap visible and invisible each time within the loop.

   Generate both 16-bit and 32-bit versions of each program. Run them both on a 32-bit operating system and record the times. Which program benefits more (that is, which has the highest percentage improvement) from taking advantage of 32-bit support—the processing-intensive program or the graphics-intensive program?

   Run both the 16-bit and 32-bit versions of other sample programs covered in earlier chapters, including the variable and math sample programs. Which areas show the biggest improvement when run as 32-bits applications? Which show the smallest improvement?

2. Write a program that simply consists of one form and a command button that displays a message saying "Hello World!" Generate an EXE for this program from both 16-bit Visual Basic 4.0 and 32-bit Visual Basic 4.0. Then use the 16-bit Setup

Wizard that comes with Visual Basic to generate setup disks for the 16-bit EXE file. The screen at the end of the generation has a details button you can use to view file details of the setup. Note the number of files required for the program and the total size required. Next use the 32-bit Setup Wizard and repeat the same process to generate setup disks for the 32-bit EXE file. Again note the number of files required and the total size required. How do 16-bit requirements compare to 32-bit requirements?

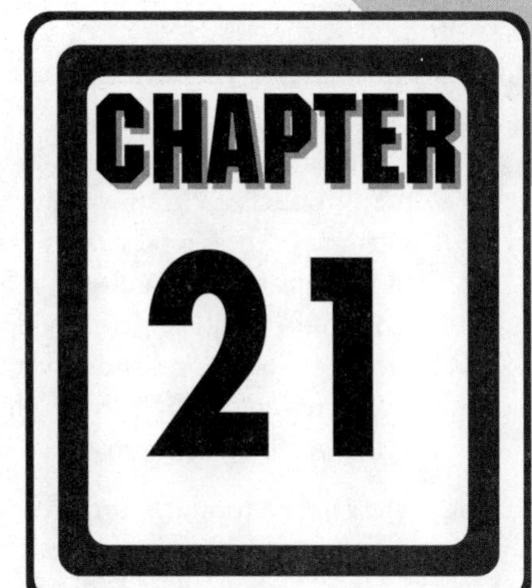

Jet Engine/ Access

Databases provide a very powerful means for programs to store and manage data. However, these capabilities come at the cost of performance. Chapter 19, "File I/O," discusses file input/output and the fact that reading and writing information from disk inherently slows the operations. Regardless of how a program is written, it takes more time for the system and its underlying hardware to carry out the movement of information between a permanent storage medium and RAM than to perform a calculation or update a value already in RAM. In addition, databases introduce another layer of code for a program to interact with. Database software can be very complex, and when your program makes use of database services, that layer of unseen code becomes part of your program and part of its performance as well.

Fortunately, database use is so critical to programming that sophisticated-yet-efficient database products are readily available. The Jet Engine is the most well-known layer of database software in the Visual Basic world. Jet comes with Visual Basic and provides access to the native Access-format databases, which are stored in database files with the well-known .mdb extension. In addition, Jet provides access to a wide variety of other databases. Among those on the list are both local and server databases. Jet allows database interaction at the open database connectivity (ODBC) level. This is a standard approach that is now supported by nearly all major databases and provides a significant degree of database independence in source code.

The range of options in the database realm is very large, and procedures to upgrade database performance are very specific to the particular database to be used. In that light, database performance tuning could fill a book in itself. *Database Developers Guide with Visual Basic,* by Roger Jennings (Sams Publishing), is one book that contains much helpful information. This chapter focuses primarily on optimization techniques for the Jet Engine, using an Access-format database for the sample program. Important techniques for enhancing database performance are illustrated through a series of examples. First we will examine the speed of operations using standard data access objects. That will be followed by a comparison of using the OLE data control for the same operations. Next we will consider the speed of the same data access object approach when operations are grouped into transactions. Finally we will discuss specific tradeoffs in the use of tables versus dynasets, field reference techniques, the `Seek` method, and a delete query.

This chapter's example focuses on a simple one-table database so that key concepts are clearly highlighted in the simplest approach possible. Be aware that many complexities of database programming, such as table normalization and joins, will confront the programmer who must implement a more sophisticated database. If you will carry out extensive database programming, you should plan on further research and experimentation. The tips offered here, like all the tips in the book, should be considered suggestions. In all areas of performance—but particularly database programming—it is difficult to provide iron-clad guidelines that are applicable in every situation. The best database approach will be very specific to the project at hand. Even performance results such as those presented in this chapter can vary drastically from system to system. Memory, caching, disk speed, network activity, the size of a database, and other factors can all greatly influence database speed, and the sample timings presented might not be duplicated on your system. Therefore, view these samples and guidelines as a starting point rather than an ending point. Always test your own database-optimization alternatives thoroughly to arrive at the best performance-tuning decision.

Database Operations

A sample program is used to carry out tests for a series of data operations. There are four groups of tests carried out: data access object operations, data control operations, DAO objects using

transactions, and DAO objects with refined techniques. Within each group of tests, a database will be populated, modified, and searched, and then deletes will take place to return the default database to its original size. The sample program is built on the database DbTest.mdb, which is on the CD-ROM that comes with this book. One table, tblPatientInfo, is used for the tests to follow. That table is shown in Figure 21.1.

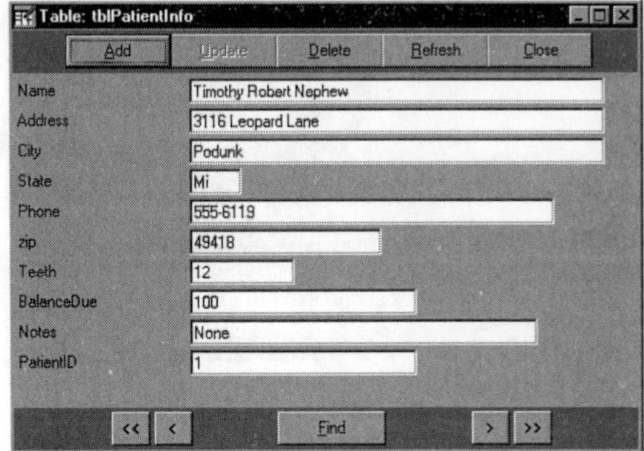

Figure 21.1.
Table layout.

The table has typical information fields, such as name, address, city, state, zip code, and phone. A patient ID field contains patient identification numbers. This is an indexed field, which means that the database indexes information in this field and can take advantage of this index for certain operations such as sorts and retrievals. As this implies, the database layer does more overhead work to manage the index when records are added. However, the benefit comes when records are sorted or retrieved. Refer to the *Visual Basic Programmer's Guide* for more details on indexing.

> **TIP:** Define field indexes if you need to maximize the speed of sorts and searches. This will come at the cost of update speed, as more overhead occurs when records are added to keep the index current.

This table starts out with nine records in it to simulate a pre-existing database. The populate operation will increase the size by adding the number of records you specify. The update function will modify some data on all the newly added records. The search technique will search for certain criteria. And the delete technique will delete all new records except the original nine. The program is shown in Figure 21.2 and is available on the CD-ROM in file Db32.exe. A 16-bit version of this program, Db16.exe, is also available on the CD-ROM.

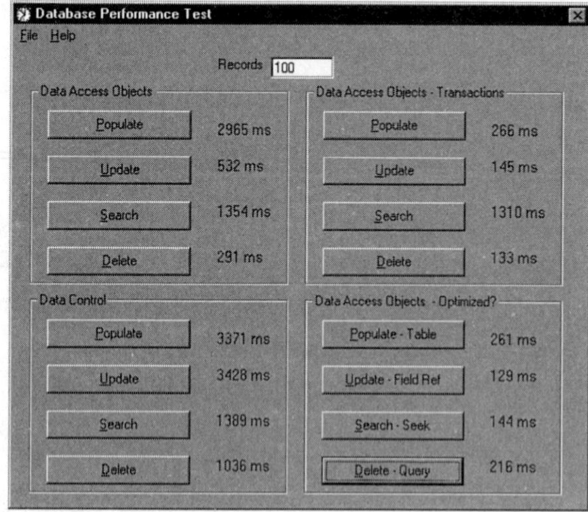

Figure 21.2.
The 32-bit DB test program.

Data Access Object Operations

Data access objects provide a programmatic interface to data in a database through the Jet Engine. The data access object 3.0 library, which can be referenced through the Visual Basic Tools|Reference menu choice, makes use of the highly optimized Jet Engine 3.0. However, this avenue is only open to 32-bit programs. 16-bit programs must use the data access object library 2.5 and Jet Engine 2.5. DAO 2.5 provides similar services to DAO 3.0, but provides them in a 16-bit package. It also does not provide replication support. Some of the syntax supported in DAO 2.5, including that used to create databases and recordsets, is obsolete in DAO 3.0. However, conceptually the approach is the same, and there is a Data Object Library 2.5/3.0 that can be used with 32-bit programs. This reference allows you to use older-style syntax even though the program uses the 3.0 engine.

The 32-bit sample program Db32.exe on the CD-ROM references the data access object 3.0 library to carry out a series of tests. One test populates that database with the number of records specified by the user, another test modifies records, another carries out searches, and another test deletes all records in the database. The code for the test to populate the database is shown in Listing 21.1. This code is carried out when the user selects the command button Populate from the data access object section. Records are initially added into a dynaset or a copy in memory of the data rather than into the table itself. Changes to the dynaset are reflected back into the underlying table. This will be examined in more detail later in the chapter, when an alternative table-based technique is used to carry out the same database population. The Workspace object is used to reference the working set for the data. This syntax is unique to the data access object 3.0 layer, and essentially provides working sessions with data access.

Listing 21.1. A populate operation using a data access object.

```
Private Sub cmdPopulate_Click()

Dim dbCurrent As Database
Dim rsCurrent As Recordset

Call Common_StartTimedTest

Set dbCurrent = DBEngine.Workspaces(0).OpenDatabase(DBName)
' Opened as dynaset so we can contrast with table in another test case
Set rsCurrent = dbCurrent.OpenRecordset("tblPatientInfo", dbOpenDynaset)

For i& = 1 To Val(txtMaxRecords)

    rsCurrent.AddNew
    rsCurrent!Name = "Ms. " & Str(i&)
    rsCurrent!Address = Str(i&) & " Lane "
    rsCurrent!City = "VBLand"
    rsCurrent!State = "Mi"
    rsCurrent!Zip = "48419"
    rsCurrent!Phone = "000000000"
    rsCurrent!Teeth = i& Mod 20
    rsCurrent!BalanceDue = i&
    rsCurrent!PatientID = 20 + i&
    rsCurrent.Update
Next

rsCurrent.Close
dbCurrent.Close

Call Common_EndTimedTest(lblElapsedTime(0))

End Sub
```

After these records are added to the database, another test can modify them. The code for that test is shown in Listing 21.2. This code is carried out when the user selects the command button Update from the data access object section. Notice that field references are in the form of *Field("Name")*. This type of field reference will be contrasted with the *Field!Name* technique in an example later in the chapter.

Listing 21.2. An update operation using a data access object.

```
Private Sub cmdUpdate_Click()
Dim dbCurrent As Database
Dim rsCurrent As Recordset

Call Common_StartTimedTest

Set dbCurrent = DBEngine.Workspaces(0).OpenDatabase(DBName)
Set rsCurrent = dbCurrent.OpenRecordset("tblPatientInfo", dbOpenTable)
```

continues

Listing 21.2. continued

```
Do While Not rsCurrent.EOF

     ' Update non-default patients i
     If rsCurrent!PatientID > 20 Then
        rsCurrent.Edit
        rsCurrent("Teeth") = 15
        rsCurrent("BalanceDue") = 200
        rsCurrent("Notes") = "This patient has been updated now."
        rsCurrent.Update
    End If
    rsCurrent.MoveNext

Loop


rsCurrent.Close
dbCurrent.Close

Call Common_EndTimedTest(lblElapsedTime(1))

End Sub
```

Code that carries out a series of searches for specific records is shown in Listing 21.3. This code is carried out when the user selects the Search command button from the data access object section. Because the search takes place against a predefined set of records, the search is repeated in a loop to extend the duration of the test. This will be contrasted with the use of a table `Seek` method later in the chapter. The dynaset `FindFirst` method is used to navigate the database table.

Listing 21.3. A search operation using a data access object.

```
Private Sub cmdSearch_Click()
Dim dbCurrent As Database
Dim rsCurrent As Recordset
Dim strSearch As String
Dim i%

Call Common_StartTimedTest

Set dbCurrent = DBEngine.Workspaces(0).OpenDatabase(DBName)
Set rsCurrent = dbCurrent.OpenRecordset("tblPatientInfo", dbOpenDynaset)

 ' Carry out looped test to extend duration
For i% = 1 To Val(txtMaxRecords \ 5)


        For j% = 1 To 100 Step 4
            strSearch = "PatientID = " & Str(j%)
            rsCurrent.FindNext strSearch
        Next j%

Next
```

```
rsCurrent.Close
dbCurrent.Close

Call Common_EndTimedTest(lblElapsedTime(2))

End Sub
```

The final routine in this group of tests is one to delete any records that have been added. The code that carries out the deletions is shown in Listing 21.4. This code is carried out when the user selects the Delete command button from the Data Access Object area of the window pictured in Figure 21.2. This code traverses the records in the database, visiting every record with the `MoveNext` method to locate the next record and then carry out the delete. This approach is contrasted with the use of a single `Delete` SQL query later in the chapter.

Listing 21.4. A delete operation using a data access object.

```
Private Sub cmdDelete_Click()

Dim dbCurrent As Database
Dim rsCurrent As Recordset

Call Common_StartTimedTest

Set dbCurrent = DBEngine.Workspaces(0).OpenDatabase(DBName)
Set rsCurrent = dbCurrent.OpenRecordset("tblPatientInfo", dbOpenTable)

Do While Not rsCurrent.EOF

     ' Always leave default patients in db
     If rsCurrent!PatientID > 20 Then
        rsCurrent.Delete
    End If
    rsCurrent.MoveNext

Loop

rsCurrent.Close
dbCurrent.Close

Call Common_EndTimedTest(lblElapsedTime(3))

End Sub
```

OLE Data Controls

The next series of tests comprise the same populate, update, search, and delete operations on the same table, but this time an OLE data control is used to access the data. The data control is provided on the main form in the program and is named Data1. The data control database name is assigned in the `Form_Load` event by updating the data controls `DatabaseName` property with the appropriate location.

The use of the data control eliminates the need for the data access object declarations and database-initialization steps that were required for the data access object tests. In one sense, the way these tests are structured is not a direct comparison of equivalent techniques. This is because the data access object test timings include the time on each test to initialize the database and recordset. With the data control, this price is paid just once, at form load, and is not reflected in the timings for a test. However, the data access object initializations are included in every test for the sake of clarity because the skew introduced with the small database is minimal. This also simulates how these two alternative approaches might be used in actual programs. A data control is likely to serve as a global object reference. An approach based on data access objects is more likely to have repeated creations of recordsets as needed. The data access object tests could be modified to open the database once at form load and to close the database once at form unload in order to provide a more equivalent test. This is presented as a Workshop exercise at the end of the chapter.

The code to populate the database using the data control is shown in Listing 21.5. This code is carried out when the user clicks on the Populate button in the Data Control group of command buttons.

Listing 21.5. A populate operation using a data control.

```
Private Sub cmdDCPop_Click()

Call Common_StartTimedTest

For i& = 1 To Val(txtMaxRecords)

    Data1.Recordset.AddNew
    Data1.Recordset!Name = "Ms. " & Str(i&)
    Data1.Recordset!Address = Str(i&) & " Lane "
    Data1.Recordset!City = "VBLand"
    Data1.Recordset!State = "Mi"
    Data1.Recordset!Zip = "48419"
    Data1.Recordset!Phone = "000000000"
    Data1.Recordset!Teeth = i& Mod 20
    Data1.Recordset!BalanceDue = i&
    Data1.Recordset!PatientID = 20 + i&
    Data1.Recordset.Update
Next

Call Common_EndTimedTest(lblElapsedTime(5))


End Sub
```

Listing 21.6 shows the code to carry out updates using the data control. This code is carried out when the user clicks on the Update button in the Data Control group of command buttons. The code is similar to the data access object technique except that references are made using the data control instead of object declarations.

Listing 21.6. An update operation using a data control.

```
Private Sub cmdDCUp_Click()

On Error GoTo cmdDCUp_Err

Call Common_StartTimedTest

' Must start at beginning of set
Data1.Recordset.MoveFirst


Do While Not Data1.Recordset.EOF

     ' Update non-default patients
     If Data1.Recordset!PatientID > 20 Then
        Data1.Recordset.Edit
        Data1.Recordset("Teeth") = 15
        Data1.Recordset("BalanceDue") = 200
        Data1.Recordset("Notes") = "This patient has been updated now."
        Data1.Recordset.Update
    End If
    Data1.Recordset.MoveNext

Loop


Call Common_EndTimedTest(lblElapsedTime(6))

Exit Sub

cmdDCUp_Err:

Call Common_EndTimedTest(lblElapsedTime(6))

If Err = 3167 Then
    ' Normal err indicating deleted record placeholder was encountered
    Resume Next
Else
    MsgBox "Error: " & Error$, , "Unexpected Database Problem"
    Exit Sub
End If

End Sub
```

Listing 21.7 shows the code to carry out the searches using the data control. This code is carried out when the user clicks on the Search button in the Data Control group of command buttons. Once again, the code is similar to that in the data access object technique except that references are made using the data control instead of object declarations. The data control recordset supports the same `FindNext` method that was used with the object recordset.

Listing 21.7. A search operation using a data control.

```
Private Sub cmdDCSearch_Click()
Dim strSearch As String
Dim i%

Call Common_StartTimedTest

' Start at beginning of set
Data1.Recordset.MoveFirst

For i% = 1 To Val(txtMaxRecords / 5)

        For j% = 1 To 100 Step 4
            strSearch = "PatientID = " & Str(j%)
            Data1.Recordset.FindNext strSearch
        Next j%


Next

Call Common_EndTimedTest(lblElapsedTime(7))

End Sub
```

Listing 21.8 shows the code to carry out the deletes using the data control. This code is carried out when the user clicks on the Delete button in the Data Control group of command buttons. Just like the data access object test case, this test case uses the `Delete` method to delete each record. Like the original test, this test must move to each record with the `MoveNext` method to carry out the delete operation.

Listing 21.8. A delete operation using a data control.

```
Private Sub cmdDCDel_Click()


Call Common_StartTimedTest

Data1.Recordset.MoveFirst

Do While Not Data1.Recordset.EOF

     ' Always leave default patients in db
     If Data1.Recordset!PatientID > 20 Then
        Data1.Recordset.Delete
    End If
    Data1.Recordset.MoveNext
```

```
Loop

Call Common_EndTimedTest(lblElapsedTime(8))

End Sub
```

As the representative timings in Figure 21.2 show, the data control is slower than the same tests using data access objects. Update and delete operations were significantly slower.

> **NOTE:** A detailed comparison of all the database techniques addressed is provided later in this chapter in the "Results" section. Full normalized results appear there in Table 21.1.

Data Access Objects Versus Data Controls

The data access objects offer clear advantages over the data control. However, the data control enables fast and convenient programming. A data control can be used with other "bound" controls to automatically fill controls with database values. This data control does offer much better performance than the data control of Visual Basic 3.0 and Jet Engine 2.0. The difference in timings in Figure 21.2 is the result of repeated loops of testing. A specific application's performance penalty may not be this large, or it may be larger, depending on the application. If performance penalties are within the range of 20–30 milliseconds per user operation, this is a penalty you may be willing to pay in exchange for the programming convenience of the control. The data control approach is likely to be fully adequate in many situations. If you are doing extensive database operations, then you might gain your user a second or more for some operations if you use the data access objects. Once again, the performance testing has highlighted a situation where the programmer can achieve faster performance at the cost of more coding effort.

> **TIP:** Use data access objects rather than the OLE data control for faster performance when you are willing to sacrifice the data control's convenience.

Data Access Objects Using Transactions

The next series of tests repeats the original tests involving data access objects, with one key difference. The next tests use methods from the workspace for the database session to provide transaction control. The `BeginTrans` method tells DAO we are in the process of a series of transactions and not to "commit" or save the results until we are through that series. When we get

to the end of that series, we can use the `CommitTrans` method to cause the saves to take place. Alternatively, we could have used the `RollBack` method to cancel any saves from that series. Without transactions, saves and the corresponding database-management overhead would take place on every statement. Our original DAO tests used no transactions and paid this overhead price. Here we use transactions to avoid that penalty.

Listing 21.9 shows the modified code to populate the database. It uses the transaction statements to treat the addition of all the new records as one transaction. This code will be carried out when the Populate button is selected from the Data Access Objects–Transactions group of buttons.

Listing 21.9. A populate operation using a transaction.

```
Private Sub cmdPopTrans_Click()
Dim dbCurrent As Database
Dim rsCurrent As Recordset
Dim wsCurrent As Workspace

Call Common_StartTimedTest

Set wsCurrent = DBEngine.Workspaces(0)
Set dbCurrent = wsCurrent.OpenDatabase(DBName)
Set rsCurrent = dbCurrent.OpenRecordset("tblPatientInfo", dbOpenDynaset)

' Start the transaction
wsCurrent.BeginTrans

For i& = 1 To Val(txtMaxRecords)

    rsCurrent.AddNew
    rsCurrent!Name = "Ms. " & Str(i&)
    rsCurrent!Address = Str(i&) & " Lane "
    rsCurrent!City = "VBLand"
    rsCurrent!State = "Mi"
    rsCurrent!Zip = "48419"
    rsCurrent!Phone = "000000000"
    rsCurrent!Teeth = i& Mod 20
    rsCurrent!BalanceDue = i&
    rsCurrent!PatientID = 20 + i&
    rsCurrent.Update
Next

' End the transaction
wsCurrent.CommitTrans


rsCurrent.Close
dbCurrent.Close


Call Common_EndTimedTest(lblElapsedTime(9))


End Sub
```

The same transaction approach is used to instruct the DAO to treat all of the updates as one transaction. Listing 21.10 shows the modified code to update the database. This code will be carried out when the Update button is selected from the Data Access Objects–Transactions group of buttons.

Listing 21.10. An update operation using a transaction.

```
Private Sub cmdUpTrans_Click()

Dim dbCurrent As Database
Dim rsCurrent As Recordset
Dim wsCurrent As Workspace

Call Common_StartTimedTest

Set wsCurrent = DBEngine.Workspaces(0)
Set dbCurrent = wsCurrent.OpenDatabase(DBName)
Set rsCurrent = dbCurrent.OpenRecordset("tblPatientInfo", dbOpenTable)

' Start the transaction
wsCurrent.BeginTrans

Do While Not rsCurrent.EOF

     ' Update non-default patients i
     If rsCurrent!PatientID > 20 Then
        rsCurrent.Edit
        rsCurrent("Teeth") = 15
        rsCurrent("BalanceDue") = 200
        rsCurrent("Notes") = "This patient has been updated now."
        rsCurrent.Update
    End If
    rsCurrent.MoveNext

Loop

' End the transaction
wsCurrent.CommitTrans


rsCurrent.Close
dbCurrent.Close



Call Common_EndTimedTest(lblElapsedTime(10))

End Sub
```

This transaction approach is again used around the search operations. A transaction isn't as relevant to a search operation, since no updates take place and thus there is little benefit to deferring saves. Nevertheless, transaction statements are used so we have a complete set of comparison results for every test. Listing 21.11 shows the modified code. This code will be carried out when the Search button is selected from the Data Access Objects–Transactions group of buttons.

Listing 21.11. A search operation using a transaction.

```
Private Sub cmdSearchTrans_Click()

Dim dbCurrent As Database
Dim rsCurrent As Recordset
Dim wsCurrent As Workspace
Dim strSearch As String

Call Common_StartTimedTest
' Open the db as readonly to improve access
Set wsCurrent = DBEngine.Workspaces(0)
Set dbCurrent = wsCurrent.OpenDatabase(DBName, True, True)
Set rsCurrent = dbCurrent.OpenRecordset("tblPatientInfo", dbOpenDynaset)

' Start the transaction
wsCurrent.BeginTrans


For i% = 1 To Val(txtMaxRecords / 5)

        For j% = 1 To 100 Step 4
            strSearch = "PatientID = " & Str(j%)
            rsCurrent.FindNext strSearch
        Next j%

Next


' End the transaction
wsCurrent.CommitTrans


rsCurrent.Close
dbCurrent.Close


Call Common_EndTimedTest(lblElapsedTime(11))

End Sub
```

The transaction approach is also used for the delete operation. All deletes are treated as one transaction. Listing 21.12 shows the modified code. This code will be carried out when the Delete button is selected from the Data Access Objects–Transactions group of buttons.

Listing 21.12. A delete operation using a transaction.

```
Private Sub cmdDelTrans_Click()

Dim dbCurrent As Database
Dim rsCurrent As Recordset
Dim wsCurrent As Workspace

Call Common_StartTimedTest

Set wsCurrent = DBEngine.Workspaces(0)
Set dbCurrent = wsCurrent.OpenDatabase(DBName)
Set rsCurrent = dbCurrent.OpenRecordset("tblPatientInfo", dbOpenTable)

' Start the transaction
wsCurrent.BeginTrans


Do While Not rsCurrent.EOF

     ' Always leave default patients in db
     If rsCurrent!PatientID > 20 Then
        rsCurrent.Delete
    End If
    rsCurrent.MoveNext

Loop

' End transaction
wsCurrent.CommitTrans


rsCurrent.Close
dbCurrent.Close


Call Common_EndTimedTest(lblElapsedTime(12))


End Sub
```

As the representative timings in Figure 21.2 show, transactions offer very significant performance improvement when used to group operations that update the database. In addition to this type of code triggered transaction processing, a certain level of automatic transaction handling takes place as well. DAO 3.0 and Jet Engine 3.0 provide transaction support that occurs automatically even if transaction statements do not appear in your source code for certain sequences of operations. However, as the sample program showed, even with this built-in automatic level of transaction support, there is still additional benefit to applying transactions to the areas of your choice. Transactions offer a degree of speedup that for many applications will certainly be perceived by the end user. This is also a relatively easy technique to use. However, it does require additional code statements. Likewise, a good transaction management strategy should include use of rollback methods to cancel transactions that are aborted, and careful thought should be given to how big of a series of statements to wrap up in a transaction. Transactions essentially defer database saves and temporarily cache results in memory rather than write to disk. Therefore, transactions consume memory, and large transactions can consume considerable memory. So this is an area that offers big payback to programs, but as usual, comes with the price tag of at least some additional programmer coding effort. Still, the potential benefits are so great that the use of transactions is generally recommended. For most programs, it will be well worth the effort of using transactions.

> **TIP:** You can use database transactions to significantly enhance performance in database operations.

Data Access Objects with Optimized Techniques

The final group of tests again repeats the original data access object tests, with minor changes. This group of tests is structured to demonstrate a variety of additional database optimization techniques. In order that comparisons can be made against a common frame of reference, the tests are based on the original no-transaction DAO approach. Then, for each test, a different optimization step is carried out. This potpourri of techniques is somewhat unrelated, so each is addressed individually.

The first optimization technique is to simply populate the database using a table rather than the dynaset of the original DAO test. This test will be carried out when the button labeled Populate–Table is selected from the Data Access Objects–Optimized? group of buttons. The modified listing appears in Listing 21.13. The table approach turned out to be significantly faster. If you compare the results of the populate operation for Data Access Objects and for Data Access Objects–Optimized? in Figure 21.2 you will see that the record creations occurred in less than 1/10 the time of the original method. For most simple operations, tables can offer significantly faster performance than dynasets and snapshots. This advantage is not present for more complex operations, such as sorts, filters, and joins.

> **TIP:** For simple operations (operations other than sorts, filters, and joins) use tables instead of dynaset or snapshot recordset objects to significantly enhance performance.

Listing 21.13. A populate operation using a table.

```
Private Sub cmdPopEl_Click()

Dim dbCurrent As Database
Dim rsCurrent As Recordset

Call Common_StartTimedTest

Set dbCurrent = DBEngine.Workspaces(0).OpenDatabase(DBName)
Set rsCurrent = dbCurrent.OpenRecordset("tblPatientInfo", dbOpenTable)

For i& = 1 To Val(txtMaxRecords)

    rsCurrent.AddNew
    rsCurrent!Name = "Ms. " & Str(i&)
    rsCurrent!Address = Str(i&) & " Lane "
    rsCurrent!City = "VBLand"
    rsCurrent!State = "Mi"
    rsCurrent!Zip = "48419"
    rsCurrent!Phone = "000000000"
    rsCurrent!Teeth = i& Mod 20
    rsCurrent!BalanceDue = i&
    rsCurrent!PatientID = 20 + i&
    rsCurrent.Update
Next

rsCurrent.Close
dbCurrent.Close

Call Common_EndTimedTest(lblElapsedTime(13))


End Sub
```

The next test is a comparison of update field reference methods. This test will be carried out when the button labeled Update–Field Ref is selected from the Data Access Objects–Optimized? group of buttons. This test, shown in Listing 21.14, uses explicit field reference with the `!` (exclamation point) operator. This is in contrast to the first DAO test, which used the field name delimited in quotations nested in parentheses. That prior method of referencing a field was *`recordset("FIELDNAME")`*, while the method used for this test is *`recordset!FIELDNAME`*. The results in Figure 21.2 show that the `!` reference method is significantly faster. The other method took more than four times as long. Because there is little program-maintenance advantage to the other method, routine use of the `!` operator appears to be warranted.

> **TIP:** For significantly faster performance, use the exclamation operator in the format *`recordset!FIELDNAME`* rather than the parentheses operator in the format *`recordset("FIELDNAME")`* to reference recordset field names.

Listing 21.14. An update operation using ! field references.

```
Private Sub cmdUpEl_Click()
Dim dbCurrent As Database
Dim rsCurrent As Recordset

Call Common_StartTimedTest

Set dbCurrent = DBEngine.Workspaces(0).OpenDatabase(DBName)
Set rsCurrent = dbCurrent.OpenRecordset("tblPatientInfo", dbOpenTable)

Do While Not rsCurrent.EOF

     ' Update non-default patients i
     If rsCurrent!PatientID > 20 Then
        rsCurrent.Edit
        rsCurrent!Teeth = 15
        rsCurrent!BalanceDue = 200
        rsCurrent!Notes = "This patient has been updated now."
        rsCurrent.Update
    End If
    rsCurrent.MoveNext

Loop


rsCurrent.Close
dbCurrent.Close

Call Common_EndTimedTest(lblElapsedTime(14))

End Sub
```

The next test is a comparison of search methods. This test will be carried out when the button labeled Search–Seek is selected from the Data Access Objects–Optimized? group of buttons. This test, shown in Listing 21.15, uses the `Seek` method to search for search targets. `Seek` is a method that can only be used on tables. Therefore, the database recordset had to be created as a table rather than a dynaset for this test. By contrast, the first DAO test used a dynaset and the `FindNext` method for searches. In other respects the tests are identical.

Listing 21.15. A search operation using `Seek`.

```
Private Sub cmdSearchEl_Click()

Dim dbCurrent As Database
Dim rsCurrent As Recordset
Dim i%, j%

Call Common_StartTimedTest

Set dbCurrent = DBEngine.Workspaces(0).OpenDatabase(DBName)
Set rsCurrent = dbCurrent.OpenRecordset("tblPatientInfo", dbOpenTable)
```

```
For i% = 1 To Val(txtMaxRecords \ 5)

        ' Set the index to use in the seek
        rsCurrent.Index = "IDIndex"

        For j% = 1 To 100 Step 4

            ' This string assignment is left in so this will be a "fair" comparison
            '    to other tests which had to set up string.
            strSearch = "PatientID = " & Str(j%)
            rsCurrent.Seek "=", j%
        Next j%

Next

rsCurrent.Close
dbCurrent.Close

Call Common_EndTimedTest(lblElapsedTime(15))

End Sub
```

The `Seek` method must be used in conjunction with a field that has been defined in the database to be an index field. An index field is a field for which the database maintains special information, for optimal lookup of records based on the contents of that field. Because multiple indexes can exist, you must specify which is to be used with `Seek`. You do this by setting the recordset's `Index` property with the name of the indexed field. Then the `Seek` method will seek against that field. You supply the condition and value to `Seek` when it is used. For example, this:

```
recordset.Seek "=", 5
```

would carry out a search for the next occurrence of the numeral 5 in the field indicated by `recordset.Index`.

Results in Figure 21.2 show that `Seek` takes approximately 1/10 the time of the original DAO test. This is an expected result, because we know that `Seek` is using the optimized index method of lookup.

> **TIP:** Use the table `Seek` method for the fastest search time. This approach is significantly faster than the recordset `FindNext` and `FindPrevious` methods.

The final test is a comparison of deletions. This test will be carried out when the button labeled Delete—Query is selected from the Data Access Objects–Optimized? group of buttons. This test, shown in Listing 21.16, uses a `DELETE` query to delete records from the database. By contrast, the original DAO test visited every record and used a delete method on each record.

An SQL DELETE query lets us give instructions for this delete in one statement to Jet, rather than having to repeatedly request a delete for each record.

To carry out the DELETE query, we must define a query object and assign our deletion string to it. Queries can be added permanently to the database for easy future reference if we define a query name in the first parameter of the CreateQueryDef method. In the case of this test, we simply need a temporary query, so we supply no name in the first parameter. The second parameter is used to specify our SQL string. Our use of SQL here is really using a language within a language. SQL (Structured Query Language) represents instructions that will be passed on to the database for processing rather than acted on directly by the Visual Basic interpreter. After creating our temporary query definition, we can execute it with the Execute method for carrying out queries.

Listing 21.16. A delete operation using a query.

```
Private Sub cmdDelEl_Click()


Dim dbCurrent As Database
Dim qryCurrent As QueryDef

Call Common_StartTimedTest

Set dbCurrent = DBEngine.Workspaces(0).OpenDatabase(DBName)
Set qryCurrent = dbCurrent.CreateQueryDef
   ➥("", "DELETE * FROM tblPatientInfo WHERE PatientID > 20")

qryCurrent.Execute

qryCurrent.Close
dbCurrent.Close

Call Common_EndTimedTest(lblElapsedTime(16))


End Sub
```

The results in Figure 21.2 show that the DELETE query performs faster than the individual-record deletion approach. The difference is relatively slight here. However, if you experiment with the program and repeat the tests with more records specified, you will find that the advantage of the DELETE query increases as the program deals with larger record sizes.

Just as DELETE queries provide performance advantages, so do UPDATE queries. UPDATE queries work in much the same manner to update all records fitting a specified criteria. Refer to the *Visual Basic Professional Features* book for further details.

> **TIP:** DELETE and UPDATE queries can offer performance advantages over traversing a recordset and individually updating or deleting records.

A query that is given a name can even be compiled into an intermediate format for optimal processing at runtime. Then the text string representing the SQL does not have to be processed, but a quicker intermediate format can be acted upon by the database engine. According to the Visual Basic documentation, such compilation will take place if you run the query in the Visual Basic development environment before generating the EXE file.

> **TIP:** Be sure to run any code that uses a named SQL query from within the Visual Basic environment before making your executable. This causes the SQL text string to be "compiled" into an optimal format for fastest processing at runtime.

You can also define queries directly in your database. This requires the database product to go into database-design mode. Alternatively, you can write a Visual Basic program to carry out this query storage. Then you can save the queries directly to the database with your query saving program. This allows you to refer to queries by name from programs you run from then on, instead of supplying the SQL query text. This offers some administrative advantages, because queries are then defined and maintained in your database. From another perspective, the Visual Basic source code then embodies less information, and part of the virtual program "logic" is shifted to the database, so maintenance could be viewed as more difficult. Considerations of the pros and cons of program maintenance on this issue are subjective, depending on whether your view of the world is database administrator-centric or application programmer-centric. However, there are clear performance advantages to having the SQL query pre-stored in the database, regardless of your philosophy on the administration issue.

> **TIP:** Define stored queries directly in the database for faster performance. Programs can then reference the stored queries instead of supplying them dynamically.

In general, anyone who is doing significant database programming can benefit greatly from a thorough understanding of the database-oriented SQL language. If you know how to use SQL effectively, you can often use a simple step to carry out what you might otherwise have to implement with a great deal of code.

> **TIP:** Learn SQL if you do a lot of database programming. There are many advanced SQL techniques that can be used in conjunction with Visual Basic database operations to eliminate much of the code that would be required if you did things "the brute force" way. This in turn can lead to faster performance.

Results

Table 21.1 is a summary of normalized results for the populate, update, search, and close operations for each of the four groups of tests. The results shown in Figure 21.2 are representative timings from a series of tests that were carried out. Keep in mind that results (including the relative order of results) may differ significantly when carried out on your own system, depending on your system memory, disk controller, system activity, and other factors.

Table 21.1. Normalized results.

Data Control	*DAO with Transactions*	*OCX with Optimization*	*DAO Regular*	*DAO Special*
Population	23.0 (dynaset)	26.1	2.1 (dynaset)	2.0 (table)
Update	4.1 `rs("field")`	26.6 `rs("field")`	1.1	1.0 `rs!field`
Search	10.5 `FindNext`	10.8 `FindNext`	10.2 `FindNext`	1.1 `Seek`
Delete	2.3 per record	8.0 per record	1.0 per record	1.7 with query

Several important assumptions can be made from these results. Faster performance can generally be achieved by using the data access objects rather than the OLE data control. The data control provides great convenience in programming, eliminating the need for data object declarations. However, this convenience does come at a price. The use of transactions offers performance speed-ups over the equivalent DAO approach without transactions. This technique also requires more lines of code and more thought on the part of the programmer regarding how many statements a transaction should be wrapped around.

The performance value of specific individual optimization techniques is also evident in this table. These techniques have already been discussed in the chapter and include approaches such as using tables instead of dynasets, referencing field names with the explicit `!` reference indicator, using seeks on indexes, and carrying out queries rather than individual operations

Comparison of Database Speed in 16-Bit and 32-Bit Programs

The same series of tests carried out with Db32.exe was also carried out with a 16-bit version of that program. The 16-bit version is named Db16.exe and is also available on the CD-ROM that comes with this book. This program uses the same source code as the 32-bit version,

except that it makes use of a different database. That is carried out at form-load time, as shown in Listing 21.17.

Listing 21.17. A form-load operation to use the appropriate database.

```
Private Sub Form_Load()
    Common_CenterForm Me

#If Win32 Then
     ' 32-bit can use Jet Engine 3.0
     DBName = App.Path & "\DBTest.mdb"
#Else
     DBName = App.Path & "\DBTest16.mdb"
#End If

    ' Set data control location
    Data1.DatabaseName = DBName

End Sub
```

The 16-bit version is different not only in that it requires the 16-bit Visual Basic interpreter, but also in that a 16-bit program cannot use the DAO 3.0 library that provides access to the 32-bit Jet Engine 3.0 functions. Rather, it must use DAO 2.5 and the Jet Engine 2.5. According to Visual Basic documentation, DAO and Jet Engine 2.5 support nearly all the functionality of Jet 3.0, except an area called replication. However, function aside, a 16-bit program inevitably entails different performance behavior as well, as discussed earlier in this book. The results from DB16.exe appear in the program window shown in Figure 21.3. The normalized results are shown in Table 21.2. The comparable Db32.exe ratios are indicated in the table by square brackets directly below the corresponding Db16.exe times.

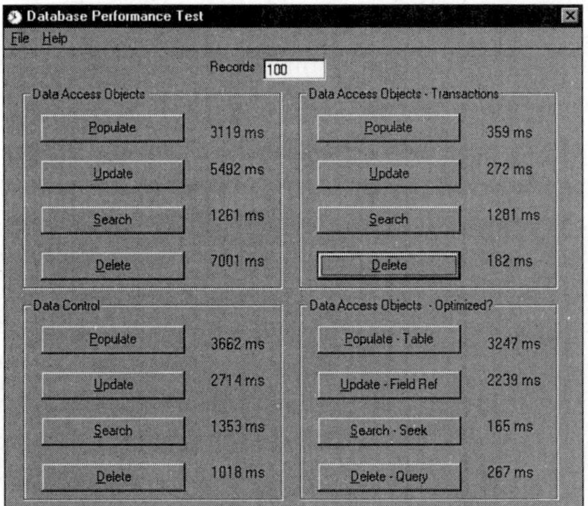

Figure 21.3.
The 16-bit DB test program.

Table 21.2. Normalized results for Db16.exe; Db32.exe times are in [].

Data Control	*DAO with Transactions*	*OCX with Optimization*	*DAO Regular*	*DAO Special*
		Population		
16-Bit	24.1	28.4	2.8	25.1
32-Bit	[23.0]	[26.1]	[2.1]	[2.0]
Notes	(dynaset)		(dynaset)	(table)
		Update		
16-Bit	42.6	21.0	2.1	17.4
32-Bit	[4.1]	[26.6]	[1.1]	[1.0]
Notes	`rs("field")`		`rs("field")`	`rs!field`
		Search		
16-Bit	9.8	10.5	9.9	1.3
32-Bit	[10.5]	[10.8]	[10.2]	[1.1]
Notes	`FindNext`	`FindNext`	`FindNext`	`Seek`
		Delete		
16-Bit	54.3	7.9	1.4	2.1
32-Bit	[2.3]	[8.0]	[1.0]	[1.7]
Notes	per record	per record	per record	with query

A comparison of the 16- and 32-bit results makes it clear that the 32-bit approach and Jet Engine 3.0 offer clear performance advantages. The 16-bit program is significantly slower in several areas, including DAO updates and deletes. One of the greatest areas of difference is in using data access objects. Many optimizations are implemented in DAO 3.0 and Jet Engine 3.0 that help to account for faster performance, including automatic transaction handling in cases such as update operations.

The speed of searches shows little improvement between the 16-bit and 32-bit versions. After factoring out system variability, the numbers are virtually identical. This is likely an indicator that search operations within the Jet Engine were already a highly optimized operation, and there was not as much room for improvement during recent evolution. Keep in mind that we have considered just a minuscule subset of database operations in our test. There are many other areas as well that would show significant performance improvement for the 32-bit DAO 3.0 alternative. Therefore, improved speed of data access is yet another reason to encourage you to produce applications directly targeted for the 32-bit environment. If you have a legacy of 16-bit users you must continue to support, they will not be receiving the maximum performance available from today's technology.

TIP: 32-bit programs with Data Access Object 3.0 and Jet Engine 3.0 will have significantly better performance than 16-bit programs that must use older versions of database software.

Summary

This chapter examines performance issues surrounding many aspects of database performance. A sample program highlights the advantages of various database techniques. Data access objects are faster than the data control OCX, although the data control does provide convenient programming. The use of transactions considerably improves performance. Likewise, tables are faster than dynasets in the sample application, and generally they offer better performance than snapshots and dynasets. The exclamation-point reference (!) is much faster than the parentheses format when referring to field names. Finally, the use of queries is discussed. Using a delete query is faster than deleting each record from a set individually. Update queries can be used to the same effect. Queries can be predefined as stored queries in the database for optimal performance. Any programmer doing extensive database programming should learn all the intricacies of SQL, for a single SQL statement with a query can often replace many "brute force" lines of code.

This chapter also discusses 16-bit database performance issues. The same program used for the 32-bit tests is used with the 16-bit tests. However, it has to use DAO 2.5 and Jet Engine 2.5 instead of DAO 3.0/Jet Engine 3.0, because those are not available to 16-bit applications. The 32-bit programs are measurably faster, more so for some cases, such as updates, than for other cases, such as searches.

Database performance is often very intangible. Rules that apply to one situation will not apply to another, because application needs can vary greatly. Research findings that you experience in the morning may not hold true in the afternoon, because the system environment, including database size, memory, network load, and other factors, can vary greatly. The best rule is to trust nothing, test everything, and test again. You often will not find one clear answer, but you might gradually build an intricate and intuitive understanding of performance considerations that will serve you well in future development and optimization. That is the best way to ensure that you are correctly assessing the needs of you own application and environment.

TIP: The golden rule of performance testing: Trust nothing, test everything, and test again! Rarely does one set of results apply to every situation.

Obey the Signs

Beware of Falling Rocks: Don't decide to leave data controls behind and change an existing program to use the normally faster data access objects overnight.

Such a change is technically feasible, but it can involve much more work than appears on the surface. If you use many bound controls, it can take a great deal of code to remove the data control and bound controls. Code must be generated to take the place of the automatic data-update functionality served by every bound control. Painful ripple-effect-changes (accompanied by comments such as "Oops, I didn't realize that code would get broken when the bound control behavior was eliminated") are very common in such conversion activity. In many cases, the convenience of bound controls will outweigh the performance advantages of non-bound controls. In other cases, if you do plan to convert a program, allocate plenty of time. Likewise, design and map out your conversion strategy before diving in to make the changes.

Wrong Way: Transactions seem so cool that I'll put a `recordset.BeginTrans` *in my main program* `Form_Load` *and a* `recordset.CommitTrans` *in my* `Form_Unload` *and just treat everything as one big transaction.*

This is generally a bad idea. This would be a very dangerous practice. Transactions are not written to the database until a commit, so buffering large amounts of database operations provides a correspondingly high risk of data loss. If the PC is shut down or loses power, any changes that are not committed will be lost. In addition, this is not a technically feasible approach. Transactions that have not yet been committed require memory, and this approach could require large amounts of memory, depending on the database activity. Transactions should generally be targeted for much smaller periods of activity, such as an `Edit...Update` sequence.

Q&A

Q Can I use the `Seek` method with dynasets?

A No, the `Seek` method is only available with table objects.

Q Is there a way to change every value in the field of a database all at once without having to traverse every field, much like I can change every occurrence of a word in a word processor?

A Yes, the `UPDATE` query will allow you to do that. It works much like the `DELETE` query discussed in this chapter in that you can specify a SQL string. The string can indicate the fields to be replaced with a new value. Refer to `UPDATE` in the Visual Basic help file for further information.

Workshop

1. The use of the data control eliminates the need for the data access object declarations and database initialization steps that were required for the data access object tests. However, in one sense, the way those tests are structured is not a direct comparison of equivalent techniques. This is because our data access object test timings include the time to initialize the database and recordset. With the data control, this price is paid just once, at form load, and is not encompassed in the timings for a test. Modify the test programs so that the data access object initialization is carried out just once at program startup, and close the recordset and database just once at program termination. Does any speedup of tests result? (The difference will normally be quite small.)
2. Write a test to measure how much combined time the database and recordset initialization take. Is the amount of time required large enough to be perceptible to a user?

Moving Code to DLLs

The primary objective of this chapter is to discuss when and how to move code to a DLL. Often, critics of the performance level of Visual Basic simply say, "Well, just move it to a DLL." Even though there are times when moving code to a DLL is necessary, this chapter points out that it is not always appropriate or necessary to give up on Visual Basic and do so. When it is necessary, however, you need to understand the process required to do so and the ramifications of the results.

This chapter begins by discussing the reasons for both transferring functionality from Visual Basic to a DLL and for originating functionality in a DLL. Building upon this foundation, the chapter proceeds to address the mechanics of declaring a DLL procedure in Visual Basic and the appropriate ways parameters are passed between Visual Basic and DLL procedures. The chapter then presents a case study that takes existing functionality in a Visual Basic application and moves it into DLLs created by Visual C++, 16-bit Delphi, and both 16-bit and 32-bit Visual C++. The results of each test case are presented and compared both in terms of performance as well as the relative ease of constructing the DLLs and the mechanics involved.

After you read this chapter, you should have a much better understanding of how and why you might consider moving functionality to a DLL. You will also better understand the process you must go through in order to create a DLL. Throughout the discussion, however, you will be reminded of the alternatives that are possible *within* the Visual Basic environment before resorting to the DLL approach.

When to Consider Moving Code to a DLL

This first section describes the various circumstances and conditions under which it may be appropriate to move Visual Basic code to a DLL. The conditions are somewhat general, and specific circumstances depend on the functionality under consideration and the application that functionality is being applied in.

The Code Does Not Execute Fast Enough in Visual Basic

Often, a programmer wants to accomplish a task that Visual Basic cannot accomplish within a reasonable amount of time. In such cases, it is sometimes useful to pull out the code that is causing the performance bottleneck and place it into a DLL. That DLL, which is written in a different language, presumably will provide the functionality much faster, thereby reducing or eliminating the performance problem.

This book has examined techniques and strategies to avoid or eliminate performance problems. Still, it is realistic to concede that there may be circumstances where Visual Basic simply cannot meet performance expectations. Of course, your expectations may be too high and *no* language may be able to meet them, but it is possible that C/C++ or some other compiled language could be used to break the performance bottleneck. This is, in fact, one of the benefits of C/C++.

The Functionality Cannot Be Accomplished Using Visual Basic

It is also common to create procedures in DLLs and OLE controls that accomplish functionality that either *cannot* or cannot *easily* be accomplished in Visual Basic. This, in fact, is the reason for the huge third-party custom-control market that has arisen since the inception of Visual Basic. An OLE control, which is similar in some respects to a DLL, provides an OLE container to the Visual Basic programmer with a consistent set of functionality for ease of integration into the Visual Basic environment. Whether they be OLE controls or DLLs, these components are widely used by almost all Visual Basic programmers. While some may consider this a weakness of Visual Basic, it can actually be considered one of its biggest strengths. No language can do everything, but not all languages can enable the programmer to link functionality from *other* languages like Visual Basic can. The task under consideration here is not moving code from Visual Basic to a DLL because of a performance problem, but rather to implement functionality that is not possible to implement in Visual Basic.

The Code Is Reusable and Is to Be Shared Among Various Languages

A third condition under which using a DLL may be appropriate is when the programmer wishes to develop a component that will be used not only in Visual Basic, but among other languages as well. A programmer may, for example, develop a set of functions that perform a specific set of mathematical operations. If there are several programs that could use these functions, and those programs are all written using different languages (such as Visual Basic, Delphi, and C++), a common interface must be made available to them all. In such a case, the easiest approach is to create a DLL that allows all applications to call the DLL functions, regardless of who calls them. While one solution is to use OLE Automation to create an OLE automation server DLL in Visual Basic, it is often desirable to provide a simple set of functions in a DLL that does not use OLE technology, since the ability to exploit OLE technology may not be convenient or practical in some situations. Likewise, OLE Automation is generally slower than direct DLL calls, as discussed in Chapter 25, "OLE Automation Servers."

Interfacing a DLL to Visual Basic

You have seen that there are certain conditions under which it may be appropriate to create procedures within DLLs and to call those procedures from Visual Basic. It is important, therefore, to understand how a Visual Basic application interfaces with a DLL and to understand the performance ramifications of doing so.

How to Declare a DLL Procedure Inside Visual Basic

To Visual Basic, a DLL is simply a collection of procedures that can be called. The structure of the DLL allows Visual Basic applications to specify a procedure by name, after which the DLL makes sure the correct procedure is called and executed. All that the programmer has to do in Visual Basic is to let Visual Basic know where the procedure is, what its name is, what parameters to pass to it, and what (if any) values are returned by the procedure. This information is given to Visual Basic in the form of a *declaration* statement for the DLL. The declaration for a subroutine, which has no return value, can take the following form:

```
Private¦Public Declare Sub subname Lib libname (argument list)
```

where `Private¦Public` designates whether the procedure is available to the module it is declared in or to all the modules in the application, *`subname`* is the name of the DLL subroutine, and *`libname`* is the name of the DLL. If, for example, you had a subroutine called `UpdateDatabase` and this subroutine was contained in the DLL called DBCALLS.DLL, the declaration statement may look like this:

```
Declare Sub "UpdateDatabase" Lib "DBCALLS.DLL" (ByVal svdbName as String)
```

In the case of a function, the declaration is slightly different, because a function returns a value. In such a case, the declaration would take the form

```
Declare Function fcnnname Lib libname (argument list) as RetType
```

where *`fcnname`* is the name of the function and *`rettype`* is the data type of the variable that gets returned from the function. An example of a function called `CheckDBStatus` may be declared as

```
Declare Function "CheckDBStatus" Lib "DBCALLS.DLL"
➥(ByVal svdbName as String) as Long
```

which requires a string argument and returns a long integer. Visual Basic also allows the programmer to set up alias names for functions. This and other details can be found in Visual Basic help or in the *Visual Basic Programmer's Reference.*

How to Correctly Pass Arguments to a DLL Procedure

It is very important to properly specify the arguments in the argument list of a declaration. If they are not specified properly, several things may happen when Visual Basic executes and the function attempts to run. In one case, Visual Basic will see a mismatch between the argument specifications that have been given to Visual Basic through the declare statement and the DLL's internal representation. This would cause VB to give a "Bad DLL Calling Convention" error when the function attempts to execute.

Another possibility is that the function will be called, but because a parameter was not passed properly, Windows may stop the application dead in its tracks. Once you step outside the confines of the Visual Basic environment and start to use external procedures in DLLs, you open up the possibility of your application stopping in an abnormal way. With Visual Basic, those problems are very rarely present, but when you are using DLLs, they can be commonplace if you don't have a clear idea of what's going on.

Therefore, it is very important to ensure that the parameters are defined and passed to the DLL procedure properly. The easiest way to handle this is to determine the data type of each argument. If the argument is a pointer, a 32-bit address must be passed. If, on the other hand, the argument is a data type, the data type must be clearly known both for Visual Basic and C++, including the number of bytes the DLL expects to get passed. A few simple rules of thumb can be used to make this process easier.

First, you must know whether the DLL expects a pointer to the variable you are passing it or the actual contents of the variable. If the DLL expects the actual contents of the value, you should use the `ByVal` keyword. If a pointer is expected, the `ByVal` keyword should not be used. When working with strings, the `ByVal` keyword should be used when passing a string to a DLL that is expecting a string in a format acceptable to C, specifically a "null-terminated C string." Only when a procedure expects a string with the special Visual Basic format should the `ByVal` keyword not be used.

Next, you must know how to convert the data type of the Visual Basic variable into the data type of the DLL, or vice versa. Table 22.1 may be helpful in determining how Visual Basic data types translate to C/C++ data types, and vice versa.

Table 22.1. Common data-type conversions.

VB Data Type	*C/C++ Data Type*
`Byval x as Integer`	`int x`
`Byval x as Integer`	`short x`
`Byval x as Integer`	`UINT x`
`Byval x as Integer`	`unsigned short x`
`Byval x as Integer`	`BOOL x`
`Byval x as Integer`	`WORD x`
`Byval x as Integer`	`BYTE x`
`Byval x as Long`	`DWORD x`
`ByVal x as Long`	`LONG x`
`ByVal x as Single`	`float x`
`ByVal x as Double`	`double x`

continues

Table 22.1. continued

VB Data Type	*C/C++ Data Type*
`ByVal hWnd as Integer`	`HWND hWnd` (16-bit)
`ByVal hWnd as Long`	`HWND hWnd` (32-bit)
`x as Integer`	`int *x`
`x as Integer`	`short *x`
`x as Integer`	`UINT *x`
`x as Integer`	`unsigned short *x`
`x as Integer`	`BOOL *x`
`x as Integer`	`WORD *x`
`x as Integer`	`BYTE *x`
`x as Long`	`DWORD *x`
`x as Long`	`LONG *x`
`x as Single`	`float *x`
`x as Double`	`double *x`

Therefore, if the C/C++ DLL procedure has an argument such as

```
float CalcChecksum( int count, char* szString, float* data);
```

you would declare the function in VB as

```
Private Declare Function "CalcChecksum" Lib "DBCALLS.DLL" (count as Integer,
➥ ByVal szString as String, data as Single)
```

Even though the rules seem clear, there can inevitably be confusion when you are trying to get the argument list right. Keep examining the variables carefully until the program runs correctly. Fortunately, you should be able to tell immediately whether the arguments are correct, and you can test the function call to make sure.

Creating the DLL—The 16-Bit Case Study

Before discussing the specific details of how a DLL can be created and used, it must first be noted that this book is not really intended to *teach* you how to create a DLL. This book focuses on the performance benefits of doing so, not necessarily on *how* to do so. Therefore, as you read and study the process in this chapter, keep in mind that there are a great many references that can be consulted on the nuts and bolts of creating a DLL and interfacing it to Visual Basic. A list of some useful references are in Appendix B, "Sources of Information."

In this case study, the application contains a function that performs a matrix division of two 1000-element, long-integer arrays. The result of the division of these arrays is then displayed to the user. This procedure requires 1000 division operations, and division is one of the most time-consuming arithmetic operations. Therefore, you should assume that the operation turns out to be a performance bottleneck when implemented directly within Visual Basic. Also assume, for the purposes of this study, that no further optimization techniques can be carried out on the function in Visual Basic.

The first test case is carried out using 16-bit DLLs and a 16-bit Visual Basic application. This is done so that Delphi, which can only produce 16-bit DLLs at the time of this writing, can be compared with Visual Basic and Visual C++. Consider the Visual Basic application Ldr16.exe, shown in Figure 22.1.

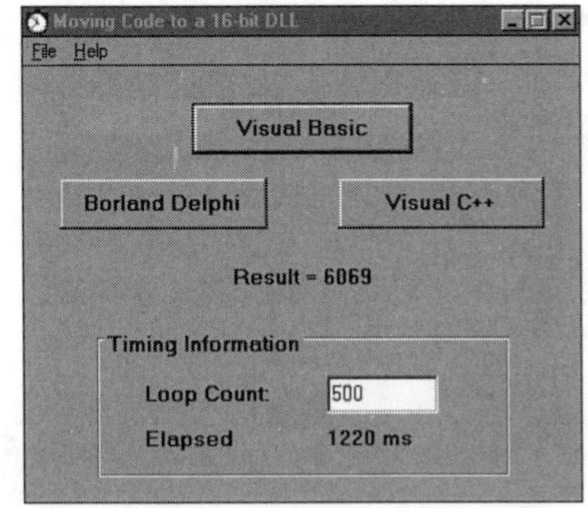

Figure 22.1.
The Ldr16.exe application testing the 16-bit Visual Basic implementation with `Loop Count` *set to* `500`.

The application contains three command buttons—one for Visual Basic and the other two for Visual C++ and Delphi. The result of the functions executed in each language is shown in a results label, and the number of times the function is called and the elapsed time for those calls are contained in the Timing Information frame.

Each command button carries out the matrix-division via a DLL function or a Visual Basic function, as denoted by the caption on each button. The command button that is labeled Visual Basic, for instance, calls the function `VB_MatrixDivide`, which is implemented directly inside Visual Basic using a simple function call. The code for the Visual Basic command button `Click` event is shown in Listing 22.1.

Listing 22.1. The Visual Basic matrix-divide calling event.

```
Private Sub cmdVB_Click()

    ' This event records the elapsed time for the matrix
    ' divide function called within Visual Basic. The
```

continues

Listing 22.1. continued

```
    ' number of times the function gets executed is
    ' determined by the user.

    Dim i&                          ' Index value
    Dim Result&                     ' Result value

    ' Declarations for the two arrays which will be divided
    Dim a(1 To 1000) As Long
    Dim b(1 To 1000) As Long

    ' Initialize arrays
    Call InitArrays(a(), b())

    ' Start the timer
    Call Common_StartTimedTest

    ' Call the DLL function however many times user specifies
    For i = 1 To txtLoopCount
        Result = VB_MatrixDivide(a(), b())
    Next

    ' Stop the timer and post the elapsed time
    Call Common_EndTimedTest(lblElapsedTime)

    ' Display the result of the function call
    lblResult = "Result = " & Result

End Sub
```

The subroutine first declares the two arrays to be divided. Both are dimensioned to 1000 elements. These arrays must be initialized with meaningful data, which is the purpose of the `InitArrays` subroutine, shown in Listing 22.2.

Listing 22.2. The Visual Basic array initialization subroutine.

```
Private Sub InitArrays(a() As Long, b() As Long)

    ' This simple function initializes the two arrays to be
    ' divided, simply by filling them with data

    Dim i As Integer

    For i = 1 To 1000
        a(i) = 1000 - i
        b(i) = i
    Next

End Sub
```

After the arrays are initialized, the timer is started and the division function is called as many times as you requesting order to obtain a large enough number of iterations to make the

timings more meaningful. As stated previously, the function `VB_MatrixDivide` is part of the application; this is the Visual Basic implementation.

The command button that is below and to the right of the Visual Basic command button is labeled Visual C++. When the user clicks this button, Visual Basic makes a call to a DLL written in Visual C++ that contains the matrix-division function. The click event for this command button is shown in Listing 22.3.

Listing 22.3. The Visual C++ matrix-divide calling event.

```
Private Sub cmdVC_Click()

    ' This event records the elapsed time for the matrix
    ' divide function using a Microsoft Visual C++ DLL.
    ' The number of times the function gets executed is
    ' determined by the user.

    Dim i&                          ' Index value
    Dim Result&                     ' Result value
    Dim ArrDim&                     ' Array Dimension

    ' Declarations for the two arrays which will be divided
    Dim a(1 To 1000) As Long
    Dim b(1 To 1000) As Long

    ' Initialize arrays
    Call InitArrays(a(), b())

    ' Store the upper limit of the array in a variable
    ArrDim = UBound(a)

    ' Start the timer
    Call Common_StartTimedTest

    ' Call the DLL function however many times user specifies
    For i = 1 To txtLoopCount
        Result = VC_MatrixDivide(a(1), b(1), ArrDim)
    Next

    ' Stop the timer and post the elapsed time
    Call Common_EndTimedTest(lblElapsedTime)

    ' Display the result of the function call
    lblResult = "Result = " & Result

End Sub
```

This event code looks quite similar to that of the Visual Basic command button shown in Listing 22.1 except that the function `VC_MatrixDivide` is used rather than `VB_MatrixDivide`. The `VC_MatrixDivide` function is out in the Visual C++ DLL rather than inside the Visual Basic application. In addition, the first element of the array is passed as a pointer rather than the entire array. This convention is used whenever passing an array of elements into a DLL created using C/C++.

The third command button, labeled Borland Delphi, invokes the matrix-divide function created using Delphi. The `Click` event for the Delphi command button is shown in Listing 22.4.

Listing 22.4. The Delphi matrix-divide calling event.

```
Private Sub cmdDelphi_Click()

    ' This event records the elapsed time for the matrix
    ' divide function using a Borland Delphi DLL.
    ' The number of times the function gets executed is
    ' determined by the user.

    Dim i&                          ' Index value
    Dim Result&                     ' Result value
    Dim ArrDim&                     ' Array Dimension

    ' Declarations for the two arrays which will be divided
    Dim a(1 To 1000) As Long
    Dim b(1 To 1000) As Long

    ' Initialize arrays
    Call InitArrays(a(), b())

    ' Store the upper limit of the array in a variable
    ArrDim = UBound(a)

    ' Start the timer
    Call Common_StartTimedTest

    ' Call the DLL function however many times user specifies
    For i = 1 To txtLoopCount
        Result = DP_MatrixDivide(a(1), b(1), ArrDim)
    Next

    ' Stop the timer and post the elapsed time
    Call Common_EndTimedTest(lblElapsedTime)

    ' Display the result of the function call
    lblResult = "Result = " & Result

End Sub
```

As you can see, the click-event procedure for the Delphi DLL is almost identical to the one for Visual C++, except that the Delphi DLL function is called rather than C++ or the Visual Basic functions. Both the Visual C++ and Delphi functions must both be declared in the Visual Basic application because they are external to Visual Basic. The functions are declared in the Declarations section of the main form, as shown in Listing 22.5.

Listing 22.5. Declarations for external functions of Ldr16.exe.

```
Option Explicit

' Declarations for matrix divide functions for
' Microsoft Visual C++ and Borland Delphi
Private Declare Function VC_MatrixDivide Lib "VCDLL16.DLL"
➥(x As Long, y As Long, ByVal size As Long) As Long
Private Declare Function DP_MatrixDivide Lib "DPDLL16.DLL"
➥(x As Long, y As Long, ByVal size As Long) As Long
```

The function declarations for the two external functions are virtually identical, except for the name of the functions and the DLLs they are contained in. Note that the Visual C++ function is called `VB_MatrixDivide` and is in VCDll16.dll, while Delphi's function is called `DP_MatrixDivide` and is in DPDll16.dll. Now that the click events for each matrix-division function have been shown, the matrix-division functions themselves will now be presented in their own respective programming languages.

Implementing the Matrix Division Function Using Visual Basic

The Visual Basic command button calls the function `VB_MatrixDivide`, which is a function inside, or internal to, the Visual Basic application. This function, which is contained in the form module, is shown in Listing 22.6.

Listing 22.6. The `VB_MatrixDivide` function.

```
Private Function VB_MatrixDivide(a() As Long, b() As Long) As Long

    ' This is the Visual Basic implementation of the
    ' array division function. The procedure is very
    ' simple, contained in one loop.

    Dim Result As Long
    Dim i As Integer

    For i = 1 To UBound(a)
        Result = Result + a(i) \ b(i)
    Next

    VB_MatrixDivide = Result

End Function
```

As you can see from Listing 22.6, a simple division of each array element into the other is carried out across the entire length of the array. A significant number of divisions are required in order to derive the answer, all of which must be added to obtain the final result.

Using a C++ DLL Function

The second implementation of the matrix-divide function was carried out in Visual C++ in order to improve performance. Keep in mind that it is not necessarily the purpose of this book to show the reader how to create a DLL, but rather to explain the performance results of doing so. Turn to one of the references cited in Appendix B for further information on this useful topic. The first important file is the header file for the DLL. This is shown in Listing 22.7.

Listing 22.7. The 16-bit `VC_MatrixDivide` DLL header file.

```
// File Name:          VCDLL16.H
// Description:        Matrix Division DLL Header file
// Author:             Tim Koets
//
// This code module contains the functions prototypes and definitions
// necessary to create a DLL using Microsoft Visual C++. The functions
// prototyped in this header file are described below:
//
//  WEP
//         WEP, which is short for "Windows Entry Point", is a
//         function which gives the DLL an entry point to Windows
//         so that functions within it can be used.
//
//  LibMain
//         This function is also used to allow other programs to
//         call functions within this DLL
//
//  VC_MatrixDivide
//         This function can be called from any application which
//         can DLL functions.

#include <windows.h>

// Definitions

#define  EXTINT    extern "C" int _far _pascal
#define  EXTLONG   extern "C" long _far _pascal

// Global Variables

HINSTANCE ghInstance;

// Function Prototypes

EXTINT _export WEP(int nShutDownFlag);

EXTINT LibMain(HINSTANCE hInstance, WORD wDataSeg,
           WORD wHeapSize, LPSTR lpszCmdLine);

EXTLONG _export VC_MatrixDivide (long a[], long b[], long arraysize);
```

As you can see from the header file, two functions (`WEP` and `LibMain`) are necessary in creating a DLL (in addition to the actual functions that will be called from other applications). Listing

22.8 presents the actual source code file. In this code module is the function that is actually called in Visual Basic, `VC_MatrixDivide`, which is denoted in boldface type.

Listing 22.8. The 16-bit `VC_MatrixDivide` DLL source code file.

```
// File Name:       VCDLL16.CPP
// Description:     Matrix Division DLL Code Module
// Author:          Tim Koets
//
//
// This code module contains the functions necessary to create a DLL
// using Microsoft Visual C++. The functions in this module are
// described below:
//
//  WEP
//        WEP, which is short for "Windows Entry Point", is a
//        function which gives the DLL an entry point to Windows
//        so that functions within it can be used.
//
//  LibMain
//        This function is also used to allow other programs to
//        call functions within this DLL
//
//  VC_MatrixDivide
//        This function can be called from any application which
//        call DLL functions.

#include "vcdll16.h"

EXTINT _export WEP(int nShutDownFlag)
{
    return 1;
}

EXTINT LibMain(HINSTANCE hInstance, WORD wDataSeg,

WORD wHeapSize, LPSTR lpszCmdLine)
{
     if (wHeapSize > 0)
     {
        UnlockData(0);
     }

     ghInstance = hInstance;
     return 1;
}

EXTLONG _export VC_MatrixDivide (long a[], long b[], long arraysize)
{
   int i;
   long result = 0;

   for (i = 0 ; i < arraysize ; i++)
        result += a[i] / b[i];

   return (result);
}
```

As you can see from the source code, this function is very similar to the Visual Basic function, except that it is written using C syntax rather than Visual Basic. The last important file to include when creating a DLL using Visual C++ is the DLL's definition file. This file is shown in Listing 22.9.

Listing 22.9. The 16-bit `VC_MatrixDivide` DLL definition file.

```
LIBRARY    CIELAB
EXETYPE    WINDOWS
CODE       PRELOAD MOVEABLE DISCARDABLE
DATA       PRELOAD MOVEABLE SINGLE
HEAPSIZE   1024
EXPORTS
           WEP PRIVATE
; To implement your own Windows Exit Procedure add the following
; function to your application (referring to it in the .def file is
; not required.)  The extern "C" is only required if module is C++.
; extern "C" int FAR PASCAL _WEP(int)
; {
;       /* Your WEP functionality goes here */
;  return 1;
; }
```

The definition file contains important memory-management information that is beyond the scope of this book. These three files, along with the appropriate makefile and compiler settings, constitute the required elements for creating a DLL using Visual C++.

Using a Delphi DLL Function

The third implementation of the matrix-divide function was carried out using Delphi to create a DLL. With Delphi, two files are necessary to create a DLL. The first file is the DPR file, or *Delphi project file*. This file contains the library declaration and functions to be exported in the DLL. The project file in this application, named DPDll.DPR, is shown in Listing 22.10.

Listing 22.10. The `DP_MatrixDivide` DLL project file (DPDll.DPR).

```
library DPDLL16;

uses
  DLLProj in 'DLLPROJ.PAS' {No Form Used};

type typArray = array[1..1000] of Longint;

function DP_MatrixDivide(a,b: typArray; arrsize: Longint): Longint; export;
var i: integer;
begin
     Result := 0;
     for i := 1 to arrsize do
     begin
```

```
        Result := Result + a[i] div b[i];
    end;
end;

exports
  DP_MatrixDivide;
{$R *.RES}
begin
end.
```

The second file is the PAS, or *Pascal* file, which consists of an object of the class `Tform`. Delphi must have at least one form associated with an application, even if it is a DLL. Even though the form is not used or brought into existence when the DLL function is called, it must be included in the project. So the file DPDll.PAS is a dummy file that is not explicitly used. The file, called DPDll.PAS, is shown in Listing 22.11.

Listing 22.11. The `DP_MatrixDivide` DLL Pascal file (DPDLL.PAS).

```
unit DLLProj;

interface

uses
  SysUtils, WinTypes, WinProcs, Messages, Classes, Graphics, Controls,
  Forms, Dialogs;

type
  TForm1 = class(TForm)
  private
  public
  end;

implementation

{$R *.DFM}

end.
```

These two files, along with the appropriate compiler and project settings, can be used to create the Delphi DLL file DPDll16.dll, which contains the appropriate matrix division function, `DP_MatrixDivide`.

Obtaining and Comparing the Results

Now that all the DLLs have been created and the Visual Basic application is aware of and able to call each function, timings can be carried out. Refer to the main form of the application, shown in Figure 22.1. A performance analysis was carried out using 500 iterations of the loop that calls each function, respectively, in the `Click` event of its command button. The results in

Figure 22.1 are for the Visual Basic implementation. Refer to Table 22.2 for each of the implementation results.

Table 22.2. Results of Ldr16.exe with `Loop Count` set to 500.

Language	*Function Used*	*Normalized Time*
Visual Basic	`VB_MatrixDivide`	2.84
Delphi	`DP_MatrixDivide`	1.68
Visual C++	`VC_MatrixDivide`	1.00

The results obtained in this case study indeed meet our expectations; Visual C++ is the fastest, followed by Delphi, and then Visual Basic. These results speak well of Delphi, which is comparable in performance to Visual C++ with respect to mathematical operations. This is not too surprising, considering that both Delphi and Visual C++ do not need to work through an interpreter and can therefore carry out the multiplication loop much faster. Visual Basic is not as efficient with floating-point arithmetic, particularly division operations. (Refer to Chapter 10, "Math," for more information on math in Visual Basic.)

In order to give you some idea of the amount of work involved for each solution, a simple table is provided that shows the authors perception of the relative ease in coming up with each solution. We use a numerical scale, with 10 being extremely difficult and 1 being very easy. The conclusions are shown in Table 22.3.

Table 22.3. How easy was it to implement the solution?

Solution	*Ease*
Visual Basic	3
Delphi	7
Visual C++ (16-bit)	9
Visual C++ (32-bit)*	5

* The 32-bit DLL was written using Visual C++ 2.2 with the help of the MFC DLL Wizard.

While these results are quite subjective and depend on the programmer's skill level, it seems clear that Visual Basic is by far the easiest solution. The programmer never has to leave Visual Basic, can implement the function in the same language, and can easily make changes to the function if necessary.

When using Delphi, you basically have to switch environments and load the project that created the Delphi DLL in order to use it. You must be familiar with Delphi, which can take time and effort, particularly when attempting to build a DLL. The Delphi help and documentation is not especially geared for helping programmers through DLL construction, so it takes some searching and experimentation to get a DLL to work properly. Once a DLL has been created, you must switch back to Visual Basic and test the DLL. If the DLL doesn't work properly or there is a problem in the declaration or parameter definitions of either language, anything from a "Bad DLL Calling Convention Error" to an application crash can result. This can get quite annoying when you are attempting to get a DLL to function properly.

Finally, when you're using C++, the same activities must be carried out, only it is much less intuitive and requires more skill to create a DLL in C/C++. The language is certainly the most powerful in terms of the type of parameters it can accept or return, but it is a lower-level language with unclear instructions on how to create a DLL. Although much of Visual C++ is becoming automated with wizards, the help support is not especially geared for those who are creating DLLs. So, once again, the user is left to experiment and potentially experience crashes and other problems until the DLL is working properly.

It appears, then, that the more work and difficulty in creating the DLL, the better the performance, at least for the type of function created in this case study. While this may not be true for *all* cases, it certainly holds true in this one. The programmer, the available resources, and the needs of the user are ultimately the determining factors in whether to consider using a DLL. Creating DLLs and getting them to work with VB applications may appear simple, but there is often a different "gotcha" involved every time a DLL is created. This can cause a lot of frustration and waste a lot of time. Before thinking about creating a DLL, consider the alternative approaches detailed in the next section.

Creating the DLL—The 32-Bit Case Study

The 32-bit test case uses a minor variation of the Ldr16.exe application and compares the performance of the matrix-division directly in the 32-bit Visual Basic application Ldr32.exe to a function call to a 32-bit Visual C++ DLL. Delphi could not be used in this comparison because, at the time of this printing, Delphi could not create 32-bit applications.

The main form for the Ldr32.exe application is shown in Figure 22.2. Note that it is essentially the same except that it lacks the Delphi command button.

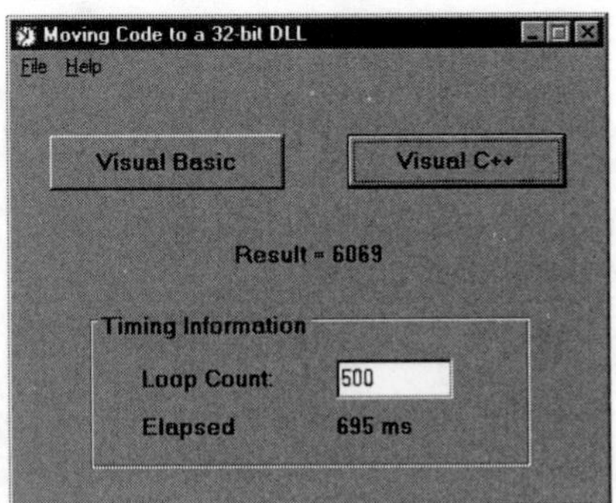

Figure 22.2.
The Ldr32.exe application testing the 32-bit Visual C++ implementation with `Loop Count` *set to* `500`.

Again, all the functions are the same in the application. The only difference other than the lack of the Delphi test is the declarations section of the main form. Since this is a 32-bit application, the 32-bit DLL must be used instead. The declaration for this DLL is shown in Listing 22.12.

Listing 22.12. Declarations for external functions of Ldr32.exe.

```
Option Explicit

' Declarations for matrix divide functions for Microsoft Visual C++

Private Declare Function VC_MatrixDivide Lib "VCDLL32.DLL"
➥(x As Long, y As Long, ByVal size As Long) As Long
```

Note that the name of the DLL is VCDll32.dll, not VCDll16.dll, which was used in the previous test case. The 32-bit DLL was written using Visual C++ 2.2 with the help of the MFC DLL Wizard. The primary files of interest are the VCDll32.CPP file and the VCDll32.DEF files. In this case, no header file is required. The source and definition files are shown in Listings 22.13 and 22.14, respectively.

Listing 22.13. The 32-bit `VC_MatrixDivide` DLL source code file.

```
// File Name:       VCDll32.CPP
// Description:     Matrix Division DLL Code Module
// Author:          Tim Koets
//
//
// This code module contains the functions necessary to create a DLL
// using Microsoft Visual C++. The functions in this module are
// described below:
//
// This file defines the initialization routines for the DLL as well
// as the DLL functions themselves. These functions are described below:
//
//  DLLMain
//        This is the entry point function for the DLL.
//
//  VC_MatrixDivide
//        This function can be called from any application which
//        call DLL functions.
//

#include "stdafx.h"
#include <afxdllx.h>

#ifdef _DEBUG
#undef THIS_FILE
static char BASED_CODE THIS_FILE[] = __FILE__;
#endif

static AFX_EXTENSION_MODULE VCDll32DLL = { NULL, NULL };
```

```
extern "C" int APIENTRY
DllMain(HINSTANCE hInstance, DWORD dwReason, LPVOID lpReserved)
{
    if (dwReason == DLL_PROCESS_ATTACH)
    {
        TRACE0("VCDLL32.DLL Initializing!\n");

        // Extension DLL one-time initialization
        AfxInitExtensionModule(VCDll32DLL, hInstance);

        // Insert this DLL into the resource chain
        new CDynLinkLibrary(VCDll32DLL);
    }
    else if (dwReason == DLL_PROCESS_DETACH)
    {
        TRACE0("VCDLL32.DLL Terminating!\n");
    }
    return 1;   // ok
}

long VC_MatrixDivide (long a[], long b[], long arraysize)
{
    int i;
    long result = 0;

    for (i = 0 ; i < arraysize ; i++)
        result += a[i] / b[i];

    return (result);
}
```

Listing 22.14. The 32-bit `VC_MatrixDivide` DLL definition file.

```
; VCDll32.def : Declares the module parameters for the DLL.

LIBRARY      VCDLL32
DESCRIPTION  'VCDLL32 Windows Dynamic Link Library'

EXPORTS
    VC_MatrixDivide
```

Any additional details regarding the 32-bit implementation are not provided here because, if not otherwise stated, it is identical to the 16-bit implementation. Therefore, we can proceed directly to the results, which are summarized in Table 22.4.

Table 22.4. The results of Ldr32.exe with `Loop Count` set to `500`.

Language	*Function Used*	*Normalized Time*
Visual Basic	`VB_MatrixDivide`	1.56
Visual C++	`VC_MatrixDivide`	1.00

The results for the 32-bit test case are similar to those for the 16-bit test case: The Visual C++ approach provides a faster solution. Note, however, that in the 32-bit case, the two approaches are much closer together in time than they were in the 16-bit implementation—due in part to the improved performance of the 32-bit Visual Basic interpreter. Even so, Visual C++ is faster, which is to be expected in either 16-bit or 32-bit operating environments, because the floating-point division is more dependent on the arithmetic efficiency of a language rather than specific 16-bit and 32-bit considerations. Keep in mind, however, that this may not be the case in the future.

Alternatives to the DLL Approach

Before considering the DLL approach, you should make sure that all other possible alternatives have been explored, particularly if you does not have the skill and/or time to go through all the work of creating and debugging a DLL. Therefore, this section presents a series of possible alternatives to once again remind the programmer that there are other approaches that may require less time and effort and produce the same, or perhaps even better, results for the user. With this important point in mind, the following sections describe some of the alternative approaches to creating a DLL.

Apply Optimization Techniques

Make sure you have explored all possible optimization techniques in Visual Basic before moving to a DLL. As you can see from the material presented earlier in the chapter, a great deal of effort must be put into creating a DLL and getting Visual Basic to interface properly with it. It is important to try and eliminate the performance bottleneck in Visual Basic *first* before moving to the DLL solution.

Use the API and DLLs Already Available to Accomplish the Task

It is often possible, particularly where you are trying to accomplish a task that is not possible for Visual Basic, to take advantage of existing third-party OLE controls and DLLs to accomplish the task for you. By using functions or controls that are already available, you avoid doing all the work yourself, plus you may get a more robust and functional procedure than you could have built yourself (unless, of course, you are actually the incredible, dynamic programmer everybody thinks you are). A wide variety of OLE controls and DLLs exist that can supplement your functionality or replace it altogether, thus freeing you of the need to create a DLL.

In addition to providing the functionality you need, you may also find that DLL procedures and OLE controls can improve performance over a Visual Basic solution. You may be implementing the functionality "manually," which could be done more efficiently using a

preexisting commercial routine or control. Not only do you avoid re-inventing existing functionality, but you also have a more robust and efficient routine.

Eliminate the Need for a DLL By Modifying the Functionality

Finally, you may be able to eliminate the need to write or move code to a DLL by eliminating the functionality completely. On occasion, a task may be very time-consuming in Visual Basic but also very complex. The added time required to create, test, and debug a DLL to provide the functionality may not be worth the effort, particularly when you're not really sure how much faster the DLL approach will be. Therefore, it may be better to drop the functionality altogether rather than invest too much time in other alternatives. For some pieces of functionality, this simply may not be possible, but for others, it may need consideration under tight budget or time constraints.

Summary

In this chapter, Visual Basic, Visual C++, and Delphi are used to illustrate the methods and results of moving code out of Visual Basic and into a DLL. Several important points are emphasized in this chapter. First, it is important to realize that moving Visual Basic code into a DLL typically involves more time and effort than sticking with a Visual Basic solution, particularly for beginning programmers. Therefore, it is important to know when it is appropriate to move code to a DLL and when it is not. This chapter points out three cases where it can be appropriate: when the code does not execute fast enough in Visual Basic, when the functionality cannot be accomplished using Visual Basic, and when the code is reusable and is to be shared among various languages.

The chapter then discusses the requirements to interface a DLL to a Visual Basic application, particularly the declarations required and the comparison of the Visual Basic data types to the C/C++ data type set. This section also discusses the importance of using correct data types, since the program is likely to crash or bring up an error if the data types are not matched properly between Visual Basic and the DLL function that is being called.

The chapter presents two case studies in which a function is placed into 16-bit DLLs created using Microsoft Visual C++ 1.5 and Borland Delphi, and into a 32-bit DLL created by Microsoft Visual C++ 2.0. The results show that for the functionality being considered, the C/C++ solution is the fastest, followed by the Delphi solution and then the Visual Basic solution. While this is clearly dependent on the functionality being implemented and is not universally true in every case, it does show the benefit of moving code, when necessary, to a DLL.

The performance results of moving code to a DLL may not be consistent across languages, since they depend a great deal on the type of functionality being implemented. The type of function used in this chapter is very well suited for a compiled language such as Delphi or C/C++. Keep in mind, however, that other operations, such as complex string manipulations, may be much easier to implement in Visual Basic and may yield timings that are totally different from the ones presented in this chapter.

The chapter also points out that, while the C/C++ and Delphi solutions provide better performance in this case study, it takes a considerable amount of time and effort to create the DLLs, test them, interface them with Visual Basic, and test the application using the DLL. This additional work may not be worth the performance boost, particularly if the program has a release deadline or there are limited resources and hours to tackle the problem. In such cases, it may be better to keep the functionality in Visual Basic and look for ways to improve performance within the environment.

The chapter concludes by presenting several such alternative solutions. The first, which is to apply the optimization techniques presented in this book, is perhaps the most practical way to improve performance in an application where a bottleneck exists. Depending on the functionality, it may be possible to use other DLLs and the Windows API to integrate and/or supplement the functionality in Visual Basic. Finally, it may be better to modify or even eliminate the functionality if the performance negatively affects an application. (This is true when you are using *any* language.)

While the goal of the chapter is not to *teach* you how to create a DLL, the chapter does present some of the means and consequences of doing so. This discussion should give you a clearer idea of what's involved and what some of the alternative options are if you do not have the extra time to create a DLL. As was mentioned earlier, a great deal of material is available that can provide more information on creating a DLL. Refer to Appendix B for more information.

Obey the Signs

Wrong Way: It's very quick and easy to put a DLL together once you get the hang of it.

It seems that once you've put together a DLL, it should be trivial from that point on. But beware! A great many little gotchas are out there that can take a lot of time to iron out. There always seems to be a new, little problem every time you write a DLL.

Beware of Falling Rocks: Do not give up on trying to fix performance bottlenecks without considering a DLL.

While writing a DLL can be time-consuming and somewhat difficult, it is often a very effective way to circumvent a performance problem or, at the very least, minimize its impact. It is wise to get to know other key programming languages so that you can, if necessary, create DLLs when needed. The more experience you gain, the easier it will become.

Q&A

Q Where do I go for more information on building DLLs?

A It depends on the programming tool, but if you use either Microsoft Visual C++ or Borland Delphi, a variety of references exist. The latest 32-bit version of Visual C++ contains a DLL wizard for when you are creating a DLL based on MFC. Refer to Appendix B for a complete list of references.

Q Don't the performance results depend on what the function does?

A Absolutely. This is why results can vary significantly depending on the function being implemented. One language might be better suited to some operations than another. Therefore, expect results to differ.

Q Can Visual Basic create DLLs?

A Yes. With Visual Basic 4.0, you can create OLE Automation server DLLs (which still require the Visual Basic runtime interpreter). These allow other applications to take advantage of Visual Basic, which acts as a server, serving any client application that is calling it. This is a very powerful, new feature of Visual Basic that is treated extensively in Chapter 25.

Workshop

Consider an existing application that has a particular performance bottleneck you would like to reduce or eliminate. Can that functionality be separated out of the application and placed into a DLL? What information must you give to and receive from the function? If you have a working knowledge of C, C++, or Delphi, and you have the necessary tools, create a function inside a DLL, and use Visual Basic to call the function. What are the results? Did the boost in performance justify the effort?

Optimization Strategies: Object Creation and Manipulation

This section addresses the powerful object capabilities of Visual Basic 4.0. Visual Basic provides a clear object model for the programmer to work with. This includes the ability to create classes and objects based on those classes. It also encompasses the ability to incorporate object containers into an application. Object-based program components can even be shared by OLE Automation server technology. With any object, it is important to understand the available properties and methods well. Sometimes the manner of using an object can have a drastic impact on performance. Each of these areas is covered in turn.

Chapter 23, "Objects," discusses the use of classes and class modules to define objects. The use of classes makes software easier to design, implement, maintain, and document. Furthermore, it provides for better code reusability. This chapter focuses on performance issues related to classes and objects. This includes a look at optimization of object references and dealing with collections of objects.

Chapter 24, "Object Linking and Embedding," considers OLE object containers, which allow an object to be directly embedded into a Visual Basic application. Strategies for incorporating such object containers are discussed, as are the performance ramifications of making use of these containers.

Chapter 25, "OLE Automation Servers," examines performance issues relating to OLE Automation servers. A relative comparison is provided of performance trade-offs between the same code directly in an Visual Basic application, bundled into an out-of-process OLE Automation server, or incorporated into an in-process OLE Automation server. Corresponding guidelines on when to use each type of server are provided. Performance strategies for using Remote Automation servers are also considered.

Chapter 26, "Know Your Objects: The OLE Graph Control Sample," illustrates how vital it is to understand the properties and methods of an object to make optimal use of it within your program. In this case, the object examined is the 32-bit Graph OLE customer control, or OCX. Optimization techniques that focus on the `AutoInc` property and the `Draw` method are provided. The samples show that intelligent use of properties unique to one object or custom control can be very important.

Part VII will provide you with insight into how to tailor your Visual Basic applications for optimal performance with respect to objects, classes, and OLE Automation servers. With the guidelines in this section, you should be able to incorporate an efficient object strategy into your application development, with clear insight into the performance trade-offs inherent in such an approach.

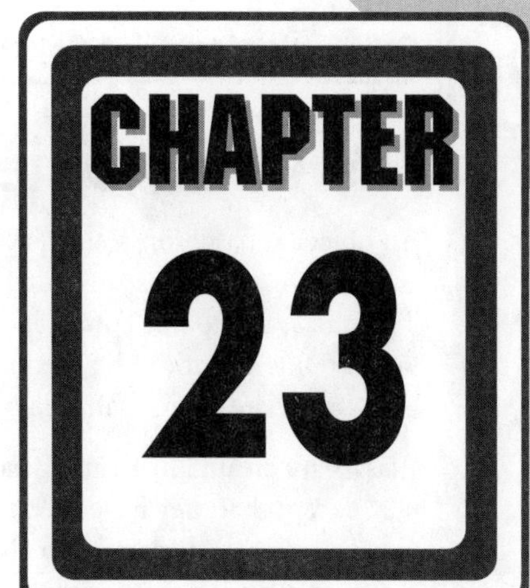

Objects

One of the most exciting new capabilities of Visual Basic 4.0 is the ability to create classes and objects based on those classes. This capability enables the programmer to produce applications that are more object oriented, which has many programming advantages. The use of classes makes software easier to design, implement, maintain and document. Furthermore, it provides for better code reusability. These benefits were greatly lacking in previous versions of Visual Basic.

Some of the key performance issues related to classes and objects are discussed in this chapter. While it is not the goal of this chapter to make you an expert at programming with objects, it does provide you with suggestions for how to maximize performance when using them in your Visual Basic applications.

The Class/Object Relationship

An object is based on a class. A commonly used analogy in the industry is to view classes as cookie cutters. Classes are related to objects the same way a cookie cutter is related to a cookie. The class is the cookie cutter; it defines the characteristics of the object, that is, the cookie. The same cookie cutter can be used to cut as many cookies as necessary, just as a single class can be used to declare more than one object.

Classes are created in Visual Basic using *class modules.* Class modules are similar to code modules, except that they have specific characteristics that distinguish them from the other module types. A variable declared in a class module, for example, serves as a property of the class. Procedures within a class module serve as methods of the class. These should be familiar concepts if you use controls such as a textbox control. The textbox control has properties, such as `Text`, `Left`, and `Width`, as well as methods, such as `Move` and `SetFocus`. When you place a textbox control on a form, you create another object of the textbox *class.* The control you place on the form can be thought of as a textbox *object,* of which many can be placed on a form. In the same way, objects derived from user-defined classes can be created and used throughout an application.

You can declare properties in a class module by declaring a variable in the declarations section of the class module. This becomes a property for the class. If the variable is declared as `Public`, the property that variable represents can be set but without any validation or intervening code. If, for example, you have a class with a property that only allows for an integer in the range 1 through 100, you would want to disallow the user from stepping outside the boundaries of that range. If you used a public variable in your declaration, you would have no way of validating that property as part of the class.

Fortunately, Visual Basic contains three special procedures in a class module called *property procedures.* These are the `Property Let`, `Property Set`, and `Property Get` procedures. The `Property Let` procedure is called whenever a specified property is set. The code in the procedure can then be used to assign the value to the actual property variable, which can be declared private rather than public. This ensures that some type of validation can be performed before the actual property is set. In the preceding example, the `Property Let` function would be used to ensure that the value the user enters is in the acceptable range and, if so, it would assign the value to the actual property variable.

The `Property Set` procedure is a special case of the `Property Let` procedure. It is used to set a variable whose data type is an object rather than one of the standard Visual Basic data types like the integer, single, or string data types. The `Property Get` procedure is called whenever the program reads a property from an object. In this manner, the property can be formatted or calculations or data conversions can be carried out. Together the property procedures ensure that the class has control over validating and properly representing the properties contained in the class.

Visual Basic 4.0's capability to use objects and user-defined classes from which objects can be created introduces the traditional performance trade-off: power and flexibility versus performance. Objects are very powerful, and applications which use them are usually easier to maintain and develop. However, ease of development often comes at the expense of performance. Objects open the door to more powerful application designs, and they may spark very good ideas for layers of code to ensure data encapsulation that would not otherwise be utilized. The `Property Get` procedure, which can be defined in a class so that that code will be carried out whenever a given property value is retrieved, is such an example. This code might do some data massaging or integrity checking. If a global variable was used rather than an object, this integrity checking would not be possible. Using the object enables the programmer to use integrity—checking code every time the program attempts to assign a new value to the property of the object.

A very complex design based on hierarchical object implementation and built on layers of collections and objects may have a more adverse performance impact than a flatter, simpler implementation that would require less interpretation time. The performance impact is very application specific, and in most cases, the development benefits outweigh the performance penalties. The best way to assess this is to simply take performance measurements throughout the development life cycle rather than being surprised at the end of a complex project where performance is being considered for the first time.

Declaring Objects

An important consideration when working with objects is to use the most specific means possible of declaring an object. The more specific the declaration, the faster the performance when that object is accessed. The following assignments give examples of slow and fast object-declaration pairs:

```
Dim MyForm as Form                    ' Slower
Dim MyForm as frmPreviouslyDefined    ' Faster - uses existing form

Dim MyThing as Object                 ' Slower
Dim MyThing as New MyObjectClass      ' Faster - uses class module def.

Dim MyControl as Control              ' Slower
Dim MyControl as Textbox              ' Faster - uses control class
```

The improved performance resulting from one of the optimal access references is relatively small, but performance will be noticeably faster as the number of accesses to that object increase. In an object-intensive program, the cumulative effect can be noticeable and possibly quite significant. There are no significant maintenance disadvantages to this approach, and the more specific declarations could even be regarded as a better programming practice. Therefore, this approach should be used as standard practice.

To illustrate this principle, consider the application ObjDec32.exe, which is contained on the CD-ROM that accompanies this book. The main form of this application is shown in Figure 23.1.

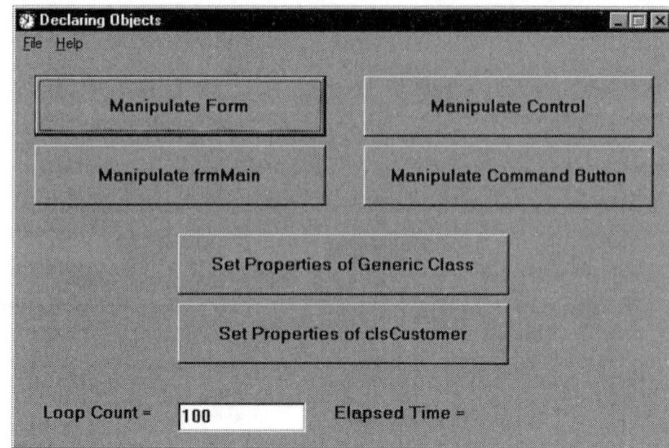

Figure 23.1.
Running the ObjDec32.exe application.

As you can see, the form contains six command buttons, a loop counter, and a label showing the elapsed time of the procedure represented by each command button. The first test case considers using a generic form versus a specific form. The first two command buttons in the upper-left corner of the form are used for this test case. The procedure for the `Click` event of the top command button, labeled Manipulate Form, is shown in Listing 23.1

Listing 23.1. The `Click` event for the Manipulate Form command button.

```
Private Sub cmdGenericForm_Click()

    Call Common_StartTimedTest

    Call Manipulate_Generic_Form(Me)

    Call Common_EndTimedTest(lblElapsedTime)

End Sub
```

The procedure for the command button labeled Manipulate frmMain is identical with the exception of the call made within the loop. Rather than calling `Manipulate_Generic_Form`, this procedure calls the subroutine `Manipulate_frmMain`. Both of these procedures will now be examined.

The `Manipulate_Generic_Form` subroutine is shown in Listing 23.2.

Listing 23.2. The `Manipulate_Generic_Form` subroutine.

```
Private Sub Manipulate_Generic_Form(ByVal frm As Form)

    Dim i&       ' Index value

    For i = 1 To txtLoopCount * 100
        frm.Tag = frm.hwnd
    Next

End Sub
```

Note that `Manipulate_Generic_Form` requires one argument of type `Form`. Now consider the `Manipulate_Main_Form` procedure, shown in Listing 23.3.

Listing 23.3. The `Manipulate_frmMain` subroutine.

```
Private Sub Manipulate_frmMain(ByVal frm As frmMain)

    Dim i&       ' Index value

    For i = 1 To txtLoopCount * 100
        frm.Tag = frm.hwnd
    Next

End Sub
```

This subroutine is identical to the first, except that the argument now uses the specific form object as a data type rather than the generic object. The same basic principles are used in the other two sets of command buttons.

The second test case considers using a generic control versus a specific control. Listing 23.4 shows the procedures used in this test case, which is conducted using the two command buttons located in the upper-right corner of the form. The differences between the generic and specific procedures are shown in boldface type.

Listing 23.4. Generic versus specific control subroutines.

```
Private Sub cmdControl_Click()

    Call Common_StartTimedTest

    Call Manipulate_Generic_Control(cmdControl)

    Call Common_EndTimedTest(lblElapsedTime)

End Sub
```

continues

Listing 23.4. continued

```
Private Sub Manipulate_Generic_Control(ByVal ctrl As Control)

    Dim i As Integer
    Dim svOldCaption As String

    svOldCaption = ctrl.Caption

    For i = 1 To txtLoopCount
        ctrl.Caption = i
        ctrl.Tag = ctrl.Parent.hwnd
    Next

    ctrl.Caption = svOldCaption

End Sub


Private Sub cmdCommandButton_Click()

    Call Common_StartTimedTest

    Call Manipulate_CommandButton(cmdCommandbutton)

    Call Common_EndTimedTest(lblElapsedTime)

End Sub

Private Sub Manipulate_CommandButton(ByVal ctrl As CommandButton)

    Dim i As Integer
    Dim svOldCaption As String

    svOldCaption = ctrl.Caption

    For i = 1 To txtLoopCount
        ctrl.Caption = i
        ctrl.Tag = ctrl.Parent.hwnd
    Next

    ctrl.Caption = svOldCaption

End Sub
```

The second test case considers using a generic object versus a specific object based on a user-defined class. The user-defined class that is used in this test case is `clsCustomer`, which is defined in a class module and is referenced within the procedures shown in Listing 23.5. As in the previous listing, the differences between the procedures using specific object references and the generic object are highlighted in boldface type.

Listing 23.5. Generic versus specific object subroutines.

```
Private Sub cmdNewObject_Click()

    Dim MyObject As Object

    Call Common_StartTimedTest

    Call Manipulate_Generic_Object(MyObject)

    Call Common_EndTimedTest(lblElapsedTime)

End Sub

Private Sub Manipulate_Generic_Object(ByVal obj As Object)

    Dim i&

    Set obj = New clsCustomer

    For i = 1 To txtLoopCount
        obj.Customer_Name = "George"
        obj.Address = "111 Parkway"
        obj.Age = 35
        obj.Employer = "Acme Inc."
        obj.Phone = "222-3333"
    Next

End Sub



Private Sub cmdExistingClass_Click()

    Dim MyObject As New clsCustomer

    Call Common_StartTimedTest

    Call Manipulate_clsCustomer_Object(MyObject)

    Call Common_EndTimedTest(lblElapsedTime)

End Sub

Private Sub Manipulate_clsCustomer_Object(ByVal obj As clsCustomer)

    Dim i&

    For i = 1 To txtLoopCount
        obj.Customer_Name = "George"
        obj.Address = "111 Parkway"
        obj.Age = 35
        obj.Employer = "Acme Inc."
        obj.Phone = "222-3333"
    Next

End Sub
```

The results for each of the three test cases is summarized in Table 23.1.

Table 23.1. Results of the ObjDec32.exe application with `Loop_Count` set to `100`.

Reference	*Form*	*Control*	*Object*
Generic	1.08	1.31	6.00
Specific	1.00	1.00	1.00

The results show that the specific implementations are faster than the generic implementations. The performance difference is particularly significant in the case of objects. This is because the `Manipulate_Generic_Object` subroutine must set the generic object passed to it to the `CommandButton` type before its properties can be used. With the `Manipulate_clsCustomer_Object` subroutine, this was not required because the subroutine knew at the outset what sort of object it was dealing with. The extra step of setting the object to a specific class added a considerable amount of overhead to the procedure. The results presented in Table 23.1 show the benefit of being as specific as possible when assigning object types to variables.

The results will, of course, vary depending on the controls, objects, and forms that are used and the ways they are manipulated, but the use of specific object types whenever possible will make your applications run faster.

> **TIP:** For faster performance, always use the explicit class name rather than the generic one when declaring objects.

Using Object Collections

A very powerful feature of Visual Basic 4.0 is the ability to create collections of objects, including collections of objects defined from user-defined classes specified in class modules. Managing objects is much easier when those objects are grouped into collections. Programmers can apply both `Add` and `Remove` methods to collections, and collections can be indexed by item. There are many inherent advantages to these methods; for instance, when an item is removed from a collection with the `Remove` method, the collection is automatically compressed. You don't have to worry about opening holes left from deleted items, nor do you have to worry about shifting the data to eliminate those holes through statements such as `ReDim`.

The use of collections does come at a performance cost that, as usual, will vary depending on the specific application. To evaluate the impact of classes on performance, consider the test application ColArr32.exe, which is included on the CD-ROM that accompanies this book.

This application consists of six operations: the creation, modification, and deletion of a *collection* of objects, and the creation, modification, and deletion of an *array* of objects. The main form of the application is shown in Figure 23.2.

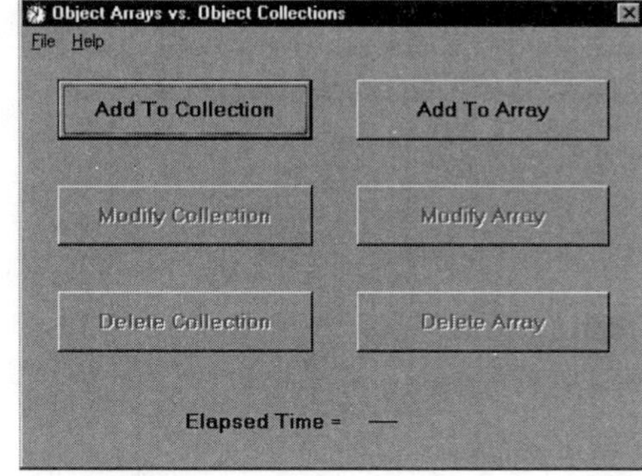

Figure 23.2.
Running the ColArr32.exe application.

Notice the Declarations section of the main form:

```
Private colRunners As New Collection
Private arrRunners() As RunnerClass
Private ArrayCount As Long
```

The first line creates a *collection* of objects called `colRunners`. The second line creates an *array* of objects called `arrRunners`. The number of elements in this array is counted using the `ArrayCount` variable, which is declared last. The `RunnerClass` class module consists of the following properties, as defined in the declarations section of the class module Collect.cls:

```
Public Name As String
Public age As String
Public BestMarathon As String
Public BestMile As String
```

The class also contains initialization code that sets some of the properties to initial values, as follows:

```
Private Sub Class_Initialize()

    BestMarathon = "None"
    BestMile = "None"

End Sub
```

We will first examine the command button in the upper-left corner of the form, labeled Add To Collection. The code listing for the `Click` event of this command button, and the procedure it calls, is shown in Listing 23.6.

Listing 23.6. Procedures used to add objects to the collection.

```
Private Sub cmdAddCollection_Click()

Call Common_StartTimedTest

    For i% = 1 To 200
        Call MakeAnotherColItem(i%)
    Next i%

    Call Common_EndTimedTest(lblElapsedTime)

    cmdModifyCollection.Enabled = True
    cmdDeleteCollection.Enabled = True

End Sub

Sub MakeAnotherColItem(ByVal Indx%)

    Dim Runner As New RunnerClass

    Runner.Name = "Mr. " & Indx%
    colRunners.Add Runner

End Sub
```

The `Click` event procedure calls `MakeAnotherColItem` 200 times. The `MakeAnotherColItem` procedure then creates a new object of class `RunnerClass` and adds it to the collection `colRunners`. This entire process is timed and reported to the user.

In the case of the array of objects, consider the command button labeled Add To Array. Its `Click` event code and the procedure it uses are shown in Listing 23.7.

Listing 23.7. Procedures used to add objects to the array.

```
Private Sub cmdAddArray_Click()

    Call Common_StartTimedTest

    ReDim Preserve arrRunners(ArrayCount + 200)

    For i% = ArrayCount To ArrayCount + 200
        Call MakeAnotherArray(i%)
    Next i%

    Call Common_EndTimedTest(lblElapsedTime)

    ArrayCount = ArrayCount + 200

    cmdModifyArray.Enabled = True
    cmdDeleteArray.Enabled = True

End Sub
```

```
Sub MakeAnotherArray(ByVal Indx%)

    Set arrRunners(Indx%) = New RunnerClass
    arrRunners(Indx%).Name = "Mr. " & Indx%

End Sub
```

As you can see, the click event redimensions the array in increments of 200 as more runners are added. The collection, on the other hand, has a built-in count property that automatically keeps track of this for you. When the `MakeAnotherArray` subroutine is called, a new object is created based on the `RunnerClass` class and is assigned to the array.

The second row of command buttons modifies the collection of objects and the array of objects, respectively. These modification subroutines are shown in Listing 23.8 and 23.9.

Listing 23.8. Procedures used to modify the objects in the collection.

```
Private Sub cmdModifyCollection_Click()

    Call Common_StartTimedTest

    For i% = colRunners.Count To 1 Step -1
        colRunners(i%).Name = colRunners(i%).Name & " Phd."
    Next i%

    Call Common_EndTimedTest(lblElapsedTime)

End Sub
```

Listing 23.9. Procedures used to modify the objects in the array.

```
Private Sub cmdModifyArray_Click()

    If ArrayCount > 0 Then

        Call Common_EndTimedTest(lblElapsedTime)

        For i% = ArrayCount To 0 Step -1
            arrRunners(i%).Name = arrRunners(i%).Name & " Phd."
        Next i%

        Call Common_EndTimedTest(lblElapsedTime)

    End If

End Sub
```

Both procedures essentially accomplish the same task, namely to append a string to the name property of the objects contained in either the control or the array. The command buttons used to delete the objects inside the collection or array are shown in Listing 23.10 and 23.11, respectively.

Listing 23.10. Procedures used to delete the objects in the collection.

```
Private Sub cmdDeleteCollection_Click()

    Call Common_StartTimedTest

    For i% = colRunners.Count To 1 Step -1
        colRunners.Remove i%
    Next i%

    Set colRunners = Nothing

    Call Common_EndTimedTest(lblElapsedTime)

    cmdModifyCollection.Enabled = False
    cmdDeleteCollection.Enabled = False

End Sub
```

Listing 23.11. Procedures used to delete the objects in the array.

```
Private Sub cmdDeleteArray_Click()

    If ArrayCount > 0 Then

        Call Common_StartTimedTest

        ReDim arrRunners(0)

        Call Common_EndTimedTest(lblElapsedTime)

        ArrayCount = 0

        cmdModifyArray.Enabled = False
        cmdDeleteArray.Enabled = False

    End If

End Sub
```

In the case of the collection, the `Remove` method can be easily and conveniently used. In the case of the array, every object can be removed at once by redimensioning the array to zero. The results of creating, modifying, and deleting a collection of these objects versus an array of these objects are shown in Table 23.2.

Table 23.2. Normalized results of manipulating objects in collections versus in arrays.

	Normalized Results	
Operation	*Collection*	*Array*
Creation of all instances	1.75	1.00
Modification of all instances	1.00	5.07
Deletion of all instances	1.50	1.00

The results show that it is faster to *place* objects in an array than in a collection, but it is much faster to *manipulate* those objects in the collection. It is also faster to delete the objects out of the array than it is to delete them out of the collection.

These results make sense when you consider what happens when an object is created in a collection. The `Add` method requires more overhead because it must update other properties of the collection, such as the `Count` property. In other words, the collection has extra "intelligence" that a simple array does not have. That extra intelligence, in the form of properties and methods, slows down the filling and emptying processes of the collection. In the case of the array, it is simply redimensioned and the extra element is set as an object. When you're working with the objects, however, the situation changes. The results show that it is considerably slower to work with the array than with the collection.

If the addition and deletion of objects does not take the bulk of the processing time in an application, collections are preferable. They provide a much cleaner interface to the programmer. The use of collections is particularly beneficial if a great number of manipulations are carried out on the objects within the collection. If, on the other hand, the opposite is true, the arrays are better to work with. As a general rule, however, the collections are a better choice, simply due to their structure and their performance in manipulation.

TIP: Object manipulation is faster when objects are stored in collections than in arrays. While the creation and removal of objects can be slower in collections, the advantage of faster manipulation, coupled with a cleaner interface, makes collections the optimal choice in most cases.

Summary

The ability to create user-defined classes and objects based on those classes is an exciting new feature of Visual Basic 4.0. This chapter examines some of the ways to make programs run faster when they use this new object capability. Two specific techniques are presented.

First, when declaring objects, use the specific name of the class rather than a more generic one. The use of a generic class sometimes offers more flexibility, particularly when you're creating subroutines that can accept objects based on any number of classes. The results of a simple test program, however, show a considerable boost in performance when objects are declared with a class as specific as possible. The trade-off in doing so is reduced modularity in procedures and other areas of code where you wish to leave the type of object open-ended. If you can tie down those ends, however, your application will benefit from increased performance.

The second technique explored in this chapter involves storing groups of objects. Visual Basic 4.0 provides the ability to store objects in collections that are specifically designed to store them. An alternative technique is to simply store the objects in an array that is declared with the class of the objects being stored in it. A code example shows that collections are faster for manipulating objects but not for creating and deleting them. Arrays are faster when you're creating and deleting entries, but they are not as robust and present a messy alternative to the programmer. The chapter concludes that collections are more desirable not only for performance, but for code maintenance, legibility, and structure.

Much more could be said about objects, because they are extremely powerful and relieve the Visual Basic programmer of the many workarounds that were necessary with earlier versions of the product. These techniques will help you achieve the maximum performance in object creation and manipulation, resulting in a faster, more appealing application.

Obey the Signs

Wrong Way: Use public variables in class modules all the time to maximize performance.

This is not good general advice, because the property `Let` and `Set` procedures should not necessarily be avoided in favor of public variables. Don't think that you must avoid property procedures in order to maximize performance. The overhead of calling the procedure is quite small, and it really depends on what goes inside the property procedure, not the mere fact that it exists.

Beware of Falling Rocks: There are times when it is not appropriate to declare objects with references to specific classes.

This chapter points out the benefit of declaring variables with classes that are as specific as possible to the variable. While this dramatically improves performance, there are times when it is not practical to do so. Sometimes you may have procedures that must be able to manipulate several different types of objects at once. Be careful not to sacrifice or break down the beauty of the object-oriented model unless performance can be dramatically improved. Sometimes code structure can outweigh the benefits of increased performance.

Q&A

Q How do Visual Basic objects improve the overall performance of applications?

A Objects make life easier for you primarily because you can structure code in a more object-oriented fashion. Before objects were available, Visual Basic programmers had to create forms and hidden controls to duplicate some of the object-oriented capabilities that are now more fully available (such as encapsulation). Using objects rather than workaround solutions may not dramatically improve performance, but it will most certainly make life easier for you and those who maintain your application. Objects can result in performance penalties if they result in more layers of code to be processed than a non-object architecture, but this tradeoff is very specific to the design of each application.

Q Is it faster to use public variables in class modules to represent properties, or is it better to make them private and create property procedures?

A Public variables are usually faster than property procedures because any validation code or calculations you supply when a property is set in a property procedure add more time to the application than simply setting a variable. This means you have a trade-off between performance and functionality (a familiar concept). Depending on what your property procedures do, performance is usually worse when using a property procedure than when using a property variable. One exception to this rule is when you write a lot of code in the code that sets a variable to simulate a property procedure for a simple variable. You may actually be better off, in this case, using a property procedure instead. Even when a property procedure provides a performance penalty, the penalty is typically very slight and often not in the realm of time that would be perceptible to a user.

Workshop

Write an application that uses a user-defined class to create objects. In your application, assign values to the properties of those objects. Compare the use of public variables declared within the class module to represent properties with the use private variables and property procedures. In your property procedures, try just assigning the value passed in to the procedure to the private variable. Then try using validation code. What are the impacts on performance?

CHAPTER

24

Object Linking and Embedding

A powerful advantage of Visual Basic 4.0 is the level of integration that a Visual Basic app can achieve with other applications through OLE—specifically, embedding or linking data with the OLE container, directly inserting OLE objects, or using OLE automation objects to control other applications. OLE provides easy access to other application objects from a Visual Basic app, painless incorporation of other objects directly into a Visual Basic application through the OLE object container control, and the ability for a Visual Basic application to likewise make itself available as a server. Therefore, the only limit to what a Visual Basic application can now achieve is the developer's initiative and creativity. This world of object sharing does raise some important performance considerations, however.

This chapter focuses on objects that are incorporated into your program through the container control. Chapter 25, "OLE Automation Servers" focuses on OLE automation. The container control provides a doorway for your application into other objects. The performance considerations related to the container control are for the most part external rather than internal, meaning that performance is more dependent on how the object you are connecting to behaves than how your application uses it. Your party is affected the most by who you let in the door, and so it is with the OLE container control. The purposes for which you use the OLE container control and the type of objects with which it interacts can be major factors in your application's performance.

This chapter takes a slightly different approach from the chapters preceding it. The focus in this chapter is on providing an understanding of the overall ramifications of the control itself, independent of the object linked to it, rather than a specific performance test case. This is because any test would be very specific to the object inserted into the container. There are some important performance considerations to be aware of when using OLE container controls that apply regardless of the object inserted. Even if you can't do much to prevent them, an awareness of these issues can help you make defensive design decisions. That is where we turn our attention now.

The Performance Penalty from Other Objects

When you use the services of another application, you inherit its performance characteristics. OLE performance in Visual Basic 4.0 is much improved from earlier versions, but nevertheless, there is a lot more overhead involved with supporting OLE than if an application simply had internal code to achieve the same result with no external dependencies.

The OLE container provides several powerful capabilities for your applications. You can use it to either *link* or *embed* objects created by other applications. With either approach, it also enables the activation and control of objects contained in other applications from within your own application.

An object in the object container provides a collection of actions, or *verbs,* that cause operations to take place on the object. You can trigger these actions in your code, and therefore control the object's application, through the use of the object's `DoVerb` method. If the object's `AutoActivate` property is set to `True`, your user will automatically be presented with a list of verbs that apply to an object in the container control whenever the right mouse button is clicked. The object and its application can also be controlled and activated in this manner. The activation can consist of starting up the application that contains the object in a separate window, just as if that application had been started independently with the appropriate data file already loaded.

The activation could even occur alternatively "in place," displaying the object data within the OLE container and giving users the perception that they are working with the data as a window in your program. Menu items that are relevant to the activated object can be provided on your application's menu bars. Thus, OLE can be used to give the impression that those objects *and* their external applications are a part of *your* application. This can be both good and bad. If your user clicks on an OLE container to bring up a picture and then is disappointed by the display time of that picture from its host application, the user may very well perceive that it is *your* application that has the problem.

You as a developer must fully assess the performance of the integrated piece of software before settling on it as an acceptable solution. You adopt that software object as your own when you incorporate it into your application, because from the standpoint of the user, it *is* part of your application. Sometimes there will be nothing you can do about the poor performance of an object driven through OLE automation. Often, however, you can improve performance by gaining a better understanding of the object.

Case Study: Bill's OLE Container Control Nightmare

Before planning to provide an object in your application with the OLE container control, carefully consider the pros and cons. If the performance of the object's parent application will be perceived as unacceptably slow to your users, you may wish to reevaluate the decision. More than a few Visual Basic programmers have paid the price for good intentions. For example, consider the hypothetical OLE container control experience of Bill, the programmer of our earlier case studies.

Suppose Bill has the task of writing a small employee database for in-house use at his company. The company simply needs to give all its employees the ability to quickly access employee information such as name and office phone number. Since Bill has some free time and has a reputation as someone who has been experimenting with Visual Basic and databases, he is given the task. After months of fending off criticisms from his C++ biased co-workers, Bill is anxious to show them the wonderful things Visual Basic can do, particularly with database applications.

Bill attends a planning meeting for the new system with his bosses. In Bill's enthusiasm to showcase the abilities of Visual Basic, he blurts out that he can provide user-editable pictures of every employee in the database with virtually no extra effort. Of course, his boss thinks this sounds pretty neat, so she pats Bill on the back and tells him to go for it. Bill comes away from the meeting excited about the support he receives. He decides to really showcase the OLE container control in his application. He not only provides an OLE container control that is bound to employee pictures in the database, but he also provides controls to contain special-format pictures of each employee's office location that can be viewed with a photo viewer application. Still not satisfied, he adds another OLE container control to contain WAV files of employee voices, which he pulls from voice mail. For a final flourish, he even rounds up floor plan diagrams of each employee's office, which are in a special data format that can be used only with one specific floor plan viewer application. He then adds an OLE container control for the floor plans as well.

Finally, the day comes when Bill unleashes his system on users. It is less than a smashing success. Bill had an inkling that the performance of his application was mediocre as he developed it on his Pentium. The outcry from his users is deafening as they try to run it on their slower machines. The main form shows information for one employee at a time. Users want to use the new application to quickly scroll from one employee's information to another. However, with the OLE container controls, information is somewhat slow to scroll and the program itself is very slow to load. Even activating the objects is perceived to be slow. Bill has placed all four database-bound container controls on the main form. Because of this, the application takes a considerable amount of time to load the first form and to change from one form to another.

Bill receives many complaints about his application having very poor performance in its handling of the photo viewer. This puzzles Bill because the photo viewer is a slow application, but it is not his application. The slowness that his users experience in viewing the photo objects that contain the office pictures is the fault of the photo viewer application, and nothing he has any control over. Bill cannot understand why his users are blaming him.

Likewise, he receives complaints about the paint program, which is the application associated with employee pictures. It really doesn't take the paint program much longer to load from Bill's application than if it were started as a separate package. However, it appears to take longer because the users subconsciously expect the response time of the object's activation to be on par with the response of the other command buttons in Bill's application. They don't stop to think that an entirely separate application must be loaded when they activate an object—they just know they must wait.

There are other problems as well. Several users who had never even realized they didn't have sound cards have suddenly stormed into the boss's office demanding one so they can fully use the latest software. And many users have become very irate when they attempt to work with the floor plan diagrams in the database and find that their system cannot activate those objects because they don't have the appropriate applications installed.

Bill must now slink to and from the water cooler, dodging the accusatory "I told you so" glances of C++ programmers as he plans a major design overhaul of his application. The problem, he realizes, wasn't Visual Basic. It was that Visual Basic made it so easy and so tempting for him to incorporate many more objects than he really needed. He could support the objects, but he had to pay a performance price. His co-workers really would have been happier and more impressed with a simpler database that appeared to have a snappier performance and caused them fewer frustrations. Instead, they have a slow employee database that causes them some puzzlement as they attempt to activate the objects they don't have experience with. There are several important lessons that Bill has learned the hard way.

TIP: If you use an OLE container control to provide an interface to an object, your application will pay a performance penalty when forms containing the OLE container control are displayed, but particularly at load time. Users may even perceive more performance problems than really exist, because when they activate an object they might subconsciously expect application command button–type response time and overlook the fact that they have to pay the price of waiting for the embedded or linked object's application to load.

TIP: Sluggish performance can tarnish the usability of an application, whether it is caused by your code or not. Recognize that when you enable an application to embed an object or you incorporate an application into your own app through in-line activation, users will regard the external application's performance as that of your own.

TIP: If you provide an object container for standardized purposes, you must consider whether all your users will have the necessary software to work with that object. In some cases, object support in an application may even make users realize they need more hardware, such as sound cards or additional memory. If your users don't all have the required systems, consider the decision carefully. You must decide if the importance of that feature is such that it will be worth it to end users to endure the cost, or worth it to you to endure the complaints, of those who will need to upgrade their capabilities because of your application.

These tips are not meant to discourage you from using OLE containers. It is a powerful technology whose time has arrived. However, the use of OLE containers should not be undertaken lightly just to add another bell or whistle to an application. The technology is sound. Most of the lessons that Bill has learned relate more to the psychology of user perceptions of performance than to the technology. This generation of computer users is still getting used to the concept of an application incorporating components of other applications and the performance ramifications this entails. For now (and probably forever), any such undertakings should be carefully planned, prototyped, and performance tested in advance…a lesson Bill will be sure to remember when he finds his next job.

TIP: OLE container controls can greatly extend the capabilities and power of your application. They can also impose a performance penalty. Since they allow you to incorporate another application into your application, it may take some

experimentation to understand all the ramifications. Make sure you schedule plenty of time to investigate and prototype when you work on a new design based on incorporation of OLE container controls.

Verb Considerations

Earlier discussion addresses the fact that you can write code to interact with an embedded or linked object and its application. You programmatically control the actions of the object in an OLE container control through its `DoVerb` method. This replaces the `Action` property of Visual Basic 3.0. (Backward compatibility is provided.) You can query the verbs by examining the `ObjectVerbs` array of the object. There you can find additional functions beyond the standard actions (in-place activation, activation as a separate app, and hiding). The standard actions can be carried out by setting `DoVerb` to the appropriate value as documented under the `DoVerb` portion of the Visual Basic help file. In addition, the other verbs that a unique object supports may give you better performance alternatives for some of the tasks you need to carry out. Study an object's verbs carefully before deciding how to use it. You may discover that more optimal actions are available than what you would otherwise program.

Beware of Added Storage Demands

When you open the door for your users to easily incorporate embedded objects into an application (particularly document-centric objects), disk-space consumption can be dramatically affected. If your database users are able to add wav files, video files, and pictures of their latest family reunion to the form that they use for their weekly status report, they are likely to do so. You can have a lot of additional data once you open this door. This is not necessarily a bad thing. After all, that's what the container control is intended for. However, you should consider the performance impact in advance.

> **TIP:** When you provide users with the capability to add embedded objects into an application through an OLE container control, your storage needs may increase considerably and performance may be affected. Large volumes of data can be generated when objects are made convenient and accessible.

Linking Versus Embedding Objects

When you insert an object into a container control, you can control whether it is linked or embedded. You can do this several ways, including doing so programmatically by using the OLE container control's `CreateLink` method or by checking the link check box at runtime on the insert dialog box that the container provides. An embedded object is initially stored in the application source file, but when modified can be stored in a separate embedded file. Forms with container controls storing linked objects appear to load slightly faster than those with embedded objects. In testing carried out with `WordDoc` objects containing pictures, forms with linked objects as opposed to embedded objects seemed to load about 12 percent faster. These results will, of course, be very application and object specific.

TIP: Form load times for forms containing OLE container controls will vary greatly depending on the objects and the applications. However, in one series of tests carried out, forms with locally linked objects loaded slightly faster than forms with objects embedded directly in the container controls.

There are other important considerations for the performance of linked objects. An object is quite likely to be linked across a network if it must be shared on more than one PC. Load and access times in this case would be less than for an embedded object where data is stored locally on the PC. If you provide an application where you must make the same data available to all your users, but that data will never change, consider providing the data through an embedded object to safeguard your users from the penalty of network performance.

TIP: If you provide linked data that is shared across a network in an OLE container control, users will pay the price of the network performance penalty. Access will be faster if the object data is embedded and stored in the local application file, if you know the object data will never change.

Another property that you might think could pertain to load speed when skimming the OLE container control property list is the `DisplayType` property. When `DisplayType` is set to `0`, the contents of the container control are displayed. When `DisplayType` is set to `1`, only the icon for the object is displayed. It might seem intuitive that it would be quicker to load and display just the icon rather than the contents. Surprisingly, testing seemed to show that there is no penalty for displaying contents. In fact, in a series of tests, forms with only controls displaying object icons loaded slightly faster than forms with controls that displayed object contents. While the difference was not great enough to be statistically significant, it does tell you that switching to a `DisplayType` of icon will not alleviate form load performance problems.

TIP: Displaying the objects stored in OLE container controls on forms as icons seems to offer no performance loading advantages over displaying the entire contents for the object. Therefore, use the technique that makes the most sense in the context of your user interface.

The `SizeMode` property seems like another likely candidate that might affect the form load performance of a form containing many controls. Setting the `SizeMode` property of an OLE container control affects how the contents are represented within the container. Possible options include clipping, stretching, autosizing, and zooming. Constants for each of these property values are documented in the Visual Basic help file. A series of tests showed no clear relation to these settings and overall form load time for a form containing many OLE container controls. It is likely that there is an image calculation and painting performance difference between these techniques, but that the time is so small in the face of overall form load time and timing fluctuation that it is not a statistically significant factor.

Enhancing Speed By Using Memory Instead of Temporary Disk Space

The OLE container control has a property called `MiscFlags`. `MiscFlags` can be set to carry out some advanced features for the control. One of those features is very important to performance. That feature is the ability to use memory rather than temporary disk space for working storage for a loaded object. Since OLE container control objects can have large quantities of data associated with them, the data size can get quite large. Therefore, this setting should only be used when you are sure that there will be plenty of memory available. The default setting of the container control is to use temporary disk space rather than memory. The syntax for setting this property to direct the control to use memory over temporary disk space is

```
oleMyObject.MiscFlags = vbOLEMiscFlagMemStorage
```

The constant `vbOLEMiscFlagMemStorage` that appears in this code is a predefined Visual Basic constant. This one-line statement is all it takes to cause memory to be used instead of disk space. Performance savings can be substantial. On one test carried out, this cut control access time in half. Results will, of course, be very application and object dependent.

Summary

This chapter provides a conceptual discussion of OLE object container controls. When you provide an OLE control in your application, your application is then subject to the performance impact of supporting that contained object and, in some cases, it inherits the behavior of its associated application, as well. Users will perceive the performance of contained objects as that of your application. Therefore, you must use OLE container controls judiciously.

OLE container controls will cause a form to take longer to load. Embedded objects in container controls seem to take more of a toll than linked objects, although the difference is slight. The OLE container control's `MiscFlags` property can be set to tell the control to use memory for storage of loaded objects rather than temporary disk space. This can provide noticeable performance improvements within an application.

Often when an OLE object container control is provided, it is for uses such as storing information in a database and accessing that information from a database front end. Providing such an opportunity for users can result in large volumes of data. If you add an object container control to a heavily used database so users can store graphic images, for example, you may find that users enjoy the convenience so much that 80 percent of new entries now contain pictures in the container control. That, in turn, will place heavy storage demands on your system, which you may not have anticipated. The best guideline is to be cautious, plan ahead, and carry out extensive performance testing using the container control.

Obey the Signs

Wrong Way: Container controls sound intimidating, so I'll avoid them for now.

Wrong attitude! Container controls add amazing capabilities to your application. They open the door to a whole world of possibilities, including better use of multimedia. While there can be some performance drawbacks with incorporating them, you won't know how extensive they are until you investigate. The container control is a technology that has finally come of age, and will be of great use to those who put in the work to understand and exploit it.

Beware of Falling Rocks: Don't get so carried away with container controls that you add them frivolously.

Container controls can add important touches to an application. On the other hand, it is easy to go hog wild and end up with an application that is needlessly loaded with container controls and stuffed full of "documents." Use a container control when it adds important functionality to your program. If you are tempted to do so for spice rather than function—for example, adding WAV files that make animal sounds when your user logs off—reconsider. It is not likely to be worth the performance penalty.

Q&A

Q I used to use the `Action` property under Visual Basic 3.0. Does it still work?

A The `Action` property is still supported but not recommended. The `DoVerb` method is a much better way to control action. It has supporting properties such as `ObjectVerbs` that can be used to find out the list of actions that an object can support. And don't forget that clicking the right mouse button will provide a list of verbs for the object in the selected OLE container control, as long as that control's `AutoVerbMenu` is set to `True`.

Q Are you saying that objects can have their own actions? I thought they all worked the same.

A Every object supports default actions, such as open, hide, and activate in place. However, objects can also have their own actions. You can query these programmatically by looking at the `ObjectVerbs` property array.

Workshop

Write a program that assesses the performance of opening an object in a separate application window (`object.DoVerb vbOLEShow`), and write another test to open it with in-line activation (`object.DoVerb vbOLEUIActivate`). How does the performance of the two programs compare?

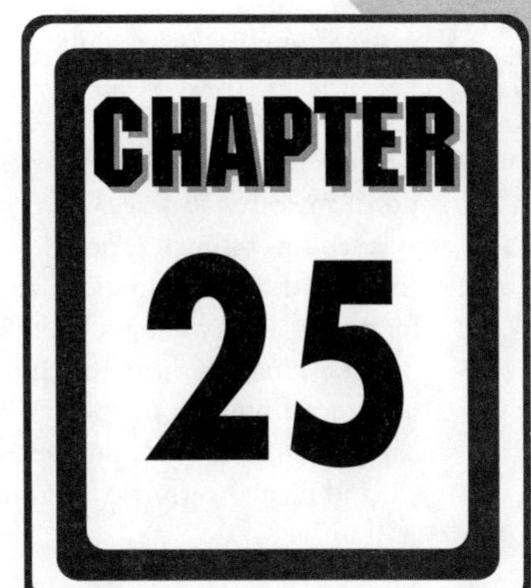

OLE Automation Servers

One of the most powerful capabilities available for implementing advanced Visual Basic architectures built on shared services and reusable components is the ability to define OLE Automation servers. You can create OLE Automation servers in Visual Basic that provide exposed properties and methods to other applications. The magic of this service-sharing architecture is accomplished through system OLE services. Fortunately, Visual Basic 4.0 makes it so easy to create such servers that little OLE-specific knowledge is needed. These servers can be bundled in convenient EXE or DLL packages.

Chapter 23, "Objects," discusses how your application inherits the performance characteristics of any external object it incorporates. The same principle in reverse applies when you provide services through exposed objects such as OLE servers. Since any OLE Automation server code you develop is intended to be shared with other applications, there is an additional need for performance tuning. Others will certainly be using the application, and they will encounter the additional overhead that using an OLE Automation server entails. You should assess performance from this perspective with relevant test applications before considering any object complete and ready for public use. The issues of the overhead of using OLE Automation servers, and related performance tuning guidelines, are the focus of this chapter.

In-Process Versus Out-of-Process OLE Automation Servers

With the 32-bit version of Visual Basic 4.0, two types of OLE Automation servers can be implemented: in-process and out-of-process OLE servers. An in-process server is built from Visual Basic source code into a DLL; an out-of-process server is built as an executable file. As the name implies, an in-process server can be run in the same address space as its calling application. An out-of-process server incurs the overhead of a separate address space. Therefore, the use of in-process servers, which are available to 32-bit programs only, can provide considerable performance benefits. Comparative performance of in-process versus out-of-process servers is examined in the sample function call program shown in Figure 25.1. This program, UseSvr32.exe, is available on the CD-ROM that comes with this book.

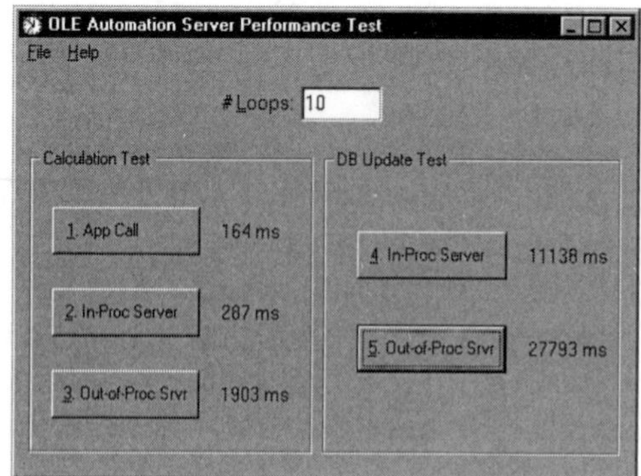

Figure 25.1.
Calculation call test case results after the first trial of each test.

Calculation Call Tests

The first series of tests we will consider are those enclosed in the frame labeled Calculation Test in Figure 25.1. These tests exercise a calculation that is called from within the same Visual

Basic program, from an out-of-process OLE Automation server, and from an in-process OLE Automation server, respectively.

The Same Program Call

Listing 25.1 shows the code for the first test case, a standard call to a function defined within the same program.

Listing 25.1. A call to a function in the same program.

```
Private Sub cmdAppCall_Click()
' This routine tests speed a call to a calculation routine within the same app


    ' This event records the elapsed time for the matrix
    ' divide function called within Visual Basic.  The
    ' number of times the function gets executed is
    ' determined by the user.

    Dim i&                         ' Index value
    Dim Result&                    ' Result value

    ' Declarations for the two arrays which will be divided
    Dim a(1 To 1000) As Long
    Dim b(1 To 1000) As Long

    ' Initialize arrays
    Call InitArrays(a(), b())

    ' Start the timer
    Call Common_StartTimedTest

    ' Call the function as many times as user specifies
    For i = 1 To txtMaxLoops
        Result = VB_MatrixDivide(a(), b())
    Next


    Call Common_EndTimedTest(lbl1Results)

End Sub
```

This calculation function that is called in all test cases is the same one that was used in Chapter 22, “Moving Code to DLLs,” to carry out comparative analysis of Visual Basic code with C++ and Delphi dynamic link library code. Here we use the calculation routine to perform the same comparison for OLE Automation server calls. The calculation routine `VB_MatrixDivide` is shown in Listing 25.2. This routine is defined locally within the Visual Basic main form module for the first test case. The subroutine `InitArrays` carries out the initialization of arrays prior to this call.

Listing 25.2. The calculation routine.

```
Private Function VB_MatrixDivide(a() As Long, b() As Long) As Long

    ' This is the Visual Basic implementation of the
    ' array division function.  The procedure is very
    ' simple, contained in one loop.

    Dim Result As Long
    Dim i As Integer

    For i = 1 To UBound(a)
        Result = Result + a(i) \ b(i)
    Next

    VB_MatrixDivide = Result

End Function
```

An In-Process OLE Automation Server Call

The next test is structurally very similar, as shown in Listing 25.3. However, instead of a call being made to a local function to carry out the calculation, a call is made to the same routine contained inside an in-process OLE Automation server.

Listing 25.3. An in-process OLE Automation server call test.

```
Private Sub cmd2_InProc_Click()

' This routine tests speed a call to a calculation routine in an InProc Server


    ' This event records the elapsed time for the matrix
    ' divide function called within Visual Basic.  The
    ' number of times the function gets executed is
    ' determined by the user.

    Dim i&                      ' Index value
    Dim Result&                 ' Result value

    ' Declarations for the two arrays which will be divided
    Dim a(1 To 1000) As Long
    Dim b(1 To 1000) As Long

    ' Initialize arrays
    Call InitArrays(a(), b())

    ' Start the timer
    Call Common_StartTimedTest


    Dim objInfo As CalcIn  ' Server class
```

```
    ' Create the new instance of this object
    Set objInfo = New CalcIn


    ' Call the function as many times as user specifies
    For i = 1 To txtMaxLoops
        Result = objInfo.OLEServer_MatrixDivide(a(), b())
    Next


    Set objInfo = Nothing

    Call Common_EndTimedTest(lbl2Results)

End Sub
```

The calculation used in this test case is contained in the objInfo object's `OLEServer_MatrixDivide` method. This method is defined in the class `CalcIn`, which is the basis for this OLE Automation server object. This calculation is therefore available as a method for objects instantiated from that class. The server was defined and compiled from a separate Visual Basic project than our test program. The OLE Automation server project and resulting executable files are available on the CD-ROM as CalcIn32.vbp and CalcIn32.dll. The OLE Automation server project is declared with appropriate settings for the project and class library and contains a class module that defines the `OLEServer_MatrixDivide` method. That class module appears in Listing 25.4. Refer to the *Visual Basic Programmer's Guide* for full details on creating automation servers. An in-process server is built from this project and its class definition. This results in the ClassIn32.dll. To use this class from a Visual Basic program after the in-process server is built, you simply need to add the appropriate reference, `Calc Sample—InProc 32-Bit`, under the Visual Basic Tools | Reference menu. Then the class can be directly referenced in that project's source code by referring to the class name `CalcIn`, as shown in Listing 25.4.

Listing 25.4. The OLE Automation server class module.

```
' Note - these properties are settings stored in the text file, some
'        are settable through the Class Module property sheet window
VERSION 1.0 CLASS
BEGIN
  MultiUse = -1  'True
END
Attribute VB_Name = "CalcIn"
Attribute VB_Creatable = True
Attribute VB_Exposed = True
Option Explicit

' Note - this is method defined in class module

Public Function OLEServer_MatrixDivide(a() As Long, b() As Long) As Long

    ' This is the Visual Basic implementation of the
```

```
    ' array division function.  The procedure is very
    ' simple, contained in one loop.

    Dim Result As Long
    Dim i As Integer

    For i = 1 To UBound(a)
        Result = Result + a(i) \ b(i)
    Next

    OLEServer_MatrixDivide = Result

End Function
```

NOTE: Another application can only use the services of an OLE Automation server if that application references the server when the application is built. OLE Automation servers must be defined in the system registry for their classes to be exposed as an available reference. This procedure is carried out automatically when you install the sample programs from this book's CD-ROM. However, if you experience problems or wish to redefine the programs to the registry, simply rebuild each automation server through Visual Basic, and the servers will be automatically registered. Server project files used by this test program are CalcIn32.vbp, CalcOt32.vbp, LogIn32.vbp, and LogOut32.vpb. There are other methods that can also be used to register server programs. Simply running the executable file of a Visual Basic out-of-process OLE Automation server will cause it to register itself. Similarly, the utility RegSvr32.exe, which comes with Visual Basic, can be used to register an in-process OLE Automation server DLL.

An Out-of-Process OLE Automation Server Call

A test case almost identical to the in-process server test is used to check the performance of an out-of-process OLE Automation server. This server has the available reference name `Calc Sample—OutProc 32Bit`, which the project references, and the class name `CalcOut`, which is referenced by the test program source code. That test case is shown in Listing 25.5. The only difference in the test program code is that a different class is used to reference the out-of-process server than the in-process server. The calculation code is defined as a method in the out-of-process project's class, just as it was for the in-process project's class. The only differences between the in-process server `CalcIn` and out-of-process server `CalcOut` are that a different class name, a different project option name, and a different reference name were used so that the servers could be uniquely distinguished. The `CalcOut` server is built from project CalcOt32.vbp into file CalcOt32.exe. By virtue of building `CalcIn` as a DLL and `CalcOut` as an EXE, the servers were designated as in-process or out-of-process.

Listing 25.5. An out-of-process server test case.

```
Private Sub cmdForNext_Click()

' This routine tests speed a call to a calculation routine within an
'   Out of Proc OLE Automation Server


    ' This event records the elapsed time for the matrix
    ' divide function called within Visual Basic.  The
    ' number of times the function gets executed is
    ' determined by the user.

    Dim i&                        ' Index value
    Dim Result&                   ' Result value

    ' Declarations for the two arrays which will be divided
    Dim a(1 To 1000) As Long
    Dim b(1 To 1000) As Long

    ' Initialize arrays
    Call InitArrays(a(), b())

    ' Start the timer
    Call Common_StartTimedTest


    Dim objInfo As CalcOut   ' Server class


   ' Create the new instance of this object
    Set objInfo = New CalcOut


    ' Call the function as many times as user specifies
    For i = 1 To txtMaxLoops
        Result = objInfo.OLEServer_MatrixDivide(a(), b())
    Next


    Set objInfo = Nothing

    Call Common_EndTimedTest(lbl3Results)

End Sub
```

Comparison of Results

Results from running this test program will be different when you exercise each test for the first time compared to when you execute it subsequent times. Initialization of the OLE servers seems to incur overhead that is not present on following accesses. Typical timings for a first trial are shown in Figure 25.1. Representative timings for subsequent trials are shown in Figure 25.2. The timings drop significantly.

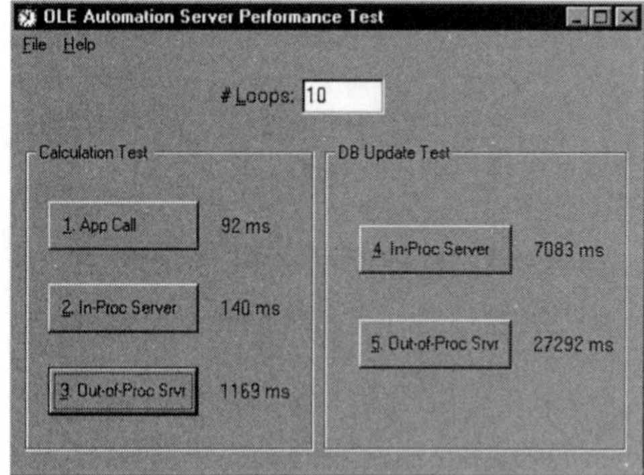

Figure 25.2.
Calculation call test case results after repeated trials of each test.

This calculation test is the same as the one used in Chapter 22 when we looked at the speed of a C++ dynamic link library. A representative trial of that program is repeated here as well to show the C++ DLL performance. That result is shown in Figure 25.3.

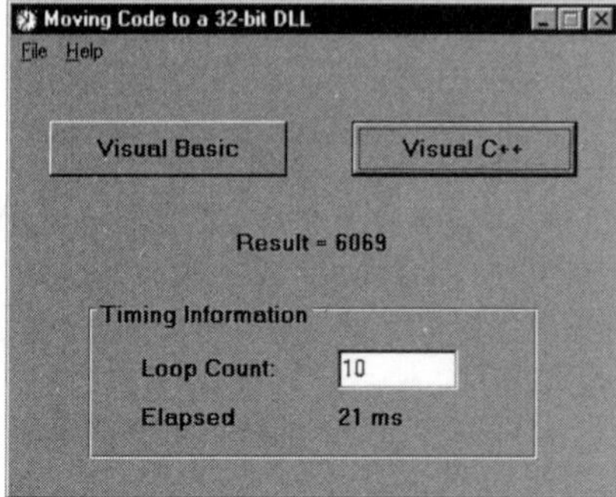

Figure 25.3.
Results from a DLL call.

Normalized timings for these trials are provided in Table 25.1.

Table 25.1. Calling a calculation routine from a Visual Basic application.

Test Case	*Normalized Result*
C++ DLL call, first trial	19.0
VB app call, first trial	7.8
In-process server call, first trial	13.7
Out-of-process server call, first trial	90.6
C++ DLL call, subsequent trials	1.0
VB app call, subsequent trials	4.4
In-process server call, subsequent trials	6.7
Out-of-process server call, subsequent trials	55.6

Table 25.2 shows these results sorted from best to worst.

Table 25.2. Results of calling a calculation routine from a Visual Basic application, sorted from best to worst.

Test Case	*Normalized Result*
C++ DLL call, subsequent trials	1.0
VB app call, subsequent trials	4.4
In-Process server call, subsequent trials	6.7
VB app call, first trial	7.8
In-process server call, first trial	13.7
C++ DLL call, first trial	19.0
Out-of-process server call, subsequent trials	55.6
Out-of-process server call, first trial	90.6

The usual disclaimer applies that results will be very application dependent for such trials. Still, a general trend emerges that can be expected to largely hold true regardless of application-specific considerations. The C++ DLL is clearly the fastest call method for a calculation. Calling the calculation routine inside Visual Basic proves to be the second fastest approach. This approach is significantly faster than calling an in-process server method.

Even though an in-process server shares the address space of the calling application, it still incurs OLE overhead at each call that is not present in a direct Visual Basic function call. An in-process DLL is *not* the same as a regular C++ DLL. A Visual Basic–produced in-process OLE Automation server DLL requires the runtime interpreter when it is carried out. Even though it is packaged as a dynamic link library, it is still interpreted. Additionally, unlike a traditional C++ DLL, the in-process DLL provides its services under the auspices of OLE by exposing classes, properties, and methods. Significantly more overhead is involved than with a simple call to a compiled DLL function call. The out-of-process time is far behind the times of the other methods.

Next we carry out a similar test to get a more well-rounded view of performance and to offset any application-specific skew. For the second test we again compare in-process and out-of-process times. The server we use for these test cases is a modified version of the Performance Time Log server utility described in Chapter 7, "Supporting Utilities for Performance Analysis."

Our test code uses the in-process server LogIn32.dll and the out-of-process server LogOut32.dll. These servers advertise their services in the Visual Basic Tools | References window as Sample Log—OutProc 32-Bit DLL and Sample Log—OutProc 32-Bit EXE, respectively. They are referenced by class names `clsInProcTimeEntries` and `clsOutProcTimeEntries` from within the code of the UseSrv.exe test program.

The test code calls database functions contained in the server that result in adding a timing record to the database. This code is shown in Listing 25.6.

Listing 25.6. The in-process server timing database update test case.

```
Private Sub cmd4_InProc_Click()
' This routine tests speed a call to an in-proc server that makes db updates


    Dim i&                                    ' Index value

    Dim objTimeInfo As clsInProcTimeEntries   ' Server class


    ' Start the timer
    Call Common_StartTimedTest

    ' Call the function as many times as user specifies
    For i = 1 To txtMaxLoops

        ' Create the new instance of this object
        Set objTimeInfo = New clsInProcTimeEntries

        ' Insert a simulated timing, using loop index
        '   First set up four properties of this object, then
        '   call the method "AddTiming" to cause object to add
        '   this new entry to the underlying database.
        lngLastDuration = lngLastDuration + 1

        objTimeInfo.NewCollection = "DBSPEED"
        objTimeInfo.NewStartTime = 0
        objTimeInfo.NewEndTime = lngLastDuration
        objTimeInfo.NewDuration = lngLastDuration
        objTimeInfo.AddTiming

        Set objTimeInfo = Nothing
    Next

    Call Common_EndTimedTest(lbl4Results)

End Sub
```

The out-of-process test case is very similar; the only difference is that it refers to the class of the out-of-process server rather than the in-process server to cause the correct server to carry out the update. That code is shown in Listing 25.7.

Listing 25.7. The out-of-process server timing database update test case.

```
Private Sub cmd5_OutOfProc_Click()


' This routine tests speed a call to an in-proc server that makes db updates
```

```
    Dim i&                                     ' Index value

    Dim objTimeInfo As clsOutProcTimeEntries  ' Server class


    ' Start the timer
    Call Common_StartTimedTest

    ' Call the function as many times as user specifies
    For i = 1 To txtMaxLoops

        ' Create the new instance of this object
        Set objTimeInfo = New clsOutProcTimeEntries

        ' Insert a simulated timing, using loop index
        '   First set up four properties of this object, then
        '   call the method "AddTiming" to cause object to add
        '   this new entry to the underlying database.
        lngLastDuration = lngLastDuration + 1

        objTimeInfo.NewCollection = "DBSPEED"
        objTimeInfo.NewStartTime = 0
        objTimeInfo.NewEndTime = lngLastDuration
        objTimeInfo.NewDuration = lngLastDuration
        objTimeInfo.AddTiming

        Set objTimeInfo = Nothing
    Next

    Call Common_EndTimedTest(lbl5Results)

End Sub
```

The results from these test cases are shown in Figures 25.1 and 25.2. Normalized results for these two methods are shown in Table 25.3.

Table 25.3. Normalized results for in-process versus out-of-process server calls.

Test	*Normalized Result*
In-process, first trial	1.6
In-process, subsequent trials	1.0
Out-of-process, first trial	3.9
Out-of-process, subsequent trials	3.8

The results here are slightly different from those in the first calculation test. The performance gap between the two types of servers is actually smaller. The out-of-process server was around four times slower in the calculation tests. While this is a significant slowdown, it is less than that of the calculation test. This is more evidence that every performance test is application and trial specific. In performance tuning, no results should ever be viewed as absolute. There are too many factors that keep us from isolating every area affecting performance. In this test, we can surmise that at least part of the difference is because the behavior profile of database code is different from calculation code.

> **TIP:** In-process OLE Automation server performance is slower than that of the same code directly called in a Visual Basic program. Likewise, out-of-process OLE Automation servers have substantially slower performance than their in-process counterparts.

Out-of-Process Server Performance

The out-of-process server clearly comes out at the back of the pack when it comes to performance in every case. Input/output takes many times longer than any of the other methods on the system used for the test. Results will vary based on factors such as the system, available memory, and the type of application. But regardless of the variations, the out-of-process server will not approach the performance levels of the other methods. It is constrained by several factors, including OLE overhead, interpreted code, and a non-shared address space.

You may wonder at this point why anyone would use an out-of-process server. There are several good reasons. OLE Automation servers, whether in-process or out-of-process, provide a wonderful code-packaging mechanism. Simply distributing component executables and DLLs is much easier than rebuilding and redistributing an entire application for every small change. Likewise, at a programmatic level it is easier to write code that is built on the class/object model of the automation servers than to write a normal collection of modules, routines, and variables. An out-of-process server (which must be generated by an EXE file) can also present a user interface when called as a standalone program, while an in-process server cannot be directly invoked as a standalone program. Thus, any regular application can make its services available as an out-of-process server. Exposing services, or making available the properties and methods of an object to another calling component, is the core of OLE Automation servers. The ease of exposing services is one great benefit of this technology. It would be a daunting task to write other-language DLLs to accomplish this same level of information sharing.

> **TIP:** Even though OLE Automation servers impose some overhead penalties, they offer substantial benefits in terms of code design, development, and maintenance. For timing-critical code, they should be used with discretion; but otherwise, potential server benefits should be considered.

Remote Automation Servers

Another big advantage of out-of-process servers is that they can be used as remote automation object (RAO) servers, whereas in-process servers cannot. RAO servers reside across the network from calling programs. The servers execute in a different CPU than the program that calls them. This can provide great performance boosts to the calling programs. The calling program doesn't have to wait for the remote automation server to complete but rather can continue with other processing. The RAO can notify the calling program when its results are finished. Depending on the type of calling program, this speedup can be significant. Even if the RAO code executes a little slower than some of the other call techniques, benefits will still be present since that RAO code can be carried out on a different PC than the PC where the client program resides. The client can continue on with other useful work even as the RAO server PC is still processing a prior request. Since the calling client program has eliminated the processing burden from its CPU and can simply collect results when they are available, that client program can potentially execute much more quickly.

> **TIP:** Remote automation objects can provide significant performance improvements by off-loading tasks to a server CPU across the network and allowing the calling client program to continue processing even as the server collects results.

Therefore, the RAO is a very important performance-enhancing tool in client/server environments. Visual Basic client/server performance is a very broad area and the possible subject of a separate book in its own right. However, there are two immediate considerations that bear highlighting here. When the RAO approach is used, the speed of the network and the speed of the server CPU can be constraining factors on performance. When you enter the client/server world of computing, forces that are external to your PC (and often out of your control) will make your program run faster or slower. We have already seen what a tremendous challenge performance tuning can be in a standalone environment, with the great variability and flux in system performance from one time span to another. With client/server computing, this factor is multiplied many times over.

> **TIP:** Remember that once you incorporate a strategy based on remote automation objects, your program performance will be influenced by external factors such as network load and server CPU.

OLE Server Busy Time-outs and Perceived Performance

When you make use of another application's exposed objects through OLE, you are counting on that OLE server application to be available to service your requests. However, if that application is already responding to the requests of yet another client application, your application must wait its turn. Likewise, if your application requests some action of the server that the server application is not able to fulfill because of its current state (for example, if it is already displaying a modal error message to an interactive user), the server will not be able to immediately respond to your application.

In both of these cases, Visual Basic automatically keeps trying to fulfill your request by continually retrying to pass the request to the server, in hopes that the busy period is a temporary condition. Visual Basic continues these repeated efforts until a given time-out period has expired, and then it displays the "Server Busy" message to the user.

The retry duration is controlled by your application through the `App.ServerBusyTimeout` and `App.RequestPendingTimeout` properties. The `ServerBusyTimeout` property has a default of 10 seconds, and `RequestPendingTimeout` has a default of 5 seconds. OLE communication establishment and contention is not an area you can directly control since it depends on the state of the PC at any given time. However, this is an area that may be a perceived performance issue to your users because they will be very aware that they are waiting on the software at these times of contention.

The time-out properties raise an interesting performance question for the developer. Is it better to consider an operation to be timed out as quickly as possible? This allows you to have the fastest possible time-out feedback to the user, but also increases the likelihood that a time-out message may be generated before all operations have a chance to succeed. On the other hand, if a time-out condition is only declared after very long periods of time have gone by and you've given your code every chance to communicate, you will have subjected your user to a longer wait before time-out error messages are presented.

Will your users' perceptions of the program be better if they occasionally have to wait long periods of time but rarely have the application give them a busy (failure) message? This will probably be the case if they are in an environment where OLE communication establishment is likely to be slow or marked by contention. If so, you may want to increase the time-out periods even more. Or, is it more likely that situations when the OLE server is tied up will be very infrequent? In this case, perhaps your user would like immediate feedback in the very rare cases when the server is busy, rather than be subject to much longer waits to see the same "busy" error message. As you probably suspected, there are no stock answers to these questions. A time-out strategy that works well for one user on a blazing-fast Pentium with little OLE server contention may seem to impose insufferable waits on another user on a turtle-slow 386 where there is much contention for OLE services due to the other software being used. In general, the Visual Basic defaults serve as an effective starting point, but depending on your specific OLE server needs and target user base, you may need to tweak these to satisfy your users' needs.

> **TIP:** Consider user perceptions when deciding on a server time-out strategy.

Summary

This chapter examines performance issues surrounding OLE Automation servers. A comparison of server performance is carried out for both calculation-based services and database services. Testing shows that C++ DLLs offer the best performance, followed by native Visual Basic application calls. In-process servers perform measurably slower than the native Visual Basic calls. Even though they share the same address space as the calling application, they are encumbered by OLE overhead not present in a direct-call approach. Likewise, out-of-process servers relegated to a different address space offer performance that is many times slower.

In-process servers are fundamentally different from C++ DLLs because they expose their services through OLE rather than direct calls. The code is also interpreted code and requires the runtime interpreter when carried out, unlike C++ DLLs. However, both in-process and out-of-process servers offer substantial benefits. They allow a packaging of code that can be highly effective in streamlining your development, maintenance, and support efforts. The exposed object model can facilitate development efforts and opens the door to more sophisticated software design.

Remote automation objects offer tremendous advantages and flexibility in implementing a client/server application approach. Additionally, even though RAOs must be out-of-process servers rather than in-process servers, they can lead to performance improvements for calling client applications. They enable client applications to off-load processing. Client/server performance tuning is a challenging area, and there are many factors to consider in the client/server performance arena not present in standalone performance optimization, such as network load and server speed.

Finally, the chapter covers time-out considerations for OLE Automation server objects. Settling on a time-out strategy may involve psychological considerations regarding users' reactions to various methods of time-out handling in addition to the usual performance considerations.

Obey the Signs

Beware of Falling Rocks: Don't settle on a long server time-out setting to ensure your user's chances of success without considering the ramifications.

If your user's environment is one in which time-outs are rarely encountered, it may be better to give them more immediate feedback. If they rarely get a time-out condition, when problems are encountered it may be unlikely that making them wait longer (at the expense of their patience) increases the chance of recovery.

Wrong Way: Assume that any code will be significantly faster if packaged as an in-line OLE Automation server DLL rather than as direct Visual Basic code.

This is not true! Code that's left within a Visual Basic application will be faster than code that's called from a server. However, there are many advantages to a server approach, which are outlined in this chapter.

Q&A

Q Which is faster, an in-process OLE Automation server or an out-of-process OLE Automation server?

A An in-process server is significantly faster because it shares the address space of the calling application.

Q What is faster, an RAO or a local out-of-process OLE Automation server?

A It depends on the application. It may benefit your application's performance to not have to do the local processing, but if it is a very small task, the network overhead and the administrative burden of using a remote call might overshadow the performance benefit.

Workshop

Write an in-process server that has two methods. Call one method repeatedly from a test program. From the calling program, create the object at the start of each loop and set it to the `Nothing` keyword at the end of each loop within the loop. (Note: Setting objects to `Nothing` frees the memory for that object.) This technique is used in this chapter and is described in detail in Chapter 18, "Multitasking and Memory." Obtain a timing for this approach. Then modify the program so that the object is created just once outside the loop and is cleaned up just once after the end of the loop. Capture another timing. How much improvement is there from this second approach? Is it enough to be perceptible to a user?

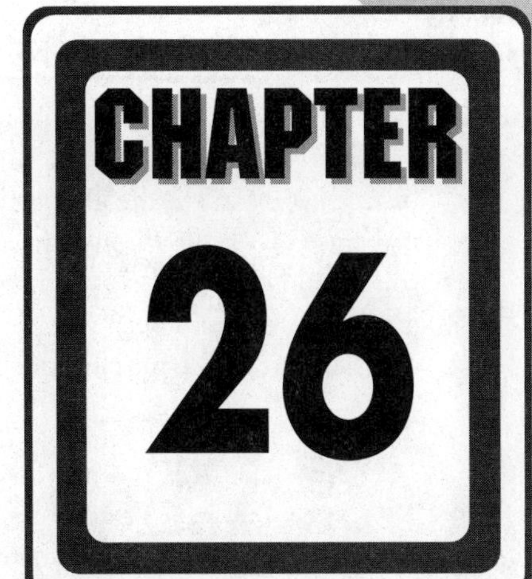

Know Your Objects: The OLE Graph Control Sample

Since Visual Basic is largely a component-glue tool, ultimately the use of your specific components will have as much of an impact on your application's unique performance as anything. Every component has unique properties or methods that can dramatically affect performance. This chapter illustrates the importance of knowing your controls intimately through a look at the OLE graph control.

Many programs need to display data in a graphical format. Data that is presented in a bar graph or pie graph can convey important statistics clearly.

Fortunately, the Visual Basic programmer does not have to build such graphs from scratch. Instead, you can use the OLE graph control that comes with Visual Basic to quickly and easily make use of VB's graphing capabilities. However, there are many performance considerations you should keep in mind when using the OLE graph control. Many of these are not obvious to the novice user and become clear only after experimentation with the properties and methods of the control. The purpose of this chapter is to highlight such considerations.

> **NOTE:** The OLE graph control comes with Visual Basic and is stored in file Graph32.OCX for the 32-bit version, and file Graph16.OCX for the 16-bit version. An enhanced advanced version of the graph control, with significantly advanced features, is also available from Pinnacle Publishing.

Specifically, this chapter looks at the time that is required to present data in a bar graph. The first example looks at a bar graph with values assigned at design time. Next, the amount of time required to generate the graph at runtime is compared. Then the same graph is generated using the control's blit technique to draw the graph data. This technique, called the *bit-blit-technique* because it provides some capabilities of the Windows API `BitBlit` function, builds the graph in memory before doing a mass copy to the display. Finally, the chapter examines the potential advantages of using the `AutoInc` property.

These examples provide a good general examination of issues affecting the OLE graph control. Every graph situation a programmer encounters is likely to be unique, but this chapter provides an approach for analyzing graph capabilities that can be applied to specific situations.

The OLE Graph Control Sample Program

The concepts in this chapter are illustrated by the sample program on the CD that accompanies this book, Gr_Ocx32.exe. A 16-bit version of the program, Gr_Ocx16.exe, is also available on the CD-ROM. The program's user interface is shown in Figure 26.1. The program has option buttons to display various types of graphs, each of which corresponds to a test case. Test cases consist of bar graphs that have properties assigned at runtime, bar graphs that use predefined design time settings, bar graphs that are drawn using the bit-blit technique to move the graph to screen, and bar graphs that have data assigned using the `AutoInc` property. Clicking on the button for a test case choice results in displays of the graphs and the time it takes to generate them. Each test case displays training data for four different runners in a separate graph, so four graphs are generated for every test case. The same runner training data sets are plotted for each of the test cases to ensure consistency. In this way, you can see direct head-to-head comparisons of the time for each technique.

When the test program starts, a blank window that displays no graphs is initially displayed. The graphs for each test case are hidden with a `Visible` property of `False` until they are used for a particular test. Eight graph controls are defined on the form. Four of the controls are used for each of the test cases that do not require preassigned property values. The other four of the graph controls are used for the test case that does require preassigned property values. When a specific test case is carried out, the `Visible` property of the appropriate control is set to `True` to display the plotted data.

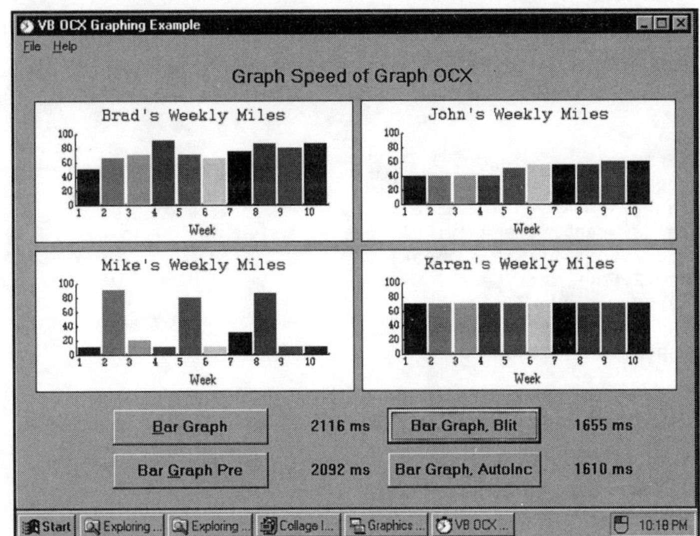

Figure 26.1.
The OLE graph control test program.

The Runtime Assignment Bar Graph Test Case

When clicked, the bar graph command button generates a bar graph of weekly running mileage for each of four runners. This is done using standard OLE graph controls and setting all essential values at runtime. The code for this test case is shown in Listing 26.1.

Listing 26.1. Bar graph generation.

```
Sub cmdBarGraph_Click ()
Dim i%

Call ClearGraphs

Call Common_StartTimedTest


' Graph 1

graph1.NumPoints = MAX_POINTS
graph1.NumSets = MAX_SETS
```

continues

Listing 26.1. continued

```
graph1.GraphTitle = "Brad's Weekly Miles"
graph1.BottomTitle = "Week"
graph1.FontFamily = 2 ' Modern
graph1.YAxisMax = 100
graph1.YAxisStyle = 2
graph1.YAxisTicks = 5

For i% = 1 To MAX_POINTS
    graph1.ThisPoint = i%
    graph1.GraphData = g_arrBradMiles(i%)
Next i%
graph1.DrawMode = 2
graph1.Visible = True


' Graph 2
graph2.NumPoints = MAX_POINTS
graph2.NumSets = MAX_SETS
graph2.GraphTitle = "Mike's Weekly Miles"
graph2.BottomTitle = "Week"
graph2.FontFamily = 2 ' Modern
graph2.YAxisMax = 100
graph2.YAxisStyle = 2
graph2.YAxisTicks = 5

For i% = 1 To MAX_POINTS
    graph2.ThisPoint = i%
    graph2.GraphData = g_arrMikeMiles(i%)
Next i%
graph2.DrawMode = 2
graph2.Visible = True


' Graph 3
graph3.NumPoints = MAX_POINTS
graph3.NumSets = MAX_SETS
graph3.GraphTitle = "John's Weekly Miles"
graph3.BottomTitle = "Week"
graph3.FontFamily = 2 ' Modern
graph3.YAxisMax = 100
graph3.YAxisStyle = 2
graph3.YAxisTicks = 5

For i% = 1 To MAX_POINTS
    graph3.ThisPoint = i%
    graph3.GraphData = g_arrJohnMiles(i%)
Next i%
graph3.DrawMode = 2
graph3.Visible = True


' Graph 4
graph4.NumPoints = MAX_POINTS
graph4.NumSets = MAX_SETS
graph4.GraphTitle = "Karen's Weekly Miles"
graph4.BottomTitle = "Week"
```

```
graph4.FontFamily = 2 ' Modern
graph4.YAxisMax = 100
graph4.YAxisStyle = 2
graph4.YAxisTicks = 5

For i% = 1 To MAX_POINTS
    graph4.ThisPoint = i%
    graph4.GraphData = g_arrKarenMiles(i%)
Next i%
graph4.DrawMode = 2

graph4.Visible = True

' Ensure paints are complete before taking final timing
me.refresh

Call Common_EndTimedTest( lblBarGraphTime)

End Sub
```

The code shows that arrays of data are assigned to the graph. These arrays contain the raw graph data, which consists of the weekly running mileage for four different runners. This data is assigned to the array when the form loads so that it can be used for subsequent tests. This initialization procedure is not part of the timed test but is a prerequisite to carrying out any test. Therefore, the initialization procedure is called when the program starts its `Form_Load` event. A partial listing of the initialization procedure is shown in Listing 26.2.

Listing 26.2. Graph data array initialization.

```
Sub Init_Arrays ()


g_arrBradMiles(1) = 50
g_arrBradMiles(2) = 65
g_arrBradMiles(3) = 70
g_arrBradMiles(4) = 90
g_arrBradMiles(5) = 70
g_arrBradMiles(6) = 65
g_arrBradMiles(7) = 75
g_arrBradMiles(8) = 85
g_arrBradMiles(9) = 80
g_arrBradMiles(10) = 85

g_arrJohnMiles(1) = 40
g_arrJohnMiles(2) = 40
g_arrJohnMiles(3) = 40
g_arrJohnMiles(4) = 40
g_arrJohnMiles(5) = 50
g_arrJohnMiles(6) = 55
g_arrJohnMiles(7) = 55
g_arrJohnMiles(8) = 55
```

continues

Listing 26.2. continued

```
g_arrJohnMiles(9) = 60
g_arrJohnMiles(10) = 60


g_arrMikeMiles(1) = 10
g_arrMikeMiles(2) = 90
g_arrMikeMiles(3) = 20
g_arrMikeMiles(4) = 10
g_arrMikeMiles(5) = 80
g_arrMikeMiles(6) = 10
g_arrMikeMiles(7) = 30
g_arrMikeMiles(8) = 85
g_arrMikeMiles(9) = 10
g_arrMikeMiles(10) = 10


g_arrKarenMiles(1) = 70
g_arrKarenMiles(2) = 70
g_arrKarenMiles(3) = 70
g_arrKarenMiles(4) = 70
g_arrKarenMiles(5) = 70
g_arrKarenMiles(6) = 70
g_arrKarenMiles(7) = 70
g_arrKarenMiles(8) = 70
g_arrKarenMiles(9) = 70
g_arrKarenMiles(10) = 70

End Sub
```

The code for the bar graph button–click event simply assigns data for each runner using each of the four arrays in a `For` loop. Then the graph is generated using the `DrawMode` property. Characteristics such as the graph title are also set within this code by assigning values to the properties of the graph control.

The main activity of this code, then, is to assign all relevant properties to each graph (such as title, number of points, and number of sets), assign data to each graph from the corresponding global data set array, and then show the graphs. This is carried out for each of four graphs, which correspond to the four sets of runner mileage data that are used in this sample program.

Several properties are set for each graph. `NumPoints` defines the maximum number of data items on the graph, and `NumSets` defines how many concurrent sets of data are used. For this example, the value of the `NumSets` property is set to `MAX_SETS`, which is predefined to be `1`. We only map one set of data per graph. Each of the four runners' data is shown on a separate graph. We could have graphed every runner's weekly mileage bars on just one graph with overlapping data sets by setting this property to `4`. For clarity in this example, however, `NumSets` has been restricted to `1`.

The properties called `GraphTitle` and `BottomTitle` control the titles that appear on the graph. `FontFamily` is set to `2` to indicate the modern font. `YAxisMax`, `YAxisStyle`, and `YAxisTicks` all define the characteristics of the Y axis in terms of range and increments.

Note that this property information is set once for each graph and then does not change as the graph is presented. This indicates that it could have been set statically at design time rather than set dynamically at runtime. The approach of setting up the information dynamically is sometimes used because it makes for clearer programming documentation. For example, the programmer can tell at a glance at the source code what the properties of the control are being set to without having to refer back to the control property window itself.

Next we will consider the `For` loop. The `For` loop encompasses every point of data. Notice the statement `Graph1.ThisPoint = i%`. The purpose of this statement is to indicate the current data point to be processed by the graph control. The `NumPoints` property is used to indicate the overall number of points the control must accommodate. The `ThisPoint` property indicates which of those points is currently active and will be referred to in subsequent data handling property assignments. An illustration of how this property applies is shown in the following statement:

```
Graph1.graphdata=G_arrBradMiles(i%)
```

This statement assigns data to the current data point of the graph object. Our data to be graphed has to be moved from the global array into the graph control for the control to graph it. This assignment to the `GraphData` property will move the array data into the data slot indicated by the control's `ThisPoint` property. In this manner, every data point is transferred to the graph control for subsequent graphing. There are significant performance ramifications related to this approach. Every data point that we wish to graph has to be transferred over with such a statement. Before each such transfer the `ThisPoint` property must be updated to reflect the data point we want the graph control to treat as the current point. These statements, of course, consume processor time. Finally, after all the graph properties are set and all the data has been moved over to the graph data property, the graph is drawn. A property setting causes the graph to be drawn, as illustrated in the following statement:

```
Graph1.DrawMode = 2
```

This statement sets the control's `DrawMode` property to indicate the type of drawing desired, which causes the control to produce the graph onscreen. This graph control will plot the graph data and show the updated image using standard techniques. Then finally the graph is made visible.

This example is built on the standard Visual Basic OLE graph control. This component is not a standard part of the Visual Basic toolbar or a built-in control but rather an OLE control that can be added to the toolbar. Depending on your configuration, it may be added by default. If not, you can add it through the Tools | Custom Control menu item to make the graph control available. Figure 26.2 shows the tool indicator for the graph OCX in the bottom-right column of the toolbar.

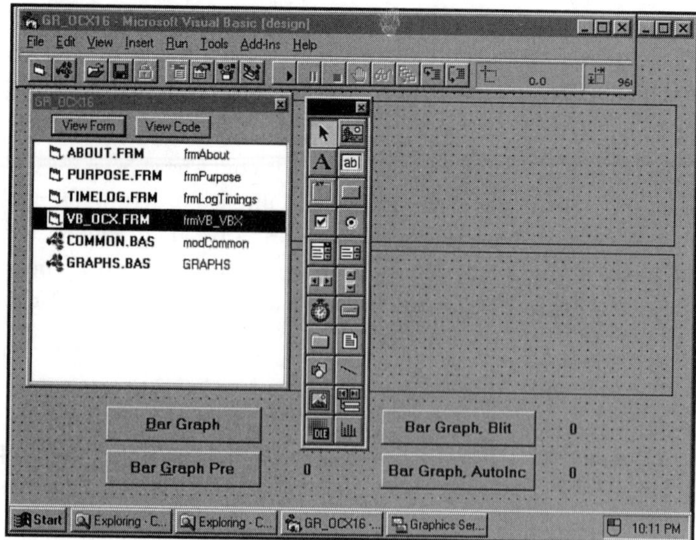

Figure 26.2.
The OLE graph control in the Visual Basic design environment.

The results of this test are shown in Figure 26.1. The code generates and displays a graph for each of four runners. Our code sample uses the COMMON.BAS start-time and end-time calls to capture a time for this process. That time is then displayed to the right of the bar graph button. As the figure shows, this took approximately 2.3 seconds on our reference PC. The next step is to generate the same graphs by setting properties at design time where possible rather than runtime. This will tell the performance impact of the runtime property assignments.

The Preassigned Property Bar Graph Test Case

The code that is associated with the Bar Graph Pre command button to carry out the preassigned property test case is much the same as that used for the runtime assignment test case. The difference is that this code does not have to set up property values for properties that do not change at runtime since those properties have been preassigned. The code is shown in Listing 26.3. The code uses the same `For` loop to move data from the data set array to the `GraphData` property for each graph control. This is followed by a `DrawMode` method to generate the graph and a `Visible` statement to show it on the screen. What is absent from this sample that was in the first, however, is the setting of all the `NumPoints`, `NumSets`, `GraphTitle`, `BottomTitle`, `FontFamily`, and Y-axis properties for each graph control. These do not have to be set in this case because they have been set at design time. Each graph control was selected at design time and the corresponding property sheet was brought up. Within this property sheet window, the same property settings that previously were carried out at runtime were made so that they will be in effect when the program starts. This eliminates the need for statements that make these settings in our code. Removal of these statements means that there are fewer statements for the Visual Basic runtime interpreter to process, and execution time should therefore speed up accordingly.

Listing 26.3. Bar graph generation with design-time property settings.

```
Sub cmdBarGraphPre_Click ()

Dim i%


Call ClearGraphs

Call Common_StartTimedTest


' Graph 1

    For i% = 1 To MAX_POINTS
        grapharray(0).ThisPoint = i%
        grapharray(0).GraphData = g_arrBradMiles(i%)
    Next i%
    grapharray(0).DrawMode = 2
    grapharray(0).Visible = True


' Graph 2
    ' Must create a new control if not the first control
    For i% = 1 To MAX_POINTS
        grapharray(1).ThisPoint = i%
        grapharray(1).GraphData = g_arrMikeMiles(i%)
    Next i%
    grapharray(1).DrawMode = 2
    grapharray(1).Visible = True


' Graph 3
    ' Must create a new control if not the first control
    For i% = 1 To MAX_POINTS
        grapharray(2).ThisPoint = i%
        grapharray(2).GraphData = g_arrJohnMiles(i%)
    Next i%
    grapharray(2).DrawMode = 2
    grapharray(2).Visible = True

' Graph 4
    ' Must create a new control if not the first control
    For i% = 1 To MAX_POINTS
        grapharray(3).ThisPoint = i%
        grapharray(3).GraphData = g_arrKarenMiles(i%)
    Next i%
    grapharray(3).DrawMode = 2
    grapharray(3).Visible = True

' Ensure paints are complete before taking final timing
me.refresh

Call Common_EndTimedTest(lblBarArrayTime)

End Sub
```

The most relevant question for this example is how much of a speedup do we really get? It has been mentioned that it is a common practice to set these properties at runtime for programming convenience and, in some cases, clarity. We can improve execution by moving these statements to design time, at the cost of program clarity. Is the speedup worth the effort? The result is shown in Figure 26.1. In the case of our reference PC, we derived a speedup of 41 milliseconds, or less than 2 percent. Such a small speedup is not likely to be perceptible to the user. However, it does point out that speedup can be gained in this manner. In some cases, if you need to extensively tailor a graph, you may need to carry out many more property settings than were used here. Likewise, you may have cases where you assign values to many more graph controls than just the four used here. In either case, the advantages of this technique would be amplified, and should be considered. Moving the property setting to design time will enhance speed, particularly if you have to make the same assignments multiple times. However, as in this case, eliminating the 32 runtime statements (4 graphs times 8 statements each) will not have a major impact on program speed.

The Blit *DrawMode* Bar Graph Test Case

The code associated with the Bar Graph Blit command button is exactly the same as the code in previous example, which generated the bar graph with predefined property settings, except for one small but significant difference. The difference is in the technique used to generate the graph through the `DrawMode` property. Whereas in previous examples `DrawMode` was set to `2` to generate the graph, in this case it is set to `3`. The code for this approach is shown in Listing 26.4. A value of `2` for the `DrawMode` property tells it to draw the graph using conventional methods. By contrast, a value of `3` tells the graphics server to build the bitmap in memory first, so it is not visible to the user, and then move it to display it all at once with the Windows API `BitBlit` operation.

Listing 26.4. Bar graph generation with the blit-type `DrawMode` property.

```
Sub cmdBlit_Click ()
Dim i%


Call ClearGraphs

Call Common_StartTimedTest


' Graph 1

    For i% = 1 To MAX_POINTS
        grapharray(0).ThisPoint = i%
        grapharray(0).GraphData = g_arrBradMiles(i%)
    Next i%
    grapharray(0).DrawMode = 3
    grapharray(0).Visible = True
```

```
' Graph 2
    ' Must create a new control if not the first control
    For i% = 1 To MAX_POINTS
        grapharray(1).ThisPoint = i%
        grapharray(1).GraphData = g_arrMikeMiles(i%)
    Next i%
    grapharray(1).DrawMode = 3
    grapharray(1).Visible = True


' Graph 3
    ' Must create a new control if not the first control
    For i% = 1 To MAX_POINTS
        grapharray(2).ThisPoint = i%
        grapharray(2).GraphData = g_arrJohnMiles(i%)
    Next i%
    grapharray(2).DrawMode = 3
    grapharray(2).Visible = True

' Graph 4
    ' Must create a new control if not the first control
    For i% = 1 To MAX_POINTS
        grapharray(3).ThisPoint = i%
        grapharray(3).GraphData = g_arrKarenMiles(i%)
    Next i%
    grapharray(3).DrawMode = 3
    grapharray(3).Visible = True

' Ensure paints are complete before taking final timing
me.refresh

Call Common_EndTimedTest( lblBlit)

End Sub
```

Note that the graph is redrawn at runtime only when the DrawMode property is set to 2 or 3. Property value changes that affect the graph's appearance will not be visible until this DrawMode property is set. Therefore, the choice of a DrawMode setting could be significant, because it will be used every time you want to display a new graph image. The choice of a drawing technique will also be affected by design considerations such as whether you are always leaving a graph visible by setting its Visible property to True, or just displaying it when desired and hiding it at other times, as with our test programs. If your graph is always displayed, it is even more likely that you would want to use the blit DrawMode technique to ensure smooth graph generation. The blit style of DrawMode displays the graph all at once, whereas the conventional DrawMode generation will show the graph as it is generated. In terms of raw performance, we can see the results by comparing this test case with DrawMode set to 3 to our previous test case with DrawMode set to 2. The results are shown in Figure 26.1.

This approach took slightly more than 1.8 seconds, whereas the conventional method took more than 0.5 seconds (or 30 percent) longer. Where this is not a gigantic difference, it could be even greater depending on the data set generated. This brings us to the first significant observation of this chapter: If you have no reason to do otherwise, display graph results with a `DrawMode` setting of `3` to take advantage of the `BitBlit` API for faster performance.

> **TIP:** If you have no reason to do otherwise, display graph results with `DrawMode` set to `3` to take advantage of the `BitBlit` API for faster performance.

The AutoInc Bar Graph Test Case

The code associated with the Bar Graph `AutoInc` command button is once again architecturally similar to that of the previous test case. So that a relevant comparison can be made to the previous technique, the blit-style `DrawMode` property setting is used in this test case as well. This code is shown in Listing 26.5.

Listing 26.5. Bar graph generation with `AutoInc`.

```
Sub cmdAutoInc_Click ()
Dim i%


Call ClearGraphs

'This test must be carried out with AutoInc On, this could
'  also have been set at design time.
For i% = 0 To 3
    grapharray(i%).AutoInc = 1
Next i%

Call Common_StartTimedTest


' Graph 1

    For i% = 1 To MAX_POINTS
        '*** Not needed with AutoInc! ==> grapharray(0).ThisPoint = i%
        grapharray(0).GraphData = g_arrBradMiles(i%)
    Next i%
    grapharray(0).DrawMode = 3
    grapharray(0).Visible = True


' Graph 2
    ' Must create a new control if not the first control
    For i% = 1 To MAX_POINTS
        '*** Not needed with AutoInc! ==> grapharray(1).ThisPoint = i%
        grapharray(1).GraphData = g_arrMikeMiles(i%)
    Next i%
    grapharray(1).DrawMode = 3
    grapharray(1).Visible = True
```

```
' Graph 3
    ' Must create a new control if not the first control
    For i% = 1 To MAX_POINTS
        '*** Not needed with AutoInc! ==> grapharray(2).ThisPoint = i%
        grapharray(2).GraphData = g_arrJohnMiles(i%)
    Next i%
    grapharray(2).DrawMode = 3
    grapharray(2).Visible = True

' Graph 4
    ' Must create a new control if not the first control
    For i% = 1 To MAX_POINTS
        '*** Not needed with AutoInc! ==> grapharray(3).ThisPoint = i%
        grapharray(3).GraphData = g_arrKarenMiles(i%)
    Next i%
    grapharray(3).DrawMode = 3
    grapharray(3).Visible = True

' Ensure paints are complete before taking final timing
me.refresh


Call Common_EndTimedTest(lblAutoInc)



' Turn off this setting so it doesn't effect other tests
For i% = 0 To 3
    grapharray(i%).AutoInc = False
Next i%

End Sub
```

The difference in this example is the way that the current point of the graph control is referenced. As you have seen in previous examples, the graph's `ThisMode` property was incremented to indicate which of the graph's data points to update. Then a specific update to the graph's data was carried out by setting the graph's `GraphData` property. Assigning a value to the `GraphData` property updated the data point indicated by the `ThisPoint` property. Therefore, in previous examples, `ThisPoint` and `GraphData` properties have been used in tandem, with `ThisPoint` to move the current data pointer and `GraphData` to receive the data itself.

If we know that our data points will be addressed in sequential order, there is a property setting that instructs the OCX to automatically increment the current data point after every assignment to `GraphData`. This eliminates the need to update the `ThisPoint` property. In other words, the graph control resets its own current graph point by doing the equivalent of updating the `ThisPoint` property. With this approach, there is no need for a code statement to update `ThisPoint` each time we shift to a new data point. Therefore, while the control still carries out the work of automatically shifting the data point for us, we no longer need to use a statement in our Visual Basic source code for this purpose. The statement in your Visual Basic program that updated `ThisPoint` can be eliminated, reducing the number of statements that a runtime interpreter must execute. Because ThisPoint was previously updated every time through the loop that assigns data for each of the four graphs, the number of statements eliminated by this technique is significant. For our example, we eliminate 40 ThisPoint assignments (4 graphs times 10 data points each), which the interpreter no longer has to execute for this test case, compared to earlier techniques.

The property that instructs the graph control to do this automatic incrementing is named, appropriately enough, AutoInc. When AutoInc is set to 0 by default, no automated incrementing takes place. When AutoInc is set to 1, the graph control will automatically do this incrementing. Although our example deals with graphs containing just one dataset each, AutoInc even handles the case of multiple datasets per graph in the same manner. In our sample program, the AutoInc property is set to 1 to turn it on for each of our four graphs before we start our timed test. Normally if you chose to use the AutoInc property, you would set it once at design time, but it is set at runtime here to illustrate this property setting. Likewise, there is a loop through all four graphs after our time test is complete at the bottom of this code segment, a loop that sets AutoInc to False to turn off the automatic incrementing. This step would not be necessary in a normal program, but for the sake of our test program we turn the property back off so that it will not affect subsequent tests. In the main body of timed code, the code statements are identical to those of the blit technique, except we no longer need to update the current point ThisPoint property for each data point assigned. Therefore, that statement has been removed from the For loop for each of the four graphs.

The results of this test case are shown in Figure 26.1. The AutoInc technique was 33 milliseconds faster than the blit DrawMode technique. The only difference between these two cases is the use of AutoInc. This is a marginal improvement but one that comes at no cost to code maintenance or developer impact. It is likely that much of this savings is due to the smaller number of statements processed by the runtime interpreter because it now has a smaller code path to interpret.

> **TIP:** Use AutoInc when assigning sequential data points to a graph to reduce the number of statements the interpreter must process.

Interpreting Performance Impact

Now that we have seen several settings and techniques that affect performance, it is time to put them into perspective. The blit technique (setting DrawMode to 3) was identified as a technique that was likely to give the user perceptible program speedup. Because this technique involves building a graph image in memory, it is reasonable to assume that the more extensive or complicated the graph and the greater the graph draw time, the more significant the speedup we will witness with this technique. Likewise, each of the other savings areas should be considered in this perspective.

Using predefined properties that are set at design time offers a slight improvement over the runtime technique. In this example, the speedup was real but not likely to be perceptible to the user. However, because this speedup comes from not having to set property values and reducing the number of statements for the interpreter, we can safely assume that the more properties that can be set at design time, the more speedup we will have. Therefore, a general guideline for graphs that must be optimized is to set properties at design time rather than runtime for the graph to achieve speedup. The more properties that must be established on the graph, the more significant the improvement will be, although speedup is generally slight from this technique.

We should likewise analyze the speedup from the `AutoInc` property in the same light. We must consider what's behind the speedup to extrapolate how significant savings can be. `AutoInc` provides speedup because there are fewer statements required in our source code to assign data points. Therefore, it is logical that the more data points we are generating on our graph and the more runtime statements that are required to assign those data points, the more payback we will get from using `AutoInc`. The greater the number of data points processed, the more significant the speedup.

All of these areas of graph speedup should be carefully considered with respect to application-specific needs. For example, if a graph title must change based on current global settings of the program, then the graph title property will have to be generated at runtime and cannot be set at design time. This speedup technique therefore would not be an option for that property. Likewise, if you must generate your graph data in nonsequential order, skipping among data points as data is generated, then `AutoInc` would not be a feasible option. Even with `DrawMode` set to `3` technique, there may be occasions not to use the optimal settings. It is conceivable that a program might need to generate a graph in an incremental rather than non-instantaneous presentation manner because of user interface considerations. With every performance-enhancing technique comes a trade-off. In some cases, you gain performance at the cost of flexibility.

Performance Discrepancies

An important theme in measuring performance is that performance timings are relative and will differ from one timing to another. Therefore, the most relevant performance testing is the one that most closely simulates your application. This variance in timing is especially evident when we are measuring the performance of the graph control. The timings that have been presented in this chapter are representative timings that were produced when the graphs were drawn repeatedly in succession. While the relative performance merits of the graphing techniques remain constant, the absolute timings can differ significantly. For example, the Bar Graph AutoInc command button code always performs the fastest. Relative to the other techniques, it is always the best. However, the amount of time that this technique takes from one test to another can vary significantly.

The OLE graph control takes some special performance hits when the first graph instance is generated. This makes intuitive sense from a programming standpoint because it is reasonable to expect that there may be initialization and memory-management overhead.

The important lesson here is that timings vary, depending on the sequence of operations. If your application is going to generate a graph just once, then you should analyze initial graph-generation times. On the other hand, if your application will generate graphs repeatedly, the in-succession generation time will be of more concern to you. Fortunately, the relative performance merits of the approaches remain the same, regardless of the varying overhead penalty.

Summary

This chapter looks at the performance ramifications of various OCX graph-generation techniques. A sample program generates a standard bar graph of mileage for four different runners. Then similar test code uses design-time property settings (where feasible) rather than runtime settings. A small improvement was shown from this method. Next, the same bar graph is generated using the blit technique by setting the `DrawMode` property to `3`. This shows a more significant performance improvement. Then the same code was carried out using the `AutoInc` property to automatically set the current graph data pointer rather than incrementing it manually with the `ThisPoint` property. This also shows small performance gains.

The payback from all of these techniques depends on the type of graph generated and the number of data points to be graphed. There is a noticeable initialization-overhead penalty when a graph is generated for the first time. Subsequent generations of a graph will be quicker. As with most areas of performance, you should carefully consider the graphing needs of your own application and measure the most relevant areas of performance.

Obey the Signs

Wrong Way: Performance will generally not differ by much from the first generation of a graph to the tenth generation of a graph if the same techniques are used.

This is a fallacy. As this chapter shows, performance can differ significantly from the first generation to subsequent graph generations. Additional initialization overhead is incurred when the graph is generated for the first time.

Wrong Way: Because setting `AutoInc` to `True` is a faster approach, it should be a mandatory standard for every project.

This is not a good practice. The `AutoInc` method will be faster for programs that assign the graph data in exact sequential order. However, there are some circumstances in which it may be necessary to have a program generate graph data for data points out of order, in a nonsequential fashion. In such a case, setting `AutoInc` to `True` would have undesired results, as the current graph data pointer would not correspond with the intended update. The best approach is to ensure that programmers thoroughly understand what the `AutoInc` property does, and then they can use it when performance benefits are possible without changing the intended effect of the code.

Q&A

Q Will the `AutoInc` property be turned on by default when you create a graph control?

A No. The default setting for `AutoInc` is `Off`. This property must be set to `On` to have the OCX take care of automatically setting the current graph data point.

Q Why is a graph setting of `DrawMode` equal to `3` called the blit technique?

A When this property setting is put into effect, the control uses the `BitBlit` Windows API or a similar technique to move all of the image that has been completely constructed in memory to the display at one time rather than incrementally.

Quiz

Modify the code associated with the first bar graph command button so that it uses the blit technique rather than the standard technique of drawing.

(This change can be carried out simply by setting `DrawMode` to `3` rather than to `2`. This property setting causes the OLE graph control to use the blit technique when drawing the graph.)

Workshop

Modify the sample program in this chapter to assign 200 weeks of training or data points to each runner instead of just 10 weeks of training. Rerun the `AutoInc` test. Likewise modify and rerun the similar blit `DrawMode` test, which does not use `AutoInc`. Notice the performance benefit of `AutoInc` in this case. Is the speedup more significant now that we have increased the number of data points?

Epilogue

This section provides you with an overview and summary of each chapter in the book. Parts I and II present optimization concepts for understanding and applying optimization. The main concepts of each chapter are summarized in this section. Parts III through VII present actual optimization strategies that you can apply to your applications. The techniques and conclusions made in each chapter of every section are summarized for your reference.

The Epilogue not only serves as a wrap-up of all the concepts discussed in this book, but it also serves as a useful reference to all the techniques presented. As you optimize your applications, you can use the Epilogue as a quick reference of fundamental concepts and techniques that will enable you to make your programs operate as efficiently as possible.

Epilogue

Performance and optimization is not a small topic. The vast body of experience and knowledge that has been accumulated over the years with respect to performance is massive indeed. A good guide to that information is essential. This chapter recaps the important themes throughout this book, both in the "Optimization Concepts" and "Optimization Strategies" material. You can use this chapter as a handy reference, particularly if you want to see a quick summary of the important points on any specific subject area.

Part I: Optimization Concepts: Understanding Optimization

Part I introduces you to the world of performance tuning and optimization, focusing on a complete definition of optimization, followed by when and where to optimize your applications. The goal of the chapters in Part I is to give you a better understanding of what optimization is as well as when and where it should be carried out.

Chapter 1: What Is Performance?

This chapter provides a broad and general overview into the far-reaching world of performance. Performance and optimization are defined. In addition, the consequences of poor performance and the importance of considering user perception of performance are addressed. Some background is provided on why Visual Basic programs can run into performance problem areas and why switching to another programming language should not always be the first alternative for performance tuning. The first sounding of a key refrain repeated throughout the book occurs here: "Performance assessment can be a complex and challenging task."

Chapter 2: When to Optimize

This chapter discusses some important issues to consider in determining when to optimize code. It begins by emphasizing the need for the programmer to think about the most efficient and optimal way to write code before actually writing it. In doing so, the programmer avoids writing sloppy, inefficient code that might need to be heavily optimized later. The decision of when to optimize must be made taking the cost of optimization into account. Some of the trade-offs include more difficult code maintenance, debugging, and code reuse. Furthermore, one optimization scheme can conflict with another, resulting in a lower overall performance. Each of these issues is discussed.

Optimization sometimes takes code that is fairly easy to understand and makes it more complex or difficult to follow. This, in turn, can make the program more difficult to maintain, either for you or for someone totally new to the code. While this can be minimized by careful documentation of the optimization stages, there is a trade-off between making an application efficient and making its code less cryptic and easier to understand. Likewise, optimization often makes code difficult to debug. This trade-off goes hand in hand with maintenance, since code that is more difficult to understand is typically more error prone and more difficult to debug. If the programmer is careful to test the application in light of the applied optimization technique, the chances of having fewer errors are greatly improved.

Yet another area of compromise is code reuse. The goal in Visual Basic, as in any other language, is often to write reusable components of software so that they can be applied in a wide variety of projects. Optimization strategies often include techniques that can break down the

modeling goals for code reuse, particularly the well-defined interface between modules. Care must be taken to preserve this interface as much as possible, avoiding any implied conditions for the programmer reusing the code. Often, performance can be increased by decreasing the reusability of the code. If you do this, it is very important to thoroughly document any such modifications.

Chapter 3: Where to Optimize

This chapter presents a series of general steps to determine where to optimize code. It starts by discussing the different ways of optimizing an application: improving the *actual speed* and the *perceived speed* of the application. It also discusses how Visual Basic code is executed and what performance concerns you need to consider when writing code in Visual Basic. Then, the chapter focuses on memory usage, explaining what resources are and how those resources consume memory. The importance of conserving memory is addressed.

Finally, the chapter introduces the concepts necessary to determine *where* to optimize, which essentially consist of taking a profile of every procedure in the application, logging cumulative time spent in each procedure, taking the procedures with the highest user impact and dividing them into smaller sections, and continuing to profile and subdivide those sections until easily defined optimization techniques can be applied.

Part II: Optimization Concepts: Applying Optimization

Part II provides you with information that gives you insight into applying optimization in your applications. It addresses the tools required to measure performance; the way to use those tools to obtain useful results; the factors that make those results more or less reliable; supporting utilities you can use to obtain the results; and a methodology for putting all these concepts to work in a practical way.

Chapter 4: Timing Methods

This chapter introduces the timing tools you need to take meaningful performance measurements. An introductory case study illustrates some basic timing issues and demonstrates some of the complexities inherent in carrying out even a simple series of performance tests.

This case study is followed by a discussion of timing methods, including timer precision and resolution. The ingredients that make a timing method accurate are discussed, and reasons that timing methods can be inaccurate are briefly introduced. Two vital factors, *precision* and *resolution,* are introduced and explained in the context of the Windows operating environment. Precision is a way to indicate how quickly the time is reported back when requested. The less precise the timing method, the older and less reliable the time. Resolution is a measure of the frequency with which the underlying clock or tick count gets updated. The smaller the amount of time it takes for a block of code to execute, the more important the resolution of the timer. If, for example, a timer is only accurate to the nearest 55 milliseconds, an operation that takes 30 milliseconds would very likely report 0 milliseconds total time for the measured operation. You would need a timer with a higher degree of resolution.

The chapter then focuses on the various timing methods you can use, pointing out the best timing methods to take advantage of either in Visual Basic or through the Windows API. Three functions—the Visual Basic `Timer` function, the `GetTickCount` Windows API function, and the `timerGetTime` Windows API function—are examined in some detail, and the advantages and disadvantages of using each timing method are described. Advanced timing methods are also introduced briefly for those who require more sophisticated timing analysis capabilities. In addition to the functions provided in the Windows API, profiling tools can save a great deal of time and can provide even more accurate measurements.

Chapter 5: Collecting Performance Measurements

Chapter 5 presents information on how to take performance measurements, including how to use timing methods inside an application, and how to make timings more meaningful. The chapter points out the best approaches in taking timings in event subroutines; when working with database functions; and when timing functions and subroutines, simple code groups, loops, and conditional code. Various issues to watch out for are pointed out along the way, and code listings are shown to guide you in implementing the timing measurements in your own applications.

Then this chapter discusses how to make timings meaningful and useful. Included in this discussion is an introduction to simple statistical techniques required to obtain meaningful results. Specifically, the chapter points out the necessity of taking more than one timing; taking the average, median, and standard deviation of the set of timing values; and, as the data set size increases, watching for trends in the data to determine the stability of the numbers being obtained. Ultimately, the analyst must come to the conclusion that the standard deviation has settled and the median and average agree to the point where there is enough confidence in the average timing value to use it as a benchmark for comparison. This chapter steps you through this process and gives you the skills you need to make your timing results as meaningful as possible.

Chapter 6: Factors That Affect Performance

In a perfect world, you would expect to get the same level of performance in a consistent fashion every time an application is executed. Unfortunately, life is not so simple. This chapter discusses factors that can cause an application to take a different amount of time to perform the same task each time it is run. When you are trying to assess the benefits of optimization techniques and use timing methods to do so, you are limited by these inherent instabilities of

Windows. To ensure that you are getting as accurate a set of results as possible, you must reduce the impact of all the factors discussed in this chapter.

This chapter discusses many of the problems at length, pointing out that while some variances can be solved rather easily, others are very difficult to pin down and virtually impossible to totally eliminate. The analyst must take steps to reduce these factors and ensure a consistent system state every time the application is tested for performance. Furthermore, it is important to take timings on the same system to view timings relative to each other, as well as to take absolute timings on the low-end system that is being targeted for the user. Making sure an application runs with an acceptable speed on the low-end system will help to ensure user satisfaction for those with more powerful systems.

As more of the factors that limit timing accuracy are eliminated, the timing results should become increasingly reliable. In order to determine the level of reliability, you can simply run the same test over and over again, examining the timing values. If they are increasingly consistent, you can be sure you are getting closer to an acceptable level, as is discussed in detail in Chapter 5. At that point, you can make meaningful comparisons between timings as performance optimizations are applied.

Chapter 7: Supporting Utilities for Performance Analysis

This chapter presents an overview of some of the tools available that can help in performance assessment. These tools can save time and provide more accurate performance assessment during optimization. In addition, an awareness of the types of tools available and why they are useful is provided to help raise overall understanding of performance issues, even if you will not be using these specific tools.

The first category of utilities examined is those that are on this book's companion CD-ROM. These included Watchr16, to monitor resources; Startr32, to assess program load time; Timing32, to store and analyze timing data from test programs; and common routines in the COMMON.BAS module to incorporate into your programs for general timing purposes. The second category considered encompasses commercial tools. These include those that come with the Visual Basic Enterprise Edition as well as those that are separately available commercial products. Visual Basic's WPS utility to monitor Windows 16-bit task and module status is discussed. The PView32 from Visual Basic is examined. This is a tool that allows the user to view 32-bit process and thread status.

Next, a definition of code profiling is offered and general profiling concepts are examined. These include a look at the various benefits offered by profiling—insight into code flow, insight into execution time of blocks of code, and insight into number of code hits of blocks of code. This information can be analyzed to determine which areas of an application are the best candidates for optimization. In addition, some key profiling tools are examined, including Visual Basic's

VBCP and Avanti Software, Inc.'s PinPoint, which carry out code profiling. Both tools automate insertion of profiling statements and collection of results and can serve as valuable profiling aids. PinPoint has some additional functions that aid in performance assessment, such as an easy model to master for profiling multiple applications at the same time and the ability to graphically display results. Blue Lagoon's Jet Analyzer is a very easy-to-use tool for profiling database operations of the Jet Engine.

There is a wide variety of tools available to assist in performance assessment. The value of any individual tool depends on your specific application performance assessment needs. These tools can be a great aid in evaluating performance, but the ultimate performance enhancement tool remains the judgment and analytical skill of the developer.

Chapter 8: The Brophy/Koets Optimization Methodology

This chapter looks at a specific methodology for optimization. This performance enhancement methodology is necessary to provide controlled, stepwise, incremental changes to an application during optimization. This approach is particularly necessary when dealing with performance because of the subtle nature of performance, the many variables that affect it, and the great potential for performance tweaking to affect code in ways not anticipated.

When you make performance enhancements you are assessing doing things differently than your first instinct led you to do when you developed the application. This in itself makes these changes likely to be high risk or less completely understood. The implementation methodology outlined in this chapter helps to ensure that implementing such enhancements is a safe process: You should use backups, insert one change at a time, take prechange measurements, take postchange measurements and conduct testing, and regress to the earlier source code baseline if necessary.

This chapter also talks about the need to occasionally apply a performance enhancement many places throughout the application. A technique is outlined for such situations. It consists of first implementing one case of the performance change in a controlled fashion using the regular methodology for implementing single occurrence optimizations. If that is successful, the change is applied globally throughout the application, again applying the methodology with some slight refinements.

You can take steps during implementation to pave the way for future performance enhancement implementation cycles. Building a modular collection of optimized routines is the primary way to accomplish this. This can consist of building a module of routines developed in-house that have been enhanced for performance and have ample documentation on the performance enhancements. Building collections of optimized code in OLE Automation servers is another available strategy, although the overhead of OLE Automation is always present.

All these techniques combined can lead to a more effective performance enhancement implementation phase. Less time will be spent chasing performance side effects and bug side effects, or reinventing the wheel. The end user benefits by receiving faster, more reliable applications.

Part III: Optimization Strategies: Programming

Part III begins a series of parts that focus on strategies for optimizing your applications. Part III contains chapters that deal with programming issues, including the proper use of variables and mathematical operations with those variables, and the structure of code.

Chapter 9: Variables

This chapter focuses on the best data types to use for variables in a Visual Basic application. Useful techniques are presented and demonstrated using sample applications. All of the Visual Basic data types are presented, and their common use is discussed. This is followed by a discussion of variable "containers" such as arrays and structures, as well as a brief discussion of variable scope.

The following tips are presented in this chapter:

- Use strings instead of variants whenever possible.
- Use integer-based data types rather than floating-point data types whenever possible.
- The integer and Boolean data types offer almost identical performance. Use the Boolean data type rather than the integer data type when you only need to store a True/False or Yes/No condition.
- Avoid using the currency data type whenever possible. Use another floating-point data type instead.
- Unless the set of data is very small, use user-defined types or arrays to store data sets rather than simple variables.
- Use constants instead of variables for values that do not change.
- To conserve memory, keep variable scope as tight as possible. Performance may be slightly worse as the scope tightens, but the overall maintainability and usability of the code is likely to be worth the small sacrifice in performance.

Chapter 10: Math

This chapter examines the various mathematical operations that can be applied to the data types introduced in Chapter 9. First, the chapter compares floating-point math to integer math by presenting an application that performs each basic arithmetic operation on every data type.

The results show that, in most cases, the integer data types are faster than the floating-point data types. The chapter concludes that, whenever possible, integer math is preferable to floating-point math. The chapter also shows that math using the variant and currency data types is not as efficient as using the standard integer or floating-point data types.

Next, the chapter compares the multiplication operation to division and finds that multiplication is, in general, faster. As an alternative to division, the chapter presents a technique that enables you to multiply by the inverse of a value rather than perform a standard division. This technique can, in most cases, improve performance, but it requires that the inverse be known up front or calculated in code, which may or may not improve performance, depending on the context in which it is being applied. Again, the chapter shows when and when not to apply the technique presented.

Finally, the chapter points out alternatives to the exponent operator, specifically multiplication instead of the exponent and the use of the square root function versus the 0.5 exponent value. The chapter points out that repeated multiplication of the same value to itself is usually not preferable to the exponent operator unless the variant data type is being used or the exponent (that is, the number of multiplications) is less than 3. The chapter also shows a clear performance improvement if you use the `sqr()` function in place of the exponent 0.5 when you want to take the square root of a result.

The following tips are presented in this chapter:

- Integer math is generally faster than floating-point math.
- Do not use the floating-point division operator with integer-based data types.
- The exponent operator is faster using floating-point variables than using integer-based variables.
- Avoid mathematical operations using the variant data type.
- Avoid mathematical operations using the currency data type.
- Multiplication is faster than division.
- Multiplication can be faster than the exponent operator.
- The square root function is faster than the exponent operator.

Chapter 11: Code Structure

This chapter focuses on the structure of code, the selection of specific syntactical constructs, and the impact on performance. Sample programs highlight various aspects of performance. The first focus is on packaging routines. In-line code is demonstrated to be significantly faster than procedures. The use of in-line code offers significant performance advantages, at the cost of program maintainability. Subroutines are faster than functions. Functions incur slightly more overhead in passing back return values.

The speed difference between calling procedures in the same form and calling those in another module is shown to be negligible. Decisions on the approach to use in this area should be based as much on desired program standards and conventions as on performance considerations.

`For` loops are shown to be significantly faster than `Do...While` loops. Variants should be avoided as loop indexes. Select statements are much faster than `If...Then...ElseIf` statements, and placing frequently matched conditions at the top of such selections is an important optimization tactic. Miscellaneous topics are also covered.

The execution times are shown to be slower in the Visual Basic development environment than outside it. Therefore, performance should be assessed outside the Visual Basic development environment to get the most accurate and user-relevant data, since that is the expected user configuration for most applications.

These tips provide some insight in code structuring that can result in measurable performance improvements. Some of these come at the cost of code maintainability. The value of such trade-offs will be unique to each application and programming situation. If you're armed with performance knowledge, you are at least in a position to understand these trade-offs and optimize where appropriate.

The following tips are presented in this chapter:

- In-line code performs significantly faster than calls to the same code packaged in subroutines or function calls. However, in-line code has inherent maintenance disadvantages. Therefore, use of in-line code is a good optimization approach for just those areas of a program that have particular speed demands.
- Subroutines are generally slightly faster than function calls because of efficiencies in returning data.
- Performance will generally be roughly the same to call a subroutine in either a form or a module. However, a call to a subroutine in another module could involve additional overhead to load the module into memory. Similarly, modules are loaded "on demand," so you can minimize module load time by defining related routines likely to be called together into the same modules.
- Calls with `ByVal` parameters take longer than calls without `ByVal` parameters, but the difference is very slight.
- Use `For Next` rather than `While` loops to reap significant performance benefits.
- Do not use any variables of variant data type as index types in your for loops.
- Use the `Select Case` selection method whenever possible. It offers significant performance benefits over alternative methods such as `If...Then...ElseIf`. The more selection levels down that the true condition is within the selection evaluation, the greater the performance benefit.
- Use of the parentheses expression qualifier in conditional statements makes no significant difference in performance.

- Ensure that your most frequently matched conditions appear at the front of your selection case structure, and that your least frequently matched conditions appear at the end of the choices. Likewise, put your conditions that are most likely to be true first in `If` statements. This can result in significant performance gains.
- There is little performance difference between statements on multiple lines and statements merged onto one line with the : separator. Therefore, it is recommended that separate lines be used for statements to enhance program readability and maintainability.
- The ampersand (`&`) offers a very slight performance advantage over the plus sign (`+`).
- Always run applications in EXE format rather than from within the Visual Basic environment when assessing performance. Running programs from within the Visual Basic environment can not only cause programs to run slower, it can also provide different relative performance results than you would observe outside the environment.

Part IV: Optimization Strategies: Controls

Part IV looks at issues that involve standard and custom controls. Custom controls greatly extend the capabilities of the Visual Basic programming language. This part covers issues such as performance in control loading, how best to use control properties, and performance issues related to custom controls.

Chapter 12: Control Loading

This chapter presents an analysis of control loading issues. The need for a careful approach to timing load duration is discussed. Consideration is given to tips that relate to control loading. One important guideline is that *if you can reduce the total number of custom controls your application uses, you will reduce load time.* The benefits of reducing the overall number of program controls to enhance load time are discussed. Techniques for reducing controls include just loading them on demand rather than initially and moving them to a secondary form rather than the startup form. Hiding a form for future redisplay is one way to enhance speed of secondary forms and an example is provided.

Another important guideline is to *use standard controls in lieu of custom controls where possible to enhance performance.* Standard controls load faster due to reduced disk access, memory load, and initialization overhead at load time. Among the standard controls, *lightweight controls are faster than heavyweight controls.* A sample program is used to demonstrate that lightweight image controls load significantly faster than heavyweight picture controls. These same advantages are inherent in other lightweight controls.

An important load tuning technique for many situations is to use dynamic control creation. *Runtime-control-array–created image and picturebox controls load faster than design-time–created*

controls. The dynamic creation of such controls and the performance advantages this offers is covered in detail.

Controls have their own initialization techniques, resource considerations, and related performance impact. The best you can do to understand all the load implications of such controls is to use techniques outlined in this chapter to perform your own load time analysis. Armed with this information, you can make decisions on the merits of avoiding controls to improve form load time and performance, at the cost of the rich functionality that controls provide.

The following tips are presented in this chapter:

- If you can reduce the total number of custom controls your application uses, you will reduce load time.
- Use standard controls in lieu of custom controls where possible to enhance performance.
- Lightweight controls are faster than heavyweight controls.
- To improve startup load time, only load controls that are initially required. If other controls may be required later but are not required initially, they can be created when needed using a control array `Load` statement. Graphics controls that display bitmap images are the most likely candidates for deferred creation. These controls can be created on demand with a control array `Load`, with their corresponding bitmap images loaded from a resource file or from a bitmap file, or assigned from another image control.
- If you're loading a picture or image control on demand, assign the picture from a resource file compiled into your project exe with the `LoadResPicture` statement, or just reassign from the picture property of a previously existing picture or image control when possible. This will offer faster performance than loading the image directly from a bitmap file with the `LoadPicture` statement, as well as eliminate the need to distribute that file with your application.
- Move controls to secondary forms rather than the main form to improve the user's perceived load time.
- If a secondary form loaded from the main form must be repeatedly loaded and unloaded, the load time will be the slowest the first time it is loaded. Consider the time of the first load of a form to evaluate worst-case performance.
- If you have a secondary form that is frequently accessed by the user and contains many controls, you can substantially improve the redisplay speed of that form by hiding it rather than unloading it when the user closes the form. It will remain in memory and subsequent `Form.Show` statements will quickly reactivate/repaint it rather than carry out the more time-consuming reload. Time savings of a second or more can result, depending on the type of form displayed.
- If a form requires many identical image and picture controls, runtime-control-array–created controls provide faster program loads than do design-time–created controls.

The more identical image or picture controls you have, the greater the speedup you stand to gain from this technique. If you have shape controls, it will be faster to lay them out at design time than to dynamically create them.

Chapter 13: Control Properties

Every control brings with it unique performance considerations based on the unique code behind that particular control. Each control may have its own performance bottlenecks and resource and memory constraints awaiting your discovery. Some significant performance savings can be realized through an informed use of control properties. Under Visual Basic 3.0, savings could be realized if you used *default values* of controls. However, under Visual Basic 4.0 use of default values does not provide this advantage, and is even slightly slower than explicit reference of properties.

The most significant way to enhance control property–related performance is to store control properties in variables if you will reference those properties frequently in code. Variable access that is 30 times faster than property access is demonstrated in the sample program in this chapter. A little more code effort is required, but the performance payback is substantial.

The use of the `With` control reference construct is also examined. There is a slight performance benefit to referencing properties within the context of `With`. Finally, the label caption and textbox text property are compared. The `Label` caption property updates dramatically faster than the `Textbox` text property. This highlights the important point that every control and its properties will have different performance considerations.

The following tips are presented in this chapter:

- Behavior and performance of Visual Basic 4.0 programs is significantly different from those of Visual Basic 3.0 programs in some areas. Some optimization steps that are relevant for Visual Basic 3.0 are not relevant for Visual Basic 4.0. For instance, using the default property when assigning the value of a standard control property no longer offers significant time savings.
- Using the default property of a standard control offers no significant performance advantages over explicitly referencing the property.
- Using the default property of an OLE custom control results in slower performance than explicitly referencing the property. Avoid the use of default properties when working with OCX controls.
- Store control properties in variables if you will reference those properties frequently in code. Substantial performance savings can result.
- There is no performance penalty for referencing control properties via the `With` construct. `With` even seems to be marginally faster than referencing controls via the full control name and property.

Chapter 14: Custom Controls

The chapter begins by stating the difference between a *standard control* and a *custom control.* A standard control is built in to the Visual Basic environment, whereas a custom control is a separate file that must be included in the project as a standalone component, much like a DLL. Standard controls are usually more limited than custom controls, while custom controls offer a richer suite of functionality or provide functionality otherwise unavailable in the Visual Basic environment. The increased functionality of a custom control often comes at the cost, however, of reduced performance and increased memory usage. Standard controls are usually more limited in functionality than custom controls, but have the benefit of taking less memory and performing better since they are inherent to Visual Basic.

The three primary uses of a custom control are (1) to provide functionality that is not possible in Visual Basic using a standard control; (2) to enhance or otherwise extend the functionality of an existing standard control; and (3) to provide functionality more easily through the use of a custom control than with Visual Basic code. In any of these cases, the trade-off between performance and functionality must be considered.

Often the programmer wishes to use only a subset of a control that provides a wealth of functionality. It is often unnecessary to use a custom control that slows the application down and requires a great deal of memory if, for example, only 25% of the control's functionality is ever used. The programmer can often use existing standard controls and code techniques to "simulate" the custom control to the extent of functionality that the programmer desires. This comes at the cost, however, of development, maintenance, and debugging time.

A sample application demonstrates that the manual implementation is faster than the custom control implementation. The more complex and feature-rich the control, the longer it typically takes to manipulate and exercise the control. If, on the other hand, controls are simpler and have less functionality, the execution time typically improves as well. It is often advantageous to use code and standard controls. This does not mean that custom controls should not be used, but that the best tool should be chosen for the task at hand. Often, the solution does not necessarily have to involve custom controls.

The performance of one custom control versus another is not just related to its feature set and complexity. Custom control performance also depends, of course, on how well the control was written and how efficient its underlying code is. The programmer is wise to experiment with all of the control options at his/her disposal, comparing each in terms of performance and functionality to arrive at the best decision.

The following tip is presented in this chapter:

- There are viable alternatives to custom controls which can often eliminate many of the negative side effects custom controls impose.

Part V: Optimization Strategies: Graphics

Part V discusses performance issues for Visual Basic applications that use graphics in one way or another. This includes a very large percentage of the applications written with Visual Basic, so this issue is of prime importance to the Visual Basic programmer. The proper use of graphics methods, controls, and the Windows API is discussed, and each approach is compared to the others in terms of performance and implementation. This part also discusses how to display pictures in the most efficient manner and how the programmer can cause graphics to paint and redraw to the screen as efficiently as possible.

Chapter 15: Graphics Controls, Methods, and the API

The chapter examines the three fundamental techniques the programmer can use to create graphics: Visual Basic graphics controls, Visual Basic graphics methods, and the Windows API. Applications are written for each of the three techniques to evaluate their performance. The results indicate that placing shape controls on forms at design time is faster than creating them dynamically at runtime using code. The results also show that design-time shape controls are faster than graphics methods but that graphics methods are faster than dynamically created shape controls. The Windows API is also compared to methods and controls, and the performance is comparable to that of graphics methods.

The evaluation of performance in this chapter is based primarily on the load time of the form on which the graphics are drawn. When you're simply considering the amount of time it takes to display graphics on a form initially, static, lightweight controls perform better than dynamic controls or methods. When you're considering the API, methods and controls can be faster in some cases and comparable in others. This does not always mean that static controls should be used. Often, graphics must be loaded dynamically because different numbers and types of graphics may be required based on user actions. In such cases, it may not be practical to design every type of graphics control up front that you might need.

The Windows API can provide any level of functionality Visual Basic provides, and much more. Although this chapter does not delve into the wide flexibility and functionality of the API, you should note that the API can often be used to extend graphics capabilities far beyond those of which Visual Basic is capable of performing. Finally, the chapter briefly discusses the issue of display speed versus printer speed. Outputting graphics on a printer is almost always much slower than outputting them to a video screen, so the programmer should always provide graphical display output as well as printed output.

The following tips are presented in this chapter:

- Graphics controls load faster if explicitly defined at design time than they do dynamically at runtime.

- Graphics created at design time using controls are faster than those using graphics methods at runtime.
- Standard Windows API graphics functions do not provide significant performance advantages over graphics controls and graphics methods implementations that provide the same functionality.
- Printing graphics to a printer takes longer than displaying those graphics on the screen.

Chapter 16: Displaying Pictures

This chapter starts out by introducing the reader to the standard graphics files and their formats. These graphics files are used to load and store pictures into Visual Basic applications. Certain types of graphics file formats are inherently faster than others. After discussing the various graphics file formats and their optimal use, the chapter introduces the controls used to display pictures, namely the *image* and *picture box* controls. Their strengths and weaknesses are discussed, and sample applications are presented that compare the amount of time it takes to load each control with a picture. The image control can be loaded with a picture faster than can the picture box control.

While the image control is faster, it is not always the control of choice. The picture control has additional functionality that the image control does not have, such as the ability to store child controls, DDE/OLE support, and the ability to process events that the image control is never notified of. The added features of the picture box control might make up for the loss in performance. On the other hand, you might not be taking advantage of the picture box control and might be just as well off using the image control. In such a case, performance will improve and application overhead will drop. The balance between functionality, ease of use, and performance must be carefully determined to arrive at the best compromise.

The chapter presents strategies for maximizing the performance of both the image and picture box controls. The `LoadPicture` function, which is used to load graphics into a control at runtime rather than at design time, is introduced. The use of this function enables the application to load much faster and take less space for the executable file. An application loads much faster if the graphics are loaded dynamically. This is important for optimization when you wish to cut down on the amount of time an application takes to load initially. Often, if the perceived speed of an application can be reduced, the user is much more impressed with the application.

The following tip is presented in this chapter:

- Image controls are faster than picture box controls.

Chapter 17: Painting and Redrawing

This chapter discusses several practical techniques for maximizing the efficiency of a Visual Basic application when painting and redrawing graphics on forms and picture box controls. The two fundamental properties relating to this topic, `AutoRedraw` and `ClipControls`, are both described, and techniques are presented that relate to each property.

The `AutoRedraw` property determines whether the "back" layer of a form or picture box control is saved in memory so that when the form needs to be repainted, Windows can simply use a predefined bitmap. When the property is set to `True`, Visual Basic stores the image in memory and redisplays it as necessary. While this frees the developer from worrying about redisplaying graphics generated using methods, the process consumes memory and can ultimately degrade performance. If, however, the property is set to `False`, the extra memory is freed up at the expense of the programmer redrawing the graphics in the `Paint` event of the form or picturebox control. Again, depending on the condition, this may or may not improve performance.

The `ClipControls` property determines whether a "clipping region" is created for the back layer of the form that is used for graphics methods. If a form has a large number of controls on it and very few methods are used, it is best to set the `ClipControls` property to `False`. If, on the other hand, a large number of graphics methods are used, it may be desirable to define a clipping area so that the graphics produced by those methods are drawn efficiently and time is not wasted drawing to the form where graphics at higher layers overwrite what gets drawn in the "back" layer. Again, the decision about whether to set the property to `True` depends on the situation. These guidelines are presented in general terms, and the developer must experiment to make the right decision.

Finally, the chapter presents a technique used to minimize the number of repaints necessary in Visual Basic applications. The technique is to hide controls that are changed in ways that affect they way they are displayed. Often, if many changes must be made to a single control or if the same change is to be made across many controls, it is desirable to hide the control or controls while those manipulations are taking place. By hiding the controls and then doing the manipulations, the programmer can potentially save a repaint for every modification and only require one repaint to hide the control(s) and one repaint to redisplay the control(s). A sample application is presented to illustrate the benefits of doing so.

The following tips are presented in this chapter:

- Set `AutoRedraw` to `False` if graphics methods are not used to create graphics in a container.
- Set `AutoRedraw` to `False` whenever you can quickly re-create the graphics using graphics methods in the `Paint` event and/or when the graphics change often.
- Set `AutoRedraw` to `True` when the container has a lot of complex graphics that are difficult to reproduce and/or when the form doesn't change very often.

- Set `ClipControls` to `False` if the form has a lot of controls on it and graphics methods are not used. If graphics methods are used, it may still be beneficial to turn `ClipControls` off, but this must be determined on a case-by-case basis.
- Minimize the number of repaints by setting controls to be invisible when they're being manipulated.

Part VI: Optimization Strategies: System Environment and Interaction

There are many ways that your Visual Basic programs can interact with the system and are affected by the nature of the operating environment. To understand this interaction, you must look above and beyond the standard constructs of the Visual Basic language and have some understanding of the system itself. Such considerations include the use of memory, the nature of a multitasking system, file generation, the differences between a 16-bit and 32-bit operating system environment, Jet Engine database capabilities, and the incorporation of other-language DLLs into an application. Part VI examines each of these concepts and offers strategies for maximizing the efficiency of Visual Basic applications in each area.

Chapter 18: Multitasking and Memory

One of the objectives of this chapter is to provide reasons for using the `DoEvents` statement and the performance ramifications of doing so. First, an example is provided to highlight the necessity of the `DoEvents` function. Without this statement, programs under Windows 3.1 can temporarily lock out other applications as well as lock out all other events within the same application. An easy-solution sample program simply places a `DoEvents` statement in every loop, and each time through the loop this statement will give other events a chance to be processed. The sample program in the chapter shows, however, that such an approach carries with it a nontrivial performance penalty. The use of a `DoEvents` statement can nearly double the execution time of a simple loop in some cases.

A tactical workaround to this approach is illustrated. If the `GetQueueStatus` API call indicates that a message is present for the application, `DoEvents` is called to deal with that message. If `GetQueueStatus` indicates that no messages are present, `DoEvents` is not called within the loop.

This chapter also looks at memory considerations related to form unloading. Three main techniques are examined to remove forms that have been loaded through an array of form objects. The first technique is to hide forms. This is shown to be an expensive memory operation compared to the alternatives.

The next technique is to unload the loaded forms rather than hiding them. The form unload method does not unload a form's code from memory, but simply clears out the form, so some memory loss would normally be expected after just loading/unloading a form. The unload technique shows similar execution time to the hiding approach, has no memory savings, and results in slower redisplay of the form.

The final technique illustrated is to unload forms and set the form object variables to the `Nothing` keyword. This approach is almost as quick as the plain unload approach, and it provides significant memory savings. As for the best overall approach to remove arrays of form objects, the hide approach is best for applications that must maximize form redisplay speed, and the unload/set to nothing approach is best for applications that must minimize memory consumption.

The discussion of these techniques is followed by a general look at memory issues. Memory management can be heavily influenced by system activity levels and concurrent use of programs. Such activity can affect test results for these sample programs, as well as user programs. In addition, the "out of memory" error that can occur on form loading is addressed. A technique to trap this error and allow a program to recover is provided.

All the techniques provide important background for dealing with memory-related Visual Basic issues in general. Every application will have unique performance considerations for which the best approach is simply to have a well-grounded understanding of the complexities of the memory-management aspects of Visual Basic and Windows.

The following tips are presented in this chapter:

- The `DoEvents` statements consumes nontrivial amounts of time even if there are no events to respond to.
- The `GetQueueStatus` API is a safe and quick way to allow response to other events when coupled with `DoEvents`. A `GetQueueStatus` with `DoEvents` is faster than using `DoEvents` alone.
- Loading then hiding forms is a memory-expensive operation and should be used only if later speedy retrieval of forms is desired.
- When dealing with arrays or collections of form objects, hide forms to enhance redisplay speed at the cost of increased memory consumption. Alternatively, unload forms and set the form object to `Nothing` to optimize memory use at the cost of form redisplay speed. The best approach is application specific.
- Object variables should be set to `Nothing` after object use is complete. The potential memory conservation benefits normally outweigh the negligible cost of extra processing time.

Chapter 19: File I/O

This chapter looks at performance of various file I/O techniques. Different techniques have advantages for different types of data storage and retrieval. The sample program in this chapter demonstrates performance of the file access methods across various types of storage and retrieval models. In any implementation, the choice of the best file I/O technique is very dependent on

the application and data. Nevertheless, the examples in this program show some general performance trade-offs when the performance of each file access method for the sample is examined.

This chapter illustrates that different file I/O techniques will have performance advantages depending on the application. Random file I/O is especially strong for unordered record-based file manipulations. Binary file I/O is speedy and requires more implementation work, but may be particularly suited to managing large amounts of data. Sequential file I/O is in some respects the easiest to use but does not provide the random data access capabilities of random or even binary file I/O with as much ease.

Likewise, the Windows API INI profile function calls do not execute as quickly as some of the other techniques. The advantage of these calls is in ease of use at a programming level. They also allow data to be retrieved quite easily with no concern to file layout or order of data in the file, but this comes at the expense of performance. If an application has simple file I/O needs, the APIs might provide an easy programming solution. If data needs are more complex, the APIs could likely introduce noticeable negative performance impact.

The additional overhead of a particular database approach may be slower than file I/O. However, it provides advantages in data management. Again, if quantities of data are vast, the programming and data management effort will be greatly simplified with a database technique. A database is an additional layer laid on top of file I/O, and that in and of itself imposes an overhead performance penalty that would not be present if you used file I/O directly. However, today's databases come highly optimized so this penalty is not necessarily a big enough barrier to justify file I/O.

The following file I/O tips are presented within this chapter:

- The `Print` statement generally offers significantly faster file I/O speed than the `Write` statement.
- Use `LINE INPUT` rather than `INPUT` for line-oriented file I/O. The line-at-a-time retrieval of `LINE INPUT` is much faster than the variable-based `INPUT` retrieval approach.
- If you need to read a series of values from a line into variables, `INPUT` will offer similar or better performance than using `LINE INPUT` to read the whole line, if you take into account the extra time you must spend parsing the string with that approach. `INPUT` also makes for more maintainable code with its clearer code-eliminating approach.
- Sequential I/O is faster than binary I/O when you're reading or writing a line at a time sequentially. If you need to write or read from various nonsequential locations, binary or random file I/O will be the only feasible approach.

Chapter 20: 16-Bit Versus 32-Bit Code

This chapter presents some of the key points and strategies concerning 16-bit versus 32-bit applications. Differences between 16-bit and 32-bit Visual Basic applications can be viewed in two categories: those you can't see reflected in your source code and those you can. Differences you can't see relate to the fact that a 32-bit Visual Basic application will exploit the underlying 32-bit operating system, regardless of your program structure. This has some architectural advantages over the less-sophisticated 16-bit operating system. Even 16-bit programs that run under the 32-bit system will still use an interpreter whose code is targeted for the less-sophisticated 16-bit environment.

The other area considered is references that can be viewed in source code that are unique to 32-bit Visual Basic programs. Such references reflect the more powerful programming model and capabilities available to the author of the program made possible by the operating system. These areas include the ability to create and use in-process OLE Automation server DLLs, to use the more optimal Jet 3.0 layer based on threads, and to create and use remote data objects that bypass the Jet layer, among others. Some capabilities offered by 32-bit programs, however, do not spell tangible performance improvement. 32-bit OLE automation control or OCX load time is one such area. Overall, 32-bit programs perform noticeably faster than equivalent 16-bit programs if both are run on a 32-bit environment. As with all performance testing, though, results can be expected to vary by application.

Chapter 21: Jet Engine/Access

This chapter examines performance issues surrounding many aspects of database performance. A sample program highlights the advantages of various database techniques. Data access objects are faster than the data control OCX, although the data control does provide convenient programming. The use of transactions considerably improves performance. Likewise, tables are faster than dynasets in the sample application, and generally offer better performance than snapshots and dynasets in most cases. The exclamation point (`!`) is much faster than the parentheses (`()`) when you're referring to field names. Finally, the use of queries is discussed. Using a delete query is faster than deleting each record from a set individually. Update queries can provide the same type of speed advantages. Queries can be defined as stored queries in the database for optimal performance. Any programmer doing extensive database programming should learn all the intricacies of SQL, because a single SQL statement with a query can often replace many "brute force" lines of code.

16-bit database performance issues are also addressed. The same program used for the 32-bit tests is used with the 16-bit tests. However, it uses DAO 2.5 and Jet Engine 2.5 instead of DAO 3.0 and Jet Engine 3.0 since those are not available to 16-bit applications. The 32-bit programs are measurably faster, especially more so in some cases (such as updates) than in other cases (such as searches).

Database performance is often very intangible. Rules that apply to one situation will not apply to another because application needs can vary greatly. Research findings you experience in the morning may not hold true in the afternoon as the system environment, including database size, memory, network load, and other factors, can vary greatly. The best rule is to trust nothing, test everything, and test again. You often will not find one clear answer, but will gradually

build an intricate and sometimes intuitive understanding of performance considerations that will serve you well in future development and optimization. That is the best way to ensure that you are correctly assessing the needs of you own application and environment.

The following tips are presented in this chapter:

- Use data access objects rather than the OCX data control for faster performance when you are willing to sacrifice the data control's convenience.
- Use database transactions to significantly enhance performance in every area of database operations.
- For simple operations (operations other than sorts, filters, and joins) use tables instead of dynaset or snapshot recordset objects to significantly enhance performance.
- Use the exclamation operator `recordset!FIELDNAME` rather than parentheses operator `recordset("FIELDNAME")` to reference recordset field names for significantly faster performance.
- Use the table `Seek` method for fastest search time. This approach is significantly faster than the recordset `FindNext` and `FindPrevious` methods.
- `DELETE` and `UPDATE` queries can offer performance advantages over traversing a recordset and individually updating or deleting records.
- Be sure to run any code that uses a named SQL query from within the Visual Basic environment before making your executable. This causes the SQL text string to be "compiled" into an optimal format for fastest processing at runtime.
- Define stored queries directly in the database for faster performance. Programs can then reference the stored queries instead of supplying them dynamically.
- 32-bit programs with Data Access Object 3.0 and Jet Engine 3.0 will have significantly better performance than 16-bit programs that must use older versions of database software.

Chapter 22: Moving Code to DLLs

In this chapter, Visual Basic, Visual C++, and Delphi are used to illustrate the methods and results of moving code out of Visual Basic and into a DLL. Several important points are emphasized in this chapter. First, it is important to realize that moving Visual Basic code into a DLL typically involves more time and effort than a Visual Basic solution, particularly for beginning programmers. Therefore, it is important to know when it is appropriate to move code to a DLL and when it is not. This chapter points out three cases in which it can be appropriate: when the code does not execute fast enough in Visual Basic, when the functionality cannot be accomplished using Visual Basic, and when the code is reusable and to be shared among various languages.

The chapter then discusses the requirements to interface a DLL to a Visual Basic application, particularly the declarations required and the comparison of the Visual Basic data types to the C/C++ data type set. Having presented important interface concepts, the chapter presents two case studies in which a function is placed into 16-bit DLLs created using Microsoft Visual C++ 1.5 and Borland Delphi, as well as a 32-bit DLL created by Microsoft Visual C++ 2.0.

The results show that for the functionality being considered, the C/C++ solution is the fastest, followed by Delphi and then Visual Basic. While this clearly depends on the functionality being implemented and is not universally true for every case, it does show the benefit of moving code, when necessary, to a DLL. The performance results of moving code to a DLL may not be consistent across languages, since they depend a great deal on the type of functionality being implemented. The type of function used in this chapter is very well suited for a compiled language such as Delphi or C/C++. Others may not fit as well.

The chapter also points out that, while the C/C++ and Delphi solutions provide better performance in this case study, it takes more time and effort to create the DLLs, test them, create the Visual Basic interface to them, test the interface, and test the entire application using the DLL. This additional work may not be worth the performance boost, particularly if the program has a release deadline or there are limited resources and hours to tackle the problem. In such cases, it may be better to keep the functionality in Visual Basic and look for ways to improve performance within the environment.

The chapter presents several solutions. The first, which is to apply the optimization techniques presented in this book, is perhaps the most practical way to improve performance in an application where a bottleneck exists. Depending on the functionality, it may be possible to use other DLLs and the Windows API to integrate and/or supplement the functionality in Visual Basic. Finally, it may be better to modify or even eliminate the functionality if the performance so negatively affects an application, which is true using *any* language.

While the goal of the chapter is not to *teach* you how to create a DLL, the chapter does bring out some of the ramifications, procedures needed, and results obtained from doing so. This discussion gives you a clearer idea of what's involved and what some of the options are should you not have the extra time and effort to create a DLL.

Part VI: Optimization Strategies: Object Creation and Manipulation

Part VI addresses the powerful object capabilities of Visual Basic 4.0. Visual Basic provides a clear object model for the programmer to work with. This includes the ability to create classes and objects based on those classes. It also encompasses the ability to incorporate object containers into an application. Object-based program components can even be shared by OLE Automation server technology. With any object, it is important to understand the available properties and methods well. Sometimes the manner of using an object can have a drastic impact

on performance. Each of these areas is covered in turn, including the use of standard objects, OLE embedded objects, and in-process and out-process OLE Automation servers.

Chapter 23: Objects

The ability to create user-defined classes and objects based on those classes is an exciting new feature of Visual Basic 4.0. This chapter examines some of the ways to make programs that use this new object capability run faster. Two specific techniques are presented in this chapter. The first technique is to use the specific name of the class rather than a more generic one when declaring objects. The use of a generic class sometimes offers more flexibility, particularly when creating subroutines that can accept objects based on any number of classes. The results of a simple test program, however, show a considerable boost in performance when objects are declared with a class as specific as possible. The trade-off is reduced modularity in procedures and other areas of code where you wish to leave the type of object open-ended. If you can tie those ends down, however, your application will likely bound forward in performance.

The second technique explored in this chapter involves storing groups of objects. Visual Basic 4.0 provides the ability to store objects in "collections" that are specifically designed to store them. Another technique is to simply store the objects in an array that is declared with the class of the objects being stored in it. A code example shows that collections are faster when you're manipulating objects, but not when you're creating and deleting them from the collection. Arrays are faster when you're creating and deleting entries, but they are not as robust and present a messy alternative to the programmer. The chapter concludes that collections are desirable, not only for performance, but for code maintenance, legibility, and structure.

The following tips are presented in this chapter:

- For faster performance, always use the explicit class name rather than the generic one when declaring objects.
- Object manipulation is faster when objects are stored in collections rather than arrays. While creation and removal of objects can be slower in collections, the advantage of faster manipulation, coupled with a cleaner interface, makes the choice of collections optimal in most cases.

Chapter 24: Object Linking and Embedding

A very powerful technical capability of Visual Basic 4.0 is the level of integration that can be achieved with other applications through OLE, specifically embedding or linking data with the OLE container, directly inserting OLE objects, or using OLE Automation Objects to control other applications. With easy access to other application objects from a VB application, and now the ability for a VB application to likewise make itself available as a server, the only limit to what a VB application can achieve is the developer's initiative and creativity. This world of object sharing does impose some important performance considerations, however. That is the topic of this chapter.

When you use the services of another application, you inherit their performance impact. OLE performance is much improved from early versions, and superior to DDE in most cases, but nevertheless, there is a lot more overhead that goes on to support OLE than if an application simply had internal code to achieve the same result with no external dependencies.

OLE allows you to easily embed objects into your application. You can also provide in-place activation to activate other applications within your application when an object is selected. Menu items relevant to the activated application can be provided on your application's menu bars, and they can edit or work with an activated document within a window in your application. OLE can be used to give your user the impression, look, and feel that those objects are a part of *your* application! However, using OLE objects can be a double-edged sword. If a user is using your application and clicks on an OLE container to bring up a picture, and then is dismayed at the bring-up time of that picture in its host application, the user may very well perceive that your application is the one with the problem.

The developer must assess performance of the integrated piece of software before settling on it as an acceptable solution. You adopt that software object as your own when you incorporate it into your application, because from the standpoint of the user it *is* part of your application.

The following tips are presented in this chapter:

- If you use an OLE container control to provide an interface to an object, your application will pay a performance penalty when forms containing the OLE container control are displayed, but particularly at load time. Users may even perceive more performance problems than really exist, because when they activate an object they might subconsciously expect application command button-type response time and overlook the fact that they have to pay the price of waiting for the embedded or linked object's application to load.
- Sluggish performance can tarnish the usability of an application, whether it is caused by your code or not. When you enable an application to embed an object or you incorporate an application into your own app through in-line activation, users will regard the external application's performance as that of your own.
- If you provide an object container for standardized purposes, you must consider whether all your users will have the necessary software to work with that object. In some cases object support in an application may even make users realize they need more hardware, such as sound cards or additional memory. If your users don't all have the required systems, consider the decision carefully. You must decide if the importance of that feature is such that it will be worth it to end users to endure the cost, or worth it to you to endure the complaints of those who will need to upgrade their capabilities because of your application.
- OLE container controls can greatly extend the capabilities and power of your application. They can also impose a performance penalty. Since they allow you to incorporate another application into your application, it may take some experimentation to understand all the ramifications. Make sure you schedule plenty of time to investigate

and prototype when you work on a new design based on incorporation of OLE container controls.

- When you provide users with the capability to add embedded objects into an application through an OLE container control, your storage needs may increase considerably and performance may be affected. Large volumes of data can be generated when objects are made convenient and accessible.
- Form load times for forms containing OLE container controls will vary greatly depending on the objects and the applications. However, in one series of tests carried out, forms with locally linked objects loaded slightly faster than forms with objects embedded directly in the container controls.
- If you provide linked data that is shared across a network in an OLE container control, users will pay the price of the network performance penalty. Access will be faster if the object data is embedded and stored in the local application file, if you know the object data will never change.
- Displaying the objects stored in OLE container controls on forms as icons seems to offer no performance loading advantages over displaying the entire contents for the object. Therefore, use the technique that makes the most sense in the context of your user interface.

Chapter 25: OLE Automation Servers

This chapter examines performance issues surrounding OLE Automation servers. A comparison of server performance is carried out for both calculation-based services and database services. In-process servers perform measurably slower than the native Visual Basic calls. Even though they share the same address space as the calling application, they still are encumbered by OLE overhead not present in a direct call approach. Likewise, out-of-process servers relegated to a different address space offer performance that is many times slower.

In-process servers are fundamentally different from C++ DLLs since they expose their services through OLE rather than direct calls. They also are interpreted code and require the runtime interpreter when they're carried out, unlike C++ DLLs. However, both in-process and out-of-process servers offer substantial benefits. They allow a packaging of code that can be highly effective in streamline development, maintenance, and support efforts. The exposed object model can facilitate development efforts and opens the door further to sophisticated software design.

The related remote automation objects (RAOs) offer tremendous advantages and flexibility in implementing a client/server application approach. Additionally, even though RAOs must be out-of-process servers rather than in-process servers, they can lead to performance improvements for calling client applications. They enable client applications to offload processing. Client/server performance tuning is a challenging area, and there are many factors to consider in the client/server performance arena not present in standalone performance optimization (for example, network load and server speed).

Finally, time-out considerations are discussed for automation objects. Settling on a time-out strategy may involve psychological considerations of users' reactions to various methods of time-out handling as well as performance considerations.

The following tips are presented in this chapter:

- In-process OLE Automation server performance is slower than that of the same code directly called in a Visual Basic program. Likewise, out-of-process OLE Automation servers will have substantially slower performance than their in-process counterparts.
- Even though OLE Automation servers impose some overhead penalties, they offer substantial benefits in terms of code design, development, and maintenance. For known timing critical code, they should be used with discretion, but otherwise potential server benefits should be carefully considered.
- Remote Automation Objects can provide significant performance improvements by offloading tasks to a server CPU across the network and allowing the calling client program to continue processing even as the server collects results.
- Your program performance will be influenced by external factors such as network load and server CPU once you incorporate a strategy based on Remote Automation Objects.
- Consider user perceptions when deciding on a server time-out strategy.

Chapter 26: Know Your Objects: The OCX Graph Control Sample

This chapter looks at the performance ramifications of various OCX graph-generation techniques. A sample program generates a standard bar graph of running mileage for four different runners. Then, similar code is carried out, but it uses design-time property settings where feasible rather than runtime settings. This method yields a small improvement. Next, the same bar graph is generated using the Blit DrawMode property setting. This shows a more significant performance improvement. Then, the same code is carried out using the AutoInc property to automatically set the current graph data pointer rather than incrementing it manually through the `ThisPoint` property. This also shows small performance gains. The payback from all these techniques depends on the type of graph generated and the number of data points to be graphed.

In addition, the variance of timings of graph generation is discussed. There is a noticeable initialization overhead penalty when a graph is generated for the first time. Subsequent generations of a graph are quicker. As with most areas of performance, especially for the graph OCX, you should carefully consider the needs of your own application and measure performance of those areas.

The following tips are presented in this chapter:

- If you have no reason to do otherwise, display graph results with `DrawMode` equal to 3 to take advantage of the Blit API for faster performance.
- Use `AutoInc` when assigning sequential data points to a graph to reduce the number of statements the interpreter must process.

Putting It All Together

The objective of this book is to address the major themes of performance and optimization for Visual Basic programming and to provide advice and techniques on how to apply them to your present and future programming projects. One of the important themes emphasized throughout the book is that absolute performance of any given segment of code can vary greatly from one trial to another, since there are so many factors that can influence its execution speed. Not only can timings vary on the same system, but certainly the performance of a segment of code will vary from one PC to another. This book avoids presenting you with absolute timings because they are of little value. What is really of concern to you in the optimization process is the methodology for analyzing performance and how one performance technique compares to another technique, regardless of the platform. Therefore, the focus of this book in comparing performance alternatives is to look at *relative* timings rather than absolute timings.

Timings are carried out under controlled circumstances to minimize system flux and ensure that the environmental conditions are as similar as possible between two comparable tests. In addition, repeated timings are collected and the average results are calculated to lessen the influence of aberrations during measurements caused by moments of system fluctuation. Results are for the most part (except when considering form load) provided as *normalized* results, where the time for each approach is shown as a multiplier of the best approach. This provides for easy interpretation as well as ensures that the timings are considered in a relative light.

The more performance testing you carry out, the more you will realize how greatly Windows performance can fluctuate from one moment to another. This factor is observed throughout testing. Likewise, there are drastic differences in behavior between 16-bit programs running under Windows 3.1 and under Windows 95. Windows 3.1, Windows for Workgroups 3.11, and Windows 95 all have different behavior profiles. Visual Basic 3.0 and Visual Basic 4.0 certainly do as well! In some cases, the most optimal techniques under Windows 3.1 with Visual Basic 3.0 are the least optimal techniques under Windows 95 with Visual Basic 4.0. Likewise, differences in performance between 16-bit and 32-bit programs are very significant at times. Similarly, programs run within the Visual Basic environment with its heavy intervention can have drastically different performance profiles than programs run outside the environment. To provide the clearest findings, all results provided in this book are for Visual Basic 4.0 32-bit programs run as executables outside the Visual Basic Integrated Development Environment, unless otherwise noted.

Do not rely on these timings as the final word in performance. The point of this book is to enable you to carry out your own performance assessments. In that light, please question these results and carry out your own verification of any techniques that are important to your own optimization efforts. Source code and executables for test programs have been provided to make that as easy as possible. Ultimately, you must be the final judge, jury, private investigator, and executioner of your program's optimization. The timings presented here should be viewed as carefully documented pieces of evidence for you to consider in your performance optimization task that serve as your starting point, rather than the final verdict.

You now have the conceptual tools and code utilities to better analyze performance bottlenecks, as well as the tools and techniques to reduce their impact or eliminate them altogether. We hope that, through the discussion of concepts and the use of the tips and techniques presented in this book, you will be able to use this book as a reference guide and mentor when programming, and by doing so you will write faster, more efficient Visual Basic applications. Visual Basic is a breakthrough in programming tools, and its proper use can and will continue to have rich benefits for Windows programmers and developers everywhere.

Appendixes

This section provides appendixes summarizing reference information that may be of interest. This includes a recap of sample programs used throughout the text, as well as a summary of performance information.

Appendix A, "Summary of Programs and Environments," summarizes all the sample programs that have been presented throughout the book. A short description of each program is provided. In addition, the environment used to run the program for relative performance study is summarized. Since timings will vary greatly from one environment to another, and the emphasis of this book is on providing you with the background to carry out your own performance research, rather than to present any absolute timings or ultimate relative rankings of techniques, timings are not summarized. Rather, you are encouraged to use this appendix as a guide to the sample programs and build up your own collection of timing results unique to your own test environment!

Appendix B, "Sources of Information," provides a summary of various resources for Visual Basic information, tools, and components. This information is intended as a representative sampling of the very large variety of Visual Basic resources available. Included on this list are some of the vendors of performance-related products that provided evaluation material during the research for this book, as well as many other well-known resources that were not directly involved in research for this book but have products of general interest.

These appendixes provide a brief summary of what's in this book and resources to supplement the book in the future. This material provides a convenient bookend to this work with a look at where you've been and where you may yet venture. The authors hope that this book serves as the starting point to your own quest for highly tuned, optimal Visual Basic applications. The information in this book and the resources mentioned here can serve as oars on this journey, but ultimately your own research and analysis will determine the direction in which you head. Good luck!

Summary of Programs and Environments

This appendix provides you with a summary of the programs contained in each chapter in this book, which demonstrate the validity of nearly every technique presented in this book. This appendix contains a summary of the hardware platforms that were used to carry out the research presented in each chapter as well as the filenames and descriptions of those programs. Specific test timings themselves are not provided because the focus of this book is not to present absolute timing results. Rather, it is to provide you with a methodology for carrying out performance research. You are encouraged to run all programs in your own user environment, collect timings, modify the programs as needed, and draw your own conclusions.

You will find that the findings summarized throughout this book will be generally supported, but each environment may introduce its own specific skew. Such is the nature of performance!

In all cases, identical source code is used for 16- and 32-bit programs with a conditional compile handling the few differences between the environments. There are, however, different 16- and 32-bit project make files to simplify the task of building the executables for you. 32-bit programs use a 32-bit in-process server to store timings, whereas 16-bit programs use a 16-bit out-of-process server. Additionally, the database program in Chapter 21 uses the Jet 3.0 engine. Having two separate project files enables you to reference them easily and in the appropriate manner. It also makes clear, at a glance, whether a program can run in a given environment. For example, the OLE Automation server test program of Chapter 25 is available only in 32-bit format.

You are welcome to use the programs and source code for these programs for your own purposes, but recognize that it is research-and-development software crafted to guide you through experimentation. It is intended to be used along those lines for future performance insights. As such, this software carries with it no warranties of any kind—except that you can count on seeing some interesting and useful results when you begin to carry out your own performance assessments.

Chapter 4: Timing Methods

Hardware Configuration

90MHz Pentium with 16MB RAM

Programs Included

Bill32.exe (Bill16.exe)

This application is used to compare the accuracy of the various timing methods available for making performance assessments.

BillEn32.exe (BillEn16.exe)

This application also is used to compare the accuracy of the various timing methods available for making performance assessments. This application is an enhanced derivative of the Bill32/Bill16 application.

Chapter 7: Supporting Utilities for Performance Analysis

Hardware Configuration

N/A. This section presents utilities you can use in performance tuning tasks; relative timings are not provided.

Programs Included

Strtr32.exe (Strtr16.exe)

This is a utility that can be used to launch a Visual Basic program and capture a load time for that program, if that program has been modified as described in Chapter 7.

Watchr16.exe

This is a 16-bit utility to monitor Windows 3.1 resources and memory. The utility can present an alarm when memory or resources dip below a certain threshold. The utility can also provide memory and resource information under Windows 95, although it is less pertinent there.

Timing32.exe(Timing16.exe)

This is a utility that allows you to view and modify timing statistics that can be automatically collected as each performance test on the CD-ROM is carried out. Timing32 invokes a 32-bit in-process OLE Automation server, PerfLog.dll, to provide this function. Timing16 is a 16-bit out-of-process OLE Automation server that provides this function directly. Timings are stored in a database on the system, stored by default at installation time in directory C:\vbperf\source\timedata.

Common.BAS

This is not program that can be run directly. Rather, it is a Visual Basic BAS module collection of routines that can be used in performance assessment. These routines are used in all the sample programs throughout the book.

Chapter 9: Variables

Hardware Configuration

90MHz Pentium with 16MB RAM

Programs Included

StrVar32.exe (StrVar16.exe)

This application compares the performance of assigning values to fixed-length strings, variable-length strings, and variants.

IntAll32.exe (IntAll16.exe)

This application compares the performance of assigning values to integers; long integers; Booleans; bytes; and single, double, currency, and variant data types.

CurAll32.exe (CurAll16.exe)

This application compares the performance of assigning values to the currency data type versus all other data types. Specific emphasis is placed on monetary calculations.

Contnr32.exe (Contnr16.exe)

This application compares the use of user-defined types, arrays, and simple variables to store sets of data.

GlbVar32.exe (GlbVar16.exe)

This application compares the performance of assigning values to public (global) variables versus using constants.

VarScp32.exe (VarScp16.exe)

This application compares variable assignments of various scopes, including public versus private variables of application, module, and form scope.

09Quiz32.exe (09Quiz16.exe)

This is the Quiz problem posed at the end of the chapter.

Chapter 10: Math

Hardware Configuration

90MHz Pentium with 16MB RAM

Programs Included

MthCmp32.exe (MthCmp16.exe)

This application used every fundamental arithmetic operator to compare the performance of simple arithmetic for each standard Visual Basic data type.

MltDiv32.exe (MltDiv16.exe)

This application compares the performance of multiplication versus division for all relevant data types.

MltExp32.exe (MltExp16.exe)

This application compares the performance of multiplication versus the exponent operator for positive integer exponents. Comparisons are made for each relevant data type.

SqrExp32.exe (SqrExp16.exe)

This application evaluates the use of the exponent operator where the exponent = 0.5 to the square-root function. Comparisons are made for each relevant data type.

1001Qz32.exe (1001Qz16.exe)

This is the first Quiz question posed at the end of the chapter.

1002Qz32.exe (1002Qz16.exe)

This is the second Quiz question posed at the end of the chapter.

Chapter 11: Code Structure

Hardware Configuration

50MHz 486DX2 with 12MB RAM

Programs Included

callty32.exe (callty16.exe)

This application examines various ways in which a block of code can be called, whether it be in-line, in a function within the form, in a subroutine within the form, or in another module.

callar32.exe (callar16.exe)

This program compares the performance of passing various arguments to procedures. Tests include function and subroutine calls with and without the `ByVal` keyword.

loop32.exe (loop16.exe)

This application compares the performance of various loop schemes, including `DoWhile...Loop`, `Do...LoopWhile`, `For...Next`, and `For...Next I%`. Comparisons are made not only on the loop constructs themselves, but also on the index used in the loop. Indexes of various data types are compared.

select32.exe (select16.exe)

This application compares various methods for making selections in code. The `Select Case`, `If Then...Else`, `If Then...ElseIf`, and `If () Then...ElseIf` constructs are compared.

Misc32.exe (Misc16.exe)

This application evaluates the performance of some miscellaneous functions of lesser importance. Tests are made on multiline assignments, blank lines, continuation symbols, multiline and single-line constructs, and string concatenation methods.

Chapter 12: Control Loading

Hardware Configuration

50MHz 486DX2 with 12MB RAM

Programs Included

BigLd32.exe (BigLd16.exe)

This application illustrates how slow a program can be when many controls are placed on it.

LoadCt32.exe (LoadCt16.exe)

This program loads a startup form that can then be used to load a control-intensive form. This illustrates the load-time penalty of a control-intensive form.

Dt_Img32.exe (Dt_Img16.exe)

This application calculates the load time of a form with 30 image controls on it created at design time.

Dt_Pic32.exe (Dt_Pic16.exe)

This application calculates the load time of a form with 30 picture controls on it created at design time.

Rt_Img32.exe (Rt_Img16.exe)

This application calculates the load time of a form with a control array of 30 image controls created at runtime.

Rt_Img32.exe (Rt_Img16.exe)

This application is a derivative of Rt_Img32. It calculates the load time of a form with a control array of 30 image controls created at runtime. Rather than calculating and assigning all control location properties in a loop, it explicitly assigns precalculated values.

Rt_Pic32.exe (Rt_Pic16.exe)

This application calculates the load time of a form with a control array of 30 picture controls created at runtime.

Quiz1_32.exe (Quiz1_16.exe)

This is the Quiz problem posed at the end of the chapter.

Chapter 13: Control Properties

Hardware Configuration

50MHz 486DX2 with 12MB RAM

Programs Included

PropDf32.exe (PropDf16.exe)

This application compares the performance of using a default property of a control versus the specific property.

PropVr32.exe (PropVr16.exe)

This application compares the performance of updating the properties of a control by using the property directly or using a variable.

Quiz1_32.exe (Quiz1_16.exe)

This is the Quiz problem posed at the end of the chapter.

Chapter 14: Custom Controls

Hardware Configuration

90MHz Pentium with 16MB RAM

Programs Included

MhGage32.exe (MhGage16.exe)

This application evaluates the time required to load and manipulate the MicroHelp Gauge control.

MyGage32.exe (MyGage16.exe)

This application evaluates the time required to load and manipulate a manual simulation of the MicroHelp Gauge control to compare performance to the MhGaug32.exe application.

Chapter 15: Graphics Controls, Methods, and the API

Hardware Configuration

90MHz Pentium with 16MB RAM

Programs Included

Ctl32.exe (Ctl16.exe)

This application evaluates the load time of a form that contains multiple controls that are placed upon it at design time.

CtlArr32.exe (CtlArr16.exe)

The CtlArr32.exe application evaluates the load time of the form used and the time required to display multiple controls created using a control array at runtime on that form.

Method32.exe (Method16.exe)

This application evaluates the time required to create and display graphics on a form created using graphics methods at runtime.

Api32.exe (Api16.exe)

This application evaluates the time required to create and display graphics on a form using the Windows API at runtime.

15Quiz32.exe (15Quiz16.exe)

This is the Quiz problem posed at the end of the chapter.

15AnsA32.exe (15AnsA16.exe)

This is the first solution for the Quiz problem posed at the end of the chapter.

15AnsB32.exe (15AnsB16.exe)

This is the second solution for the Quiz problem posed at the end of the chapter.

Chapter 16: Displaying Pictures

Hardware Configuration

90MHz Pentium with 16MB RAM

Programs Included

Bmp32.exe (Bmp16.exe)

This application evaluates the load time of a form that contains a series of picture controls that store bitmaps that are created at design time.

Img32.exe (Img16.exe)

This application evaluates the load time of a form that contains a series of picture controls that store bitmaps that are created at design time.

BmpLd32.exe (BmpLd16.exe)

This application evaluates the load time of a form that contains a series of picture controls that store bitmaps that are created at design time and loaded at runtime using `LoadPicture`.

ImgLd32.exe (ImgLd16.exe)

This application evaluates the load time of a form that contains a series of picture controls that store bitmaps that are created at design time and loaded at runtime using `LoadPicture`.

16Quiz32.exe (16Quiz16.exe)

This is the solution for the quiz problems posed at the end of the chapter.

Chapter 17: Painting and Redrawing

Hardware Configuration

90MHz Pentium with 16MB RAM

Programs Included

NoMeth32.exe (NoMeth16.exe)

This application evaluates the time to redisplay graphics on a form where no graphics methods are used and graphics controls are used exclusively.

Meth32.exe (Meth16.exe)

This application evaluates the time to redisplay graphics on a form where graphics methods are used exclusively.

ClipT32.exe (ClipT16.exe)

This application evaluates the time to redisplay graphics on a form where graphics methods are used along with standard controls. The `ClipControl` property is set to `True` to evaluate the performance of controls and graphics in mixed layers.

ClipF32.exe (ClipF16.exe)

This application evaluates the time to redisplay graphics on a form where graphics methods are used along with standard controls. The `ClipControl` property is set to `False` to evaluate the performance of controls and graphics in mixed layers.

RePnt32.exe (RePnt16.exe)

This application evaluates the time required to move several controls across a form when first hiding the controls and then moving them versus keeping them visible throughout. This shows the performance benefits of minimizing the number of repaints.

17Quiz32.exe (17Quiz16.exe)

This is the solution for the Quiz problems posed at the end of the chapter.

Chapter 18: Multitasking and Memory

Hardware Configuration

50MHz 486DX2 with 12MB RAM

Programs Included

DoEvnt32.exe (DoEvnt16.exe)

This application evaluates the penalty imposed by using the `DoEvents` statement various ways in code.

forms32.exe (forms16.exe)

This application compares three techniques for manipulating forms when finished with them: hiding the form, unloading the form, and unloading the form and setting the form object to `Nothing`, thereby deallocating memory.

Chapter 19: File I/O

Hardware Configuration

50MHz 486DX2 with 12MB RAM

Programs Included

FileIO32.exe (FileIO16.exe)

This application provides a comparison of various sequential and binary read and write operations.

Chapter 20: 16-Bit Versus 32-Bit Code

Hardware Configuration

50MHz 486DX2 with 12MB RAM

Programs Included

This chapter considers the performance of 16- and 32-bit versions of programs from other chapters.

Chapter 21: Jet Engine/Access

Hardware Configuration

90MHz Pentium with 32MB RAM

Programs Included

Db32.Exe (DB16.Exe)

This application compares the performance of data access objects and the OLE data control and demonstrates various optimization techniques such as the use of transactions.

Chapter 22: Moving Code to DLLs

Hardware Configuration

90MHz Pentium with 16MB RAM

Programs Included

Ldr32.exe (Ldr16.exe)

These programs are used to call functions stored in 32-bit and 16-bit DLLs, respectively. Various DLLs are called to compare the performance of various languages versus Visual Basic in the context of calling DLL functions.

VCDll32.dll

This is the 32-bit DLL created using Microsoft Visual C++ 2.0 and called by the Visual Basic application Ldr32.

VCDll16.dll

This is the 16-bit DLL created using Microsoft Visual C++ 1.5 and called by the Visual Basic application Ldr16.

DPDll16.dll

This is the 16-bit DLL created using Borland Delphi and called by the Visual Basic application Ldr16.

Chapter 23: Objects

Hardware Configuration

90MHz Pentium with 16MB RAM

Programs Included

ObjDec32.exe (ObjDec16.exe)

This application compares the use of declaring variables using general object, form, and control class declarations versus using specific class declarations.

ColArr32.exe (ColArr16.exe)

This application compares the performance of storing and manipulating objects in a collection versus in an array.

Chapter 24: Object Linking and Embedding

Hardware Configuration

50MHz 486DX2 with 12MB RAM

Programs Included

This chapter doesn't contain any programs; it focuses on a philosophical discussion of the ramifications of embedded objects. The Chapter 25 test program shows related concepts.

Chapter 25: OLE Automation Servers

Hardware Configuration

50MHz 486DX2 with 12MB RAM

Programs Included

UseSvr32.exe

This application compares the performance of in-process versus out-of-process servers.

CalcIn32.dll

This file is the in-process calculation server used by the UseSvr32 application.

CalcOt32.exe

This file is the out-process calculation server used by the UseSvr32 application.

LogIn32.dll

This file is the in-process database-update server used by the UseSvr32 application.

LogOut32.exe

This file is the out-of-process database-update server used by the UseSvr32 application.

Chapter 26: Know Your Objects: The OLE Graph Control Sample

Hardware Configuration

50MHz 486DX2, with 12MB RAM

Programs Included

Gr_Ocx32.exe (Gr_Ocx16.exe)

This program evaluates the graph speed of the OLE graph control for various graph types.

Vb_Vbx16.exe

This program evaluates the graph speed of the Graph VBX for various graph types.

Sources of Information

This appendix presents a list of books, articles, and software that are representative of what is available as tools or reference works. Some of these were referred to in this book. Demo versions of most of the tools mentioned here, as well as many more not referenced in this appendix, are provided on the CD-ROM that comes with this book. The material covered here is a sampling of just some of the many tools and sources of Visual Basic information available. You might want to consider any or all of these for additional information.

Performance Tools and Other Utilities

SpyWorks

Desaware
5 Town & Country Village, Suite 790
San Jose, CA 95128
(408) 377-4770
Fax (408) 371-3530

This utility enables you to take more advantage of the Windows messaging system and API by providing subclassing and callback capabilities as well as direct message manipulation.

VBTools 4.0

MicroHelp
4359 Shallowford Industrial Parkway
Marietta, GA 30066-1135

This product is a series of very powerful custom controls that can greatly enhance the capability of your applications.

VB Compress

Whipplewhare
20 Cedar St
Charlestown, MA 02129
Tech Support (617) 242-2511
Orders (800) 241-8727
Fax (617) 241-8496

This powerful utility cleans up your code, eliminating any variables that are not declared and procedures that are not called. Redundancies are eliminated, and your resultant executable is smaller and cleaner. This process ultimately improves the performance of your application.

Visual Basic Code Profiler (VBCP)

Microsoft Corporation
One Microsoft Way
Redmond, WA 98502-6399

The Visual Basic Enterprise and Professional Edition profiler (included on the Visual Basic CD-ROM) measures the frequency and the time of execution of code throughout your application. The profiler automates the process of modifying your programs with timing statements to collect this information, and clearly summarizes and presents results. That information can then serve you by identifying performance bottleneck areas in your code and prime candidates for optimization.

PinPoint

Avanti Software, Inc.
3790 El Camino Real, Suite 347
Palo Alto, CA 94306
(415) 329-8999
Fax (415) 329-8722
e-mail `76260.266@compuserv.com`

PinPoint's Avanti enables the user to carry out the same basic profiling capability that VBCP does, but with many additional features. Like VBCP, PinPoint can automatically insert procedure-based timing statements throughout an entire project. Then, when the program is executed, the procedure-by-procedure timings can be captured, displayed, graphically represented, and saved in a profiler application. They can also be logged directly to a file. A very helpful trace of program flow is available for viewing in the results window. All of these features combine for a very effective analytical tool that can provide a quick and accurate application flow/performance trace.

Jet Analyzer

Blue Lagoon
6047 Tampa Avenue
Tarzana, CA 91356
(818) 345-2200

The Jet Analyzer is a tool that profiles the speed of the various operations of the Jet Engine database, which is somewhat of a "black hole" in terms of its internal workings. The Jet Analyzer shines light into this black hole and puts some responsibility for database performance back in the hands of the developer. There are many alternative database-implementation approaches that you can use for a specific series of database operations. Modifications to database code can often result in vastly improved performance if you know which area to modify and where your expensive database operations are. Jet Analyzer profiles your database operations to tell you the expense of all database operations. An ODBC analyzer offers similar capabilities for ODBC.

Rocket

SuccessWare
27349 Jefferson Avenue
Temecula, CA 92590
(909) 699-9657

Rocket is a very fast database engine. It is a collection of DLLs and visual controls that provide speed, power, and flexibility in xBase database approaches. It is an attractive alternative for those with high-speed database needs.

Visual Basic Programming Books and References

Real-World Programming with Visual Basic 4, Sams Publishing, Mann

Teach Yourself Visual Basic 4 in 21 Days, Sams Publishing, Gurewich & Gurewich

Visual Basic 4 Unleashed, Sams Publishing, various Visual Basic authors

Visual Basic Database Programming, Sams Publishing, Jennings

Visual Basic Programmer's Journal, Fawcette Publishing

Microsoft Visual Basic Programmer's Guide

CompuServe Forums

This is a very valuable resource for the exchange of Visual Basic information. The Microsoft-supported forum can be reached at

```
GO MSBASIC
```

The forum supported by *Visual Basic Programmer's Journal* can be reached at

```
GO VBPJ
```

Index

Symbols

A

INDEX
I

B

INDEX
I

INDEX
I

INDEX
I

INDEX
I

J-K

L

M

INDEX
I

INDEX
I

P

INDEX
I

Q

R

S

T

U

W-Z

Add to Your Sams Library Today with the Best Books for Programming, Operating Systems, and New Technologies

The easiest way to order is to pick up the phone and call

1-800-428-5331

between 9:00 a.m. and 5:00 p.m. EST.

For faster service please have your credit card available.

ISBN	Quantity	Description of Item	Unit Cost	Total Cost
0-672-30837-1		Visual Basic 4 Unleashed (book/CD)	$45.00	
0-672-30620-4		Teach Yourself Visual Basic 4 in 21 Days, Third Edition	$35.00	
0-672-30728-6		Visual Basic Programming in 12 Easy Lessons (book/disk)	$39.99	
0-672-30440-6		Database Developers Guide with Visual Basic 3 (book/disk)	$44.95	
0-672-30779-0		Real-World Programming with Visual Basic 4 (book/CD)	$49.99	
0-672-30640-9		Master Visual Basic 4, Second Edition (book/CD)	$49.99	
0-672-30470-8		Teach Yourself Delphi in 21 Days	$29.99	
0-672-30736-7		Teach Yourself C in 21 Days, Premier Edition	$35.00	
0-672-30499-6		Delphi Unleashed	$45.00	
0-672-30474-0		Windows 95 Unleashed	$39.99	
0-672-30717-0		Tricks of the Doom-Programming Gurus (book/CD)	$39.99	
		Shipping and Handling: See information below.		
		TOTAL		

❑ 3 ½" Disk

❑ 5 ¼" Disk

Shipping and Handling: $4.00 for the first book, and $1.75 for each additional book. Floppy disk: add $1.75 for shipping and handling. If you need to have it NOW, we can ship product to you in 24 hours for an additional charge of approximately $18.00, and you will receive your item overnight or in two days. Overseas shipping and handling adds $2.00 per book and $8.00 for up to three disks. Prices subject to change. Call for availability and pricing information on latest editions.

201 W. 103rd Street, Indianapolis, Indiana 46290

1-800-428-5331 — Orders   1-800-835-3202 — FAX   1-800-858-7674 — Customer Service

Book ISBN 0-672-30796-0

CD Install

Installing the CD-ROM

The companion CD-ROM contains software developed by the authors, plus an assortment of third-party tools and product demos. The disc is designed to be explored using a browser program. Using Sams' Guide to the CD-ROM browser, you can view information concerning products and companies, and install programs with a single click of the mouse. To install the browser, here's what you do:

Windows 3.1 Installation Instructions:

1. Insert the CD-ROM disc into your CD-ROM drive.
2. From File Manager or Program Manager, choose Run from the File menu.
3. Type `<drive>\setup` and press Enter, where `<drive>` corresponds to the drive letter of your CD-ROM. For example, if your CD-ROM is drive D:, type `D:\SETUP` and press Enter.
4. The installation creates a program manager group named VB4 Performance. To browse the CD-ROM, double-click on the Guide to the CD-ROM icon inside this Program Manager group.

Windows 95 Installation Instructions:

1. Insert the CD-ROM disc into your CD-ROM drive. If the AutoPlay feature of your Windows 95 system is enabled, the setup program will start automatically.
2. If the setup program does not start automatically, double-click on the My Computer icon.
3. Double-click on the icon representing your CD-ROM drive.
4. Double-click on the icon titled Setup.exe to run the installation program. Follow the onscreen instructions that appear. When setup ends, the Guide to the CD-ROM program starts up, so that you can begin browsing immediately.

Following installation, you can restart the Guide to the CD-ROM program by pressing the Start button, selecting Programs, then VB4 Performance and Guide to the CD-ROM.

> **NOTE:** The Guide to the CD-ROM program requires at least 256 colors. For best results, set your monitor to display between 256 and 64,000 colors. A screen resolution of 640×480 pixels is also recommended. If necessary, adjust your monitor settings before using the CD-ROM.